PENGUIN BOOKS

# *Friends in Youth*

'A clear-eyed look at two friends who took pivotal roles in the war that split the nation . . . The triumph of *Friends in Youth* is that it doesn't conceive of itself as a joint biography of two important men set against a background of "History". Instead, it is History that is front and centre . . . [Dinshaw finds] fascinating human-interest stories among the large cast of minor characters' Kathryn Hughes, *Guardian*

'An outstanding dual biography, and a meticulous ground-level view of the complex network of shifting allegiances that led to England's most dramatic upheaval . . . Dinshaw's book is profoundly entertaining, startling in its depth, and a necessary cautionary tale about the human cost of political division' Daniel Brooks, *Daily Telegraph*

'An elegant and humane work of considerable literary and historical polish . . . a book of engaging originality, covering one of the most traumatic and formative eras in British history' David Robinson, *Country Life*

'An original take on the issues that divided friends and families in the opening stages of the English Civil Wars' Jackie Eales, *History Today*

ABOUT THE AUTHOR

Minoo Dinshaw lives in London and is the author of the highly acclaimed *Outlandish Knight: The Byzantine Life of Steven Runciman*.

# *Friends in Youth*
## *Choosing Sides in the English Civil War*

# MINOO DINSHAW

PENGUIN BOOKS

PENGUIN BOOKS

UK | USA | Canada | Ireland | Australia
India | New Zealand | South Africa

Penguin Books is part of the Penguin Random House group of companies
whose addresses can be found at global.penguinrandomhouse.com

Penguin Random House UK,
One Embassy Gardens, 8 Viaduct Gardens, London SW11 7BW

penguin.co.uk

First published by Allen Lane 2025
Published in Penguin Books 2026
001

Copyright © Minoo Dinshaw, 2025

The moral right of the author has been asserted

Penguin Random House values and supports copyright.
Copyright fuels creativity, encourages diverse voices, promotes freedom
of expression and supports a vibrant culture. Thank you for purchasing
an authorized edition of this book and for respecting intellectual property
laws by not reproducing, scanning or distributing any part of it by any
means without permission. You are supporting authors and enabling
Penguin Random House to continue to publish books for everyone.
No part of this book may be used or reproduced in any manner for the
purpose of training artificial intelligence technologies or systems. In accordance
with Article 4(3) of the DSM Directive 2019/790, Penguin Random House
expressly reserves this work from the text and data mining exception.

Typeset by Jouve (UK), Milton Keynes
Printed and bound in Great Britain by Clays Ltd, Elcograf S.p.A.

The authorized representative in the EEA is Penguin Random House Ireland,
Morrison Chambers, 32 Nassau Street, Dublin D02 YH68

A CIP catalogue record for this book is available from the British Library

ISBN: 978–0–141–98651–7

Penguin Random House is committed to a sustainable future
for our business, our readers and our planet. This book is made from
Forest Stewardship Council® certified paper.

To my two Fs

Alas! they had been friends in youth;
But whispering tongues can poison truth;
And constancy lives in realms above;
And life is thorny; and youth is vain;
And to be wroth with one we love
Doth work like madness in the brain.

                                        Samuel Taylor Coleridge, *Christabel*

# Contents

| | |
|---|---|
| *List of Illustrations* | xi |
| *Historical Background* | xv |
| *On Texts, Dates, and Names* | xxix |
| *Maps* | xxxiii |
| Prelude: The Pit's Brink | 1 |
| 1. The Making of the Moderates | 25 |
| 2. The Lawyers' Interlude | 62 |
| 3. Tragedy, Adventure, and Romance | 78 |
| 4. Prelates, Predestination, and Parliament | 108 |
| 5. Pulling Down Cobwebs | 137 |
| 6. Differences in Opinion | 163 |
| 7. A Tedious Debate | 184 |
| 8. Sober Men, Authors of Counsels | 206 |
| 9. Hurry and Smoke | 241 |
| 10. Vulgar Intelligence, Vigorous Defence | 276 |
| 11. The Percy's Peace and the Poet's Plot | 309 |
| 12. Our Utmost Endeavours | 357 |
| 13. England Commits | 404 |
| *List of Notable Characters* | 425 |
| *Further Reading* | 457 |
| *Acknowledgements* | 473 |
| *Index* | 477 |

# List of Illustrations

1. Bulstrode Whitelocke, unknown artist, 1634, National Portrait Gallery (via Wikimedia).
2. Edward Hyde, Adriaen Hanneman, unknown date, most likely 1623–39, National Portrait Gallery (via Wikimedia).
3. College Farm, Purton, photographed by Robin Webster, 2012 (via Wikimedia).
4. John Selden, studio of Peter Lely, seventeenth century, Yale University Art Gallery (via Wikimedia).
5. Apotheosis of Buckingham, Sir Peter Paul Rubens, 1620–24, National Gallery (via Wikimedia).
6. Lucius Cary, 2nd Viscount Falkland, Cornelius Johnson, c. 1633, Montacute House, National Trust Collections (via Wikimedia).
7. Lettice, Lady Falkland, Cornelius Johnson, c. 1633, Indianapolis Museum of Art (via Wikimedia).
8. Burford Priory, photographed by Charles Latham, 1894, published in J. Alfred Gotch, *Architecture of the Renaissance in England*, vol. 1 (via Wikimedia).
9. Sir Kenelm Digby, Sir Anthony van Dyck, 1630s, National Maritime Museum (via Wikimedia).
10. Philip Herbert, 4th Earl of Pembroke, Daniel Mytens, 1634, Hardwick Hall, National Trust Collections (via Wikimedia).
11. Charles I and Henrietta Maria, King and Queen of England, Scotland and Ireland, Sir Anthony van Dyck, 1632, Kromeriz Archdiocesan Museum (via Wikimedia).
12. Sir Thomas Aylesbury, Bt, William Dobson, before 1646, National Portrait Gallery (via Wikimedia).
13. William Laud, Archbishop of Canterbury, Sir Anthony van Dyck, c. 1638, Fitzwilliam Museum (via Wikimedia).

## List of Illustrations

14. Thomas, 1st Baron Wentworth (later 1st Earl of Strafford), with his secretary Sir Philip Mainwaring, Sir Anthony van Dyck, c. 1636, Birmingham Museums Trust / Lady Juliet Tadgell (via Wikimedia).
15. John Pym, Edward Bower, c. 1644, Blickling Hall / National Trust Collections (via Wikimedia).
16. William Lenthall, Cornelius Johnson, seventeenth century, Palace of Westminster (via Wikimedia).
17. George, Lord Digby and William Russell, later 5th Earl of Bedford, also known as 'War and Peace', Sir Anthony van Dyck, 1637, Althorp House (by permission of Earl Spencer).
18. Charles I, Daniel Mytens, 1628, Palace of Holyroodhouse (via Wikimedia).
19. Robert Devereux, 3rd Earl of Essex, William Faithorne the Elder, 1643, National Portrait Gallery (via Wikimedia).
20. Prince Rupert of the Rhine and Officers, William Dobson, c. 1644, Ashdown House / National Trust Collections (via Wikimedia).
21. Sir John Byron, William Dobson, before 1646, Tabley House / University of Manchester Collections (via Wikimedia).
22. Sir Edmund Verney, after van Dyck, c. 1640, lent by a private collection, National Portrait Gallery (by permission of the National Portrait Gallery).
23. Charles II as Prince of Wales, William Dobson, 1642, Scottish National Gallery (via Wikimedia).
24. Sir Edward Hyde, William Dobson, c. 1643, private collection, formerly Weiss Gallery (via Wikimedia).
25. Bulstrode Whitelocke, unknown artist, c. 1650, National Portrait Gallery (via Wikimedia).
26. Algernon Percy, 10th Earl of Northumberland, as Lord Admiral, after van Dyck, 1640, private collection, formerly Sotheby's (via Wikimedia).
27. Dorothy, Lady Spencer (later Countess of Sunderland), Sir Anthony van Dyck, c. 1639, Petworth House (by permission of Lord Egremont).

28. Lucy, Countess of Carlisle, Sir Anthony van Dyck, *c*. 1635–7, Petworth House (by permission of Lord Egremont).
29. Sir Henry Vane the Younger, Gerard Soest, *c*. 1655, Dulwich Picture Gallery (via Wikimedia).
30. St Michael's and All Angels parish church, Great Tew, photographed by Bill Boaden, 2015 (via Wikimedia).

*Endpapers*: engraving depicting the armies of King Charles I and Sir Thomas Fairfax exhibiting the exact order, preparatory to the Battle of Naseby, 1645 (Copyright © National Army Museum / Bridgeman Images).

# Historical Background

Bulstrode Whitelocke and Edward (Ned) Hyde, the two principal subjects of this book, were both born after the accession, in 1603, of King James VI of Scotland to the English and Irish thrones as James I. They grew up in a country that had consumed the formative legends of the Elizabethan age, tales of Gloriana, the Faerie Queene who had conquered the Armada, seemingly beyond the point of surfeit. To the uncertainty of an all too uneternal Virgin Queen, self-evidently the last of her line, there succeeded a fecund royal family of indisputable, long-standing status, its male issue comparatively inexhaustible. Dynastic insecurity was to give way to patriotic, political, and religious tensions, but, at the outset of Stuart rule in England, such conflicts did not pose inevitably insurmountable or decisive problems.

If James represented a return to the reassuringly traditional model of male royal succession, in religion he also perpetuated Queen Elizabeth's most stable and successful policy. The Elizabethan compromise of Protestant doctrine and conservative hierarchy suited him perfectly. Although the new King's aesthetic tastes were a little plainer than those of his predecessor and godmother, and his appetite for theological disputation considerably greater, James adopted the episcopal structure he had inherited with an enthusiasm that court-inclined families like the Hydes noted with relief. Rumours that his Catholic mother, Mary, Queen of Scots, or his Presbyterian upbringing might have tugged James to one extreme or the other on the religious spectrum proved ill-founded.

After the shock of the Gunpowder Plot attempted by Catholics against both King and Parliament in November 1605, the nation and monarch seemed bound together behind the Church of England's median settlement. The Whitelockes admittedly lay a degree outside this consensus, being broadly identifiable by the slippery term of 'Puritans', by no means joyless in their personal habits, but tending towards hotter Protestantism and lukewarm about the role of bishops in both church and state government. At the opposite pole of religious dissension, Captain Edmund Whitelocke, Bulstrode Whitelocke's turbulent uncle, managed to fall under suspicion of involvement in the Gunpowder Plot (he was indeed to be implicated in practically every conspiracy of note during his lifetime), only a few months after serving as a riotously voluble godfather to the young Bulstrode.

The new King's advantages as royal paterfamilias and moderate religious continuity candidate were offset both by his Scottish origins, and his irritation with the institution of the English Parliament, honed over the previous century as the preeminent instrument of Tudor royal governance. Bulstrode's father, James Whitelocke, and Ned Hyde's paternal uncles, Nicholas and Lawrence, all three ambitious and industrious lawyers, rose to distinction as MPs, with Nicholas Hyde initially, James Whitelocke persistently, in opposition to the court.

The dazzling career of George Villiers, later Duke of Buckingham, from 1614 increasingly dominated King James's patronage, policy, and popular image. The Hydes, among many other courtly families such as the Carys, soon Viscounts Falkland, partook of the bounty that flowed towards those willing to serve the new favourite's interests alongside their own. James Whitelocke continued to criticize the court, and also Buckingham, as long as this was reconcilable with his own professional ascent, but eventually he allowed himself to be brought into the ever-extending Villiers clientele through his friends in Buckingham's following, men such as Humphrey May and William Laud.

Laud, like May, had been an Oxford contemporary and friend of James Whitelocke, and felt for him a warm regard that was returned not without reservation. Laud later extended this feeling, benign if at times overbearing, to James's son Bulstrode as an undergraduate and then a rising young lawyer; he was also to become Ned Hyde's most important early professional patron. At heart Laud was a bibliophile, politician, and aesthete rather than a theologian. For political and personal rather than doctrinal reasons, he veered away from the Church of England's existing Calvinism, with its beliefs in predestination, salvation by faith alone, rather than good works or ritual, reserved for a limited few (the 'elect'), and absolute identity of the Papacy with Antichrist.

Like many English prelates Laud was instead moving closer to the group of tenets that had in Holland acquired the name of 'Arminianism', including a greater role for free will, works, and sacraments. To its traditionally Calvinist, 'Puritan' opponents such thinking seemed tantamount to Catholic backsliding. But to Laud, to Buckingham, and to Prince Charles – King James's heir since the death of Charles's popular, conventionally and militantly Protestant elder brother Henry in 1612 – the home-grown English strand of 'Arminianism' represented instead the ideal architecture by which a strong Crown and dignified Church stood tall together. James himself veered between grandly pacific intellectual projects for the reunification of Christendom itself, or for the English Church to find allies as far afield as Venice or Greece, and caution about letting 'Arminian' churchmen appear too influential. While James ruled, Laud and those of his mind were to some extent leashed.

In 1619 both theological and political developments on the continent were to raise the religious temperature. At the Dutch Synod of Dordrecht, better known in English as Dort, Protestant clergymen from the Netherlands, Germany, Switzerland, England, and Scotland met to determine the validity of Arminianism and unanimously condemned it. But this granitic verdict concealed considerable dissent, including among the British contingents. One English cleric present, John Hales, later one of the eminent company of theologians to be found as guests at Lord Falkland's manor of Great Tew, and as such a revered friend of Ned Hyde, declared he 'bid John Calvin good-night' as a result of the Synod's extreme judgement.

Meanwhile in Germany, the Calvinist Elector Palatine, Frederick V, married to the Stuart princess Elizabeth (sister of Charles), a cynosure of poetic celebration and popular Protestantism as her deceased brother Henry had been, accepted the Crown of Bohemia from a Protestant faction of nobles, in defiance of the Catholic Habsburg candidate, Ferdinand, who had recently become Holy Roman Emperor. Frederick's unwarlike father-in-law James VI watched his daughter's elevation to so precarious a crown with alarm, and his characteristic timidity was soon to be vindicated by the overthrow of the 'Winter King and Queen' at the hands of invading Habsburg armies. Frederick soon lost not just his sudden kingdom but his hereditary patrimony of the Palatinate, and King James and his heir Charles would both henceforth be under immense patriotic and religious pressure to restore their exiled relatives to at least some territory by force or (the old King's preference) negotiation.

Prince Charles had once been hurt by his father's doting deferral to the favourite Buckingham, but Buckingham was too instinctive a courtier to let this feud last and managed to become all but as inseparable a friend to the heir as to the monarch. As King James devoted his waning powers to seemingly interminable negotiations with Habsburg Spain, essentially trying to gain both a Spanish bride for Charles and the Palatinate's return to the exiled Elector, Buckingham convinced Charles to burst the dam with an extraordinary diplomatic intervention, and the pair of them travelled to Madrid incognito. This escapade, which sabotaged James's peaceful policy beyond redemption, was also psychologically crucial in the formation of the future Charles I. The young prince, like Laud a natural, hierarchical aesthete, readily absorbed the Spanish Habsburg conceit of splendidly elevated monarchical dignity during the months he spent at Madrid, Toledo, and elsewhere in Spain.

In 1625 the old King at last died, amid hysterical rumours of poisoning by Buckingham with Prince Charles's connivance. Nevertheless, real power still lay with the irresistible Buckingham. Despite marrying in the year of his accession the young, passionate-tempered French princess Henrietta Maria, the new King Charles soon found himself at war with France and Spain. These Catholic realms, normally bitterly at odds with one another, were each alone considerably more powerful than the British kingdoms. Theoretically Charles waged war in the popular, martial Protestant interest; while Buckingham, now advanced to Lord Admiral, believed himself a hero destined to capture the nation's still elusive heart by way of victory.

But victory was to prove an equally elusive mistress. Parliaments raised early in the reign to secure funds for the prosecution of war increasingly proved more interested in bringing down the ever more hated Buckingham. At the brief, truculent Parliament of 1626, the now Sir James Whitelocke, Judge of the King's Bench, found a Commons seat for his son Bulstrode by the contrivance of his courtier friend, and Buckingham's ally, Sir Humphrey May. Yet the younger Whitelocke himself still gravitated as a green MP towards the movement for Buckingham's impeachment.

In the aftermath of Buckingham's utterly courageous yet lethally incompetent attempt to relieve besieged French Protestants at the Île de Ré off the Atlantic coast of France, young Ned Hyde remembered London as filled with dissolute, swaggering soldiers. Most veterans were seldom or never paid, and in 1628 one of them, a depressive wounded officer, John Felton, passed over for promotion and drawn to religious and political radicalism, at last ended Buckingham's 'reign' with a stab through the heart in a Portsmouth inn. Ned Hyde and Bulstrode Whitelocke, by now close friends and jocular sparring partners at the Inns of Court, expressed, respectively, courtly horror at and prevalent national sympathy for the deed.

For King Charles the loss of his best friend and chief minister was simultaneously a crippling sorrow and a fresh start. His so far jagged relations with his French consort changed rapidly into a deep love, through which Queen Henrietta Maria acquired access to profound influence (over the succeeding years she would consistently charm Whitelocke and infuriate Hyde). The King had had enough both of ill-starred wars and of the Parliaments that had so irregularly paid for them. From 1629 onwards he ruled peacefully, alone and, at last, to many if not all his subjects, with some aplomb.

Young Hyde and Whitelocke came to maturity amid a broad picture of national prosperity. In 1634, encouraged and probably selected by John Selden, the older lawyer and antiquary they both respected most, they helped to arrange *The Triumph of Peace*. This was a masque laid on by lawyers both old and young, oppositional and courtly, to express the loyalty and gratitude of the Inns of Court to King, Queen, and their pacific foreign policy alike. It also served to disassociate the entire legal profession from its most tactless son, the vehemently prolific pamphleteer William Prynne, who had recently implied that the Queen was a 'Notorious Whore' because of her fondness for amateur theatricals. Prynne had been prosecuted at Laud's urging through the Star Chamber, a court of appeal operating under the royal prerogative alone, on whose overmighty abuses Hyde, Whitelocke, and their friends among the young lawyers, whatever they thought of the obnoxious Prynne, were wont to compose satirical, probably beer-inflected orations.

By now Hyde was often to be found at Great Tew, the house of young Lord Falkland within convenient reach of Oxford, an intellectually eclectic, doctrinally ecumenical atmosphere where an affinity of bookish friends mingled, debated, and joked with light hearts, free consciences, but serious and idealistic intentions. Here divergent attitudes to the Church of England, to Laud, to the King's court and government, to Parliament, to power and to literature, were to be found and enjoyed in refreshing variety.

Falkland himself exemplified this group's complexity. He was politically sceptical of Laud's influence and of the reasserted lay powers of English bishops. He had developed from university Calvinism towards subtler, less combative Arminianism. The fanatical family decisions of his intellectually brilliant Catholic mother had dissolved his initially tolerant courtesy towards Catholicism. He disapproved strongly of the juridically obscure means by which the King raised money without Parliament's consent, especially Ship Money, the extra-parliamentary levy controversially extended by Charles from coastal regions to the whole country. Yet Falkland remained fundamentally, fatefully loyal to the Crown.

Although Hyde had connections at court through two marriages and both he and Whitelocke had achieved success in their profession, they chafed, like Falkland and so many other Englishmen of birth, means, and talent, at their continuing exclusion from the share in their country's counsels that their fathers and uncles had long possessed. Whitelocke and Hyde were both personally well-disposed towards Laud, one of Charles's dominant counsellors and since 1633 Archbishop of Canterbury, but they also knew his faults as a man and politician better than most. For other leading royal ministers, especially Thomas, Lord Wentworth, a bitter enemy of Buckingham whose hard-line, 'Thorough' competence by now made him most plausible as the slain favourite's successor, these friends' attitudes veered between hostile respect and personal loathing.

The chance for the younger generation to enter history proper came with the rebellion in Scotland, from 1637, against the Anglicized Prayer Book, in greater uniformity with the Church of England, imposed north of the border at Laud's urging. Neither Hyde, Whitelocke nor Falkland actually sympathized with the Scots rebels, to Whitelocke 'a foreign nation' in rebellion against their natural prince; Falkland went so far as to volunteer to fight under the Earl of Essex against the Scots. But many English peers were in fact in secret communication with the Scots 'Covenanters' (so-called for the National Covenant they had sworn to uphold a Presbyterian Scots Kirk), regarding them as politically and religiously more sympathetic than an exclusive, Arminian, Catholic-tinged royal court.

After the poor performance of the royal army raised against the Scots without parliamentary assent or funds in the First Bishops' War of 1639, which retreated without daring to engage the enemy, the King was left with no choice but to summon Parliament for the first time since 1629. Hyde obtained election to the body that assembled in April 1640, and regarded its swift dissolution – it would become known as the Short Parliament, especially by contrast to its epochal twenty-year-long successor – as a tragically squandered opportunity for governmental cooperation. The summer brought an even more humiliating defeat by the Covenanters, with a Scots army invading England and occupying Newcastle. Hyde and (after an electoral squabble) Whitelocke sat in the second, December, Parliament of 1640, the future Long Parliament.

## Historical Background

This new Parliament was dominated by the verbosely managerial John Pym. Pym, like his immensely rich and ambitious patron, the Earl of Bedford, regarded the Scots not principally as enemies, invaders, or rebels but as pragmatic and religious allies whose armed presence at Newcastle was useful, indeed essential, for putting pressure on the King. Hyde, Whitelocke, and Falkland initially accepted Pym's seniority and his extensive reforming programme, especially his determination to bring down Thomas Wentworth, lately made Earl of Strafford, now the King's paramount minister after returning from a controversial but successful term as Lord Deputy of Ireland. Strafford had urged Parliament's recall but also tough handling of the Scots. Partly because of political antipathies that reached back to the sway of Buckingham, Whitelocke, Falkland, and Hyde all played more or less prominent roles, with differing degrees of regret, in Strafford's prosecution and eventual execution. The demise of Strafford in the State had its counterpart in the Church with the downfall of Archbishop Laud, though Laud was for the present only imprisoned.

In the first half of 1641 a number of political reforms favoured, at least at the time, by Whitelocke, Hyde and Falkland resulted. They included the abolition of several prerogative courts such as the Star Chamber; a bill to ensure Parliament could not be dissolved without its own consent; the condemnation of Ship Money; and the exile of ministers involved in Charles's Personal Rule. But a series of initiatives, to which Hyde was party, for the reformers themselves to become Charles's leading counsellors, broke down with the death of Pym's noble protector, the ambitious but tactful Bedford.

Moderate unanimity regarding reform began to wane over the question of Church government, with Hyde stalwart for the ancient historical lay rights of the bishops (with the support of his and Whitelocke's long-time intellectual mentor, John Selden), Whitelocke among many others working with Pym and his faction (soon known as 'the Junto') against the bishops, and Falkland wavering between the two sides. In this context the King, who in the summer of 1641 was about to depart to seek political support in the apparently unlikely turf of his native northern realm, reached out to Hyde and made a tentative beginning to what would become for both of them a life-defining alliance.

That autumn the stakes rose sharply with news of a fresh rebellion in Charles's third kingdom, Ireland. In the absence of Strafford's heavy but effectual hand as the former Lord Deputy there, Catholics in Ireland had decided to drive the sort of hard bargain so successfully practised by Scots Presbyterians. These new rebels could only be stopped by an army that, by ancient, definitive tradition and law, answered to the king. Pym and his allies, horrified by the idea of such an expedition in royal hands, exploited rumours that the Catholic rebels were secretly sanctioned by the Queen, the King, or both. The 'Junto' argued that this crisis warranted the transferral of the King's ability to appoint and control generals to the Lords and Commons, shepherded by itself.

In December 1641 emerged the decisive reckoning of the debate over the Grand Remonstrance, a bitter catalogue of grievances addressed by the Commons, under Pym's leadership, notionally to the King, but increasingly, in reality, to the wider country. Whitelocke, quite as much as Hyde and Falkland, recognized the Grand Remonstrance as an act of political sabotage, scuppering any potential cooperation between the court and Parliament – an indication of Pym and his allies' true intent no longer to counsel the King, but to take over his powers. Almost a whole night of rhetorical struggle ensued, at the end of which the party sympathetic to the King, of which Hyde had by now become the most crucial leader and organizer, lost by only eleven votes. But this was enough to set Parliament and country alike continuing on the way to irretrievable confrontation.

In the aftermath of the Remonstrance's narrow passage, the King took the leading moderates who had fought to block it, including Hyde and Falkland, into his inner circle, but almost simultaneously succumbed to counsel that his new moderate advisors wholly abhorred. On 4 January 1642 King Charles attempted to arrest Pym, four other anti-court MPs, and a 'popular' peer, in one of the violent-seeming but incompetently managed operations that were all too characteristic of the King's unsteady career. This overreach lost the King support in London, as it was to turn out permanently, and he retired initially to Hampton Court, in due course as far as York.

Nonetheless, Pym's case to supplant the King's lawful control over the realm's armed forces was no more watertight, however unpopular Charles had now made himself in the capital. At a crucial debate over the status of the militia in February, Hyde was one of the minority in the Commons to assert the King's rights, while Whitelocke delicately framed a more equivocal position. After the debate's conclusion Whitelocke courteously declined an invitation from Hyde and another court-inclined friend to leave the Commons for the King's side.

It took until May for Hyde to slip away, on a medical pretext, to the King's makeshift court. Whitelocke was in the meantime engaged in the drafting of the unyielding Nineteen Propositions, stripping the King of most of his prerogative powers. Internecine hostilities truly began in August, after a last-ditch appeal for peaceful accommodation by Whitelocke. While Hyde remained a civilian advisor, ultimately based in the King's longest-term alternative capital at Oxford, Whitelocke, still an MP at Westminster, found time to 'trail a pike', raise troops, kidnap one Royalist notable, and offer to his cause his copious opinions on law, diplomacy, strategy, and theology.

In October 1642 a surprisingly numerous and well-led Royalist army confronted Parliament's scarcely superior forces at the Battle of Edgehill in southern Warwickshire, the only field of the war to be witnessed in person by Hyde. An apparently decisive royal victory was flung away partly by Prince Rupert, the exiled younger son of Elizabeth, Queen of Bohemia and so the King's nephew, of whose haughty, hot-headed aggression Hyde and Falkland greatly disapproved. An advance on London urged by Rupert but opposed by Hyde followed, in the course of which Whitelocke's estates near Henley were despoiled with cruel specificity by the Prince's cavalry.

Rupert's subsequent sack of Brentford and the retirement of the King's army from Turnham Green were to reveal, as Hyde had feared, that the Royalists had the strength to panic and further alienate London, but not to conquer it.

The following year of 1643 at first brought a gradually improving situation for the King, and correspondingly serious attempts by Parliament to treat for peace. As a result Whitelocke, dispatched by Parliament as one of the moderately inclined members both best suited and most eager to undertake peace negotiations, encountered his old friend Hyde once more, soon to be elevated as Sir Edward Hyde, Chancellor of the Exchequer.

Overlapping with such official overtures was a more discreet and mysterious set of Royalist intrigues based on winning back majority opinion in London. After the failure and exposure of these schemes they would be dubbed Waller's Plot, after Edmund Waller, the deep-pocketed poet who incompetently steered some of them. Waller had been one of the friends assembled at Great Tew and was operating with the knowledge and cautious support of his former host Falkland, now the King's Secretary of State.

After neither diplomacy nor subterfuge succeeded in curtailing the war, the Royalists began, after a high summer when Prince Rupert took Bristol, to lose momentum. Their siege of Gloucester was an ill-chosen, mishandled failure for which Falkland bore some blame and felt much guilt. Royalist attempts also overseen by Falkland to keep the Scots neutral gradually, inexorably failed, while the understanding that the King reached with the Irish rebels, privately deplored by Hyde, did more harm to his reputation than good to his armies. The English Civil War was on the point of becoming British when Falkland, who had long since become Hyde's moral and political ideal as well as his inseparable closest friend, fell at the Battle of Newbury in September. Falkland perished in a state of evident despair, leaving Whitelocke a ring in his will, eulogized and lamented by many of his moderate parliamentary opponents.

The war's intensification in 1644 saw the Royalists under Prince Rupert beaten in July at Marston Moor in Yorkshire by an alliance of English Parliamentarians and Scots Covenanters, the battle at which Oliver Cromwell's legend and power together came into being. Yet that September the King partly made up for this by his conclusive defeat of the Earl of Essex at Lostwithiel, while at the same time Scots and Irish Royalists under the Marquess of Montrose were menacing the heartlands of Parliament's new Covenanter allies.

Parliament showed its teeth with the execution in January 1645 of Whitelocke and Hyde's former patron Archbishop Laud, but immediately afterwards it returned to the negotiating table at Uxbridge. Here both old friends united for one final, weary, jaundiced and desperate but genuine effort to achieve a peace against very long odds. Three deputations, Royalist, Parliamentarian, and Covenanter, attended, and despite several obviously incompatible interests, all showed genuine desire to achieve breakthroughs on the major subjects of religion, the militia, and Ireland. But no amount of willingness by those involved in the Treaty of Uxbridge could alter the fundamental irreconcilability of their political masters.


This is the story of how two close friends, themselves divided by few if any serious differences of political opinion, united both by generous measures of idealistic vision for their country's better governance and reasonable ambition for their own personal distinction, inadvertently contributed to their country's division, and gave their all, in vain, to calm the ensuing turmoil.

Whitelocke and Hyde's joint, industrious, conscientious human failure in 1640–45 forms only the first part of the wider historical saga that led approximately to the institutions that still govern Britain. Whitelocke at the elbow of Cromwell, and then Hyde, by then Earl of Clarendon, beside Charles II, would take their turns again to bequeath to their country a workable political settlement, in days of greater power, grandeur, experience, and influence. On their second, mature failures would be built the eventually long-lasting, if not always edifying, monument of 1688, namely parliamentary sovereignty patchily gilded by constitutional monarchy.

## Historical Background

But this book concerns an earlier, more sombre and, I believe, less familiar story: how Whitelocke and Hyde came to be, from their early youth in 1628, united by their friends and ideals, part of a consistent group of 'liberal-minded' and 'sober men', thinking and acting very largely in harmony as rising statesmen; yet how, entirely against their wills, they were, with their England, wrenched apart. In these friends' instinctive likeness, and their gradual, reluctant estrangement, is to be found a tragedy as revealing of their times as sadly instructive to ours.

# On Texts, Dates, and Names

## The 'Diary' and 'Memorials' of Bulstrode Whitelocke

Bulstrode Whitelocke's journal, or 'Diary' as its rediscoverer and editor Ruth Spalding chose to call it, was commenced after the Restoration (and Whitelocke's involuntary retirement from public affairs) in 1660, and continued until his death in July 1675. Its narrative of the decades preceding its writing are thus largely, but not entirely, a retrospective reconstruction; it clearly, at times explicitly, incorporates notes and letters that were written either prior to or during the civil war. The *Diary*'s intended audience is stated to be Whitelocke's many children, continuing and elaborating the family tradition set by his father Sir James Whitelocke's *Liber Famelicus*, though the reader will often feel that the 'diarist' cannot help soliciting the longer-term attention of posterity.

These writings were, however, first published in 1681 as the *Memorials of the English Affairs*, only six years after their author's death, extensively edited by (or at the behest of) the Anglo-Irish politician Arthur Annesley, Earl of Anglesey. Compared to the manuscript unearthed centuries later by Spalding, the *Memorials* reveal a smoother style and an increased tendency towards political moderation. The versions differ as to detail, each at different points providing more meat and salt than the other. Even before being compared to the more unspun-seeming *Diary*, the *Memorials* have generally received a mixed press from historians, who tend to discern in them more of their editor's accommodations than their author's experience. However, Anglesey's career, ideals, and character had much in common with those of Whitelocke, for whom in his preface he expresses wholehearted admiration. The extent of Whitelocke's own involvement in, or nature of his attitude to, preparing his account for publication before his death, is neither known nor recoverable. I find value in both the *Diary* and the *Memorials*, and do not discount the possibility that the more nuanced opinions of the latter reflect authorial development as probably as politically motivated interference.

Whitelocke would be knighted in 1656 by Oliver Cromwell as Lord Protector, then in 1658 briefly dispatched as Lord Whitelocke to Cromwell's Other House, but neither elevation concerns our story or complicates the writer's nomenclature.

## *The 'History' and 'Life' of Edward Hyde, Earl of Clarendon*

The historical writings of Edward Hyde, later Earl of Clarendon, are more copious, more renowned, and greatly more historiographically complicated than those of his friend. Like Whitelocke, Hyde was a prodigious amateur devotee of history in early youth, though his ambitions as an author were also more literary and poetic. Whitelocke as a young man dabbled in historical writing (and musical composition) for pleasure, but acknowledged no public or private work. Hyde, by contrast, wrote a comparison between Robert Devereux, Earl of Essex, and George Villiers, Duke of Buckingham, scarcely a year after the duke's murder in 1628, and at the time of Hyde's own marriage into the Villiers family, and his description passed from hand to hand at court until it reached the notice of Charles I himself.

Hyde's older friend Ben Jonson was right, if resentful, in noticing the young man's distraction from his considerable literary potential by his profession, the law, and the ensuing 'business' of politics. It was only after the serious reversal in the first English Civil War to the cause Hyde had reluctantly but, eventually, fully embraced – in 1646, after all the events of this book – that he found the time and the will to concentrate on beginning his *History of the Rebellion* in earnest. Although the (much later) published text claims to have been begun in 1640 and evidently draws upon even earlier material, such as the Buckingham essay, the first part of the *History*, which ends with the events of March 1644, is fundamentally a creation of Hyde's years in political exile on Jersey in 1646–8. The *History* was at this point, at least theoretically, written primarily for the eyes and counsel of Charles I, defeated, imprisoned, but still alive, often defiant, and by no means altogether despairing. Hyde courteously analyzes the past mistakes of the King and his advisors, and warns him against possible future ones, whether failure to compromise or concessions in the wrong direction.

Called back to politics by the executed king's son Charles II, Hyde would return to his historical vocation almost exactly two decades later, after undergoing extremes of fortune unusual even by the standards of the mid-seventeenth century. As Lord Chancellor in exile, Hyde oversaw the exiled young king's policy, political education, and spy network, from 1651 until the Restoration of 1660. After in large part engineering his royal charge's astonishingly seamless return to power that year, Hyde became the restored monarchy's de facto prime minister. Shortly afterwards he found himself the unwilling father-in-law of the Duke of York and heir presumptive to boot, a dubious honour that also resulted in Hyde's 1661 elevation as Earl of Clarendon. In 1667 Clarendon's enemies succeeded in scapegoating him for the government's failures in peace and war, and Charles II, with singular but characteristic ingratitude, contentedly acquiesced in his mentor and minister's banishment, one that would turn out to be permanent. Exiled in France, tormented by gout, Clarendon took up his pen again, now writing from a more personal and intimate perspective, without the aid of state papers or the remniscences of friendly fellow counsellors and talkative soldiers in defeat. The resulting *Life* occupied him between 1668 and 1670. From 1671 until his death three years later he resumed the *History* from 1644 onwards, uneasily fitting the *Life* within it.

Unlike Whitelocke, Clarendon in his second exile self-confessedly wrote for a reading public in some unknown future, deliberating carefully over what to include and what to omit. But like his former friend, he would not live to oversee his work's publication, undertaken by his younger son, the gifted and opportunistic Tory politician Lawrence Hyde, Earl of Rochester. The *History*, encompassing the *Life*, first emerged in two volumes during 1702–3, in the reign of Clarendon's granddaughter Queen Anne, as part of a party-political paper war between Whigs and Tories. Whitelocke's *Memorials* were frequently cited on the contrary side, further occluding the considerable common ground the two erstwhile friends had in fact shared.

Hyde composed the first part of the *History* on Jersey as Sir Edward Hyde, but all the rest as Earl of Clarendon, his title after 1661, and his historical writing was published under this later style. I have called him 'Clarendon' when referring to later historical writing, thinking it useful to keep his prevalent post-Restoration point of view in mind.

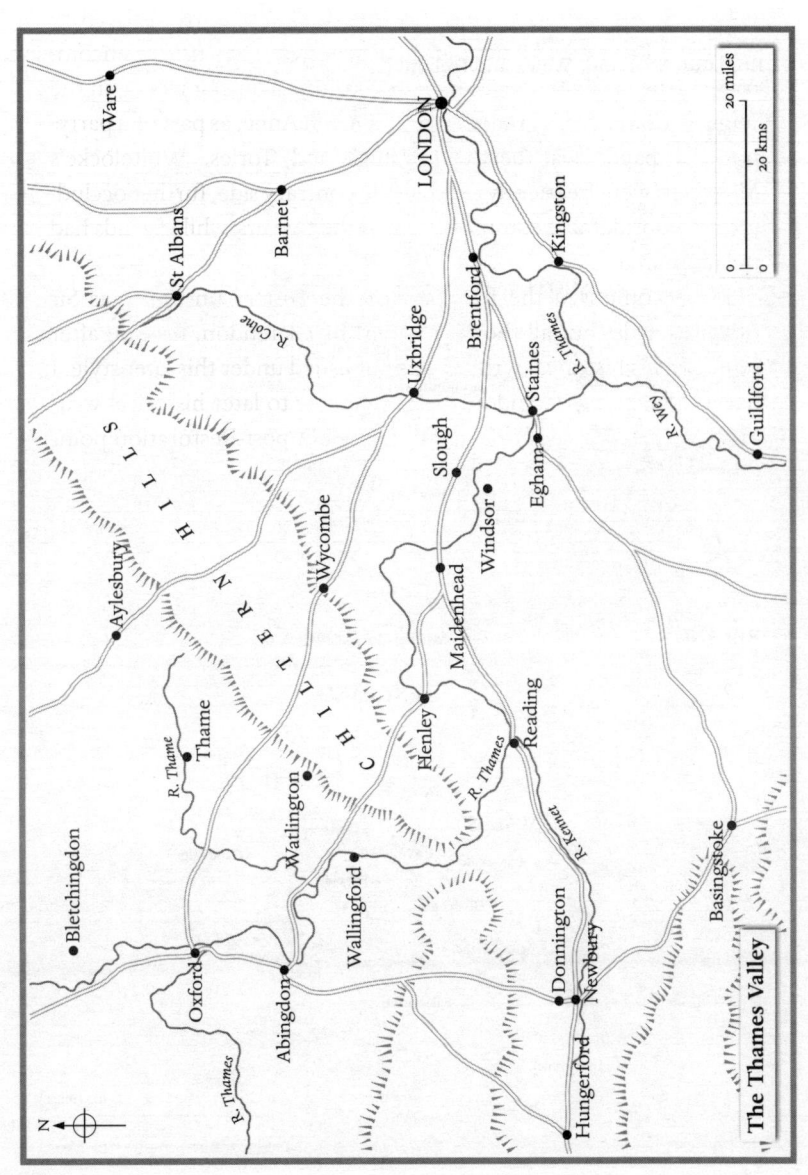

# Prelude: The Pit's Brink

*If all men, by thy great Example lead,*
*Would that prepared way to Vertue tread . . .*

George Sandys, 'A Panegyrick to the King',
*Ovids Metamorphosis Englished*, 1640

## In Pursuit of 'Purer Air': Near Ditchley, Oxfordshire, May 1642*

The traveller from London now sticking to the obscurer county byways scarcely gave the impression of being a desperate cavalier, or even a particularly practised horseman. He was still in his early thirties, but his carefully composed dignity and stubborn paunch already gave him an older, statelier appearance. Both his unflustered bearing and his costume, sober but well-made and presentable, the dark garb of an industrious lawyer, expressed his adequate means. His eyes, bulging from a precociously crimson face, were often bright by nature whether with amusement or impatience, but now he appeared to have them mastered, dulled, sealed away from undue attention. Only his voice was impossible to dress down with any such assumed modesty. It was the one extravagant thing about him, melodious in timbre, courteous on the whole, argumentative when necessary, but always innately persuasive.

A cynical, reasonably well-informed observer might have taken this slightly comical-looking fellow for a sensible man clearing out of the capital, seeking refuge ahead of the foreboding rumour of civil war. But there were those in Oxfordshire, and especially in the

---

* All dates will, for simplicity's sake, be rendered in New rather than Old Style.

university city, who could have guessed at the much more dramatic narrative urging on such an apparently respectable figure. For this prosperous gentleman was Edward Hyde, familiarly known as Ned; the offshoot of a distinguished legal dynasty, himself a highly successful Middle Temple barrister, and Member of Parliament for the far-off Cornish town of Saltash (a seat bestowed upon Hyde by his original political patron the Earl of Pembroke, to which he had no personal connection). Hyde's present journey was, in fact, a risky adventure, and one that marked a point of no return.

Hyde had told the Speaker of the House of Commons, his old acquaintance William Lenthall, that his journey was necessitated by urgent medical advice. The renowned physician Dr Thomas Winston had recommended that the overworked member for Saltash, troubled by a gallstone, should take a country rest-cure at Purton, the modest Wiltshire estate Hyde had inherited from his father. Speaker Lenthall, a very rich, temperamentally prudent lawyer, had recently become a national hero by his refusal to deliver up five rebellious members of the House of Commons to the ire of their vengeful king, Charles I. Lenthall, not in fact himself a fervid political idealist, had probably not interrogated Mr Hyde's excuses in an especially sceptical spirit. Just as the Speaker had shielded John Pym, John Hampden, Denzil Holles, Arthur Haselrig, and William Strode from King Charles in January, so he now quite as easily condoned Hyde's evasion, in turn, of the by now ascendant Pym and company. Hyde, who had once counted among Pym's most active and articulate younger supporters, had become his faction's enemy and, increasingly, its target. Lenthall probably assumed, with both humane relief and political satisfaction, that Hyde was now prudently, with any luck permanently, withdrawing from the national stage.\*

Hyde's journey took him ten miles north of Lenthall's own

---

\* Dr Winston's covering testimony would have greatly assisted this impression. This well-to-do physician excelled in assuring all his most prominent patients that he shared their political sympathies, and so had a good enough reputation with Parliament.

## Prelude: The Pit's Brink

Oxfordshire estate at Burford, purchased almost a decade previously from a much closer personal and political friend of Hyde's. This was Sir Lucius Cary, 2nd Viscount Falkland, since that January one of the King's Secretaries of State. The complexities of Stuart politics had made Falkland, born at Burford into a West Country courtly family, a Dublin graduate, a Scots peer, and an English MP. Like his friend Hyde, Falkland occupied a pocket borough. Saltash had been presented to Hyde by the powerful, equivocal Earl of Pembroke, while Falkland's seat, Newport on the Isle of Wight, was arranged at the behest of the Earl of Portland, a personally proud, politically cautious Catholic sympathizer. Both royal office and parliamentary business detained Falkland for the present in London.* Since Burford's sale to Lenthall, Falkland's remaining Oxfordshire manor was Great Tew, even closer to Hyde's immediate destination. There, Falkland, Hyde, and other like-minded friends – two of them about to prove instrumental to the officially ailing Hyde's true mission – had passed their happiest, most rewarding years, in sympathetic, scholarly tranquillity. In the words of the learned gossip, John Aubrey, the company at Great Tew had constituted 'all the excellent of that peaceable time'. Hyde himself would later liken the atmosphere of this interlude, one of both essential formative importance and lasting, sustaining pleasure, to that of 'a college situated in a purer air'.

Earlier in Hyde's journey from London, he had passed by Henley-on-Thames, where the principal property holder, another lawyer

---

\* The Secretary of State held a prestigious, powerful, and difficult position, running the King's diplomatic correspondence, advising his foreign policy, and superintending the government's intelligence. The remote ancestor of the modern Foreign Secretary, the role had evolved under Henry VIII in various masterful and opportunistic hands, in particular those of Thomas Cromwell. It had increasingly become considered a place that required two colleagues. Falkland had accepted this demanding honour in the first days of 1642, very much at his friend Hyde's insistence. He succeeded Sir Harry Vane the elder, whom the King had (with good reason) come to distrust to the point of loathing. Falkland's senior colleague, Sir Edward Nicholas, was an old family friend of the Hydes.

MP, was an older friend even than Falkland. This was Bulstrode Whitelocke, whom Hyde had lately urged to take a similar path. Whitelocke instead stayed in Parliamentarian London, and would soon prove a loyal and diligent representative of its cause, yet this decision would not, now or for several war-torn years to come, put him personally at odds with his old friend.

Bulstrode Whitelocke and Ned Hyde were steadfast companions, who had already stood by one another in law and love, in sociable, aesthetic, marital, and political concerns. Nonetheless they were now fixed – more irreversibly than either would, for some years, wholly accept – on not merely divergent, but directly opposed courses. Neither man had, as yet, profoundly changed; both continued to believe in many of the same ideals, to desire similar outcomes, through much of the eventful period to follow. Whitelocke had entered politics in earnest with Hyde's explicit encouragement and assistance. These two talented, ambitious, conscientious lawyers had in common friends, patrons, tastes, and inclinations, all acquired during the peaceful years of their youth and early maturity. Whitelocke and Hyde had benefited from the eerie calm of the eleven years (1629–40) when Charles I ruled without Parliament, while keeping their eyes candidly open to defects in the Crown and the Church's government that they had hoped, in vain, together to reform. Despite their complete lack of antagonism, for all their continuing private friendship, they were now fated to contest the consequences of such failures.

## 'Arcanum Imperii': *Westminster, February/March 1642*

Since the previous autumn, the already quarrelsome House of Commons had been confronted with a fresh emergency: the rising of Ireland in armed, bloody rebellion. The facts of the crisis were grim enough, the stories it fomented even, and ever, wilder. The leaders of the parliamentary opposition to the court of Charles I, King of England, Scotland, and Ireland, now had all too much to lose or gain. Their sincerely felt horror of the Irish rebels, religiously and racially inflected, combined with their solemn awareness of the opportunity before them. Although the House was genuinely united in its desire to address the crisis, the question of that resolution's shape soon proved to be extremely divisive.

The Irish revolt had rapidly accumulated a momentum that could be arrested only by countervailing force. A fresh English army needed to be raised, paid for, and commanded. The right to raise forces belonged by tradition to the King, to the extent that it all but defined his office. But Parliament was increasingly certain it had permanently wrested from royal control the right to raise money to pay for war. The question of leadership was the most opaque, and urgent, of all. The King had briefly advanced the startling suggestion that he himself should lead the Irish expedition; one of many manoeuvres towards his real objective, appointing commanders of his own choosing. But the leaders of the prevailing majority in the House of Commons were still more determined to pick their own nominees in control of any army – regardless of the infringement of anciently established law and custom that this entailed.

Since the reign of England's firmly Protestant boy-king, Edward VI, almost a century earlier, the Commons had been permitted to meet in St Stephen's Chapel within the Palace of Westminster. This cramped precinct made the endemic absenteeism among members something of a necessity for the smooth running of normal business. Only the Speaker, the clerk, and his assistant could be guaranteed physical seats. While the rest of the members jostled for places in the chapel's pews, those who had already gained a name for themselves (or been born to one) had better chances of securing a suitable perch from which to catch the Speaker's glance. The 'House' of Commons was not really a building at all, but a political conceit: its unity both essential to and definitive of its proper function.

The generally accepted master of the Commons, by virtue of his long parliamentary experience and instinct for political procedure, was John Pym. Pym, a Somerset minor gentleman and former

Exchequer official on the cusp of old age, possessed a prodigious capacity for industry, and useful familial and professional connections besides, which just about counteracted his alarming debts and lack of finesse. In the House, Pym spoke with unrivalled passion and stamina, but could not lay claim either to a euphonious style or invariably consistent reasoning. In 1640, when Parliament was recalled after eleven years of rule by the King alone, Pym had instantly been recognized as the effective leader of the 'anticourt' party. He maintained this primacy with the invaluable support of his smoother, richer associate, John Hampden, and of Oliver St John, wiliest of the many lawyers among their adherents. St John, showing remarkable and characteristic flexibility, had accepted office as the King's Solicitor-General in January 1641, and still purported to represent the true royal interest.

Ned Hyde had entered Parliament as one of Pym's most promising supporters, a personal friend of Hampden, and a connection by marriage of St John. But after a period of productive and significant collaboration with this dynamic troika, Hyde had become disenchanted by his associates' increasing radicalism. In midwinter 1641–2 he entered fully into the professional and personal orbit of the King. Both prudence and preference at first inclined Hyde to limit his activities to anonymous drafting on Charles's behalf, accompanied by backstage bargaining towards some kind of accommodation. In the debates over control of the militia, Hyde was far from the conspicuous oratorical standard-bearer he would later, in his subsequent role as a historian, claim to have been. During the most decisive debate on the militia question it was not Hyde but his old companion Whitelocke, the member for Great Marlow in Buckinghamshire, who came forward and dared to express an elegant, logical, and lasting solution to the deadlock.*

---

* Great Marlow, unlike Hyde's seat at Saltash and Falkland's at Newport, was by no means a pocket borough. Whitelocke had secured it by way of what was, for its time, an unusually democratic knife-edge tussle, in which, however, Hyde among others had played a discreet but decisive part.

*Prelude: The Pit's Brink*

Whitelocke presented a much more outwardly impressive carriage than the plump and sedentary Hyde. Four years his friend's senior, he looked rather younger, tall and slight, with striking black hair and a pale complexion, a fashionably pointed beard, a faint but intriguing scar near his mouth, and the sort of immaculately tailored, Frenchified black garments whose glistening sobriety was intended to be noticed. He walked with a slight limp, and as a result did not generally dance. Following the chase on foot in his Oxford days – the undergraduate Whitelocke was as yet no affluent man about town – in the company of William Juxon, the kindliest and grandest of High Church dons, young Whitelocke had suffered a serious and permanent leg injury. Despite this setback, he grew up as game as ever for physical adventure, engaging in a couple of picturesque escapades assisting the elopements of his friends, then later his own, and at one point coming close to accepting a French cavalry commission. Women ranging from rural landladies to Queen Henrietta Maria herself found Whitelocke an interesting conversational prospect. Those men who thought his confidence tinged with pomposity sometimes teased him by implying he looked like a clergyman. A tactful man, Bulstrode Whitelocke generally chose not to take such sport amiss.

On this occasion Whitelocke began mellifluously, if a little ponderously, telling the House of Commons what they hardly needed to learn, that the matter under question was 'of the greatest concernment'. He widened his address to 'us all, and our posterity after us', displaying the instinct both of the lawyer he was and the memoirist he was to become. It was in deploring the expedient now before the House – while admitting its possible necessity – that Whitelocke's caution became touched with rhetorical fire:

> . . . I do heartily wish that this great word, this new word, the Militia, this hard word might never have come within these walls: But that this House may be as the Temple of Janus, ever shut against it . . .

According to legend, the temple to the two-faced god in the ancient forum at Rome had been raised by Numa Pompilius, the city's most pious king and lawgiver. The temple gates were open in times of war, shut during ever rarer spells of peace. The emperor Augustus boasted of having closed them three times. Whitelocke, in transferring the temple to London and the Commons, would have brought to mind two axiomatically peaceful periods in living memory, the whole reign of the late King James, and the controversial, but undeniably pacific, personal rule of his son Charles.

After a little legal badinage Whitelocke proceeded to the crux of his argument:

> I humbly apprehend that this power of the Militia, is neither in the King only, nor in the Parliament; and if the Law hath placed it anywhere, it is both in the King and Parliament, when they join together.

The matter, Whitelocke contended, was perhaps a fine, difficult, and puzzling one, but there were benefits to be drawn from its inexactly defined mystery:

> ... it is a wise Institution of our Law, not to settle this power anywhere ... that the People might be kept in ignorance thereof as a thing not fit to be known, not to be pried into. It is the great *Arcanum Imperii*, and the less it is meddled with, the less acquaintance we have with it, the better it will be for all sorts of persons, both for King and People.

Here Whitelocke spoke like the specifically English common lawyer he was, wedded to the ineffable, organic meandering of a system based upon precedent and adaptability. He displayed both his suspicion of the executive and his scepticism of rule by demagoguery, and suggested that the law's apparent lack of clarity protected monarch and populace both from one another and themselves.

Whitelocke went on to illustrate that not merely principles but practical considerations gave rise to his attitude:

> ... if the power of the Militia should be in the King, yet the power of money being in the Parliament, they must both agree, or else keep the sword in the scabbard, which is the best place for it. It is true, that the King by his tenures may require the service in war, of those that hold of him [i.e. the monarch's feudal inferiors, that is, all English, Scots, and Irish subjects]; but if they stay above forty days with him, unless he give them pay they will stay no longer.

Expressing his widely shared yearning for the preservation of peace, Whitelocke then demonstrated that his doctrine of royal and parliamentary cooperation made war a more distant prospect. He was not even quite willing to specify that King and Parliament acting together necessarily possessed the automatic legal right to command military force: 'neither in the King alone, nor in the Parliament: but *if anywhere* in the eye of our Law, it is in the King and Parliament both consenting together.'

Whitelocke's intervention was not quite as perfectly balanced as it was designed to appear. From his rich larder of legal examples, and historical or scriptural instances, he selected a pair – the Jewish Sanhedrin and the laws of King Edward III – that tended to undermine the royal as opposed to the parliamentary position. With a clear majority in the House, Pym's side was evidently, at last, about to prevail and seize control of the kingdom's military apparatus. Yet Whitelocke trained most of his fire on the large Royalist minority, which included many friends of his, Ned Hyde being the closest and most prominent. Nor was the application of Whitelocke's advice to the Irish situation particularly useful to the weary members; he spoke incidentally of the well-established right of local sheriffs to put down domestic disturbances – hardly sufficient to meet the demands of a rebellious island kingdom. His avowed solution was more of a polite request. He declined on this occasion to support Pym's Militia bill, instead suggesting:

> ... that we yet again should petition his Majesty, that the Militia may be settled in such hands as both he and you shall agree upon

whom you may trust; and who I hope will be more careful to keep it sheathed than to draw it.

The peripheral relationship of the actual Irish rising to Whitelocke's whole line of thought is revealing. Every man in the Commons and Lords by now knew that the militia question had widened to determine the lasting superiority in the government of England. Whitelocke was all too aware that both sides were now simply trying to grab whatever arms lay to hand. His real desire was to preserve some threadbare form of peace and collaboration, without drawing too much ire from the dominant Pym faction that he sought to moderate from within.

Ned Hyde might have disagreed with certain points of theory here advanced by Whitelocke. He would soon state in private and in published writing his own preferred, more traditional model of the 'mixed monarchy', with the King as head of the body politic, ruling in concert with Parliament, but undoubtedly its superior. But between the political preferences of Whitelocke and those of Hyde's other closest friend, Falkland, there was not even this delicate distinction. Unquestionably Hyde, as much as Falkland, would have welcomed, even if he had not actually encouraged, Whitelocke's speech, and still entertained hopes that it might be the portent of a favourable settlement.

Such hopes were not to flourish. In the early days of March 1642, Pym's impatient House of Commons presented a new Militia Ordinance, taking hold of the right to raise troops. Hyde, along with Geoffrey Palmer – another old Middle Temple friend of his and Whitelocke's, renowned as a barrister for his courtly politesse, yet in the Commons a rowdier, more open, and resolute Royalist than even Hyde as yet chose to appear – determined to leave London as soon as the Ordinance had, inevitably, passed. Hyde and Palmer begged Whitelocke to accompany them, united as of old, in their youthful days as carefree students of the law. But their friend now claimed to be persuaded by 'the solemn protestations of the most powerful and active members' that Pym and his

## Prelude: The Pit's Brink

allies would only use their new power defensively, and that war upon the King by Parliament was still unthinkable. Although Whitelocke was to confess in his later writings that he was at this point 'not yet clear of this opinion', he had been particularly convinced by the support for the Militia Ordinance of the Lord Keeper, Edward Littleton, the senior legal authority in the country. Whitelocke consequently decided to vote, after all, in favour of the Ordinance.

Behind Whitelocke's invocation of Lord Keeper Littleton in his excuses to Hyde, there hung unspoken another name, not so exalted in the formal legal or political hierarchy of England, but far more honoured by the learned men of Europe. John Selden, lawyer, Parliamentarian, pioneering secular historian, and antiquary, had been the most important influence upon the young Whitelocke and Hyde, less as a legal or even literary authority than as both a family and a personal friend, a generous host, giver of wise counsel, arranger of influential meetings, and model of civilized conduct. Like Whitelocke, Selden had openly expressed his doubts about the Militia Ordinance; like Whitelocke, he would stay in London and offer Parliament carefully nuanced support. As a protégé of Selden, Hyde had become a fairly close friend of the Lord Keeper Littleton, another of Selden's powerful friends, of a similar age and approximate political position. By stoutly quoting Littleton to Hyde, Whitelocke was really reminding him of the painstakingly moderate policy of Selden. But even so old and close an associate as Whitelocke was not to guess that Hyde's own friendship with the Lord Keeper, like his bond to Falkland, and, increasingly, even to the King himself, would shortly assume an independent, momentous, and partisan form.

Whitelocke thus offered in answer to Hyde and Palmer, his dismayed Royalist friends, not just an appeal to political trust – none of these men were so naïve – nor to political hierarchy, for neither were they pure conformists; but to a personally rooted idealism, a continuing quest after peace, wisdom, and compromise within Parliament. Hyde, for one, now considered, with great regret, that this position was too optimistic. Besides, it was impossible for him personally to adopt it, since he was already too far committed to a riskier path. The choice for him now lay between danger allied to influence on the King, and danger in obscurity and finding himself alone.

Hyde also suspected that Whitelocke's fine reasoning was motivated by fear: for influence, safety, fortune, most of all for the large inherited Whitelocke estates near Henley, close to the capital and the centre of parliamentary power. Having already launched himself upon the highest and most secret intrigues in pursuit of the elusive moderate settlement that all his friends desired, Hyde might reasonably have felt some contempt for Whitelocke's graceful neutrality. But then, again, his own, smaller Wiltshire patrimony was more distant, safer in the predominantly Royalist west.

Like the friends' common mentor Selden, Whitelocke still enjoyed continuing credit with both sides. When forced to make a definitive choice, he understandably, and in the main sincerely, held to the safer path. His reward, had he gone along with Hyde and Palmer, might at this point have been more immediately spectacular. Although a natural courtier, he would have been a surprising as well as an eloquent recruit for the King's party. But in resisting whatever lure of ambition or appeal to friendship he may have felt, Whitelocke committed himself to a career path that would prove for almost two decades to be more stable and powerful than those of his old associates.

Whatever disappointment they felt or expressed, the Royalist lawyers parted from Whitelocke as still avowed friends. Whitelocke remained on such intimate terms with Palmer that they were soon, in defiance of open civil war, living together as fellow tenants of a handsome and convenient town house. But, after Hyde contrived to leave London in May, it would be eight months before he and Whitelocke met again, both by then committed to opposing sides, Whitelocke as a Parliamentarian Peace Commissioner and Hyde as a Royalist counsellor.

## Prelude: The Pit's Brink

### *'Time too swift'*: Ditchley to Nostell, May 1642

After a fleeting stop at Oxford to conspire with Gilbert Sheldon, Warden of All Souls, his closest friend among the dons and another intimate of Great Tew, Ned Hyde headed for the manor of Ditchley, his next breathing-space on his way to his true destination: King Charles's makeshift court at York. His route was, contrary to his excuse to William Lenthall, by this point all too obviously northern rather than western, should it be discerned by unfriendly observers. Ditchley was a less obvious refuge than, for instance, Great Tew itself, where Hyde's presence if noted could have caused complications for its owner Falkland, who was obliged to remain for now in London.

The recently widowed Lady Lee, chatelaine of Ditchley, had been born Anne St John. She was a cousin of Oliver St John, the King's unfaithful Solicitor, Pym's legal left-hand man. The house was thus on the face of it an unlikely stopping point for a runaway Royalist MP. But Lady Lee was also a relative of Hyde's own deceased first wife, another Anne (née Ayliffe). That match had been suitable, impassioned, and brief; cut short by the pregnant Anne Hyde's death from smallpox after six months of happy marriage. Hyde had mourned his first wife conspicuously and, even after his remarriage, remained devoted to her family. His and Falkland's trust in the connection was now wholehearted.

Unlike his friend Whitelocke, Hyde was not particularly musical, but as he neared the great Elizabethan manor house of Ditchley, even he might have remembered the words of an old song by a hack poet, set to John Dowland's lute music:

> *His golden locks Time hath to silver turn'd;*
> *O Time too swift, O swiftness never ceasing!*
> *His youth 'gainst time and age hath ever spurn'd,*
> *But spurn'd in vain; youth waneth by increasing:*
> *Beauty, strength, youth, are flowers but fading seen;*
> *Duty, faith, love, are roots, and ever green.*

*Friends in Youth*

For Ditchley, as much as anywhere in England, encapsulated the nostalgic memory of Queen Elizabeth's reign; a memory of whose legend Hyde was personally somewhat sceptical, but whose continuing appeal to most of his countrymen he recognized. While Burford and Great Tew, to either side of Ditchley, had in the old Queen's day been subject to the exacting proprietorship of Falkland's widely hated Tanfield grandparents, Ditchley itself had been built by a glamorous and popular landlord. Sir Henry Lee had held the ceremonial, chivalric post of Queen's Champion. At Ditchley, Lee had once entertained the Queen (twice, he had complained, would have altogether worn out his resources), lived in sin with one of her court ladies, and commissioned one of Gloriana's most famous portraits. *'His golden locks'* had been scribbled to commemorate the Champion's retirement from the tourney lists. It was this Sir Henry's namesake, cousin, and heir whose widow now, with whatever trepidation, gave Ned Hyde shelter.

Lady Lee was a woman whose high intelligence, firm religious principles, and formidable character would become more conspicuous later in the century, in her dealings with her youngest child, the libertine poet Lord Rochester. Her marriage to Rochester's boozily gallant father, Henry Wilmot, still lay in that unknown, martial future soon to descend upon her, Hyde, and everyone else in the three Stuart kingdoms. In both religion and in politics Lady Lee closely fitted the widespread label of 'Puritan', arguably nearer in sympathy to, for example, Bulstrode Whitelocke than to his friend, her sudden guest, Ned Hyde. Lady Lee's 'Puritanism', or 'high Calvinism', was, in fact, the traditional position of the Elizabethan aristocracy: sceptical about royal prerogative power and bishops who presumed to meddle in politics. But she did her duty towards Hyde. After a few days spent successfully lying low, while usefully employed in drafting royal negotiations with Parliament, Hyde was tracked to her house not by any hostile authority, but two reliable friends.

The first of these confidential visitors to the leisurely Oxfordshire fugitive came at Hyde's own request, and Falkland's command. *Pace* his medical account to Lenthall, it was a doctor of theology whom

## Prelude: The Pit's Brink

Hyde had summoned to his side. Dr William Chillingworth, another bookish equestrian, galloped over to Ditchley from Trinity College, Oxford. He was a small man of intoxicatingly rapid speech, his eyes unsteadily gleaming, destined to enter the gallery of Hyde's most vital and evocative pen-portraits:

> ... a man of so great a subtlety of understanding ... so rare a temper in debate, that, as it was impossible to provoke him into any passion, so it was very difficult to keep ... from being a little discomposed by his sharpness and quickness of argument ...
>
> Such a levity, and propensity to change, is commonly attended with great infirmities ... but the sincerity of his heart was so conspicuous, and without the least temptation of any corrupt end ... that all who knew him clearly discerned, that all those restless motions and fluctuations proceeded only from the warmth and jealousy of his own thoughts ...
>
> ... all his doubts grew out of himself, when he assisted his scruples with all the strength of his own reason, and was then too hard for himself ...
>
> ... a man of excellent parts ... of a cheerful disposition ... of a very public heart, and an indefatigable desire to do good; his only unhappiness proceeded from his sleeping too little, and thinking too much; which sometimes threw him into violent fevers.

Chillingworth was generally a man more likely to be called upon for intellectual than practical assistance. His unorthodox brilliance had led him into perilous, and ludicrous, scrapes before and would do so again. But it had occurred to both Hyde and Falkland that Chillingworth was the right man for the present difficulty. Like his godfather, William Laud, Archbishop of Canterbury, Chillingworth came from a huge family of well-to-do provincial drapers and farmers. Ties of blood, of collegiate and clerical life lent him access to safe houses from Oxford 'almost as far as Yorkshire'.

What Lady Lee made of Chillingworth, whose theoretical and experimental boldness of mind – as convinced of the absolute power of princes as of the free will of human souls – represented the antithesis of her own cast-iron country outlook, is sadly unrecorded. Before too long, urgent news followed the doctor to Ditchley, brought by a second close friend. Of John Ayliffe little is known except that Hyde 'dearly loved' him, which are not much-lavished words in Hyde's huge corpus of memoir. Ayliffe may not have been identical with Hyde's brother-in-law of the same name, but he was surely in some way related to the first Mrs Hyde, and therefore also to Lady Lee. He brought a dire warning from Falkland and another of the Great Tew friends, Dr George Morley.

Dr Morley, though certainly no Puritan in the stereotypical, joy-averse sense, was, like Lady Lee, a conventionally pious Calvinist, Reformed, or 'hot' Protestant; committed to belief in double predestination, whereby the elect few are saved, and the rest damned, according to divine foreknowledge. He was at odds with Archbishop Laud and, more amiably, with many of his companions at Great Tew. Under Chillingworth's influence Falkland and his friends, including Hyde, were coming to look with favour on the Arminian doctrine, increasingly favoured at court, which placed more emphasis upon salvation by divine grace and human free will. As asserted by a somewhat younger contemporary, the ever-gossipy but often well-informed writer John Aubrey, Chillingworth became Falkland's 'most intimate and beloved favourite'. They were indeed sometimes labelled, usually by hostile Calvinists, as 'Socinians' (or even 'Pelagians'), rejecting the doctrines of original sin and the Trinity; and there would come to be a certain amount of truth in such rumours, since Chillingworth encouraged flexibility, adventurousness, reason, and speculation, above all in spiritual and philosophical matters.

But at this juncture Dr Morley's more run-of-the-mill reputation proved of great use to Falkland and Hyde. Confident of Morley's Calvinist credentials, 'a person of great authority in the Parliament' approached him as he loitered in Westminster on the lookout for news. This ally of Pym, assuming that the godly Dr Morley was a man of his own political outlook, hurriedly informed him that the Lord Keeper of the Great Seal – Lord Littleton, the de facto Lord

## Prelude: The Pit's Brink

Chancellor and highest legal office-holder in the land, the dignitary whose opinion in favour of the Militia Ordinance had formed Whitelocke's pretext for eventually supporting it – had just fled for the King's court at York. Worse still, Littleton had sent the Great Seal, required for the normal functioning of government and the law, ahead of him by royal messenger. Parliament quickly and correctly surmised that the person responsible for swaying the hitherto timid Lord Keeper Littleton was none other than the supposed convalescent, Ned Hyde. Although Littleton had proved so pliable an instrument of Pym in the contention over the militia, he was also known to have lately been much in the company of the absent member for Saltash. Hyde's leave of absence on medical advice now stood revealed, three days after his departure from the capital, as a blatantly political sleight of hand.

Pym and his supporters were accordingly determined upon a course they had increasingly desired, but for which they had until now lacked proper grounds – the prosecution of Hyde, their former associate now gone irredeemably renegade, for high treason. Dr Morley at once informed Falkland, then galvanized the swiftly mounted John Ayliffe to alert Hyde. Ayliffe carried a hasty letter from Falkland advising Hyde to make for the north immediately, and delivered it to Ditchley that same night, ahead of Parliament's rumoured retribution the next morning.

In the plans that followed, those unlikely co-conspirators, the Puritan Lady Lee and the practically heretical Chillingworth, played leading parts. Hyde's and Chillingworth's horses were sent ahead thirty miles north to a farmhouse near Coventry, home to one of the theologian's innumerable brothers. Meanwhile the erstwhile riders travelled by a smoother road and a more comfortable, as well as secure, means, hidden in her ladyship's six-horsed closed coach, sheltered by the unimpeachable character of the crescent-mooned Lee escutcheon.

When the travellers and their mounts had rested sufficiently to return to the road, Chillingworth superintended another feint, guiding his friend on an unexpected tack east to the Leicestershire village of Lutterworth. One of Lutterworth's previous rectors had been John Wycliffe, the medieval forerunner of English Protestantism; his successor in 1642 was of a more flamboyant doctrinal disposition, and another of Chillingworth's admirers. He gave the pair of fugitives a handsome reception. Since the outlawed Hyde was now reluctant to take the risk of enjoying another leisurely pause, Chillingworth directed him 'by unusual ways' another thirty miles north through Derbyshire, till they reached a more impregnable refuge than the rector's hearth.

Sir John Wolstenholme the younger was, like his lately deceased father, one of the King's favoured financiers and tax farmers. His father had purchased, among other estates, Nostell Priory by Wakefield in Yorkshire, one of the medieval foundations dissolved and disbursed by Henry VIII. Wolstenholme, like Falkland, was staying at this time in London waiting upon events, but, following the King's own wishes, he had made his north-country residence ready to receive Ned Hyde. This royal order was the result of Hyde's continuing detachment; he was as eager to remain independent for the time being from the temporary royal court at York as he was to be sheltered from the avenging spirit of Parliament, 'in some private place near York . . . till [the King's] affairs absolutely required [Hyde's] presence . . . there being many reasons that he should be concealed in those parts as long as might be convenient'. In the comfort, security, and privacy of Nostell Priory, Hyde was soon joined by his wife Frances and their four children, the youngest born only that March.

The position of Wolstenholme's private affairs revealed, even on the edge of conflict, how intertwined in amity and business both sides still were. For this royal financier's principal legal counsel was still that precarious Parliamentarian, Bulstrode Whitelocke.

## *'Like a cast at dice': Westminster, July 1642*

As spring turned to summer, King and Parliament failed to come to terms in a correspondence that formed a public analogue to

Whitelocke and Hyde's separated friendship. Hyde and Falkland, now settled at the royal court in the north, drafted the King's proposals, while Whitelocke chaired the committee that considered and replied to them. But despite the depth of potential goodwill thus embedded within both camps, matters continued to degenerate towards the hard-line, bellicose positions passionately denounced by the friends on either side.

Privately Whitelocke continued his immaculately moderate conduct. Wolstenholme was but one among several Royalist clients on his books. Whitelocke and Hyde's fellow Middle Temple lawyer and close mutual friend Geoffrey Palmer, the Royalist who, with Hyde, had urged Whitelocke's flight from London, was excused from attending the House of Commons at Whitelocke's request. But Hyde's more high-profile defection, with its evident connection to the flight of the Lord Keeper and loss of the Great Seal, meant Whitelocke was powerless to stop Parliament from now excluding Mr Hyde, the truant former member for Saltash, from any future pardon.

When the King was driven to raise his own forces through a feudal, extra-parliamentary mechanism called the Commissions of Array, Parliament's Militia Ordinance was bound to be put to the test. Whitelocke, after months loyally negotiating to strengthen Parliament's hand, baulked at a final commitment to an open conflict he had never favoured, and now delivered a speech to the Commons more impassioned, if perhaps less practical, than his earlier proposed compromise:

> The question which was last propounded about raising of forces, naming a general, and officers of an army, hath been very rare before this time, in this assembly, and it seems to me to set us at the pit's-brink, ready to plunge ourselves into an ocean of troubles and miseries, and if it could be, into more than a civil war brings with it.

'More than a civil war' is a striking and perhaps prophetic turn of rhetoric; Whitelocke appeared to dread worse than the apparent worst, an overthrow of the deepest nature of things.

Bulstrode Whitelocke had form in pursuing this particular theme. As a schoolboy at the Merchant Taylors', he had once been chosen to make a Latin address to the masters and boys of St Paul's school, signifying the end of a street-fight between the young scholars of the rival establishments (a fight in which Whitelocke hints he had himself played a venturesome part). Much as he must have done on that occasion, he now asked leave 'to consider this unhappy subject in the beginning, progress, and issue of it'. He quoted Julius Caesar, remarking that the Roman dictator 'knew as much of civil war as any man before him'; Caesar was generally regarded as the aggressor in the wars that overturned the Roman Republic, and Caesar's name was common parlance for the King's. Whitelocke appealed to the wild anti-Catholicism that was Pym's chief instrument in mobilizing the populace, arguing that at Papal Rome 'nothing will more advance their empire, than our divisions. Our misery . . . is their joy . . . our distractions will be their glory.' That other, more urbane, Whitelocke who delighted in French and Italian music, garb, and culture, whose person and talents notably impressed Henrietta Maria, the French, and Catholic, Queen of England, was for the moment lain aside.

But Whitelocke, in a vision uncannily reminiscent of his friend Hyde's later historical writing, could hardly help praising, at least by implication, the extended, aesthetically refined, prosperous sense of quiet that England had enjoyed over the eleven years in which the King had lately reigned without Parliament: 'God blessed us with a long and flourishing peace.' He identified the increasing likelihood of war with divine retribution for the nation's sins, 'to make us executioners of divine vengeance upon ourselves'. His usually clear, legal mind now became fuddled by intensity of emotion. He could not exactly now break ranks with Pym's belligerent policy, but neither could he bring himself to welcome the extreme, cauterizing or killing cure of civil conflict upon the ailing body politic.

Yet Whitelocke struggled through this tension to capture the precise mood of the moment:

## Prelude: The Pit's Brink

> It is strange to note, how we have insensibly slid into this beginning of a civil war, by one unexpected accident after another, as waves of the sea, which have brought us thus far: and we scarce know how, but from paper combats, by Declarations, Remonstrances, Protestations, votes, messages, answers and replies: we are now come to the question of raising forces, and naming a general, and officers of an army.

There had always been an army and a general in question – the force to be sent to contain the continuing Irish crisis – but Whitelocke and all his auditors in the by now reduced, Pym-led Commons knew that England and not Ireland would experience the depredations of the army now to be mustered. Whitelocke himself had been as deeply implicated in the 'paper combats' as Julius Caesar in the Roman civil wars. His speech possesses the astonished authenticity with which he awoke to the full consequences of his handiwork. Whitelocke was correctly proud of the 'paper combats' passage, replicating his inspired stroke of national ventriloquism in a sententious, contemporaneous letter to his ever-understanding wife.

After another raid on Roman precedent with a dip into Lucan, the great Latin laureate of civil strife – whose most famous work had been translated into English by Thomas May, another literary crony of both Selden and Hyde – Whitelocke glossed in blazing terms the poet's meaning for some of his less learned parliamentary colleagues. In consequence of such a war as was now contemplated:

> We must surrender up our laws, liberties, properties and lives into the hands of insolent mercenaries, whose rage and violence will command us, and all we have, and reason, honour and justice will leave our land; the ignoble will rule the noble, and baseness will be preferred before virtue, profaneness before piety.

Here Whitelocke spoke both as the punctilious city lawyer and the established Buckinghamshire squire. His point was as national as it was personal, and in both terms, again, prophetic: 'Of a potent people we shall make ourselves weak.' He added some further flourishes on the lamentations of widows and orphans, but his practical case was made.

Despite himself, Whitelocke could speak with greater imaginative impact as a historian than as a politician, and he demonstrated the application of historical thinking to the ostensibly unknowable future:

> What the issue of it will be, no man alive can tell, probably few of us now here may live to see the end of it. It hath said, *He that draws his Sword against his Prince, must throw away the Scabbard:* those differences are scarce to be reconciled; these commotions are like the deep seas, being once stirred, are not soon appeased.

In a sense both Whitelocke and Hyde would live to see the conclusion of the civil wars, the monarchy subjugated, thrown down, and at last restored. But neither would witness the mostly decisive settlement, at the accession in 1688 of William III and Mary II by parliamentary fiat, of the abstract question at stake – whether, in the last resort, King or Parliament was in both civil and military affairs sovereign.

Whitelocke then pondered the description of England once made by the French duc de Rohan: 'That it is a great Creature, which cannot be destroyed, but by its own hand.' Rohan was a particularly poignant and loaded authority to invoke. A heroic Protestant soldier, and the godfather of King Charles, he had only four years previously fallen in battle during the interminable and internecine war in Germany, begun over the rights of Charles's brother-in-law, the King of Bohemia. The final point in Whitelocke's appeal was simply that a resort to force would raise the stakes, eliminate the hope of any judicious compromise, and leave total victory or defeat to mere chance: 'The issue of all war is like a cast at dice.'

Trained as he was, like his friend Hyde, to display even-handedness through the exigencies of the legal profession, Whitelocke could not commit his entire intellect to the pacific preferences that obviously ruled his heart. He made haste – prudent haste – by way of reassuring those who might still consider him a waverer, to insist that:

> I am not for a tame resignation of our religion, lives and liberties, into the hands of our adversaries, who seek to devour us. Nor do I think it inconsistent with [Parliament's] great wisdom, to prepare for a just and necessary defence of them.

He understood, Whitelocke continued, that to prove Parliament was in earnest about its military preparations might well increase its bargaining power in further negotiations with the King. All the more reason, surely, to embark on such negotiations once again, 'so that there may be no strife between us and those of the other party, for we are brethren'.

Whitelocke's plea came too late to have any likelihood of prevailing; John Pym and his closest associates had despaired of any further trust in the King and were now bent on war. But the manner in which Whitelocke made his case well illustrates the cast of mind then to be found throughout much of the reluctantly rebellious Parliament, as well as in the closest counsels of the King, and all over the wider, unaligned, and apprehensive country. How different things had been at the dawn of Whitelocke and Hyde's close friendship, during what had seemed the dusk of English parliaments: the late 1620s, when what the land had lacked in political opportunity it had readily proffered in good company, for those fortunate or talented enough to attain it.

# I.

# The Making of the Moderates

*These prompt to Vertue, those from Vice affright;*
*All fully mingling Profit with Delight.*

George Sandys, 'Argument',
*Ovids Metamorphosis Englished*

## The Middle Temple of the 1620s

The first glimpses to be found of Edward Hyde and Bulstrode Whitelocke in one another's company share the performative style so characteristic of Whitelocke, who later preserved them. Whitelocke came to be the friend in whose interests it was to remember the relationship's earliest period. Hyde preferred to forget, elide, or actively censor its existence: whether by simple omission, or by emphasizing other characters and events. So the story of this friendship – itself a personal history of a pivotal time – begins from Whitelocke's perspective, in his hand.

His journal first paints the amused, cursory, slightly wistful group portrait of a talented and opinionated clique of young lawyers. These mainly Middle Temple sparks were not perhaps quite so well-ordered and hard-working as they liked to think of themselves, but they possessed certain principles in common and, not long before Parliament was dissolved by King Charles in 1629, a measure of courage to express them. Clarendon's *Life* provides some parallel testimony, its character sketches more psychologically revealing, or at least internally curious, than the scenes and company summarized by Whitelocke. But their scene and its concerns similarly wind around the fringes of the courts of law and of the royal court itself.

Whitelocke's first mention of Hyde places his friend among the young lawyers encountered at the Middle Temple on his arrival there in late 1622:

> . . . Mr [Bartholomew] Hall, Mr Geoffrey Palmer afterwards a Baronet & the King's Attorney, Mr Maynard, afterwards a Baronet and the King's Sergeant, Mr [i.e. Edward] Hyde, afterwards Lord Chancellor & Earl of Clarendon . . . Mr Robert Hyde [Edward Hyde's older cousin], afterwards Lord Chief Justice of the King's Bench, Mr Lisle, afterwards one of the Commissioners of the Great Seal [under the Commonwealth, alongside Whitelocke himself] . . .

Geoffrey Palmer's name is not a familiar one, but he is particularly important at various points in the lives of both Whitelocke and Hyde; he also seems to have been regarded by the Whitelocke family as their cousin. Whitelocke continues the catalogue with another list of eminent contemporaries, those who resided at different Inns of Court: Harbottle Grimston, Matthew Hale, John Fountaine, and Thomas Widdrington. Taken as a whole this second group exemplifies a milieu of skilful legal practice and conscientious, moderate opposition to royal policy, mirroring Whitelocke's own sympathies and career. The destinies of Whitelocke's and Hyde's more intimate Middle Temple friends of the first list were to be more various, dramatic, and polarized.

But about Edward Hyde himself, Whitelocke's memory, a little tellingly, betrays him. At the end of 1622 Hyde was, in fact, still in his early teens. Far from being a companion at the Inns of Court, he had scarcely begun his (none too distinguished) Oxford career. Whitelocke's over-prompt invocation of his younger comrade is, however, more of a clue than a mere slip. It gives a sense of how inextricable Hyde was from Whitelocke's broad memory of his earliest days as a Middle Templar, despite Hyde's being four years younger and then much less conspicuous than Whitelocke. It also carries an ironical charge, given Whitelocke's own circumstances when, in the mid-1660s, he compiled this list of friends, his mood embittered, wounded, and regretful.

Whitelocke – whose hitherto spectacular professional and political success had been, to him, unjustly and prematurely curtailed after the Restoration of 1660 – dwelt now with a sour, half-proud relish on the catalogue of friends who had profited in the legal practice they all shared. Some had (at least notionally) shared his side in the civil wars, some opposed it, while an agile few had successfully changed allegiance at least once. In these score-settling meditations, Edward Hyde featured as the supreme exemplar of Whitelocke's eminent but ungrateful old acquaintances. At the time Whitelocke wrote his retrospective account of 1622–3, Hyde, as Lord Clarendon, was Lord High Chancellor of England, the supreme legal authority in the kingdom, Charles II's universally recognized chief minister. Whitelocke could not then have known – though he might just about have speculated, hardened as he was by the two most eventful decades of statecraft his country had ever endured – how much sardonic sport the muse of history was still to play with Edward Hyde, Earl of Clarendon, that erstwhile younger companion who by then appeared to have made so permanently, maddeningly good.

## The Boyhood of Bulstrode and Youth of Ned, 1605–28

Bulstrode Whitelocke had always been everybody's darling. His parents, James Whitelocke, a brilliant, self-made advocate, and Elizabeth Bulstrode, a Puritan gentlewoman sprung from two old and well-connected families, the Bulstrodes and Crokes, both brimful of lawyers, were high-minded, high-powered, intelligent, and indulgent. They lavished attention, education, and affection on their son (we hear comparatively little of Bulstrode's two sisters). Bulstrode Whitelocke was set apart from the outset by that interesting Christian name, euphoniously peculiar even in an epoch of astonishingly florid examples. It had been imposed at his baptism by his godfather and uncle, Captain Edmund Whitelocke, a charming, incorrigible soldier, parasite upon various rebel earls. At the Merchant Taylors' school the rising lawyer's son stood out (by his own account at least) for charismatic leadership and rhetorical ability. The powerful family friends, stars of the cloth and the robe, judges of the day and to come, authorities, advocates, and archbishops, who lingered at the Whitelockes' convivial, musical hearth, at first in Fleet Street and then, as James Whitelocke's practice prospered, in the country, were amused by their conversations with his bright-eyed boy, Bulstrode.

At Oxford, young Whitelocke was rapidly taken up by two inseparable Williams, the university's most powerful pair of dons, Laud and Juxon, soon to emerge as the kingdom's leading politician-prelates. Laud was James Whitelocke's old college friend, though not necessarily his unvarying ally in political or religious profession. In 1626, at the age of twenty-one, Bulstrode Whitelocke first sat in the House of Commons, at around the same period as his more probably accurate first acquaintance with Ned Hyde, just arrived at the Middle Temple. Young Whitelocke's election had been casually arranged by his father, by now Sir James Whitelocke, a judge of the King's Bench, and consummately connected throughout the political world.

Edward, familiarly known as Ned, Hyde was born into a cadet branch of a legal and political dynasty more thrustingly court-inclined than the Whitelockes, Bulstrodes, or Crokes. Like Bulstrode Whitelocke, Ned Hyde benefited from the support of a devoted and civilized father, Henry Hyde the Elder, yet he made no such unerring debut. Ned had grown up in the wake of an elder brother, Henry, their father's namesake and heir, intended for the family profession of the law. He also had sisters; like the Whitelocke daughters their presences are shadowy, though one, Susan Hyde, was destined to find in those shadows a tragic end.\* Ned Hyde, seemingly fitted

---

\* Susan Hyde's brief and ill-fated career as a Royalist spy run by her brother in a desperate hour, and his guilty suppression of her perilous service and terrible fate, lies beyond the confines of the present book.

## The Making of the Moderates

by both temperament and destiny for a second surviving son's quiet, clerical lot, joined his brother at Oxford, but only gained admittance to the small and shabby Magdalen Hall, not, as was by now traditional for Hydes, the great college of the same name.* He overlapped with his elder brother Henry just long enough to be startled, and against his better judgement quite impressed, by the quantity Henry habitually drank, 'too much corrupted in that kind'. Then, in 1626, Henry Hyde the younger died suddenly at twenty-five. Ned Hyde, now his father's only surviving son, expected to become the hopeful young lawyer among his line and generation of Hydes, was removed from further study at Oxford and dispatched instead to the Middle Temple. It is easy to infer from the respectful phrases of his formal, pious later narrative that young Hyde was not enthusiastic about this turn of fortune. Alhough in his *Life* Clarendon professed gratitude to his father for detaching him from the louche circles and circumstances of his brother's university life and death, he 'always reserved a high esteem' for Oxford, a city with which he would be intimately linked again in coming years of pleasure, of adversity, and, eventually, power.

Ned Hyde loved and obeyed his father in all respects. He called the elder Henry Hyde 'an excellent scholar' who 'took pleasure in conferring with him, and contributed much more to his education than the school did'. Equally, he had responded well to his father's personal tutelage – humane, theological, historical, literary, but certainly not legal. He found that:

---

* One of Magdalen Hall's earlier, more intellectually distinguished sons was Thomas Hobbes, who arrived there at some point in 1601–3 and was admitted BA in 1608, a year before Ned Hyde's birth. According to his friend and admirer John Aubrey, an unstimulated Hobbes spent much of his time as an undergraduate trapping jackdaws with cheese parings, lead weights, and quicklime, fascinated by 'such sharpness of sight in so little an eye'. Hobbes and Hyde, both Wiltshire men, appear to have been acquainted from early in Ned's life. They would become closely associated at Great Tew, before their later actions and writings decisively estranged them from one another.

## Friends in Youth

... he could not bring himself to an industrious pursuit of the law study, but rather loved polite learning and history, in which, especially in the Roman, he had always been conversant.

Bulstrode Whitelocke was also to note that he had followed his father's example 'in studying the English history wherein he was most exact & perfect', but this accomplishment has the appearance of a mere afterthought, whereas to young Hyde history manifested itself early as a ruling passion, laboriously tamed.

Ned Hyde knew that his father had himself, as a young man, evaded the family business of the law as long as he could, by every conceivable method – perilous foreign travel in Catholic Europe, parliamentary service, and at last a lucrative marriage and a benevolently squirearchical Wiltshire existence. It was not Ned's easy-going father, but his stern, industrious uncle, Nicholas Hyde (soon to be knighted and made Lord Chief Justice after his part in defending the Duke of Buckingham from parliamentary impeachment), who was on hand to sponsor his entry into the learned society of the Middle Temple in 1626. Sir Nicholas kept a sharp eye on young Hyde's activities there subsequently, and 'almost every night put a case to him in law'.

Ned Hyde's health was far from robust during these first years of legal study. The very evening after his introduction to the Middle Temple he collapsed from quartan fever while attending prayers with his uncle at the Temple Church. Readers of his autobiography may be inclined to scepticism about the literal timing of such a dramatic ailment, but it seems to reflect accurately enough Hyde's gloomy feelings about the path that had now been chosen for him. In the summer of 1628 the young Hyde set out on his first, and as it would turn out only, attempt at 'riding the circuit', accompanying the itinerant judges of the realm and watching them furnish their sentences at rural assizes. At Trinity College, Cambridge, where the judges and their attendants were lodged, he contracted the smallpox, and scarcely escaped with his

## The Making of the Moderates

life.* The memory of his dissolute elder brother, who had bequeathed this burdensome career, might have haunted these early, faltering steps. Young Whitelocke's first adventure riding the circuit, in 1625, had been more active but scarcely less accident-prone, culminating in a nearly disastrous river-crossing, from which the aspiring advocate tellingly recuperated by trying his hand at writing a historical treatise.

In spite of avuncular vigilance or medical setbacks, young Hyde now embarked upon certain extracurricular interests with potentially dangerous enthusiasm. As young King Charles waged simultaneous wars against France and Spain, 'the town was full of soldiers'. In 1627 George Villiers, Duke of Buckingham, England's omniglamorous royal favourite, patron of Hyde's family among many another, and the ultimate source, even, of young Whitelocke's parliamentary seat the previous year, valiantly yet incompetently led an expedition to attack the Ile de Ré off France's western coast. Buckingham had aimed to relieve French Protestants under siege by their own king's forces at La Rochelle on the mainland, hoping thus to attain the popularity as a Protestant hero that had long eluded him. Of the 7,000 English troops involved, 4,000 did not return; the rest, among a throng of hypothetical heroes who claimed to have been at Ré or at least to have intended to be, filled every watering-hole in London with heady discourses of militaristic self-pity, punningly styling the recent fiasco 'the Ill Array'. Young Hyde found himself all too drawn to the swaggering company of such men of action, whether actual or apparent. Perhaps they reminded him of his superior, sottish elder brother. The impetuous claims of braggart swordsmen would

---

* Hyde was attended, and probably saved, by the famous Cambridge apothecary John Crane. Crane is of rich biographical interest quite apart from his evident talent as a physician: he seems to have been brought up female in childhood owing to abnormalities at birth, and subsequently lived in a discreetly homosexual quasi-marriage with his medical mentor and financial benefactor, William Butler.

not hold axiomatic appeal for Sir Edward Hyde during the subsequent course of his long, unexpectedly adventurous career, but at this point there were many lessons the younger man had yet to learn.

At some point in 1628 Ned Hyde acquired a new, larger set of rooms in the Middle Temple, and decided to accommodate a lodger. The rising poet and playwright Will Davenant was twenty-two, three years Hyde's senior, and equipped with an inventory of varied experience that bedazzled his impressionable host. He had left a wife and son at the lodgings of his tailor, Urswick; family and tradesman went alike unremunerated.

Davenant, who like most of London's chancers at this time affected military airs, had in truth seen less perilous, if probably, to Hyde, more intriguing service. He had been a page to Fulke Greville, Lord Brooke, a survivor from the already legend-tinged days of Queen Elizabeth, and a celebrated political, philosophical, and literary sage. Davenant, an Oxford publican's son who claimed to be William Shakespeare's godson, bastard, or both according to mood, maintained that Greville, most famous as the best friend of the fallen poet and Protestant hero Sir Philip Sidney, often wished to be remembered 'under no other notion than of Shakespeare's and Ben Jonson's Master'. Ned Hyde would quite soon come to befriend both Ben Jonson himself, along with a more respectable early critical champion of Shakespeare than Davenant, the 'Ever Memorable' scholar John Hales.

By way of Sir Lawrence Hyde, yet another powerful uncle, the Queen's Attorney-General, Ned passed on a wild pirate-hunting scheme of Davenant's to the Secretary of State, Lord Dorchester. When Davenant's second play, *The Tragedy of Albovine, King of the Lombards*, was grandiloquently printed in 1629, among the commendatory verses that preceded it was one by Mr Edward Hyde: Ned Hyde's only extant experiment in verse, one all too worthy of the drama to which it was attached. Once he had spread his literary wings in prose, however, Hyde never found himself impelled to mention this remarkable early friendship in his later writings.

## 'The villain hath killed me', London, 1628-32

Will Davenant seems to have attached himself to Ned Hyde not long after witnessing the unwholesome murder of his celebrated former patron. Lord Brooke was stabbed at the end of September 1628 by a disaffected manservant, who, spared pursuit on his wounded employer's orders, then quickly dispatched himself. John Aubrey notes, with Davenant as his authority, that the deed was done as its culprit 'was trussing up his Lord's [breeches] coming from Stool'. Brooke perished four weeks later, finished off partly by his own over-investigative instructions to his physicians. This death was symbolic as the end of one of the last great Elizabethans; Brooke's faintly sodomitical reputation lent it sinister gossip value; and it had too some larger importance, as the dead man's seat in the Lords and huge fortune passed to his cousin and adopted heir Robert Greville, who held severely Puritan religious, commercial, and political interests. Nonetheless this murder was 'quite drowned', as Aubrey says, and 'scarce taken notice of' by comparison to the outcry, chaos, national jubilation, and opportunistic scrambling at court that had exploded following the demise of a higher-ranking victim that summer.

Late August found the Duke of Buckingham at his defiant, debonair best, handsomely lodged at the Greyhound Inn in Portsmouth, whence he was superintending the outfit of a fresh expedition against France. Although fully aware of his own unpopularity, having recently lost his favoured physician to a public lynching, he disdained, like Caesar, any extraordinary measures for self-protection. But as Buckingham stood splendidly Caesar-like, he failed to notice an embittered ensign like *Othello*'s Iago, one John Felton. Crippled in one hand during the 'Ill Array', passed over for promotion, and faced with permanent unemployment without a pension, Felton had finally been spurred to action by unwontedly political reading matter, especially a copy of the Petition of Right, the recent parliamentary reproach to Buckingham and the King.

When Felton's ten-penny, three-inch knife pierced the duke's left breast, the stabbed Buckingham could only gasp out 'The villain hath killed me', before his swift, almost painless end: the old soldier knew his business better than Lord Brooke's manservant. Felton could probably have made his escape in the anti-French panic that now ensued, directed at several luckless Huguenot aristocrats present as allied commanders. Instead he identified himself with a pride many of his compatriots soon shared: 'I am the man.'

The Catholic adventurer Sir Kenelm Digby heard the news far away in the Ionian Islands west of Greece, hungry Europe's only source of currants, yoked to British markets via the Levant Company, a corporation that had benefited from the eloquent counsel of Bulstrode's father, Sir James Whitelocke. Digby abandoned his promising debut in piracy and made for home.* Buckingham's death would change everything: for the Digbys, hitherto blocked by the great favourite from courtly preferment, evidently for the better; for the Hydes, who had risen to prominence as the duke's legal facilitators, probably for the worse; for Sir James Whitelocke, who had made his name opposing the court, and his precocious son Bulstrode, who had just sat in the Commons at Buckingham's pleasure, in a manner that remained to be seen.

The very name of John Felton held immediate significance for the historically inclined young Hyde. Clarendon's *Life* recalls that 'he was often wont to say' how he had been reading from William Camden's *Annals* to his father at the moment when the news reached Henry Hyde's estate at Purton. According to this clearly oft-burnished tale, Ned Hyde had just reached Camden's consideration of an earlier John Felton, or Johannes Feltonus: the Catholic enthusiast who, in 1570, had nailed to the door of the Bishop of

---

* If Aubrey is to be believed, Digby owed to the late favourite his own 'goodly handsome', unpiratical person. King James, understandably terrified of naked steel after being exposed to it both *in utero* and on several occasions during his frequently nightmarish Scottish reign, nearly jabbed Digby's eye out from sheer panic while knighting him, a disaster only averted by the lithe-limbed Buckingham.

London's palace a copy of the papal bull excommunicating Queen Elizabeth and denying her right to the throne of England. But it was no mere nominative determinism that attracted Hyde to the coincidence. Both Feltons represented religious fanaticism, albeit in different confessional forms (the duke's assassin, Hyde adds in the *History*, was stirred to his deed by 'some popular preachers in the city', as well as his own innate 'melancholy nature'). Hyde saw both men as republican rebels against the Crown and malcontent outsiders from the state Church. He was to spend most of his career defending his ideal *via media* with respect to Crown, Parliament, and Church from the extremities of both Rome and Geneva, often causing both Papists and Puritans to forge cynical alliances against him.* It is not surprising that the second Felton's resemblances to the first seemed to him to proffer a crucial and consistent lesson.

Both Whitelocke and Hyde describe Felton's trial, at which Whitelocke was actually present; he notes in his journal that:

> ... Felton who killed the Duke ... though at his apprehension he said he did it, because the Duke was an enemy to his Country, yet at his Trial he showed remorse, he was hanged in chains for it.

Whitelocke's sympathy for the defendant – albeit expressed at a safe distance in time from the deed – is clear enough. Hyde did not share it, but even he showed some respect for Felton's consistency of purpose and eventual contrition.

---

* Hyde's habitual position is well represented by one of George Herbert's lyrics, 'The British Church':

> *A fine aspect in fit array,*
> *Neither too mean, nor yet too gay,*
> *Shows who is best.*
> *Outlandish looks may not compare,*
> *For all they either painted are,*
> *Or else undress'd.*

*Friends in Youth*

In the *History* that Hyde composed in his first exile on Jersey after Charles I's defeat in the First Civil War, with the King himself expressly conceived as his primary reader, his account of the murder is well suited to the naval backdrop of wartime Portsmouth, complete with a swashbuckling battle royal worthy of the French novelist Alexandre Dumas. After Felton identified himself as the killer, Hyde relates:

> Thereupon some of those who were most furious suddenly ran upon the man [Felton] with their drawn swords to kill him; but others, who were at least equally concerned in the loss and in the sense of it, defended him; himself with open arms very calmly and cheerfully exposing himself to the fury and swords of the enraged, as being very willing to fall a sacrifice to their sudden anger, rather than to be kept for that deliberate justice which he knew must be exercised upon him.

This is in some ways an intriguingly ambivalent picture. Hyde, scion of a family of Buckingham clients, naturally portrays the duke's bereft attendants in a mainly complimentary light – half of them righteously, passionately, perhaps understandably bent on hot-blooded vengeance, the other (by implication, the more Hydean?) group carefully attentive to legal due process, and heroic in its defence. But at the same time Hyde is realistic about the reasons for these courtiers' differing reactions: they are 'equally concerned in the loss and the sense [i.e. significance] of it', motivated by the same political and economic forces that, conversely, now propelled Sir Kenelm Digby homewards across the Mediterranean. With Buckingham's death many careers appeared to be extinguished, but in the aftermath of his murder still more struggled to be born.

Like Buckingham's grieving friends, in Hyde's version Felton displays both commendable and self-interested aspects. On the one hand he shows a courage and forebearance that may appear explicitly Christlike: 'himself with open arms very calmly and cheerfully exposing himself to the fury and swords of the enraged, as being very willing to fall a sacrifice'. Certainly many of Whitelocke's and Hyde's countrymen saw Felton in exactly this way – as a heaven-sent redeemer who had selflessly accepted death to rid his fellow Englishmen of Buckingham's oppression.

Oxford was then a university riven between 'high Calvinist', Puritan-inclined Protestant orthodoxy on the one hand, and counter-reformist, royally sponsored theological tendencies on the other. At Trinity College a visiting schoolmaster, Alexander Gill the younger, was overheard drinking Felton's health, and reported to William Laud; that surprising old friend of Sir James Whitelocke, the young king's long-standing favourite among his clerical advisors, recently appointed Bishop of London. Gill was harshly sentenced by Laud acting through the ominous Court of the Star Chamber, though he was later pardoned. Davenant told Aubrey that the false friend who shopped Gill to the authorities was Laud's godson, William Chillingworth, who in 1642 would be Hyde's accomplice on his flight from London to York.

In 1632, Edward Hyde married his first wife. The match was, as he is at pains to inform us in his *Life*, one of exemplary suitability: made 'with his father's consent and approbation'. The bride, Anne Ayliffe, was 'a young lady very fair and beautiful, the daughter of Sir George Ayliffe, a gentleman of a good name and fortune in the county of Wiltshire, where [Hyde's] own expectations lay, and by her mother nearly allied to many noble families in England'. This was no exaggeration, for Anne was a cousin of the late Duke of Buckingham. Ned Hyde had thus become not just a client or ally, but a relation of the dead duke's huge, still influential, voracious Villiers family.

## *Bulstrode Blooded: Parliament, Mr Selden, the Middle Temple Revels and Mrs Percy's, 1626–9*

During the latter 1620s Bulstrode Whitelocke was more skilful than his younger friend Ned Hyde in combining amiable pleasures with

## Friends in Youth

professional advancement. Since his mishap on the banks of the river Wye he had ridden the circuits more successfully. Young Whitelocke made his name for courage as well as diligence by accompanying and assisting his father in adjourning the court sessions in London at a time of plague. During the same years he assisted two friends and fellow students of the law, John Pyne and Harbottle Grimston, in pre-matrimonial crises. Whitelocke helped to spirit Pyne's willing *inamorata* from her obstructive uncle's house, then spoke up for Grimston, who sought, and, as a result of Whitelocke's intervention, successfully won, the hand of one of his friend's cousins, the daughter of his maternal uncle Judge Croke.

As a Parliamentarian Whitelocke enjoyed a less promising apprenticeship than as a lawyer, partly because of the difficulties that institution was then undergoing. The Parliament of 1626, Charles I's second, sat for only five months between February and June. Its House of Commons was massaged towards docility by the appointment of several previously oppositional MPs as sheriffs, marooned in their counties and unable to stand for Parliament. Nonetheless, it still passed little in the way of constructive royal policy. Bulstrode found himself in an innately confused position. His father had fixed his seat through Sir Humphrey May, Chancellor of the Duchy of Lancaster, who had been the elder Whitelocke's and Laud's boon companion at Oxford; but less directly, by the compliance of May's patron, Buckingham himself. Yet all the energy and chance of distinction in the House was evidently to be at Buckingham's expense. Whitelocke describes the guidance he received both from May and his father; he represents his reins as loose and, within these parameters, his behaviour as filial yet freethinking:

> Whitelocke by his father's means was returned a Burgess of Parliament for Stafford, & also . . . for Boroughbridge in Yorkshire by Sir Humphrey May . . . ancient & trusty friend of the Judge [Whitelocke the elder] by whose direction Whitelocke waived Boroughbridge and elected to serve . . . for Stafford . . . thus early did his father provide for his best education, & gave him good

counsel concerning his demeanour in Parliament, and though he disliked his sitting in the Gallery [the elevated part of St Stephen's Chapel], then esteemed the resort of mutineers & wished him to leave that place, yet as to the giving of his vote (which was seldom with the Court party) he left him to the liberty of his own conscience & judgement, advising him to follow the dictates thereof, & not to be engaged in any party or faction whatsoever.

The reader perceives young Whitelocke acclimatizing with mild bafflement to the peculiar rules that handed him electoral success in two separate seats without any particular exertion, and then obliged him to choose between them on tactical grounds, on the advice of the experienced politician and courtier Sir Humphrey May. Judge Whitelocke, once a 'mutineer' himself, the defender of the Levant Company against the Crown and briefly, in 1613, held by royal command in the Fleet Prison, shows himself as a mature conservative, advising his adored boy to stay away from the troublemakers as much as to know his own mind or follow his heart. Over the two decades of his later, consecutive parliamentary service, Whitelocke indeed evaded consistent identification with any one political clique, as his father had counselled. But in this earlier trial run, he allowed himself on the whole to be absorbed into the rebellious majority shepherded by the 'three Johns' – Eliot, Pym, and Hampden. These now became an alternative set of older mentors.

The Commons still functioned as a theoretically, at best actually, unified and unanimous body, harking back to the efficient instrument of royal government it had once been, honed in the long reigns of Henry VIII and Elizabeth I. Even conversational references to political divisions over the House's business were technically serious breaches of order, verging upon the treasonous in their implications. No losers' consent was necessary, for the House's voice and decisions were regarded as singular. This crucial convention was by now in decline, but would not be tested to its destruction for another fifteen years, in an episode Whitelocke was to witness all too closely.

Bulstrode Whitelocke's consciousness of his own greenness in 1626 is encapsulated in his summation of Parliament as 'the best school in Christendom'. Clarendon's *Life* recalls Edmund Waller, another precociously fixed MP also present in the 1626 Commons, as having boasted of and deprecated his early debut in equal measure, in a similar manner to Whitelocke's journal, claiming to have been 'nursed in parliaments'. Whitelocke professes to have been as industrious in Parliament as he had been upon the legal circuits during this 'beginning in public action'. 'Business he constantly attended both in the house and at Committees, & took notes of what passed, & by this he gained much knowledge & experience in the public affairs'. This is interesting, as taking such notes in the Commons was theoretically out of order, though it seems to have been quite frequently, and to posterity most gratifyingly, indulged. Whitelocke's notes survive, another faint intimation of the occasional historian and voluminous memoirist to come.

Whitelocke's memories of the 1626 Parliament, however, are not wholly to be relied upon. In his later, post-Restoration journal he remembers being 'admitted into particular acquaintance' with Sir Edward Coke and Sir Thomas Wentworth. Coke, the greatest legal panjandrum in the land, yet another friend of Sir James Whitelocke, was already well known to Judge Whitelocke's son. Wentworth, a proud, capable, and eloquent Yorkshire landowner, was a leading figure in the opposition and by this point a particular opponent of Buckingham. Both men are thus perfectly convincing as associates of the young Whitelocke as he flirted with the 'mutineers', yet in truth neither were MPs or even in London in 1626, as they were among those awkward former MPs whom the Crown had thwarted by appointing them sheriffs. Most of the other members Whitelocke lists as 'particular acquaintances' are likely enough; Eliot, Pym, and Hampden, emerging as leaders of the parliamentary dissidents; Sir Dudley Digges, a disappointed applicant for Buckingham's favour, by now bitter in pursuit of the favourite's impeachment; and the three distinguished older lawyers, William Noy, Edward Littleton, and John Selden.*

Both Bulstrode Whitelocke and Ned Hyde would have been well aware of Selden long before they fell under his civilizing spell. Selden was, it need by now hardly be mentioned, a friend of Sir James Whitelocke. He was also a dogged yet good-humoured legal and political jousting partner of Hyde's uncle Sir Nicholas. But more importantly, both these lettered young men would have innately regarded the man Whitelocke later called 'that prodigy of learning of his age' with bookish awe. Young Whitelocke was constantly in Selden's company from 1623, soon after his entry into the Middle Temple, and Hyde likewise, from his own entry two years later. Both friends describe an all but identically affectionate, intellectual shaping spirit. Whitelocke 'grew so much into [Selden's] affection, that he allowed him the free use of [his] library, & showed him the way for gaining of the Oriental tongues, wherein himself was excellent . . . Whitelocke gained great improvement by his rare study and conversation.' Notable among the 'Oriental tongues' was Hebrew, of which language Selden was England's greatest exegete. But as with his recollections of his first parliamentary experience, Whitelocke's emphasis is on the faculties he developed at Selden's feet, rather than Selden himself.

It is to Clarendon's *Life* that the reader turns for the human portrait:

> Mr. Selden was a person whom no character can flatter, or transmit in any expressions equal to his virtue. He was of so stupendous learning in all kinds and in all languages (as may appear in his excellent and transcendent writings) that a man would have thought he had been entirely conversant amongst books, and had never spent an hour but in reading and writing; yet his humanity, courtesy and

---

* Whitelocke also more surprisingly names Sir John Savile and Sir Edwin Sandys, both partisans of Buckingham, implying his father's advice, to make friends on all sides and stay above party divisions, had sunk in after all.

affability were such, that he would have been thought to have been bred in the best courts, but that his good nature, clarity, and delight in doing good, and in communicating all that he knew, exceeded that breeding.

This complementary – and complimentary – description, of a scholar who appears to have devoted himself entirely to private learning, and simultaneously a courtier polished in every outer accomplishment, is a traditional device. The editor of Whitelocke's *Memorials*, Arthur Annesley, Earl of Anglesey, would even construct a similarly praiseworthy juxtaposition about Bulstrode himself. Clarendon twists the passage out of cliché by his rueful, knowing afterthought – that Selden possessed better manners and a truer capacity both for friendship and for the passing on of knowledge than any princely court could usually boast. He then dwells in more detail on the characteristics of Selden's writing, proving that his use of the word 'transcendent' earlier was perhaps itself a courtier-like initial sidestep:

> His style in all his works seems harsh and sometimes obscure; which is not wholly to be imputed to the abstruse subjects of which he commonly treated, out of the paths trod by other men; but to a little undervaluing the beauty of a style, and too much propensity to the language of antiquity: but in his conversation he was the most clear discourser, and had the best faculty of making hard things easy, and presenting them to the understanding, of any man that hath been known.

Any reader tempted to charge Clarendon, master of the baroque sentence, with calling the kettle black, need only compare Selden the antiquary to the same man's *Table Talk* – a collection of aphorisms so pithily homespun that their attribution to Selden was long if vainly contested. Examples include 'Jumping upon things at first dash will destroy all', and 'when we talk of our children, we mean ourselves'. Clarendon finishes his survey of Selden's personal

## The Making of the Moderates

qualities with another lovingly repetitious claim – 'Mr. Hyde was wont to say, that he valued himself upon nothing more than having had Mr. Selden's acquaintance from the time he was very young.' The conflict of humility and vanity here reveals not just Selden's kindness, but Edward Hyde to his core.

Selden shared some of the ambivalence of Hyde's own father towards practising as a barrister. But he proved able to exploit his real interests by offering lucrative counsel to other barristers and clients, while continuing to pursue voracious and limitless private antiquarianism. He thus in his hours of pleasure half-invented secular history in England. His earnings were supplemented by the patronage of his friend the Earl of Kent, who seemed not to mind in the least that his much richer wife, born Elizabeth Talbot, was widely and probably correctly thought to be Selden's lover.* The two surviving contemporary oil portraits of Selden convey his physical attractiveness to a surprising degree, caught in his long, doleful, witty, and unusual, if hardly handsome face.

It was in fact his historical enquiries that had first stirred Selden into political activity, when, in 1618, his *History of Tithes* was suppressed at the instigation of King James's episcopate, much affronted by his unintimidated attention to the sources of, and authority for, their revenues. In 1621, not yet himself an MP, Selden framed a Protestation in favour of free speech in Parliament, even on matters of foreign policy. He was consequently imprisoned, though he endured a relatively gentle incarceration; Selden's gaoler-cum-host, the Sheriff of London, shared his interest in Anglo-Saxon manuscripts.

Selden's old friends and fellow lawyers, William Noy and Edward Littleton, named alongside Selden in Whitelocke's summary of his parliamentary baptism, would help to shape both Whitelocke's and Hyde's careers in active, unexpected ways. Selden's influence on the

---

* On account of Selden's lax attitude to his formal profession, his inheritance from the Countess of Kent and his possible secret marriage to her, Aubrey stated, as admiringly as irreverently, that Selden 'got more by his Prick than . . . by his practice'.

lives of his younger protégés was different. His was a consistent, if often background, presence; many of Whitelocke's and Hyde's most pivotal introductions and friendships can be persuasively traced to his connective ability. His hospitality was as pleasant as his personal habits were contained. Aubrey says he 'kept a plentiful table', and was 'never without learned company', while himself being 'temperate in eating & drinking'. He also details the antiquary's practice of draping a 'kind of false carpet' over his undisturbed papers and books while entertaining, so that he might show courtesy to his visitors but 'needed not to displace his papers or books'. Selden was his younger friends' intellectual and moral touchstone, both an approachable patron and a lofty ideal.

Whitelocke's journal concludes his narrative of his first Parliament in a tone of high satisfaction:

> These occasions increased his confidence & procured him favour, & in all the great transactions of that stout Parliament, wherein he was an Actor and a constant attender, he was neither swayed by Court flattery, nor by popular vanity, but followed clearly that light & reason which God had given him.

The 1626 Parliament, short-lived, petulant, and ineffectual, was 'stout' only in obstructiveness and discord. But this passage is a retrospective declaration of Whitelocke's political creed, rather than a contemporary record of his actions or views. In fact, in the same entry it is clear enough that he chose 'popular vanity', and this had its consequence. Having irritated his father and expended (for now) his credit with Sir Humphrey May, Whitelocke was not elected to the Parliament that assembled in 1628, missing its significant developments (and denouement).

Perhaps he hardly minded. At the Christmas prior to the 1628 parliamentary elections he received a more exciting and pleasurable, if also expensive, elevation, being named the Middle Temple's Master of Revels. Whitelocke, the austere retired statesman and godly worshipper of the 1660s, remembered his reaction to this coup in a manner hard to reconcile with the ambitious, smart young man about town he had once been:

> ... by the unanimous consent of the young gentlemen of the Middle Temple chosen Master of the Revels ... with much importunity, & reluctancy for diversion of his study, he at length was prevailed with, to accept ...

Yet the Bulstrode Whitelocke revealed in this same journal, merrily fixing up his companions' marriages, leaping on and off carriages and riverbanks, delighted by the praise both of wise elders and young blades, surely embraced his new position and its flattering opportunities. He was now the obvious leader, in 'courtesy, justice, & ... mettle', of his legal cohort. At school and at Oxford he had been the favourite of the masters and the dons; now he was the popular choice of his own contemporaries. Whitelocke claims to have bound his fellow Revellers to avoid 'debauchery ... swearing, or the like disorders, though they met almost daily at Taverns,' he adds quickly, 'to consult and practise about their revelling'. He also says he stilled duelling among the young lawyers, who, like all fine gentlemen, habitually carried swords, fairly adjudicating all their quarrels. The revels themselves, jolly displays of costumed dancing to music, became, he says, famed for 'excellent order, handsome gentlemen & good dancers'. Courtiers of both sexes attended as well as a German Graf, who 'discoursed much in Latin', declaring that 'there were no such Colleges as [the Inns of Court] in Christendom'. Most excitingly, Whitelocke 'was often sent for to bring some of his Revellers to the Court, to dance with the great Ladies there'.

In the journal entry describing the summer vacation of 1628, six months after his inauguration as Master of the Revels, Whitelocke provides the first real glimpse of Ned Hyde among their other companions:

Whitelocke had excellent conversation in ... the house of one Mrs Percy in Fleet St, with Mr Palmer, Mr Hyde, Mr Grimston, Mr Hall,

*Friends in Youth*

> Mr Chaloner & others, where they exercised their wits & learning in the imitation of Star Chamber proceedings, & sentencing with ingenious speeches, those of their company who transgressed their orders by swearing, ill speaking, or the like . . . There the use was instead of drinking, which they contemned . . . sometimes to put cases, to inquire of public affairs . . . whereby they improved their knowledge, & were the more fitted for public services . . . but detested all scurrility and debauchery.

In old age Bulstrode Whitelocke continues to assure his readers, including in the first instance his children and grandchildren, of his clean-living start as Master of the Revels. Surviving records of his payments at this time imply a somewhat different milieu, at least touching the consumption of wine and beer. Clarendon's tactic when approaching such passages of his youth is the opposite of Whitelocke's protestations of innocence, harping upon his 'fancy sharp and luxuriant' as a young man. It almost becomes possible to suspect not only that Whitelocke is censoring his dirty linen, but that Clarendon exaggerates his own. Yet this second temptation should be resisted. Young Ned Hyde was after all living alongside Will Davenant, who would be prostrate with syphilis two years later. Whether Mrs Percy was a motherly landlady of Puritan religious preferences or another sort of mistress of another sort of house is unknowable. Among Whitelocke's and Hyde's comrades, Grimston collaborated, after his marriage to Bulstrode's cousin, in presumably well-refreshed horseplay involving Bulstrode disguising as his coachman, while Thomas Chaloner was an infamous sot by the 1650s and is unlikely to have been entirely sober as a carefree young law student two decades earlier.*

---

* Tom Chaloner would later be associated with the most intellectually, politically, and privately free-spirited of the Parliamentarians, Thomas May, Henry Marten, Henry Neville, and John Harrington. May and Marten, as well as Chaloner, were friends of Ned Hyde before the civil wars, and continued to have good relations with Whitelocke thereafter. Aubrey sums Chaloner up thus: 'as far from a Puritan

## The Making of the Moderates

The fledgling political opinions of these youthful legal students were to be more career-defining than their personal conduct. They were imitating Star Chamber speeches not out of mere professional desire someday to deliver them as judges, tamely fatted instruments of the royal voice, but in a spirit of bold irreverence, pillorying the system for the present and hoping, one day, to pull it down. For the Star Chamber, together with the other courts outside the regular judicial system of the common law – the courts of the Councils of the North, Wales, and the Marches, the Earl Marshal, and the High Commission (under the archbishop of Canterbury, for ecclesiastical affairs) – was one of the furthest and most hated extensions of royal prerogative power. Of the friends engaged in light mock-oratory at Mrs Percy's, one in particular would play a crucial later part in the dismantling of most of these courts – not any of the future supporters of Parliament during the civil wars, Whitelocke, Grimston, Hall or Chaloner, but the man who would go down in history as an arch-Royalist, Edward Hyde.

The Parliament of 1628–9, Charles I's third and for many years his last, from which Bulstrode's susceptibility to the 'mutineers' had excluded him, was a more decisive affair than its predecessor, not in principle opposed to the King, but thoroughly disgusted by the ascendancy and incompetence of Buckingham. Under the leadership of Sir John Eliot and Lord Wentworth it passed the Petition of Right, restricting many of the perceived abuses for which the King and Buckingham, in scraping up men and money for their ill-fated continental adventures, had been responsible. King Charles reluctantly accepted the Petition, framing it as a statement of the existing constitutional balance rather than a concession. He was to regret this forced tolerance when a copy of the Petition was found sewn into John Felton's hat after Buckingham's murder. But however unwilling, this royal consent was shrewdly granted, winning Charles

---

as the East from the West . . . of the Natural Religion [meaning something akin to paganism in morals, and agnosticism in metaphysics] . . . one who loved to enjoy the pleasures of this life.'

the support of the ambitious Wentworth, from now on one of the most capable agents of royal government. Then, when the King decided to dissolve the still uncooperative Parliament in 1629, a group of MPs resisted by holding down the Speaker of the Commons, Sir John Finch, keeping him in his chair. This led to the arrest of nine recalcitrant MPs, among them the ringleader Eliot, who would soon die in gaol, and Whitelocke and Hyde's host and mentor, John Selden. The judges who soon condemned these nine MPs to continued imprisonment, of varying harshness, included Ned Hyde's uncle, the Lord Chief Justice Sir Nicholas Hyde, Bulstrode Whitelocke's uncle Judge Croke, and, more intimately yet, Bulstrode's own father, Sir James Whitelocke. Judge Whitelocke might have been Selden's old friend, but on this occasion his obligations to his courtier associates, such as Sir Humphrey May and William Laud (in his private, literary life, another of Selden's fond and fascinated correspondents), clearly carried the day.

## *The Apollo Chamber, Devil and St Dunstan's Tavern, Fleet Street, c. 1629*

Somewhere between the Inferno of his sub-tenant Will Davenant, full of plans and plays, gunpowder and mercury, and the cooling intellectual Elysium of John Selden's library, Ned Hyde about this time located a third, far more famous model, whose huge mental, creative, and physical bounty encompassed attributes of both the others. As Clarendon proclaims:

> Ben Jonson's name can never be forgotten, having by his very good learning, and the severity of his nature and manners, very much reformed the stage; and indeed the English poetry itself. His natural advantages were, judgment to order and govern fancy, rather than excess of fancy, his productions being slow and upon deliberation, yet then abounding with great wit and fancy, and will live accordingly . . . surely as he did exceedingly exalt the English

language in eloquence, propriety, and masculine expressions, so he
was the best judge of ... poetry and poets, of any man who had
lived with, or before him, or since ...

Despite Clarendon's stout belief in his immortal reputation, since Jonson's heyday his stature has waned. As a playwright and poet he is eternally and unfavourably bracketed with Shakespeare; even if Jonson's judgement as a critic is respected almost as highly as Clarendon predicted, that is largely because of the polite verse in which he prophetically praised his deceased contemporary, friend, and rival as a poet 'for all time'. When young Ned Hyde met him, though, things were different. Jonson was by the late 1620s a little on the slide, retired from the popular stage, his primacy as deviser of the court's masques ever less of a given, occasionally derided as past his prime by the clever young men who called themselves 'Sons of Donne'. Nonetheless he was still generally considered to be the greatest poet and playwright of the country's recent, glorious Elizabethan past: Shakespeare's supremacy was insisted upon only by a few less classically minded eccentrics like Davenant and John Hales.

Ned Hyde was a poet only in his own conceit and, counter-intuitively, in prose, but like many other such writers and readers, he cared profoundly about poetry in general. He naturally gravitated to the Apollo Room of the Devil and St Dunstan Tavern on Fleet Street – the street of Bulstrode Whitelocke's birth, locale too of Mrs Percy, hostess to Whitelocke, Hyde, and their friends in the summer of 1628 – and the company of the various scribblers and gadflies who considered themselves 'sealed to the tribe of Ben'. The *Life* implies that Hyde's friendships with Selden and Jonson began about the same time, but then this is the same work in which Clarendon altogether effaces his early friendships with Davenant and even Whitelocke. Selden could easily have introduced Hyde into Jonson's company, but so too could the racier poetic circle around Davenant. Whatever his entré, this was a new, thrilling world for young Hyde; one to which his friend Whitelocke, so much more promising by the end of the 1620s as a lawyer, courtier, even possibly politician, never attained (or sought) the same degree of access. Clarendon wryly articulates the difficulty for any young lawyer of staying in with the poets – especially the prickly old Jonson himself – while continuing to take his own profession seriously:

> ... [Jonson] had for many years an extraordinary kindness for Mr. Hyde, till he found he [i.e Hyde] betook himself to business, which he [i.e. Jonson] believed ought never to be preferred before his company.*

Jonson, Clarendon quietly suggests, was interested chiefly in compliant disciples; but Hyde already had in Selden a more useful, less demanding master. He was drawn to the Tribe of Ben not merely by its chieftain, but by its wider atmosphere: '[Jonson's] conversation was very good, *and with the men of most note* [my italics].'

What Whitelocke pursued at Oxford, in the 1626 Parliament, and as Master of the Revels in the Middle Temple and at court, was the acquaintanceship of men (and indeed, at court, women), of whatever age, who possessed power, or the promise of it to come. When, at the turn of the year 1628–9, an attempt was made by envious fellow Middle Templars to oust Whitelocke and other Revellers from offices to which they had been chosen within the Middle Temple that Christmas (Whitelocke had become its Treasurer), Whitelocke saw them off with a 'solemn speech', and emerged with his 'interest so increased that whatever he & his Revellers proposed found a clear passage in their Parliament [i.e. the Middle Temple's Presiding Council]'. It is unclear from Whitelocke's journal whether this was a genuine contention, or entirely a 'custom of the [Middle Temple] Society', to 'imitate the course of the house of Commons, & take liberty of speech, the better to enable them to serve their Country'. Ned Hyde, though also of the Middle Temple, appears to

---

* Aubrey suggests that Jonson had a particularly acerbic opinion of the legal profession.

have taken no notable part in this debate, if he even attended it. While the talent for leadership, even government, that Bulstrode had displayed since his Merchant Taylors' schooldays was with him still, Hyde at this time preferred over the pursuit of power the acquaintance of friends who were famous, talented, amusing, original, above all 'of note', memorable.

The friends of Jonson at the Apollo Room who first attracted Hyde's interest included two poets a generation younger than their 'father' Ben, a pair of poetic and debauched Toms, May and Carew; as well as Sir Kenelm Digby, the sometime pirate who had returned to England on hearing of Buckingham's murder. Both May, whose translation of Lucan would come to furnish Whitelocke's oratory, and Digby, a natural philosopher among his other varied accomplishments, were prodigious in their learning; Digby additionally presented a heroic figure of danger, adventure, and glamour. Carew might be a courtly scapegrace, but he was a poet of gleaming calibre, who garnered fresh gossip from the highest, not excluding royal, sources. All possessed worldly and literary experience, flair, and range that Ned Hyde would not have discovered in the more earnest crowd of students at law to be found at Mrs Percy's.

## Enter Sir What-Care-I, 1629–30

Since the courtly poet Thomas Carew was, Clarendon emphasizes, 'very much esteemed by the most eminent persons in the court, and well looked upon by the king himself', it was perhaps through him that the Sons of Ben first heard of Lord Falkland's recall from Ireland. Henry Cary, 1st Viscount Falkland, Lord Deputy of Ireland since 1622, was one of Jonson's most long-standing, generous, and (at least notionally) powerful remaining patrons. But, as the rumour now ran, the viscount's short-tempered but ineffectual record in Dublin had persuaded King Charles to prefer a firmer hand – that of the former opposition leader, Sir Thomas, now Baron, Wentworth. Wentworth had already made a great success of running his own part of the world for the King's government as the Lord President of the Council of the North, a position in which he excelled at exploiting the arguably arbitrary, irregularly judicial power that Whitelocke, Hyde, and their friends so deplored. Falkland's loss of power meant that an old and open-handed friend of Jonson would now have a much leaner purse. But consolation was coming to London in the form of Falkland's promising eldest son, Sir Lucius Cary, expected any moment to join the Tribe of Ben at the Devil and St Dunstan tavern.

Lucius Cary was the heir of a family whose complexities exemplified those of the three British kingdoms. His parents were an unlucky match, their marriage a mistaken gamble on conjoined prospects and resources. The 1st Lord Falkland was a brave but unsuccessful soldier, a charming but spendthrift courtier (yet another Buckingham client), a discerning reader but a hot-headed, unwise politician. Lucius's mother, Elizabeth Lady Falkland, neé Tanfield, brought a much greater fortune to the marriage – materially, as the sole heiress of her tight-fisted Oxfordshire family, but also, what turned out to be still more significant for her progeny, intellectually and spiritually. Her unsympathetic but perceptive lawyer father had noticed that from an early age Elizabeth's 'spirit' was 'averse from Calvin'. Lady Falkland initially estranged herself from her parents by financial recklessness on her husband's behalf; the Tanfields settled their estates to descend after both their deaths to Lucius, their eldest grandson. In 1626 Lady Falkland alienated her husband, too, by her public and vocal conversion to Catholicism. Lucius was educated as far as possible from her influence, at the rigorously Calvinist Trinity College Dublin, under James Ussher, an axiomatically traditional Elizabethan Protestant. King Charles put Lady Falkland under house arrest in what was intended as a sharp but brisk rebuke, then for some weeks, characteristically, forgot to inform her she was at liberty. Ben Jonson, himself sporadically Catholic, doubtless took an understanding view of all these goings on.

When Lucius Cary returned to London in 1629 – a congenial stop on his way to visit the Oxfordshire estates of Burford and Great

Tew, just left to him by his recently deceased Tanfield grandmother – he brought with him his dearest friend, Sir Harry Morison. Morison, who had been knighted and made a captain alongside Lucius by Lord Falkland, was a humanistic scholar as well as a soldier, another enthusiastic aspirant to the Tribe of Ben. But Morison could not make a long stay among the Apollo Room company, being called away back to garrison duty in Ireland; the smallpox caught up with him on the road, and he died on the Welsh shore. Jonson wrote a long-celebrated Pindaric Ode in commemoration of his young acquaintance's loss, 'To the Immortal Memory and Friendship of that Noble Pair, Sir Lucius Cary and Sir Henry Morison'. This replied to a far less disciplined elegy, its structure and tone throughout disordered by raw emotional pain, rapidly composed by Cary himself. Neither Sir Lucius's tormented outpouring in verse, nor Jonson's cool, Stoical answer, allayed the bereft Cary's intense grief over the loss of his great friend. It would soon be expressed in deeds, not words.

This extreme turmoil in Sir Lucius Cary's emotional background, at the same time and in the very setting when he first encountered Ned Hyde, treated with the utmost poetic seriousness by their mutual friend Jonson, makes one of Hyde's statements about the young Cary in his *History* either oddly mistaken, or deliberately occlusive to the truth:

> His education for some years had been in Ireland . . . so that when [Cary] returned into England, to the possession of his fortune, he was unentangled with any acquaintance or friends . . . and therefore was to make a pure election of his company; which he chose by other rules than were prescribed to the young nobility of the time.

Thus Hyde completely omits the existence of Harry Morison, just as Clarendon's *Life* actively suppresses his own early relations with Davenant and Whitelocke (among others). It is possible that Ned Hyde and Harry Morison never happened to meet under Jonson's aegis, but even then hardly probable that Hyde was totally unaware of Morison's significance, particularly given subsequent events. It seems that Hyde, soon in turn to become Cary's closest friend, did not care to dwell on his short-lived predecessor.

Nor did Hyde, either as Sir Edward in the *History* or Lord Clarendon in the *Life*, choose to discuss Cary's rash acts following Morison's loss to smallpox. When Sir Lucius gathered that his (wholly honorary) command of a troop of horsemen had been revoked along with his father's office, he sought out the blameless professional soldier who had succeeded to the captaincy and challenged him to a duel, getting himself clapped in gaol at the end of 1629 as a result. His father had to beg the King to let him out, and the quarrelsome young Cary was mocked all over London by the barely punning sobriquet of 'Sir What-Care-I'.

The impetuous son was soon to land his unlucky father in another, more serious imbroglio, one whose consequences even Hyde in his most hagiographical mode did not attempt to launder. The first Lord Falkland, having exhausted both his own and his wife's possessions in maintaining his courtly rank and then his high office in Ireland, relied entirely on arranging a prosperous match for his heir to avoid complete financial disaster. Sir Lucius, financially independent, indeed rich, since his Tanfield inheritance, though at twenty not yet formally of age, had other concerns.

At the conclusion of his heartbroken elegy to Morison, Lucius had turned to his lost friend's family: 'you, his aunt and sister, him being gone / Shall be to me my Harry Morison.' This was no idle thought. Still fresh from the Fleet, Sir Lucius immediately married Lettice Morison, Harry's sister, pious, shy, and penniless, without consulting Lord Falkland. Clarendon, as always effacing the lost brother and best friend between the married couple, describes Lettice courteously as 'a lady of the most extraordinary wit and judgment . . . [of] the most signal virtue and exemplary life, that the age produced', 'passionately loved' by her new husband. Her portrait by the Anglo-Dutch artist Cornelius Johnson resembles a high-minded, long-faced young man.

From the *Life* it can be deduced that Ned Hyde first encountered

## The Making of the Moderates

Sir Lucius Cary late in 1629, at about the time of Harry Morison's death. His immediate impression of Cary was not at all favourable:

> His person and presence . . . was in no degree attractive or promising. His stature was . . . smaller than most men; his motion not graceful; . . . his aspect so far from inviting, that it had somewhat in it of simplicity; and his voice the worst of the three, and so untuned, that instead of reconciling, it offended the ear . . . sure no man was less beholden to nature for its recommendation into the world . . .

In its denial of the conventional, romantic looks that would come to typify the 'Cavalier' – and which the portraits of Lucius Cary duly portray – Hyde's impression seems charmingly naturalistic. Yet it should be treated with some wariness, first because of the mature Clarendon's writerly love of antithesis – he goes on to declare how 'that little person and small stature was quickly found to contain a great heart' – and second, his semi-conscious tendency to attribute aspects of his own thought, character, and experience to Cary, the lost hero of his writings, instead. The still youthful, unproven, bulky Ned Hyde, earning his place at Jonson's board mostly by lending a devoted ear, is in evidence here as much as any accurate depiction of the future 2nd Viscount Falkland, the moderate Royalist paragon to come. Most interesting and convincing in its specificity is Clarendon's detail about Lucius Cary's harsh (perhaps Dublin-tinged?) voice, especially as Hyde's own always seems to have been noticed for its unusually, even incongruously pleasant melody.

After his precipitate marriage Sir Lucius Cary was as completely estranged from his father as his mother had become at her conversion to Rome. Lord Falkland had intended a different Lettice for his son, the very well-dowered daughter of the first Earl of Cork, an immensely rich Anglo-Irish super-intriguer. Her sister, Katharine, Lucius's childhood playmate, remained his friend after her marriage to Viscount Ranelagh, and would also become fond of Ned Hyde. Clarendon claims that Sir Lucius attempted to settle at least one of his late grandparents' Oxfordshire estates on his father, in recompense for his unfilial and, considering his father's assiduity in getting him released from gaol, ungrateful course of action. But this proposed gift would have involved legal complexities enough to tantalize young lawyers like Hyde and Whitelocke. The Carys could certainly not now afford such intricate embroilment, which is presumably (abundant wounded pride aside) why the first Lord Falkland refused to consider any such offer, if it was indeed made. Lucius's father, so recently as Lord Deputy of Ireland the next thing to a king in Dublin, was soon reduced to a London debtors' prison. Sir Lucius had thus managed to propel first himself and then his exasperated father into imprisonment. The newly married young Carys departed for the Low Countries, where Sir Lucius had a typically idealistic plan to volunteer as a soldier in the Protestant cause, the sort of paladin he had thought Sir Harry Morison was destined to be. But like so many of Sir Lucius's fantastic schemes during this interlude of not-quite-maturity, his Dutch commission failed to materialize. He and his wife were soon back in England, where they chose to reside next at Great Tew, the manor that would capture Hyde's heart and inspire his pen.

## *Marriages and Partings, Early 1630s*

The early 1630s were highly, but separately, eventful for Bulstrode Whitelocke and Ned Hyde. From 1634 up to (and even beyond) the definitive outbreak of civil war in England eight years later, the two men are connected through plentiful documentation, well-corroborated events, and a wide range of people – letters from Hyde quoted in the Whitelocke papers, references in Whitelocke's journal, independently verifiable political and private dealings, and an increasingly intellectually coherent, numerous, and celebrated constellation of mutual friends. Yet in the five years preceding this dramatic time both men, as far as the remaining documentation is concerned, appear peculiarly absent from one another's lives.

This drifing apart seems to have been the natural result of the

## The Making of the Moderates

two friends' trajectories up to this point. By 1630 Whitelocke had become conspicuous, and was evidently ambitious, as a lawyer and, potentially, through his new connections as Master of the Revels, as a courtier. He began to practise as a barrister, with his father Judge Whitelocke's approval, to help pay the onerous bills necessitated by the distractions and displays of the Revels.

Meanwhile Judge Whitelocke was making exploratory manoeuvres around the marriage market on Bulstrode's (and his sisters') behalf. After a couple of false starts in 1627 and early 1629, both apparently foundering upon details of the marriage settlement, early in 1630 Sir James Whitelocke identified and secured a seemingly ideal bride for his son. Rebecca Bennet was the niece of none other than Sir Humphrey May, the fixer of young Whitelocke's parliamentary debut. Her deceased father had been an Alderman of London. At twenty-one, four years younger than Bulstrode, Rebecca came with an almost suspiciously generous marriage portion, £3,000 (the equivalent of over £350,000 in purchasing power today). She impressed her projected groom at their first meeting as a 'proper comely young gentlewoman, of a good carriage and disposition'. The wedding day was fixed for the summer of 1630, at Mortlake, where Mrs Bennet kept a country house incorporating a chapel. No one appeared much discouraged by the death shortly before the appointed ceremony of the ingenious matchmaker Sir Humphrey. The mourning adopted by both the Whitelockes as family friends and the Bennets as close kin was considered rather fashionable, suiting the groom's dramatic pallor and black hair. Young Whitelocke journeyed to his nuptials upriver by barge from the Temple, reporting his feelings as 'gallant enough'.

Such expectations were to receive a sharp, immediate check. In the aftermath of what turned out (for reasons to receive proper attention later) to be a nightmarish wedding, Whitelocke distracted himself by providing counsel for John Selden and the other MPs whom the King had imprisoned after the dissolution of Parliament in 1629, and 'constantly attended all the debates on these matters in the Courts of Justice'. But over the next few years domestic sorrows rather than professional battles were to absorb most of his activity. The rapid and uncomplicated birth of a son, named James after his grandfather the Judge, in 1631 was outweighed first by his wife's extreme psychological delicacy, and then by the deaths of Bulstrode's parents, his mother's the same year and Judge Whitelocke's in 1632. Although now left a rich man – in today's terms just about a millionaire – Whitelocke appeared for the moment frustrated in his formerly bustling career. In 1633 he failed to obtain a position as a Master of Requests – a lucrative and honourable post dealing with chancery law – when the incumbent 'answered magisterially, that he would not sell the King's favour'.

At Michaelmas 1633, Whitelocke was summoned by his father's old friend and his own early protector, William Laud, lately made Archbishop of Canterbury and on his way to attend the King at Oxford, of whose university he was Chancellor. They met in Henley, close to Whitelocke's house at Phyllis Court; the archbishop was lodged at the Bell, a large, handsome, reputable, comfortable inn that Whitelocke was soon to add to his father's already huge local portfolio. Whitelocke urged the archbishop to accompany him home, but Laud stayed put, saying he only wished to ask his former Oxford charge a few questions as to his future, 'upon the great change in his fortune by his father's death'. Whitelocke expressed the desire to continue with his legal career, if, that is, His Grace the archbishop approved. His Grace did so, very well:

> . . . having at Oxford had the care . . . of Whitelocke he desired to see him do well having an affection for him, and therefore counselled him to go on in his profession, but his father having left him a competent provision for a gentleman, he wished him not to sweat too much at it . . . & promised if it should lie in his power that he would be a friend to him, & endeavour his good & preferment.

This was surely not just a kindly offer but a polite warning. It was now four years since the King had dissolved Parliament; Laud was among the most influential pillars of the personal royal government, dubbed the 'Thorough' administration by his colleague Thomas, Lord Wentworth. The archbishop followed his advice with touching praise of his late friend the judge, and laid on supper for Whitelocke at the inn, where he 'treated him with so much kindness, & respect, that all his own people, and strangers took great notice of it . . . he was pleasant at supper, as he used to be at meals'; in other words, Laud treated him with the same lightness and fondness he had shown to his friend's son at Oxford. Whitelocke must have known himself to be both wooed and cautioned by the King's government in archiepiscopal form.

As for Ned Hyde, from early 1630, the approximate beginning of his attachment to the Carys and their friends, his life appeared to be developing in a direction that would leave his title to the legal bar almost as purely decorative an honour as Lucius Cary's lost troop of horse. In 1631 his chief patron at the Inns of Court, that sometimes intimidating but extremely useful relative, his uncle Sir Nicholas Hyde, died 'of a malignant fever, gotten from the infection of some gaol', depriving Ned of his most formidable supporter in his scarcely chosen career. At the same time his ripening involvement with the Cary circle was drawing him out of London to Oxfordshire, where he was to discover friendship and conversation even more to his taste than Selden's or Jonson's. He also fell madly in love.

In 1632 Hyde married Anne Ayliffe almost as swiftly, if less controversially, as Lucius Cary in his conjunction with Lettice Morison. Anne was a Wiltshire neighbour from a greater family, another force drawing Hyde out of the city for all her family's courtly credentials. Despite Clarendon's carefully stuffy description of Anne's excellent wifely qualities (including the mumbled aside that she was 'very fair and beautiful'), of her important familial affinities, of his own easy-going father's total approval, between the lines the marriage was evidently a love-match. Had it lasted, perhaps Hyde would have replicated the example of rural domesticity and decent obscurity set by his father. In fact Anne's death from smallpox five months after the wedding, still pregnant with their first child, left Hyde as grieving as Sir Lucius Cary after the death of that other smallpox victim, Harry Morison, and all the more fatefully bound to his influential, charming, contentious marital kin, the families of St John and Villiers.

Hyde 'bore [Anne's] loss', Clarendon would recollect, writing three and a half decades later and immediately after the death of his second wife, 'with so great passion and confusion of spirit, that it shook all the frame of his resolutions'. His despair manifested itself quite similarly to Cary's; he was tempted to give up 'all thoughts of books' (that is, his in any case half-neglected legal progress) and travel 'beyond the seas to enjoy his own melancholy'. The difference lay in Ned Hyde's relationship with his father; his 'entire duty and reverence' to Henry Hyde the elder kept him in England whatever he might have preferred.

Probably as a compliment to his wife's extended family, Hyde had at about the time of his wedding composed and circulated his first effort in historical writing, a comparison of two royal favourites, Elizabeth's Earl of Essex and the late Duke of Buckingham, distinctly in the latter's favour. By implication Hyde also defended the kingdom's present and recent past against those religious and political malcontents who tended to dream of the Elizabethan era as a vanished golden age. This well-judged essay flew fast and high, confirming Ned's position in the affections of the Villiers family and, though he would not find this out for several years, attracting the interest of the King himself. A year after his first wife's death, still determined not to remarry, Ned Hyde found himself, to his deep discomfiture, enlisted as a source of advice in a delicate court intrigue concerning the honour of the house of Villiers.

After Anne's death Hyde had received a kindly letter from her aunt, Barbara Villiers, vouchsafing that 'I was so daily a witness of your affection to her that you may ever command me . . . your most assured loving Aunt'. But soon enough matters were on quite the other foot. Aunt Barbara's daughter, Eleanor Villiers, a maid of honour to Queen Henrietta Maria, was impregnated by the Queen's acknowledged favourite, Harry Jermyn (who, according to a rumour attributed to, among others, Hyde's scurrilous, courtly poet friend Tom Carew, was also the lover of the Queen herself). When Jermyn refused to take responsibility and offer marriage, Eleanor's intelligent but hot-blooded brother, Lord Grandison, was all for confronting him in a duel. Hyde attempted to intervene by more peaceable means in the summer of 1633, telling his father, 'My Lady Villiers [Aunt Barbara] believes that I may be of some use.' But to another Villiers sister who had already become a close friend of his, Anne, Lady Dalkeith, Hyde wrote after the visit to Greenwich at which he witnessed Aunt Barbara's dispiriting interview with the King and Queen, that 'the Queen stood by without any great sense of what had or could be said . . . never poor Woman [meaning Aunt Barbara] had less favour nor deserved more pity'. The account of the scandal that Clarendon later included in his *Life* is carefully sparing with names, while seeming to locate in this cynical microcosm of the courtly world the source of the whole coming civil dissension: 'much of that faction grew out of it, that survived the memory of the original . . . to shew us how from small springs great rivers may arise'.*

Such then were the early 1630s for Ned Hyde, leaving aside the ever more sustaining comfort of Great Tew: total detachment from an unloved profession, romantic marriage followed by pulverizing bereavement, and disillusioning experience at close quarters of the courtly nobility, the King and especially the Queen not excluded. But, in an episode he never later chose to recall, it was by Bulstrode Whitelocke's side that he returned to the glaring light of history.

---

* Briefly banished from court, Jermyn returned from a comfortable French exile within the year and was soon high in royal favour again. Eleanor Villiers, her reputation irretrievably tarnished, died unmarried. Nothing more is heard of their child.

## 2.

# The Lawyers' Interlude

*There be, who our Delights despise*
*As Shadows, and vain Phantasies.*

George Sandys, 'Urania to the Queen',
*Ovids Metamorphosis Englished*

## The Histrio-mastix and the Triumph of Peace, 1632–4

The former companions Whitelocke and Hyde were to be reunited early in 1634, in the most ostentatious fashion, through the actions of two lawyers named William – the prolific pamphleteer and hot Protestant, William Prynne, and his nemesis, William Noy. Noy, one of Whitelocke's impressive older acquaintances at the 1626 Parliament, had in that assembly been counted among the royal government's opponents, but in 1631 he accepted the post of the King's Attorney-General. Some time after this he took particular notice of Whitelocke, complimenting the up-and-coming lawyer for his advice concerning a tricky parliamentary impasse. Speaking of the resulting Bill and young Whitelocke's part therein, Noy commented that 'there were good wits as well as good Lawyers in the framing of it'. Furthermore he 'used Whitelocke with the ceremony of a Lord Treasurer [a compliment to Whitelocke's continuing reign as Treasurer of the Middle Temple]', and made the intriguing prophecy that Whitelocke 'would be a greater man than King's Attorney'.

In the winter of 1632–3, *Histrio-mastix: the players scourge, or actors tragedie*, a 'pamphlet' in name alone since it ran to over 1,000 pages, became the latest work from the indefatigable hand of William Prynne to fascinate the capital. Prynne, a barrister of Lincoln's Inn in his early thirties, was becoming known less for his legal practice than his passionate enthusiasm in print and austerity in religion. Although *Histrio-mastix*, Prynne's most significant work to date, condemned the writing and acting of plays, and attending them, Prynne actually approved of the *reading* of plays in a godly cause. Nor was his work untouched by the influence of the dramatic genre he ostensibly reviled. He appears to have pilfered his treatise's unwieldy, bastard-Greek title from a 1599 play of the same name by John Marston, a playwright whose bitter temper might well have appealed to Prynne's saturnine disposition.

Whether by unfortunate accident, as Prynne was soon to plead, or by ideological design, the emergence of *Histrio-mastix* closely coincided with a masque at court in which Queen Henrietta Maria herself, addicted as she was in every way to performance, was due to sing, act, and dance. For some six months before the publication of *Histrio-mastix*, as all London well knew, the Queen, her ladies, and friends had been rehearsing *The Shepherd's Paradise* by the courtier, incipient Catholic, and part-time secret agent Walter, or Wat, Montagu; and one of Prynne's very latest additions to his text had been an index reference containing an egregious swipe at *all* female dramatic performers, regardless of rank, as 'notorious whores'. Prynne was arrested for seditious libel late in 1633, and brought to trial the following year.

Prynne was prosecuted by William Noy, urged on by Archbishop Laud, in the unpromising surroundings of the Court of the Star Chamber – the same high-handed institution that Whitelocke, Hyde, and their friends had mocked at Mrs Percy's in 1628.\*
Early in the century Judge Whitelocke's friend, the eminent jurist

---

\* Laud's distaste for Prynne seemed half aesthetic, half outrage at the pamphleteer's obsessive anti-Jesuit paranoia, so often directed at the archbishop himself. Laud wrote of the offender's 'long meagre face' and 'head which is stuffed with Plots'.

Sir Edward Coke, had praised the Star Chamber, with one vital caveat, as 'the most honourable court (our Parliament excepted) in the Christian world'. By January 1634 the Star Chamber had presided without parliamentary restraint for four and a half years; aspects of the institution that had once felt versatile and efficient were now regarded as instruments of unaccountable royal will. More conspicuous even than the eponymous stars glinting from the chamber's ceiling were its four tapestries portraying each season, stitching the inevitability of royal justice into the passing of time itself.

As Prynne awaited his verdict amid such awe-inducing splendour, he could hardly have guessed how soon he would live to see these seasons and stars stripped of their vaunted power. But that time was not yet at hand. Prynne was inevitably convicted, heavily fined, his degrees revoked and his ears sentenced to cropping (a light trim of the lobes, given this first offence). In 1628 Prynne had produced a slighter pamphlet than *Histrio-mastix* on *The Unloveliness of Lovelocks*, denigrating the style of lengthily tressed hair that the King had adopted and popularized in men as 'unseemly and unlawful unto Christians'. There he had asked rhetorically of courtiers, 'Would they not rather have the commonwealth disturbed, than their hair disordered?' Now he had to adopt lovelocks himself to hide his punishment's consequences, consequences that would, in time, play their part in the commonwealth's disturbance.

But in 1633 itself, public opinion was little moved by the horribly comical plight of this blabber-mouthed killjoy who had insulted the pretty Queen and her innocent theatricals. Neither Ned Hyde nor Bustrode Whitelocke approved of the processes by which the Star Chamber operated and had arrived at its verdict. Yet when it came to Prynne, neither young man dissented from the prevailing, unfriendly opinion. Hyde's *History* dismissed Prynne as a person 'most notorious' for 'declared malice against the government of the Church by bishops', and not of 'interest or any esteem with the worthy part' of the legal profession, 'looked upon . . . under character of reproach'.* Whitelocke left no sign of any personal reaction to the Prynne incident. His maternal family seem in fact to have been 'hotter' Calvinist Protestants than Prynne, who was essentially a curmudgeonly, traditionalist, nostalgic Elizabethan thinker. But the respectable judge and his wife had not lived to see very far into this daring, aesthetic, sophisticated new era. Their son was certainly not going to waste time or prospects by acting on any inconvenient sympathy between his presently somewhat unfashionable family creed and any man in Prynne's position. The would-be-martyr was not only a trifle ridiculous, but a dangerous radical condemned by the government, detested by Whitelocke's old family friend and patron Laud, and held in contempt by what seemed to be the entire legal establishment in which Sir James Whitelocke had made the family name, a name that the younger Whitelocke hoped only to burnish.

According to Whitelocke's journal, the young lawyers of the Inns of Court, and in particular himself and his friend Ned Hyde, quickly became instrumental to Noy's efforts to remedy Prynne's libel against the Queen. Early in 1633, before Prynne had even been arrested:

> A design was laid for the four Inns of Court joining together to present a Royal Masque to the King & Queen . . . showing their difference of opinion from Mr Prynne's new book of *Histriomastix* against interludes. It took well with all the Inns of Court, especially the younger sort of them . . .

But the later, slightly variant account in Whitelocke's *Memorials* places the initiative elsewhere, not emanating from the Inns of

---

* Hyde was surrounded, as he composed the first version of his *History* in exile on Jersey, by islanders who would have remembered their infamous, unmistakable prisoner. After 1637 Prynne was kept in lonely, inkless confinement at the Castle of Mont Orgeuil on the island, to staunch his writings more effectually than the Tower of London had done.

Court, rather being conveyed more or less subtly towards them from the royal Court itself at Whitehall:

> This was hinted at in the Court and by them intimated to the chief of these Societies, that it would be well taken from them, and some held it the more seasonable, because this action would manifest the difference of their opinion, from Mr Prynne's new learning . . .

The two versions are not wholly irreconcilable. William Noy, both a fixture at court and a pillar of his Inn, might easily have transmitted a whim or suggestion from an enterprising courtier, even from the King himself, without appearing to compromise the Inns' intellectual independence. The lawyers were no doubt eager enough to find an excuse to scour off the stigma of their brother-barrister Prynne's *Player's Scourge*, and fond enough of an extravagant entertainment anyway.

It is hardly surprising that Noy picked Whitelocke – as the Middle Temple's Master of Revels and Treasurer a prominent and influential young talent, and already a great favourite of the Attorney-General – to form part of the committee tasked with arranging the Inns of Court's Masque for the King and Queen. The appearance of Ned Hyde alongside Whitelocke after several years of professional obscurity is less expected. Hyde's relations with Noy do not seem to have been good. Like many others, he took a dim view of Noy's smooth trajectory from parliamentary critic to Attorney-General, and would report in his *History* that:

> The Court made no impression upon [Noy's] manners; upon his mind it did: and though he wore about him an affected morosity which made him unapt to flatter other men, yet even that morosity and pride rendered him the most grossly liable to be flattered himself.

But Hyde himself was not without connections at court. They included Tom Carew; Sir Lucius Cary, now Lord Falkland, who jokingly claimed Carew as his kinsman; Wat Montagu, a more genuine, marital connection of Falkland and the author of the Queen's Masque; Will Davenant, by now one of the Queen's gadfly hangers-on; and the Villiers tribe in general. More significantly still, the older members of the Committee included Selden, now released from house arrest after a personal apology to the King for his involvement in the restraint of the Speaker in 1629. Selden, surely, would have spoken in favour of Hyde's inclusion.

In a remarkable show of unity that must have been deliberately contrived by the cunning Noy, the Speaker of 1629, Sir John Finch, also agreed to serve on the committee alongside Selden, his former assailant. In Hyde's view Finch 'had much that the other [Noy] wanted, but nothing that the other had . . . Having led a licentious life in a restrained fortune . . . set up upon the stock of a good wit and natural parts, without the superstructure of much knowledge in the profession.' Whitelocke lightly dubbed the older lawyers of the committee – Noy, Finch, and Selden – 'the Grandees', a Spanish term for high nobility whose English application was just coming into use to mock the leaders of the opposition to the court, both in the Commons and the Lords.

Lawyers young and old being now assembled, Whitelocke begins to describe the mechanics behind the masque:

> These met together and consulted about the business, & made sub-committees, one for the poetical part, another for the properties of the masquers and antimasquers and other actors, another for the dancing, & to Whitelocke in particular was committed the whole care & charge of all the music . . .

The 'antimasques' constituted subordinate and subversive actions within the wider masque, often written in a lower, more informal, comical register, with subversive rather than idealizing intent, forces of rebellion to be crushed amid the grace and harmony of the conclusion; the most familiar parallel to the modern theatregoer might be the Caliban, Stephano, and Trinculo sub-plot in Shakespeare's *The*

*Tempest*. It may have alerted Noy's colleagues to something curious going on that the King's Attorney-General now took chief responsibility for the antimasques, traditionally a sphere of minor importance hardly befitting the most senior member of the committee.

The poet that the Inns of Court commissioned, James Shirley, was a double-sided choice. On the one hand, Shirley was rumoured to share the Queen's Roman Catholic religion, and was a playwright particularly favoured and enjoyed by the King. But he was also his own man, a friend to the Inns of Court as a gentleman boarder of (Finch's) Gray's Inn, and a professional writer for the public stage. The lawyers chose Shirley over a courtly amateur like Wat Montagu, in whose *Shepherd's Paradise* the Queen and her company had precipitated the Prynne scandal, or the then favoured court masque versifier, Hyde's friend Tom Carew. The experienced Shirley justified the lawyers' confidence, insisting on a unique degree of independence from the famous, flattering scene-designer loaned by the court, Inigo Jones. The lawyers had found a writer whom both King and Queen were likely to accept, without their being able altogether to dominate him.

In allotting the masque's musical side to young Whitelocke, Noy perhaps remembered the widespread reputation for euphony of the Whitelocke parents' household. Prynne in *Histrio-mastix* had condemned equally 'Dancing, Music, Apparel, Effeminacy, Lascivious Songs' and 'Laughter' as 'universal overspreading still-increasing evils' across the kingdom. But not all 'Puritans' resembled Prynne. Elizabeth Whitelocke's deep Calvinism in religion was sterner and less insular than Prynne's; she spoke excellent French, after all Jean (John) Calvin's mother tongue. Her son now gathered forty lutenists, 'besides other instruments and voices in consort together', collecting musicians from the various nations to be found in the cosmopolitan city. They practised at his townhouse in Salisbury Court, west of St Paul's Cathedral and jostled by competing theatres. Whitelocke had acquired this busy city bridgehead to suit his wife Rebecca, who had rapidly manifested her discontent at being left behind in Berkshire.

## The Lawyers' Interlude

Especially swift to engage the court composers Simon Ives and Will Lawes in the business of the Inns' masque, Whitelocke was not however going to deny himself the pleasure of dabbling in a little composition himself. Will Lawes and his elder brother Henry, an equally famed musician, masquer, and composer, had, incidentally, almost certainly known Ned Hyde from infancy; they came from Wiltshire, where Henry Lawes was born at Dinton, a manor whose notably benevolent squire was Henry Hyde the elder, father of Ned. The autumn after the masque in which his brother Will composed airs for Whitelocke and the lawyers, Henry Lawes was busy at Ludlow Castle on the verge of north Wales, helping the young John Milton with the masque now generally known as *Comus*.

Whitelocke knew that his employment of Ives and Lawes would be especially pleasing to the Queen, and also selected four singers from her own, Roman Catholic, chapel: he seems to have chivalrously and astutely identified that Henrietta Maria, not King Charles, was the most important patron to impress, and to have acted on this observation without religious prejudice. In contrast to their implied backgrounds as members of, in Whitelocke's case, a Puritan family and, in Hyde's, a dynasty of courtly lawyers, Whitelocke was calculating what melodies would please the French Queen, while Hyde, the Eleanor Villiers affair still fresh in his thoughts, already had good reason to distrust her.

The theme that Shirley, with his usual talent for pleasing the King's ear, selected for the lawyers' masque was *The Triumph of Peace*. No other four words could have conveyed so precisely how King Charles liked to portray his policy since the dissolution of his third Parliament in 1629. Since 1618, central and northern Europe had been riven by what would prove to be the Thirty Years War, an avowedly religious struggle that became increasingly political. Charles I's family was directly involved; his brother-in-law, the Calvinist Elector Palatine, married to Charles's dangerously popular sister Elizabeth, had set the whole catastrophe in motion by his rash acceptance of the Bohemian Crown from that kingdom's Protestant nobility, in defiance of the far more powerful Catholic Habsburgs.

After the demise of the swashbuckling, silken-sworded Buckingham, Charles managed to emulate his own peace-loving father, eschewing serious military commitments on the continent, if at a concomitant price to his martial and religious credibility.

England's unexpected neutrality left a void into which, in 1630, galloped the King of Sweden, Gustavus Adolphus. Hailed as the greatest general of his age, this 'Lion of the North' succumbed to a mysterious shot directed from his own ranks two years later. He left lamenting admirers in every Protestant land, including the English poet and sometime court masque librettist Aurelian Townshend. In one of his few specifically political works, Townshend urged his fellow poet Tom Carew to join him in mourning the fallen Protestant hero Gustavus. Some of Townshend's lines on the slain Swedish King veered close to what might have sounded to King Charles like sedition:

> Princes ambitious of renown shall still
> Strive for his spurs to help them up the hill;
> His glorious gauntlets shall unquestioned lie
> Till hands are found fit for a monarchy.

Clearly the King of England is by implication the lesser prince, struggling in vain to fill the dead Gustavus's gloves. The reference to 'the hill' is particularly sharp as it alludes to 'the hill of fame' on which King Charles had been seated in *Chloridia*, Ben Jonson's last masque of 1631. Jonson had been replaced as the court's masque-writer the next year by none other than Townshend; now, only months later, Townshend dared to criticize the royal peace policy while subtly undermining his predecessor. But Carew, shortly in turn to replace Townshend as the King's masquer, answered him in a supremely apt strain. Townshend is indeed now mainly remembered as the poet to whom Carew addressed this rejoinder, an unparalleled evocation of the peaceful 1630s:

> Tourneys, Masques, Theatres better become
> Our Halcyon days; what though the German Drum

> Bellow for freedom and revenge? the noise
> Concerns not us, nor should divert our joys;
> Nor ought the thunder of their Carabins
> Drown the sweet Airs of our tun'd Violins . . .

Neither Townshend nor Carew's positions are quite as clear as they at first seem. Townshend, personally neither Calvinist nor Puritan, may have been lobbying on behalf of his particular patroness, the Catholic Queen Henrietta Maria, for pro-French intervention against the Habsburgs; while the ambiguity of Carew's character and thought has its role to play in the development of his friend Ned Hyde's opinions and friendships. But in choosing to write for the lawyers a spectacle entitled *The Triumph of Peace*, the professional poet Shirley was evidently showing his loyal sympathies in relation to a pre-existing controversy about foreign policy at court.

The committee's younger lawyers were now dispatched by Noy on a ticklish errand, handling altogether weightier persons than poets, as Whitelocke relates:

> Hyde & Whitelocke were sent to the Lord Chamberlain & Sir Henry Vane the Controller, to advise with them & to see things fitted for the scene & Masque in the Banqueting house at Whitehall against Candlemas night, when it was intended to present the Masque to conclude Christmas . . .

The Lord Chamberlain was Philip Herbert, 4th Earl of Pembroke. He had won the favour of old King James as a teenager by his good looks and sedulous attention to the chase, for which, Hyde acidly observed, Pembroke neglected any more sedentary education: 'He pretended to no other qualifications than to understand horses and dogs very well, which his master loved him the better for.'* This

---

* Worse things were said by some of the 4th Earl; Aubrey reports a story, which must thus have been in contemporary circulation however unlikely its facts, that Pembroke had really been born of an incestuous affair between his mother, the

bookish dig notwithstanding, Lord Pembroke had, with his older brother, been the dedicatee of Shakespeare's First Folio. He also supported his cousin George Herbert through his gift of the benefice of Bemerton, which lay conveniently near his poetically famed palace at Wilton in Wiltshire.

Although well known for frequent violent tantrums, Pembroke was cordial enough to the Inns of Court's emissaries on this occasion. But the Comptroller of the Royal Household, Sir Harry Vane, was less amenable; quite another proposition:

> There being a difference of opinion betwixt Sir Henry Vane & Whitelocke, Sir Henry gave harsh and proud words to Whitelocke [to] which he retorted smartly as esteeming the honour of the Inns of Court concerned therein, but the Lord Chamberlain took up the matter for the present, & what Whitelocke had said, was approved by his fellows . . .
>
> . . . Sir Henry who had as great pride as parts, and a scornful way of expressing himself, expected according to the name of his office, to be Comptroller of all other men's judgements, & . . . appeared to hold himself who was a great officer and a privy Counsellor, to be undervalued, in a young Lawyer's difference of opinion from his wisdom.

Hyde remembered Vane at about this time as 'a busy and a bustling man, who had credit enough to do his business in all places, and cared for no man otherwise than as he found it very convenient for himself'. With Pembroke, on the other hand, Hyde seems to have established a rapid understanding. He would soon accept his first sinecure from the earl, and even after many political differences had disenchanted him would still acknowledge 'having been formerly beholding to him for many civilities when there was so great a

---

celebrated Mary, Countess of Pembroke, poet and patroness, and her even more famous brother, Sir Philip Sidney: 'but he inherited not the wit of either brother or sister'.

distance between their conditions'. Five years after this first courtly meeting, Hyde would enter the House of Commons as one of a group of MPs loosely affiliated with Pembroke's interests. The Banqueting House whither both young lawyers now proceeded was the overpowering scene of Whitehall's most dignified occasions, completed by Inigo Jones in 1622, to house, among other things, the masques whose machinery he contrived for King and Court.*

The *Triumph of Peace* was presented on the night of 3 February 1634, just after Candlemas. The procession of masquers set out from Ely House in Holborn towards Whitehall, by way of Chancery Lane, Temple Bar, and Charing Cross. Each Inn of Court was represented by its own 'Roman triumphant chariot', the order to be determined by lot. But the seats, Whitelocke recalled, were carefully crafted 'of an oval form to prevent questions about precedence', with four lawyers riding in each chariot, assisted by a coachman. Finch and Shirley's Gray's Inn came first, its chariot draped with silver and orange; then Whitelocke and Hyde's Middle Temple, bedecked in silver and blue, of a light shade known as 'watchet'. These chariots had been preceded by the royal marshal and his truncheon-men to clear the path, then by the Inns' brightest sparks, 'a hundred gentlemen on horseback, each of them having a page and two lackeys', and finally by the actors and musicians in still more expressive chariots that displayed their parts to best advantage. So many were the torches of resinous wood and flambeaus of waxen wicks, in honour of the festival just passed, that some witnesses (not very credibly) declared that midnight had been transformed to noon.

Whitelocke did not himself take a seat in the Middle Temple's chariot, but provided its coachman, and in subsequent years regarded silver and blue as his own heraldic colours. It is easy to

---

* The Banqueting House's splendid if all too soon ironical ceiling by Rubens, showing the apotheosis of King James and an allegory of the birth of King Charles, would not be completed until 1636 (Rubens sketched the design during his visit to London in 1630, then executed the painting in Antwerp).

imagine that this stylish, extroverted, ambitious young man would have enjoyed the attention of riding in the procession, but his and Hyde's duties now obliged otherwise. It was back to Whitehall for them, showing itself to its most impressive and ingratiating advantage; Whitelocke's journal shows him much affected:

> Hyde and Whitelocke went before to Whitehall to see all things in readiness & found the Banqueting house so crowded with Lords, Ladies & gentlemen all richly clothed, & the Ladies glistening with rich garments and richer Jewels, & the room so full that they scarce left room for the King and Queen to enter, the Lord Chamberlain carried Hyde and Whitelocke to his daughter Carnarvon's chamber, who was a lady of excellent wit and discourse . . .

Lady Caernarvon's husband was another devotee of the chase, the Queen, the gaming tables and the Catholic Church. Hyde would later come to esteem him, somewhat to his own surprise. Carnarvon's wife, Lady Anna Herbert by birth, did not share her husband's and the Queen's religion, but it is still worth noting Whitelocke's ease and pleasure in her courtly company. At the same time, his description of those jam-packed and bejewelled environs carries a trace of Puritanical distaste; it could easily be compared to the similarly gorgeous House of Pride in Edmund Spenser's Protestant romance, *The Faerie Queene*. There is a faint political charge, a sceptical vigilance towards courtly sycophancy, discernible in Whitelocke's naturalistic observation that Charles and Henrietta Maria could hardly push themselves through their hordes of adorers.

The first contingent of masquers now performed the antimasque devised by Noy, watched by the royal party and the two younger lawyers from the Banqueting House's great window. At its head was an actor attired as a bat-winged 'Phansie', a herald of disconcerting thoughts about to be sanctioned before the royal presences. Among Phansie's troubling evocations came a gang of beggars and cripples riding on spavined horses; a knot of small boys representing scavenger birds, a magpie, a crow, a jay, and a kite, somewhat mysteriously pecking at an owl; and, with increasingly evident political bite, a series of parodic representations of patent-holders and monopolists, one particularly noticeable for the bunch of carrots in his hat and the fat capon (a castrated cockerel) perched on his fist as if it were a hawk. Later on in the proceedings a group of menial craftsmen, like the mechanicals of *A Midsummer Night's Dream*, interrupted the masque's action and demanded their fair share of it, before taking flight in the hope that the court would think their presumption 'was meant for an Antimasque'.

Whether Charles I and Henrietta Maria displayed an enlightened, rueful sense of humour for which subsequent historians have given them small credit, or whether they concentrated their attentions on the more conventional elements of Shirley's masque, such as the concluding song inaccurately prophesying the eternal flourishing of their progeny, they evidently enjoyed the procession, action, and music alike. The masque was requested to trail its way around Whitehall's Tilt Yard so as to double the royal party's time inspecting it. Henrietta Maria and her ladies joined in the dancing at the act's conclusion – a satisfying seal upon the outrage of the incarcerated Prynne – which lasted 'till almost the morning'. The masquers and lawyers were afterwards entertained at a huge banquet of a breakfast, 'after which they all dispersed, & thus this worldly pompe & glory, if not vanity, was soon gone & past over as if it had never been' – Whitelocke's recollections are once again torn between the courtier's pride and the Puritan's guilt.

The Queen particularly noticed one air, according to its composer, Whitelocke himself; she was astonished that 'Whitelocke's Coranto' was not composed by a Frenchman, considering it 'fuller of life and spirit than the English airs use to be'. There is little reason to doubt this admittedly immodest account. Whitelocke was a genuinely gifted amateur composer, and the Coranto's widespread surviving notations are consistent with his boast that it remained in fashion all over England for 'nearly thirty years'. Those were decades, one might otherwise have thought, when political upheaval quickly overshadowed musical fashion, but given the shape of

Bulstrode's primary, public career, a measure of popularity lasting until shortly after the Restoration actually makes sense. More immediately, an encore for the Queen was arranged for ten days later, at the hall of the composer's *alma mater*, the Merchant Taylors'. There was one unfortunate consequence – the master of the King's Music, Nicholas Lanier, took offence at being displaced by mere City men, and Whitelocke had to write a diplomatic apology.*

Sir John Finch, Whitelocke, and Hyde were deputed by Noy's committee to undertake the masque's final formality, attending court once more 'to give their Majesties humble thanks for their gracious acceptance of their service in the Masque'; this rite too proceeded smoothly. By this time the King and Queen had also been presented with Carew's masque *Coelum Britannicum* ('British Heaven'), a more restrained but wittier production than Shirley's *Triumph of Peace*. Among its most delighted spectators was Hyde's more recent bosom friend, young Lord Falkland. Carew's masque portrays an extended debate between the dignified messenger-god Mercury and the anarchic deity Momus, patron of satire. It concludes with the entire pantheon of pagan gods resigning their power in Charles and Henrietta Maria's favour.

Whitelocke, too, could now be found at the Apollo Chamber where Hyde had first met Jonson, Carew, and Sir Lucius Cary, but characteristically Whitelocke tended there to musical, not poetic company. He entertained his recent collaborators Simon Ives and Will Lawes, treating them to munificent gifts of gold under pewter platters. The other (Catholic) musicians of the Queen's chapel also attended this celebratory evening; Whitelocke was still choosing to

---

* Lanier was one of that fascinating kindred, of mixed Huguenot, Jewish, and Venetian lineage, that had served as musicians for English monarchs since Henry VIII's day. His aunt Aemilia Bassano, spectacularly identified by A.L. Rowse as the Dark Lady of Shakespeare's Sonnets, was the first recorded professional female poet in England (as opposed to Elizabeth, Lady Falkland, the first published amateur female poet).

## The Lawyers' Interlude

ingratiate himself with the Queen's party, if by appealing to its musical aesthetics rather than, necessarily, its politics or religion.

'But black night overtakes the glorious day,' Whitelocke concludes his journal entry on the masque with unwonted lyricism, 'the fairest calms have storms in their bosom, & the chain of earthly things, for one link of joys have two of sorrows.' Passing from lament into homily, he hastily appends 'and it is best so, least the constant smiles of this world should allure us too much into love of it, & cause us to forget God'. There is rather less pious resignation in the loving pairings of nouns that follow – 'this high pleasure & jollity, this honour & favour, this joy & gallantry, as to Whitelocke's particular concerns, was soon plunged into the depth of grief & misery'. In the trials Bulstrode Whitelocke was about to undergo, Ned Hyde, his younger, more miscellaneously connected and already bereaved friend, would fully prove the resilience of their bond of friendship.

3.

# *Tragedy, Adventure, and Romance*

> *Fire, Aire, Earth, Water, all the Opposites*
> *That strove in Chaos, powrefull Love unites . . .*
>
> George Sandys, Argument,
> *Ovids Metamorphosis Englished*

## *A Bride and the Mother, Mortlake, and Phyllis Court, 1630–31*

After the dissolution of the 1626 Parliament had left the younger Whitelocke once more at a loose end, his father Sir James twice sought, each time in vain, to match his heir to a suitable wife. First Judge Whitelocke enquired after the heiress of a rich City merchant; next he identified the beautiful and good-natured daughter of a Hertfordshire knight. According to his son's journal, both suits fell through during discussions over the marriage settlement. But what traces of Sir James's negotiations survive in the older Whitelocke's *Liber Famelicus* give little sign of avaricious wrangling. Three years earlier the canny old lawyer had matched Bulstrode's elder sister Elizabeth well, among the Mostyns of Wales, later to be ardent Royalists, when the girl was twenty (about average for a gentle, rather than noble, marriage). Perhaps the real stumbling block was one the younger Whitelocke would have found more painful to acknowledge, even in the journal he composed for both his own and general posterity – his lasting lameness, incurred in his unlucky Oxonian hunt with William Juxon.

The answer Sir James Whitelocke found, early in 1630, to the problem of his beloved son's matrimonial prospects was located by the same man who had granted the youthful Bulstrode his first chance in politics: Sir Humphrey May, Chancellor of the Duchy of Lancaster. For all the younger Whitelocke's parliamentary unbiddability, Sir Humphrey apparently retained sufficient fondness for the young man, or for his eminent father, to interpolate Bulstrode into his own family. Sir Humphrey had a sister of strong character and large estate, Dorothy, widow of a City alderman, Thomas Bennet; and among their children was a daughter, Rebecca, who appeared to be in a similar position to Bulstrode's, being, despite considerable outward charm, unaccountably difficult to match. The prospect of a lucrative alliance with Sir Humphrey's City kin must have come as a relief and a prize that, for both Whitelockes, thoroughly made up for that bygone squib of a Parliament.

But what the revellers would find on the appointed wedding day, a fine summer's morning in 1630, after a pleasant trip by boat upriver to Mrs Bennet's house at Mortlake, much dismayed the groom at their head:

> ... there he met with an unexpected disturbance, the bride was exceeding ill, deprived of her senses and reason, by the distemper she was in, which some said was caused by the fever then upon her, others said, by a violent fit of the mother she fell into upon the thoughts of the great change of her life ... all wondered at it ...

The 'fit of the mother' refers to the universal mother of the womb, not to Mrs Bennet. Whitelocke means by it a hysterical episode, or panic attack. It may now seem surprising that the adverse reactions of cloistered daughters, confronted by sexual initiation and family life with near-strangers, were ever received with 'wonder'. Yet here, most probably, lay the answer to Rebecca's sizeable dowry and her family's almost suspiciously rapid acceptance of young Whitelocke. Mrs Bennet, whom subsequent events were to reveal as not overscrupulous, was certainly aware of her daughter's delicacy.

Everyone, including Rebecca once she recovered herself, remained set on the marriage going ahead, and if, as Whitelocke implies, he himself had second thoughts, he stifled them. Rebecca was busy 'expressing sorrow for the trouble of her servant', meaning in chivalric terms her betrothed groom; Whitelocke's 'father and his friends persuading him, but his affection more, he proceeded in the marriage'. But, the wedding party having once dispersed, the trouble returned:

> ... the night was far spent, the bride put to bed, her bridegroom soon came to her, & expecting marriage joys met with strange discomforts, his bride fallen into new fits ... so violent that her bridegroom was fain to leave her bed to call for help for her, thus she continued all night, and gave more expectation & fear of her death, than hopes of her recovery.
>
> Thus strange & full of sorrow was the beginning of the settlement of Whitelocke's fortune, & so different from that which new married men look for & enjoy.

Recounting the fiasco more than three decades later, Whitelocke appears to have had immediate access to the confusing, raw emotions he felt at the time, more human, perhaps, than attractive. He had been taught by his parents that he deserved, and would shortly, doubtless with the help of industry and morality, attain all good things. He had experienced occasional physical mishaps in his youth, but his internal life, certainly compared to that of Ned Hyde, appears to have been untroubled. He was now tied for life – someone's life, at any rate – to a girl apparently in bodily and mental agony from a complaint he was unequipped to understand.

In 'sharp grief' Whitelocke now consulted 'him who orders all things', offering the prayer that 'these unusual beginnings in sorrow, might be returned in future comforts'. The next morning Rebecca showed some improvement but also seemed 'troubled at her husband's cause of sadness', as if not remembering, or accepting, the virulence of her attack. The newly married couple successfully consummated their marriage within at most two months of the wedding, as their son James, his Whitelocke grandfather's namesake, was born in July 1631.

The first surviving letter from husband to wife, written halfway through Rebecca's pregnancy, combines awkward formality with genuine solicitude. In Oxford on business with his maternal uncle Edward Bulstrode (another lawyer, more diffident in his profession than his brother-in-law and nephew), Whitelocke wishes Rebecca:

> . . . health, courage and freedom from fear, which she may well enjoy considering her security and the stillness of rogues at that time.

In fact after their son's birth Rebecca made a much swifter and fuller recovery than her vigilant husband perhaps expected. In August Whitelocke wrote to his father that '[Rebecca] is ready for her journey [from Mortlake to Fawley Court in Buckinghamshire] sooner than he thought', though he considerately noted a plan to pause at Horton should her strength prove overtaxed.*

Early on in the marriage Whitelocke was, according to his journal, reading widely, both in the Scriptures and among 'heathen philosophers, whose constancy & rules in adversity . . . may shame some Christians'. From Epictetus, the Stoic, he extracted the motto *Quodcunque evenerit optimum*, which he translated and elaborated into English as 'Whatever happens is best – *if I make it so*'. He composed lute music and a lyric on this theme:

> *The comforts of this life are fading joys,*
> *Pleasures are toys,*
> *Honours are vapours, riches fly away*
> *And friends decay . . .*
> *Then let our fortunes rise or fall*
> *Happen what will 'tis best of all.*

---

* Horton would five years later become the home of the young John Milton (in 1631 living with his father in Hammersmith), where many of his early poems were composed.

> ... *If thou are disappointed in the things*
> *Which thy hope brings*
> *Ne'er to fruition, if the joys of love*
> *Afflictions prove* ...
>
> ... *Happen what will, 'tis best of all,*
> Quodcunque evenerit optimum.

Whitelocke demonstrates in this song an unfailing ear, traditional Calvinist doctrine, and an accordingly sententious mode of thought. No amount of Stoical resolution could have prepared him for the shape not only of his marriage, but ultimately too his public life, from which disappointing vantage point he would compose his journal.

## 'University in a less volume': The Great Tew of the Early 1630s

At the end of 1630, as Whitelocke weathered his domestic tribulations, Sir Lucius Cary at last entered into his new Oxfordshire estates, 'resolving to retire to a country life, and to his books; that since he was not like to improve himself in arms, he might advance in letters.' Cary thus arrived in the country as a hermit in flight from failure and frustration – his father's fall, his own disgrace, his consecutive estrangement from both his parents, and his brief, uneventful, anticlimactic sojourn in the Low Countries. But in this rural retirement Cary, soon to become 2nd Viscount Falkland, was, perhaps to his surprise, about to discover the sense of purpose and joy of fulfilment that had seemed to elude him throughout 1629–30.

Falkland's manor at Great Tew no longer survives. His other seat and likely birthplace at Burford has had better luck, but this he had to sell to an old family friend, the future Speaker of the Commons William Lenthall, in 1633, after the first viscount died unreconciled to his son, leaving his title encumbered by enormous debts. The damage inflicted on Great Tew during the civil wars was compounded by

## Tragedy, Adventure, and Romance

eighteenth-century neglect, then sealed by nineteenth-century demolition. No drawings of the old house's structure have survived. Fitting monuments are left in its adjoining parish church, but more importantly in the memoirs of literary and historical gossips – John Aubrey, Anthony Wood, and, supremely, those of Clarendon himself. Typically as terse about landscape as he is elaborate in characterization, Clarendon nonetheless conveys a consistent, refreshing impression of Great Tew:

> ... [Falkland's] house being within ten miles of Oxford ... the most polite and accurate men of that university ... frequently resorted, and dwelt with him, as in a college situated in a purer air; so that his house was a university in a less volume; whither they came not so much for repose as study ...
>
> ... the company that was always found there [were] all men of eminent parts and faculties in Oxford, besides those who resorted thither from London; who all found their lodgings there, as ready as in the colleges; nor did the lord of the house know of their coming or going ... till he came to dinner, or supper, where all still met; otherwise, there was no troublesome ceremony or constraint, to forbid men to come to the house, or to make them weary of staying there; so that many came thither to study in a better air ...

The 'purer' or 'better' air is partly literal, for both Oxford (as opposed to its surrounding country) and London were infamously hospitable to plague and noxious to weak chests. But it is more profoundly moral, theological, and political. At Falkland's open house, unlike at court, in the capital, or in the university, free minds might dispute safe from conformist disapproval. According to Hyde, Falkland himself preferred to abstain from reading, despite his increasingly famous library, whenever his scholarly friends visited, except in cases when a specific point needed to be looked up.*

---

* The contrast with Selden's habit, as reported by Aubrey, of keeping his books and papers set aside for use but concealed, presents an amusing and perhaps

Otherwise, general conversation, studded with the allusions supplied by his visitors, sufficed.

By now Falkland had matured beyond his courtly but luckless father, and instead resembled his bibliomaniac, spiritually preoccupied mother. The variety of Falkland's intellectual friendships kept him from either adhering to or reacting overmuch against the dowager Lady Falkland's Catholic dogma. He was in fact too genuinely 'catholic' to become either Roman Catholic or violently anti-Papist. The younger Falkland's disturbed times would force him, as his friendship with Ned Hyde lured him, into a political career, but his keenest natural abilities evidently lay in open-minded, amiable religious disputation.

Politically, Hyde would come to see Falkland as something of a naïf in his idealism, gently deprecating his 'reverence to parliaments', and his 'jealousy and prejudice towards the court', which Hyde shrewdly diagnosed as stemming from the first Lord Falkland's theoretically high-flying, actually accident-prone, career. Hyde was in talent and direction in some ways Falkland's opposite, the necessary complement to offer the friendship its intense attraction, at the same time as both men aspired to similar ideals. Hyde's Christianity was traditional and social rather than spiritual and inward. His passions tugged him on the journey upon which he would encourage both his closest friends, Falkland and Whitelocke, towards people and their science, the journey of politics.

In his *Life* Clarendon is expansive upon the friendships he formed at Great Tew; pre-eminently with Falkland himself, but also with many others who would have, in some cases, an even longer-lasting influence upon his life and career. There was William Chillingworth, Laud's godson, Falkland's guide down the heady path of experimental theology (as, later, Hyde's through the byways of the Midlands); Chillingworth's best friend from their undergraduate days, the more rigid, conventional, but superbly capable and

---

revealing comparison between the venerable lawyer-antiquary and the noble young patron, both so famous for their private libraries.

self-confident Gilbert Sheldon; the witty John Earle, the 'Ever-Memorable' John Hales, and the sardonic George Morley. These are the men whom Clarendon wished posterity to remember as his most cherished companions.

In a separate, if related, category Clarendon places several figures equally, or in some cases even more spectacularly, gifted, but who would turn out to lack the personal and political fellowship and loyalty exhibited by the Great Tew pantheon proper. He recalled the seeming friendship of such men largely to regret their shortcomings, lament their fickleness, or refute their pronouncements. These included the mellifluous, hugely rich poet, Edmund Waller, the worldly courtier Tom Carew, the severe, heavy-drinking scholar, translator, historian, and poet Tom May, the future Catholic priest Hugh Cressy, and Thomas Hobbes, an apparently orthodox, if prodigious, scholar who was to become the greatest intellectual renegade of the age.

Although Whitelocke as well as Hyde counted Falkland among his most admired acquaintances, his allusions to the scholarly young nobleman are relatively distant and deferential, indicating that they knew each other mainly in a political context and, especially, through Whitelocke's professional services as a barrister. Far more committed than Hyde to their common profession, after 1628 Whitelocke badly needed to counteract his debts from liberal expenditure as the Middle Temple Master of Revels. Much later, Whitelocke was however to describe 'that ingenious Lord Falkland' as his 'great friend', seemingly regarding Falkland, no less than Falkland's actual bosom friend Hyde, as a crucial, poignant, and symbolic worthy – worthy of honour and remembrance, as well as, perhaps, a useful acquaintance to recall after the Restoration.

In 1650, seven years after Falkland's death fighting with the Royalists at the Battle of Newbury, Whitelocke was to acquire an example of his writing that he describes as an 'excellent piece', later 'unhappily mislaid'. He also offered ample employment to the source of this literary bounty, Thomas Triplet, one of the late viscount's many clerical protégés, during what were, for Anglican divines like

Dr Triplet, the years of hardship during the Commonwealth. Whitelocke's account of Falkland's last battle would become almost as influential as Hyde's. He complained of the ingratitude of Falkland's son when the latter became a political enemy. But none of this quite amounts to the sort of mutual personal warmth, interest, and involvement that bound Falkland and Hyde on the one hand, Hyde and Whitelocke on the other.*

The closeness of Hyde and Falkland's personal and political friendship from the early 1630s until, and indeed in some ways beyond, Falkland's death in 1643 is both evident and significant. But early in the same period, between the miserable decline of Whitelocke's first marriage and the dramatic inception of his second, Ned Hyde also unquestionably and faithfully played the part of Bulstrode's dearest friend. Whether to his former friend's credit, as a reproach, or both, Whitelocke wished his own children to remember Clarendon's bygone affection, copying down some of the other's letters into his journal 'to let you see the kindness and correspondence that was between this gentleman and me in these times'.

## To France, by Way of Bow, and Back, April–June 1634

By 1634, after four years of marriage, the younger Whitelockes displayed an outwardly lively and contented household to the world. Like her marital relations, Rebecca took great pleasure in music. In company, her looks, like her husband's, were generally admired. Her health was still a little delicate – in 1633 Whitelocke had sought and easily obtained a licence allowing Rebecca to eat meat on days forbidden by the established Church on these grounds – but her husband's own constitution, after all, also had its occasional eddies. Her parents-in-law had, however, continued to worry about the effects of her 'melancholy fits' upon their cherished son. Elizabeth

---

* By an uncanny coincidence Whitelocke would drag out his last years in involuntary retirement at Chilton Foliat, the Wiltshire seat of Falkland's Cary ancestors.

Whitelocke died the spring after the marriage, and her husband followed her in the summer of 1632. At his only meeting with his grandson and namesake, born in 1631, Judge Whitelocke, 'to try the child's natural inclination, put a piece of gold' into little James's hand. When the baby reasonably enough dropped it, his grandfather made the dubious if eventually accurate joke that this might set the tone for the family fortunes in the third generation.

Growing bored at Phyllis Court, the subsidiary Whitelocke country house near Henley, while her husband rode the rural justice circuits, Rebecca persuaded her husband to acquire the smart town house at Salisbury Court, near St Paul's Cathedral and several theatres, that so proved its worth during the masque rehearsals. Not long after the masque's performance, Ned Hyde, in the letter that marks his regular return to his old friend's company and archive, wrote to Whitelocke of his pregnant wife's contrasting desire for rural peace; she had chosen to bear her latest child at Cranbourne Lodge in Windsor Forest, which her father held for life as a royal warden. The rapidly shifting allegiances of civil war would in the fateful year of 1649 allot this delightful place to the enjoyment, instead, of Bulstrode and Rebecca Whitelocke's son, James Whitelocke the younger, by then a captain under Oliver Cromwell. In fortunate ignorance of revolutions to come, Hyde appealed to his friend for a gift of cider to be sent into the depths of the woods for his own patriarchal refreshment.

The aftermath of the *Triumph of Peace* had left Bulstrode the darling of lawyers as well as a fairly well-known amateur composer noticed by the Queen. His start at court offered him an equivalent extralegal sphere to his friend Hyde's standing welcome at Great Tew. But, that April, before Whitelocke could make much use of these advantages, disaster struck in the form of his beautiful, haunted wife. Her latest attack came on her 'in far greater violence than in any time before'; words wholly failed Whitelocke the later memoirist: 'if the manner thereof should be related, tears would blot the paper . . . Never poor creature had a more dismal sickness . . . never man . . . a sharper affliction.'

In the midst of Rebecca's drastic deterioration, months into an urban married life that had seemed to afford her greater happiness than before, her formidable mother Dorothy Bennet and the rest of her family took over from her young, baffled husband. Young Mrs Whitelocke was sent east to Bow, under the care of a Dr Bartlett 'famous for the cure of such distempers'. This doctor was indeed well known to the Bennets. One of Rebecca's married sisters, suffering from a similar complaint, about which neither Whitelocke nor his father had been told anything salient, was already Dr Bartlett's patient. The physician charged £200 for his cure and 50 shillings a week for Rebecca's board (respectively worth about £24,000 and £250 today). Whitelocke demurred less at the price than at the doctor's stipulation that 'none of [Rebecca's] friends, nor her mother, nor her husband himself must see her' for almost half a year, 'for that he affirmed would disturb her so as wholly to hinder his cure'. Mrs Bennet, supported by two of her sons, persuaded Rebecca's reluctant husband to accede to this perverse-seeming advice.

'Being thus banished from her company whom he most loved,' Whitelocke writes with perhaps forgivable melodrama, 'he took a sudden & rash resolution, that in regard he must not see his wife, he would not stay in the kingdom where she was.' Elsewhere he makes out less hot-bloodedly that Dr Bartlett had himself suggested that the forcibly separated husband might find distraction by a journey into France. Whatever the truth, it seems Whitelocke was not eager to let Mrs Bennet know about his planned trip. He did not initially give details of the enterprise even to close friends and family – neither to Hyde, who since the masque had, it seems, picked up once again his close association and regular correspondence with Whitelocke, nor to his own sisters and their husbands. As his fellow traveller Whitelocke chose Robert Cole, a Middle Temple lawyer of his own age, not brilliant or rich but whose character was soon to be proven excellent. The passport for travel beyond the seas required of English subjects was acquired from the Lord Chamberlain, Pembroke, who had just been so obliging about the lawyers' masque. After a tiresome wait for fair wind at Rye in Sussex ('This town is not very eminent'), the lawyers and their servants embarked on a safe, swift passage to Dieppe.

Ned Hyde's father, Henry, had ventured overseas out of curiosity half a century earlier. Continental travel was not much easier in 1634 than it had been during the reign of Elizabeth. This was Whitelocke's own first excursion abroad, though one of his father's brothers was a merchant settled in Germany. Whitelocke had arrived in the France of Louis XIII, or in other words of Cardinal Richelieu; Pembroke had furnished him with letters of introduction to the Cardinal, the French-born English Resident at Paris, Réné Augier, and other useful dignitaries.*

Whitelocke found Dieppe 'a convenient Sea Town', an improvement at least on Rye. He struck up what would turn out to be a lasting epistolary friendship, 'for many years after' with the town's governor, Colonel de Montigny, 'an Eminent Soldier . . . of good quality'. These letters have vanished, to history's great loss, as M. de Montigny remained at his cross-channel post until after the Restoration and must have witnessed many interesting English visitors of various allegiance flitting past his watch. The governor was not, however, the most intimate friend Whitelocke struck up at Dieppe. At the inn where the travellers broke their journey, he noticed, or as he insists was noticed by, the hostess, who was much intrigued by his elegant appearance and sad story (gleaned from Cole's French manservant):

---

* Augier, a Huguenot lutenist from the Dauphiné, had married the daughter of a French merchant based in London, and then started his diplomatic career in 1619 as Secretary for the French Tongue to Lord Herbert of Cherbury, ambassador to Paris and brother of the poet George Herbert. Like Whitelocke, Augier was favourably regarded by Queen Henrietta Maria, but he fell into disgrace in 1640 after squabbling with his colleague, a Guernseyman. Perhaps partly on account of his friendly 1634 dealings with Whitelocke – always appreciative of musical talent – Augier's career was resuscitated, though seldom remunerated, with his appointment in 1644 as English Agent in Paris for Parliament, and, later, the Protectorate.

> She being a handsome well-spoken and well fashioned woman, habited . . . like a Lady . . . came to Whitelocke's chamber, highly complimented him, told him the ill effects of Melancholy, entreated him for his own and his friends' sake to cast it off . . . Whitelocke was able to answer her language, but not her own arguments of reason and courtesy . . .

If the doctor at Bow really did advise the French trip to Whitelocke, perhaps a few enchanting French landladies were exactly what he had in mind as a distraction. This encounter at Dieppe appears to have been the first of a few similarly pleasant acquaintanceships.

Whitelocke and Cole rode by coach to Rouen, where Whitelocke enjoyed visiting the cathedral, and wrote down a story that amused him about the English Duke of Bedford, who was buried there. The French King Henri IV – father of Queen Henrietta Maria – had apparently reproached a courtier for vandalizing Bedford's effigy with his sword. The King had warned the offender to keep his blade for living enemies of France, doubting 'if the Duke of Bedford had been alive, the young gallant would so fiercely have assaulted him'.

On the way to Paris, Whitelocke, like Henry Hyde before him, fell into that most scandalous company in English terms, befriending a Catholic divine, the prior of a Celestine monastery.* With airy resourcefulness Whitelocke claimed to be a Catholic himself, 'meaning the true sense of Catholic' – belonging to the universal Church (thus articulating the basic position of Great Tew, as well as anticipating that of nineteenth-century Anglicans). The prior proved extremely inquisitive about English 'laws, customs, and government', as well as geography, an interest Governor de Montigny at Dieppe had also shown. Whitelocke's reader begins to wonder if Richelieu had arranged for him to meet all the Cardinal's best secret agents consecutively.

---

* At Rome, Henry Hyde had often and controversially been noticed in the company of William Allen, later a cardinal, the most notable English propagandist to support the endeavour of the Spanish Armada.

Whitelocke states with an increasingly worldly and connoisseurial eye that 'the mien of [French] women far exceeds others of their condition in other countries'. From Paris he sent to a trustworthy servant for a huge quantity of colourful ribbon, 'such as gentlewomen usually wear in knots . . . for a Lady here to whom I am much engaged'. At Paris, too, Whitelocke was finally able to exploit some of the credit he had earned with the Queen and her suite at the masque. Pierre de la Mare, one of the 'four most excellent Musicians of the Queen's Chapel' recruited by Whitelocke earlier that year to assist with *The Triumph of Peace*, had furnished his erstwhile employer with introductions to musicians in Paris with connections to the English court. These included Balthasard de Montgison, an elderly Parisian bourgeois who had been a close friend of Charles I's childhood dancing instructor, as well as M. Richard, who might have been any of the six musicians of that family to have entered Queen Henrietta Maria's service.

Montgison excused himself from lodging Whitelocke, Cole, and their servants in his handsome town house on the grounds that a 'Mr Mayherne' was staying there for the next fortnight. This was certainly not the all too distinguished Huguenot royal physician, Sir Theodore Turquet de Mayerne, baron d'Aubonne, whose services were considered too valuable, and whose contacts too internationally seditious in their potential range, for King Charles ever to let him leave England; it may well have been Henry d'Aubonne, Mayerne's sickly, improvident son.

Passing Frenchmen commented on Whitelocke's costume, 'of English cloth without lace, the cloak lined with suitable plush', and purported, surely not sincerely, to find it preferable to the French style. There then apparently followed Whitelocke's most dizzying if unfortunately least well-documented French social conquest; an invitation from Cardinal Richelieu himself for Whitelocke to become his 'Secretary for the British Affairs'. Whitelocke claims to have prudently replied neither yes nor no, while of course rendering many thanks. He wriggled out of this dangerously eminent offer by signing up instead in some capacity to command a troop of

French horse in Picardy, a quixotic-seeming move that recalls Sir Lucius Cary's unavailing quest for a Dutch mercenary command in 1630.

It was not in Whitelocke's nature – or in accord with his neo-Stoic motto – to linger in grief while there were strange sights to be sought and possible opportunities to be seized. But he wrote often to Dr Bartlett at Bow, oftener still to a trusted friend and former servant of his father's, John Cely, who kept him informed of business affairs at London and domestic life at Fawley Court in Buckinghamshire. To Cely he professed that 'All my comfort is in my child's health', a phrase whose anxious solicitude seemed to apply as much to his wife Rebecca as to their son. Whitelocke instructed his clerk to see that young James received a present of two French coats, 'one for every day, the other for holidays', but also to conceal the garments' Parisian origin; he still wished to be a vanished man as far as word in England went at this time. Another letter to Cely contains an early sign of trouble to follow: 'I would fain know what particular scandals my wife's mother lays upon me.'

Although Mrs Bennet was thus clearly still supposed to be ignorant of the whole French sojourn, word seems to have reached her of her son-in-law's whereabouts by late May. Ned Hyde, among a few other Middle Temple friends, established contact with Whitelocke about this time, and of all the letters Whitelocke now received from England, in his journal he lists the frequent communications from 'his intimate friend Mr Edward Hyde' first. In the earliest of these letters Hyde reproached his friend for not telling him of the French scheme, but his tone remained, despite increasingly alarming circumstances, one of consistent lightness and good cheer. Hyde visited the Whitelocke household in the absence of both its master and mistress, and sent Whitelocke happy news of young James, whom he called his 'little friend'. He expressed scepticism about Whitelocke's self-imposed exile: 'Paris has as few antidotes against a troubled soul as London'. Hyde probably referred in the first instance to the swirling political intrigue of both capitals. But he was also well qualified to offer his friend comfort and advice of a more private and interior kind; his first wife's death from smallpox was still only two years past. Perhaps this understanding contributed to his fondness for Whitelocke's boy James, deprived of his mother by her illness and his father by travel. Whitelocke showed his appreciation of Hyde's acts of friendship by arranging, even at the distance of Paris, the gift to him of a certain manuscript by the hand of their mutual acquaintance, Izaak Walton, an occasional Great Tew guest. In 1634 Walton had not yet published his first book, a life of John Donne. He would later attain fame with *The Compleat Angler*, his contemplation of retired rural pleasure amid the political rigours of the 1650s.

From Dr Bartlett, Whitelocke at first heard good news of his wife's progress. Rebecca's high spirits and happy temper, once her attacks had passed, were consistent. The doctor's strategy of isolation, harsh though it had sounded to her husband, seemed to be working, 'which gave [Whitelocke] great joy and hopes of comfort'. But, as Whitelocke had written in his song for the lute upon the mysterious and all-powerful divine principle, 'He turns our joys to grief'. In mid-May he first hinted to his colleague Bartholomew Hall of a sudden and disastrous development in Rebecca's treatment, one quite contrary to Dr Bartlett's prescription: 'She has fallen much worse upon sight of her mother.' Although Mrs Bennet had insisted on the isolation cure being followed to the letter, she had not herself hesitated to breach it. Early in June, only six weeks into the intended six months of Rebecca's confinement, Whitelocke scribbled an account of the catastrophic sequel for his sister Elizabeth:

... hearing of the hopeful way her daughter was in of recovery ... [Mrs Bennet] went to the doctor's house with a most earnest desire to see her daughter [Mrs Bennet also had two other married daughters similarly afflicted and living under Dr Bartlett's roof at this time] ... and notwithstanding divers denials, at last was brought to speak with [Rebecca]. Immediately whereupon, whilst her mother was with her, my wife fell into a relapse and increased to the highest extremity and raging, without taking any sustenance for twelve days together, and the fourteenth after . . . she died. The news of the saddest affliction of my life, came to me in a strange country.

The account in Whitelocke's journal suppresses some of this emotional charge, while being clearer about his view of his mother-in-law's malign impact:

. . . being admitted, the mother & daughter spake kindly & rationally one to another, the daughter enquired very affectionately for her husband, how he did and where he was, & lamented her sickness that kept her from him. Her mother took her aside and discoursed privately with her for about an hour together, whereupon, even whilst her mother was with her, the daughter's weak spirits being thus tired and oppressed, she then fell into a relapse . . . at this time what her mother said was not made known, nor could Whitelocke ever hear it . . .*

Coupled with his earlier fear of his mother-in-law spreading 'scandals', it is probable that Whitelocke's belief, confided to his children much later if not to his sister at the time, was that Rebecca would have recovered regardless of her mother's visit – had not Mrs Bennet maliciously suggested to her daughter that she had been permanently abandoned by her husband.

When he heard the first news of his wife's once again worsening condition, Whitelocke himself – then about to take up his captaincy in the French horse – fell dangerously ill. Perhaps reports of this reached England quickly; maybe Mrs Bennet needed no such prompting. The next letter Whitelocke received from Hyde postdated Rebecca's death. Hyde, never enthusiastic about the French excursion, urged his friend's immediate return, as his mother-in-law was now spreading word that her daughter's husband had died

---

* An example of Whitelocke's sometimes jarringly Caesarian, distant third person in the journal.

abroad. Mrs Bennet intended to petition the Crown to claim custody of young James Whitelocke in light of both his parents' decease, and with it the entire Whitelocke estate, Fawley and Phyllis Courts, their adjoining land, and the City property. Whitelocke praises Hyde for his 'letters of comfort'. He also mentions the crucial ministrations of 'his loving companion' Cole, who held him in his arms and 'many times expected that he would die' before the sickness passed.

Whitelocke concludes his account of his first wife with a touchingly formal threnody: 'She was tall & comely of a tender & sweet disposition, of ingenious & rational discourse, when her parts were not eclipsed by her distemper . . . just & faithful, pious & charitable, & most affectionate to her husband.' Hyde, by contrast, when writing of his own earlier deceased and passionately loved first wife Anne Ayliffe, concentrated on his own distressed state – 'He bore her loss with so great passion and confusion of spirit, that it shook all the frame of his resolutions' – before bustling on into the court allegiance into which his family-by-widowhood was to draw him.

When Whitelocke was well enough to travel he, Cole, and their servants started for England, 'chiefly for the sake of his child', taking their homeward path through that same stretch of Picardy in which Whitelocke and, it seems, Cole had been on the point of volunteering as French auxiliary cavalry officers. It was no country for civilians; the Englishmen had to ride through the night 'to avoid the danger of straggling soldiers'. Several times they came under fire by accident. From the depths of grief Whitelocke, displaying some of the historical consciousness he shared with Hyde, was stirred, as at Rouen, by the resonance of the landscape to what he termed 'the English story'. He had immediately donned mourning, while Cole was in splendid military scarlet. Wherever they stopped Whitelocke was given the first fresh horse and a cup of wine, and they realized he was being taken for a priest.

The Englishmen sailed from Boulogne after about thirty-six hours on horseback. Whitelocke tells a story that, brooding on Rebecca's loss, he overheard a plot by the French mariners to exact vengeance for Buckingham's attack on the Ile de Ré seven years earlier, by murdering the Englishmen and looting their possessions. Whitelocke claims to have offered them some tobacco and attempted to have a reasonable discussion about international foreign policy, in which 'grandees' and not 'the people of each Nation' were to blame for hostilities. The Frenchmen at first prosecuted their case 'with their usual earnestness', but Whitelocke's gifts eventually smoked them back into relative neutrality. Thus ended the young lawyer's first continental foray with a narrow escape and safe arrival into Dover.

Given what had transpired between Whitelocke and Mrs Bennet – she seems to have regarded him as having at the very least abandoned her daughter and at worst had perhaps got wind of his various French dalliances, while he could charge her with having caused his wife's death, broadcast his own, and plotted to steal his estate and child – peace was somehow made with astonishing rapidity, 'according to advice of friends, & his own inclination to quiet'. Which friend might have counselled such a wisely cautious response Whitelocke at once signals, by the addition that 'none seemed more delighted' with his return 'than Mr Edward Hyde'.

## Ned Hyde as Bulstrode's Cupid, July–November 1634

Ned Hyde had another reason for delight. After about two years of widowhood – he feelingly remembered them later as three – he married in July 1634 his second wife, Frances Aylesbury. She would be a spouse of Penelopian patience for thirty-three eventful years, and the mother of at least eight, possibly nine Hyde children. Although Clarendon began his *Life* not long after he had lost Frances in turn, he does not give the impression of having been so entirely overcome by passion in his second match as his first. In the case of his first wife Anne Ayliffe, the first particular Clarendon describes is her surpassing beauty, before proceeding with a rhetorical cough to her supremely advantageous family connections. The memory of his wedding to Frances does not elicit any such outburst. Here Clarendon harrumphs about why his younger self had determined to remarry for marriage's sake; he missed the comforts of the marital state, and he required some domestic spur to keep him practising the law (quite different in this to his own father, who had married an heiress as a final escape from his loathed profession). Then Clarendon marches into his second father-in-law's credentials, 'Sir Thomas Aylesbury, baronet, master of requests to the king'.*

The Aylesburys were, like the Hydes (and, in origin, like Falkland's higher-climbing Cary family), gentry grown fat in the Duke of Buckingham's service. Since Anne Ayliffe had been a Villiers cousin herself, Frances Aylesbury was a less socially prestigious bride, Hyde's equal rather than superior. But Sir Thomas was, both materially and personally, an ideal father-in-law: affectionate, amusing, a gifted mathematician and imaginative patron, generous and rich. He was clearly a fond father, writing to Henry Hyde that Frances was 'a child that none could have from me but a good man'. Ned Hyde had no need to fear any similar embarrassment to poor Whitelocke's Bennet saga from such a quarter.† His own parents did not travel to London for the wedding, his mother cleaving fast to her detestation of the capital, while old Henry Hyde's health, succumbing as he was to recurrent attacks of angina, kept him even from his beloved estate of Purton, bound to the town of Salisbury, musing on the plot reserved for his grave beside the cathedral.‡

---

* The Master of Requests was the judge in charge of the Court of Requests, a lesser, cheaper alternative to the common-law courts, by Aylesbury's time much undermined and on its way out, but still of great use to Hyde as most of his commercial practice as a barrister lay within it.

† Hyde's brother-in-law Will Aylesbury was a less reliable figure: a wit and translator of Italian who charmed King Charles, became tutor to the Duke of Buckingham's sons, expressed fiercely anti-Parliamentarian views in 1640, but died in 1656 as a Cromwellian administrator in Jamaica.

‡ Hyde's mother Mary, whose unwillingness to come to London was the only element of her personal character he chose to record, was yet translated in death, by her son's eventual eminence, to eternal rest in Westminster Abbey.

The ringing phrases in which Clarendon describes Frances's virtues suggest he came to value her highly but gradually, as the wife 'by whom he had many children of both sexes, with whom he lived very comfortably in uncomfortable times, and very joyfully in those times when matter of joy was adminstered'. Frances herself, no apparent partner of her husband's scholarly enthusiasms or political activity, possessed more practical and financial sense than her husband, and was greatly esteemed by many of Hyde's most discerning, capable, and worldly friends. She may also, as Clarendon suggests he had hoped at their marriage, have been more professionally ambitious for Hyde's legal career than he himself had previously been. Certainly it was immediately after their wedding, as Clarendon remembers, that Mr Hyde 'laid aside all other thoughts but of his profession, to the which he betook himself very seriously', no longer, the reader infers, worshipping at the feet of Jonson in the Apollo Room, and certainly sparing no more time for the likes of Will Davenant. Hyde's profounder bonds, however, with Falkland and the Great Tew circle, with Selden, and at this time perhaps with Whitelocke above all, were only strengthened by this more emotionally settled and legally industrious mode of life.

That same September saw the death in his early seventies of Henry Hyde the elder, whom Ned Hyde, his last surviving son, called 'not only the best father, but the best companion and the best friend he ever had or could have' and 'the wisest man he had ever known'. Henry Hyde bore out this devoted assessment in his last hours, commending his daughters solemnly to their brother's loving care. A less reliable later tale from the interested pen of Bishop Burnet maintains that Henry Hyde also warned his son always to look to the public good, even if this meant defying his prince. Burnet, a Scot and a Whig, had every reason to paint Clarendon the English Tory dignitary and historian as a deeply dyed renegade. But the source he cites, Falkland's lifelong friend Lady Ranelagh, of moderately Parliamentarian sympathies, is itself of interest as showing the lasting political nuance with which Clarendon and his circle were remembered.

Meanwhile Whitelocke was, for the first time since becoming Master of Revels for the Middle Temple in 1628, submitting himself to a period of retrenchment. He gave up the house in Salisbury Court, after all acquired at his late wife's behest, and determined, just as his friend Ned Hyde was resolving similarly, to work harder at the Bar. Whitelocke was (both by his own account and by the corroboration of his career) unusually well-suited to the role of assiduous urban go-getter, and, simultaneously, of beneficent rural squire. At Fawley Court his tenants were as friendly, loyal, and informal with him as they had been with his father the judge. Whitelocke represents himself as taking the advice of a certain tenant farmer, William Cooke, unusually seriously – advice that was fiscal, moral, even, on occasion, political. He records his long, frank, and instructive conversations with Cooke in detailed dialogues, almost Platonic in form, plain and pragmatic in import. While Cooke occasionally has the appearance of a composite, all but allegorical figure, he was a genuine and competent retainer-cum-family-friend of the Whitelockes. In time his quick-thinking action would ensure the family's security. At this time, however, Cooke the farmer's counsel sometimes has an uncanny ring of Hyde the lawyer's counsel.

According to Whitelocke's journal Cooke, on being consulted by Whitelocke in general terms about 'the present ordering of my affairs', started to muse about his fondness for 'my little young landlord', namely three-year-old, motherless James Whitelocke, before coming out with the aphorism that 'odds will beat any gentleman'. In other words: 'Sir, you want skill in ordering the affairs of a house to the best advantage. There wants a woman to govern those things.'

The same pressure that Hyde applied to himself for remarriage was now, scarcely months after Rebecca's final crisis and death, upon Whitelocke. It is to Cooke that Whitelocke attributes the credit for naming 'the Countess's niece, Mistress Willoughby by name'.

Ned Hyde had carried on a certain amount of business and pleasure among the high aristocracy of the kingdom since his marriage into the fringes of the Villiers clan in 1632. Bulstrode Whitelocke was slightly more of a novice in such circles. His father the judge had encouraged him to think that only physical peril and moral worthlessness were to be found in overmuch recourse to the company of the court. The paramount example of this precept had been Bulstrode's uncle and godfather, Captain Edmund Whitelocke, he who had bestowed upon the boy his eye-catching Christian name. Captain Whitelocke had made an art of tippling with earls, attaching himself to their lordships of Rutland, Northumberland, and Sussex consecutively. Yet now William Cooke recommended that his landlord woo the niece of another Earl of Rutland.

Captain Whitelocke's patron, Roger Manners, 5th Earl of Rutland, had rashly joined the Essex rebellion of 1601, along with two of his younger brothers, Francis and George; these unruly Manners brothers were all imprisoned by Elizabeth, but forgiven by King James. At the time when Bulstrode Whitelocke, at his tenant's suggestion, began to cast about for a second wife, the third of these brothers, George, was the seventh earl. Although Lord Rutland leaned towards Puritanism in his religious observances, this, as so often, implied no dolorousness in his personal character. Whitelocke described him as:

> ... about sixty years old [actually fifty-five when Whitelocke first encountered him], & had been a handsome man ... stooped to old age ... a little disfigured with the loss of one of his eyes ... of good and pleasant discourse ... understood business well, & managed it prudently when he would be troubled with it, but (like other great men) he trusted his servants & minded more his pleasures ... hunting, hawking, bowling & racing ... he delighted to see young people dance & be frolic wherein he would sometimes go too far in example.

Whitelocke knew well that to Rutland he would count as one of those able servants who spared the earl his business, not the gentle sprigs who might dance with, or wed, his nieces.

The niece in question was Frances Willoughby, the daughter of Rutland's sister (also named Frances), and of the late Lord

Willoughby of Parham. Frances lived at Hambleden with her aunt, another Manners sister, the Countess of Sunderland, within an hour's walk of Fawley Court. Lady Sunderland's late husband, a light-touch, Catholic-inclined President of the Council of the North, had at his resignation five years previously left a record and legacy of chaos. Dying soon afterwards in 1630, the earl had bestowed his fortune, such of it as remained unfrittered, upon several illegitimate children. It was this defunct rogue's widow to whom Whitelocke now had to appeal to approach the 'comely and housewifelike' young Frances.

Whitelocke paid a carefully innocent first visit to Lady Sunderland, returning a dredging device that some of his servants had borrowed to drain an 'unwholesome' moat. Still in mourning black, he left his bedraggled beard unshaved. But his real intentions were suggested by the young henchman he brought with him, a monoglot but melodic French lutenist called Piccart, recruited in Paris, who had recently had the benefit of practice with Whitelocke's friend, the Queen's composer and the fellow progenitor of the Coranto, Simon Ives. The page Piccart was an ornament of continental sophistication, an assistant if it came to serenading, and an accomplice who lacked the linguistic capacity to gossip.

In his journal Whitelocke set down how he first remembered Frances Willoughby, with a fastidious, prim, but undeniable appreciation:

> Mistress Willoughby came into the room; her habit was plain but neat, her person was most beautiful and lovely, so that upon first sight of her, Whitelocke was strangely surprised, & struck with high affection . . .

The disjuncture in the social ranks of the lovers aside, this courtship, as Whitelocke presents it, was more plausible than exciting. Frances appears in his telling as a nice, orderly girl living with an agriculturally benevolent widowed aunt, both of them from a family of good, godly credentials in the Puritan sense.

But, as befitted the deceptive context of a noble family during King Charles's outwardly placid, latently tumultuous personal rule, there were deeper and more unsettling matters at play. The Manners family boasted a complex and, from Whitelocke's point of view, disreputable background. The sixth earl had become an out-and-out Catholic, a rite in which he was joined with varying discretion by his daughter the Duchess of Buckingham, his brother-in-law the rascally Earl of Sunderland, and his sister the Countess of Sunderland, aunt of the virtuous, godly English maiden to whom Whitelocke now paid court.

Beyond religious difference, other skeletons rattled noisily in the comital cabinet; the sixth Earl of Rutland's baby sons were well known to have been murdered by witchcraft, and then there was poor Lady Sunderland's penury on account of her unlamented husband's bastards. But most importantly, and at the point where the role of Ned Hyde stands, just perceptibly, behind that of the good-natured tenant William Cooke, is the connection of the whole family to that ouroboros of Caroline patronage, the Duke of Buckingham and his ubiquitous Villiers kindred.

Sir James Whitelocke had for many years operated specifically and defiantly from outside the Buckingham camp, once characterizing a rival for a lucrative post as a 'hangby and pettifogger' of the Villiers clan. The younger Whitelocke had observed the condemnation of Buckingham's assassin without relish; he was not at ease amid the graceful cynics of the Villiers conglomerate, including the Manners family. Buckingham himself had married a Catholic Manners daughter, and a favourite kinswoman of that very same Duchess of Buckingham was the trusted old gentlewoman companion of Lady Sunderland, one Theodosia Thynne.

Mrs Thynne was the daughter-in-law of Sir John Thynne of Longleat, whose man of affairs had been the first Lawrence Hyde, Ned Hyde's grandfather. Rather like Juliet's Nurse, Mrs Thynne managed Whitelocke's communications with his chosen bride when no one else could have done. She was one of several well-wishers within the Manners extended family likely to have been conciliated by Whitelocke's close friendship with Hyde. Mrs Thynne was also the audience for a joke by Frances that reveals a livelier character behind her unadorned chastity; Frances later admitted to Whitelocke that she had remarked to the gentlewoman of her aunt Lady Sunderland, 'Come, let us go see the widower, perhaps we may have good of him.'

With such an ally as Mrs Thynne assured, all proceeded well enough, at first. The countess offered the widowed Mr Whitelocke a standing welcome to Hambleden. Before long the three of them (not counting Mrs Thynne, or the French boy) went fishing on the Thames. On their return Whitelocke, Piccart the page, and Lady Sunderland herself entertained Frances with lute music. After one opportunity to speak to Frances alone had been thwarted, Whitelocke employed Mrs Thynne to pass to her a note addressing her as his chivalric 'mistress', vowing that his love was 'as unfeigned as can lodge in the breast of any man'.

Soon Lady Sunderland permitted intervals of conversation tête-à-tête with Frances. Whitelocke ascertained what Frances herself thought of the match, and only then approached her aunt. Although neither felt authorized to give definite assent, they seemed 'not displeased with the notion'. Whitelocke's flair at fishing had prevailed. Even better, Bulstrode soon realized he had caught his son a perfect stepmother. The now four-year-old James, uninhibited by the societal boundaries that restrained his father, 'did strangely court Mistress Willoughby, as if he had known his father's desires and affections towards her whom the child called his Lady'.

There yet remained three potential obstacles to Bulstrode Whitelocke's betrothal to Frances Willoughy; his prospective bride's widowed mother, the Dowager Lady Willoughby, Frances's brother Francis, 5th Baron Willoughby of Parham, and most important and doubtful, her uncle and principal trustee, Lord Rutland. The friendly Lady Sunderland soon persuaded her sister Lady Willoughby to look kindly on the alliance. Ned Hyde, with the help of his first wife's kinsman Lord Grandison, Buckingham's nephew and his own close friend, pledged to work upon Frances's fiery brother,

Grandison's frequent companion at court. Francis, Lord Willoughby, exactly the same age as Whitelocke, shared much political common ground at this point with both the lawyer friends. The century's troubles would reveal him as a man of ambition and vision, if little steadiness.

At this delicate moment in his suit, Whitelocke found himself summoned to London for reasons of which he gives two barely reconcilable accounts. On the one hand, it seems that he was answering a charge of disloyalty to the established Church, probably connected to his position as recorder of Abingdon, a town teeming with religious non-conformists in whose service he had been popular, diligent, and bold. At the same time, Whitelocke claims to have been briefing the Privy Council about the details of the French and Flemish coasts, information he implies he had gathered secondhand rather than through his own recent voyage; his likeliest highly placed source would appear to have been Colonel de Montigny at Dieppe, who was, he says elsewhere, still his frequent correspondent at this time. As Whitelocke relates, his dispatch was appreciated but he 'grew weary' of such machinations, because they 'brought no profit'. Both these shadowy incarnations, Whitelocke as dissident and government secret agent, do however point to the same powerful figure, Archbishop Laud. Laud's interest in his deceased, ambivalent old friend's son had apparently been entirely benevolent up to this point, and he was certainly Whitelocke's most obvious Privy Council patron, yet the course of Whitelocke's private life was about to change this.

Perhaps tipped off by way of the City, the court, or even Lambeth Palace, two furious visitors arrived at Fawley Court while Whitelocke was otherwise detained in London. They were young Lord Willoughby and the Earl of Rutland, respectively Frances Willoughby's mercurial brother and her ruddily precipitate, all-powerful cyclops of an uncle. They cross-questioned William Cooke, handily present as so often, about Whitelocke's substance and character, and what they heard seems to have been more honest than satisfactory: Rutland forbade the marriage forthwith.

Unaware of these developments, Whitelocke called by at Hambleden on his way home from town, his beard newly trimmed, apparelled in his City best, only to find Lady Sunderland sadly obliged to refuse him the house whose freedom she had so lately proffered. Yet, with the help of Mrs William Cooke and an apple-basket that served to conceal discreet epistles, Whitelocke divined that Frances herself still favoured him, while Mrs Thynne stood ready for further employment.

Whitelocke scrupulously carried out a cross-examination of himself. Its conclusions proved his rectitude in the matter, and what was more Lord Rutland's villainy, to his own complete contentment. 'He considered that in this business he had used no indirect or unlawful means' (the common law being silent on apple-baskets), '. . . that her brother was a young lord who had not the disposing of his sister, that her uncle had his niece's portion in his hands, & occasions for the use of it'. In this analysis of the case Whitelocke's equally learned friend Ned Hyde evidently concurred.

Rebecca had died in June; Whitelocke had, with unconvincing reluctance, begun his suit of Frances in September. On the night of 8 November he recruited his six burliest tenants, packed them into a coach, and was guided by Mrs Thynne to a rendezvous he and Frances knew. Whitelocke left his bucolic bravoes a short distance away as an emergency reserve, but put into practice the executive part of the plan, he tells us, alone. Frances was waiting with a maid and the two dodderiest of her aunt's gentlemen. 'After salutations, Whitelocke told his mistress that the weather was cold & bad for her to walk, & entreated her to make use of his coach.' The startled pair of old gentlemen, like Mrs Thynne 'decayed in their fortunes', but unlike that enterprising lady ignorant of what was afoot, 'suspecting somewhat began to bustle', whereupon Whitelocke clapped his hand to his hilt and politely advised the countess's gentlemen pensioners that his intentions were as honourable as the gentlemen's continued presence was superfluous. The countess's Pensioners agreed, with no need for Whitelocke to summon the six Adonises of Henley. So Whitelocke 'came away not slowly to Fawley carrying this rich treasure', namely Frances Willoughby, 'with him'. The gates slammed behind them and they were married in the judge's Puritan chapel by Whitelocke's hand-picked parson with little ceremony beyond, perhaps, spirited lute music from Piccart. 'After a short breakfast they took coach & drove apace to London to handsome lodgings near the Temple' (the Ship Inn, still open), 'whither divers of their friends came to them, & rejoiced with them'.

There is no evidence as to whether or not Ned Hyde was present at his friend Whitelocke's first marriage; but at this second alliance, which he had done so much to promote, his participation can be taken as read. Only four months into his own contented second marriage to one Frances, Hyde had helped to manage Whitelocke's more romantic runaway union with another. Nor did Hyde rest idle after the celebrations, rushing to wait upon the clique of young noblemen, including his friend Lord Grandison and Whitelocke's sudden, unknowing brother-in-law Lord Willoughby, 'with whom his power was considerable'. 'Chiefly by [Hyde's] ingenuity and contrivance,' according to Whitelocke's journal, Willoughby at least was persuaded to become 'well acquainted' with Whitelocke, showing 'respect and brotherly kindness' and promising to attempt to win their uncle Rutland 'to a right understanding'.

The court was, in general, delighted at the elopement's novel theatricality. King and Queen alike remembered Whitelocke as the graceful contriver and composer of the lawyers' masque less than a year before. Still more to the point, the affronted Rutland was all too well known to the King: before his inheritance George Manners had been an obstructive Puritan MP in the 'Useless Parliament' of 1625. King Charles was heard to pronounce that 'he knew not but that it might be well for both parties'. The widowed Duchess of Buckingham, whether on account of Mrs Thynne or perhaps through Hyde, approved of the match, as did the ladies of the court in general.* The great lords at worst held their peace, though surely

---

* Lady Katherine Manners's betrothal and marriage to Buckingham had itself been brought about amid her father's fury, Villiers' sharp practice, and the bride's

most would have reacted with bloody rage if Whitelocke had flouted their decisions as he had Rutland's. The Lord Chamberlain Pembroke in particular continued to show goodwill to the up-and-coming lawyer; he 'said publicly that he was glad of [the marriage], & he thought his cousin [meaning Frances, a very distant relative] had done better for herself than any of her friends would have done for her'. Lord Pembroke was then, it should be remembered at this point, the most powerful aristocratic patron of Mr Edward Hyde.

---

independent desire. In 1635, the spring after the Whitelocke elopement, the widowed duchess entered into a romantic and, most thought, imprudent second marriage to the handsome, meretricious Irish Earl of Antrim.

4.

# Prelates, Predestination, and Parliament

*Two equall Zones, on either side, dispose*
*The measur'd Heavens; a fifth, more hot than those.*

George Sandys, Book I,
*Ovids Metamorphosis Englished*

## Bishops in Play: The Charm of John Williams, 1619–35, and the Temper of Archbishop Laud, 1634–5

Not only the King and the nobility, but the two most ubiquitous, mutually antipathetic power-players in the higher clergy now concerned themselves in Bulstrode Whitelocke's marital fortunes. The first, John Williams, Bishop of Lincoln, had form as a smoother-over of difficulties for both the Whitelocke and Manners families. Williams was a rich and aristocratic Welshman, proud to be of more exalted lineage than were most Caroline bishops. The old-fashioned, competent portrait painter Gilbert Jackson catches Bishop Williams at ease, powerful and worldly, in a tall black hat and assertive ruff, his face all foxily beady eyes, neat courtier's beard and conspicuously secular whiskers. Williams had proved himself to be useful and amenable to old King James, professing the unfussy Calvinism that James consistently preferred in his episcopacy. Williams's enemies accused him in whispers of sharing with his monarch amatory as well as theological preferences. He once told Buckingham that he was 'unmarried, and inclining so to continue', a state unusual in a firmly Protestant cleric with large estates in Wales and great pride of blood. His chaplain's hagiography, describing Williams as 'chast perforce' due to a youthful accident, employed a pretext often used to veil then unspeakable predelictions.

In 1619, Williams – a little tardy in responding to the stratospheric ascent of George Villiers over the previous five years – made up for lost time, settling the thorny problem of the then Marquess of Buckingham's much-desired marriage to Lady Katherine Manners, the sixth Earl of Rutland's only daughter.* The lady and her father were both uncompromising Catholics (having converted at the suggestion of Lord Rutland's Catholic second wife about ten years earlier), and King James refused to let his favourite marry into a family that rejected his ecclesiastical authority. Dr Williams applied himself to the difficulty and:

> . . . brought the Earl [of Rutland] about so dexterously with his art and pleasant wit, that his lordship put it into his hands to draw up all contracts and conditions . . . which he did to the fair satisfaction of both sides.

He also took Lady Katherine's religious instruction in hand, with the result that she undertook a brief conversion to the Church of England before her marriage, quite evidently for form's sake, and returned to her father's rite not long after it. Promotion for Williams in both Church and State, as Bishop of Lincoln and Lord Keeper of the Great Seal, followed in 1621. But four years later, at the accession of Charles I, Williams lost the Great Seal and, for the moment, his confident grasp on royal amity.

In 1631 Bishop Williams came to Fawley Court to consecrate the chapel of his old friend Judge Whitelocke. Also in attendance was his fellow bishop, Robert Wright of Bristol, along with 'several knights, esquires, doctors, gentlemen & ministers'. Williams undertook

---

* Francis was the middle brother between Roger, the fifth earl and Captain Edmund Whitelocke's patron, and George, the seventh earl, Bulstrode's second wife's uncle and trustee.

this kindness in the face of his superior Archbishop Laud's vociferous disapproval of private chapels. When Judge Whitelocke followed his wife to the grave in 1632, it was to Williams that the younger Whitelocke applied for permission to establish a consecrated graveyard at Fawley. Authorization was immediately forthcoming, so that Whitelocke was able to erect a handsome monument for his parents in what had been their own garden.

Following Whitelocke's elopement with Frances in November 1635, Williams outdid himself with a sleekly charming epistle to the runaway bride's mother, the Dowager Lady Willoughby:

> If your daughter ... had been married to the greatest subject in England I should have esteemed him worthy of the fortune. But considering these casualties often come to pass by God's providence and permission ... it is wisdom ... not to make these accidents worse ... by our unprofitable and unreasonable impatience. Peradventure Mr. Whitelocke ... is not so well known ... unto your good ladyship as he is unto me ... I know him thoroughly, his friends and his fortunes. He is a gentleman of fair descent both from the father's and mother's side ... Your daughter shall lead as happy a life, for his person and usage, as she could have done in any other place wheresoever ...
>
> He is a counsellor at law, indeed, and therein the more to be approved of, but a gentleman besides richly and plentifully provided for ... such a one ... in all respects, as your ladyship may have comfort of and a bishop be bold to mediate for to any personage in England.

Here is fully displayed the sinuous rhetoric that so appealed to King James and would later sway even his less flexible successor. Syrupy flattery is seasoned by judicious Calvinist nostrums; cautious reproach by yet more syrup. Personal affection, convenient interpretations of ancestry, and considerations of hard cash are all invoked; underlying the whole, Bishop Williams offers Lady Willoughby a wager – that Bulstrode Whitelocke is a coming man. This bet paid off, both for him and his addressee; Lady Willoughby allowed herself to be persuaded. Her brother the choleric Lord Rutland, and at last even Lady Sunderland, who though so amiable a neighbour had been deeply hurt by Whitelocke's underhand management of the elopement, then followed their sister in adjusting to the existing state of affairs.

The second prelate to express his view on Whitelocke's sudden second marriage was Archbishop Laud himself, whose intervention Whitelocke described with considerable understatement as 'another difficulty'. Laud's headmasterly missive was not now an enticement to a slap-up supper at Whitelocke's local Bell Inn, nor a grandly confidential invitation to attend the Privy Council, but an official summons amid forbidding archiepiscopal splendour to Lambeth Palace. There Laud, all but incoherent with fury, 'chid him for marrying above his rank, & without acquainting [Laud] with it, & contrary to an order, that no child of a nobleman should marry without particular leave of the King, or the archbishop'.

This convention did exist but was very patchily applied, and the King himself had already shown that in this instance he did not mind in the least about the marriage. Laud's over-punctiliousness here was emotional rather than calculated, the touchy little cleric simply losing his temper, rather than employing the deviously technical mental capacity that had once skewered William Prynne's defence. Whitelocke's rejoinder was smooth but sharp. He:

> ... excused himself from not acquainting his Grace with the business beforehand because of the haste of it, & pleaded his ignorance of the order [that is, regarding the marriage of noblemen's children], & that he thought it no disparagement for the younger daughter of a Baron, to marry the eldest son of a Judge.

Feeling both that the archbishop in his well-known wrath was beyond reason, and that he himself had been treated 'more like a porter than a gentleman', Whitelocke departed with dignity and promptitude. After the intervention of Richard Baylie, Laud's successor as President of St John's, the archbishop actually climbed down and apologized to his former pupil, inviting him back to dinner where he deigned 'to excuse his passion for him, & that it was in love to him & promised all readiness to do him good'.

Ned Hyde was also contacted by Laud owing to his second marriage, but in a very different context and temper. In March 1635 the widely loathed Lord Treasurer Portland at last died after a protracted illness; Hyde had long joked to Whitelocke of the anticipation with which the legal and political worlds awaited the preferment possible at this demise. King Charles now put the Treasury into the collective charge of a commission of peers, naming his trusted Archbishop of Canterbury as the First Lord Commissioner. Laud thus amassed a new combination of ecclesiastical and secular powers about which Hyde was, both at the time and in retrospect, politely but volubly critical. Nonetheless, when Laud found himself in need of fresh legal advice in relation to his new duties at the Treasury, he listened to gossip that Hyde had been retained by a group of merchants, pleading valiantly but ultimately without success against the late Lord Treasurer's corrupt support of a monopolistic wharfinger.* One of these merchants, Daniel Harvey, described Hyde as 'a young lawyer of the Middle Temple, who was not afraid of being of council with [the merchants], when all men of name durst not appear for them'.

This was a mixed compliment, underlining the fact that Hyde, for all the flim-flam of the royal masque, had not yet become a 'man of name' in his profession. But his father-in-law, Sir Thomas Aylesbury, undoubtedly then was; early in 1645 gossip even reported that the King was considering placing Aylesbury on the Privy Council. Laud accordingly went to Aylesbury, and was greeted with the characteristically genial answer that the young Hyde couple were at that moment living in the Master of Requests' own town house, and that Aylesbury's promising son-in-law would be delighted to

---

* This was a certain Sir Abraham Dawes, Farmer of the Customs and Lord Portland's 'minion', whose name today gilds a sheltered housing scheme in Putney.

wait upon Laud without further ado. What followed was a Lambeth Palace interview both parallel with, and opposite to, Whitelocke's dressing down. Laud had no personal connection to, no theological or political predisposition for or against, Hyde. At this time Hyde, quietly inclined to be sceptical of Laud's power and policy in Church and State, was yet both open to discussion and eager for employment. But most simply, surprisingly, and importantly, the already old, short-tempered archbishop in a hurry and the 'liberal-minded' young lawyer at once found that they liked one other.

Hyde remembered that Laud 'received him civilly according to his manner, without much ceremony', understanding and forgiving the archbishop's infamous brusqueness. Laud met him in the vernal intimacy of the archiepiscopal garden, where Hyde rendered honest answers about the case of the crooked wharfinger. While he referred to Portland's 'asperity', he showed none himself. Laud confessed that as a prelate he had accepted the whole burden of leading the Treasury Commission with the utmost reluctance. So says Clarendon at any rate; his reader may suspect either the historian or the archbishop's reliability on this point. Laud, though he soon gave up his place on the Commission, would fight hard to ensure the Treasury went to his ally (or, as some said, subordinate) and fellow clergyman Bishop Juxon. At any rate Hyde then loosened up, complaining of Portland's 'indecent rage', and delivered the papers that Laud required of him.

The warm friendship that now came into being was, like the archbishop himself, deeply, paradoxically, imperfectly human. The tenth child of a prosperous draper, Laud was tiny, busy, and learned, fluent in writing and speech, in personality far more individual and easy-going than the caricature later drawn by partisan defenders and enemies alike. In religious doctrine he was no zealot. As a friend he could demonstrate both humility and wit. But as an adversary he was prickly to the point of what appeared to be paranoia, though events would ultimately justify it. Privately Laud wrestled with his conscience over urges he perhaps shared with his enemy Williams, but was more vulnerable to political attack over his perceived sympathy towards Catholicism, however sincerely and justly he thought of himself as a consistent opponent of papal authority.* After his elevation to Canterbury, Laud was offered a cardinalate by a secret papal envoy. He rejected this approach with the thoughtful and nuanced realization that 'something dwelt within me which would not suffer that, till Rome were other than it is', but by the same token he evidently did not share the conventional Calvinist identification of the Papacy with Antichrist.

Laud's greatest failing, as Hyde saw from the start, was his absolute belief in his own powers, his certainty as to the rectitude and benefit of the discipline he dealt out. Clarendon was to sum him up as 'a man of great courage and resolution, and being most assured within himself, that he proposed no end in all his actions or designs, than what was pious and just . . . he never studied the best ways to those ends.'

## The Teachings of Arminius, and the Archbishop's Godson – William Chillingworth, 1630–37

At Leiden in the late sixteenth century an unworldly Dutch scholar, Jacobus Arminius, had begun to teach that the central tenet of Calvinism – Double Predestination, whereby the Elect are divinely ordained to reach Heaven while the rest are born irrecoverably damned – was gravely mistaken, and that Christians did after all possess the free will to determine their own destinies. Strict Calvinists condemned Arminius' ruling as a halfway-house towards Catholicism, sliding back to salvation by way of good works, not

---

* In 1625 Laud dreamt thus of King James's beautiful favourite: 'That night in a dream the Duke of Buckingham seemed to me to ascend into my bed, where he carried himself with much love towards me, after such rest wherein wearied men are wont exceedingly to rejoice; and likewise many seemed to me to enter the chamber who did see this.'

faith alone. The 'Arminians' attracted further opprobrium by their rational, untribal opinion that Roman Catholics were members of an imperfect and corrupted, but valid Church. Many dreamed of eventual reunion. 'Arminianism' appealed to, or coincided with, the instincts of some of the most fashionable, learned, and ambitious English prelates and theologians. Both Archbishop Laud and Charles I favoured this tendency less for intellectual or theological, than political and aesthetic reasons. Laud saw in the loose Arminian drift a potential instrument for the restoration of benevolent clerical power and overwhelming 'beauty of holiness'; Charles saw in the counsel of Laud the readiest way to a stronger, more magnificent regality. In 1625 the diminutive new King translated the still smaller prelate, then Bishop of St David's, a poor Welsh diocese in which Lord Keeper Williams had kept him penned as long as possible, to the see of London. In 1633 Charles I at last appointed Laud Archbishop of Canterbury after the long-awaited death of George Abbot, a traditional 'high Calvinist' and inadvertent murderer.*

Such English 'Arminians' as were genuinely attracted to the movement's theological and philosophical, rather than disciplinary and ceremonial, implications, in fact constituted a running irritant to Laud. Foremost among them was his own godson, William Chillingworth, soon to become Lord Falkland's favourite sage and Hyde's admired friend. Chillingworth, who shared the small stature of his godfather Laud and his future patron Falkland (Clarendon later pointed out 'it was an age in which there were many great and wonderful men of that size'), appalled Laud, then still Bishop of London, by converting to Catholicism and fleeing to France to train as a Jesuit. The brilliant young scholar embarked upon this drastic course in 1630, about the time when Ned Hyde met Sir Lucius Cary and young Cary embarked on his own parallel series of

---

* Archbishop Abbot had, in 1621, accidentally shot dead one of Lord Zouch's gamekeepers, while hunting deer with a crossbow. His chase-addicted, high Calvinist monarch King James insisted that 'an angel might have miscarried after this sort'.

adventurous indiscretions. Chillingworth paid scant attention to the pleas of his godfather or those of his own profoundly conventional best friend, Gilbert Sheldon, yet still returned home in short order after becoming dissatisfied with Roman doctrine on his own account.*

Too tricky a young man for himself, let alone others, readily to understand, Chillingworth possessed an ascetic, rigorous delicacy of thought, not always matched by morally scrupulous conduct. On paper an obsessive, addicted seeker of truth, he had a tendency to leave many of those he dealt with in words and deeds feeling the more deceived. John Aubrey had judged Chillingworth guilty of 'the detestable crime of treachery' for informing on Alexander Gill to his powerful godfather. Chillingworth's duplicitous behaviour in 1633, through which he first came to Falkland's notice, is a matter of more definite record.

Chillingworth entered the household of Falkland's prodigious, now all but penniless, Catholic mother as tutor to the Dowager Lady Falkland's daughters, also being educated as Catholics. The young man gave his new patroness to understand that he shared her religion, even though he had left the English Jesuit hothouse at Douai three years earlier as a disillusioned, doctrinally restless layman. Not unreasonably, Lady Falkland felt deeply betrayed when she discovered Chillingworth earnestly, secretly at work undermining the Cary girls' faith in papal supremacy. Dismissed in disgrace by the dowager, this geographically and theologically itinerant scholar instead found a warm welcome with her eldest son at Great Tew, educating not Lord Falkland's Catholic sisters but his two youngest brothers, Patrick and Henry.

In his formal role of tutor to the younger Carys at Great Tew,

---

* The Jesuit who briefly 'turned' Chillingworth, Percy alias Fisher, also claimed the Duke of Buckingham's mother, almost captivated the favourite himself, and confirmed the lifelong Catholic allegiance of the scientist-scholar-pirate Sir Kenelm Digby, perhaps the most flamboyant of all Ned Hyde's wide acquaintance.

Chillingworth proved a still more spectacular failure. His conceptual somersaults were not at all suited to catch the interest of two headstrong young boys; Chillingworth, for his part, occupied himself more with his employer's matchless library than his inattentive pupils. Of Chillingworth's religious instruction Patrick Cary later recalled that 'I knew no other distinction then, between the Catholic and Protestant [Churches] . . . but that my mother was of that, my father of this.' When, in 1636, the Dowager Lady Falkland arranged for her younger sons to be snatched away to France, and Catholicism, from underneath Chillingworth's distracted nose, the boys departed willingly, delighted by the adventure.*

This was not, as might be imagined, a disaster for the tutor, rather a turning point for his employer. Instead of blaming Chillingworth, Falkland saw his own former willingness to tolerate the priestly vagaries of his mother's establishment as weakness, where he had intended only politeness. He henceforth took the duty of refuting the exclusive claims of Roman Catholicism far more seriously, a battle in which he identified Chillingworth as his armourer, Great Tew as his fortress. For Chillingworth was, with his patron's wholehearted approval, now engaged in a more solemn task than the education of scapegrace Cary cadets. His book, the fruit of Great Tew's library, *The Religion of Protestants*, published in 1637, was to express the entire religious and intellectual position of the Falkland circle. In it he included an account of his own doctrinal wanderings as an evocative parable:

---

* A plausible view of Chillingworth's conduct in both Cary households, attractive by later standards though shocking to his contemporaries, is that he saw the theological differences between Lady Falkland's Catholicism and the ever more Arminian, or even Socinian, Protestantism he came to share with her son, as 'inessential', and hardly cared either way about the children's allegiance. A few years later the young Milton would encounter Patrick Cary, still beneath the age of discretion, at the English College at Rome. Patrick, a more considerable poet than his eldest brother, was destined to lapse, accept minor employment under Cromwell, and perpetuate the line leading to the present Viscount Falkland. His sisters, as gifted and less wavering, would live, write, and die as nuns.

> I know a man that of a moderate Protestant turned a Papist, and the day that he did so . . . was convicted in conscience, that his yesterday's opinion was an error, and yet thinks he was no schismatic for doing so . . . The same man afterwards upon better consideration, became a doubting Papist, and of a doubting Papist, a confirmed Protestant. And yet this man thinks himself no more to blame for all these changes; then a traveller, who using all diligence to find the right way to some remote city, where he had never been, (as the party I speak of had never been in Heaven,) did yet mistake it, and after find his error, and amend it.

Through many subtle contortions and an exponentially widening mass of reading, Chillingworth had come to reject papal authority, accept the Arminian doctrine on grace, free will, and salvation, but go further in his distaste for conventionally firm teaching on the doctrine of the Trinity. For him the exact form of the Church, or the mysteries of Trinitarian doctrine, were 'inessential' matters of opinion; stern rulings on such subjects led to unnecessary schism. All that was needed was to apply reason to Scripture, and to permit latitude throughout an ideally reunified universal Christian Church.

## 'Grateful to all kind of company' – Great Tew in the Mid-1630s

Although Whitelocke almost certainly never visited Great Tew, and never mentions Chillingworth, he was later to write in slightly bemused approval of both Falkland's theology and that of Falkland's follower, Thomas Triplett. Their basically Chillingworthian ideas would have appealed to Whitelocke by their doctrinal latitude and practical tolerance. Like Falkland and Chillingworth, Selden and Hyde, Whitelocke was politically Erastian, believing that the Church should be properly subjected to the State.

Falkland's particular milieu at Great Tew allowed religious and political innovations to coalesce as distinct ideas, at a time when they were otherwise prone to blur. The productive mixture of clergy and laymen gathered by Falkland included sophisticated theologians with simplistic political positions, meeting, enjoyably halfway, worldlier, perhaps more realistic political minds not over-interested in theological adventure. On a certain occasion, one of the less doctrinally up-to-date guests cut into a bristling discourse on the problem of predestination, and asked to be reminded what view exactly the Arminians held. 'They hold all the best bishoprics and deaneries in England', came the reply from George Morley, one of Falkland's more traditionally Calvinistic Oxford friends. The riposte inevitably reached Archbishop Laud, and Morley's cooling career froze fast.

So much criticism of Laudian policy emanated, one way or another, from Great Tew that it at times seems to resemble a circle of Elizabethan Calvinists, irritated by the archbishop's tampering with both the religious and political status quo. On the other hand, Falkland's friends displayed so many, such uncoincidental, personal connections to Laud, such articulate attraction to Arminian theology, and such loyalty, with very few exceptions, to the King in the wars that lay ahead, that the opposite picture of Great Tew can equally be assembled, as a liberal wing of the Laudian platform. There is plenty of evidence for both conclusions, precisely because neither is wholly, even mainly, true. Once the religious and political sympathies of these Oxfordshire friends and disputants are separated out, this loose circle, so varied in its intellectual freshness, is revealed in a subtler, more resilient hybrid form.

In religion Hyde let Falkland take the lead, and Falkland was in turn enthralled by the scepticism, reason, liberty of conscience, and Arminianism he imbibed from Chillingworth. So the friends ended up theologically close to the archbishop and the court's fashionable doctrine. But politically, Falkland acknowledged Hyde as his superior in experience, legal knowledge, and judgement, and, just as Falkland followed Chillingworth in theology, so Hyde admired Selden in politics, exalting as his highest ideal the 'mixed monarchy'. This entailed Crown, Parliament, and State Church all operating in harmony, through traditional, limited, interlocking roles – roles and limits Charles and Laud found all too constraining. The beliefs of Great Tew's leading spirits, apparently contradictory, were thus specifically consistent: supportive of Arminian theology, but preferring it to be expounded by reasonable discussion rather than governmental arm-twisting; critical of Archbishop Laud's and the Church's political influence; eager enough for the calling of a new Parliament to sympathize on occasion with the most radical Calvinists.

Throughout the wider circle of connections to Tew, this Janus-faced philosophy – theology facing in one direction, politics in another – recurs, notable in an age so often characterized in terms of these two disciplines' inextricability. Chillingworth himself was as rigid a Royalist as he was theologically supple, believing any resistance to royal authority whatsoever to be unlawful rebellion. His friend Sheldon was provocatively quick to the mark in espousing the Laudian position that the Pope was not Antichrist, yet fiercely resisted an attempt by Laud himself to meddle in the temporal affairs of his Oxford college, All Souls. Selden, the great theorist of parliamentary liberties, personally admired Laud, with whom he regularly exchanged books and letters, and would soon defend the presence of bishops in the House of Lords. And the outspoken Dr Morley, like a large proportion of supporters of the King in the wars that ensued, was a quite straightforward Calvinist.

Morley was credited with introducing the poet-politician Edmund Waller into the Great Tew circle. Waller was born in 1606, three years before Hyde and one year after Whitelocke, to a much greater fortune, if less exalted rank, than Falkland. He was elected an MP at just eighteen, three years younger than Bulstrode at his parliamentary debut, even then considered a beginning precocious to the point of impropriety. The Great Tew companions first heard of Waller as a shrewd heiress-hunter, vaguely oppositional political dilettante, and modest but committed devotee of poetry. Waller obtained full admission to the company at Great Tew by his generous and shrewd settlement of a debt owed by Morley. He may also have interested Falkland independently. Quite apart from his poetic facility, Waller's first cousin was John Hampden, the experienced, eloquent, and extremely rich Parliamentarian, leader (advised by none other than Whitelocke) of the resistance to the King's most notoriously arbitrary tax, 'Ship Money', which Falkland had also refused to pay. Hyde, whom later political developments were to prejudice firmly against Waller, allowed the poet to be 'a very pleasant discourser, in earnest and in jest, and therefore very grateful to all kind of company, where he was not the less esteemed for being very rich'.

Waller himself claimed Edward Fairfax, translator of Tasso and illegitimate great-uncle of the future Parliamentarian cavalry commander, as his chief poetic model. But in the company of Falkland and his friends, he was present at a debate about the standing of a now much better-remembered poet: the occasion, retold by the younger poet John Dryden, when John Hales, 'the Ever Memorable', oldest, most pacific, perhaps best loved of the great talkers at Great Tew, argued, then radically, in favour of the definitive superiority of Shakespeare over both Jonson and the classical poets.

Hales had spent most of a delicately self-effacing career secluded in bibliomaniac peace as a Fellow of Eton; one of relatively few scholars of reputation attached to that college in its first 300 years of existence, though various notable men to whom the Crown owed impossible debts were appointed its Provost. He would have known Bulstrode's father while James Whitelocke served as Eton's Steward. Hales seems to have been genuinely uninterested in any preferment that removed him from his library. He had experienced enough of the world beyond it to disappoint him in 1616, at the Synod of Dort in the Netherlands. This debate between Calvinists and Arminians was disgracefully fixed in the former party's favour, prompting Hales to bid the conference, and Calvin, 'good night'. Hales had a horror of sexual immorality, according to Clarendon rebuking Tom Carew for his lasciviousness even on the courtier poet's deathbed. But his loathing for religious schism was still more extreme, and he denounced it in his writings with passionate elegance. Archbishop Laud remembered Hales with affection from their university days, and was inclined to overlook his various theological unorthodoxies.

After Hales's library, Selden's, and Falkland's, one of the greatest in England was considered to be that of the wily Bishop Williams. When Williams fell more than usually foul of Charles I in the summer of 1637 and was sent to the Tower under the ire of the infamous Star Chamber, Ned Hyde was offered first refusal on the Williams collection by a government informer looking for a fat commission. Hyde, obviously irresistibly tempted, wrote to his purer-hearted friend Falkland to justify the purchase, but Falkland successfully appealed to his better nature, and Hyde, doubtless with a sigh, refused the offer.*

## 'Fierce tempests breed' – The Crisis in Scotland, 1637–9

The year 1637 was personally one of happiness for Hyde, bringing the birth of his adored first child Anne. During the two previous years the Whitelockes had produced a daughter and a son, filially and dynastically named Frances and William after their mother's noble parents. The two fathers exchanged fond letters, presents, and arch greetings to each other's children, 'my little wench' (Anne Hyde), and 'my little friend' (James Whitelocke, the younger). For the next few years Frances Whitelocke reinforced the family nursery with astonishingly annual regularity, and Frances Hyde followed suit more often than not. Ned Hyde's first son, named Henry for Ned's dearly loved late father, was born in 1638.

In August 1637 the world of letters lamented the passing of Ben Jonson. The egregious William Davenant, Hyde's former tenant

---

* Whitelocke's morals were later to be similarly tested in determining the destinies of two libraries – that of his Royalist legal colleague and friend Richard Lane, and the Royal Library itself. In both cases his conduct was of disputed quality.

and cast-off acquaintance, would be referred to unofficially but ubiquitously as the court's new Poet Laureate from the next year (disappointing, in particular, another of Hyde's literary friends, Tom May). But 1637 is remembered above all for the action of a probably mythical, symbolically indispensable Edinburgh 'herbswoman', Jenny Geddes, who hurled her stool at the unfortunate Dean of St Giles's Cathedral. This unfortunate clergyman, James Hannay, was attempting to introduce the King's new Laudian prayer book, intended to regularize Scottish devotion in line with Anglican ritual south of the border. Devotions turned to riot; riot, two years later, ripened into war; the herbswoman had, as tradition has it, personally initiated the cycle of armed conflict that would wrack the three British kingdoms for fourteen years. The Scots, rallying to Presbyterian nobles, and ably led by mercenary captains returning from continental employment to defend their motherland and Kirk, defied Charles with a National Covenant to protect their Calvinist national Church, from which the insurgents took their name of Covenanters.

When the King sought volunteers in men and subsidies in cash for an extra-parliamentary war against his native, but less biddable kingdom (in his *History*, Hyde called Scotland in relation to England 'but the wilderness of that garden'), among the gentlemen of his chamber now obliged to set a martial example was Tom Carew, Ned's old friend from the Jonson circle. A reluctant combatant, Carew wrote one of his last poems in the aftermath of the Scottish campaign of 1639, an epistle addressed to 'Ghibi', probably Gilbert North, another courtly de facto conscript. Carew writes from Wrest Park, seat of the scholarly invalid Earl of Kent, employer and friend of his wife's rumoured lover, John Selden. Selden and Carew, intimate friends of Falkland and Ned Hyde (and also, in Selden's case, Bulstrode Whitelocke), can thus be connected to the same great house at the historical moment when settled peace was slipping into unremitting war.

Carew provides an unequalled pawn's-eye-view of the 1639 Scottish venture's grim pointlessness:

> I breathe (sweet Ghibi) the temperate air of Wrest
> Where I no more with raging storms opprest,
> Wear the cold nights out by the banks of Tweed,
> On the bleak Mountains, where fierce tempests breed.
> And everlasting Winter dwells; where mild
> Favonius, and the Vernal winds exiled
> Did never spread their wings: but the wild North
> Brings sterile Fern, Thistles, and Brambles forth.

Carew's 'temperate air', like the 'purer air' with which Hyde credited Great Tew, evokes a moderate, peaceful, civilized political climate, now impinged upon by the grim, relentless landscape of war (and Scotland). Already close to his obscure death, Carew seems prophetically bleak, exhausted by unwonted military and meteorological rigours in a sick cuckold's house, his poet's glance much sharper and more original on the natural, vernacular encumbrances of the north than the conventional, classically figured amenities of the south. As for 'Ghibi', the poem ends with a parting that rebukes as much as compliments him:

> Thus I enjoy myself, and taste the fruit
> Of this blest Peace, whilst toil'd in the pursuit
> Of Bucks, and Stags, th'emblem of war, you strive
> To keep the memory of our Arms alive.

With the shadow of more to come so strenuously kept from the hearth at Wrest Park, the poet seems to ask, why bother playing at battles in the chase? It is a sentiment that Selden, Whitelocke, and most of Falkland's accustomed visitors at Great Tew would have instinctively endorsed.

Both Hyde and Whitelocke were gloomily critical of the King's conduct of the war against the Scots, but neither, unlike some English Puritans, especially northerners, approached sympathy with the aims of what remained to them an exterior enemy force. Neither the Wiltshire squire's son nor the city-born judge's had any

Scottish connections or sympathies. Hyde initially thought of the Scottish crisis as 'a small, scarce discernible cloud'. Whitelocke referred to the Covenanting rebels as 'a foreign nation, proud and subtle, against their natural Prince'. 'Natural' was an apt word; Charles Stuart, unlike his loyal subjects, those profoundly English lawyers Whitelocke and Hyde, was a Scotsman born and reared at Dunfermline, in whose speaking voice a light accent still persisted. But the King's tragedy was that he was especially distant from his native kingdom in his preferred religious rite, whereas many of his English subjects resembled the Scots only in theirs.

Late in 1638 Whitelocke sent Hyde a gift of cider. Hyde's letter of acknowledgement reflected relatively glumly on the northern front:

> We talk of nothing but Law in the [Middle Temple] Hall and of war in the Town . . . my Lord Traquair [a shifty Scots peer at this time professing to be on the King's side] brings nothing but despair from Scotland . . . even the victory is like to prove melancholic enough.

Yet by anticipating a royal victory of any kind Hyde was in fact still over-optimistic. The toy war with the Scots in the summer of 1639, in which Falkland served as a volunteer, a farcical sequence of forgettable brawls and undignified withdrawals, was yet significant for what failed to occur. The Scottish leadership would prove its calibre over the years to come – fighting on both sides – but at this point the royal army outnumbered the rebels, and was better supplied and equipped, with substantially more cavalry. If King Charles's peacock of a commander, the Earl of Holland, had shown a little more gumption, victory could, even should, have been his.* Instead

---

* Lord Holland was an extremely well-connected, charming, and unreliable man. He knew and got along with both Hyde and Whitelocke, as well as almost anyone else he considered to be of any possible consequence. Whitelocke had endeared himself to Holland particularly successfully both by their religious common ground, Puritan by doctrine if not by stereotypical temperament, and, probably more importantly, by the gift of a handsome horse.

Holland disastrously fell for a ruse arranged by the hardened Scots mercenary, General Alexander Leslie, and retreated before inferior forces rigged up to alarm him near Kelso.

## *'Friends at London' – The Search for Parliamentary Seats, Early 1640*

Happily ignorant of the long-term significance of his chosen general's blunder, King Charles was at last seriously considering a recourse he had long dismissed or postponed. The Lord Keeper whom Charles had swiftly appointed in the place of Bishop Williams, Thomas, Lord Coventry, a friend and patron of Sheldon and Chillingworth, had for some time argued in vain for the summons of a Parliament. He died in January 1640. But the still more influential Thomas, Lord Wentworth, that ruthless Yorkshire magnate who had replaced the first Lord Falkland as Lord Deputy of Ireland, had raised considerable funds and arms by steering a biddable Dublin Parliament. He now successfully urged that his royal master should follow suit.

The new Parliament had very broad support. It united the hopes of Ned Hyde's closest friends from both sides of his life, the Bar and Great Tew – Selden and Whitelocke on the one hand, Falkland and Waller on the other – as well as the remaining experienced malcontents of the 1620s, led by the two surviving rebellious Johns (minus Sir John Eliot, dead in gaol), Pym and Hampden. Whitelocke himself claimed some indistinct blood tie to Hampden; he would use the suggestion of cousinage as a device signalling willingness to enter into a political alliance on other occasions. Since 1626 Whitelocke had been retained by Hampden in the latter's attempt to demonstrate the illegality of 'Ship Money'. This extra-parliamentary tax had occasionally been raised by English monarchs from coastal regions to cover naval defence. Charles I's regular recourse to it over the whole kingdom was unprecedented, if not explicitly law-breaking.

Remembering his father's judgement in the case of Bates and the Levant Company, Whitelocke had advised his client not to pay the tax in its new form, to avoid setting a perilous precedent towards the unlimited bloating of the Crown's power. Hyde was of the same opinion, wary of Ship Money as 'a spring and magazine that should have no bottom', while Falkland had also refused to pay the levy on his inland estate. The case brought Whitelocke great credit among the embryonic opposition to the court.

In the run-up to the Parliament of April 1640, the first since the notorious assembly of 1629 that had ended in Speaker Finch's restraint and the imprisonment of Selden, Eliot, and the other rebel members, Hyde wrote to Whitelocke to ensure he was abreast of developments and conveniently placed to stand. Whitelocke allowed himself to be convinced to put himself forward as the burgess (non-knightly member) for Abingdon in Oxfordshire, the town of which he had been since 1632 a popular and indeed, in religious terms, boldly populist Recorder. At heart, though, Whitelocke felt less sanguine than his friend, and was:

> ... not very ambitious of the place, foreseeing the danger of the times, but his friends at London & the Anticourt party upon the argument of public good, & many letters coming to him from Abingdon of their confidence to carry the election for him he was persuaded to stand for it.

Perhaps, though, this prophetic pessimism was mere self-protective hindsight, for, in an unaccustomed political setback, Whitelocke was this time baulked of his seat, Abingdon being more or less bought by its Justice of the Peace Sir George Stonehouse. Whitelocke would bitterly recall that Stonehouse:

> ... wrought by more effectual means on the vulgar people ... employed his butcher, brewer, vintner, tailor, shoemaker, & other like instruments to labour for him ... above all other arguments ... prevailed by his beef, bacon, & bag pudding, & by permitting as

many as them as would to be drunk at his charge . . . & by these laudable and honourable means he convinced their judgements that therefore he was the ablest person to serve as their Burgess in this Parliament.

Whitelocke was, however, in excellent company in this defeat. Another friend of Hyde and Falkland who tried and failed to find a seat in the first Parliament of 1640 was Thomas Hobbes.

Hyde, unlike Whitelocke, in 1640 contested a seat in Parliament for the first time. Yet Whitelocke undoubtedly had Hyde, the future Royalist, in mind when referring to his 'friends at London' of the 'Anticourt party'. Hyde became member for Wootton Bassett in Wiltshire, a few miles from his estate at Purton, with the help of his St John in-laws, and under the aegis of the still amiable Earl of Pembroke. Among Hyde's other closest friends, Waller and Falkland – who as a merely Scottish peer was eligible to sit among the English Commons – assumed their seats as a matter of course. Selden, for some reason, perhaps a variation on the unease Whitelocke professed to feel, preferred to bide his time for the moment.

So, in April 1640, Hyde and Falkland followed their precocious friend Waller to their first Parliament, while Whitelocke, who intended to appeal against the Abingdon result as soon as he could, awaited further developments at the Covent Garden house of his Willoughby in-laws. His mother-in-law Lady Willoughby soon found herself the only person on hand to deliver her daughter Frances's baby daughter Anne, the Whitelockes' fifth child in under six years.

## *Hyde's Debut under Pym's Wing: The Short Parliament of 1640*

Ned Hyde was always to remember making his maiden address to Parliament on the morning after a speech by John Pym. Pym was perhaps the most experienced, capable, and diligent orator the newly elected Commons could boast:

> The long intermission of parliaments having worn out most of those who had been acquainted with the rules and orders observed in those conventions. And this gave him some order and reverence amongst those who were but now introduced.

Such novices included Hyde, Falkland, and even, effectively, their friend Waller, who had played no significant part in the Parliaments into which his fortune had propelled him before the Personal Rule.*
In Pym, Hyde was initially reassured to find a long-standing stalwart of the Middle Temple, 'of private quality, and condition of life'. He viewed the much older man with mingled admiration and condescension; Pym was clearly not a character whose talents had been tempered at university, or who would have suited the company at the Apollo Room or Great Tew, 'his parts rather acquired by industry, than supplied by nature, or adorned by art'.

But at the same time Hyde recognized the force of Pym's character, granting that he 'appeared to be the most leading man' present. He at first willingly succumbed to the rhythm of a rhetoric whose motives he would doubt only with hindsight:

> ... he had a very comely and grave way of expressing himself, with great volubility of words, natural and proper; ... understood the temper and affections of the kingdom as any man; ... had observed the errors and mistakes in government; and knew well how to make them appear greater than they were.

Pym was noted at the beginning of the Parliament as a would-be reformer of church government, furiously opposed to the accumulation of secular power by Archbishop Laud – in which the friends of Great Tew quite agreed with him – and almost irrationally

---

* All in all, 167 of the 332 MPs – just over half – were elected for the first time.

prejudiced against Arminian doctrine – but that did not yet seem so germane to matters then under discussion. For the moment Pym stuck prudently to the world and not the spirit, and 'recapitulated the whole series of the grievances and miscarriages which had been in the state'. Here too Hyde and his friends could happily support him.

Whitelocke and Hyde's all but boyhood antipathy to the Star Chamber had established for them both, but especially Hyde, a principled opposition to all the other irregular, high-handed law courts that operated outside the Common Law – the courts of the Councils of the North, of Wales and the Marches, of the High Commission and the Earl Marshal. Hyde did not, however, object to his father-in-law's Court of Requests, nor to any of the other Courts of Chancery, which represented a tangled forest of their own with altogether too much commerce at stake.* Instead Hyde chose as his first target the most antiquated and even slightly absurd of these institutions, the Earl Marshal's Court, or Court of Honour, regulating questions of chivalry and heraldry.

In this body Hyde located the 'one grievance' against the royal government omitted by 'that worthy gentleman' (Pym), with ornamental modesty wishing it had been 'remembered by some man who might with more lustre and advantage have presented it to the house'. Defenders of the Court of Honour – generally clients of the Earl Marshal himself, Lord Arundel – pointed to its venerable origin in at least the fourteenth century. But Hyde characterized the Earl Marshal's Court as no hallowed and harmless heraldic sanctuary, rather an institution that had flourished at Parliament's expense during the Personal Rule – sitting far more regularly than was necessary and inflicting over-punitive penalties, to the corrupt engorgement of the Crown's revenue. Hyde and Whitelocke's legal mentor Selden, as the author of *Titles of Honour* (1614), which laid

---

* Whitelocke would eventually emerge as the great defender of the courts of Chancery against the impatient, unlawyerly populist instincts of Protector Cromwell.

out the higgledy-piggledy, arbitrary origins of the English peerage, would doubtless have approved of his protégé's piquant style of attack.

Hyde cited one particularly evocative anecdote concerning a London merchant who had been fined of all he possessed and cast into gaol after a squabble with a boatman over a fee. The worthy citizen had made the mistake of calling the swan on the boatman's livery, signifying his service to an earl, a mere goose. Hyde silkily called the reigning Earl Marshal 'a great and honourable person', and disarmingly insisted he was sure Lord Arundel himself would be most eager to reform his own so patently flawed and hated court. In truth Hyde's relations with Arundel, a famous connoisseur but a proud and solemn stick of a man, were signally curt; in his *Life* Clarendon would comment that Arundel 'thought no other part of history considerable but what related to his own family'.

Hyde knew he had cut a memorable and enjoyable figure in his first parliamentary outing. No one who had witnessed an unblooded young lawyer beginning to discourse on the purlieu of an obscure lesser court could have expected to be very interested – the matter had not even troubled the attention of that comprehensive reformer Pym – let alone amused, but the mirth and pleasure Hyde elicited was general. He was conscious of himself as an apprentice, but successful, theatrical performer: 'this being the first part he had acted upon that stage, brought him much applause; and he was ever afterwards heard with great benignity.' As a barrister Hyde was already a practised speaker, his very voice (unlike Falkland's) harmoniously pleasing to the ear, but at the House he had entered and mastered a crucial new arena. The Commons was now both the only court and the only stage he desired to command.

Unlike Whitelocke, Hyde had not regarded *Triumph of Peace* as a triumph of his own. His first glimpse of courtly life pre-dated the masque, and he had then discovered enough to be wary of tempting charm and apparent praise from that quarter. Instead he won the satisfaction that shaped his destiny at this moment, as a new MP with a spectacular maiden speech. Whitelocke, in exactly the

## Friends in Youth

converse situation, had entered Parliament by his father's devising early – almost too early – and quickly learned not to be oversentimental about the House; but he was extremely beguiled by the court's glory at the time of the masque. And just as Whitelocke had been rent from the lure of the court by his wife's illness before he could solidify his triumph there, so the victory Hyde had won on his ingress into the House of Commons was to be quickly overshadowed, though in his case by a more general rather than personal reverse.

Hyde, better informed at court than in the House of Commons itself at this time, foresaw and dreaded the coming crisis, and:

> ... observed by the several discourses of many of the court ... of near admission to the king and queen ... that they believed the king would be so much displeased at the proceedings of the house, that he would dissolve them; which [Hyde] believed would prove the most fatal resolution could be taken.

Hyde privately pleaded with Archbishop Laud himself to intercede with the angered King, insisting that the 'desperate counsel' of a dissolution 'would produce great mischief to the king and to the church'. Furthermore, 'he was confident the house was as well constituted and disposed, as ever house of commons was or would be: that the number of disaffected to church or state was very small.' Laud agreed with Hyde's worrying forecast, but not with his assurances of the sitting Parliament's loyalty, and said he would not advise the King in either direction.

It is easy to imagine why Hyde clung to the Parliament he had entered with such pleasure and flair; his own later testimony admits that some of his grounds for optimism were then mistaken. Like Falkland, he put too much faith in Pym and Hampden's assurances that they aimed at only moderate and necessary reform. But when, three weeks later, King Charles indeed dissolved what was inevitably afterwards dubbed the Short Parliament, he did indeed rid himself of a relatively Royalist and cooperative body, by comparison with what was to follow.

According to Hyde, the King's political opponents celebrated the dissolution as a clear royal blunder. In the *History*, Hyde describes meeting 'within an hour of the dissolving' one of his first wife's innumerable relations, Oliver St John, a Lincoln's Inn barrister and associate of Pym and Hampden. St John, who, Hyde says, 'had naturally a great cloud in his face and very seldom was known to smile', was looking uncommonly cheerful, and merrily remarked on the usually jovial Ned's own gloomy countenance. He then assured Hyde that 'all was well . . . it must be worse before it could be better . . . this Parliament would never have done what was necessary to be done'; a sentiment that Hyde might have found more persuasive at the time than he was later willing to admit.

## *The King's Misfortunes, Lord Saye's Wrath, Whitelocke's Toehold, Summer 1640–January 1641*

Whitelocke returned to Fawley Court without any probable hope of a parliamentary seat, treating the bruise to his pride with a healthy dose of admiration for his own good character. Although as Recorder of Abingdon he might, Whitelocke considered, have proven a bad enemy for the townspeople who had spurned him, he generously refrained from vengeance, instead labouring to continue his father's successful combination of the roles of assiduous city advocate and kindly country squire. In summer the return of the campaigning season reminded England's worthies that they were still at war with the Scots, a war that Whitelocke, Hyde, and many of their fellows did not consider a civil conflict, rather a foreign invasion in the mould of many another incursion from across the Border before the Union of the Crowns. Along with several neighbouring squires, Whitelocke stocked up a private arsenal in case of any necessary emergency. He noted that while 'men differed much in opinion touching the war, most wished it had not been begun'.

After the Short Parliament's failure to provide him with subsidies from conventional taxation, the King relied on the extra-parliamentary sources of money he had garnered over the last decade, and on private donations, to prosecute another Scottish war. Command of the royal force fell to the learned voluptuary and gossip Lord Conway, a friend of Selden with considerable military training, some experience but, it turned out, rather less ability or courage. The Scots Covenanters' General Leslie continued to show his capacity for psychological warfare as much as swift manoeuvres, entertaining Royalist officers to dinner so that they might report back on his army's by now genuine superiority. At the Battle of Newburn (Tyne and Wear) in August he easily routed Conway. Hyde, showing ill-informed disdain for the Scots even as fighters, believed that the royal commander must have been bribed to withdraw so precipitately. But the numerical and qualitative disadvantages Conway faced would have taxed much abler generals. Leslie then took Newcastle and, in the autumn, forced King Charles to sign the Treaty of Ripon, wherein the king pledged to pay the Scottish army, with money he had largely spent already in his ineffective resistance, to occupy County Durham. Having lost all hope of asserting his religious and political policy, Charles still needed money, and a new Parliament, merely to maintain his battered position.

This time Whitelocke (like Selden) was entirely determined to get into the House of Commons. Whitelocke first hoped to become knight of the shire for Oxfordshire, alongside the Presbyterian soldier and Caribbean investor Sir William Waller.* But Waller and Whitelocke faced stiff and prickly competition, especially from James Fiennes, heir to a powerful Puritan peer, Viscount Saye and

---

* Knights of the Shire were the members of the Commons for large rural constituencies, of higher standing than the burgesses who sat for towns. They were not obliged to be actual knights – in this case Waller was, but not Whitelocke or either of their opponents.

Sele. Whitelocke had just decided to give way to young Fiennes, as he broadly agreed with that family's opposition to the court and to Ship Money, when he heard that Lord Saye himself 'wondered that an upstart lawyer should contest with his son in that country'.

Whitelocke was goaded into the spirited reply that though he honoured Lord Saye as a peer and a patriot, he also honoured his own legal profession, then declared that there had been gentlemanly Whitelockes and Bulstrodes in Oxfordshire long before any upstart Fienneses were heard of there. 'This caused a distaste from his Lordship to Whitelocke,' the latter ruefully remembered, 'and more strangeness than formerly.' Whitelocke's proud and sharp response recalls both his refusal to be bullied by Sir Harry Vane during the preparations for *The Triumph of Peace*, and his rapid rejoinder to Laud when the archbishop reprimanded him for marrying above his rank, to the effect that his father, a judge, was worth any old nobleman. On points like these this polished, ambitious, usually tactful man on the make sometimes revealed a raw spot.

Whitelocke had thus seriously damaged his relations with the reforming party in Parliament whose actual principles he favoured; on the advice of his friends, neighbours, and kinsmen, he endeavoured to make some amends by giving way after all in the Oxfordshire election. He did so with a less than perfect grace, and decades later insisted that 'at the Election, his name was so cried up, that if he had appeared, he had carried it'. Yet perhaps the unexpected sequel suggests there was something in this. By his own account Whitelocke was completely surprised when 'the honest people of Great Marlow', their emissary 'a plain country fellow in mean habit [though in fact a lawyer] called Toucher Carter', suddenly chose him as one of their burgesses, apparently owing to a general belief that he had been wronged at both Oxfordshire and Abingdon. Although this election too was a contested and murky business, the enemies Whitelocke accrued by it were smaller fry than the Fienneses, and crucially unconnected to the 'Anticourt Party'. In the final count Whitelocke gained the seat. In this way he scraped into the Commons three months after the second 1640

Parliament's first meeting, partly as a result of Hyde's influence, along with that of another Middle Temple mutual friend of theirs, John Maynard.

Ned Hyde had not been returned again for Wootton Bassett – perhaps because some of the reformers distrusted his known personal closeness to Laud – but he quickly found another seat at Saltash in Cornwall through a Middle Temple connection, and so was among the members who assembled that November. It is revealing of the nature of these two friends that whereas Hyde passes over the slightly sticky nature of his political transition, or transaction, in dignified silence, Whitelocke leaves an extended, even comical account of his own belated and bumpy success in returning to Parliament. Thus when the friends were at last united in their first mutual Parliament, at Whitelocke's entry in January 1641 – the Parliament that would become the Long Parliament, the most momentous gathering in the protracted history of that eventful institution – Hyde was occupying his second pocket borough, while Whitelocke sat as a genuine, if accidental, tribune of the people.

# 5.
# *Pulling Down Cobwebs*

*Coronis, now a Crow, flyes Neptunes fright.*
*Nyctimene is made the Bird of Night.*

George Sandys, Argument to Book II,
*Ovids Metamorphosis Englished*

## *The Earl's Rise and the Duke's Ghost, January–Autumn 1640*

Charles I's lack of patience with the first Parliament of 1640 is perhaps best understood by contrasting that assembly's recalcitrance with the more effective support and service he had obtained elsewhere. Thomas, Lord Wentworth, the ambitious Yorkshireman who had once been one of the King's most formidable parliamentary opponents, and who still elicited little personal warmth in Charles's breast or, as importantly, that of his queen, had steadily proven himself as the royal government's most capable minister. First on his own territory as Lord President of the Council of the North – overseeing one of the extralegal courts so detested by Hyde – and then as Lord Deputy of Ireland, a role that had hitherto defeated most comers, Wentworth had appeared to vanquish all dissension. His religious preferences were stern and plain; he benefited from an exalted reputation for tough competence even among Puritans otherwise suspicious of the Crown; crucially, he was able to extract funds for the Crown from a thoroughly cowed Irish Parliament. The godly diplomat Sir Thomas Roe wrote to the King's piously Calvinist, at times threateningly popular sister, Elizabeth, the exiled 'Winter Queen' of Bohemia, that 'The lord deputy of

Ireland doth great wonders and governs like a king, and hath taught that kingdom [Ireland] to show us an example of envy, by having parliaments and knowing wisely how to use them.'

Both Roe and Elizabeth evidently hoped that Charles I might learn from his minister's Irish policy by returning to effective, traditional royal government, authoritarian yet parliamentary. In January 1640 the King heeded Wentworth's advice to call both English and Irish Parliaments, elevating Wentworth to the rank he had long and vainly sought as Earl of Strafford, and advancing him from Lord Deputy of Ireland to Lord Lieutenant of Ireland. This distinction permitted the new Lord Strafford to leave behind in Ireland a deputy of his own (his mild-mannered, faithful friend and underling, Christopher Wandesford) and come to his King's assistance in England, and, as Charles ultimately intended, Scotland. Although the earldom's glory turned out to be brief, Wentworth is still known to history as Strafford, the title under which he played the last and most memorable part of his belligerently active career.

Strafford was a particularly warm friend to Laud, despite a religious gulf between them of which the archbishop was creditably aware. Laud, whose secretly jocose nature found a match in Strafford's dry northern palate, once remarked to the Yorkshire Puritan that 'Pastors and Elders and all [i.e. Calvinist, Presbyterian church government, without bishops, as in Covenanting Scotland] will come in if I let you alone.' Strafford was just one of Laud's many incongruous, revealing friends, including the irenic, unambitious John Hales, the subtle polymath Selden, the theologically plain, politically anti-court and worldly Erastian antiquarian and lawyer Judge Whitelocke, and Ned Hyde and Bulstrode Whitelocke themselves, would-be reformers also drawn towards certain circles at court. Yet both Hyde and Whitelocke, despite their separately cordial personal histories with Laud, resolutely if courteously opposed the rough-and-ready Strafford, already dubbed by his many enemies 'Black Tom Tyrant'. Most importantly Falkland, already the keeper of Hyde's conscience, was bitterly disposed against Strafford.

The reason for Strafford's unacceptability to many of the Great

Tew companions did not really concern either political or religious principle. Strafford's tendency towards plain, old-fashioned Puritan aesthetics was accompanied by an unusually practical attitude, for his day, to the frequently divergent interests of Church and State, sometimes resembling Great Tew's thinking at its clearest. His nostalgia for the balanced days of Queen Elizabeth's settlement, his loyal service to the Crown, and especially his belief that the monarch should cooperate with a respectful Parliament, were all quite compatible with the opinions held at one time or another by Falkland and his friends, or even, in theory, with the ideals of Pym, St John, and Hampden.

Nor was the group alienated from Strafford merely by personal shortcomings on either side. Archbishop Laud, who had, despite bristling, maintained his long family friendship with the Whitelockes, father and son, who charmed Selden with his learning and Hyde with his honesty, was generally far more difficult to get on with than Strafford. Strafford's political allies, underlings, and kinsmen were devoted to him with an affection scarcely to be found amid affairs of state of this period – indeed almost the only comparison is the friendship to be found in Falkland's circle. Strafford could be pompous – after suffering the earl's long-winded boasting about his descent from John of Gaunt, a Welsh peer had much entertained old King James by quipping 'if Wentworth ever becomes King of England, damme if I don't turn rebel'. But he was also well educated and more than passably humorous. He liked to doodle or 'vandyke' caricatures of his fellows on the Privy Council, and he compared his fickle personal enemies and pretended friends in Ireland to the sea nymphs to be found in Ovid's *Metamorphoses*.

The real division between Strafford and the up-and-coming young lawyers and thinkers who included Whitelocke, Hyde, and Falkland derived from the wider politics of family and faction. As so often in the courtly landscape that preceded the civil wars, the pivotal figure was George Villiers, Duke of Buckingham, assassinated more than a decade before the calling of the Long Parliament, but living on in the memory and allegiance of influential clans and individuals. To Buckingham the Hydes and Falkland's family of Cary owed, respectively, their legal prominence and their courtly advancement; to Buckingham's family both Hyde and Whitelocke had become connected by marriage, friendship, and business; and Buckingham, while he dominated the court, had consistently barred the ambitions of the able, proud, power-hungry Thomas Wentworth.

When Buckingham and Prince Charles urged war with Spain at the very end of the old King's reign, Wentworth advocated peace. After the favourite's killing and his own sudden arrival in office, first in the north and then in Ireland, Wentworth supplanted and insulted Buckingham's former creatures wherever he found them. He brashly announced his intention easily to outdo his three immediate predecessors at Dublin Castle put together; of these the last two had been Buckingham's marital connection the first Viscount Grandison, and then the favourite's friend and nominee, the first Lord Falkland. It was one of Wentworth's officers that young Sir Lucius Cary had intemperately challenged to a duel. Around the same time Ned Hyde was further tightening his Villiers connections through both his marriages – into Buckingham's St John kin and then the murdered duke's Aylesbury clients – and composing his prose defence of Buckingham's posthumous reputation.

Bulstrode Whitelocke, though his father had patchily opposed the policies of the favourite early in a long legal and political career, had first been elected to Parliament at the behest of Buckingham's close ally Sir Humphrey May. Whitelocke was now vocally proud of being the husband of a cousin of Buckingham's widow. But perhaps most importantly, like John Pym and very unlike Strafford, Whitelocke clearly favoured a foreign policy of alliance with France over Spain. His personal relations with Strafford, however, characteristically seem to have been more cordial than the enmity towards Strafford nursed by Hyde and Falkland, despite Whitelocke's similar factional distance from the Lord Lieutenant.

But business was business. The state's affairs, and any chance to shape them, were always to be placed before outward courtesy by any capable and ambitious young man, such as Wentworth himself had once been as a rising leader of the parliamentary opposition to Buckingham. When the new Parliament reassembled, with Pym an even more dominant spirit within it – urging as the first necessity the downfall of Strafford – Falkland, Hyde, and Whitelocke were all more than willing to give ear to his case.

## 'New Treason that I never heard of', November 1640–January 1641

At Ned Hyde's first arrival in the new Parliament of November 1640, his effective party leader of the previous session, Pym, made sure of the younger man's convictions. He followed on where his ally Oliver St John had left off, urging Hyde that:

> They must now be of another temper than they were the last parliament . . . must not only sweep the house clean below, but must pull down all the cobwebs which hung in the top and corners, that they might not breed dust . . .

Hyde himself had already identified, to general acclaim, one particularly low-hanging cobweb, the Earl Marshal's Court; together with, by broader implication, the other courts operating outside the common law at Whitehall (the Star Chamber itself), York, Dublin (the Lord Deputy or Lieutenant's Star Chamber equivalent, the Elizabethan Court of Castle Chamber), the Lord President of the Marches' court at Ludlow, and at Lambeth Palace the Archbishop of Canterbury's Court of the High Commission. Hyde made this particular cause his own with great boldness, for its wider principle extended in an unavoidably dangerous, partisan, and committed direction. The last pillar of the King's government, Thomas Wentworth, Earl of Strafford, formally exercised his power both as Lord President of the Council of the North, overseeing his own prerogative court at York,

*Friends in Youth*

and now as Lord Lieutenant of Ireland, even in absentia commanding another court at Dublin.*

Yet, by the inception of 1640's second Parliament, Strafford was already a waning force. Although the Irish revenues he had raised for the Crown at his Dublin Parliaments had provided King Charles with one of his few military resources, the Short Parliament had demonstrated all too obviously that Strafford had erred in asserting that the king could successfully adapt this tactic to England. Strafford's contribution to Charles I's second Scots war was also disappointing at best. More soldierly in his bearing than his record, 'Black Tom Tyrant', in his late forties beginning to ail from overwork, fell ill at the worst possible moment, leaving the whole campaign to Lord Conway, that sympathetically hapless scholar-epicure. But despite these setbacks, Strafford remained King Charles's most formidable, gifted, and trustworthy minister.

Pym, who at this point still professed and may even in some sense have intended entire loyalty both to the King's person and office, chose for the present to regard Strafford as the spider responsible for all of the cobwebs he had it in mind to sweep away. Hyde reproduces Pym's 'long, formed discourse' on the first day of the new Parliament as follows:

> We must enquire from what fountain these waters of bitterness flowed . . . there was one more signal in that administration than the rest, being a man of great parts and contrivance, and of great industry to bring what he designed to pass; a man who in the memory of many present had sat in that house an earnest vindicator of the

---

* The other wielder of conciliar power beyond the reach of the common law was the Earl of Bridgewater, Lord President of the Council of Wales and the Marches, for whom Milton wrote *Comus*. Although Hyde attempted to dismantle this office too, Whitelocke regarded Lord Bridgewater as a potential patron, generally well thought of and respected for his impeccable legal training, tolerance towards religious dissenters, and fair disposal of justice. His lukewarm support for the King petered out into pessimistic neutrality during 1640–41, while his office and its powers became an anomalous survival until 1689.

laws... and champion for the liberties of the people; but that it was long since he turned apostate from those good affections, and according to the custom and nature of apostates, was become... the greatest promoter of tyranny, that any age had produced...

With stirring inevitability Pym named Strafford, accusing him of tyrannical actions in both his northern and Irish offices, and 'all other provinces wherein his service had been used by the King', an ominous first allusion to the war with the Scots. In Pym's speech as Hyde frames it, not only is hatred for Strafford discernible – hatred rooted in resentment of Wentworth's 1628 switch from opposition to office after Buckingham's murder – but an admiring sort of fear. Pym, himself exceptionally able and ambitious, saw in Strafford the severest threat both to his political programme and to his personal survival. As Hyde makes clear, this is because Pym initially aimed at re-enacting Strafford's journey to power, using opposition to the court as an audition for government office.

In the autumn of 1640 Hyde was one of many rising, often youthful Parliamentarians who shared in and supported Pym's hopes, aspiring to share with their ringleader the fruits of Strafford's downfall. Clarendon is strikingly honest in his later *Life* about the milieu of Mr Hyde the reformist MP at this time, a constant guest at Pym's table. There Hyde also befriended Hampden, whom he initially considered even more persuasive but would come to distrust over the next year. Hyde must have known Oliver St John, through local, legal, and family contexts, longer and better than any of the other leaders of Pym's 'Junto', yet he seems to have liked him the least; a telling exception to the usually, to Hyde, sacred ties of his first wife's Villiers and St John kin. To Pym himself, for now, Hyde continued to show every mark of sincere admiration.

Hyde's *History*, written during the continuing partisan struggles of the civil war, and in theory primarily for the perusal of Charles I, takes a retrospectively tough, Royalist line on the case against Strafford. Hyde notes various rambling, illogical speeches by Strafford's local Irish and northern enemies, all packed into the Commons by

Pym. Hyde emphasizes an intervention by his political soulmate Falkland, who, though 'very well known to be far from having any kindness for [Strafford]', raised a scrupulous objection against Pym charging him for any offence before assembling the (doubtless, Falkland implied, abundant) evidence for the prosecution. Falkland was overruled by Pym on the 'ingenuous and frank' grounds that this would allow Strafford time to escape, and did not press his point, probably made for form's sake. Hyde as Lord Clarendon, writing his *Life* in exile, is more measured. He admits his own impersonal but important role in the erosion of Strafford's position, and the hard yet rewarding work chairing the committee that overhauled the conciliar courts, chipping away, slowly and inexorably, at the power of the president's Court at York.

Having earned the respect of his colleagues so early, Hyde had been voted to chair several parliamentary committees. One of them, more incidental to his interests than the abuses of Earl Marshal and the Council of the North, arbitrated a dispute between Lord Manchester and some of his Cambridgeshire tenants, protesting against their common land's enclosure. Striving to maintain order, Hyde fell into an acrimonious exchange with the petitioners' MP, Oliver Cromwell. 'Every man would have thought,' Clarendon in the *Life* recalled of this first clash between himself and the future Lord Protector, 'that as their natures and their manners were as opposite as it is possible, so their interest could never have been the same.' Cromwell was noticed at the same period by the courtly MP Philip Warwick for the rusticity of his dress, appearance, and voice. Clarendon calls him on this occasion 'contrary, offensive, tempestuous and insolent'. It is irresistible to imagine Hyde as already Cromwell's greatly contrasting adversary: plump, comfortable, consensual, mellifluous, well turned out, a peacemaker, but a stickler for the proper rules. Clarendon not wholly convincingly claims that this dispute gave rise to Cromwell's constant antipathy, ripening into persecution, towards him ever after. In fact neither man would have much to do with the other, or achieve decisive preeminence in their eventual causes, for several more eventful years.

On 11 November, Strafford, on his way to the House of Lords, where he had hoped to claim parliamentary immunity, was arrested by the Gentleman Usher of the Black Rod. Once lodged at the Tower on 25 November, the prisoner sent a message to his young third wife to 'continue on the family as formerly'. Pym now argued of Strafford, more ingeniously than logically, that 'the habit of cruelty in himself is more perfect than any act of cruelty he hath committed'. Lord Ranelagh, one of the Irishmen whom Strafford had mocked as fickle 'Sea-Nymphs', the husband of Falkland's childhood friend Lady Katharine Boyle, added his voice to Strafford's opponents. Strafford shrugged him off, protesting contemptuously of the charges against him that 'Almost every article set forth a new treason that I never heard of before.'

As autumn turned to winter, while Hyde kept his head usefully down amid his committee work on the extralegal courts, Pym and his friends continued to find Strafford a maddeningly effective disputant. In the new year they turned in their frustration to a newcomer to the House of Commons, an excellently connected lawyer celebrated for wit, dash, industry, and courtesy, the burgess for Great Marlow, Bulstrode Whitelocke, freshly confirmed on 5 January 1641.

## *Judge Whitelocke's Ghost on Trial; The Prosecution and Acquittal of Strafford, January–March 1641*

Before he could properly recommence his parliamentary career Whitelocke, to his great surprise and dismay, found himself obliged to defend both his father's judicial reputation and his own inheritance. Worse still, he was put in this position by perhaps the last person he would have expected – his and Hyde's mutual shaping spirit and one of the acutest minds in Parliament, John Selden; Judge Whitelocke's old friend, someone from whom the younger Whitelocke had hitherto received only kindness, friendship, and wisdom. But Selden had not forgotten his imprisonment, along with eight other members, after the dissolution of 1629. Now, correctly judging the new Parliament's mood, he joined with the other surviving former prisoners – William Strode, Denzil Holles, Sir Walter Long, and Benjamin Valentine – in claiming substantial compensation from the estates of the judges of the King's Bench who had condemned them, Whitelocke's father (and Hyde's uncle Sir Nicholas) among them.

As the only son and heir of one of the accused judges, Whitelocke's position was as politically invidious as materially precarious, but he managed to navigate it to his own advantage and credit. One of the judges of the King's Bench from 1629, Bulstrode's great-uncle George Croke, had already been specifically excluded from blame by Selden and the other plaintiffs, and Whitelocke now argued that his father's posthumous memory deserved the same consideration. He struck a cleverly deferential note, emphasizing that he was motivated by care for his father's good name, 'though but a new Parliament man, and of little experience', this characteristic insistence on family honour and his own filial love and duty helping to render more respectable his no less important pecuniary interest. Whitelocke kept his address short, modest, yet morally forceful, and resumed his seat to resounding shouts of 'well moved'. He must have felt tremendous relief when he was seconded by no less a person than John Hampden, his fairly newly claimed distant kinsman. It was soon decided to exonerate Judge Whitelocke alongside Croke.

Although this matter did not seem to affect Whitelocke's deep friendship with Selden even at the time, it genuinely threatened his estate, fortune, and fledgling public career. Whitelocke had only recently gained his seat, without the backing of any powerful patrons; Lord Saye, one of the great Puritan 'popular peers', continued to loathe him, as he would demonstrate both by subsequent words and deeds. Strafford, when first accused of treason, had tried to counterattack by accusing Saye (fairly) of collusion with the rebellious Scots. It may be that Whitelocke's unfortunate new feud with Saye had led at least some of the reformers to fear that this novice MP might actually support the court and Strafford, and so to try at this early stage to effect Whitelocke's financial and political ruin. By emphasizing his father's own record as an 'anticourt' rebel in his time, Whitelocke evidently reassured Hampden in particular. As for Selden, he seems to have been genuine in his desire for compensation – he was still seeking damages from the other judges' estates six years later – and it is therefore tempting to wonder if this known grievance had been exploited by the vengeful Lord Saye.

It seems that this discomfiting experience, and, perhaps, ideological test, proved sufficient to earn Whitelocke what was then arguably the most notable, and perilous, role in the House of Commons. Scarcely two months after his entry into Parliament, Whitelocke was appointed chairman of the select committee of the whole House considering the evidence for Strafford's impeachment and prosecution for high treason. He did his best to shirk this high mark of his colleagues' regard, but in vain: 'they called him to the chair & would not excuse him though he laboured to avoid it'. The committee's work was dangerously confidential; its deliberations proceeded 'under an engagement of secrecy because of the nature and greatness of the business'. After Whitelocke received the necessary papers he 'made solemnly ... a Voluntary Oath', along with his fellow committee members. The commitment required was also punishing in its intensity; Whitelocke's presence was almost constantly required. He moved his wife and children into temporary lodgings at Dean's Yard in Westminster, where they were neighbours of Ned Hyde's father-in-law Sir Thomas Aylesbury, and thus, often enough, of the young Hyde family too.

Each of Whitelocke's colleagues on the committee rewards a closer look, and together they form a variously intriguing composition. Pym and Hampden were, in truth, in charge. Then came Denzil Holles and William Strode, both arrested with Selden in 1629, and so Whitelocke's recent adversaries; Lord Digby, the charming, gifted, mercurial heir to the thoughtful, moderate, reform-minded Earl of Bristol; the godly Sir Walter Erle, an obsessive sniffer-out of papistry; and a strong contingent of legal expertise – Selden himself, Oliver St John, the Welsh lawyer John Glynne, and Whitelocke's and Hyde's Middle Temple friends Geoffrey Palmer and John Maynard. Maynard had, with Hyde, helped to ensure Whitelocke's eventual return to Parliament that January.

Some of these committee-men, like Whitelocke himself, had doubts about the whole case. Selden, probably the most learned authority in Parliament, was not at all satisfied with Pym's charges, or their all-too opportunistic threads of substantiation. Denzil Holles's sister had been Thomas Wentworth's second wife. Although her accidental death had been accompanied by ugly rumours, Holles and his family, now convinced of Strafford's innocence both in the private and public spheres, were concerned to protect the inheritance of their relatives, Strafford's children.* Lord Digby would soon prove to be playing an altogether more elaborate game.

Several of Strafford's would-be prosecutors came from a milieu with which Hyde was more familiar than Whitelocke. Hyde, not Whitelocke, was at this time regularly in Pym and Hampden's company. Through his adventurous and intellectual cousin Sir Kenelm Digby, Lord Digby was already an intimate friend of both Falkland and Hyde. Although Palmer and Maynard were the Middle Temple cronies of both Hyde and Whitelocke, St John and Glynne were

---

* Wentworth's second wife Arabella, mother of his son and heir and two daughters, was pregnant with a fourth child in 1631 when she leant forward to bat a buzzing insect from her husband's coat, tripped, and fell. A premature labour ensued, which she did not survive. Wentworth was already on bad terms with his Holles in-laws over their political differences since his adherence to the court, and the family for some time proved receptive to a false story that he had knocked his wife over in a fit of rage, effectively murdering her and their child. Wentworth did not help matters by quickly identifying an attractive young woman, Elizabeth Rodes, who would, he thought, serve adequately as a stepmother to his children. Since her rank was respectable rather than exalted, he absorbed Elizabeth into his household without confirming the fact of their marriage. On all available evidence he was acting from cold pragmatism, but his enemies – and in-laws – quickly accused him of hot crime. By the time of the Strafford trial in 1641, however, it seems that these terrible accusations had been rebutted to the Holles family's satisfaction.

connected mainly to Hyde, by marriage and by Lord Pembroke's patronage respectively. Hyde would thus, in fact, have been a more obvious and experienced choice for committee chairman than Whitelocke. His personal and political animus against Strafford, as a result of his consistent loyalty to the Buckingham faction and his friendship with Falkland, was a less tepid driving force than Whitelocke's courteous parliamentary scrupulousness. Hyde was already openly working against Strafford by attacking the Presidential Court at York.

Hyde was, however, all too well known as a personal friend of Archbishop Laud, whom Parliament committed to the Tower in March 1641. The sixty-eight-year-old prelate, his health indifferent, was abruptly and uncomfortably accommodated, but the deprivation of which he complained most feelingly was his separation from his books and even pen and ink, a penalty he had once cheerfully visited upon the pamphleteer William Prynne. No serious attempts were as yet carried out to prosecute the archbishop. With the more immediately important case of Strafford under way, as long as Laud was confined in the Tower rather than holding sway at court or voting in Parliament, Pym and his partisans could rest content; they included, despite friendly considerations, Whitelocke and Hyde, respectively Laud's past and recent protégés.

Whatever his individual feelings, Hyde, like Falkland, was in politics consistently opposed to Strafford and Laud's authoritarian governmental combination (what Strafford termed 'Thorough' rule). But he would remain cautious about committing himself prominently or irrevocably throughout his involvement with the 'anticourt' reformers, heartfelt and industrious though that involvement seems to have been.

If Hyde, despite his ties to Laud, had been approached about joining, let alone chairing, the Strafford committee, he would almost certainly have ducked it; and conversely Whitelocke's acceptance of the role was bold to the point of rashness. It came both with a near certainty of offending the court, and, worse still, with the risk of drawing envious attention from fellow members of the opposition. Whitelocke had already acquired in Lord Saye a grim enough adversary. Holles and Whitelocke were soon at odds over how friendly Parliament should be towards the Scots still occupying the north and exacting tribute from the Crown (Holles was particularly close to the Covenanters both in politics and religion). Unsurprisingly, Whitelocke's worst, most open enemy on the committee was Lord Saye's placeman, Sir Walter Erle, who was also all too tempting a target for some of Whitelocke's drier drolleries. It seems that the committee in general suspected their novice chairman of too much softness, perhaps even active goodwill towards Strafford, as the process continued to be hampered by the lack of convincing evidence against the King's minister.

The trial opened in the most ancient chamber of Parliament, Westminster Hall, on 22 March 1641. King Charles and Queen Henrietta Maria (herself still no friend to Strafford) watched almost throughout from a curtained royal box. Hyde says they meant to be 'untaken notice of', but he is probably being deliberately obtuse to conceal his own anti-Straffordian perspective. In fact, by witnessing Strafford's trial in 'secret' as conspicuously as possible, the King made it more difficult – though not, as it would turn out, impossible – to override an acquittal.

A crucial witness for the prosecution came forward after a fortnight's wrangling stalemate: Sir Harry Vane, the haughty courtier who as royal comptroller had annoyed Whitelocke in the run-up to *The Triumph of Peace* seven years earlier, now the King's Secretary of State. As Strafford's fellow Privy Counsellor at the time of the Short Parliament's dissolution, Vane attested, not very confidently, that Strafford had advised the King as follows: 'You have an army in Ireland; you may employ it to reduce this kingdom.' Vane's not-quite-implication was that 'this kingdom' meant not Scotland but England.* His minutes of the Privy Council meeting were then

---

* Hyde emphasizes the unappealing but plausible story that Vane wanted Strafford dead over a minor title, Baron Raby, assumed by Strafford but claimed by the Vanes.

retrieved and offered to the committee by his son and namesake, but after that the relevant papers went missing for some time.* The committee correctly suspected that the papers had been leaked to Strafford's defending counsel, and Whitelocke was blamed by some of his fellow members. He cleared his name for the time being amid further 'solemn protestations'. In due course a quite different culprit would stand revealed.

Whitelocke pressed Vane for as much clarity as possible, considering that these charges constituted 'matters of a very high nature'. The results left him unsatisfied, and he privately reported to the committee that it might, 'for the honour of the House', prove better to omit this particular charge. Sir Walter Erle spluttered back that the honour of the House was but poorly served when 'gownmen', in other words lawyers, interfered in military matters. Erle thus repeated the slur of his patron, Saye, upon Whitelocke's legal calling. Whitelocke replied with silky fury, 'that he held his profession no diminution but an honour to him, & not rendering him the less intelligent of military affairs, but he thought he had as much, and had been as long a soldier as Sir Walter Erle'.

Of course Whitelocke had never been a soldier at all, though he had toyed with the idea during his French sojourn. His point was that the abrasive Sir Walter, who boasted of his brief Dutch military record and reputedly enjoyed playing with miniature models of besieged fortifications, was no more a real soldier than himself. But as in the case of Lord Saye, once Whitelocke had delivered his stinging riposte he yielded on the actual political question. Having himself no wish to press a case he felt was evidentially unsound, he cheerfully left its presentation before the Commons to Erle in particular, 'who had undertaken to make proof of it without witnesses'. Whitelocke waspishly, but also doubtless sincerely, thanked Erle for

---

* Hyde (reasonably) assumed that the younger Vane was acting on his father's behalf; Whitelocke either believed or pretended to believe the (tenuous) account of the Vanes, that father and son offered the verbal and then the written evidence separately, without the elder Vane in any way authorizing the younger.

freeing him from this onerous task. Digby, Hampden, and Maynard all expressed uneasiness as to how Erle might perform, but Whitelocke washed his hands of the sequel: 'I shall acquit myself if any slur happen by it.'

The next day Erle, beginning 'with much gravity and confidence', soon became 'blank and out of countenance', faced with the inadequacy of the testimony in his case's favour. Strafford 'lost no advantage' and mocked his inquisitor with elaborate good manners, 'rising from his seat with a low obeisance', and referring merrily to the 'fresh and furious assault' of the 'worthy knight'. Like Erle, Strafford liked to play the soldier, and his portraits show an impressive figure in black armour suggestive of the victories he never really won; but unlike his unfortunate prosecutor, he was a Parliamentarian and orator of the first rank. Contrary to his subsequent reputation for humourlessness (in this respect like his friend Laud), he could be exceptionally and cruelly amusing. When Erle tried to urge the real and present danger of Strafford's planned Irish invasion, Strafford successfully implied that Sir Walter was unaware of the existence of the Irish Sea.

Rebutting the Vane evidence, Strafford's eloquence reached particularly resonant heights:

> If words spoken to friends . . . shall be brought against a man as treason, this . . . takes away all the comfort of human society . . . it will be a silent world; a city will become a hermitage.

No one could now deny that the accused was playing a spectacular part upon what Whitelocke specifically called the case's 'theatre'. Despite, or in combination with, his craggy, dark looks, in his hour of need Strafford still seemed airier in his wit than anyone else in Westminster Hall. Even the Queen found herself noting the beauty of his long hands. Selden, Holles, and Digby all felt confirmed in their misgivings about the prosecution. Highly placed old sparring partners of Strafford, including the Chancellor of the Exchequer, Lord Cottington, who had long tried to block his rival's rise, and

Lord Bristol, Digby's father, whom Strafford had mocked as 'the Scots' Mercury' because of his eagerness to make peace with the rebels, clearly signalled their willingness to intervene on the side of the accused. Cottington even testified against Vane's ever more tentative version of events at the Privy Council.

As Erle came to another embarrassed halt after displaying his total ignorance, for all his martial preening, of how royal commissions for generals worked, Pym covered up for his collapsing colleague by referring to his simple 'mistake'. Lord Digby more facetiously than helpfully suggested Erle's speech was a 'superfoetation', the medical term for a pregnant woman's redundant second conception. The Queen joined in the merriment, joking in her adventurously accented English that Sir Walter Erle, the 'Water Cur', 'did bark but not bite'. By contrast she remarked of the committee chairman, whose Coranto she had once so enjoyed, that 'she never heard any man speak so clearly . . . with so little gaping'. More reconciled than her husband to Strafford's fall, she thought Whitelocke and the rest 'did bite close'.

Hyde in the *History* singled out his and Whitelocke's mutual friend Geoffrey Palmer for the 'modesty and decency' of his language towards Strafford, 'though the weight of his arguments pressed more upon the earl than all the noise of the rest'. He did not mention Whitelocke in the context of the trial at all, but as Palmer, unlike Whitelocke, became a Royalist, he has probably garnered the credit Hyde would have extended to both men at the time. Whitelocke himself records a comment of Strafford's to an unnamed friend, 'That Glynne & Maynard used him like Advocates, but Palmer & Whitelocke used him like gentlemen, & yet left out nothing material to be urged against him, & he spake many respectful words of Whitelocke.'

Once again Whitelocke's preoccupation with coming across as both a professional and a gentleman is noticeable, but the suggestion also matches with Hyde's impression of Palmer (and so perhaps, elliptically, of Whitelocke), while showing Whitelocke's eager respect for Strafford's opinion. In any case the blundering of Sir

Walter Erle had made more of an impact than all the smoothness his legal colleagues could provide, even before Strafford embarked upon his remarkable defence.

The accused's closing oration stirred the emotions even of an unfriendly Scots observer, possessing all the brooding force of prophecy:

> Beware you do not awake these sleeping lions by the raking up of some neglected, moth-eaten records . . . be not you ambitious to be more skilful, more curious than your fathers were in the art of killing.

Impeachment and high treason now seemed remarkably distant prospects. The imprisoned peer had gained in stature and won himself more influential friends throughout his mishandled trial, even if the city crowd outside, well-primed by the prosecution, remained bent on his ruin. Pym and Hampden knew that to accept their defeat would be to face personal financial catastrophe, political failure, and very likely prosecution and even execution in their turn. They needed another strategy, and in fact two plans now emerged for a resolution. The discreet, able, sympathetic, but not yet, for all that, decisively committed Mr Hyde was well placed to observe the development of both.

## 'Stone-dead hath no fellow' – The Threat of Attainder and the Hope of Compromise, March–May 1641

Pym and Hampden quickly arrived at the momentous decision to proceed against Strafford by way of an Act of Attainder; the medieval instrument for judicial murder by parliamentary will. Such an Act required a simple majority in both Commons and Lords, sealed by the royal consent, to demand its victim's head without further cavil. Debate over whether to resort to this extreme expedient occupied the Commons for the whole week after the failure of the conventional impeachment charge. While neither Hyde nor Whitelocke played a prominent part in this argument, Hyde's confrere Falkland deployed a witty and in the end decisive line of attack. Falkland rose to his scant height and asked a question calculated to raise smiles: 'how many hairs' breadths make a tall man?' It was a dramatic and paradoxical start but its import soon became clear:

> How many make a little man no man can well say, yet we know a tall man when we see him from a low man; so 'tis in this, how many illegal acts make a treason is not well known, but we well know it when we see it.

Like Pym's earlier attempt, Falkland's argument employed little logic, but it drew upon a human, rather than legalistic, image and sentiment. Coming from a man of Falkland's well-known public spirit, selflessness, and virtuous repute, it served its purpose more effectively than most of the preceding passages of legal chicanery put together. 'In equity,' Falkland concluded with uncharacteristic brutality, 'Lord Strafford deserves to die.'

In the division of the House on 21 April, only fifty-nine members of the Commons dared to resist the Bill of Attainder (not, till the King had assented to it, formalized into an Act); City pamphleteers instantly damned this brave minority as 'Straffordians, enemies of justice, betrayers of their country'. They included John Selden, the delicate-minded diarist Philip Warwick, both previously opponents of Strafford, and, most suddenly and unexpectedly, George, Lord Digby, the cautious Earl of Bristol's all too eloquent heir. By an ardent volte-face in Strafford's defence, referring to the attainder as 'but murder with the sword of justice', Digby won the permanent gratitude of the King, shattered his more careful father's reputation as a 'popular peer', and fairly clearly revealed himself as the rogue member of Whitelocke's committee who had leaked to Strafford's defence counsel details of the prosecutors' proceedings, and of the younger Vane's mislaid minutes.* But Whitelocke, Falkland, and Hyde, despite the decisions of their friends and colleagues Selden and Digby, unhesitatingly voted with the majority for the merciless attainder.

That did not imply that they all three necessarily desired Strafford's death. Hyde in particular evidently remained conflicted. He was outraged by the violation of parliamentary privilege committed by the dissemination and blackening of the Straffordians' names. Also, like many other far-sighted members, Hyde did not see how the King himself could ever now credibly consent to his minister's execution, after allowing the court to know of his pledge to avert any harm to Lord Strafford's life, possessions, or honour at all costs. But most importantly of all, Hyde already saw the outline of an alternative, to him much more attractive, solution.

On 26 April 1641, as Hyde tells the tale in the *History*, he was taking a turn at bowls in fashionable Piccadilly, at 'a fair house for entertainment and gaming, and handsome gravel walks with shade'. He was doubtless in need of recreation, after a gruelling session in Parliament overseeing the abolition of the northern Presidential Court at York. But if his resort to walking and bowling was a pleasant diversion now, it was surely not an accidental one. Hyde was aware he was lingering upon a green 'whither very many of the nobility . . . resorted', and he now encountered the particular great nobleman who regarded himself as the lynchpin of a proposed compromise.

The Bill of Attainder had cleared the Commons on 21 April, but not, as yet, the Lords. While 'King Pym' ruled in the House of Commons, matters were very different in the Lords, of which body Hyde's Piccadilly companion was then arguably the most experienced, influential, and widely trusted member. Francis Russell, 4th

---

* Nonetheless Whitelocke remained under lasting suspicion to some as the rumoured source of the leak, until Digby's guilt was proven by the capture of the King's papers after the Battle of Naseby in June 1645. Whitelocke's openly equivocal political position and his friendship with two of Strafford's advocates, Matthew Hale and Richard Lane, contributed to the gossip.

Earl of Bedford, was later described by Hyde as 'A wise man . . . of too great and plentiful a fortune to wish a subversion of the government . . . [Bedford] only intended to make himself and his friends great at court, not to lessen the court itself.' But in the spring of 1641, Hyde would have proudly counted himself among Bedford's friends. Furthermore, as Hyde was to his own parliamentary patron Pembroke, so Pym was to Bedford. Moderate-minded Bedford might be, but he held one of the most powerful, outwardly hottest radicals in his hand, and seemed easily capable of assuaging him to support a reasonable settlement. Bedford's tendrils now reached into the Straffordian faction too, for Digby was his son-in-law. Exemplifying Hyde's model of the educated, responsible aristocrat, Bedford loved the poetry of Donne and Herbert, dipped into the most advanced current theories of natural philosophy, enjoyed justifying his real political ambition by astute allusion to historical precedent, and indeed was once heard to regret that the study of history did not possess the stature of an established profession.

At first Bedford and Hyde conversed safely about Hyde's disposal of the court at York, and Bedford paid Hyde several pretty compliments about his diligence in its dismantlement. Then they turned to business. Bedford portrayed the whole Strafford affair as 'a rock, upon which we should all split . . . the passion of the parliament would destroy the kingdom . . . the king was ready to do all they could desire, if the life of the earl of Strafford might be spared'. Perhaps Bedford felt he actually had to convince Hyde, who had after all voted for the Act of Attainder, but more likely both were already of the same opinion, with which Hyde the historian's narrative voice entirely agrees.

Like Hyde, Bedford felt that the King could hardly be induced to act against what all knew was his private belief, even leaving aside the authority of his royal promise to keep Strafford safe. Bedford, who had no liking for Strafford, for himself would have happily voted through the attainder, but given the sentiment of the King he simply found this course of action impracticable, especially compared to the benefits of a sensible deal. Strafford could be 'banished, or imprisoned for his life, as they chose', 'a remedy proposed by the king; which he thought might be rendered so secure, that there need remain no fears of that man's ever appearing again'. Bedford used the same word, 'passion', to describe the over-zealousness of his own man, Pym, and the excesses of the royal minister Strafford, urging a more rational middle path by force of contrast.

With Strafford (and Laud) permanently removed from the King's favour, opportunities for office, public service, preferment, profit, and glory lay open. Bedford himself, Hyde says, intended to occupy the potentially preeminent place of Lord High Treasurer, replacing Laud's feeble nominee Bishop Juxon. Pym would succeed the ageing and amenable Cottington as Chancellor of the Exchequer. Indeed the first step of this programme had already been put into practice, with the appointment of Oliver St John as solicitor-general. Among the many other promotions to be handed out in such a bloodless revolution, Hyde and his friends might expect all manner of good things. As he discreetly put it in the *History*, 'I was at that time no stranger to the persons of most that governed, and a diligent observer of their carriage.'

Bedford professed himself especially delighted to have found Hyde there disporting himself at bowls, as there was a friend of his 'who needed his counsel'. This turned out to be the Earl of Essex, a flinty, stolid soldier, sidelined by courtiers in the lacklustre Scottish wars. In 1639 Lord Falkland had served under Essex as a volunteer. Hyde, too, knew Essex well enough, having once unsuccessfully intervened to effect a reconciliation between him and Archbishop Laud. With Essex on the Piccadilly green was his brother-in-law, the Earl (soon after Marquess) of Hertford, another, warmer high-ranking acquaintance of Hyde. Bedford explained that Hertford was trying, without success, to bring Essex into line over the question of Strafford's fate, and wondered if Hyde's advice might tip the balance.

Hertford now left Hyde alone to try his best with Essex, who seemed oddly, perhaps dangerously cheerful. He teased Hyde that he had 'that morning performed a service, which [Essex] knew

1. Bulstrode Whitelocke at just under thirty, painted in the year he would triumph at court, travel to France, lose one wife and win another.

2. Edward (Ned) Hyde in the plain apparel of his legal profession, relatively youthful if already looking somewhat older than his years, well-fed and ebullient.

3. Purton 'College Farm', the Wiltshire Hyde cadet property to which Ned Hyde's father, Henry Hyde the Elder, moved from Dinton around 1626, and which Hyde inherited from him in 1634.

4. John Selden, lawyer, Hebraicist, antiquarian, parliamentarian, lover and wit, and an ideal mentor and host, played a formative part in Whitelocke and Hyde's private lives and public ideals.

5. George Villiers, 1st Duke of Buckingham, patron of the Hydes, the Carys and many others, was murdered scant years after this celebratory vision was painted by his great protégé, Rubens.

6. Sir Lucius Cary at about the time he inherited the Falkland viscountcy from his estranged, extravagant father, early in his friendship with Ned Hyde.

7. Cary impulsively married the penniless, pious and, Hyde says, beautiful Lettice, sister of his deceased bosom friend Sir Harry Morison, early in 1630.

8. Lucius Cary was born at Burford, and inherited it along with Great Tew, but sold Burford to William Lenthall, later Speaker of the Commons, to pay his father's debts.

9. Sir Kenelm Digby, natural philosopher, romancer and pirate, was one of various remarkable figures the young Ned Hyde got to know in the circle of the ageing poet Ben Jonson.

10. The 4th Earl of Pembroke as Lord Great Chamberlain, the capacity in which he first encountered Whitelocke and Hyde. He soon became Hyde's patron, and would remain politically sympathetic to both friends.

11. The King and Queen, soon to reject Hyde's suit on a matter of honour at Greenwich, but shortly thereafter to receive Whitelocke and Hyde graciously at Whitehall.

12. Sir Thomas Aylesbury, patron of mathematics, Surveyor of the Navy, Master of Requests and then of the Mint, was from 1634 Ned Hyde's affectionate and useful father-in-law.

13. William Laud, Archbishop of Canterbury, a longstanding if interfering family friend to Whitelocke, became Hyde's most important employer, and had a close though often double-edged interest in the Great Tew friends.

14. Thomas Wentworth, ultimately Earl of Strafford, was, along with Laud, said to 'govern England like the sun and moon'. He was to be brought down by a coalition including Hyde, Falkland and a more reluctant Whitelocke.

15. John Pym, the universally respected de facto leader of the reformers in the Parliaments of 1640, gradually forfeited Hyde's support by his deliberately obstructive radicalism.

16. William Lenthall, initially regarded as a timid Speaker, showed both civility and calibre at Charles I's attempted seizure of the Five Members. Later he inadvertently abetted Hyde's flight to the King.

17. The mercurial, divisive, over-talented and spectacularly devious George, Lord Digby (*left*), who first drew Hyde into direct if discreet royal service, painted alongside his more cautious brother-in-law.

[Hyde] did not intend to do'; that all his excellent work against the court of York would remind peers of Strafford's many abuses of power, and encourage them to vote for the attainder. Essex evidently understood that Hyde, like many other prudent MPs, had voted for Strafford's execution without actually wanting it to take place. Hyde soberly put forward a recapitulation of Bedford's plan to enforce 'so severe a censure, as would determine [i.e. terminate] all the activity of the earl of Strafford that might prove dangerous to the kingdom . . . or mischievous to any particular person'. But Essex had little time for Hyde's lawyerly reminder that Strafford's enemies would be safe from prosecution if the minister was exiled or imprisoned. He cut Hyde off with the memorable snarl, 'Stone-dead hath no fellow.' Essex had no faith that Strafford would stay out of royal favour, and cease to be a threat, as long as he still lived. When Hyde pressed him as best he could, Essex declared with polite but definite hauteur that he was too tired to talk further.

## *'Our good pen will harm us'* – Who Killed Strafford?

Not long after Hyde's Piccadilly intrigue, the Bill of Attainder passed through a thinly populated, intimidated House of Lords. The bishops, usually the block vote upon whom the royal government relied, absented themselves from offering an opinion either way on a charge punishable by death. Strafford went to the scaffold on 12 May 1641. The panicked King had repeatedly and ineffectually schemed to free his minister by unofficial military means, thus further alienating his subjects. That supplest of clerical politicians, Whitelocke's family friend Bishop Williams, soon to become Archbishop of York, persuaded the King, contrary to the earlier promise from which Strafford had ostentatiously but perhaps insincerely released him, to sign the fatal Act of Attainder. Williams had convinced Charles that this was the only way to protect himself and his family, especially his Catholic consort, from the people's wrath. On his way to his death Strafford was blessed by his faithful friend, and

*Friends in Youth*

fellow prisoner of the Tower, Archbishop Laud. The fall that united them effaced the different religious inclinations they had hitherto upheld. Once these two had, the Puritans feared, 'struck a league, like moon and sun, to govern day and night, religion and state'. Now one was annihilated, the other at the scant mercy of their enemies. Before his execution Strafford delivered one last warning to the crowd to 'consider seriously whether the beginnings of the people's happiness should be written in letters of blood'.*

Strafford had been determinedly hunted to the grave by the reforming party he had once himself led. But he was also destroyed by the men who would later be famous as voices of compromise and reason. Hyde and Falkland, themselves connected to the Buckingham faction that Strafford had replaced, had some friends in the half of Yorkshire that hated Strafford, others with rival interests to 'Black Tom Tyrant' in Ireland. Beyond the thundering pedantry of Pym's prosecution, the voices that rose in support of it – often to greater effect – evoked a convivial party of relatives, companions, and clients. Lord Essex, who had expressed the desire to see Strafford 'stone-dead' over bowls with Hyde, had been Falkland's commander in Scotland. The Irish Boyle faction, Lords Cork and Ranelagh, old if unsteady friends to Falkland's father, whom Lucius Cary had known for most of his life, spoke up loudly against Strafford. Falkland himself – despite the opposition of two old friends from the company to be found both around Ben Jonson and at Great Tew, Selden and Digby – dealt Strafford his killing blow, in his sophistical argument for the attainder.

Hyde's subsequent writings, composed with careful Royalist purpose, obfuscate his and his friends' part in the anti-Straffordian web. Hyde offers Strafford a stiff-necked, grudging tribute: 'very few wise men were equally employed with him ... scarce any whose faculties and abilities were equal to his'. By comparison his

---

* Strafford also left a tender parting letter for his son and heir, who would eventually grow up to speak in remembrance of his father's unjust fate during the impeachment of a later royal minister, none other than Lord Clarendon.

remembrances of the glorious popinjay Buckingham are overflowing with praise. When it mattered Hyde, Falkland, and the considerable body of learned, unaligned, moderately reforming opinion that they led, helped Thomas Wentworth, latterly Earl of Strafford, to a traitor's grave. They did so for reasons that related only faintly to actual political differences, more substantially to political ambitions, and most decidedly to factional grievances dating back to the ascendancy of Buckingham.

Hyde and Falkland emerged from the crisis of the attainder as figures of temporarily enhanced power and reputation. But Philip Warwick, one of the few members of the Long Parliament stubborn and brave enough to vote in Strafford's defence, records a prescient contemporary opinion of these carefully moderate men's policy, which he attributes to an unnamed 'wise Lord, who had great influence on them all'. This lord:

> ... would complain that [Hyde's and Falkland's] wit and elegancy, as it was very delightful, so it would not long last useful ... would beget rather a frowardness in men to see such things treated of with elegancy and irony ... 'Our good pen will harm us'.

The likeliest candidates for the 'wise Lord' are Lord Bristol, father of the rash turncoat Lord Digby, and Hyde's cautious bowling companion Lord Bedford. Bedford himself died three days before Strafford, of smallpox, without attaining the power he sought, or witnessing the sequel that both he and Strafford had all too shrewdly anticipated. For those, like Hyde, who had hoped to rise alongside him, Bedford's arbitrary natural death was freighted with bitter disappointment.

In the aftermath of Strafford's execution, Hyde and Falkland appeared to be careful, well-thought-of, useful, and considerate members of the Long Parliament's governing party. Bulstrode Whitelocke both deserved and gained more, at a perhaps less severe price to his conscience. He had done his duty fairly, competently, and impartially. If some colleagues still suspected him of too much partiality towards the Parliament's victim, more praised his industrious and unobjectionable conduct; while the court, particularly the Queen, still noticed his style and intelligence without resenting his good service to their opponents. For his own part, Whitelocke had learned a haunting moral lesson from the show trial and politically motivated death sentence handed down to the legally and obviously innocent Earl of Strafford.

# 6.
# *Differences in Opinion*

> *So in our Theater's solemnities,*
> *When they the Arras raise, the Figures rise . . .*
>
> George Sandys, Book III,
> *Ovids Metamorphosis Englished*

## *Vast and Fatal Consequence: The Act for the Perpetual Parliament; Bulstrode Whitelocke, May–June 1641*

The attainder that had been used to destroy the Earl of Strafford was an ancient legal device applied in a new and controversial manner. But alongside it was passed a more radical bill by far, 'of almost as fatal a consequence to the King and kingdom', Hyde thought, 'as [the attainder] was to the earl'. This was the Act by which Parliament refused to be dissolved by any authority except its own, soon dubbed by aghast supporters of the court the 'Act for the Perpetual Parliament'. Hyde does not mention that the rather reluctant author of this hurriedly drawn-up, unprecedented Act was his old friend Bulstrode Whitelocke.

While Whitelocke believed, as in the matter of Strafford's attainder itself, that it was his duty to put his services at the disposal of the reforming party, he had grave doubts about what he was being asked to do: 'too hasting [sic] a proceeding in the making of a law, especially of so vast consequence as this was', thus re-echoing Hyde's ominous, many-faceted noun, 'consequence'. Yet Whitelocke was proud, also, that his 'pen began to please the house', and such conspicuous public distinction overcame his private reservations. Whatever his instinctive concerns about recent events, by first leading the prosecution of Strafford, and then confirming the life of the Parliament for the foreseeable future, he had arrived in triumph upon the national stage. Whitelocke was not now merely professionally well regarded, but, at last, a figure of his father the judge's stature. 'Whensoever I stood up to speak to any question I was heard before others.'

Many of Whitelocke's legal and political clients, friendly acquaintances and relatives were moderate King's men looking to protect themselves against the worst that might now befall them. Whitelocke's great-uncle, Judge Croke, hitherto consistently excluded from Selden's accusations of high-handed practice, now wrote to Whitelocke humbly asking him to restrain his hotter colleagues in the Commons from 'too severe censure' against judges and bishops. Sir John Wolstenholme, the royal financier also on excellent terms with Ned Hyde, asked Whitelocke for mysterious favours relating both to Parliament and 'his country in the business of the customs', and, it would appear, acquired whatever it was he was after.*

## 'Inseparable friends divided' – The Battleground of the Bishops; Edward Hyde, May–June 1641

Contrary to the *History*'s implication, at the time of his friend's bill for the Perpetual Parliament, Hyde neither made, nor, almost certainly, felt any objection. He showed more interest than Whitelocke in the provision's second, if scarcely secondary purpose – to protect the financial, as opposed to the political, position of sitting MPs. If this Parliament had shared the fate of its predecessor, so quickly dismissed by the King, and if another period of personal rule had ensued, those MPs already eye-deep in debt would have been all but ruined. Hyde himself, though less rich in fortune or estate than Whitelocke, was solvent enough; but the greatest power in the House, John Pym,

---

* Wolstenholme, like many court-aligned MPs, had been elected to the Short but not the Long Parliament.

## Differences in Opinion

whose political guidance and programme Hyde still at this point accepted, owed notorious sums in every direction. Not long after the passage of the 'Perpetual Parliament' Act, Pym's material position had been worsened by the death of the Earl of Bedford, his chief aristocratic patron. He must have been especially relieved at the certainty provided by Whitelocke's jerry-built legislation, keeping Pym snug within Parliament *sine die*, safe from prosecution for debt.

After the execution of Strafford, Hyde briefly convinced himself into a cautiously optimistic state of mind, judging the mood of the Lords, Commons, city, and country at large to have grown 'marvellous calm and composed'. He congratulated himself with the bringing to fruition of the legislative programme he had always pursued with more wholehearted vigour than the whole distressing, if possibly necessary, Strafford business. The King consented with astonishing, listless resignation to the final abolition of the remaining extra-parliamentary courts that Hyde had vocally condemned: the Earl Marshal's Court, the archbishop of Canterbury's Court of the High Commission, and the Star Chamber (the Council of the North having already been dispatched). Whatever satisfaction these achievements brought Hyde was, however, diluted by the death of Bedford, the lodestar of ambitious yet moderate reform, which 'left all those who expected offices and preferments desperate in their hopes', Hyde not least among them.

Hyde was then keeping a closer eye than Whitelocke on the distribution of government posts. In the *History* he rarely admits where he stood in relation to promotions, dismissals, and quarrels, whereas Whitelocke's journal is almost endearingly frank in remembering especially such political gossip as directly related to him. More deeply entrenched and implicated within English aristocratic factions than Whitelocke, Hyde offers more detail on the goings-on in the Lords. When, for example, a quarrel between Lord Pembroke and the son of Lord Arundel led to Pembroke's replacement as Lord Chamberlain by the Earl of Essex, Hyde knew all the men involved personally, and could read the King's motive, in this case an attempt to win over the popular Essex to the courtly interest.

*Friends in Youth*

With Strafford at last safely 'stone-dead', Parliament had moved on to the question of bishops' voting rights in the Lords. Hyde's *History* states that there was no majority in the Commons against the bishops, and only two peers in the Lords, Lord Saye and Sele and Lord Brooke, who were 'positive enemies to the whole fabric of the Church', opponents of the very existence of bishops in either Church or State. Pym himself, Hyde acutely notes, 'was not of that mind'. Neither, at first, had been his richest, closest Commons ally Hampden, nor many of the most important oppositional noblemen. Many northern English MPs who had eagerly collaborated with Hyde in the bringing down of the Council at York were also 'pleased with the government [i.e. the existing episcopacy] . . . of the church', as were 'the lawyers who drove on most furiously with [Pym]' (another of Hyde's few, elliptical references to Whitelocke's standpoint). Yet the most radical party now persuaded many more pragmatic reformers to see the benefits of a first step, depriving the bishops of their seats in the Lords, as the bishops almost always voted in the Crown's interest, so constituting a mitred barrier to any progress for the 'anticourt' opposition.

Both Hyde and Whitelocke had now proved their calibre and usefulness to Pym as allies. But Hyde was also already being assessed by the reforming group as a possibly dangerous future opponent. As summer passed into autumn, he found himself being wooed, and tested, by Pym's more definite partisans. Clarendon's *Life* records two attempts at a more complete recruitment, the first by Nathaniel Fiennes, second son of Lord Saye and Sele, avowed enemy both to bishops and Bulstrode Whitelocke. Fiennes himself was in Hyde's view the most committed bishop-baiter in the Commons with the possible exception of Sir Harry Vane the younger, the subtler-minded son of the bad-tempered, ambitious, and treacherous courtier of the same name, involved, with his father, in Strafford's failed impeachment. One night after dinner at Pym's lodgings, Fiennes half-urged, half-threatened Hyde to fall in line with the plan to eject the bishops from Parliament. As Clarendon claims in the *Life*, Hyde answered that he supported the bishops for

## Differences in Opinion

reasons both of conscience and reason, and that he saw no realistic alternative put forward by the reformers for a new kind of government in Church or State; to which Fiennes curtly replied that 'there would be time enough to think of that'.

Hyde's second half-flattering warning resulted from an apparently accidental encounter with a cheerier character than Fiennes, but with, to Hyde, a far more shocking conclusion. Walking in the churchyard of Westminster Abbey, Hyde recognized Harry Marten, a raffishly genial fellow barrister MP whose chambers lay near his own, and the two fell into friendly badinage. Marten (seemingly) joked that by defending the court – in the form of the bishops – Hyde would 'undo himself'. Hyde insisted he 'had no relation to the court', and only supported good government and the law of the land. Marten then admitted, in response to Hyde's counter-probe, that though he considered 'the men who governed the house', that is Pym and company, mere 'knaves', and shared little of their 'opinion or nature', he supported them both out of self-preservation, and because of his own secret preference for republican rule, still at this time a rare and dangerous position in England. Both Fiennes and Marten, according to Clarendon's *Life*, were openly ready to resort to armed conflict.

Hyde, like both his close friends Whitelocke and Falkland, was not at this point an unmodulated defender of the bishops, either in their political or religious role (contrary to what he would later imply and assert). But he seems to have felt that the humiliation of the Lords Spiritual had now gone too far. His personal friend and patron Archbishop Laud, a collateral casualty of the revolution that had overcome the hated Strafford, and swept away, to Hyde's own satisfaction, the archbishop's Court of the High Commission, remained in the Tower. For now it suited Hyde well enough that Laud remain there, impotent but unmolested. Meanwhile John Selden, no superstitious traditionalist, invincibly upheld the undeniable and ancient legality of the bishops' voting rights. Unlike Falkland and Whitelocke, Hyde never favoured the loss of the bishops' votes. But neither was he, nor his preceptor Selden, at this stage eager to go to the wall in the cause of the status quo.

When the bill on the bishops came to a vote in May, it had been reshaped into a seeming compromise, engineered by Hampden, whereby bishops would lose their place in the Lords, clergy would be barred from secular employment, but the reformers would pledge to stop there and leave the episcopate its place in Church government. Falkland and Whitelocke accepted this deal and voted with Hampden against the bishops, but Hyde and Selden, increasingly unconvinced by the reformers' attempts at reassurance, were among the opposition. The bill came to a decisive stop in the Lords, an inevitable fate while the bishops still clung to their seats, leaving the reformers in an angrier temper, ready now to insist on the total 'Root and Branch' abolition of the episcopate.

Falkland and Hyde were already celebrated in the House as an indivisible pair, displaying their personal and political alliance by invariably sitting together in the chamber. Their sudden divergence much amused a portion of the Commons, as Hyde reports in the *History*:

> ... a difference in opinion between two persons who had never been known to differ in the House ... which administered much pleasure to very many who loved neither of them ... so marvellously delighted to see the two inseparable friends divided in so important a point, that they could not contain from a kind of rejoicing ... the more because they saw Mr Hyde was much surprised with the contradiction ...

But if Falkland had dismayed his friend and startled the wider Commons, Hyde's conduct, too, had been noticed in a more elevated place.

## *A Discreet Conversation, June 1641*

Later that summer, during a lull in parliamentary business, Hyde was quietly approached by an unexpected and probably unwelcome figure. Henry Percy, MP for Northumberland, younger brother of

*Differences in Opinion*

that county's eponymous earl, Algernon Percy, was one of the House's most controversial members. A favourite of the Queen, Percy had involved himself in one of the doomed army plots to rescue Strafford from the Tower, then confessed the scheme to his powerful, cautiously Parliament-inclined brother Northumberland. Both the 'anticourt' group and the fiercest Royalists thus despised him, but the King himself still favoured him: both on Queen Henrietta Maria's account, and in recognition of the fact that Henry Percy had absorbed much odium that might otherwise have seeped nearer to the royal person. Hyde's personal relations with Percy were not warm. As a young courtier-soldier, Percy had been a Strafford placeman, and an enemy of Falkland.

So when Percy told Hyde that the King wanted to see him that evening, Hyde, whether from prudence or genuine astonishment, mumbled excuses. He protested that he was personally unknown to His Majesty: could Percy mean the other Edward Hyde in the Commons?* But Ned Hyde had attended the Court at Greenwich to help intercede in the case of Eleanor Villiers's pregnancy, had been presented to the King and Queen at the lawyers' masque, was a frequent enough attendant at the fringes of court life to have helped his friend Whitelocke by influencing Lords Grandison and Willoughby in the matter of Bulstrode's elopement, and, most importantly, had written and privately circulated a prose defence of Buckingham that was noted and admired by Charles. That the King should now seek him out was not so inconceivable as the peril of the moment made Ned Hyde momentarily assume or pretend, and when Percy insisted he had the right man, there was naturally no question of any longer evading the royal audience.

Percy led Hyde into a Whitehall far more intimate, spacious, and aesthetically delicate than the crowded glimpse he and Whitelocke had experienced seven years before at the time of *The Triumph of*

---

* This was not a convincing evasion; the other Mr Hyde, or Hide, was a profoundly obscure member – and just about the only Hyde in public life who was not Ned's relative.

*Peace*. They proceeded through an outer chamber, and then the Privy Gallery, into the Square Room. Here Percy left Hyde for a 'very short time' alone, or without, at least, human company. A painting of Tarquin and Lucretia hung opposite him, believed by the King, perhaps erroneously, to be by Titian, a thing of menacing beauty in any case; Lucretia meditative, Tarquin behind her in the shadows. Hyde, always more intellectual than visual, can be forgiven in the circumstances for failing to notice it. Percy returned with the King, whose hand Hyde hurriedly kissed. By the time he had straightened up, Percy had slipped out, leaving Hyde in the intimidating glory of a private royal audience.

The two men looked and sounded very different. Ned Hyde was the larger in body and personality. Although he dressed with more care and ornament than, for example, the rustic Cambridgeshire MP Oliver Cromwell, his appearance was as plain as his voice was, incongruously, courtly. Charles presented against the world a diminutive, fragile stalactite of faultless taste. For all his recent troubles with his northern kingdom, the King's voice retained a trace of the soft accent of his Dunfermline birth, his commanding words haltingly delivered in his notorious stammer. It is hard to imagine his appearance without the layers of later Cavalier portraiture, with a plumed hat at a rakish angle and all the equipage of horsemanship, the hunt, and the battlefield. For Charles I's peacetime, courtly incarnation, his 1628 portrayal by Daniel Mytens is more helpful. This presents a richly doubleted exterior, rather Shakespearean to the modern eye, somewhere between a romantic lead like Bassanio in *The Merchant of Venice* and a just ruler like Duke Theseus in *A Midsummer Night's Dream*; closest of all, not unsuitably, to the lovelorn prince of Illyria, Duke Orsino in *Twelfth Night*, that melancholy, idle lord of drunkards and Puritans alike.

Despite the closeness to the Queen of his intermediary Henry Percy, Hyde had, significantly, been conducted into the presence of the King alone. Mr Hyde had after all distinguished himself to his monarch by his defence of the bishops of the Church of England, for whom the Catholic Henrietta Maria had more antipathy than

*Differences in Opinion*

concern. She surely knew of this meeting through Percy, but probably gave it little thought. She would quite soon come to rue its fruit.

Clarendon's account attributes most of the conversation to the King. Hyde was not a man given to social nerves, no matter how intimidating his sourroundings; his assumed narrative detachment as a historian probably conceals a mutually animated exchange. Charles declared that 'he heard from all hands how much he was beholden to Hyde', praising him above 'all his servants in the House of Commons'. Commending Hyde's 'affection to the church', he hinted at considerable rewards to come. The mature Clarendon emphasizes in the *Life* that, just as with louring Fiennes and joshing Marten, Hyde insisted he had acted out of principle rather than political expediency. This possibly sincere line of argument also made an excellent impression on the King.

Charles then lamented 'the passion of the house', sounding uncannily like the late Lord Bedford, once Hyde's hoped-for political chief, regretting the 'passion' of both King and Commons over bowls in Piccadilly. He asked Hyde if he thought the Root-and-Branch Bill against the bishops was likely to pass. Hyde doubted that it would, at any rate not without a long and hard struggle. No part of the reformers' parliamentary programme that year had yet been halted; but then, no part of it had hitherto been opposed by him, Ned Hyde, with the moderate body of reforming opinion he felt himself to represent. Furthermore, Hyde believed that the most talented and forceful of the reformers, Pym himself especially, cared far less about the episcopacy than about the secular overhaul of the government.

For his part, the King had already determined to go north to his native kingdom, Scotland, and somehow parlay some support from the rebels who, as Hyde must have thought but could hardly say, had already several times beaten Charles both in battle and in negotiation. All Mr Hyde had to do now, the King instructed, was to make sure the bill against the bishops did not pass before his return to the capital. Hyde smilingly replied that in that case, 'by the grace of God, [the church] will not be in much danger'. Charles took this careful joke as one of the compliments to which he was accustomed.

Hyde executed his half of this operation with a success that justified the King's confidence. By August the bishops were, for the time being, preserved from 'Root and Branch' reform, Falkland the most notable of many members won back to the court's side by Hyde's private persuasion. Indeed Falkland now refuted Hampden's argument in person during the ensuing debate, coining the ringing adage 'If it is not necessary to change, it is necessary not to change.' But in private, Hyde recalls, Falkland joked with some acerbity about the all too lukewarm camp he had just re-entered: 'They who hated bishops hated them worse than the Devil, and they who loved them loved them not so well as they did their dinners.'

The King, who was making less progress with putative supporters in Edinburgh, wrote to Hyde through his Secretary of State Edward Nicholas (himself an old friend of the Hyde family), with congratulations and thanks. As with Archbishop Laud and John Pym alike, Hyde had proved himself a capable and genuine friend to a powerful patron, this time, at least in theory and for the time being, the most powerful of all.

Extremists like Fiennes and, for all his joviality, Marten now had still greater reason to distrust Hyde, while the moderates, his close friends Selden, Whitelocke, Falkland, and Waller, but also more distant and less innately sympathetic men like the hot-blooded Sir John Colepeper, began to see in Hyde a possible leader. Most of all, the King and Secretary Nicholas had marked out Ned Hyde as the very man they needed.

Pym and his most powerful colleagues, Hampden and St John, did not even now entirely despair of Hyde's support, but, noting his consistent effectiveness, first as a reformer and then as an emergent 'Episcopal party' champion, they watched him with greater vigilance. For himself, Hyde himself was still determined to please as best he could both the court and what he was not yet willing to define as its opposition.

## 'A kind of consternation' – The Irish Rebellion, October–November 1641

The autumn of 1641 brought another of Charles I's three realms, Ireland, to rebellion. Strafford's rule in Ireland had given that nominal kingdom and always restive province some semblance of order, if harshly imposed then at least as heavily upon the powerful as the powerless. Christopher Wandesford, the trusted assistant whom Strafford had left as his Deputy on his departure for London, had died of a fever; and the Earl of Leicester, the compromise candidate who should, King and Parliament had agreed, now replace Strafford at Dublin, reluctant to act on this dangerous elevation, tarried in England. Into the void rushed the old discontented humours of Ireland's subject people, and their penalized Roman Catholic faith. Rebels under the leadership of Catholic gentlemen, with the incompletely tacit backing of the 'Old English', and scant remaining Gaelic Irish, Catholic high aristocracy, tried and failed to take Dublin Castle by surprise, then turned on the plantations of Protestant 'New English' and (especially) Scots colonists in Ulster.

Whitelocke's journal was typical of contemporary English opinion both in and out of Parliament, calling the rising 'so horrid, black and flagitious a rebellion as cannot be paralleled in the stories of any other nation'. Hyde in his *History* suggests, for his time less conventionally but more accurately, that from the moment members of the Commons were informed of the crisis, a strain of paranoiac fantasy was set loose:

> There was a deep silence in the House, and a kind of consternation, most men's heads having been intoxicated . . . with imaginations of plots and treasonous designs through the three kingdoms.

Estimates of Protestant casualties soared amid a national mood of rising panic and ghoulish titillation. Whitelocke was quickly named to the Commons committee appointed to respond to the Irish crisis, the first notable political part he had played since drafting the bill protecting Parliament from dissolution. But he had scarcely entered upon this latest duty when he was laid low by a dangerous illness. Just so, Whitelocke might have reflected, had Pym's patron Lord Bedford, that great hope of Ned Hyde and other moderates, been stymied on the eve of political glory by sudden sickness quickly ripening to death.

Whitelocke believed he was preserved from Bedford's fate by an unlooked for and esoteric art. Shortly before his malady he had encountered William Lilly, a long-faced, cunning-eyed recovering depressive, who claimed to possess a mastery of astrology. Lilly had been a back-room dogsbody to a north-country MP and court stooge, William Pennington; he had arrived in London that September, in flight from a fierce wife and a tedious provincial existence, with his eye to any opportunity. Whitelocke did not let notional political differences or ungenerous gossip inhibit his interest in Lilly's professed skill, and in this serious sickness he sent for him, with excellent results.

Returning to the Commons, Whitelocke found the talk of Irish horrors all the more inflamed. During a discussion as to whether or not Ireland counted as a 'conquered nation', Whitelocke now maintained:

... that the English were never conquered by Duke William of Normandy, but received him by compact as their King, & that he never styled himself Conqueror, but the flattering monks did it, nor claimed the Crown but as heir by the Will of Edward the Confessor, from whom he received the laws of England into Normandy, so far was he from introducing the laws of Normandy into England, & with this kind of learning, the house seemed to be much pleased.

Whitelocke, more than his preceptor and probable source for this line of thought, Selden, was at this point less a historian in pursuit of the past than a politician wedded to the present. By arguing that William of Normandy was not a tyrant above the native law but an heir in accordance with it, he defended the established state of things, Crown, Parliament, and common law working in concord, in both England and Ireland. It was, he doubtless hoped, a reasonable and conciliatory position to which King Charles himself could not possibly object.

## A Parliament of Diarists, October 1641

Such conciliation was not, however, persuasive to the boldest of the parliamentary reformers. Pym's 'violent party' (to use Hyde's later term in the *History*) rejected the qualified offers of a part in the royal administration that the King felt compelled to extend to them. Their confidence in the support of the City crowd was rising, aided by the bloody tales pouring out of Ireland and reports, some partly accurate, many deliberately confected, of various royal skulduggeries: the attempted kidnap or murder of rebellious nobles in Scotland, links between King Charles and the Irish rebels, or schemes for Catholic support from abroad through the Queen. Hyde's *History* gives a good idea of how these rumours:

> . . . made more impression upon the minds of sober and moderate men . . . who till then had much more disliked the passionate proceedings of the Parliament, than could be then imagined or can yet be believed, so great a prejudice . . . was universally contracted against the Court, especially towards the Queen, whose power and activity was thought too great.

Hyde's frank choice of the word 'universally' embraces, where Ireland and Queen Henrietta Maria were concerned, the historian himself.

The proceedings of the Long Parliament in the autumn of 1641 were dramatically and profusely documented. Besides the mass of emergent, polemical newsprint, several members, against a notional rule to the contrary, kept detailed written notes on debates. By comparison to Hyde's *History* such accounts can be jagged, incoherent, repetitive or quotidian, but also less susceptible to the aesthetic, partial finessing of a political veteran whose sensibility was almost as literary as historical.

Most exhaustive of the diarists is Sir Simonds D'Ewes, a moderate supporter of Pym, and himself one of the most industrious members and prolix speakers in the House. While sharing the historical and antiquarian tastes of Selden, Whitelocke, and Hyde, D'Ewes was nonetheless somewhat suspicious of Selden in particular, calling him 'more learned than pious'. D'Ewes became a baronet in July 1641, following either an attempt by the royal camp to procure his allegiance or a simple cash purchase. His general position was similar to that of Whitelocke, loosely aligned with Pym in his actions, occasionally sceptical of the reformers in theory. Another diarist aligned in outlook to Whitelocke and D'Ewes, if more cautious and less active than either, was Sir John Holland, whose chief hope was to put 'a period to our unhappy troubles'. The last and least of these accounts is that of Sir Thomas Peyton, a committed Royalist of limited patience and, according to his witty sister-in-law, Dorothy Osborne, later Lady Temple, even more scant intelligence.

From D'Ewes's perspective, Hyde was by the autumn already a consistent, if always courteous, foil to Pym. Hyde usually appears acting in concert with Lord Falkland (to the extent that D'Ewes quite often mixes up Hyde's and Falkland's speeches), as well as other defenders of the episcopacy, especially Sir Edward Dering and Sir John Colepeper, in marshalling MPs still loyal to the court. Whitelocke leaves a fainter impression on D'Ewes's pages, as a thorough, reliable legal work-horse with almost no decided or controversial opinions of his own. Such a reputation might well have suited Whitelocke, never keen to make enemies unless his honour was deeply stung.

D'Ewes noticed Whitelocke's speaking to protect parliamentary privilege in the cases of outstanding debts to City creditors, a move that would certainly have endeared Whitelocke to John Pym. Whitelocke is otherwise glimpsed managing conferences, filling out committees, occupying the clerk's chair during controversial debates, backing up the legal advice of Oliver St John, and being sent up to communicate with the Lords, seated parallel to St Stephen's Chapel in the Palace of Westminster's Painted Chamber. All of these prestigious tasks suited Whitelocke's style of eloquent facilitation, without, as yet, risking any more directly partisan intervention.

D'Ewes records Falkland and Hyde's response on 20 October to dark rumours from Edinburgh about the King's conduct there. Hyde and Falkland 'moved that we should leave the business of Scotland to the Parliament there and not take up fears and suspicions without certain and undoubted grounds'. D'Ewes himself, backed by the always excitable Sir Walter Erle, carried the House against their lawyerly caution, arguing that:

> ... those black and evil spirits which plotted this in Scotland, conveyed some of that influence hither, which wrought so effectually there ... I desire therefore that we may in time provide for our safety here, as I hope those in Scotland will look to the securing of themselves there.

On the other hand two days later D'Ewes quietly approved of another attempt by Mr Hyde to lower the temperature between King and Parliament, backing Hyde in an attempt to exculpate a drunken but not necessarily murderous Scots peer, the Earl of Crawford, who had become one of Pym's latest bogeymen.

A bill banning the clergy from secular employments – in other words, a renewed attack upon the votes of the bishops in the Lords – put D'Ewes again at odds with Falkland and Hyde. He (justly) accused them of supporting 'two sorts of motions touching this bill, first destructive to ... kill it ... second dilatory that it might lie asleep'. Hyde (or possibly Falkland; D'Ewes is unclear which) objected that to expel members of the Lords without the consent of that whole House was to infringe the Lords' parliamentary privilege; D'Ewes 'did not doubt but that most of the Lords would be as willing to be rid of them as ourselves'. The diarist gave equally little credence to Hyde (or Falkland)'s objection that the Commons was too ill-attended to pass such serious business; 'truly if when men are once elected . . . they have not so much conscience as to attend . . . I know no reason, why business of importance should be neglected by their absence.'

The bill was, once again, passed in the Commons and quashed in the Lords. But in the midst of a subsequent manoeuvre by the reformers, bringing impeachment charges against thirteen bishops, D'Ewes both picked holes in the weaselly expedient put forward by Oliver Cromwell – to suspend the bishops' votes temporarily until their seats had been safely abolished – and commended Hyde for a 'reasonable' suggestion about the timing of the debate.

Perhaps D'Ewes's most striking praise for Hyde's oratory in both style and substance came on 28 October. Hyde was replying to William Strode, one of the members imprisoned in 1629 along with Selden for the restraint of Speaker Finch, but who, unlike Selden, had never made his peace with the King; Hyde's *History* aphoristically dubs Strode 'one of the fiercest men of the party, and of the party only for his fierceness'. Strode was seconding a motion about King Charles's 'ill counsellors', 'with great violence', D'Ewes attests, 'saying all we had done this Parliament was nothing unless we had a negative voice [i.e. a veto] in the placing of the great officers of the King and of his Counsellors, by whom his Majesty was led captive'. D'Ewes, a practised judge of his fellow members' speeches, fully able to spot how well they had been written and adapted, considered Strode's intervention 'premeditated', but nonetheless in 'so extreme a strain as Mr Hyde did upon the sudden confute most of it'. Hyde's answer provides a coherent summary of his whole political attitude – passionately committed to the constitutional change delivered by the Long Parliament up to this date, but equally decidedly opposed to any further tampering with the status quo:

> . . . the choice of the great officers of the crown were to be appointed by the King being an hereditary flower of the crown: and that the passing of the three bills against the Star Chamber, the High

## Differences in Opinion

Commission Court and the ship money we had done very much for the good of the subject: and he thought all particulars were in a good condition if we could but preserve them as they were.

With this rallying-cry, both passionate and legally immaculate, D'Ewes could find no quarrel – 'For mine own part I did conceive [the choice of counsellors] was an ancient and undoubted right of the Crown.' D'Ewes preferred that 'we may lay aside' that specific controversy, essentially ceding the point to Hyde. But Hyde's wider appeal to halt the ongoing political revolution, most immediately regarding the votes of the bishops, gave D'Ewes the chance to differ from him again on religious grounds: '[Mr Hyde] thinks that all is well settled and constituted if we can but keep [bishops] as they are; truly I think the Church is yet full of wrinkles.'*

When, writing the *History* in 1647–8, Hyde contemplated the lawyers of 1641, he was remonstrating not just with Pymite sticklers like D'Ewes, or with increasingly if inexplicably estranged friends like Whitelocke, but with his own past self, that ambitious young politician who had so recently possessed far more in common with anticlerical lawyers than interfering prelates, who in many ways, in his heart of hearts, perhaps even still did.

'And here I cannot but with grief and wonder,' Hyde begins:

> ... remember the virulency and animosity expressed upon all occasions from many of good knowledge in the excellent and wise profession of the Common Law towards the Church and churchmen, taking all opportunities, uncharitably, to improve mistakes into crimes ... unreasonably, to transfer and impute the follies and faults of particular men ... to the malignity of their order and function; and so whet and sharpen the edge of the Law to wound the Church ... and at last to cut it up by the roots, and demolish its foundation.

---

* D'Ewes kept his most flamboyant show of erudition during this debate for Hyde's ally Edmund Waller, calling him a *'tungol witegan'*, the Anglo-Saxon, as he helpfully translated, for 'erring ... planetical ... prophet'.

This charge against learned and fair-minded men who ought to have known better leaves Selden on his pedestal, a model of justice and historical conscientiousness, truthful about the shortcomings of the clergy, undaunted in defence of their rights; lesser lawyer-antiquaries like D'Ewes as simply mistaken pedants; but the younger Whitelocke, Falkland, even the Ned Hyde of 1640–41 as apostates, guilty of understanding the proper balance of the constitution, willing to shut their eyes to it in pursuit of other aims.

## The 'undoubted rights' of an 'ill husband', November 1641

Hyde, seconded by Falkland, kept up his rearguard action on the King's behalf through the autumn. He also defended three hot-headed Royalist MPs, John Ashburnham, Henry Wilmot, and Sir Hugh Pollard, from Pym's accusations that they had conspired in an army plot with the soldier Sir John Berkeley, now held at Parliament's pleasure. Hyde even went so far as to defend Berkeley himself. Ashburnham was soon to become a frivolous, irksome enemy of Hyde, Wilmot a rollicking but often maddening associate, Berkeley, at first, a grateful and close friend, though eventually a bitterly personal rival.

Falkland acted as main spokesman for the emergent, cautious Royalist party in the Commons during a debate over whether to accept aid from the Covenanter Scots, lately the King's open enemies, to put down the Irish rebels. Despite his Scots peerage Falkland was, like Hyde, an Englishman with little knowledge of or sympathy for Scotland. He was particularly, and not unreasonably, averse to the spiritual and intellectual stranglehold imposed by the Scots Presbyterian Church, first north and now potentially south of the border. Falkland was lent qualified backing by Whitelocke and Hyde's Middle Temple crony John Maynard, who suggested that the Scottish troops ought to be paid by their own Parliament, not England's. But in the end the Commons agreed to accept the Covenanters' offer, paying a regiment of 1,000 Scots for Irish service, to be commanded by 'some worthy person well affected in Religion', naturally from the point of view of the ever-godly John Pym.

Pym now performed an entertainingly outrageous pivot, stating, as D'Ewes reports, that:

> . . . no man should be more ready and forward than himself to engage his estate person life and all . . . for the suppression of this rebellion in Ireland or the performance of any other service for his Majesty's honour and safety . . .

A man in his late fifties, of indifferent health, with little to his name but debt and no military experience, might risk ridicule by this gallant suggestion, but Pym was lucky in dominating solemn times, and mockery seldom gained a hearing against him. He was, in practice, far from offering his own 'estate, person, and life', threatening to withdraw Commons support for any Irish action. He now proposed to add to Parliament's latest declaration to the King the provocative rider that 'unless the King would remove his evil counsellors and take such . . . as might be approved by Parliament, we should account ourselves absolved from this [i.e. the Irish] engagement'.

Well aware that Hyde had already seen off this line of attack the previous month, Pym tried to bounce the Commons into agreeing to his measure by the back door, and many supporters arose who 'would have had it speedily assented to'. Hyde, once so carefully inconspicuous and impartial, had no alternative but to risk committing himself or see his aims in ruins, and 'stood up and first opposed it . . . said amongst other things that by such an addition we should as it were prevale [a now obsolete, even then rather technical legal term meaning, effectively, 'coerce'] the King'. Hyde now gained the swift, eloquent, but sadly counter-productive support of his and Falkland's Great Tew associate, the poet Edmund Waller.

Waller made the logically excellent but politically disastrous point that for Parliament to claim it was shot of its duties to the King because he would not agree with its choice of counsellors was an argument not dissimilar to that of the hated, now executed Strafford – that by refusing to grant the King taxations, Parliament had 'absolved [him] from all rules of government'. This identification of Pym with Strafford bit too deep. Pym exploited the fury he very likely genuinely felt, and amid the uproar Waller was forced to withdraw from the chamber, then return to ask Mr Pym's and the House's pardon. Hyde's more temperate and cool-headed rejoinder had been quite lost in the storm; but so (for the moment) had been Pym's proposed addition.

The next day, 6 November, many false rumours being spread by the rebels in Ireland were reported to the Commons. These included the rebels' claim that they were acting with royal support, and even that King Charles (in reality still in Scotland) had been driven out of England and landed at Dunluce, the stronghold of the Catholic Earl of Antrim. Pym himself saw the obvious value in associating the Irish rebels with the King, or his 'evil counsellors', and the stories – and forged copies – of a royal warrant continued to circulate, suiting both Irish rebels and the 'Junto' at Westminster. Pym's rough-spoken ally Cromwell now moved that the Earl of Essex, the most experienced soldier among the 'popular [i.e. Pymite] peers', should be granted 'power to assemble at all times the trained bands of the kingdom on this side Trent for defence thereof till further order . . . taken by Parliament'. This trenchant suggestion was the earliest form of what would eventually become Parliament's Militia Ordinance, allowing for the raising and command of forces without royal authority.

The Irish select committee – chaired by Pym and attended by D'Ewes and Whitelocke – now presented its recommendations. These included the payment and dispatch of the Scottish regiment to Ulster, though the relatively moderate Sir John Holland noted that the Scots were 'to observe the direction of the General assigned by his Majesty'. More importantly, Pym's central demand was back:

> A long Article to remonstrate to his Majesty the danger of the State from ill Counsellors, and to desire the removal of them or else that we would not be obliged to bind ourselves to relieve Ireland.

## Differences in Opinion

George Peard, one of Pym's godly diehards, seconded this latest incarnation of a long-controversial proposal – which even the generally Pym-inclined D'Ewes says 'occasioned a great deal of debate' – with a folksy parallel:

> ... we might well add this clause, for it was no more than if he had a friend or a brother an ill husband, and he should tell him he would not lend him any money or be bound for him unless he would leave his ill courses.

The King was, of course, in this construction England's 'ill husband'.

Peard was answered by Sir John Colepeper, knight of the shire for Kent, and Falkland and Hyde's increasingly frequent, always able ally. Colepeper judged Ireland to be 'a part of England', governed by English laws, and thus argued that the English Parliament was obliged to pay for Ireland's defence without imposing conditions on the King. D'Ewes, finding it hard to disagree, half-heartedly mustered a reference to the late fourteenth-century Parliaments of Richard II making political and financial support conditional on redressed grievances. But he also felt the urgency of the moment in Ireland (much more than did the pacific Falkland, who had advised that 'we should not desire assistance ... till we should know whether we did need it'), and the claims both of 'the bond of nature ... and the bond of conscience'; the Protestant Scots and English under attack were 'of the same nation ... and ... religion with us'. D'Ewes concluded by stating a ringing sentiment of loyalty to traditional royal parliamentarism:

> As I shall always be ready to assert and maintain the true liberties of the subject, so I hold myself bound in conscience and duty to assert the ancient and undoubted rights of the Crown.

This underlying doubt even in the hearts of fairly committed Parliamentarians was one to which Hyde relentlessly appealed over the years of conflict that followed.

7.

# A Tedious Debate

*Exalted voyces through the Palace ring:*
*Not like to theirs who at a marriage sing;*
*But such as menace warre.*

George Sandys, Book V,
*Ovids Metamorphosis Englished*

## Remonstrance Reborn, November 1641

The King, on his way back from Edinburgh, was shortly expected in London. In response to his anticipated arrival, Pym's hitherto sharply focused pursuit of the power to veto and replace royal counsellors widened into a more capacious programme, 'the Grand Remonstrance'. The Remonstrance, or declaration, of the people (that is the Commons), had itself been gestating for exactly a year. As a wide-ranging denunciation of royal misgovernment, it had been initiated by George, Lord Digby, the extravagantly gifted, temperamental politician who had so dramatically changed sides during the prosecution of the Earl of Strafford. Hyde explains in the *History* that the Remonstrance in this original form had overwhelming support in Parliament, including his own. Since its first proposal, however, the King's generous concessions on Ship Money, Strafford's attainder, the Perpetual Parliament, and the prerogative courts had, to many, arguably in truth even most, MPs, made any such Remonstrance redundant.

Over 1640 both the Remonstrance and Hyde himself had, however, assumed new shapes. Whatever reconciliation and cooperation

## A Tedious Debate

Hyde still personally desired, he was becoming regarded on all hands as a decisively partisan figure, the clear leader of what D'Ewes called 'the episcopal party'. The King and Sir Edward Nicholas had identified Mr Hyde as the best champion their cause possessed in the Commons. And with the King imminently expected in his capital and the Junto driven as much by panic as ambition, Pym resurrected the Remonstrance as a rambling, hyperbolic, more emotional than rational rodomontade. As Clarendon describes in the *Life*:

> [The Remonstrance] contained a very bitter representation of all the illegal things which had been done from the first hour of the King's coming to the crown to that minute, with all those sharp reflections which could be made upon the King himself, the Queen, and Council . . . all the unreasonable jealousies of the present government [i.e., of the Commons rather than of the country, not the royal administration but Pym's dominant following] of . . . introducing Popery, and all other particulars which might disturb the minds of the people . . .

Now convinced that the King would never compromise in good faith, Pym and his party had decided to raise the stakes, play for entire victory, and jettison their relations with the court altogether by a direct appeal to the people (in practice the politically active populace of the Puritan-inclining City of London). Pym, the Junto, and their mouthpieces at pulpits and printshops ardently stirred at fevered imaginings of an international Catholic conspiracy.

Hyde attempted to fight fire with fire by stoking up popular fear of a Puritan overreaction (hardly without good reason, as subsequent events would demonstrate). For this he earned an unusually witty retort from D'Ewes:

> And for that which was said by [Mr Hyde] that many sober good men were afraid the Common prayer book should be taken away . . . I durst boldly say that there were divers of the looser sort of the Clergy . . . that if they were sober to read it on the Sunday were scarce so all the six before.

Behind such spirited quips, lukewarmly Pym-inclined MPs such as D'Ewes and Sir John Holland realized that Hyde was making a powerful case. D'Ewes adds, revealingly in cipher, that a clause attacking the Book of Common Prayer was dropped from the Remonstrance, because 'we saw that the party for episcopacy was so strong'.

Hyde sensed this advantage. Clarendon's later account in the *Life* proceeds in bullish tenor:

> The House seemed generally to dislike [the Remonstrance]; many saying, that it was very unnecessary . . . all those grievances being already fully redressed, and the liberty and property of the subject being as well secured for the future as can possibly be done . . . that it was very unseasonable, after the King had gratified them with granting everything which they had desired, and after so long absence in the settling the disorders of another kingdom [Scotland], which he had happily composed, to be now welcomed home with such a volume of reproaches for what others had done amiss and he himself had reformed.

Hyde's summary shows how he had assembled an alliance to match, and perhaps at last definitely to overturn, Pym's Commons ascendancy. Hyde disowns no part of the Long Parliament's successful reforms of 1640–41, including the execution of the Earl of Strafford, who, with Archbishop Laud, is clearly included in the 'others' who 'had done amiss'. About bishops Hyde says as little as possible – the failed attempts at removing their votes and then 'Root and Branch' abolition are quietly excised from the category of 'everything they had desired'. He greatly simplifies the Scottish situation, still by no means 'happily composed', on which he had a narrow, sporadic, hostile, and dismissive perspective. Finally, Hyde employs the constitutional position of the Crown in Parliament with ingenuity and impudence, giving King Charles credit for Pym's own popular political victories.

One ally Hyde won over at about this time, a useful indicator of

## A Tedious Debate

the change of weather, was Sir Edward Dering. Somewhat similar to D'Ewes in his general background, Dering was a country baronet, an indifferently successful courtier, appealingly dotty antiquary, and discriminating book collector (he is the first customer known to have bought Shakespeare's 'First Folio'). He entered the Long Parliament after becoming 'wholly addicted . . . to the study of divinity'. Early in 1641 Dering was in the grip of an almost monomaniacal concern with reform of the episcopate. Unlike the more *politique* enemies of the bishops, he was honest, learned, and unworldly enough to propose a specific replacement scheme of his own for the church government, a compromise somewhat in the direction of Scottish Presbyterianism. Hyde found him personally a fool, irritant, and patsy, summing him up as 'a man very opposite to all [Pym & co's] designs, but . . . of levity and vanity, easily flattered by being commended'. When Dering was chosen by the hard-line reformers to put forward the 'Root and Branch' bill, Hyde acidly commented that Dering 'presented it to the House . . . with . . . two verses in Ovid the application whereof was his greatest motive'. By mid-November it seems Hyde had managed to effect a little flattery himself; Dering promptly seconded him in condemning the intemperate language of the Remonstrance.

The signs were, then, increasingly propitious for Hyde. Moderate-minded but assured Royalists, most of whom had, like Hyde himself, voted for Strafford's attainder, could be counted upon to support him as long as they bothered or dared to attend the Commons. Wavering, conflicted, conscientious natures – Selden (a rare and courageous 'Straffordian' voter as well as a proverbially scrupulous constitutionalist), Falkland, and Whitelocke – were convinced. Hardened but reasonable former rebels like Sir Benjamin Rudyerd, in his younger days another votary at Ben Jonson's boozy shrine, seemed satisfied that sufficient reform was already safeguarded. Previously unexpected fellow travellers like Dering had gradually shapeshifted into active allies. Many in Pym's outer circle, such as D'Ewes, at last wondered whether their leader had overreached himself.

## 'Good Men Amused' – The Debate's Timing Determined

In his *Life* Clarendon characterizes the reformers as now deeply alarmed, with the King almost upon them, the parliamentary stakes vertiginously risen, and their victory in jeopardy. Their resulting speeches 'appeared passionately concerned that [the Remonstrance] not be rejected', punctuated with 'high expressions', and:

> ... many insinuations 'that we were in danger of being deprived of all the good Acts which we had gained' [i.e. all the Parliament's legislative achievements since autumn 1640] ... making doubtful glances and reflections upon the rebellion in Ireland (with which they perceived many good men were easily amused [i.e. bemused, beguiled – Pym's faction were continuing to exploit Irish atrocity stories]).

The 'anticourt' faction 'in the end prevailed' in deciding that the Remonstrance should be voted upon by a grand committee of the entire Commons. Hyde depicts Pym, Hampden, and the others as disseminating two accounts among potential supporters, both reassuringly conservative; that the Remonstrance was necessary to protect the achievements of the Parliament so far, and that it was a political feint that need not ever pass beyond the walls of the chamber. The first of these assertions was debatable; the second would soon prove to be totally disingenuous. Hyde, it may be assumed, was using similar stratagems in the opposite direction.

Other factors at work in the days running up to the debate tended to irritate Pym and encourage Hyde. One of Pym's over-zealous supporters among London's myriad pamphleteers produced a broadside alleging a plot between the Catholic Earl of Worcester and the French Ambassador. This rumour emphatically did not suit Pym, who, for all his confected ire against the French Queen of England, worked in close concert with Cardinal Richelieu's

## A Tedious Debate

government against the Spanish interest.* At the same time Hyde was appointed by the House to cooperate with Whitelocke and Sir Thomas Widdrington, another of the most reputable lawyers in the Commons, to reassure the City with security for the £50,000 so far lent to contain the Irish rebellion. City and Commons thus showed their trust in Hyde's expertise and patriotism. The debt-ridden Pym appeared, by contrast, a spendthrift sensationalist.

Sensing his sliding fortunes, Pym determined to force the debate on the Grand Remonstrance to take place promptly and, if possible, cursorily. There followed a rancorous night of argument about whether the debate on the Remonstrance should go ahead, or whether Irish affairs should take priority. The embryonic Royalist party had reversed its view on this question. When the decision to be taken was over the acceptance of immediate, but, as they considered, perilously double-edged Scottish military aid in Ireland, Hyde and Falkland had favoured delay. Now they preferred to discuss the urgent matters of Ireland and let the Remonstrance rot. Pym's hold over his sympathizers was fraying; D'Ewes found the fracas over the timing too 'hot' and left the House before it concluded – decamping not for the last nor most momentous time. The House settled on dedicating an afternoon and an evening to the Remonstrance on the following Monday, 22 November; a victory for Pym in that the Remonstrance would soon be definitively accepted or rejected, but for Hyde in that it would receive proper scrutiny.

Clarendon's *Life* recalls one of Pym's most immovable confederates taking the decision with a characteristically ill grace:

> Oliver Cromwell (who at that time was little taken notice of) asked the lord Falkland 'Why he would have it put off, for that day would quickly have determined it?' [Falkland] answered, 'There would not

---

* Both Pym's following in the English Parliament and the Covenanters in Scotland relied on French political and financial support against English royal authority. The Auld Alliance rode on, in a new and subterranean form.

have been time enough, for sure it would take some debate.' The other replied, 'A very sorry one': [Pym's party] supposing, by the computation they had made, that very few would oppose it.

But he quickly found that he was mistaken . . .

Cromwell's blundering consistency of intention and impatience with impediment rings true to his later career. This moment, recollected and picked out by Hyde for its poetic symbolism – Falkland, that paragon of the moderates, juxtaposed with Cromwell, later master of the still more violent Commonwealth heirs within the 'violent party' – shows the continuing ability of this seemingly unlikely pair to mix with cordiality, honesty, and intimacy.

## 'The Narrative Part' – Debate by Day and Night, St Stephen's Chapel, Westminster, 22–23 November 1641

Sir Simonds D'Ewes reports that the debate recommenced a little late, after much time spent in discussions over Ireland marshalled by Pym. The partners in the dance had swapped again, with Pym aiming to diminish the time allotted to the debate of most real consequence. The 'many desiring to hasten to the debate of the Remonstrance' were now Hyde and his friends. Hyde, with no further need for or possibility of equivocation, opened the debate himself, followed by four of his best-known allies, of both long and recent standing, Falkland, Sir John Colepeper, Dering, and Rudyerd. Hyde also insisted that the precincts of Westminster be combed by the Serjeant at Arms, to ensure no member present in the palace missed the occasion; he evidently assumed all such absent-minded latecomers would be Royalist. At the same time Pym's assistants endeavoured to cling onto their momentum through a projection of bravado and certainty. D'Ewes heard, to his considerable, scrupulous chagrin, 'that those who wished well to the declaration [i.e. the Remonstrance] did intend to have it pass without alteration of any one word'.

Sir John Holland, a wavering Pymite, gives precise details of the debate's arguments. His pen naturally lingers on Hyde, who he says attacked the Remonstrance, in the first instance, over its tone, 'unfit expressions of more sharpness than we do intend'. He also noticed that Hyde began in a personal vein, defending the role of the Court of Requests, whose Master was his father-in-law. But the burden of Hyde's case, Holland thought, was his preference for quiet over conflict, unity over polarization:

> The mischief of a Remonstrance of ours and a contra-Remonstrance of the Lords may rise. The end [i.e. the purpose] of this Remonstrance [is] public peace; public satisfaction of those that accuse us that we had done nothing for the Commonwealth, others nothing for the King. [Hyde] alloweth a part of this declaration for satisfaction. But the narrative part he disliketh.

Hyde here sought to appear as reasonably concessive as Pym was aiming to seem heroically unyielding. He pointed out difficulties that the Remonstrance threatened to lay in store for the future, including institutional breakdown between the Houses of Parliament, because of its present form's incompatibility with its stated aims to restore, rather than break down, political harmony. Hyde still trod a balance between loyalty to Parliament and the Crown, setting out his objection (for all that D'Ewes calls his style of speech 'very vehement') in carefully measured terms.

Following Hyde, Falkland and Rudyerd encouraged the Commons to bank their gains, consider their achievements – Rudyerd declared 'We have done great things in this Parliament' – and forgive wrongs long since redressed. Falkland dubbed these matters 'fit for an Act of Oblivion'. Sir John Colepeper, according to Holland, contributed a more forceful, specific case:

> Against the form of it. This [is] a Remonstrance to the people. Remonstrances ought to be to the king for redress . . . We [are] not sent to please the people . . . we have no power but by writ and precedent . . . we have not power to do this act . . .

This conception of Parliament's constitutional position was one on which both Hyde and Whitelocke would dwell in speeches and writings to come, arguing that the balance and mystery of power, the *arcanum imperii*, required legislators to be as separate from electors as they were from the executive. Colepeper then enlarged upon Hyde's warning:

> The malignant part [i.e. the extreme Royalist faction, the 'evil counsellors', army plotters, and Papist agents or sympathisers against whom Pym's Remonstrance purported to act] will take advantages to exasperate his Majesty, and put out in his . . . name a contra Remonstrance.

Hyde and Colepeper's continuing ability and desire to distinguish themselves from the 'malignant part' around the King and, especially, the Queen, is evident and revealing. That adjective, as schism coarsened into war, would later come to be applied to every permutation of Royalism, from its moderate, constitutional shape represented by Hyde among others, to out-and-out absolutists and Papists. Like Hyde, Colepeper foresaw a 'contra Remonstrance', but unlike Hyde not specifying one from the Lords, instead from impetuous courtiers about the King. The document destined in the end to play the role of the 'contra Remonstrance' would be composed by neither peers nor courtiers, but by a narrowly thwarted constitutionalist, Hyde himself.

In the *History*, Hyde would claim that the supporters of the Remonstrance, knowing the weakness of their case (exactly as with Strafford's impeachment, and years later with the trial of Laud), all but abandoned any defence save that of majoritarian numerical strength:

> . . . the framers and contrivers of the Declaration said very little, nor answered any reasons that were alleged to the contrary; the only end of passing it, which was to incline the people to sedition, being a reason not to be given; but called still for the question [i.e. the

## A Tedious Debate

division], presuming their number, if not their reason, would serve to carry it . . .

By Hyde's reasoning Pym's objective, to commit his party to open and permanent struggle with the court, was both so obvious and so dangerous that to speak it aloud had become all but taboo. D'Ewes, on the other hand, considered that 'Pym and others answered most of the said objections'. But he also observed that Pym was forced, in answer to Hyde and Colepeper's lawyerly cunning, to specify that the Remonstrance was indeed addressed to the King, not, as it appeared by its coming first before the Commons and as every syllable of it suggested, to the people. Holland preserved a summary of Pym's response which, as so often with that great and ruthless Parliamentarian, makes up in pith for what it lacks in polish:

> The Honour of the King is the safety of his people. That [Pym] had thrust home all the plots and designs to the Court . . . time to speak plain English, lest posterity should say that England was lost and no man durst speak truth. It was time to deal plainly with the king and posterity: and come home nearer yet; since all projects have been rooted in Popery. Shall we forget that a Lord Treasurer [Richard Weston, Earl of Portland] died a Papist? that a Secretary [Sir Francis Windebank, who had fled abroad for fear of the 'anticourt' party's rise] was a Papist?

To bolster his now fading strength in numbers, Pym could still rely on the constant stoking of fear. His third asset was his disciplined endurance, always Pym's hallmark as a Commons man; in this case, Royalists and waverers alike complained, prosecuted to the point of exhaustion and starvation. Forced to confront the full debate they had resisted, unable to carry the day (or night) by either rhetorical or strategic storm, Pym and his allies resorted to a siege.

Clarendon's *Life* evokes the claustrophobic, dim atmosphere of the protracted drama:

## Friends in Youth

> ... it continued all that day ... candles being called for when it grew dark (neither side being very desirous to adjourn it till the next day; though it was evident very many withdrew out of pure faintness, and disability to attend the conclusion) the debate continued till after it was twelve of the clock with much passion ...

Both sides had struggled to delay or fashion this reckoning to serve their own ends; now, met in pitched battle, neither were willing to concede the field. D'Ewes was among those who retired wounded, faint-hearted, or simply torn:

> A little after 4 of the clock in the afternoon I withdrew out of the house foreseeing that this debate in the issue would be long and vehement ... I did the rather absent myself (being also somewhat ill of a cold taken yesterday) because there were some particulars in the said declaration which I had formerly spoken against [D'Ewes refers especially to Pym's continuing insistence that Parliament should both veto and choose royal councillors] and could not in my conscience assent unto although otherwise my heart and vote went with it in the main.

Hyde's backbencher Royalist foot soldiers showed even more frustration with this gruelling rhetorical attrition. Sir Thomas Peyton called it 'a tedious debate beyond all example and precedent'.

Bulstrode Whitelocke sat, and initially voted, with his and Hyde's vocally Royalist Middle Templar 'dear friend', Geoffrey Palmer, that other notably gentlemanly prosecutor of Strafford. Both Whitelocke and Palmer were also close enough to Rudyerd to exchange gloomy prognostications; since Rudyerd was among the first speakers to follow Hyde, it may be deduced that Whitelocke was sitting among the moderate Royalists. Whitelocke disapproved of the Remonstrance on exquisitely technical, impersonal grounds, calling it 'somewhat roughly penned, both for the matter and expressions in it' (a view unsurprisingly shared by that supremely temperate authority, Selden). Whitelocke further lamented that 'the sitting up all night caused many through weakness or weariness to leave the house'.

Hyde details and denounces Pym's blunt, relentless tactical practice:

> ... so long the debate continued, if that can be called a debate when those only of one opinion [i.e. the parliamentary Royalists] argued ... many were gone home to their lodgings out of pure indisposition of health, having neither eat nor drank all the day, and others had withdrawn themselves, that they might neither consent to it, as being against their reason and conscience, nor disoblige the other party by refusing ...
>
> ... there being not one man absent of known inclinations to the violence which then carried all before it, those of that constitution being never absent in any article of time in which anything that concerned their aims was handled; when men of moderate and sober purposes contented themselves with wishing well, and disliking what was amiss, presuming that truth would in the end prevail without their troubling themselves ...

Hyde's analysis was (with all the understandable bitterness of intense partisanship) too simplistic. D'Ewes, undeniably a man of 'moderate and sober purposes', departed on both the grounds of ill health and uneasy conscience, as alluded to by Hyde. He would have, granted the right combination of amendments, almost certainly have voted for the 'violence' of the Remonstrance had he reconciled his body and heart to hanging on in the House. That he did not shows that Hyde's resistance to Pym had been more successful than Hyde himself realized. Pym's radical true purpose, to gain lasting control of the House, alienate the court, and set the City crowd ablaze, was beginning to be recognized all too clearly. The unease of the members was reflected in a steady trickle of lesser concessions secured by the Royalists, despite the much-bruited intention of the Pym camp not to dilute the Remonstrance by a single word.

Secretary of State Edward Nicholas, watching from the gallery, just before midnight wrote to the King that he could last no longer and was leaving for his lodgings at Whitehall. He informed his master of 'diverse in the Commons House, that are resolved to stand very stiff for rejecting that Declaration, and if they prevail not then to protest against it'. Reading between the Secretary's wearied lines it seems that Hyde or one of his allies had briefed him that the numbers would narrowly tell against the King's friends in the Commons, and that it was time to consider a new and riskier manoeuvre. About two hours later, the division was finally made, with those in favour of the declaration leaving St Stephen's Chapel and those against it remaining in their seats (the interminable debate had left the chamber half-empty and no member by this point was forced to stand). The Remonstrance was carried by eleven votes (not, as Clarendon was to remember, nine), 159 ayes to 148 noes. The votes of forty members had been considered in the balance; had more MPs sympathetic to the King persevered, or half a dozen of the uncommitted chosen differently, Hyde would have tasted an astonishing last-minute triumph. Rudyerd sourly remarked to Whitelocke (both still in the chamber as Noes) that this was 'the verdict of a starved jury', a remark with which Whitelocke implicitly agreed, concurring with Rudyerd and Hyde's condemnation of the siege tactics of Pym, the just-victorious captor of the Commons.

## 'Some disorder' – The Protestation of Geoffrey Palmer, 23 November 1641

This barely decisive division turned the hitherto somewhat artificial debate – with one, slightly less numerous side making the body of the speeches and the narrow majority opposed to them doing little but stubbornly voting – into a genuine, chaotic, and frightening struggle. Hyde paints the House's scraped majority as the aggressor, saying that Hampden, 'as soon as [the result] was declared', proposed that the Remonstrance should be printed. This last-minute coup would have had the instant effect of addressing the declaration de facto directly to the people, contrary to what Pym and his lieutenants had implied both before and during the debate. It certainly went against the spirit of such a narrowly carried motion. But Nicholas's letter to the King shows that Hyde and others were probably planning to protest against the result in any case.

Protestation against what was supposed to be the will of a formally united House was an unusual and risky procedure; occasionally undertaken by proud, prickly members of the Lords, but seldom if ever in the theoretically consensual and compliant House of Commons. For Hyde, who had so cautiously and reluctantly risen to become a consistent leader of the Commons court party, to lead a protestation represented as vertiginous a raising of the stakes in his relations with the 'violent party' as was the Remonstrance itself in Pym's relations with the King. But on this occasion political expediency was to direct Pym's angry retaliation elsewhere.

Hyde's protestation against the printing of the Remonstrance seems, by the evidence both of the *Life* and of D'Ewes, to have been immediate, unambiguous, but perhaps a little perfunctory. In Clarendon's words, he 'did believe the printing it in that manner was not lawful, and he feared it would produce mischievous effects; and therefore desired that . . . he might have leave to enter his protestation.' D'Ewes records that Hyde, Colepeper, and 'divers others' among the usual suspects *offered* 'to enter their protestation', '. . . but that was gainsaid for no protestation can be entered without the consent of the house. So this matter was laid aside for a further time of debate.'

As far as D'Ewes and, certainly, Pym and the rest were concerned, protestations by a minority in the Commons were a nonsensical and dangerous concept; Hyde, Colepeper, and their friends knew that as well as anyone there, and the Royalists were merely using a parliamentary device to play for time and delay the Remonstrance's printing. The contretemps ought to have ended, at least for the night, there. That it did not was the responsibility, premeditated or not, of the man sitting next to Bulstrode Whitelocke, Geoffrey Palmer – Whitelocke and Hyde's old Middle Templar companion.

Whitelocke was horrified when his friend Palmer rose to his feet after the protestation of Hyde and the others had been refused: 'I wished him not to do it . . . and pulled him down when he stood up.' Although Whitelocke had voted against the Remonstrance and would have regarded its printing as an ominous prospect, he did not go as far as his friends in thinking it worth the trouble and dubious validity of a Commons protestation. Hyde was gratified but not, perhaps, surprised by Palmer's act. In the *Life*, Palmer is referred to as 'a man of great reputation, and much esteemed in the house'. It is probable he had been selected and prepared in advance for his controversial role, as a loyal and influential Royalist with excellent moderate connections; D'Ewes for his part calls Palmer 'a lawyer of the Middle Temple . . . whom I had long known, and knew to be learned in his profession'. What followed varies between different witnesses, and was probably in any case hard to discern amid the chamber's increasing noise. According to Clarendon, Palmer rose and spoke a further protestation solely on his own behalf, but then was 'immediately', and, Clarendon suggests, spontaneously followed by 'many' members, 'together . . . without distinction and in some disorder', all crying out that they too were protesting. If this is taken at face value, Palmer was slightly out of order but not personally guilty of fomenting the ensuing brawl.

That is not how D'Ewes interpreted it; the version he was told (it must be remembered he had left that afternoon) maintains that Palmer:

> . . . desired that a protestation might be entered in the name of himself *and all the rest* upon which divers cried *All, all,* and some waved their hats over their heads, and others took their swords in their scabbards out of their belts and held them by the pommels in their hands setting the lower part on the ground, so as if God had not prevented it there was very great danger that mischief might have been done.

## A Tedious Debate

In this narrative Palmer flagrantly and deliberately violates the peace of the House, speaking on behalf of an unspecified large group of fellow members, a move that galvanizes any restive Royalist troublemakers, the rumbustious Peytons tired of fruitless bandying of words, to resort to physical forms of argument. D'Ewes is backed by an authority who had also left the House earlier, but whose interest would presumably have been to downplay Palmer's breach of parliamentary etiquette – Secretary Nicholas, writing history after his own retirement:

> A great cry seconded [Palmer], and the spirits of those that [opposed the Remonstrance], tho' they gained not the question, appeared very high, and the others flagged, seeing so great opposition . . . there were divers that laid their Hand on their sword, and . . . resolved that they would not longer stand to be baffled by such a Rabble of inconsiderable Persons, set on by a juggling Junto . . .

Nicholas – not innately a respecter of the sanctity of majority results in the Commons – here somewhat lets the Royalist cat out of the constitutionalist bag. It seems fairly likely that, with whatever reluctance, Hyde and his friends had accepted that in the event of the Remonstrance – and more particularly its printing – narrowly passing, extreme measures would be justified in protesting in the House. After a scene of knockabout in which Hampden asked Palmer how it was he had read his fellow members' minds in order to speak for them, and Palmer insisted he had heard them shout 'All, all' *before* invoking 'all the rest' himself, it was agreed as a compromise that the Remonstrance should not – as yet – be printed.

## *Cromwell's Confidence, Hyde's Conscience, 23 November 1641*

It was now about three o'clock in the morning as the members lurched out of the House; but Falkland still retained the composure to locate Cromwell and ask him jocularly 'whether there had been a debate'. Cromwell replied in an equally amiable spirit 'that he would take [Falkland's] word another time', but then leant closer and imparted to Falkland, in a particularly earnest tone, the extraordinary confidence:

> ... that if the Remonstrance had been rejected he would have sold all he had the next morning, and never have seen England more; and he knew there were many other honest men of the same resolution.

Like Hyde's conversation with Bedford, Hertford, and Essex about Strafford's fate, culminating in Essex's killer *mot*, 'Stone-dead hath no fellow', this is one of those exceptionally vital, potentially counterfactual moments in Clarendon for which the reader has only the historian's authority. Both episodes add an almost destabilizing level of human insight to the known facts. Both are inherently plausible. In the case of Cromwell and others as emigrants, whether to the American colonies or as Protestant mercenary-crusaders in the Thirty Years War, there are plenty of precedents and parallels. Cromwell and Pym were both running short on both opportunities and funds, and had they met with political defeat just as the King returned from Scotland, their circumstances would have been more than desperate enough to merit relocation.

Both the Essex and Cromwell vignettes would have taken an exceptional degree of novelistic imagination to concoct from thin air; whether Hyde possessed such an imagination is in itself a fair and interesting question. Clarendon's emotional exclamation about Cromwell's near exile – 'So near was the poor kingdom at that time to its deliverance!' – has the ring of sincerity. Most tellingly, both Essex's refusal to compromise and Cromwell's averted flight suit Hyde's central argument in the *Life* and, especially, the *History*, addressed to a defeated, chastened monarch – that the civil wars had not begun by chance; that they need not and should not have happened at all; that repeated ways out remained, often by less than a sword's length, along roads untaken.

## A Tedious Debate

Two days after the Remonstrance's passing, Palmer was called before his fellow members, charged with inciting a mutiny in the Commons. The House voted to punish him, but was split over the penalty's severity. D'Ewes describes another extended debate lasting over the next two days, with Whitelocke unusually conspicuous as Palmer's chief defender. Whitelocke seconded Palmer's contrite but reasonable account of himself and his actions, and further pleaded:

> ... that the said Mr Palmer was a sober learned and moderate man: that his intent ... was to an end to that night's debate it being so far spent ... that he had no intention to raise any heat or combustion in the House. That he had done very good service to the House [alluding principally to Palmer's role in Strafford's prosecution] ...

After Whitelocke's intervention the members voted to send Palmer to the Tower for a short spell, rather than expelling him from the Commons, 'as his offence had deserved in a high measure', D'Ewes grumbled. At his sentencing by Speaker Lenthall, Palmer cut a distinguished figure in his barrister's gown. Soon enough Whitelocke paid a visit to his friend's new digs in the Tower, where 'we drolled about his imprisonment. He said that if he had followed my advice [i.e. avoided the protestation] he had not been a prisoner.'

In resisting Whitelocke's prudence and making his dangerous protest, Palmer had very likely instead taken the counsel of his other Middle Temple intimate, Ned Hyde. Both the *History* and the *Life* give a more complex and, in every sense, intriguing explanation of the events behind Palmer's reprimand by the Commons. Hyde's regretful conclusion appears to be that Palmer was a scapegoat, absorbing the anger of the 'violent party' that was really directed at Hyde himself; as the *History* has it:

> ... [Pym & co] being contented to compound for [i.e. make do with] Mr Palmer, and to waive questioning the gentleman who first began the protestation [Hyde] (though he was more in their

displeasure,), by reason one powerful person amongst them had taken some groundless affection to him, and declared that he would concur with them against Mr Palmer but with all his interest oppose them on the behalf of the other.

Clarendon's *Life*, written over two decades later, provides more rich and exact detail, especially on the *History*'s implausibly enigmatic claim that 'one powerful person . . . had taken some groundless affection to [Hyde]'. With the events under discussion deprived of their latent political charge by the Restoration, Clarendon could admit that he alluded not just to one mysterious patron, but to a faction with a specific identity and agenda. Clarendon is also more definite about how badly his relationship with the 'anticourt' party had broken down, though this could be ascribed to his decades as a royal minister, in exile and then in power, making him less willing or able to imagine his long-lost amity with the 'Rebellion's' leadership:

. . . this subject [i.e. the debate over the protestation] was the more grateful to [the 'anticourt' party] because they should hereby take revenge upon Mr Hyde, whom they perfectly hated above any man . . . But here they differed among themselves; all the leading violent men, who bore the greatest sway, were most glad of the occasion, as it gave them opportunity to be rid of Mr Hyde, which they passionately desired: but Sir John Hotham, Cholmely, and Stapleton, who never severed, and had a numerous train that attended their motions, remembered the service Mr Hyde had done against the court of York . . .

It was the influence, Clarendon says, of 'his Northern friends', that kept him safe and let Palmer bear the brunt of Pym's revenge – without, he emphasizes, his knowledge or consent. These friends even made to him 'signs . . . which he understood not' when Hyde started blurting out that he and not Palmer had started the protest. As for Palmer, Hyde 'loved him much, and had rather have

## A Tedious Debate

suffered himself than that he should'. Clarendon claims to have attempted to extricate his old friend from trouble on the grounds that he had been spared punishment at the original time of the offence and should not be condemned retrospectively.

Clarendon also states that many of the most extreme reformers, far from giving Palmer credit for his prosecution of Strafford, had never forgiven him for his celebrated courtesy towards the notorious defendant – a politesse for which Whitelocke had also been noticed. What Palmer underwent could very easily have befallen Whitelocke instead, had he been a step or a syllable further out of line. Hyde and Whitelocke, who had voted on the same side against the Remonstrance, only then to become countervailing voices acting upon Palmer, each go unnoticed in each other's accounts of defending their mutual friend. Clarendon's elucidation of the Palmer protestation is almost unsupported elsewhere. A single garbled newsletter reports that both Hyde and Palmer were considered mutineers by Parliament on the night of the Grand Remonstrance's passing, and that source goes on to say, incorrectly, that Hyde was held in the Tower alongside Palmer.

By at least 1647–8, when he reflected on the Remonstrance in the *History*, Hyde was all too aware that, on the day and night of 22 November 1641, he had commanded and, just, lost, the first and arguably the most decisive battle of the English Civil War that followed. He replayed its details with frustration and regret that teetered upon the obsessive, harping upon:

> ... that absurd, fatal Remonstrance, the first visible ground and foundation of that madness in the people of which they could never since be cured, [was carried].* Yet when this passed, the number in the House exceeded not three hundred [this is only just

---

* When Hyde wrote this in 1646, from the Royalist hold-out of Jersey, the King was in parliamentary custody, and no feasible Restoration (from Hyde's point of view, excepting via the Catholic or Presbyterian arms he feared worse than Parliament itself) appeared in sight.

exaggerated – 307 MPs voted, as stated above], which was not much more than half, the House consisting of above five hundred . . .

Hyde trained particular ire upon two groups of MPs – the non-voting Royalists and moderates on the one hand, and the spidery manipulators of the 'violent party', Pym above all, on the other. Of the first category he exclaimed:

> I know not how those men have already answered it to their own consciences, or how they will answer it to Him who can discern their consciences, who, having assumed their country's trust, and, it may be, with great earnestness laboured to procure that trust, by their supine laziness, negligence and absence were the first inlets to these inundations . . . which have overwhelmed us.

It was thus the first, indifferent party that had itself to blame for the second, malevolent one:

> For by this means, a handful of men, much inferior in the beginning in number and interest, came to give laws to the major part; and, to shew that three diligent persons are a greater number in arithmetic, as well as a more significant number in logic, than ten unconcerned, they, by plurality of voices [i.e. votes], in the end converted or reduced the whole body to their opinions.

Launching off that respectful but reserved adjective, 'diligent', Hyde represents in damning detail the peculiar qualities of Pym's clique; once, not so very long before the Remonstrance, in the spring of 1641 at the height of the Strafford controversy, his own friends, colleagues, models, and leaders:

> It is true, men of activity and faction, in any design, have many advantages that a composed and settled council, though industrious enough, usually have not, and some that gallant men cannot give themselves leave to entertain; for . . . they contract a habit of ill

## A Tedious Debate

nature and uningenuity [i.e. disingenuousness], necessary to their affairs and the temper of those upon whom they are to work, that liberal-minded men would not persuade themselves to entertain, even for the prevention of all the mischiefs the others intend.

These sentences, beautiful, balanced, tormented, and interminable, show Hyde still struggling to come to terms with terribly unpalatable truths.

Pym and his 'men of faction' had continued to monopolize parliamentary success, despite the considerable obstacles Hyde had toiled to place in their path, not just because of talent or industry, attributes that could be found on both sides, but *because* they had been ill-natured and disingenuous, not 'gallant' or 'liberal-minded'. Scrupulous gallantry and 'supine laziness' lay all too closely akin. If Hyde and his closest political friends – still including Whitelocke as well as Falkland – truly wished to stop the 'juggling Junto' carrying all before it, they might yet have to learn a few of the same tricks. The peroration of the *History*'s treatment of the Remonstrance reveals this realization half in spite of itself:

And whoever observed the ill arts these men used, to prevail upon the people . . . their absurd [that sclerotic adjective again], ridiculous lying, to win the affections and corrupt the understandings of the weak, and the bold scandals to confirm the wilful; the boundless promises they presented to the ambitious, and their gross, abject flatteries and applications to the vulgar-spirited; would hardly give himself leave to use those weapons for the preservation of the three kingdoms.

'Would hardly' is scarcely 'never could'. The affair of Geoffrey Palmer's protestation in particular suggests that Hyde had already reconciled himself to opposing Pym, if necessary, by means of Pymesque guile, whatever private compunction he might have felt about so doing.

8.

# Sober Men, Authors of Counsels

*Scarce could he bid farewell: sobs so ingage*
*His troubled speech; who dreads his souls presage.*

George Sandys, Book VI,
*Ovids Metamorphosis Englished*

## Dr Chillingworth's Entanglement, Westminster and the Tower, December 1641

Hyde's strategy, Falkland's emollience, Palmer's courage, and Whitelocke's caution could none of them stand long against the renewed fury of Pym's supporters. With Ireland aflame, the most important question of the moment, whether the army sent to pacify the situation would answer to King or Parliament, was still to be decided. Pym's ruthless agility in carrying critical votes at awkward hours with packed adherents won the right to print the Grand Remonstrance all over England by mid-December. Pym's following was, contrary to its leader's prior assertions, far from content merely to present its complaints to the King, nor appeased by gaining the licence to foment public fury in London. The Junto next accused 'a malignant party . . . of the Privy Council, and in other employments of trust and nearness about his majesty, the prince, and the rest of his children' – almost transparently the Queen and her favourites – of fomenting the Irish rebellion. The Pymites then renewed their campaign for the exclusion of the bishops. Still lacking any legal pretext to target Hyde or Falkland for their near-thwarting of the Remonstrance, at the end of November the 'anticourt' party settled for another scapegoat close to both the moderate leaders: William Chillingworth, Hyde's admired friend and Falkland's philosopher-in-residence.

The Palmer affair was still fresh in the minds of MPs and politically engaged gossips, particularly those of the large Royalist minority now under fire by the so narrowly victorious 'anticourt' Commons faction. One who now wrote to Hyde was Edward Kirton, steward to Lord Hertford, the great nobleman who had started as a reformer then drifted back to the court over Strafford's execution. Kirton himself was a Somerset MP cautiously inclining to the 'Episcopal party'. He warned Hyde of a riot whipped up against the bishops on 'that day on which Mr. Palmer was sent to the Tower'. Dr Chillingworth lacked Kirton's discretion, volunteering politically risky opinions to Thomas Wadland, a Clement's Inn attorney with whom Chillingworth had business connected to a Leicester hospital. Chillingworth feelingly declared to Wadland that Palmer's protest had been entirely legal. He also openly spread the story Kirton had secretly imparted to Hyde, that Pym's men were inciting crowds in London and putting pressure on MPs to abandon the bishops. Wadland promptly reported these imprudent confidences to the Commons, and Chillingworth was arrested, held, and cross-examined by MPs. Perhaps Chillingworth ruefully remembered his own denunciation of a drinking companion to his godfather, then Bishop Laud, in the very different days of 1628.

Despite a typically ingenious, disingenuous last-minute attempt to convince Pym of their common ground in criticizing the Laudian Church, on 4 December Chillingworth was imprisoned at the House's pleasure, having, as a newsletter put it at the time, 'in the behalf of Mr. Palmer . . . so entangled himself that he was sent to the Tower to keep Mr. Palmer company'. Sir Edward Nicholas reported to the King that 'some spake in his favour, and mentioned his Learning, and an Excellent Work against the Papists', namely *The Religion of Protestants*, Chillingworth's masterpiece published in 1637. Nicholas further lamented that this lettered defence was brushed aside by the reliably grim Sir Walter Erle, who called Chillingworth's book 'most light [i.e. worthless]' on the grounds that it 'found out a new Way to prove Religion, by Natural Reason'. As Nicholas complained, '. . . no sober Divine ever rejected the Evidence of Reason; and the most Ancient Fathers convinced Pagans by Reason. But [Chillingworth] is sent to the Tower.'

Chillingworth's religious writings may not have helped his case, but it was his political opinions that had landed him in the Tower, where he joined his godfather Archbishop Laud as well as Geoffrey Palmer. His words, both to Wadland in private and before the Commons in his own defence, characteristically combined clear thinking and explosive effect. According to Wadland, Chillingworth had warned 'that some members [of the Commons] were guilty of Treason, and that they should be accused within a day or two'. Almost worse, Chillingworth was said to have used the expression 'some of the other side', thus expressing the unsayable truth that the House of Commons, at this period legally obliged to act with unanimity, was profoundly divided against itself. In the end, legal and parliamentary theory would come to justify and refute both Chillingworth and his accusers. The more modern form of division and the formal system of parties allowed the Commons to evolve beyond the traditionally all-important but increasingly absurd myth of indivisible unity in the House, while enshrining the principle, so passionately and unmanageably resisted by Palmer and Chillingworth, of a losing minority's consent.

Attempting to extenuate his reported words in the Commons, Chillingworth at first, unconvincingly, denied that he had accused anyone of treason, then dared to repeat the rumours that the Pym faction had encouraged intimidation of their opponents by armed London throngs. He defended the principle of Geoffrey Palmer's protestation with two astonishingly provocative examples of protesting according to conscience: imagining first a Parliament that tried to depose a King, then one that tried, as in the reign of Mary Tudor, to reinstate the Roman Catholic Mass. Although in the context of a royal deposition Chillingworth pretended to be talking about a hypothetical scenario in France, no one was deceived, and

## Sober Men, Authors of Counsels

almost everyone was genuinely shocked at what Sir John Hotham called 'deposing a King, a Fact [deed] so horrid, as they all abhorred the thought of it'. This outrage, doubtless to some extent confected, was yet also in large part genuine. Parliament had last deposed a king a century and a half before, dethroning young Edward V in favour of his uncle Richard III, hardly a happy precedent. The republicanism expressed by Harry Marten to Ned Hyde in private was still extremely rare. Any suggestion that Parliament aimed or desired to topple Charles outright, as opposed to limiting his powers, remained both politically dangerous and, to most of Pym's partisans, sincerely horrifying.

Sir Simonds D'Ewes sharply referred to Chillingworth's 'Jesuitical position', reminding the House that, for all he might pose as a defender of the English religious *via media*, Chillingworth had once trained as a Catholic priest and was in many ways still very close to the Catholic position. He then (not unjustly) attacked his 'falsification and tergiversation here in all our hearings'. For his part Chillingworth did not deny that he had remarked to Wadland that Pym and his allies 'should be questioned for as great a Treason as the Earl of Strafford'. This was the same bold, taboo comparison that another Great Tew associate, Edmund Waller, had made on 5 November, seemingly indicative of an authentic Great Tew position, as antipathetic to the 'thorough' Strafford ascendancy as to the 'violent party' of Pym.

Although Chillingworth, like Palmer, was released from the Tower after a couple of weeks, these imprisonments constituted for Hyde and Falkland the gloomiest of portents. After so much industrious, nuanced struggle, so many useful friendships strained or sundered, all of their moderate measures for the reconciliation of King and Parliament had proven, after all, only moderately effectual. Such dispiriting outcomes partly explain Hyde's subsequent willingness to be persuaded into a more definite course by George, Lord Digby, a figure far less consensual than his familiar school of friends, Selden, Falkland, Waller, or Whitelocke.

## Enter George, Lord Digby, to Give Vent to Hyde's Indignation, December 1641

George Digby shares a famous Van Dyck 'swagger' double portrait with his brother-in-law William Russell, eldest son and successor to that Earl of Bedford in whom both Hyde and Pym had placed such lofty hopes. Dressed in soberly senatorial black satin and white lace, Digby plays the part of 'Peace' to young Russell's 'War', gleaming in military scarlet and gold. Yet the callings of these costumes are belied by their wearers' demeanours. Russell looks pudgily bland, impassive, even ingenuous. Digby bestows on the viewer, between wild leonine lovelocks and heavy, debauched eyelids, a direct glance of idle superiority, the quiet perusal of a predator wholly confident of his game.

Superficially George Digby was a curious friend for a man like Ned Hyde to have acquired, not immediately dissimilar from a voluptuary like Harry Jermyn, the Queen's dangerous but fundamentally frivolous pet, or the courtly young braggart soldier George Goring, both of whom Hyde (and Falkland) consistently detested. Like Jermyn and Goring, Digby attracted admiration and loathing in equal measure; all three were flowing-maned, reckless leaders of fashion. Both Jermyn and Digby seemed as ready with their swords as their tongues, though Jermyn tended in the final instance to evade duels, whereas Digby calmly won them.

In fact the Digby of 1641 was far more sharpened and polished than other courtly blades, in his family background, early life, education, and accomplishments to date. Reared in Spain, where his father had served as ambassador, he was an all too evidently exotic rarity among his English contemporaries. George Digby's most famous kinsman, his cousin Sir Kenelm Digby, a prodigy of science, seamanship, and sorcery, had already set a high family standard for dazzling his age. A close associate of Ben Jonson, Tom Carew, and John Selden, Sir Kenelm also had an affinity with the temper of Great Tew, and it may have been he who first introduced his cousin there. Among Falkland and the rest George Digby proved, as Harry Jermyn could never have done, their equal as a theologian and scholar. The raffish poet John Suckling, gossipy associate of Hyde's one-time lodger William Davenant, bracketed young Digby with Chillingworth himself as kindred intellectuals.

During Strafford's prosecution George Digby was more prominent and less prudent than Falkland and Hyde. His family, unlike theirs, was strongly opposed to the remnants of the Buckingham faction; the great favourite had quarrelled with Digby's father during his adventure to Spain with Prince Charles, and impeded the advancement of all Digbys ever since. But like Falkland and Hyde, Digby heartily disliked Strafford, who had in turn alienated his father, by then Earl of Bristol, for being too peaceable towards the Scots during the Bishops' Wars. Digby's suspiciously sudden change of heart, coming out so strikingly in Strafford's defence, induced King Charles to summon Digby to the Lords under his father's secondary title, thus protecting him from arrest at the hands of furious former Commons colleagues. If Digby entirely lacked Strafford's solidity, his very lightness and sharpness made him much more to Charles's personal liking.

As Clarendon tells it in the *Life*, Digby's appearance in his chambers at a decisive moment in December 1641 was entirely a matter of chance; 'the lord Digby, who had much conversation and friendship with him, coming accidentally and suddenly into the room, where he was alone amongst his books and papers'. Clarendon's consistently affectionate depictions of George Digby, even after enduring political provocations he did not forgive in others, shows the strength, reality, and longevity of their rapport. But it can hardly have been verses, theology, or any gossip bar the highest that now drew Digby to Hyde's door. He did not for a moment hesitate, 'upon the familiarity ... and ... the argument that was then between them', to rifle through his lawyer friend's writings, and what he found there delighted him.

Like Hyde, Digby knew the tactics and understood the grievances of the Pym faction from his initial, enthusiastic political debut within it. But while Hyde had maintained, even burnished his credit with the 'anticourt' or 'governing' party during the Strafford affair, Digby, as an open, vehement convert to the court, had limited his options to bold, extreme Royalist counter-attack. In Hyde, Digby saw an example of the sort of influence over the Commons he himself could have commanded if things had turned out otherwise. Now he aimed to convince his all too sensible friend to endorse his higher-stakes approach.

Digby found Hyde breathing fulminations against the Remonstrance's contradictions and extremities, and, still more promisingly, writing them down, 'only', as Clarendon remembers insisting, 'to give vent to his indignation'. The opportunistic courtier at once proposed putting this response to good use by delivering it to the King. Hyde was, as Clarendon candidly admits, horrified by this suggestion. He had gone along with the attack on Strafford partly out of self-preservation; his defence of the bishops and rejection of the Remonstrance had already used up any goodwill he had earned from Pym. He had no desire himself to become a target for the Commons' vengeance. Digby had been plucked out of danger only by acceleration to the Lords; a way of escape for an earl's heir denied to a lawyer from a family of lawyers.

Digby coolly assured Hyde that he need not worry; he would have the royal word for it that Hyde's name and reputation should be kept inviolate. Hyde thus began twenty-five years of service to the Stuarts as, effectively, the King's ghost-writer. His counter-arguments to the Remonstrance were published and disseminated with all the authority of the King's council, while their author clung to the security of the shadows.

## 'Restless Fancy' – Hyde's Friends in Office and the Attempt on the Five Members, Westminster, January 1642

In the days when they had abetted Strafford's impeachment, then his execution, Hyde and Falkland had dreamed of a broad, reforming government: projected to include Digby's father and father-in-law, Bristol and Bedford; the closely related and intermarried group of Puritan grandees, Essex and Hertford and the Rich brothers, Robert Earl of Warwick and Henry Earl of Holland; John Pym and his various Commons allies, including themselves. Bedford was now dead, Bristol's credit in eclipse with both sides after his failed attempts to compromise over Strafford, Hertford firmly with the King, the other lords even more decidedly with the opposition. Possibly in part owing to Hyde's new and covert influence upon the King, Pym was, at the beginning of 1642 and after the passing of the Remonstrance, offered promotion as Chancellor of the Exchequer. Hyde subsequently wrote that this gesture might have salvaged an accommodation if it had been tried six months earlier. As it was, Pym refused to consider the idea.

After this imaginatively over-optimistic approach, Charles I decided to settle for a more obvious expedient, promoting his most articulate current partisans, Hyde and Falkland. Both of them had until very recently been regarded as 'lukewarm' about the King's policy, but now that made them all the more useful. But Hyde was still determined to maintain his careful privacy. Falkland would rather have done the same, but Hyde persuaded his bosom friend that his duty was otherwise: Falkland's reputation might allow him to achieve the conciliation in office that Hyde still doubted his own ability to effect. So Falkland was appointed the King's Secretary of State; another leading moderate Royalist who had resisted the Remonstrance, Sir John Colepeper, a rough-hewn, rebarbative, shrewd constitutionalist, stepped up as Chancellor of the Exchequer, the office spurned by Pym himself; and Hyde continued in the manner that still suited him best, an unseen, unproven, if hardly unsuspected third man.*

---

* Falkland was appointed to serve alongside Sir Edward Nicholas, the former Buckingham protégé and Hyde family friend who had himself replaced Sir Harry Vane the elder, treacherous chief witness against Strafford, in November 1641 as Secretary of State. This post had evolved from the all-powerful role invented by

## Friends in Youth

Scarcely had the three agreed their official and actual roles when their royal master, Hyde and Falkland's glamorously infuriating friend Digby at his ear, made their positions all but untenable. Hyde had, in part, seen the trouble coming. His initial hesitation about responding to Digby's invitation had been predicated on his fear of the 'over-activity to which [Digby's] restless fancy always disposed him'. In his first, bruising involvement with the court, the Jermyn-Villiers affair, Hyde had noticed the King's vulnerability to unsteady influences (preeminently including that of the Queen). Much later he diagnosed the fatal flaw of the Stuarts – 'they trusted naturally the judgments of those . . . as much inferior to them in understanding as in quality, before their own, which,' he added, loyally and sincerely if not entirely convincingly, 'was very good'.

Now the Queen and Digby together swayed the King to combine the velvet glove of his new, moderate councillors with the iron gauntlet of sudden military force. Rashly, but not yet necessarily fatally, the King had at last decided to charge Pym, four other MPs, and one peer with high treason; a process whose conventional passage had failed partly because of Digby's own panicked silence at the pivotal moment in the Lords. Charles next swept upon Parliament accompanied by a rabble of soldiers, no more competent than those who had repeatedly failed to spring Strafford from the Tower. He brought with him his unenthusiastic eldest German nephew, Charles Louis, the exiled Elector Palatine, attempting to emanate a fictional dynastic front of royal, Protestant authority. The King aimed to arrest the five Commons men – Pym, Hampden, Arthur Haselrig, William Strode, and Denzil Holles – along with Lord Mandeville, the politically active heir of the Earl of Manchester, whom Hyde and Falkland liked and respected. The Speaker,

---

Thomas Cromwell under Henry VIII, and was by now commonly jointly held by two leading royal servants. The Chancellorship of the Exchequer carried less innate prestige or, as yet, defined power, but – as Thomas Cromwell among others had previously shown – in the hands of an able holder it had considerable potential.

William Lenthall, to whom Falkland had sold his estate at Burford, famously declined to assist the royal enquiries when Charles found 'the birds flown'. Hyde and Falkland, still on polite though wary terms with Pym and Hampden, were horrified by the attempt itself, by the feebleness of its execution, most of all that they might be associated with it. Hyde reports that they soon 'could not avoid being looked upon as the authors of those counsels to which they were so absolute strangers' and 'which they so perfectly detested'.

The King's clumsy action was undermined by his own court, whose indiscretion enabled the escape of his prey. It seems that the Earl of Essex tipped off Lord Mandeville, who warned the MPs; that left the question of who had talked to the clearly oppositional Essex. The leading candidate was soon identified as the Queen's most beautiful and infamous lady, Lucy Hay, Countess of Carlisle; Strafford's old belle, but a Percy by birth, related one way or another to most of the opposition, and now even spoken of as a secret mistress of Pym. The always equivocal French ambassador La Ferté was also blamed in some quarters for the leak. Hyde himself suspected the King's Scots Gentleman of the Bedchamber, William Murray, who according to Bishop Burnet's later, but well-placed testimony, 'had one particular quality, that when he was drunk, which was very often, he was upon a most exact reserve, though he was pretty open at all other times'. The most contorted variant of all has Digby himself – generally, with the Queen, regarded as the scheme's progenitor – telling Murray, or, even odder, leaking his own plot to Pym. Digby's effervescent, lifelong career of recreational duplicity suggests that this last theory cannot entirely be laid aside.

## 'Liberty and Sharpness' – Ned Hyde Makes His Choice: From Westminster to York, February–August 1642

The failure of the Five Members' arrest for the time being strengthened the influence of the King's new, less impetuous councillors, Colepeper, Falkland, and Hyde. Clarendon complacently remembers that at this time, whenever Falkland advised a policy, the King asked 'whether Ned Hyde were of that opinion'. Although as yet without title or office, Hyde was logistically as well as intellectually at the centre of the trio, whose secret meetings were held at his father-in-law's town house at Dean's Yard.* Hyde now urged the King to hold his nerve and stay in the capital. But Charles, alarmed by the city's fury at his breach of parliamentary privilege, and especially frightened for the safety of his Queen, fatefully opted for retreat. On 10 January the King decamped to Hampton Court, by the 12th he was at Windsor, and in March the whole court left for York. Charles was not to return to his capital until the last fortnight of his life (mid-January 1649), the city's victim, not its master.

Parliament now began at last to address the question of the army bound for Ireland, and the legal power over the militia that should control it, by tradition the very definition of the royal office. Hyde, Falkland, Palmer, and other Royalist members did their best to shore up their waning cause in spite of their master's fiasco followed by desertion, but Pym's victory was already essentially assured. Whitelocke's sophisticated and nuanced halfway position on the militia debate was a heartfelt one, but he intervened from the safe redoubt of his creditable yet limited influence, without any real prospect of moulding events.

Although Hyde, Falkland, and Colepeper considered themselves to have cast their dice with Caesar, they made no haste to follow the King in person. Hyde, upholding an ever less protective mask of neutrality, was spotted at the royal palace of Greenwich by Lords Essex and Holland, then at Windsor Castle by the Marquess of Hamilton. Hamilton, the premier Scots peer as well as an English one as Earl of Cambridge, enjoyed Charles's friendship and at times confidence. But a royal attempt during the 1641 visit to Edinburgh to kidnap or possibly murder him, involving the ever-dubious Will Murray, had shaken Hamilton's rather dubious loyalty. Hyde never

---

* Dean's Yard is now known to the pupils of Westminster School as Green (no definite article); they claim to have invented modern football on it.

liked or trusted Hamilton, the most prominent noble to have supported the Queen's debauched favourite Harry Jermyn during the Eleanor Villiers scandal. Such high-born peers as Essex, Holland, and Hamilton could exercise their right to wait upon the sovereign no matter how well-known their disaffection, but a supposedly still reformist city lawyer made for a less probable courtier unless business was at stake. Feeling the cold wind of partisanship at his back, Hyde sent his family to Cranbourne Lodge in Windsor Great Park, the royal hunting box of which his father-in-law was Keeper. In March Frances Hyde gave birth there to the couple's fourth child, Lawrence (after Anne, Henry, and little Ned, born in 1640).

In April the King formally summoned Hyde to his temporary court at York. There followed a month of frenetic drafting and negotiation, culminating in the affair of the Great Seal and its Lord Keeper, and Hyde's escape north, by turns comfortable and alarming. Safely reunited at Nostell, 35 miles south of York, with Frances and their children, he stayed there, industrious but inconspicuous, as long as he decently could, away from the troubles of both Parliament and court, while still contriving to avert or patch up by letter various strategic errors by King Charles at York.

When at last he could avoid the makeshift northern court no longer, Hyde stumbled at York upon plentiful reminders of his ambiguous career over the previous two years. He was first billeted on an attorney whose business had foundered owing to the abolition of the Council of the North, and who refused to have the architect of its downfall in his house. In the gardens of the city's Manor House, magnified by Strafford's grand pretensions, Hyde met a parliamentary delegation from London led by Lord Holland, that dressy, faithless former courtier, who warned him 'with some liberty and sharpness . . . not without menaces what parliament would do'. Falkland and Colepeper slipped away to join their colleague at York during the summer.

In August the King formally raised his standard at Nottingham. The day was dismal, the response to the banner's menacingly uninspiring motto, 'GIVE UNTO CAESAR HIS DUE', indifferent, the flag itself inclined to droop. Hyde and his colleagues were still working to restrain Charles's hesitant sword-hand. In September, Falkland sped to London and back as the King's last envoy to the Lords and Commons, a well-chosen but still unavailing messenger. Hopes of reconciliation persisted into the autumn of 1642. Notable families conspired to avoid civil war on, at least, a local level. Most spectacularly, the Parliamentarian Fairfaxes schemed with the Catholic, Royalist Belasyses to keep the whole of Yorkshire out of the fight by way of a Treaty of Neutrality, but their gentlemen's agreement was promptly rejected by Parliament.

Hyde, having freshly confirmed his worth as the chief author of the final terms to Parliament, heard that he had lost a son, his namesake, born in 1640. He received the news the morning that the King reluctantly agreed to send the much-compromised proposals south to his enemies. Hyde claimed in the *History* that the little boy's death 'did affect him, though it would not disturb him long', and that he was more concerned at King Charles's state, sleepless and heartsore at having further negotiation wrung from him. Yet Hyde referred to the short-lived Ned twelve years later, when writing a letter of condolence to a friend from the depths of penurious, hard-working continental exile.

## *An Adventure is Born – Westminster Apportions Ireland, January–February 1642*

Bulstrode Whitelocke, absent from Parliament during the royal raid of January 1642, shared the general sense of outrage at the King's action, declaring the attempted arrest of the five MPs 'much wondered at by many sober men' – sober men who included the King's luckless new counsellors, Whitelocke's friends Hyde and Falkland. Whitelocke, with his finely balanced constitutionalist sensibility, lamented not just the King's imprudent breach of parliamentary privilege, but still more its likely consequences, emboldening the extremists in the opposite camp, 'to the advantage of those that were disaffected to [the King]'. Whitelocke's own relations with the Junto remained civil rather than close. He now occupied a position not unlike Hyde's the previous year, as a man of known influence and authority whose support was greatly desired and at times menacingly sought. For now Whitelocke enjoyed the manifold advantages of being ardently wooed without risking the perils of absolute commitment.

As early as the previous December, Whitelocke had begun to invest his considerable fortune in addressing the upheavals of Ireland. Acting with none other than Geoffrey Palmer, just released from the Tower, Whitelocke had disbursed money for the relief of distressed Irish Protestants. In February, Parliament obtained the grudging consent of the absent King for an Act towards the 'Speedy Reducing' of the Irish rebels. This legislation invited private citizens to contribute funds in order to defeat the rebels, funds to be repaid when possible in Irish land seized from the Catholic insurgents.

Whitelocke, with most English Members of Parliament even loosely associated with Pym, became one of these 'Irish Adventurers', providing a handsome £400.* The list of Whitelocke's fellow Adventurers also contains certain political and even personal surprises, within a broadly coherent picture of Parliamentarian, Puritan, London largesse. As Palmer had shown in December, there were still MPs aligned with King and court (if forced to choose), who were yet sufficiently and genuinely concerned enough about the Irish situation to volunteer significant funds.

A small, rich minority – at least one in ten – of those MPs who became Adventurers inclined in general to the Royalist side. The most startling name among these was Sir John Colepeper, Hyde and Falkland's colleague and now Chancellor of the Exchequer, always attentive to Irish affairs, who outdid (or matched) Whitelocke with

---

* This would now be worth about £45,000. Whitelocke, recorded as having made a purchase of this size, himself gives a more detailed account – he says he raised £600 in total, though only a third came directly from his fortune, £300 from two associates, and £100 from the town of Henley.

£600. Another notable contributor, Sir Anthony Ashley Cooper, was an able, rich, and ambitious young baronet married into the consistently Royalist Coventry family. Sir Anthony's father-in-law, the eminent royal counsellor Thomas, Lord Coventry, had been a lawyer and Lord Keeper particularly well thought of by Hyde. Several of Lord Coventry's sons had even graced the moderating discourses of Great Tew. Sir Anthony himself now matched Colepeper in munificence towards the Irish Adventure; so did that always ambiguous dignitary, Lord Keeper Littleton. Outside Parliament one of the most flagrantly Royalist entrants among the Adventurers was Sir Nicolas Crispe. A tax farmer (and slave trader) who owed much of his wealth and its continuance to the Crown, Crispe expended £1,000 of it in the Irish enterprise.

The Adventurers incarnated a range of English – especially London – opinion across various divides beyond the merely political. In social background, they ranged from the Earl of Pembroke (£2,400), to Elizabeth Austrey, a loyal household servant of the relatively cash-strapped Cambridgeshire MP Oliver Cromwell (£200). Widows, apothecaries, lawyers, and one authoritative scholar and translator of Hebrew, Moses Wall, were also among the Adventurers. Yet doubts about the enterprise, both financial and, more occasionally (and hearteningly) moral, existed, some emitting from unimpeachably Parliamentarian sources. Sir Harry Vane the younger (who had, through 1639–40, counter-intuitively gained great wealth as an administrator of Ship Money) was alone among the Parliamentarian leaders of his radical religious and political leanings in *not* buying a share in the Adventurers' Company. The severe, scrupulous Sir Simonds D'Ewes offered £50 'without accepting any part in the rebel lands', apparently due to his anxiety that 'there was an intent to destroy' the rebels' 'women and children'.

Whitelocke, acting, as he often did, in the honourable, consensual capacity of the Commons' spokesman to the Lords, commended the Irish scheme with great enthusiasm. His speech also reflected the worsening political deadlock in England. He stated that the Irish leaders had 'falsely scandalized the Piety and Honour of His

Majesty, and of the Queen', by claiming royal authority for their uprising. While Whitelocke struggled to bridge the emerging chasm in England, he happily widened it in the distant Irish plane, eagerly identifying the rebel cause with Roman Catholicism; the English government, and Anglo-Scottish settlers, with the very 'survival' of Protestantism.

Whitelocke urged the economic as well as political benefits of this new plantation to both public and private purses, musing on the deleterious effects both of illegal Ship Money and of legal parliamentary taxation to the ordinary subject, and the superior justice and efficiency of volunteer funds being employed at a huge potential gain to the Exchequer's future revenue. He concluded in antiquarian vein, recalling the prophecy of Giraldus Cambrensis that the English would hold Ireland 'with abundant conflicts and many slaughters, by a long contest'. He cheerily, and as it would turn out disastrously, predicted that the contemplated expedition would put a 'period' on that contest. But the next few months would demonstrate what Whitelocke, as much as Hyde, already in truth feared, that the developing emergency, far from settling the old wounds of Ireland, was about to inflict fresh ones on England.

## *Provocation and Mass Songs: Public Business and Private Correspondents, Westminster, York, and Buckinghamshire, March–June 1642*

Early spring saw the maturing of the controversy over the militia, during which Whitelocke proposed openly in Parliament a compromise not dissimilar to that which Falkland, Colepeper, and (especially) Hyde were recommending to the King in private. Whitelocke was equally active in discouraging the royal party's efforts to arm itself. When the Queen, using the pretext of her daughter's marriage to the Prince of Orange, crossed to the Netherlands to obtain cash, troops, and arms on the strength of the Crown Jewels, it was Whitelocke who wrote the Remonstrance to the Dutch presented by Parliament's ambassador, Walter Strickland: a characteristic, nostalgic, historically founded reminder of English help against Spain under Elizabeth I, reprimanding fellow Protestants for siding against liberty. The jewels were pawned and Queen Henrietta Maria was equipped with money, soldiers, and weapons nonetheless.* At the end of March, Whitelocke received and, with a regret probably more personal than political, rejected Palmer and Hyde's overtures to join them in going fully over to the King.

In May, Hyde obtained his disingenuous medical leave from the Commons, and undertook his secret, meandering, and reluctant journey to join the King at York. At some carefully undated point he sent to his old friend Whitelocke a brief, cryptic, half-apologetic note. It drily commented that 'his provocation into the country' was 'not such that he is much delighted with the journey'. Yet this curt letter's form and content implies that Hyde wrote to Whitelocke before the news of his real itinerary and intentions, as opposed to his permitted rest-cure, had broken, taking Whitelocke into a potentially perilous confidence that his friend did not betray.

Without naming the King, Hyde communicates his complex present situation with great clarity. He tells Whitelocke that his clerk will vouch for how unexpected the (evidently, if not explicitly) royal summons was. Although at best a half-truth, this may have been what part of Hyde still wanted to believe. He had been actively and emotionally committed to the cause of governmental reform by parliamentary means for at least two years, if not longer. Unlike Falkland and Colepeper, he had still avoided accepting formal ministerial office from the King. He had emphatically advised against

---

* Hyde would later claim, extremely implausibly, to have been unaware of the Queen's intentions regarding the jewels. In fact he was probably as hopeful for Dutch uncooperativeness as Whitelocke and his colleagues, knowing the Queen, her funds, and her influence already to be his most unyielding and proximate obstacle.

the King's retirement from London to York. And though in his long, eventful political career Hyde would generally take the path of greatest action and risk, he always did so somewhat against an innate, lawyerly judgement that was, if not necessarily better, certainly more akin to that of his friend Whitelocke.

Hyde promised that 'if I may justify my return it shall be speedy'; this sounds like more of a wan, conditional hope than a realistic assessment. He left behind many papers 'that concern [Whitelocke's notice]' with his clerk; the context makes these sound merely legal and businesslike, though they might easily have encompassed more delicate matters. He closed with two requests, one political, one personal, both insistent. He asked that Whitelocke 'endeavour to excuse him if he is enquired after', in other words do his best to buy Hyde more time. The political outcry caused by the defection of Lord Littleton with the Great Seal in Hyde's wake would make this request impossible to fulfil, though Whitelocke did in fact carry out the same friendly service for their close mutual friend Geoffrey Palmer. Finally, the runaway asked his old companion 'however to preserve me in your own esteem'. Whitelocke notes that, for all the hurried finality of his friend's quick letter regarding his flight to the court in the north, he continued his usual amiable correspondence with Hyde throughout and beyond this period, but no such letters were to be preserved by either of the friends.

As that torrid summer proceeded, a more conspicuous, ceremonious correspondence connected Whitelocke to Hyde, Falkland, and Colepeper – Parliament's ongoing negotiations with the King. The Nineteen Propositions by which Parliament, on 1 June, courteously demanded that the King transfer to it most of the remaining powers still vested in the battered Crown, were constructed with Whitelocke's assistance and support; a draft of his alterations and additions is extant. The Propositions were initially answered – as Hyde was still on the road and only patchily available for scheming and drafting – by Falkland and Colepeper, who put forward a doctrine that Whitelocke would consistently admit in more private writing was substantially similar to his own.

According to this perspective, England's 'mixed monarchy' consisted of three Estates – King, Lords, and Commons – all of them required to act in concert to achieve harmonious government. Hyde, for his part, was taken aback by his colleagues' hurried and ad hoc constitutional statement. He cleaved, with Selden, to a more historically accurate, venerable conception of the Three Estates all residing in Parliament as the clergy (bishops), nobility (lay peers), and commons (MPs), with the King an elevated and impartial head above and beyond the rest of the body politic: ideally governing in accordance with its advice, but able, in extremity, to overrule it. Hyde's vision was thus less vulnerable to the idea that the Lords and Commons together might 'outvote' the monarch.

By mid-May the King was responding to Parliament's Militia Ordinance with his own Commissions of Array, an exercise in medieval feudal resuscitation whose erudition, at least, must have impressed Whitelocke, Selden, and, if grudgingly, D'Ewes. Word of civil disorder was at large in the country; as Whitelocke's journal describes it:

> The times began to appear very dreadful, and all discourses were of the threatening Civil War, against which Whitelocke used his best endeavours with many others, but to no effect.

In late June, Whitelocke received a spirited, teasing, yet heartfelt letter from his generally Royalist, always friendly aunt-in-law, Lady Sunderland. She thanked him for his assiduity in keeping her abreast of events; Whitelocke noted in his later journal that he was at this time expending much care and time on managing the countess's business affairs, along with those of her sister, his mother-in-law, and other Willoughby and Manners kin to Frances Whitelocke. But Lady Sunderland also lightly chided Whitelocke for not delivering better news:

> I wish you could have written me word of hopes of agreement between the King and Parliament, for as yet it seems there is none.

> If it pleases God to send good success to the English in Ireland . . .
> I hope the next good news will be of the reconciliation between the
> King and Parliament and that speedily, that your wife may have your
> company at Fawley. We want your company to sing mass songs, if
> you dare . . .

The countess, like Whitelocke in his sensible, conciliatory, all too optimistic parliamentary speeches, strongly associates a return to good order in Ireland with the resumption of normal, functioning, traditional government in England. In a sense both would live to be proven right about this in the early 1650s, though not in a way that either could have possibly anticipated in 1642. Lady Sunderland's sincere longing for a peaceful agreement as soon as possible is gracefully lightened by her gently mischievous implication that the industrious Whitelocke of Parliament is neglecting his wife, her niece. This was a reasonable complaint; at the time of this letter the heavily pregnant Frances Whitelocke was undergoing the seventh of her nine successful confinements.

Lady Sunderland's parting jest is disorienting, indeed revelatory for readers accustomed to imagining the civil wars as primarily motivated by religious differences. This fond aunt, original abettor of her niece's somewhat scandalous marriage, happily teases, and tantalizes, her nephew-in-law – Whitelocke the well-known Parliamentarian, theoretically Puritan in religious tendency, but, more importantly, the amateur composer and addictedly musical aesthete – with the prospect of joining a euphoniously and obviously Catholic household, offering the forbidden fruit of 'mass songs, if you dare'. Lady Sunderland's relaxed, untribal, irreverent idiom is the flip side of Hyde's urgent, laconic, cloak-and-dagger briskness, one, regrettably, less often invoked or remembered. Despite a rising miasma of political acrimony and universal apprehension, life in politically, religiously, and socially mixed circles of friends still persisted with natural, unforced friendliness.

## 'To Keep His Station' – Whitelocke Becomes Parliamentary Deputy Lieutenant in Two Counties, with More Trepidation than Satisfaction; Oxfordshire and Westminster, June–July 1642

Francis, 5th Baron Willoughby of Parham, was notably closer to his brother-in-law Whitelocke's politics than to those of his own Catholic and Royalist aunt. Although still under thirty and politically inexperienced, Willoughby had been for the last year the leading authority in his own family, after the death of his fearsome uncle the Earl of Rutland. As Lieutenant of Lincolnshire, from July Willoughby began to raise troops for Parliament in obedience to the Militia Ordinance. The King, distantly aware of Willoughby as a courtly tearaway and boon companion of some of the younger members of the Villiers clan, peremptorily commanded this gadfly to stop meddling with his soldiery and received a reply of both dignity and boldness: that for Willoughby to cease his levying of recruits, 'was not in his power to do without breach of that trust, which he had undertaken to the Parliament, and to which he was encouraged by the opinion of some of his Majesty's great officers, eminent in the knowledge of the laws, wherein he was not learned'.

By such 'great officers' of the Crown 'eminent in the knowledge of the laws' Willoughby no doubt alluded to Oliver St John, that most sophisticated of Pym's allies who still, in the last vestige of the Earl of Bedford's scheme for conciliation between court and Commons, held the office of King's Solicitor; more ironically, to Lord Keeper Littleton, whose pronouncement had provided Whitelocke with pivotal cover allowing him to support the Militia Ordinance, but who was now himself, thanks to Ned Hyde's persuasions, in the Royalist camp. But it is likeliest of all that in his courteous but firm adherence to Parliament, and his deference to the law of the land, Willoughby – a man on occasion both visionary and courageous, but not by nature either stable or legalistic – was listening to Whitelocke, his indispensable brother-in-law.

Whitelocke himself faced a similar dilemma on being named a Deputy Lieutenant under the Militia Ordinance, for two of the counties in which he had interests, Berkshire and Oxfordshire. Both of the lieutenants under whom he was now called upon to serve were, in different ways, discouraging as prospective superiors. William, 6th Baron Paget, Lieutenant of Berkshire, was a disappointed, anticlerical courtier, son-in-law of Lord Holland, the royal favourite turned smooth-tongued rebel. But Paget was wavering in the other direction, and, only a month after being appointed Parliamentarian Lieutenant, defected to the King.* The Lieutenant of Oxfordshire, a firmer character, was unfortunately none other than Lord Saye. He had never forgiven Whitelocke's proud response to his eldest son, or his bold comparison of the local antiquity of their respective families, while they vied for the prize of the Oxfordshire county Commons seat.

Either this unappetizing pair of superiors or his own uncommitted politics made Whitelocke hesitate to accept either Deputy Lieutenancy, as he recalled in his journal:

> ... Whitelocke was in some doubt of himself whether he should accept of these Commissions or not, but the Lord Littleton & sundry other gentlemen both of the short & long Robe [non-lawyer and lawyer MPs], having declared their opinions positively that it was Legal, & that in the case of the King's minority, sickness, or absence, the Parliament had done the like ... this being the Act of both houses, he was persuaded to accept of his Commissions, and to act upon them, chiefly there being by most of the eminent men, a solemn protestation, that they did this not to promote any war, or prejudice to the King, but for their just defence against his Evil Counsellors.

---

* Lord Paget was speedily replaced by Philip Wharton, 4th Baron Wharton, a more ideologically convinced Parliamentarian peer who confirmed Whitelocke's commission as a Deputy.

## Friends in Youth

Whitelocke still placed decisive weight upon the prior judgement of Littleton, so like him in his political moderation, his circle of friends, and his legal learning, despite the fact that Littleton had by this point, advised by Whitelocke's own friend Hyde, carried himself, his opinions, and the crucial Great Seal over to King Charles's side. Like thoughtful men on both sides, Whitelocke considered the precedents of history, though the authorities they threw up were at best dubious: Charles I was not, like Edward I, absent in the Mediterranean on Crusade, nor, like Henry VI, inarguably imbecilic, nor, like Edward VI, underage. Hence the hoary, legalistic disclaimer of Whitelocke and his 'eminent men' that they were not rebels, but acting for the good of the Crown against vaguely expressed malign influences (had such influences been specified, they would have necessarily included the Queen, diminishing any hope of accommodation).

Engaged in a lawsuit against his own conscience, Whitelocke later called as character witnesses five other leading lawyer-Parliamentarians, all of whom, he says, expressed their opinion and acted as he did on the subject of the Militia Commissions. Four of them were his intimate friends; the other had become one of the most powerful men in the country. The careers of all five, up to the summer of 1642 and afterwards, imply similar political ambiguity to Whitelocke's. The oldest and most respected of the five luminaries was, inevitably, John Selden; there followed three of Whitelocke's contemporaries, Harbottle Grimston, John Glynne, and John Maynard; finally came the sinuous, though portly, figure of Oliver St John.

All five possessed credentials acceptable to the 'popular' Pymite party. Selden had been imprisoned as a martyr to liberty; Grimston (like Whitelocke himself, Hyde, and Falkland) had helped both to condemn and abolish the King's illegal exploitation of Ship Money; Glynne and Maynard, like Whitelocke, had prosecuted Strafford; St John was Pym's foremost legal advisor. Yet Selden had defended Strafford and the bishops, and had in fact been 'invited', as Hyde had been, to join the King at York. While pleading ill health, Selden had privately assured his monarch that his 'loyal and humble affections to his majesty and his service are and shall now be as great and as hearty as any man's'. He had been almost as critical of the Parliament's Militia Ordinance as of the King's Commissions of Array and certainly did not, as Whitelocke implies, take up a commission himself.

Grimston, married by Whitelocke's contrivance to his friend's cousin, had not supported the Grand Remonstrance and only returned to the Pymite fold after the attempted seizure of the Five Members. He accepted a deputy lieutenancy on the perhaps self-deluding, but definite understanding that he would not be called upon to make war on the King. Glynne, though firmly behind the Militia Ordinance and an eager Deputy Lieutenant, was soon in the forefront of the peace party, and worked to keep the leadership of Parliament's army in moderate, aristocratic hands. Maynard, who had helped to secure Whitelocke's eventual return to the Long Parliament as member for Marlow, presented briefs for the Crown at the King's Bench for as long as it was at all compatible with remaining at Westminster, and, like Glynne, invariably worked with and for the peace party. St John, clinging to his proud title of King's Solicitor, continued to play out a double game for all it was worth with prudence, skill, duplicity, and apparent relish.

The impeccably senatorial names located by Whitelocke in support of his anguished course of action thus further illustrate his torn state of mind. But, making up that mind nonetheless, he 'resolved to keep his Station, where God had called him', namely to become a deputy both in Berkshire and in Oxfordshire, even though, in the latter case, he had to accept the odious oversight of Saye. Immediately after his tortuous self-justification, Whitelocke alludes to his continuing assistance to Geoffrey Palmer, towards whom he 'upon all occasions, did . . . the best offices in his power as a faithful and loving friend', as if unable to bring himself to admit his definite commitment to the armed Parliamentarian cause without recalling in the same breath his unaltered benevolence towards a Royalist associate.*

---

* Whitelocke's surviving papers include a letter from a courtier at York to a Royalist identifiable only as 'Sir James', apparently in high good favour with the King.

Whitelocke delayed Parliament's selection of generals and officers as long as he could manage, instead urging further attempts at treating with the King. Yet when, despite these efforts, Parliament named Essex Lord General and elected a number of officers including Whitelocke himself, he was 'somewhat unsatisfied'. The problem was not the choice of Essex, whom he respected and liked in person (as in fact did Hyde). Instead Whitelocke was irked not to have been granted the rank of colonel now bestowed on several of his colleagues: 'His command was to be only of an Independent Troop of Volunteers, & not of a Regiment, he having been a Commissioned officer for a Troop of Horse before, in the service of the French King.'

The child of a highly, if hardly uniquely, status-conscious age, Whitelocke was touched to the quick in this politically conspicuous national moment. His wholly projected rather than real military activity to date diminished his sense of military self-confidence not at all. The Deputy Lieutenancies were positions of real if local power, which despite his misgivings Whitelocke could not resist; the proposed captaincy, more chore than honour, he sidestepped with disdain. Although Whitelocke's usefulness to the parliamentary side was in fact to remain primarily civilian, at this point he was equal in standing to many potentially talented amateurs in the Lords and Commons, including Oliver Cromwell. Over his limited but not altogether nugatory military career to come, Whitelocke would make sensible suggestions, generally rebuffed through little fault of his own, did not lack courage, and saw a modicum of service.*

---

Whitelocke was apparently advising 'Sir James' in 'many troublesome businesses of law'. As late as the end of June 1642, and most probably afterwards, Whitelocke's legal practice remained ideologically indifferent.

* Listing other officers chosen by Parliament, Whitelocke rather unselfconsciously names Cromwell immediately before himself.

## 'A gallant Spirit' – Action in Oxfordshire, July–August 1642

By July, Whitelocke had returned to Fawley Court, his wife, family, neighbours, and the immediate task of arranging for all of their protection. 'The Country,' he remembered, was 'much affrighted with the news of Parliament's raising of an Army, & in most places they began . . . to provide for their own defence.' Whitelocke, while striving for peace, had efficiently planned for war since the Scottish disturbances, and Fawley Court was now 'well furnished with pikes, muskets, pistols, powder, bullet, arms & good horses . . . trained by his household servants'. His wife Frances, 'being very near her time of childbirth', was understandably 'the more frighted at the Preparations for War, but being of a gallant Spirit, & affected to the Parliament she did the better endure it'. Whitelocke makes his wife, despite her condition and the Royalist opinions of her wider family, sound more decisive about the coming confrontation than he was himself. He noticeably blames in the first instance not the actions of the King, but 'Parliament's raising of an Army', for the growing panic.

Whitelocke's civil war opened with a genuinely active, dangerous episode. In August – just after Frances had been safely delivered of a daughter, given the Scriptural, gently Puritan name of Hester – Whitelocke received word of a significant Royalist gathering being prepared at Watlington, just seven miles from his house, the first time his responsibility as Deputy Lieutenant was to be tested in combat.

The Earl of Berkshire, one of the Catholic-leaning, innumerable Howards, was due to announce the King's Commission of Array to an audience of 'divers gentlemen of principal quality in Oxfordshire'. Lord Berkshire, along with his eldest son, had in June been one of thirty-five peers to subscribe to the King's declaration, at York, that he had no intention of making war on his people, infringing their ancient liberties, or compromising their established Protestant religion.* Whitelocke quickly and properly sent word to both Lord Saye as Lieutenant, and the Commons in general, of Berkshire's imminent enterprise. From the Commons he received both orders and the strength to execute them, a troop of horse from Colonel Goodwin's regiment, and a company of infantry led by no less a Parliamentarian than John Hampden.

Whitelocke himself equipped half a dozen servants on horseback, and took them to Shirburn Hill north-east of Watlington to rendezvous with Hampden and the parliamentary reinforcements. His rank as Deputy Lieutenant pleasingly placed him in overall command, and a Royalist source would gratifyingly recount his deeds under the dread name of 'General Whitelocke'. Lord Berkshire and the Oxfordshire gentlemen, hearing of this recently irenic lawyer's sudden fire-eating approach, attempted to take refuge at the nearest manor they held, that of Sir Robert Dormer, five miles away. But Whitelocke remained determined in the chase: 'it was resolved to pursue them thither, & being summoned to yield, they fired some pistols and muskets at [the Parliamentarians] from the house, but did little hurt'. That 'little hurt' included an undignified injury suffered by the gallant lawyer turned amateur general:

> ... a blow of a pistol ... beat out many of [Whitelocke's] teeth, & loosened the rest, yet by the goodness of God, the bullet & stroke did him no further hurt, only it caused great pain ... and was a hindrance to his eating and his sleeping.

Whitelocke's teeth had not, however, suffered for naught. Rather than face the storming of the manor the small Royalist party, their honour satisfied by their brief resistance, yielded; Berkshire and 'two or three' Oxfordshire Commissioners of Array were taken,

---

* This catalogue of Royalist peers involved particularly delicate political embroidery. It included at least three earls and a baron whose support was equivocal at best, and four heirs standing in the place of their Parliamentarian, neutral, uncommitted or otherwise absent fathers.

courteously escorted in person by 'General' Whitelocke, despite his late dental mishap, to Henley. Whitelocke made, in the circumstances, heroic attempts to draw out his noble prisoner in conversation:

> ... with all Civility, but finding the Earl very proud and peevish, sullen & empty in discourse, he would not trouble himself further to accompany him, but left him ... to be convoyed to London ... there the Earl lay a long time [about a month], not enquired after nor missed or condoled ...

Ned Hyde – who tended to acidity towards the entire house of Howard – thoroughly agreed with his friend about the unfortunate earl:

> [Parliament] afterwards set [Berkshire] at liberty, as a man that could do them no harm anywhere; and then he came to Oxford, with the title and pretences of a man who had been imprisoned for the King, and thereby merited more than his majesty had to give. His affection for the Crown was good; his interest and reputation less than anything but his understanding.

In the capital Lord Berkshire's capture was largely credited to Goodwin (who had not in fact been present) and to Hampden. Hyde would, however, remember the skirmish by Watlington in his *History* as part of a consistent strategy of Parliamentarian kidnap and terror:

> For wherever [the Parliamentarians] found any person of quality inclined to the King, or but disinclined to them, they immediately seized upon his person, and sent him in great triumph to the Parliament, who committed him to prison, with all circumstances of cruelty and inhumanity ...
>
> ... Thus they took prisoner in Oxfordshire the earl of Berkshire, and three or four principal gentlemen of that county, and committed them to the Tower, for no other reason than wishing well to the King; for they never appeared in the least action in his service.

Here the propagandist comfortably outstrips the historian. Hyde's point about Lord Berkshire and his companions is obviously disingenuous. These Royalists were being preemptively apprehended in the act of raising levies against Parliament, not punished for direct military action; and in political action Berkshire was clearly implicated, by his signature to the royal declaration of June. Later in the *History*, Hyde half admitted that Berkshire had been arrested 'upon an imagination that he had some purpose to have executed the Commission of Array'. Despite these sleights of hand, Hyde's rhetoric is powerful, especially in his observation that any gentleman of influence 'inclined to the King, or but disinclined to [Parliament]' was targeted. Hyde does not anywhere mention what he must have known, that his old friend Whitelocke, an outstanding exemplar of that large, uncommitted, neutralist, and pacific category whose allegiance both King and Parliament still strove to win, had been responsible for this specific operation of 'cruelty and inhumanity'.

## A Great Prize Won and Lost – Oxford, August–October 1642

The next Royalist opponent of whom Whitelocke heard was a more formidable character than Lord Berkshire, readier to resort to 'cruelty and inhumanity' than any of Parliament's commanders at this early stage of the war. Sir John Byron of Newstead Abbey was the eldest of seven sanguinary brothers, all 'bred to arms' and ferociously devoted to the King. Sir John, who regarded the Scots rebels of the Bishops' Wars as 'vipers', had served a couple of months as Lieutenant of the Tower of London for the King. In the last days of August, Byron, with three of his brothers and the troops of horse they had quickly raised for the King, was surprised by a Parliamentarian popular rising at the dinner hour, in the Northamptonshire market town of Brackley. The newly recruited Royalist cavalry fled, abandoning not just their pride but many of their troopers and, worst of all, a quantity of much-needed treasure. Nonetheless, with 160 remaining horse, Byron retrieved this embarrassment in high style, galloping twenty miles south and seizing, for a time, a greater prize than Brackley, the university city, and future royal capital, of Oxford. As Lieutenant of Oxfordshire, Lord Saye summoned Whitelocke, among others, to assemble any troops they could find and join him in extracting Byron from his conquest.

Whitelocke raised 'a gallant Company' of 200 horsemen, this contingent alone superior in numbers if not ferocity to Byron's entire regiment. These were joined at Henley by Francis Russell, like Whitelocke an MP and Deputy Lieutenant, though his father, a successful merchant and one of the King's creditors, was still recognized by Charles and not by Parliament as Treasurer of the Navy. The younger Russell was attended by '12 servants well-horsed and armed, & all in scarlet cloaks'. Like other parliamentary gentlemen, including Whitelocke himself at the recent Watlington fracas, Russell clearly intended his men's outfit to reflect splendidly on his own conduct.

Approaching Oxford, Whitelocke – whose scouting and intelligence during this soldierly interlude was consistently efficient – received word of Byron's withdrawal. The Royalist soldier knew he could not resist the parliamentary response, now 3,000 strong under Saye, Whitelocke, and the other Oxfordshire Deputies, but had in fact already achieved his immediate aim. He departed at high speed with a splendid convoy of college silver and gold plate (whether offered voluntarily or extracted at least implicitly by force is uncertain). Lord Saye, Whitelocke, Viscount Wenman, and Baron St John of Bletso among other Deputies entered the university city on 12 September, leading horse, dragoons, and foot, 'without resistance, and were welcomed by the Townsmen, more than by the Scholars'.* It was a city of which Whitelocke and his irascible superior, Saye, had very different experiences and opinions.

Lord Saye, a cantankerous sexuagenarian who boasted of his ancient lineage, had been High Steward of Oxford University over

---

* Lord Wenman was the cousin of Falkland's late neighbour and friend Sir Francis Wenman, one of the lay disputants at Great Tew. Lord St John was a cousin both of Oliver St John and of the first Mrs Hyde.

the previous year. Yet his actual experience of the place was drastically out of date. He had briefly and haughtily attended New College, Oxford, in the reign of Queen Elizabeth, claiming the privilege of Founder's Kin on account of collateral descent from William of Wykeham, the founder of both New College and Winchester College. That Oxford of the 1590s had been a nursery of 'high Calvinism', godly Protestantism that exalted the monarchy on quietly conditional terms, as a sober champion against the Antichrist of Rome. Whitelocke's happy, industrious, conspicuous, and successful years at Oxford in the 1620s had been spent as the favourite of the future Archbishop Laud and Bishop Juxon, the grand, ritualistic, meddling don-politicians who were in the process of tilting university, Church, and State in precisely the direction deplored by Saye. By 1642 the university, its intellectual atmosphere transformed on Laudian principles – clerical, aesthetic, sympathetic to Catholic ritual, and unconditionally monarchist – had arrived at the High Church stage that was ultimately to be hardened by events into a long-standing cornerstone of Oxonian identity. The colleges and university of Oxford were administered and inhabited by men with whom Whitelocke was ideally placed to negotiate, were it not for the encumbrance of the antediluvian peer to whom he had to answer.

In his dealings with the dons Lord Saye proved surprisingly naïve, gruff in manner, but easily bamboozled. Although the scholars of Oxford in general held aloof from the parliamentary occupiers – some perhaps by nature, though political Royalism and religious Laudianism may have determined the frostiness of others – the local powerbrokers, city officials, and college heads 'protested their duty to the Parliament, & engaged to act nothing to their prejudice'. No doubt some of this conspicuous obedience was heartfelt. The city magistrates, as Whitelocke had already noted, tended to be more receptive to Parliament than was the university, while half the colleges had just been ransacked, with probably varying degrees of acceptance, by Byron's Royalist horse. But Whitelocke was less inclined than Lord Saye to take such professions of loyalty on trust, and events would bear out his caution.

## Sober Men, Authors of Counsels

According to John Aubrey, who had matriculated as an undergraduate the preceding May, Lord Saye took the opportunity of this Oxford sojourn to investigate the Protestant purity of the college chapels. Those at Aubrey's own college, Trinity, a Catholic foundation never entirely purged of its aboriginal atmosphere, *alma mater* of those anti-Calvinist troublemakers, Chillingworth and Gilbert Sheldon, felt particular consternation about Saye's unfriendly surveillance. Trinity's venerable but cunning President Ralph Kettell, before whom even Saye was a stripling, proved cool-headedly equal to the situation:

> ... the Lord Viscount Saye and Sele came (by order of the Parliament) to visit the Colleges to see what of new Popery they could discover ... In our Chapel, on the backside of the Screen, had been two Altars (of painting well enough for those times, and the Colours were admirably fresh and lively).* That on the right hand ... was dedicated to St Katharine, that on the left was of the taking of our Saviour off from the cross.
>
> My Lord Saye saw that this was done of old time, and Dr Kettell told his Lordship: 'Truly, my Lord, we regard them no more than a dirty dish-clout'; so they remained untouched ...

Kettell seems to have successfully made a distinction to Saye between 'new Popery', that is, Laudian innovation, and remnants 'of old time', of no consequence, hardly worth the effort and controversy that would attend their iconoclasm. After this wily old defender's demise, the paintings would succumb to the parliamentary Visitation of 1648.

When Saye called a council of war, Whitelocke seems to have regarded himself, and been seconded by others, as the most qualified expert on both city and university. He put a detailed, insistent case to the other Deputies and the Lieutenant:

---

* By 'those times' Aubrey could be referring to the mid-sixteenth-century reign of Queen Mary, when Trinity was founded, or to an earlier period still, if the paintings in question had survived from Trinity's Benedictine predecessor, Durham College.

*Friends in Youth*

> [Whitelocke] told them the consequence of this place, the strength of its situation, the plenty of the Country, the nearness to London, & the disaffection of the University to the Parliament [unlike Saye, he had not been taken in by the college heads' polite countenances and formal assurances] . . . that the King by his coming to Shrewsbury . . . for the conveniency of this place . . . might probably make this a principal quarter for his forces, & fortify the City, which would prove a great prejudice to the Parliament, he therefore advised the Lord Saye . . . to prevent the Scholars from supplying his Majesty . . . & place a good Garrison & Governor in it, whom his Lordship might trust with so important a piece . . .

In this context the convenient pretence that the King was not in charge of his own cause and forces, but only a pawn of 'evil counsellors', was evidently thought unnecessary to rehearse. Whitelocke openly and (as it turned out) accurately predicted the King's next move. If his advice was as flagrantly ambitious as it was strategically shrewd, it did not go unheard:

> This motion was seconded by divers of the company, & some went so far as to name Whitelocke to be a fit person to be Governor, one whom the University, & City, & the Country thereabouts did so well know, & would be the better satisfied [by his appointment] . . . chiefly the University whereof he had been a member, & who knew him to be a Scholar and a lover of them.

Whitelocke was already making the customary expressions of honoured, easily persuadable, modest demurral, the necessary prelude to his graceful acceptance, when Lord Saye – hitherto a surprisingly unproblematic commander given his unfortunate history with his Deputy – shattered both the stratagem and its proposer's dream of a civilized university governorship:

> The Lord Saye shewed no forwardness to make Oxford a Garrison especially after Whitelocke was named for Governor. And some

> private friends, informed Whitelocke that the Lord Saye remembered the former Pique against Whitelocke upon the election of the Knights for Oxfordshire . . . & that the Lord Saye had a design of making one of his sons Governor of Oxford but perceiving so general an inclination to have Whitelocke . . . [Saye] mentioned not his son, & pretending favour to the University and Country, he declined the notion of making Oxford a Garrison . . .

Whitelocke and his supporters attempted to salvage something from the wreckage of his suggestion by beseeching Saye to 'seize upon or secure' such of the college plate as had not already departed with Byron. Even this precautionary half-measure was dismissed by Saye, on the extraordinary grounds that he 'thought it not . . . probable that the King would come thither'. Saye took promises from the college heads 'that their plate should be forthcoming & not be made use of by the King against Parliament', and considered that security enough.

Lord Saye stood down his Deputies the next day, and sent their troops on to join up with Essex's army. If the Lord Lieutenant is considered to have been motivated at least in part by genuine strategic considerations, not just by venality or vengefulness on his son's behalf, then Saye must have decided to place complete faith in the coming confrontation in the field: Saye seems to have assumed that the King's defeat in battle would be so entire that he would be unable to enter Oxford. Among the Royalists there were many, whether courtiers close to the Queen or admirers of the King's bellicose nephew Prince Rupert of the Rhine, who expected an equally brisk conclusion in the other direction. Whitelocke, like his old friend Hyde in the enemy camp, hoped and worked for as swift a negotiated peace as manageable, because he rightly foresaw and dreaded a longer, closer-fought war.

During Hyde's necessarily brisk stop at Oxford the preceding spring, on his way, by carefully inconspicuous stages, to join the King at York, he had held a confidential meeting with the Warden of All Souls, Gilbert Sheldon. Hyde's and Falkland's old companion of Great Tew, and Chillingworth's closest friend and intellectual foil from their undergraduate days at Trinity, Sheldon was an irascibly determined character, an unsleeping politician, and an ever-industrious ally. In May 1642 Sheldon made to Hyde the same prediction, in the opposite political interest, that Whitelocke would urge to Lord Saye in September:

> . . . that all the colleges in Oxford, and he did believe the like in Cambridge, were very plentifully supplied with plate, which . . . lay useless in their treasuries, there being enough besides for their use . . . and he had not the least doubt but that whensoever his majesty should think fit to require that treasure, it would all be sent to him.

Sheldon proved, like Whitelocke, an accurate observer of Oxford's intentions, and also of Cambridge's, some of whose colleges outdid Oxford by far in Laudian fervour. Cambridge's attempt to convey financial succour to the King was foiled by the characteristically direct intervention of the county's MP Oliver Cromwell. But the remaining plate of Oxford was indeed sent to the King at Nottingham, not long after Saye, a frustrated Whitelocke in his train, had left the university city ungarrisoned behind him.

Had Whitelocke's admittedly self-serving proposal been heeded, leaving him in the prestigious and comfortable position of military governor over his beloved old university, the King's plight would have become desperate much sooner: with Charles denied what Whitelocke had identified as the perfect Royalist temporary capital, in terms of geography, prestige, and sympathy. The civil war would likely have been over far sooner in the Parliamentarian interest; Oxford, though deprived of its most signally romantic hour as the stronghold of monarchical loyalty, would certainly have been spared much harm both as a city and a university.

# 9.
# Hurry and Smoke

*You triple Powers, who guiltie Souls pursue,*
*Eumenides; these rites of vengeance view.*

George Sandys, Book VIII,
*Ovids Metamorphosis Englished*

## 'Wishing for the Earl of Essex', Nottingham to Shrewsbury, September 1642

King Charles had so far derived neither hope nor pleasure from his temporary capitals. The atmosphere at York had been obviously provisional, innately fractious; troubled by resurgent factions, latent under Strafford's Lord Presidency of the North, newly explosive, like Ireland, since his execution. Nottingham was tainted for the King as the site of depressingly reasonable, tiringly dogged, tediously repetitive attempts at accommodation with Parliament. The raising there of the royal standard took place amid lowering weather, inauspicious auguries, and apathetic gloom. More bad news and murmurous fears found their way there than men or funds. Although himself still invested in the progress of possible peace negotiations, Ned Hyde perceived with sympathy the King's weariness in the town 'where he had received so many mortifications'.

So, when the court and its still paltry military forces at last left Nottingham, although the King's few followers were now retreating from the heart of Charles's most important and last semi-controllable kingdom towards its western peripheries, they did so with unusual optimism and unanimity. This mood embraced the beleaguered monarch, the most hot-blooded among his officers and advisors, and even Hyde himself, conscious at last of irrevocable commitment to Charles's cause one way or another. Whitelocke noted his old friend's first exclusion at this time from any future pardon by Parliament that might result from hypothetical terms of peace. Hyde's name was listed alongside those of the courtier Sir Endymion Porter, the King's Secretaries of State Sir Edward Nicholas and Falkland, and six Royalist peers, the Duke of Richmond, the Earls of Cumberland, Newcastle, Rivers, and Caernarvon, and Viscount Newark.

This group of Royalist politicians now outlawed by Parliament had, besides its defining support for Charles, little else in common. In social class it ran from the semi-princely Stuart cousin Richmond to the legal gentry Hyde and Nicholas; in religion from the Catholics Rivers and Caernarvon to Falkland, that theologically questing, sometime anti-episcopal MP; in political tendency from the uncompromising Porter, married to a Catholic lady-in-waiting to the Queen, through the parliamentary moderates Hyde and Falkland, to the frankly tepid magnate Newark.

The previous year Porter had been scathing about the royal concessions that Hyde and Falkland had helped to extract: 'subtle designs of gaining the popular opinion . . . weak executions for the up-holding of monarchy'. Unlike either Hyde or Falkland, Porter had voted to save Strafford. Two of the Royalists condemned by Parliament had suggestive connections across the political divide. Caernarvon's father-in-law was Hyde's long-time political patron Lord Pembroke; it was Pembroke's daughter and Caernarvon's wife who had courteously received Hyde and Whitelocke at Whitehall on the occasion of *The Triumph of Peace*. Newark's younger brother, William Pierrepont, was a Pym-aligned but pacific MP, and as such a close colleague and ally of Whitelocke.

With the Earl of Essex's much larger parliamentary force rumbling behind them, the King's men cast speculative eyes on Shrewsbury, the principal market town of Shropshire. Hyde made quiet arrangements for the King's friendly reception. As an uncertain, bookish younger son, he had once expected to forge a tranquil, comfortable career in the Church of England. But while unenthusiastically finding his way as an aspirant lawyer and youth about town, he had discovered in himself a sometimes distracting, always rewarding talent for making friends. Both of these characteristics, the parsonical and the companionable, came now to the fore.

At Nottingham, Hyde had cultivated the friendship of a 'dexterous and discreet' canon (so discreet, indeed, that he still cannot be identified) attached to one of Shrewsbury's ancient collegiate churches. Innately unsympathetic to the anti-episcopal tendencies of Parliament, the canon carried letters between Hyde and Shrewsbury's mayor, Richard Gibbons, whom Hyde judged 'an old humorous fellow', unsteady in his loyalties. The canon also briefed Hyde regarding the townsmen's wider 'humour and disposition', easing the way for the King's authorization of 200 newly raised infantry under a Royalist town notable, Francis Ottley. Hyde sent Ottley a private letter assuring him of Charles's personal gratitude, then informed the King and Privy Council that, despite the unpromising appearance in Shrewsbury of a deputation of London MPs and Parliament-inclined gentlemen, the town would soon open its gates to its sovereign.

Bolstered by the prospect of a friendly western headquarters, the King's army reached Derby with increasing numbers and ascendant spirits. Hyde recalled an atmosphere of febrile but genuine bravado. The Royalists felt confident to face down their stronger Parliamentarian pursuers as soon as possible, with 'all men . . . even wishing for the earl of Essex'. Charles kept good enough order that when his forces reached Stafford in mid-September he was able to keep his men from damaging Essex's country house at Chartley, where, not quite fifty years earlier, the King's grandmother Mary Queen of Scots had been held prisoner by Essex's father, Queen Elizabeth's fatal favourite. Here the King reassured himself by drawing parallels between the rebellious Devereux family of the past and present, imagining the current emergency as another doomed rising of ambitious noblemen.

The previous April, Charles had suffered an unexpected and

humiliating rebuff, seeking entry to what had turned out to be the resolutely Parliamentarian arsenal-port of Hull. At Shrewsbury in September the disillusioned King sent Hyde ahead of him to make certain of his promising intelligence. After Hyde had confirmed all was well, Charles himself entered the city on 20 September, accepting the homage and financial support of the 'humorous' Mayor Gibbons, whom he knighted along with the stalwart Ottley, and of Dr Thomas Chaloner, headmaster of the town's Free Grammar School. Shrewsbury School, founded in 1552 by the godly Tudor boy king, Edward VI, and alma mater of the famed Protestant paladin and poet Sir Philip Sidney, was by tradition both loyal to the Crown and unerring in its Calvinism. Its adherence triumphantly confirmed the image Hyde had helped to burnish for King Charles as a moderate, responsible, wronged Protestant king.

To Hyde, Dr Chaloner's name was one to stir wry thoughts and wistful memories, of extreme youth, fierce conviction, and untroubled levity. The headmaster's witty, worldly, fiery, and dissipated younger kinsman and namesake, Tom Chaloner, had been one of the companions of the 1620s with whom Ned and Bulstrode Whitelocke had been wont to mock and rail against the Star Chamber. In 1637 young Chaloner, accused by Archbishop Laud of writing a seditious anonymous pamphlet, had escaped arrest and fled England, most likely joining an elder brother in Turkey. His cousin the Shrewsbury headmaster had entirely different political convictions. Like the college heads of Oxford, Dr Thomas Chaloner made over his institution's hoard of plate as a loan, never to be repaid, for the King's limited, ever-demanding, perpetually emptying war-chest.

Shrewsbury was, compared to York and Nottingham, secure, united, friendly, and loyal. But though the town was, Hyde recalled, 'very commodious in all respects . . . so that both Court and army were very well accommodated', 'the incurable disease of want of money could not be assuaged in either'. Some funds arrived from Oxford (those removed during Sir John Byron's first foray) and from individual Royalist magnates, but a grander recourse was needed.

Hyde was selected to implement the policy that ensued, though it was one that made him very uneasy.

Hyde's religious inclination was more consistent than (if inextricable from) his political allegiance. He had been born and reared in the Jacobean Church of England. For the Elizabethan ecclesiastical settlement Hyde felt more practical admiration than enthusiastic allegiance; his private nostalgia was located mostly in the reign of King James, whom he considered a broadly wise steward both of Church and State. Like Selden and Whitelocke, Hyde felt affection for Laud as a man but had no hesitation in criticizing him as a politician. Great Tew had whetted his powerful but conventional intellect's appetite for a more rational, or in his term 'liberal-minded' theological palate. For the Church of Rome he never entertained anything but suspicion. The Papacy was no spiritual Antichrist to Hyde, but a subversive secular force, innately opposed to England, her laws, and her kings. The Holy See had sharpened the knives of traitors against Elizabeth, the anointed English monarch. Catholic, especially Jesuit, thinkers of Europe were wont to condemn lawful Protestant princes as tyrants and quick to invoke radically 'democratic' political principles against them.

As a coming man on good terms with the court, connected to the omnipresent house of Villiers, Hyde had long counted aristocratic Catholics among his ever-extending acquaintance. His friendships, like Whitelocke's, were catholic in the wider sense, indifferent to political or religious divisions. He noticed possessors of talent, knowledge, and worldliness, as an instinctive, if not yet entirely conscious, historian, as well as an aspiring politician. By 1642 Hyde had at one time or another ranked among his personal friends the serial confessional turncoat Ben Jonson, the cynical republican Harry Marten, the political and religious radical reactionary Pym, the worldly and learned Erastian Selden, the eclectic all-but-heretic Chillingworth, and the proto-totalitarian iconoclast Hobbes. Although his closest friends, Falkland and Whitelocke, substantially, and uncoincidentally, agreed with him both in issues of Church and State, the absence of such agreement did not impede Hyde's natural approachability. This humane ability to befriend almost anyone who excited and enlivened him made Hyde an all too perfect choice to fulfil his King's next expedient.

According to Hyde in the *History*, 'some person of [Roman Catholic] inclination' 'had insinuated to the King' that the large, affluent Catholic populations of Shropshire, the Marches, and Wales would gladly supply Charles with loans or even gifts. Hyde adds that both this confidential Catholic advisor and the King himself realized the need for 'great privacy', 'very secret, to avoid the scandal of a close conjuncture with the Papists, which was every day imputed to him'. Hyde himself instantly recognized that by accepting, worse still, soliciting Catholic funds, the King risked jeopardizing Hyde's own carefully assembled programme of respectable Royalism, becoming once again all but indistinguishable from the parliamentary caricature, the Popish tyrant of the Personal Rule, whose policies Hyde had himself criticized only the previous year.

The Catholic advisor who suggested Hyde's suitability to collect Catholic contributions was probably the Earl of Worcester, the chief Catholic influence on Charles with the Queen still absent in Holland. Lord Worcester, a vastly rich Catholic convert, was about to entertain the young Prince of Wales at Raglan Castle, and be rewarded with elevation to a marquessate. His advice was locally irrefutable but strategically dubious, given sincerely, but also not without self-interest.

In vain did the greatly embarrassed Hyde protest:

> He was surprised with the information that that *classis* [i.e. sort, group, and, in this case, religious rite] of men had made choice of him for their trust, for which he could imagine no reason but that he had been often of counsel with some persons of quality of that profession [religion, i.e. Catholicism] who yet knew very well that he was in no degree inclined to their persuasion. He submitted to the King's pleasure.

The word 'profession' possesses a useful ambiguity here. Hyde used the fact of his legal profession to justify his own private good relations with prominent Catholics, despite their religious 'profession'. Disavowing any sympathy for the Roman Catholic Church with as much courtesy and sternness as his prose can fuse together, Hyde hides behind the formal shield of 'counsel', the legal advice of his calling. He paints this as his only real connection to Catholic nobles and gentlemen (though at other times he is perfectly clear that his friendships among that *'classis'* were many, personal, and genuine – as indeed was the case with Whitelocke).

Hyde evidently felt himself, and his ability to exercise a benevolent influence on king and country, to be compromised by his successful negotiations with Catholic subjects, even though this industrious service soon put thousands of pounds at the King's disposal. In the *History*, Hyde falsely cast doubt on the very existence of Catholicism among Royalist army officers. He obscured the family background and lifelong religion of the King's colonel general of dragoons, and as much as he could denied the presence of the colonel's lesser co-religionists: 'not one officer of the field ... was a papist, except Sir Arthur Aston, *if he were one* – and very few common soldiers of that religion'.

Hyde's cagey category of 'officers of the field' also allowed him to omit prominent Catholic courtiers and Royalist financial backers such as Worcester. But if Hyde massaged the true state of affairs, he was responding to a parliamentary propaganda machine bent upon the bulk production of generalizing libels: 'the Parliament in all their declarations, and their clergy much more in their sermons, assured the people that the King's army consisted *only of Papists*'.

Hyde pressed the point logically home – more logically than factually – to turn parliamentary slander against itself, conjuring the nightmare image that preoccupied him all his life of a hypocritical 'devil's alliance' of religious hardliners, Puritans and Catholics united against the national Church:

> [The Parliamentarians] themselves entertained all of that religion [i.e. Catholicism] that they could get; and very many, both soldiers and officers, of that religion engaged with them; whether it was that they really believed that that army did desire liberty of conscience for all religions, as some of the chief of them pretended, or that they desired to divide themselves for communication of intelligence and interest.

This accusation, if more intriguing than plausible or coherent, forms part of an idea in which Hyde, reflecting on his own actions early in the civil wars, needed to believe – that his old comrades who still followed John Pym had behaved quite as ambiguously as he had himself been obliged to in the King's cause. In a natural conclusion, without naming names, Hyde accused Parliament of agreeing to borrow money from prudent Catholic gentlemen in solidly Parliament-held Suffolk.

Whatever Hyde's qualms, he had proven his worth to Charles twofold, first by providing the King with the arguments that had won him a following in the country, then by managing the delicate negotiations, more than a little against both Hyde's private conscience and strategic instinct, which enabled the King to remain for the moment solvent and in the field.

## 'Hurt done by the sword', Powick Bridge, September 1642

Hardly had Whitelocke complied with the orders of Lord Saye, to retire leaving Oxford ungarrisoned, when he began to receive the bleak satisfaction of being proven right. His journal alludes to this vindication with oblique brevity: 'the King having got the start of General Essex, marched towards London'. This transformation of King Charles's position, from lurking in the west to advancing on the capital, was partly the result of the Battle of Powick Bridge, fought on 23 September, the first significant armed engagement of the English civil wars, one whose importance lay not in its trifling numbers, but its compelling narrative. The skirmish both gave birth to the legend of Prince Rupert of the Rhine, and caused the death of one of the few loose associates of Great Tew to fight for Parliament. The ferocious Royalist soldier Sir John Byron, whose career had already intersected with Whitelocke's at a critical moment, was once again a pivotal protagonist.

After hastily leaving Oxford before Lord Saye's vastly superior force, Byron, his brothers, and their thin remaining regiment of 160 horse were left in charge of a conspicuous convoy of gold and silver. Given that Byron at the opening of hostilities had been entrusted with some of the scarce royal bullion, and then lost it due to his ignominious worsting by a nocturnal Parliamentarian mob, this Oxford plate was all the more welcome, needed for the maintenance both of the royal cause and Byron's own reputation.

The Parliamentarians now aimed to block Byron and his money's return to the King at Shrewsbury, as Cromwell had managed to do at Cambridge. A cavalry vanguard about six times larger than Byron's little band of horsemen was understandably considered adequate to accomplish this mission, and dispatched a day ahead of Essex's main army to catch up with Byron near the persistently Royalist town of Worcester. In name this Parliamentarian detachment was under the leadership of Lord Saye's second son Nathaniel Fiennes, the most active, influential, and uncompromising member of his family in the House of Commons. Fiennes, though at this point of far greater importance than Cromwell as a politician, lacked his latent genius as a soldier (Hyde calls Fiennes with heavy, pleasurable sarcasm 'this doughty commander').

In truth active command over the operation lay with a more obscure professional soldier, Colonel John Brown. But Brown's own second-in-command, Colonel Edwin Sandys, was perhaps the most unexpected member of the parliamentary expedition. His uncle, George Sandys, the poet, translator, traveller, and American colonial administrator, was in complete political and theological harmony with Falkland, and well known at Great Tew. Hyde spoke warmly both of Colonel Sandys and his father and namesake, an

MP in six parliaments and three reigns, calling the younger Edwin Sandys 'son of a worthy father'. Edwin Sandys the elder had been among Whitelocke's first parliamentary mentors in 1626, Sandys's last Parliament and Whitelocke's first. The Sandyses were a large, talented, serious-minded family, sprung from the archbishop of York at the time of the Spanish Armada. Other than Colonel Edwin Sandys, almost every male Sandys active during the English civil wars bore arms for the King, in whose cause several were killed. But it was their Parliamentarian kinsman who would fight, and fall, first.

As the encounter unfolded, both sides demonstrated the inexperience of peaceful England's soldiers. The Parliamentarians failed to realize that Byron had been successfully reinforced. Fresh Royalist horse almost a thousand strong, entirely evening up the scales, were led by King Charles's recently landed German nephew, Prince Rupert of the Palatinate, with his younger brother Maurice. Rupert already had one glorious but unquestionable cavalry defeat to his name, the fiasco of Vlotho in 1638, which had ended in his capture by Imperial Habsburg forces. Now he allowed himself to be surprised while, Hyde says, 'reposing himself on the ground', accompanied by Maurice, the ubiquitous Digby, and other 'principal officers' including the Royalists' irrepressible, hard-drinking dare-devil commissary general, Henry Wilmot. The Royalist troops were tired and disordered, their junior officers were resting in Worcester, and armour had been removed by most soldiers of all ranks, when the enemy came into plain sight. Hyde conveys an impression of all-embracing, even-handed muddle.

Hyde allows credit only to a 'rebel' combatant, stating that the Parliamentarians were 'gallantly led by Colonel Sandys', 'completely armed both for offence and defence', thus giving a distinctly more efficient account of Sandys's preparations than Rupert's. Hyde then describes an almost chivalric-sounding mêlée dominated by officers, omitting a critical fusillade by the Royalist dragoons. This likely represents the version of the fight both as it was related to him and as he understood it. He also underrates the number of casualties on both sides. Yet there is a visceral touch to his statement that 'there was not on the prince's side a piece of armour worn that day, and but few pistols; so that most of the hurt that was done was by the sword'. In Hyde's mind at least, the first true exchange of the civil war in England had been uncannily traditional, a prince and his companions prevailing by sheer ferocity in close combat.

Sandys, fighting in the front line, was heavily wounded and captured by Wilmot in person. Rupert, retiring in a hurry to ensure the delivery of Byron's convoy, left the colonel, his most significant prisoner, behind at Worcester, 'charitably . . . to die of his wounds there'. The dryness of Hyde's tone here is eloquent, considering his view of Rupert both at the time and subsequently. Rupert's chaplain, Dr Watts, reported that the sinking colonel, heartily repenting of his rebellion against the King, had given permission that his change of heart be published: this it was, in a declaration signed by Falkland and Sir Edward Nicholas, which assumed, on the word of 'men of honour . . . present in the action', the Parliamentarian colonel's death.

But by 7 October, Sandys, in fact still alive, either retracted his recantation, or had his signature extorted or forged by the Parliamentarian clergy who had succeeded Watts at his bedside when Worcester fell again to Parliament.\* In a letter to the Commons, Sandys, or his ventriloquist, expressed his vehement rejection of the 'most scandalous aspersion of late raised and cast upon me, by the wicked and envious party, that I should be dead, and before my death did much repent me of taking up Arms against his Majesty, on the Parliament's side'.

The letter stuck with Parliament's legalistic party line that it was fighting 'by order from both Houses, and for the preservation of the Peace, Religion and Lawes of this Kingdom, and of his Majesty's own Royal person, with his Kingly Offspring'. It also reassured MPs

---

\* Parliamentarian clerics at other deathbeds, for example that of Chillingworth in 1644, tended to offer more acute political partisanship than religious consolation.

that the colonel's wounds were 'dangerous, but the Chirurgeons put me in comfort, not mortal'. Leaving aside the letter's authenticity, Sandys's demise that December proved its medical prognosis over-optimistic.

In his decline and death Colonel Sandys became a battlefield far more contested than the skirmish whose wounds eventually undid him. This severe young soldier was a fitting symbol of his country, with almost every aspect of his career disputed. Sandys was alternately exonerated of and blamed for acts of iconoclasm in cathedrals occupied by his troops in the summer of the war. He seems to have been on bad terms with his siblings over money and is rumoured to have first escaped justice after committing a rape, then later to have persecuted the very clergyman who had secured his acquittal. Hyde is kinder to him than most other sources, almost certainly out of regard for his father's memory, as well as continuing friendship with his uncle, George Sandys the poet.

Where Hyde was especially perceptive was in his analysis of the political importance of this chaotic affray, outside the rotting, hardly lockable gates of ancient Worcester. Both the King himself and, especially, his hot-headed German nephew had gained a significant propaganda victory:

> This rencounter [sic] proved of unspeakable advantage and benefit to the King. For it being the first action his horse had been brought to, and that party of the enemy being the most picked and choice men, it gave his troops great courage, and rendered the name of Prince Rupert very terrible . . . from that time the Parliament began to be apprehensive that the business would not be so easily ended as it was begun . . .

Here Hyde imagines, even sympathizes with, the reaction of Pym's MPs, tardily approaching the realization that had long been Hyde and Whitelocke's vocally expressed fear. At the same time, he does not exactly rejoice at the apotheosis of Rupert. And indeed Prince Rupert's buoyant fame would soon become something more than an annoyance to Hyde, Falkland, their like-minded friends, and their preferred policy of a peace arranged as speedily as possible.

## 'A great deliverance' – Ditton Park, Ivy Lane, and the Uxbridge Road, September–October 1642

Powicke Bridge, to Hyde an ominous victory involving a poignant death, was to Whitelocke and other moderately inclined Parliamentarians a predictable disaster that in some ways strengthened their hand. Nathaniel Fiennes, heir to Whitelocke's highest-ranking personal enemy Lord Saye, had been utterly discredited. As Whitelocke's *Memorials* drily describe the encounter, '. . . Colonel Nathaniel Fiennes . . . expected general Essex to second [him]; but instead of him came Prince Rupert, and slew and routed all the parliament party.'

Whitelocke seldom reported Royalist victories so emphatically or accurately, less out of Parliamentarian partisanship than because of the distorted nature of the information he received in London. But evidently there was no hiding the fiasco of Powicke Bridge from literate London gossips. Whitelocke goes on to draw a wider conclusion in blaming Lord Essex – to whom he is usually respectful and sympathetic – for the 'error of so long a stay at Worcester' in the skirmish's aftermath.

As the King's army deftly interposed itself between the Earl of Essex and London, Whitelocke remembered Parliament 'in some fright upon the King's approach', less because of the small Royalist force itself, than on account of 'the suspicion of a great party hereabouts that would join with him, and had invited him that way'. Later events indicate that Whitelocke himself was, with good reason, reckoned by many to be at least easily reconcilable to such a 'great party'. It was an ideologically uncertain moment. The ambitious young poet John Milton had published five prose tracts against episcopal church government during the previous two years, but also had proven form in adapting his poetic persona to please aristocratic, Laudian, Catholic, even Papal circles. Now he hastily composed a sonnet that is essentially a preliminary negotiation for generous terms of surrender:

> *Captain or Colonel, or Knight in Arms,*
> *Whose chance on these defenceless doors may seize,*
> *If ever deed of honour did thee please,*
> *Guard them, and him within protect from harms,*
> *He can requite thee, for he knows the charms*
> *That call Fame on such gentle acts as these,*
> *And he can spread thy Name o'er Lands and Seas,*
> *Whatever clime the Suns bright circle warms.*
> *Lift not thy spear against the Muses Bower,*
> *The great Emathian Conqueror bid spare*
> *The house of Pindarus, when Temple and Tower*
> *Went to the ground: And the repeated air*
> *Of sad Electra's Poet had the power*
> *To save th' Athenian Walls from ruin bare.*

Whitelocke witnessed this nervous mood and probably shared it. His duties, position and, crucially, the size and the very location of his estates made him more exposed to danger than young Milton, that still obscure if always self-confident poet.

Whitelocke was now instructed to raise troops and superintend scouts at Ditton Park, the house of his fellow Deputy Lieutenant and old family friend Richard Winwood, situated near the coaching village of Slough. Whitelocke's own principal properties, Phyllis Court, Fawley Court, and much of Henley, lay twenty miles further west, greatly more vulnerable to the King and his suddenly notorious German nephew. His domestic preparations for the worst were more painstaking even than the composition of a sonnet. Frances Whitelocke and her two eldest daughters Frances and Elizabeth, both still small children, were presumably considered the most at risk should they fall into the hands of uncontrolled mercenaries upon either side. In his Commons speeches urging peace negotiations, Whitelocke had often invoked ill-disciplined, irregularly paid armed men out for plunder, and he would soon gain more direct knowledge of such soldiers' depredations. He made careful and revealing arrangements for the comfortable accommodation of his wife and two eldest daughters in Ivy Lane in the City near St Paul's Cathedral, where he joined them from Ditton Park when he could.

At Ivy Lane the Whitelockes gained a landlord, Sir Thomas Fanshawe, who was not merely a Royalist but the hereditary Remembrancer of the Exchequer, chief record-keeper of royal taxation. The Whitelockes' fellow tenants were among Whitelocke's oldest Royalist friends apart from Ned Hyde himself: his grateful friend Geoffrey Palmer and their fellow lawyer Matthew Hale, men connected to each other by both marriage and politics, to Whitelocke (and to Hyde) by friendship dating back to the Inns of Court of the 1620s. Hale, a prodigious and courageous barrister, had acted, with unanswerable fairness and authority, as defence counsel to Strafford; he later did the same for Laud. Under such a roof and in such company, Frances Whitelocke and her daughters were comparatively safe from Royalist retribution. The company was cheerful, with 'good conversation & friendship among them'. Both Mrs Palmer and Mrs Hale were also in residence. Mrs Palmer was Mrs Hale's young aunt, both belonging to the legal, martial, Royalist Moore family. Mrs Hale was considered over-extravagant by her severe, though admirable, husband. No wonder Whitelocke wrote of the existence of a Royalist 'great party' in London; whenever he could get leave from marshalling county levies at Ditton Park and join his wife in the City, he lived in that party's midst.

The Whitelockes' five younger offspring, four infant girls and a six-year-old boy, stayed at Fawley Court under the care of William Cooke, the trusted tenant to whom Whitelocke partly attributed the making of his and Frances's love-match. Whitelocke's motherless eldest son and heir, his grandfather's namesake, eleven-year-old James, a future Cromwellian colonel, was left completely out of his father's reconstruction of these precautions on the home front. It is possible he was temporarily entrusted to one of his maternal uncles, all of them usefully Royalist.

In the last week of October, back at Ditton Park, Whitelocke awaited news with his fellow Deputy Lieutenant Winwood. The private army of 'Adventurers' intended for Ireland, in which Whitelocke had been among the foremost investors, had waited to cross into Ireland at Bristol under the command of Lord Wharton, Whitelocke and Winwood's superior as a hastily appointed parliamentary Lord Lieutenant (after his predecessor Lord Paget's defection). In the present emergency Parliament now ordered the Adventurers, contrary to their original purpose, to abandon plans for Ireland and reinforce Essex in the Midlands, ignoring the furious protest of King Charles at this redirection. With Wharton preoccupied elsewhere, Whitelocke and Winwood were thus directly in charge of the country between the King and London. On the Uxbridge road they awaited news with understandable anxiety. Their worst fears appeared borne out by the first report that reached them, from a beaten, panicked Scots mercenary officer in parliamentary service, Sir James Ramsay.

According to Ramsay, although he himself had, as he would later convince a court martial, 'done all that it became a gallant man to do', Essex's entire army had been completely routed at the hands of the King and Prince Rupert near a Warwickshire village named Kineton. Ramsay, who had commanded the horse on the Parliamentarian left flank, had given way before the Royalist right flank under Prince Rupert in person. This flight had in part been precipitated by the sudden battlefield defection of a troop of Anglo-Irish horsemen, part of Wharton's repurposed army of Adventurers serving under the illustratively named Sir Faithfull Fortescue, to the King's side. Fortescue, an elderly veteran whose military experience had been specifically noted in the King's protest to Parliament, had already lost two sons to the Irish Rebellion, was dissatisfied with the improvised order to march back into the heart of England, and so had readily responded to an overture from Rupert. To Ramsay's sure knowledge, the Parliament's right flank under Lord Feilding

## Hurry and Smoke

(a friend of Hyde in happier times), had collapsed after the left flank's defeat. He was certain that 'the King had routed Parliament's army, & was advancing apace towards London'.

But Whitelocke and Winwood had hardly heard Ramsay's disastrous account before it was plentifully, if murkily contradicted. Some of their own Buckinghamshire scouts returned with news 'quite Contrary, &' as Whitelocke insists, somehow only adding ambiguity as to his own feelings, 'much more welcome, That Essex had routed the Kings Army & gained a full victory'. In the flurry of rumours that then followed, Whitelocke's journal gives up on enumerating the 'many officers & soldiers posting to London, whom' he crisply adds, he and Winwood 'doubted [i.e. suspected] were not sent thither'. By now Whitelocke and his colleague were riding out together in person to pursue their enquiries, but discovering only a profusion of 'like different reports', including some from Royalist messengers who, not recognizing the identity, position, or allegiance of their road-weary and overworked interlocutors, boasted of victory. The Deputy Lieutenants despaired of obtaining a clear picture and, on the hardened politicians' assumption that the truth would arrive more quickly at the centre of power than it could settle amid the chaos of the battle-lines, sent an express rider to Westminster.

This messenger returned with a conclusion of almost Delphic pithiness and opacity:

> ... the two Armies had fought at Edge Hill, many thousands were slain, & that the Parliament's forces had a great deliverance, and a little victory, which was a true description of it.

The Battle of Edgehill's very name was as closely contested as Colonel Sandys's deathbed, Parliament's side often inclining to the name Kineton Fight after the village beside their camp. Whitelocke's 'little victory' is as elusively mild a term as his 'true description' seems unattainable. In the realm of literal, military fact, it appears very nearly the opposite of the truth. Historical consensus has long generally held that a minor tactical and potentially a major strategic advantage after the battle lay with the King. The most truthful authorities even within Whitelocke's own broad political camp, such as Lucy, wife of the parliamentary Colonel John Hutchinson, outdo Whitelocke in frankness. Mrs Hutchinson, a relation by marriage of Hyde and a historian of not wholly dissimilar mould though opposite political allegiance, recognized Edgehill, the first major set-piece battle of the English Civil War, as a symbolically futile dead heat.

Whitelocke's reaching after some kind of parliamentary gain on this basis relegates him to the eternally compromised ranks of the timeserving Parliamentarian historians exemplified by Tom May, once among young Hyde's raffish literary cronies, who painted Edgehill as triumphantly for Parliament as the stretching of the known facts could let him. But Whitelocke, unlike May, does not claim to be establishing his own superior historical account, only preserving the haphazard, third-hand reactions at the time. Read in this more modest sense, as a long past memory of an exhausted parliamentary messenger's judgement in the middle of a situation as critical as it was confusing, 'a great deliverance, and a little victory' sounds less a laboured attempt at propaganda than a mirthless, Stoical twist of gallows-humour.

As an amateur soldier (one no less experienced, much better travelled and more intellectually inquisitive than the future's irresistible conqueror, Oliver Cromwell), Whitelocke in fact held strong opinions. He felt himself entitled to be heard, and his ideas and voice to possess considerable individual merit. But in the role of military historian, Whitelocke was conservative and cautious, sceptical not just of his own ability but of anyone's to provide a truly useful and objective account of any battle. After another less ambiguous parliamentary defeat, Whitelocke would usefully articulate exactly why he felt such attempts necessarily suffered from crippling restrictions:

> By this we may see the great difference in relations of martial performances, always according to the particular interest of the relaters;

and it is certain, that in a fight the next man can hardly make a certain relation of the actions of him that was next in place to him.

For in such a hurry and smoke as is in a fight, and when a man scarce takes notice of any thing but what relates to his own immediate safety, it is hard to give any clear account of particular passages, but the general will make way for itself by the consequence and issue.

Whitelocke was not present at Edgehill and had reasonable, theoretical grounds for doubting his ability to do it historical justice. Neither of these impediments applied to his old friend in the enemy camp, Ned Hyde.

## 'The punctilio of honour' – The Way to Edgehill, Late September–23 October 1642

The King's court-cum-army proceeded still in oddly leisurely spirit, neither entirely sure nor overmuch concerned about the exact location of its more numerous pursuers under Essex. King Charles's own rising confidence was proving infectious. The army was also animated by tactical urgency and clarity, considering it, as Hyde expressed it, 'morally certain' that Essex would have to bar their way to the capital. At the same time, there were prominent exceptions to this heady, high-hearted mood, exceptions, by implication, including Hyde himself. His writings pick out several of the Royalists' more pessimistic fellow travellers, many of them connected to his pre-war life, friends, career, and sympathies.

Sir Richard Fanshawe, youngest brother of the Whitelockes' new landlord Sir Thomas, the King's Remembrancer, had chosen the Royalist side after a long, melancholy argument with his, and Hyde's, old associate, the ideologically malleable, personally Bacchic professional writer Tom May. According to Emanuel de Critz, the court painter who overheard their 'debate', 'both camps were rigorously banded' (criticized) by Fanshawe and May. Both men had long moved in the cultivated, lettered, politically ambivalent world of the Apollo Room and John Selden's ever-hospitable study. Hostile rumour, endorsed by his now politically interested former friend Hyde, accused May of hunger for the Poet Laureateship. May had dedicated his first great translations in high style to the King. He would end a compromised career and a squalid life in 1650 as the English Republic's hack historian, reviled, with immortal brilliance and some irony, by the equally slippery, then broadly Royalist Andrew Marvell, for the instability and opportunism of his political sympathies. Fanshawe, like Hyde and Falkland, was a constitutionalist and an honest critic of the Church of England's status quo. The crypto-Catholic courtier and minister Sir Francis Windebank went so far as to label him a Puritan. Hyde admired Fanshawe's literary talent, capacity for industry and private character, and in 1644 would be among a handful of witnesses at his hurried wartime wedding.

Another friend of Hyde and Falkland now with the Royalist army was Henry, Lord Spencer, who had married Edmund Waller's lost muse 'Sacharissa', Lady Dorothy Sidney. Two of Spencer's brothers-in-law, Lord Lisle and Colonel Algernon Sidney, presently over the Irish Sea attempting to suppress the Catholic revolt, were thoroughly parliamentarian in opinion. Their father Lord Leicester was another high-placed waverer, and Lord Spencer's own first sympathies had lain with Parliament, for whom he had been a highly efficient recruiting officer among his tenantry. When the King issued his summons to the north, however, Spencer, forced to make what he, like so many others, considered to be by definition an impossible and illegal choice, gloomily headed for York. He brought his monarch no men – having sent so many to Parliament instead – but a considerable fortune and a useful reputation, comparable to Falkland's, among noblemen and gentry of moderate opinions. Spencer refused any commission, choosing instead to serve among the King's Life Guards. His letters back to his wife express a particularly eloquent and human exasperation with the war's outlook:

## Hurry and Smoke

> The king's condition is much improved of late. His force increaseth daily, which increaseth the insolence of the papists. How much I am unsatisfied with the proceedings here, I have at large expressed; neither is there wanting daily handsome opportunity to retire, were it not for gaining honour; for let occasion be never so handsome, unless a man resolve to fight on the parliament side – which, for my part, I had rather be hanged – it will be said a man is afraid to fight. If there could be an expedient found to salve the punctilio of honour, I should not continue here an hour. The discontent that I, and many other honest men, receive daily, is beyond expression.

Hyde and Falkland were the two most prominent such 'honest men' in the King's councils. Falkland and Spencer were soon to be associated by their communications, both public and secret, on the King's behalf with Parliament's sometimes latent, sometimes ascendant peace party.

Sir Edmund Verney, the King's old friend and Knight-Marshal, had been appointed bearer of the Banner Royal at the glum raising of the Royal Standard at Nottingham.* His eldest son Ralph was, however, a Pymite MP and a Parliamentarian soldier. Political and religious scruples, quite as much as familial division, weighed upon the elder Verney, who thus shared the predicament of Fanshawe, Spencer, Falkland and, it may be inferred, Hyde. In the later, more personal and interior *Life*, Clarendon detailed Sir Edmund Verney's doubts at length. While outwardly differentiating his own position from Verney's, he also employed his analysis of the older man's feelings to ventriloquize his own inner conflict: '. . . Verney . . . with whom [Hyde] had great familiarity . . . a man of great courage, and universally beloved . . . told him "he was very glad to see him . . . retain his natural vivacity and cheerfulness" . . .'

Hyde responded courteously that he shared many of the other

---

* The Royal Standard's significance was ceremonial and political; the smaller, more manageable Banner Royal had a practical battlefield function in directing the Royalist army.

man's worries and felt that Verney was 'far from being as melancholic as he', whereupon Verney discharged his true confession:

> My condition is much worse than yours . . . You have satisfaction in your conscience that you are in the right; that the king ought not to grant what is required of him; and so you do your duty and your business together: but for my part, I do not like the quarrel, and do heartily wish that the king would yield . . . my conscience is only concerned in honour and gratitude to follow my master. I have eaten his bread, and served him near thirty years, and will not do so base a thing as to forsake him; and choose rather to lose my life (which I am sure I shall do) to preserve and defend those things which are against my conscience . . . I have no reverence for the bishops, for whom this quarrel subsists.

The ageing patriarch Sir Edmund Verney echoes the thoughtful young Lord Spencer's connubial letter on every point. Their reluctant actions are ultimately decided upon and motivated by 'the punctilio of honour', 'honour and gratitude'. The resemblance lends a good measure of verisimilitude to the gist, at least, of Clarendon's recollection.

Clarendon the historian and memoirist reconstructs this confidential conversation with half-conscious complexity. His Verney assumes the difference of his opinions from those of his younger friend Hyde, apparently unswervingly committed to political and religious Royalism; Clarendon's remembered younger self, in reply, all but dismisses such differences. Like Verney, the Ned Hyde of the early 1640s had limited 'reverence for the bishops'. In fact Clarendon seems to have ventriloquized Verney quite deliberately. He portrays him as the kind of ideal, loyal English worthy who would have prevented any need for civil war, had his excellent qualities been more widespread. Through the unimpeachably honourable Verney, Clarendon lets slip some of his younger self's still-torn feelings, scarcely more than a year after he had voted in the Long Parliament for the execution of the royal enforcer Strafford.

## Hurry and Smoke

None of these ambivalent Royalists adversely affected the conduct of the campaign. Fanshawe was primarily a man of peace, a linguist and diplomat. Lord Spencer had carefully avoided exercising any military responsibility. Hyde's and Falkland's own pacific hopes kept options for the King in play, options whose necessity Charles sometimes reluctantly, sometimes gladly acknowledged, of communicating with moderates still at Westminster and attempting to end the war by well-devised negotiation. Verney's gloom was, as Clarendon emphasizes, kept by this vocal old royal champion strictly to himself, as he continued to serve his monarch in a firmly individual, chivalric mode. But another, more overt dissension also broke out in the royal army's midst, a directly military clash of personalities. This argument over battlefield strategy, drawing in Falkland as an appalled bystander, involved two opposing old soldiers and the coming young paladin Prince Rupert as participants.

At about midnight on 22 October 1642, what would turn out to be the eve of the Battle of Edgehill, on the approach of Parliament's army under Essex being brought to the King's attention, Charles sent Falkland to Prince Rupert with a written order, assuming that Rupert would sufficiently respect his Secretary of State carrying a letter in his hand. But the Prince exploded at this approach by Falkland, a mere subject. Hyde states that Falkland replied in quiet tones, 'that his highness, in neglecting [the order], neglected the king'. This unpleasant exchange was an ominous portent for Falkland and his friends.

From Nottingham onwards, the commander chosen by the King had been Robert Bertie, Earl of Lindsey, an elderly Elizabethan veteran. Lindsey had remained loyal to the Stuart monarchy despite its imperfectly gracious treatment of him over the years. He knew his martial trade, and also possessed particular insight into the mind of his counterpart, Essex, a friend with whom he had served on the continent. Lindsey's plan was an old-fashioned, stolidly workable defence, dominated by infantry in closely packed 'Dutch' pike formations. But to both Rupert and another veteran of the ongoing German wars, Patrick, Lord Ruthven, this order of battle was criminally unimaginative.

## Friends in Youth

Patrick Ruthven, who had joined the King's army at Shrewsbury, was almost a decade older than Lindsey, but a livelier character: a Scots military lifer of renown, dash, and considerable competence. His passion for his adopted homeland, Sweden, was equalled by his enthusiasm for the bottle; to his German and Scandinavian officers he was 'Pater Rothwein', Father Red Wine. He shared Prince Rupert's near-idolatry of the heroically slain King of Sweden, Gustavus Adolphus, famed for devastatingly modern, aggressive cavalry tactics. Together Rupert and Ruthven persuaded the King to adopt a 'Swedish' not 'Dutch' formation, with a greater role for the cavalry under Rupert's independent command, a decision Charles promulgated at five o'clock on the morning before battle.

Lindsey, who understood that his commission as general had been fundamentally undermined by this decision, relinquished command, taking the field merely as a regimental colonel of foot. He was replaced in fact, though not explicitly in name, by Rupert (independently controlling the cavalry) and Ruthven (in overall command), with Sir Jacob Astley, who happened to be Rupert's old tutor in military matters, in charge of the foot. Falkland and Hyde entirely sympathized with Lindsey, that respectable, aristocratic, old-fashioned, markedly English soldier, in his grievance at being supplanted by the German royal cadet and the Scottish professional, with their thrusting Swedish innovations. Prince Rupert and Ruthven might well be more up to date and effectual practitioners of the latest military theory of the day, but Rupert, especially, had proven himself a tactless and dictatorial political actor.

## *'I fear them not!'* – *Edgehill, Bullet Hill, Field Hospital at King's Leys Barn, Arlescote House, 23 October 1642*

At Edgehill, Ned Hyde stood at his King's side in battle for the first and, as it would turn out, the last time in his life. Eight o'clock in the morning found him with Charles upon a ridge already suitably dubbed, after its shape, Bullet Hill. Here were stationed the largest of the King's ten precious artillery pieces. King Charles wore an ermine-lined cloak of black velvet, mourning the effusion of his people's blood, showing both his dynasty's characteristic panache in a crisis and his own peculiar, paradoxical nature. He sat on horseback among fifty mounted, loyal, well-born and elderly Gentlemen Pensioners, led by Sir William Howard.* The King, his two young sons, and their retainers, including Hyde, had a good view of a surprisingly heartening sight, that of the Parliament's soldiers assembled beside Kineton. Essex's army did not now appear much larger than the Royalist force swelled by recruiting in the rural west.

The King was accompanied by his two closest friends among the still loyal high peers of the realm, the Duke of Richmond, his own cousin, and the Earl of Dorset. Richmond was as attractive in his character as in his handsome person. Edward Sackville, Earl of Dorset, was a charming, lettered, approachable nobleman in late middle age, a racily fascinating past behind him, a surprisingly sensible, commendable future ahead. Hyde, who did not tolerate dull or ill-natured aristocrats, recalled Dorset's conversation as 'pleasant, sparkling and sublime'. Both these great lords, like Hyde, at heart desired a swift peace on terms acceptable to the King.

Hyde had been entrusted with protecting two all-important charges, the twelve-year-old Prince of Wales and his nine-year-old brother the Duke of York. Between them these Stuart princes would shape most of the triumphs and disasters of Lord Clarendon's maturity, but Hyde had not yet had a chance to observe the character of either of them in depth. This crucial civilian duty was shared between Hyde and two royal physicians. The younger of these, John Hinton, had attended the Queen since 1640. Despite his royal patroness, Hinton appears to have shared Hyde's political duality, signing a petition to Parliament urging compromise with the King

---

* The King's formal mounted Life Guards, including Lord Spencer, at their own hot-tempered insistence followed Prince Rupert on the right flank as a cavalry reserve. This whimsical knight-errantry would have serious consequences.

at the turn of 1641–2. The older and more notable physician, Dr William Harvey, was almost certainly already well known to Hyde.

Dr Harvey's elder brother, the city merchant Daniel Harvey, had seven years previously first recommended Ned Hyde's counsel to Archbishop Laud. The merchant's medical younger brother was, like Hyde, a close friend of Selden (he is mentioned in one of the somewhat enigmatic jokes preserved in the great lawyer's *Table-Talk*). Like Hyde, too, Dr Harvey knew and admired Thomas Hobbes, that restless young thinker who by the time of Edgehill was safely lurking in French exile, evading conviction by Parliament for uncomfortable opinions he had expressed about advisable limits on its pretensions to power.

Dr Harvey walked with wincing slowness, hobbled by chronic gout (a disease that lay in Hyde's future). The doctor's curious young acquaintance John Aubrey describes him in the late 1630s as already white-haired, black-eyed, pale but prone to sudden, passionate flushes, 'of the lowest stature', but 'full of spirit' and 'far from bigotry'.\* Harvey's repertoire of anecdotes of great men extended as far back as Francis Bacon, Lord Chancellor, essayist, moderate, pragmatist, and scientist. The doctor's opinions tended to be unflinching, piquant, and iconoclastic. Harvey called Man himself 'a great mischievous Baboon', loved the dark and loathed heralds, and greatly approved both of love matches and Turkish seraglios. He was one of the first habitual takers of coffee in England, which he procured in Oxford from a Greek who found it more profitable than theology at Balliol.

Hyde and the two royal physicians were mounted and armed, but unarmoured, not expecting or prepared to take part in the fighting proper. In this situation, the closest he ever approached to active

---

\* One charming later story alleges that in 1632, while the court was at Newmarket, Dr Harvey investigated a nearby suspected, and self-confessed, witch, who trusted him as a fellow magus on account of his 'very magical face'. He then cleared her name, to her sorrow, by dissecting her tame toad and proving its anatomy to be bereft of magical properties.

military experience, Hyde is revealed to be held at a quite different, perhaps though not necessarily lesser, estimation to most of his closest contemporaries, friends, and acquaintances among both the Royalists – Falkland, Spencer, Digby, Verney, Lord Grandison, the nearby Earl of Dorset – and the Parliamentarians – Bulstrode Whitelocke, Lord Feilding, Essex himself, Holland, and Hampden. Social class was doubtless one element here; Whitelocke and Hampden, appointed captain and colonel respectively, were commoners by birth, but they served on the parliamentary side where noblemen were in shorter supply and were both important men of property, Whitelocke comfortably, Hampden spectacularly rich. Military experience, actual or pretended, also played some role in propelling gentlemen onto the battlefield. Whitelocke's entirely theoretical commission as a captain of French horse appears to have been good enough for many of his colleagues. Advanced age, physical fitness or lack of it, and political importance outside fighting, were acceptable excuses to avoid the dangers of battle, but often ones discarded by proud and hot-headed gentlemen, even those, like Whitelocke, who in political frays invariably advanced prudent, peaceful counsel.

Most decisive to the willingness of an English mid-seventeenth-century politician to serve or stand aside in genuine battle seems to have been each man's individual character and self-image. Like John Selden, Ned Hyde never pretended to play the fine gallant or the venturesome knight. He was aware of and self-deprecating about his short, paunchy, lawyerly, and soft-living frame. In wooing both of his wives Anne and Frances he had been cautiously pragmatic, despite experiencing, at least in the first case, profound feeling. In courtly exchanges with friends of both sexes that at times could resemble romantic flirtation, he exerted a primarily companionate, intellectual appeal. Bulstrode Whitelocke, despite (or because of) the physical impairment left by his undergraduate riding accident, was quite different in this respect, emphatically constructing himself as a chivalric, active, virile figure whenever he could, whether in recreation, courtship, or war.

Whitelocke, three weeks after Edgehill, was to join his remote kinsman Hampden's regiment as a volunteer, wielding a pike in person. Falkland, the Secretary of State, and Colepeper, the Chancellor of the Exchequer, rode respectively under the Commissary-General Henry Wilmot and Prince Rupert. But Hyde, still without any official post, stayed back in the peppery company of Dr Harvey, overseeing the frolics of the young Stuart princes, Charles and James. The boys were more excitable than the armies. After a phantom campaign, for most of the day the commanders proved reluctant to usher in reality. Parliament, and particularly its Lord General Essex, maintained the pretext that it merely fought the King's evil counsellors (among whom Hyde was now definitely numbered), while respecting Charles's person. Now its army was militarily obliged to fire not just on Royalist troops but the King himself.

A nervous morning gave way to an agonizingly uneventful afternoon. By about two o'clock on 23 October, Dr Harvey, losing patience, ushered his royal charges out of sight of friend and foe, 'under a hedge'. Taking a book 'out of his pocket' (John Aubrey says, recalling the doctor's account in the 1650s), Harvey began to read. The doctor's interests were dizzyingly wide enough to make the subject of his perusal on this most dramatic occasion a matter of obscure speculation: quite apart from natural philosophy, he was drawn to painting, ethics, politics, and distant foreign parts. Harvey had most recently, earlier that year, finished his treatise *De Insectis*, now left at his London lodgings; he mourned its later destruction by city looters above 'all the losses he sustained . . . no grief . . . so crucifying to him'. Later that year, amid all the confusion of Royalist Oxford as a wartime court and capital, Harvey happily busied himself with experiments in ornithology.

Whatever volume Dr Harvey had begun was soon by necessity laid aside. The Parliamentarians had at last overcome their legalistic scruples. '[Harvey] had not read very long, before a Bullet of a great Gun grazed on the ground near him, which made him remove his station.' Artillery fire was now exchanged ineffectively, if no doubt alarmingly, by both sides. An anonymous contemporary letter writer testifies that 'where his Majesty and his Children were, many shots fell very near his Royal Person'.

From their crest on the hill beside the King, Doctors Hinton and Harvey, together with Hyde, witnessed the opening Royalist cavalry charges, Rupert on the right flank first. Hyde's astute if not always amiable colleague Colepeper was among the Prince's officers, and the King's Life Guards moved to support him, with Lord Spencer, honoured friend and love rival of Great Tew companions, in their glittering ranks. Then on the left flank galloped Wilmot's horse, carrying with them Falkland, repository of Hyde's keenest affection and concern. From Bullet Hill the immediate outcomes must have been confusing, especially the defection of Sir Faithfull Fortescue's Anglo-Irish troop: a tactical and psychological coup that was effective but ill-managed, as many of the turncoat cavalrymen failed to discard Essex's tawny yellow or orange sash ensigns, and were immediately shot dead by their new Royalist comrades.

Victory seemed to be as suddenly, deliriously achieved as at Powicke Bridge, when sudden, real danger careered into confused sight. Almost all the Royalist cavalry, leaving only the King's fifty brave and doddery Pensioners, had galloped out of reach, pursuing the easy fruit of the routed; but not all the parliamentary horse had been driven from the field. Essex's reserve was under Sir William Balfour, a more competent Scottish professional than Sir James Ramsay, Whitelocke's hapless subsequent informant, well routed by Rupert on the left flank. Balfour's brigade was intact, ready to menace the Royalist foot, themselves still taking with less than entire ease to Rupert's and Ruthven's new Swedish-style dispositions.

The King soon realized the emergency and took it seriously. He decided himself, virtually unprotected, to advance to the lines of his foot soldiers and rally their spirits. Meanwhile he ordered Richmond and Dorset to take the fifty Pensioners and escort the princes to safety. Characteristically, Charles found his orders disregarded, if on this occasion for reasons of love and loyalty rather than suspicion and defiance. Neither Richmond nor Dorset was prepared to be called a coward by leaving the King (Richmond declined the errand with mild Stuart grace, while Dorset expressed himself with colour, refusing to stain his reputation for courage for 'any King's Sons in Christendom'). Many of the Pensioners also insisted on accompanying their King closer to rather than out of battlefield danger.

The gouty Dr Harvey appears to have been relieved of his royal responsibilities by this point; he is not heard of again until the battle's aftermath. But the accounts of Hyde and Hinton relate this unnerving phase of the action in interestingly contrasting versions. In a private letter Hyde states that he was trusted with Prince Charles's safety at this time with only the Pensioners under Sir William Howard as protection, bound for Arlescote House a couple of miles off, where the princes and Dr Harvey had spent the previous night. In his *History*, Hyde stresses the danger in which the princes, and indeed the King, were briefly placed (though, as is his frequent habit in the *History*, he effaces himself from the episode):

> And if [Balfour's] horse had bestirred themselves, they might with little difficulty [have] destroyed or taken prisoner the King himself, and his two sons . . . being with fewer than one hundred horse and those without officer or command, within half musket shot of that body [of parliamentary horse] before he suspected them to be enemies.

This version writes out the unfortunate Pensioner commander Howard and at least one other more junior, seemingly more effective, officer who would figure in Hinton's telling, as well as being more catastrophic about the King's possible capture or even death. Hyde's purpose here seems didactic, arguing how near Royalist carelessness came to making Edgehill not an indecisive muddle but an utter disaster, while keeping his own startling personal perspective concealed behind loftily stylistic impartiality.

The younger physician Hinton's testimony is more richly, indeed irresistibly detailed. Remarkably it entirely omits the presence of Hyde. According to this account, presented to the restored Charles II and apparently endorsed by both the returned young monarch and his brother the Duke of York, Hinton found himself in charge of the princes with only a handful of Pensioners, well under the full body of fifty. As they began to withdraw they were approached by what seemed to be a much larger group of cavalry; the little group assumed it to be Royalist (presumably imagining these were the rest of the errant Pensioners), but Sir William Howard sent Prince Charles's equerry, Sir Richard Graham, to check, whereupon Graham fell injured from an enemy shot. Clarendon's *Life*, composed a few years after Hinton's version, follows it closely but ignores Hinton himself just as Hinton had previously elided Hyde. Clarendon does add one detail so evocative as to seem authoritative, that the Prince's cunning equerry Graham feigned death so well that his 'corpse' was stripped.

As Hinton tells it, the princes' retinue now identified a certain barn as a temporary refuge from the suddenly appeared parliamentarian horse, only to discover it was in use as a Royalist field hospital. The barn later acquired the name of King's Leys, because of a later Victorian myth that King Charles had spent the night before battle there. Hinton describes next a scene of high drama, implicitly supported by the authority of Charles II and explicitly corroborated in the memoirs of James II. The Prince of Wales, apparently heedless of the situation's peril, cocked his pistol and waved it at the 'rogues' and 'rebels', crying 'I fear them not!' Hinton remonstrated with him as courtesy yielded to panic, then himself fended off one of Balfour's advance-guard with sword and pistol. The Parliamentarian's old-fashioned heavy cuirass proved impervious to either until a Welsh Royalist officer, Miles Matthews, settled the matter with a pole-axe.*

Edward Hyde, at the time of Hinton's telling Earl of Clarendon,

---

* What Matthews was doing there at all is another example of the day's mystery and muddle, and of the 'hurry and smoke' with which Whitelocke so aptly described military history. Matthews, no Gentleman Pensioner, was a tough young soldier destined to be court-martialled and shot on the orders of the future regicide Colonel Horton, six years and two English civil wars later.

Lord Chancellor, and chief minister, seems to have been content to let Hinton take all going credit. His personal correspondence alludes, with pride and defensiveness, to the great honour and severe difficulty of protecting the princes from the battle with so few and such elderly bodyguards. Either a shortage of instinctive soldierly prowess at the barn if he was still present – and he had been commanded to stay with the princes – or the gravity and nearness of the princes' capture, for which he might well have found himself bearing chief blame, may, separately or in some combination, have explained his reticence.

Hyde's Edgehill thus ended rather as his war had begun, with chaos, incompetence, emergency, and flight. He must have been surprised when, on being reunited after nightfall with his friends Digby, Grandison, Spencer, and Falkland, he was informed that the King had gained at least some kind of victory. Although Hyde's personal experience of the battle was topographically and psychologically particular, in the *History* he encompassed the wider field with remarkable clarity. Chance and their own devising had placed his friends at strategic points throughout the army; colleagues with whom he was soon to be long penned in a university city and a council chamber with much opportunity for reflection and reminiscence.

From Colepeper and Spencer, Falkland and Grandison, Hyde learned to deprecate Prince Rupert's ill-discipline and the prince and Wilmot's joint penchant for looting. He described Wilmot, whom like Digby, Hyde could not entirely help liking, often against his better judgement, as 'a man proud and ambitious, and incapable of being contented; an orderly officer in marches and governing his troops. He drank hard, and had a great power over all who did so, which was a great people.'

The bellicose Wilmot faced a relatively indifferent foe, Hyde's one-time friend Lord Feilding, latterly English resident at Venice, whose own father, the Earl of Denbigh, was an old soldier and Royalist riding beside Rupert. Feilding, like Ralph Verney, thus faced the moral discomfort of fighting against his own father, and in any case led cavalry objectively outdone in calibre. Oliver Cromwell (in charge of a regiment of parliamentary cavalry that arrived too late to affect events at Edgehill) contemptuously described the quality of his side's horse early in the civil war as 'old decayed serving men and tapsters', no match for the Royalist 'gentlemen's sons, younger sons and persons of quality'. Feilding's withdrawal was a measured response to his situation, arguably wiser in defeat than his riotous enemies in victory. Of the rampant Royalist cavalry commanders only Grandison kept good order, retrieving about 100 horsemen for further operations. He did his best to take this salvaged detachment back to the centre but found himself impeded by the torrent of parliamentary fugitives.

To the mounted minds of Rupert, Byron, Wilmot, and Digby the battle indeed seemed to be over; and as the royal foot advanced many of Parliament's infantry had appeared to agree with them, beginning to quit the field. But Essex's conduct as general had differed from the King's in some decisive respects. He was surrounded not by children, tutors, clergymen, doctors, and lawyers, but by a cadre of strong strategic advisors including Charles Fleetwood and Henry Ireton, pillars-to-be of the Cromwellian military establishment. Essex did not watch with distant alarm but himself ostentatiously carried a pike in amongst his men.

In the midst of Balfour's devastating counter-attack, Hyde identifies two intensely human set-pieces; the brisk tragedy of Sir Edmund Verney, the honourable doubter, killed defending the royal standard to the last; and the rough treatment of the former Royalist commander, Lord Lindsey, wronged by the brash young Prince Rupert, fighting in the front line of his foot, only to be captured along with his son, who surrendered to stay at his father's side.

Hyde next extracts a political moral from the regaining of Verney's lost banner by one of Grandison's officers, Captain John Smith. The division between Hyde and his more pacific Royalist friends on the one hand, and their enemies, whom Hyde dubbed in scorn the 'Swordmen' on the other, was perhaps best illustrated by the ambiguous stories that clustered around the taking and retaking of the standard. Sir Edmund Verney's desperate valour in protecting the banner was to become a martyr's cult to the credit of the peacemakers. It was widely noted that Verney had refused to wear armour, and had been protected for much of the battle only by the bravery of his devoted retainer, resonantly named Jason, whose killing Verney personally avenged before his own fall. According to Hyde and other sources that shared in his lack of enthusiasm for the war (including, from the notional opposing camp, Whitelocke), Captain Smith, a Catholic, then regained the banner by straightforward courage, discipline, and prowess in combat.

The counter-narrative from the Swordmen names the hero who recovered the banner as Sir Robert Welch. While looting the parliamentary baggage-train and capturing guns, he was said to have stumbled on the banner being ushered to Essex's rear for safekeeping, and to have recaptured it by the simple expedient of pretending to be a parliamentary officer. Welch was Irish, belligerent, blindly attached to Prince Rupert, and personally obnoxious. He would live on into the inglorious, quarrelsome poverty and exile the Royalists endured in the 1650s. Smith, though a Catholic, was because of his incontestable loyalty and immaculate conduct accepted as a kind of honorary lay hero of the Church of England; he also died heroically in battle in 1644. The King made both Welch and Smith knights bannerets and struck medals in their honour, so it seems probable that both men were considered at the time to have played some part in the feat of recapturing the royal banner.

The battle's casualties were about equal, though more famous names fell on the Royalist side (an inevitable consequence of the more aristocratic extraction of their officers and command). The King's army took the field and some of Parliament's guns. But Essex's army retired more or less intact, keeping prisoners including poor Lord Lindsey and his son, Lord Willoughby, and though they left a path clear by which the King might just have retaken his capital, it was soon closed off again. Royalist reactions to this 'victory' are telling. Hyde, whose duties up to this point might be best described as covering royal propaganda, did not rejoice at the outcome of Edgehill. For him, as for friends such as Spencer and Falkland in the same camp, or Whitelocke notionally among the enemy, the battle displayed the limits of the case for war, by proving the extreme unlikelihood – indeed, as Hyde and his friends privately considered, the undesirability – of a complete victory. Taking reinforcing arguments from the uncertainty of this first great encounter of the civil war, Hyde would mount renewed appeals to the King, as Whitelocke to the Parliament, for peace.

10.

# *Vulgar Intelligence, Vigorous Defence*

*Still pressing on, he gives nor time to breathe.*
*Nor gather strength: my powers my trust deceave.*

George Sandys, Book IX,
*Ovids Metamorphosis Englished*

## *'Free intercourse with all quarters' – After Edgehill: Edgcote, Aynho, Woodstock, Oxford, Late October 1642*

The miniature court's immediate refuge in the battle's aftermath was at Edgcote House, whither Hyde had been directed to spirit the princes from the field. Sir William Le Neve, Clarencieux King of Arms, was dispatched to deliver to Essex the King's proclamation, which was Hyde's work, offering, with very few exceptions, a general pardon for rebellion. Le Neve, brusquely received and forcibly blindfolded, returned with no news except that of the death, from untreated battle injuries, of the unfortunate, captured, wronged Lord Lindsey.\*

The body of that other Royalist victim Sir Edmund Verney, to the deep distress of his Parliamentarian son Sir Ralph, could not be recovered. Word of his ghost's vigil over the field of Edgehill soon spread. Meanwhile Prince Rupert, who had so nearly won and then almost lost the battle, conducted with redemptive industry a successful minor attack on the rear of Essex's army as it left Kineton. Essex was retreating to the safety of Warwick Castle, seat of the fierce Parliamentarian

---

\* Much Royalist blame fell on Essex for failing to have Lindsey, his own old friend and former battle companion, decently attended by physicians.

## Vulgar Intelligence, Vigorous Defence

Lord Brooke, on the advice of his seasoned mercenary advisors, foremost among them the Strasbourgeois professional soldier Jan Dalbier.

Dalbier had been paymaster in the army of Count Mansfeld, one of several doomed champions of Prince Rupert's own family cause in the Palatinate. By 1642 Dalbier was confined to the debtor's prison in Southwark, whence Essex liberated him in exchange for military service. Experienced and loyal to his benefactor, Dalbier was an obscure functionary in both English and continental terms, a cautious negotiator rather than a masterful leader.

Dalbier's wary disposition suited Essex's own slow, prudent, careful temperament, while irking Parliament's gentleman volunteer commanders: more newly minted in martial practice, but animated by greater idealism and pretending to superior flair. Several of these hotter-headed Parliamentarian leaders had arrived too late for Edgehill, including John Hampden, his cousin Oliver Cromwell, Denzil Holles, and Bulstrode Whitelocke's brother-in-law Lord Willoughby of Parham. Throughout the military disputes of the month following Edgehill, Whitelocke, eager for a swift end to the war either by treaty or victory (which side's victory for the present a secondary consideration), shared and echoed the opinions of other gently born 'amateur' soldiers. Whitelocke accordingly saw more method in the Royalist strategy at its most aggressively Rupertine than did his friend Hyde, who though within the Royalist camp was committed to its most conciliatory courses.

The little court at Edgcote, for all its state of belligerent, teeming, jumpy chaos, found momentary intellectual distraction in the scientific victory of the great Dr Harvey, a much more conclusive affair than Edgehill itself. As Aubrey tells it, Harvey attended to an elderly Royalist, Sir Gervase Scrope, who had been:

> ... dangerously wounded ... and left for dead amongst the dead men, stripped; which happened to be the saving of his life. It was cold, clear weather and a frost that night; which stopped his bleeding, and about midnight, or some hours after his hurt, he awaked ... fain to draw a dead body upon him for warmth's sake ...

The remarkably preserved Scrope, found by his son Adrian, a cavalry officer, had the good luck to be brought to the attention of Dr Harvey. The physician was certainly the most advanced practitioner on the treatment of bleeding, whose discoveries regarding the circulation of the blood, first published in 1628 but still not widely accepted fourteen years later, Scrope's case so amply demonstrated.

Hyde covers this episode in a higher, more Virgilian style. Just as he had emphasized the chivalrous duty and fall of Sir Edmund Verney, and the filial surrender of Lord Willoughby of Eresby to attend his stricken and captured father Lord Lindsey, so Hyde dwells upon both Scropes' motives of public feudal honour, and private familial love:

> Young Mr. Scroope [sic] brought off his father, Sir Gervase, who, being an old gentleman of great fortune in Lincolnshire, had raised a foot company among his tenants, and brought them into the earl of Lindsey's regiment, out of devotion and respect to his lordship as well as duty to the King; and had, about the time that the general [i.e. Lindsey] was taken, fallen with sixteen wounds in his body and head . . . had lain stripped among the dead, from . . . about three of the clock in the afternoon on Sunday . . . till Tuesday evening, for it was so late before his son found him; whom with great piety he carried to a warm lodging, and afterwards . . . to Oxford, where he wonderfully recovered.

This account in the *History* buttresses one of Hyde's constant themes – the natural order of society which, if universally and lawfully observed, would have prevented civil war in England. Sir Gervase Scrope becomes an exemplar of the same type as Sir Edmund Verney, a link in a golden chain extending from the King, through Lindsey and Hyde, to his Lincolnshire tenantry, representative of the true people of the so long peaceful kingdom. His story is associated with the tragic treatment of Lindsey, by the King's nephew Rupert on the one hand and by Lindsey's own old comrade turned opposite number Essex on the other. Lindsey's and Scrope's differing fates are connected by feudal and geographical bonds, as well as the model 'piety' of their sons.

On the other hand, Hyde diminishes the part of science, and indeed of Dr Harvey, whom he leaves unnamed, referring only to 'surgeons'. He attributes Scrope's survival more to miraculous 'wonder' than medical skill, both noting and exaggerating the wounded father's long exposure. Hyde juxtaposes the story with the less edifying end of another similarly stripped, tardily discovered Royalist officer, 'one Bellingham, of an ancient extraction in Sussex'. He was a young man, not an elderly squire, and 'the only son of his father', who though cured of most of his twenty seemingly 'mortal' wounds, succumbed by the 'negligence' of surgeons to 'a wound of his thigh, of itself not dangerous, undiscerned'. This inclusion, paired with the Scrope parable, is rich in metaphorical power – the life of an old family's sole heir squandered in the Royalist cause through inattention to a minor thigh wound (minor, perhaps, but also a traditional euphemism for a genital injury).

On 26 October the court left Edgcote for Aynho, a village with an equally convenient manor house and accommodating Royalist squire, crucially halfway to Oxford. From Aynho, Hyde drafted another emollient declaration in the King's name, pardoning all the citizens of London barring an excepted few Parliamentarian city officials. By this point Hyde probably shared this proclamation's magnanimous, buoyant spirit. The court's latest itinerary represented the triumph of the policy he preferred, also favoured by such pacifically inclined counsellors as Richmond, Dorset, Falkland, and most vocally, Digby's experienced, moderate, Hispanophile, diplomatic father, the Earl of Bristol. The relentless attack now advocated by Rupert, involving a sudden lightning attempt on the capital, with the impossibly dashing stated aim of capturing both Houses of Parliament, seemed by contrast to be firmly and permanently rejected by the King, once again in accordance with his Privy Counsellors' advice.

Hyde's communications with London were still excellent. Although no more of his correspondence with Whitelocke himself survives, postdating Hyde's departure to join the King, according to Whitelocke's journal they continued to exchange regular private letters through more than a year of the civil war in England. Whitelocke's fellow tenants in Ivy Lane, the Palmers and the Hales, were prominent, committed Royalists who saw no reason as yet to remove themselves from London (in fact Hale never did so throughout the civil wars). Through such channels, Hyde was well informed about the panic and confusion in the city following Edgehill, and reconstructed it in the *History* in his most astringently comic mode. Hyde here makes the all-important point, so hard to recapture or envisage for a posterity that defines the civil wars, if at all, by dichotomy and division, that 'so many persons who were present [at Edgehill] came to the town of both sides (for there was yet a free intercourse with all quarters)'.

Events rapidly appeared to justify the decision of the King and his counsellors to head for Oxford, not London. Parliamentarian Banbury not only surrendered but defected, its considerable garrison enlisting in the Royalist army. Broughton Castle, chief seat of Lord Saye, was easily taken by storm. Charles could enjoy both the discomfiture of this personal enemy (one shared, of course, with Saye's long-suffering subordinate Whitelocke) and the magnificence of Saye's Tudor fortification, whose hospitality and hunting his father had enjoyed in happier times.

After these promising developments Charles moved through Oxfordshire not as a war commander, but as a king on a progress through his own undisputed realm. He stopped in leisurely style at the royal manor of Woodstock, cosily referred to by Hyde as '[the King's] own house', before, on 29 October, making his splendid, victorious, fateful entrance into the university city which would ever after be associated with him in politics, sentiment, atmosphere, and romance.

Oxford at this moment, assuming its single most dramatic, definitive role in its long but generally sedentary history, was caught for posterity by Hyde:

> . . . the only city of England that [the King] could say was entirely at his devotion; where he was received by the university, (to whom the integrity and fidelity of that place is to be imputed,) with that joy and acclamation as Apollo should be by the Muses.

It is a description subtly aware of its internal contradictions. Like Whitelocke earlier that autumn, Hyde was all too conscious of town-gown divisions, suppressed by the temporary presence of a royal court and army. But in his concluding flourish he articulated clearly his own feelings at the court's safe arrival in the university city that he loved.

Hyde's undergraduate career had been shadowy and undistinguished, but the roots it had planted had sprouted with new vigour and delight among the 'liberal-minded', heterogeneous divines, amateurs, philosophers, and poets of Great Tew. At Oxford the King was safe physically, but also, to Hyde more importantly, Charles was politically, intellectually, spiritually, and humanly secure. With his Catholic consort far away in the Netherlands, the King was now surrounded by the best possible influences that Hyde, Falkland, and their friends, both of Great Tew and of the Royalist peace party, could possibly have envisaged or arranged.

After all the incongruous discomforts and dangers of an itinerant court and camp, at Oxford Hyde himself was back on territory he trusted and enjoyed. If he hailed the King, via the dons, as Apollo, he counted himself among the celebrating bookish Muses. Hyde felt relief and joy not just on the King's behalf but his own. He was, as of right, lodged and entertained, along with his wife and (for the moment) their children, by his old friend Gilbert Sheldon, Warden of All Souls. Hyde would later grumble about 'troublesome' and 'chargeable' dinners in cramped and expensive accommodation, but also remember with relish the hospitality and especially the venison of college banquets.

Although Oxford was, indeed, politically and personally sympathetic to him, neither did Hyde neglect its practical advantages as

## Friends in Youth

a prestigious and strategic base for the King's cause, of which Whitelocke had vainly warned Lord Saye. At Oxford the King:

> ... found himself at good ease ... care was taken for providing for the sick and wounded and for the accommodation of the army, which was in a short time recruited there in a good measure [such recruits included the main body of the undergraduates] ... the several colleges presented his majesty with ... a very seasonable supply [their plate they had largely sent already, but they could now offer their land rents].

Hyde combines the information he gained personally at Oxford with that of his London informants to make a crucial counterfactual argument. Prince Rupert's view was that by settling at Oxford rather than storming London, the Royalists were throwing away their best, perhaps their only, chance of victory; it has never entirely been rebutted. Hyde, on good and various authority, expressed in the *History* – first written, it should be recalled, in 1646 for the defeated and captive King's specific benefit – his belief in an entirely opposite squandered opportunity.

Considering the King's movements after Edgehill, his (as Hyde saw it) morally and strategically correct resort to Oxford, and his fatal departure from it a few days later, Hyde establishes one of his most important instances of peace with honour, needlessly forfeited:

> It had been very happy if the King had continued his resolution of sitting still during the winter ... for his reputation was now great, and his army believed to be much greater than it was, by the victory they had obtained ... the Parliament grew more divided into factions ... the city [of London] appeared fuller of discontent and less inclined to be imposed upon.

Such was the judgement to which the evidence of those Royalist-leaning sympathizers such as the Palmers, the Hales, and perhaps

## Vulgar Intelligence, Vigorous Defence

even of Bulstrode Whitelocke himself, had directed Hyde, when he contemplated the mood of the capital in its still hesitant rebellion. In London, Hyde accurately reported, to describe Edgehill as a royal victory had become punishable by imprisonment. This did not indicate much confidence within the narrow, endangered Pymite elite. Among the citizens, Hyde reckoned, 'nothing' was 'so generally spoken of, or wished for, as peace'. To contemplate Whitelocke's evenings spent among moderate, learned, Royalist old friends, or Milton's panic-stricken as much as Muse-inspired sonnet, is scarcely to disagree with the as yet still unofficial royal advisor's estimate.

'They who were really affected to the King, and from the beginning opposed all the extravagances (for of such there were many in both Houses who could not yet find in their hearts to leave the company) spake now aloud,' Hyde continues, evidently thinking, among others, of his old friend Whitelocke, who had regretfully declined to join Hyde and Palmer in leaving London for the King's service that spring. More scornfully, Hyde describes the states of mind of the unprincipled and the timorous: 'half-hearted and half-witted people . . . much the major part of both Houses, plainly discerned there must be a war, and that at least the King would be able to make resistance, which they had been promised he could not do'.

Only those radicals so deeply dyed by rebellion that they could hope for no forgiveness still refused to admit of peace: 'They . . . who had contrived the mischief . . . violently opposed all motions of this kind.'

Had Charles, Hyde argues in his *History* as he and others advised at the time, sat peacefully in his hastily assumed rooms of state at Christ Church, and rested there through the winter, in accordance with standard military doctrine, then he would have had a good chance of ending the war on advantageous terms with no further loss of his subjects' lives. Unfortunately for the King, for Hyde, and, according to this reasoning, for England, Prince Rupert was to prove himself not just a superbly unconventional soldier but an all-too persuasive nephew.

## 'Strange insolences and violences upon the country' – Abingdon, Aylesbury, Reading, Henley, Fawley Court, 29 October–Early November 1642

While the King settled into his most congenial replacement capital yet, thus accepting the cautious preferences of his council, his nephew was deliberately, determinedly, and for the most part successfully exceeding his orders. Abingdon, the market town a few miles south of Oxford, famous for religious non-conformists in whose defence Whitelocke, as the town's Recorder, had played a steadfast part in the 1630s, was a natural enough target for the ascendant Royalists making sure of the university city they now claimed as their base. Aylesbury, further off into the more Parliamentarian east, was more of a stretch. Here Rupert's horse met with a rebuke around 1 November, defeated in a skirmish at the Tudor-built Holman's Bridge principally by the 'care and stoutness' of one of Whitelocke's maternal first cousins, Colonel Henry Bulstrode.

Haughtily insubordinate, Rupert undermined his uncle's clearly intended strategy, continuing the ruthless advance of his cavalry on the road to London. Whitelocke, who had responsibility for and an interest in this part of England both as a Deputy Lieutenant and in his considerable private position as a local landowner, wrote that the prince 'ranged abroad with great parties, who committed strange insolences and violences upon the country'.

These were '*strange* insolences' because Rupert was a foreigner, schooled in continental religious warfare already notorious for its cruelty. The German prince carelessly blackened his name in the earliest stages of civil war by trying, to his uncle's horror, to extract protection money from the Mayor of Leicester. His name was often anglicized to 'Prince Robert', to Parliamentarians a larcenous pun. However 'strange' by birth, Rupert was sufficiently exalted in rank, certainly in his own opinion, to circumvent his uncle's will when it suited him; a devoted volunteer and kinsman, but no subject.

He seemed to fight as much to redeem his family's misfortunes and his own impetuously mixed military record as to serve his uncle's political interest. To English observers including Falkland and Hyde quite as much as Whitelocke (indeed more so, within the grating proximity of shared royal councils), the charge of 'insolence' seemed all too apt.

But Whitelocke had a particular, intimate 'insolence' in mind: the outrage, as he clearly, lastingly felt it to be, perpetrated by freebooting Rupertine horse upon his own principal country seat, Fawley Court. In July 1642, striving his utmost to avert already inevitable civil war, Whitelocke had warned the Commons that in the event of internecine fighting in England between Parliament and King, 'We must surrender up our laws, liberties, properties and lives into the hands of insolent mercenaries, whose rage and violence will command us, and all we have'. Early that November, Whitelocke's melancholy prophecy was to materialize on his own estates.

Considering this new advance towards the capital, one that seemed to defy the King's recent decision to remain at Oxford, Hyde and Whitelocke revealingly diverge in their assessment of both Rupert's and the King's motives and judgement. For Hyde what followed was the unhappy result of poor discipline, on both sides, and an incongruously pleasant wartime autumn:

> . . . the weather growing fair again, as it often is about All Hallow's Tide [1 November], and a good party of horse having been sent out from Abingdon, where the head-quarter of the horse was, they advanced farther than they had order to do, and upon their approach to Reading, where Harry Marten was governor for the Parliament, there was a great terror seized upon [the Parliamentarians], insomuch as governor and garrison fled to London, and left the place to the party of horse, which gave advertisement to the King that all fled before them, that . . . Essex remained still at Warwick . . . and that there were so great divisions in the Parliament that, upon his majesty's approach, they would all fly, and that nothing could interrupt him from going to Whitehall . . . Reading itself was so good a post

that, if the King should find it necessary to make his own residence in Oxford, it would be much the better by having a garrison at Reading.

Upon these and other motives, besides the natural credulity in all men in believing all they wish to be true, the King was prevailed with to march with his army to Reading . . .

Hyde sees the cavalry as characteristically unruly, the King as misled by over-optimistic intelligence and delusive inward hopes. Whitelocke puts a quite different emphasis upon Charles's fresh attack: 'The king takes a resolution, *and not without grounds of reason*, to advance to London, and all his army marcheth to Reading, Henley, and those parts.'

While Hyde allows for the existence of comprehensible military reasoning for the advance, he then dismisses it as profoundly misguided: unsurprisingly, as the new dispositions overturned the policy of continuing quiet at Oxford that he and his political allies were urging at the time. Whitelocke, on the other hand, representing, perhaps, the opinions both of his fearful parliamentary colleagues and of his eager Royalist friends and co-residents at Ivy Lane, appears to have seen the King's renewed aggression as a potentially effective strategy.

Whatever his opinion of the Royalists' tactical soundness, morally and personally Whitelocke was deeply aggrieved and alienated by what followed at Fawley Court. Despite an impressively achieved high tone of impartial national concern, both in his private journal and in his more publicly polished *Memorials*, Whitelocke would never forget nor entirely forgive this scene of brigandage. The raid violated his property, purse, and pride, most of all the precarious balance of his political near-impartiality up to this point.

As Whitelocke relates in the *Memorials*, his later, more detailed, detached account of the incident:

Prince Rupert's brigade quartered at Henley, and of them a regiment of horse at my house at Fawley Court . . . Sir John Byron and his brothers commanded those horse, and gave order that they should commit no insolence at my house, nor plunder my goods . . .

This time the 'insolence' is blamed not on a royal, albeit foreign, commander, but on the more conventional target of his riotous troops. Yet Prince Rupert is not far behind, geographically or morally; he is contrasted with his more gentlemanly English officers, the Byron brothers, and evoked in the very word 'plunder', which in 1640s England was a neologism spread about by Rupert's deeds, both those remembered from the past, and experienced in the present. To both 'plunder' and 'insolence' Whitelocke returns with a vivid description:

. . . but soldiers are not easily governed against their plunder, or persuaded to restrain it; for there being about 1000 of the king's horse quartered in and about the house, and none but servants there, there was no insolence or outrage usually committed by common soldiers on a reputed enemy which was omitted by those brutish fellows at my house. There they had their whores with them, they spent and consumed 100 load of corn and hay, littered their horses with sheaves of good wheat, and gave them all sorts of corn in the straw: divers writing of consequence, and books which were left in my study, some of them they tore in pieces, others they burnt to light their tobacco, and some they carried away with them, to my extreme great loss and prejudice, in wanting the writings of my estate, and losing very many excellent manuscripts of my father's and others, and some of my own labours.

They broke down my park pales, killed most of my deer, though rascal and carrion, and let out all the rest, only a tame young stag they carried away and presented to prince Rupert, and my hounds, which were extraordinary good. They eat and drank up all that the house could afford; broke up all trucks, chests, and places; and where they found any linen or any household stuff they took it away with them, and cutting the beds, let out the feathers, and took away the ticks. They likewise carried away my coach, and four good horses,

*Friends in Youth*

and all my saddle horses, and did all the mischief and spoil that malice and enmity could provoke barbarous mercenaries to commit, and so they parted.

This is remembered only to raise a constant hatred of any thing that may in the least tend to the fomenting of such unhappiness and misery.

More than one Whitelocke is discernible in this most consciously composed tragic aria: one humanly sympathetic, one pompous and unintentionally comical, with both moods often present at the same time. There is the careful well-to-do landowner and prudent steward, preoccupied with the extent of his losses both in the quantity stolen and the severity of damage inflicted. There is the prosperous countryman, horrified at 'sheaves of good wheat' going to waste under the steaming flanks and ordure of military mounts. As the study doors are torn down we meet still more intimate, inward, and cerebral Whitelockes, the bibliophile, the proud amateur historian, even the devotedly memorializing son – but also the man of affairs still, 'wanting the writings of my estate'. If there is some amusingly injured immodesty in Whitelocke's grief for 'some of my own labours', its hurt pride is justified by the immediacy of the account: the same sense of loss shared by Dr Harvey, with his vanished entomological treatise.

The study once reduced to ashes, the soldiers and the reader proceed back outside, to the lament of Whitelocke the sportsman of considerable but not unlimited means. As with the good wheat plundered to feed the soldiers' horses, the overwhelming sensation evoked by Whitelocke is one of waste – the butchered deer, 'rascal and carrion', too young and too old, are not even fit for feasts. Whitelocke's seemly social humility is poignantly discarded as he assesses his lost kennels, every English country squire's pride, 'extraordinary good'. The loss of his coach and horses, an indispensably efficient means of travel, and an all but irreplaceable symbol of the high rank of a family and a professional's standing, was a true material setback that would soon oblige Whitelocke to contract politically revealing debts. In the 'tame young stag' presented to Prince Rupert, and, by implication, by no means declined, its thieves congratulated rather than reprimanded, Whitelocke elegantly describes, without direct bitterness, the continuing object of his real anger. The implication is that the prince, over the heads of the Byrons, not only allowed the spoliation at Fawley Court by his over-lenient treatment of ill-disciplined troops, but even encouraged it.

Behind these furious particulars, remembered for twenty years and carefully detailed in the Restoration while their princely perpetrator luxuriated in glory as the young Charles II's cousin and the country's most famous war hero, there lies Whitelocke's more significant, deeper general sense of shock and injustice.\* He acknowledges that the soldiers' pillage and destruction would have been sadly expected, 'usually committed by common soldiers upon a reputed enemy' – but he did not at this time regard himself as in any just sense the King's 'reputed enemy'. He had warned in July that with civil war would come the depredations of 'insolent mercenaries', and in his outcry over Fawley Court he states that Rupert's men equalled the worst that could be feared of 'barbarous mercenaries' – but his real sense of betrayed disgust lay in the fact that the Royalist horse themselves, unlike their prince, did not even have the excuse of being 'barbarous', or foreign. Undivided from their victims by birth or tongue, these were not mercenaries fighting for gain in a strange country, but native troops raised with undoubtedly traditional, if legally contested, authority by the King of England.

---

\* One of the mid-century's myriad oddities of political upheaval and reaction saw Whitelocke's eventual replacement, as Governor of Windsor Castle under the Commonwealth, by none other than his one-time plunderer, Prince Rupert, as the Castle's longest-presiding Restoration Constable. Whitelocke could not afford to express his old grudge in public at this time, and at Charles II's request he assisted Rupert with extensive advice on running the castle. Indeed this is one of the few acknowledgements by the restored monarchy of Whitelocke's service in any capacity. His journal and memoirs preserve Whitelocke's truer, unchanged feelings towards Rupert.

With conscientious attention (and political adaptability) Whitelocke would be as exact in recalling the looting, damage, and injustice caused by Parliamentarian troops in the years to come (especially, naturally, against his own property). His parting conclusion of 'constant hatred' of such unnecessary wartime disorder and suffering may be well-judged in its cautious non-partisanship – but it also rings absolutely true.

Next came what was nearly far worse even than the emptying and gutting of a substantial squirearchical dynasty's principal country house. In a Saturnalian reversal of peacetime domesticity, while the troopers ransacked the manor house at Fawley one of their captains, Sir Thomas Byron, chose one of the more substantial tenant's cottages as his personal billet, and happened to light on the residence of William Cooke, where Whitelocke's five youngest children were hidden. That this was a complete coincidence seems open to question, especially as Byron immediately showed a close interest in the six-year-old boy and four little girls, refusing to be deflected when Cooke loyally claimed them as his own grandchildren. Sir Thomas did not know either Bulstrode or Frances Whitelocke personally and could hardly have detected a resemblance. At any rate the children themselves, unused to such dangerous theatricals, did not succeed in passing convincingly as tenantry of tender years and soon admitted their true identities to the occupying officer, begging him for protection, or mercy.

Byron's reply was outwardly reassuring, though it bears a slightly menacing undertone in Whitelocke's recollection – 'it were a barbarous thing to hurt those pretty innocent children'. Whitelocke sincerely commends Byron's 'great generosity', adding that he 'kissed and made much of' the five children, but the proximity of the 'barbarous' deeds of Byron's soldiers at Fawley Court (admittedly against the Byron brothers' orders, and clearly beyond their patchy control) makes the scene an uncomfortable moment of atrocity only narrowly averted. Sir Thomas had saved the life of Whitelocke's Royalist maternal cousin, Captain Richard Bulstrode, at Edgehill, shooting dead a Parliamentarian infantryman about to pole-axe him from the saddle. Captain Bulstrode was a loose talker, the son of Edward Bulstrode, one of the most staid, politically inactive and trusted of Whitelocke's mother's brothers. It seems at least possible that Whitelocke confided in his uncle Edward about the details of his family's wartime disposal, that Edward Bulstrode let this slip to his Royalist son, and that the garrulous Captain Bulstrode, given the opportunity, urged the preserver of his life to act quickly to ensure the safety of his little cousins, a successful if briefly nerve-wracking family arrangement across the still very permeable lines of the civil war.*

## 'Alarum quickly came to London' – Cranbourne Chase, Colnbrook, Brentford, Chelsea, Hammersmith, 1–12 November 1642

Despite the fact that he evidently disagreed with and disapproved of the latest royal dispositions on both military and political grounds, Hyde could not in the *History* altogether suppress his ironical enjoyment at the Parliamentarians, who had outlawed him and persecuted his party, tasting discomfort on their own territory. Doubtless he would have regretted the destruction done at his old friend's country house, but, bearing in mind Whitelocke's share of responsibility,

---

* Sir Thomas Byron's discovery of Bulstrode Whitelocke's children at William Cooke's house has been occasionally argued, on fairly slender evidence, to have inspired William Frederick Yeames's 1878 historical painting, *And When Did You Last See Your Father?* The painting reveals its Romantic sympathies by inverting the parties of the aggressors and the interrogated, appearing to show a Royalist boy in archetypally van Dyckian garb being cross-examined by Puritan officials and guarded by Roundhead soldiers. There is some suggestion that Yeames may have simply misunderstood Whitelocke's allegiance, an interesting lingering legacy of the political ambiguity Whitelocke struggled, eventually in vain, to keep intact. The painting, a representative artefact of the popularly understood Cavalier/Roundhead dichotomy, thus inadvertently demonstrates the greater cultural and social fluidity of the two parties during the actual civil wars.

however reluctantly borne, for the Parliament's intransigence, such regret was not perhaps profound. Hyde would later diagnose Whitelocke's entire civil-war stance as motivated by solicitude for his large estate, considering that Whitelocke was to the legal profession and the county gentry what Lord Pembroke, who had been Hyde's patron just as Whitelocke had been Hyde's companion, was to the great nobility; a cautious timeserver who, despite his innate loyalty to the established order, had all too much to lose materially by proper adherence to the King's authority. If Hyde had at all in mind the damage done to Whitelocke's property, it did not diminish his broader *Schadenfreude*: 'This alarum quickly came to London ... received with deepest horror ... Whilst the King was at Nottingham ... [the Parliament] gave orders magisterially for war; but now it was come to their own doors, they took not that delight in it.'

Hyde's Wiltshire patrimony at Purton was at this point as exposed as Fawley Court, with parliamentary forces at nearby Malmesbury. Hyde does not, unlike Whitelocke, employ his private estate as a microcosmic image of the country's tribulations. Nor did he consider the Hyde cadet branch 'College Farm' property at Purton a reliable wartime redoubt for his family, which like Whitelocke's now divided for greater safety.

While Frances Hyde stayed beside her husband at Oxford, their children Anne (named for Hyde's ever-remembered first wife Anne Ayliffe), Henry (his Hyde grandfather's namesake), and Lawrence, still only one year old, were sent to their maternal grandfather, Sir Thomas Aylesbury, in what might at first glance have seemed to be the lion's den. Sir Thomas, deprived by Parliament of the Mastership of the Mint, was still by royal appointment Keeper of Cranbourne Chase in Windsor Forest. He was also generally liked and respected on every hand, especially as a renowned patron of mathematics. Hyde seems to have assumed that Cranbourne Lodge, his father-in-law's country retreat held for life as Keeper, would be left an inviolate refuge by both sides in the civil war, a guess that proved correct for a remarkably, tellingly long seven years, until the reign's abrupt end in 1649 changed both Windsor and the world. In this lovely green-swathed Tudor tower-house Anne, Henry, and Lawrence, respectively destined to become Duchess of York, Lord-Lieutenant of Ireland, and First Lord of the Treasury, spent their formative years peacefully swaddled in the heart of a country at war with itself.*

In November 1642, though, the war came all too close even to the green environs of Windsor. On the 3rd the King halted at Colnbrook, a few miles south-east of Slough, nearer the ultimate prize of London, but 'not so convenient' a courtly post as Reading. One of Colnbrook's superfluity of coaching inns, 'The Catherine Wheel', offered the King and his nephew the most regal lodging going; it had been standing at least since the reign of Charles and Rupert's Yorkist ancestor Edward IV, and had later accommodated Edward's grandson Henry VIII. Here uncle and nephew received the anxious messenger of an increasingly panicked Parliament, treating with Charles 'to desire him to advance no further before [Parliament] sent persons to treat with him, which they were ready to do'.

Parliament's anxiety was heightened owing to the continued absence of the Earl of Essex's army at Coventry. There the Lord General was fully occupied, endeavouring, with necessary tact and care, to rally hundreds of absent troops without damning them as deserters. For the moment Rupert's high-stakes, headlong advance had succeeded, despite the misgivings of Hyde and others, in springing the royal army between the rebellious capital and its would-be defenders.

Neither side was willing to forgo the uses of ambiguity. Charles received Parliament's message with the charm and courtesy he commanded when he chose. As Clarendon's *Life* recalls, '[the King] did return such an answer as made them believe that he would

---

* Their eviction, when it came at last by Oliver Cromwell's order seven years later, would be, by a peculiarly mocking quirk of fate, in favour of their father's old friend's eldest son and heir, Captain James Whitelocke, the boy Ned Hyde had called his 'little friend' now grown to martial, high-spending manhood.

expect them there [i.e. at Colnbrook] without moving nearer towards London'. At the same time the King delicately quibbled with the membership of the delegation that Parliament proposed to send him, objecting especially to the MP Sir John Evelyn, whom he had exempted from pardon as a declared traitor. Parliament then for its part questioned whether any man sent in Evelyn's place would be sheltered by a royal safe conduct. It suited both parties, the King's Council not wholly confident, the Parliament not entirely abject, to conduct preliminary discussions whose legitimacy could be dismissed at any moment.

Parliament did not rely on the King's receptiveness even in this relatively desperate hour, waiting for the return of the Earl of Essex, while simultaneously pleading for speedy aid from the still officially neutral Covenanters in Scotland. The King, meanwhile, offered to reside closer to London throughout formal peace negotiations, naming his own royal castle of Windsor as his base, or, in fact, his price; for Windsor was currently in the hands of Parliamentarian townsmen under the hot Pymite governor, merchant, and City of London MP, Colonel John Venn, another rebel excluded by the King from any peace treaty. In the *Life*, Clarendon retrospectively and startlingly expresses complete confidence that:

> ... if [Charles] had then stopped any further advance, and ... upon that address retired to his castle at Windsor, it would have been delivered to him ... being possessed of so considerable a place, the treaty would very probably have been concluded with good success.

Writing earlier in the *History*, Hyde was less definite as to the likelihood of Parliament ever really surrendering Windsor, but thought the gain, however unlikely, worth the game. Whitelocke agrees that the handing over of Windsor was to be effected 'that the treaty might be speeded'. This, following Charles's continued stay at Oxford after Edgehill, was for Hyde and his friends (in both camps) the King's second bloodless, pacific, golden opportunity for a constructive, if not – by the most fire-eating Royalist standards – a wholly victorious peace. It was a chance destined in the event to be squandered, like the first, by the counsel and agency of Prince Rupert.

In fact, the promise of this slender, precarious hour was disregarded by the dominant influences on both sides. As Hyde relates in the *History*, Parliament interpreted the wrangling over Sir John Evelyn's status as a peace negotiator as the 'highest breach' of its privilege, repeating the high-tempered language it had employed over the King's great original sin, the attempted arrest of the Five Members at the start of the year. 'All discourse of peace' was 'waived' by 7 November, the fifth day of the King's stay at Colnbrook, for two pressing reasons.

The Earl of Essex had reconstituted his army sufficiently to respond to Parliament's anxious enquiries, even if the resulting force was described by a waspish Hyde as 'not answerable' to its reputation. Marching from Coventry, he entered London as the popular saviour both of the capital and Parliament, immediately and wholeheartedly voted a gratuity of £5,000 by the thinly populated, greatly relieved Houses of Parliament. On the same day, the King permitted his impatient nephew to make an attempt on the prize that Parliament had failed to deliver. Rupert smashed his forces in vain against Windsor Castle, bombarding the town and driving many citizens into the royal forest.

In the *History*, Hyde calls the prince at this time 'exalted with the terror his name gave'. According to a parliamentary newsletter, 'Prince Robert's' desperadoes begged him not to waste their strength against 'stone walls, rocks and inaccessible places, where a hundred men might keep out ten thousand, all valour being useless'. The assault achieved nothing except to undermine the King's credibility at the latest talks. These had been conducted not in Colnbrook, but in slightly more commodious lodgings at Slough, further removed from London, an attempt to reassure the Parliamentarians that Rupert's battering of Windsor Castle promptly negated.

Nonetheless, when Parliament's negotiators, predominant among them the great, proud, and ambivalent Earl of Northumberland and Hyde's old patron Pembroke, at last left the doubtful delights of Colnbrook's inns on 11 November, Hyde reckoned they had reasons, some rational, some self-interested, for optimism. The trivial objection over the royal safe-conduct of Evelyn's notional replacement had been resolved with surprising logic by not replacing Evelyn at all. As for the rest of Parliament's peacemakers:

> ... those lords who had been with the petition [Northumberland and Pembroke], and some others, who thought themselves as much overshadowed by the greatness of the earl of Essex and chief officers of the army as they could be by the glory of any favourite or power of any counsellors, were resolved to merit as much as they could of the King by advancing an honourable peace.

Northumberland and Pembroke both knew the King as well as Hyde, intimately. Hyde thought them, from the beginnings of their careers in political opposition, motivated by positive ambitions and negative slights, rather than principled ideals. He maintained the consistent hope of gaining Northumberland as an active partisan for the King's party, while he no more viewed Pembroke as a real opponent than he did his old friend Whitelocke.

Although, at least when he wrote this first part of the *History* (if not later, when he came to write the *Life*), Hyde doubted whether the parliamentary earls could ever have made good their intentions about Windsor Castle, let alone wider peace, he had little or no doubt that such *were* their true and genuine intentions. Pembroke, after all, that pillar of the existing hierarchy, was – Hyde never lets his readers forget – entirely consumed by his understandable, if pusillanimous, concern to keep the great house of Wilton in his family. What could be more natural for such a man than to facilitate the return of one of the kingdom's most ancient royal castles to its rightful owner? But that owner's unleashing of his young, penniless, bellicose foreign nephew on the property in question had already done much harm, and at dawn on 12 November much worse was to come.

## Vulgar Intelligence, Vigorous Defence

As Hyde expressed it in the *History*, the King, left to his own devices, would surely have preferred to cooperate with the parliamentary grandees, greatly to his own benefit:

> If from thence [Slough] the King had drawn back again to Reading, relying on a treaty for the rest, it is probable his power would have been more valued . . . sure the King resolved to have done so, or at least to have stayed at Colnbrook . . . till he heard again from the Parliament.

Hyde's most critical point here is that the King's army, even more than Essex's half-defeated, hastily reassembled force, was in truth very far from all it was reported to be, and would have gained the dignity of mystery from keeping a well-maintained, safe distance.

But if Charles really 'resolved' to revert to this strategy, like many of his most reasonable resolutions it proved of fleeting durability. Prince Rupert, Hyde laments in the *History*, was operating on the basis of more bullish advice:

> [The Prince], trusting too much to the vulgar intelligence every man received from his friends in London . . . according to their own passions and the affections of those with whom they corresponded, concluded that the King had so great a party in London that if his army drew near no resistance would be made.

This 'vulgar intelligence', advice, Hyde adds, from 'unskilful persons', is another revealing glimpse of how constant and intact communication across the supposed divisions of civil war still remained. Hyde's closest friend within the city walls and the Parliament chamber, Whitelocke, suggests that the prince, or his informants, might not even have been entirely mistaken in their military strategy. Where Rupert, as usual, erred was not in tactics, but timing and tact. If Essex's army had still been farther off, if feelings had not already been heightened and embittered by unnecessarily 'Robertian' continental-style looting, perhaps the body of Royalist opinion that persisted in the capital (notably in Whitelocke's own Ivy Lane lodgings) would have been in a stronger position to assist the King.

It was the town of Brentford that would suffer for Prince Rupert's return to ascendancy in the Royalist councils of war. Brentford was the site of a legendary battle, formative to English identity, between Julius Caesar and King Cassivellaunus. Its Parliamentarian garrison consisted of two foot regiments. One had been raised by Denzil Holles, a complex figure: one of the Five Members, Strafford's inimical then merciful brother-in-law, future leader of Parliament's peace party alongside the very different figure of Whitelocke. The second was that of Robert, Lord Brooke, the enormously rich peer who was, alongside Lord Saye and his son Nathaniel Fiennes, the most fiercely anti-episcopal, belligerent voice in Parliament.

Neither Holles nor Brooke led their men in person on 12 November, being detained by Parliament, whose deliberations were edging in the direction of peace. Holles already inclined towards a settlement, while Brooke passionately and influentially favoured a continuation of the war. One officer who was, however, present at Brentford was Captain 'Freeborn' John Lilburne, a famous pamphleteer whose demagogic success had all but overshadowed William Prynne's. That morning Lilburne was attached to Brooke's infantry regiment, coated in princely purple, while Holles's men were in scarlet. Their mood on the 11th, what would transpire to be the eve of the battle, had been greatly lifted by the passage through Brentford of the Earl of Northumberland, open-handed and sanguine about imminent peace.

The town that Holles and Brooke guarded was unkempt but far from dour, famous, like Colnbrook, for inns, and studded with brothels besides. Brentford's most eminent innkeepers, John Lowin and Joseph Taylor, joint publicans of the 'Three Pigeons' or 'Doves', had small reason to love the soldiers of Parliament. Dilapidated former actors, as young men they had adorned Shakespeare's own company, the King's Men. Their long and glorious careers had been finally curtailed at Parliament's closure of the theatres in

## Vulgar Intelligence, Vigorous Defence

September. Lowin was an early performer of that Shakespeare role most widely loved by the playwright's contemporaries, Sir John Falstaff, who at one point in *The Merry Wives of Windsor* is persuaded to disguise himself as 'the witch of Brentford'. Taylor, who had succeeded Richard Burbage as the leading actor of the King's Men, was claimed as a personal acquaintance by the bookish, spendthrift 1st Viscount Falkland, scribbling in the Cary family's edition of the First Folio.

Whether he expressed his sincere opinion or laboured to shield the King's honour, in the *History* Hyde attributed the initiative for leading the Royalist horse upon Brentford to Prince Rupert alone, furthermore charging him with implicit tactical blackmail: 'without any direction from the King [Rupert] advanced, then sent to the King to desire him that the army might march after'. Had the King declined now to support his nephew, the horse were over-extended and the crucial royal superiority in cavalry would have been needlessly and dangerously placed at risk. In the fast-moving chaos of the campaign, chivalry and pragmatism seemed alike to urge Charles's next step: 'All things were in a hurry, and the horse [this might as well read 'Rupert'] still engaged the King to follow, so that he advanced with the whole army.' Hyde thus presents the King's yielding to Rupert as both understandable and disastrous. The conditions of the King's decision were more passive than active, rushed through and unconsidered. There was:

> . . . great oversight in making so great haste; all thoughts of a treaty were dashed; they who most desired it did not desire to be in the King's mercy . . . [they] now believed, by his majesty's making so much haste towards them after their offer of a treaty, that he meant to have surprised and taken vengeance of them without distinction. All people prepared for a vigorous defence . . .

Prince Rupert had apparently believed his advance would encourage enthusiastic participation by Royalist sympathizers within the city. But Hyde had greater personal understanding of the mentalities and politics of both sides, as well as of the stubbornly ambiguous and unaligned. He knew much of, still heard much from, Parliament's and London's natural peace party, unradical potential Royalists by preference, of whom his friend Whitelocke, Whitelocke's fellow tenant Matthew Hale, and John Selden, mentor of all three, were all outstanding examples. Hyde held with justifiable certainty that Rupert's course of action was the surest way of forcing such valuable friends, his own and Falkland's closest ideological counterparts, into active opposition to the King.

Before they had knowledge of the attack, Parliament ordered a suspension of hostilities and sent to the King hoping for similar restraint from his side. In the event their messenger proved unable to cross the renewed battle lines. As the royal army drew up on Hounslow Heath, a pair of Parliamentarian prisoners claimed to have observed the King and Prince Rupert in close conversation, the younger man looking in an ugly temper, though he had unquestionably once again got his way. Heavy morning fog enabled the Royalist horse to take the Brentford garrison almost by surprise, the King's forces having been first spotted only half a mile away.

Both sides deliberately posted to the hottest area of fighting those officers and troops who had underperformed at Edgehill, whether imposing a punishment, following military expediency given such soldiers' relative freshness, or offering a chance for redemption. The commander of the Royalist Welsh infantry, Sir Thomas Salisbury, told his poorly armed men curtly before battle, 'you lost your honour at Edgehill. I hope you will regain it here.' They soon did. Among the first Parliamentarians to flee were some inadequate cavalry under Captain Robert Vivers, who according to Nathaniel Fiennes had also been one of the first fugitives from Edgehill (Fiennes's own war record would prove little better). Vivers did not escape this time, becoming the day's first captive of rank. He was soon eclipsed by the second. As first Holles' then Brooke's foot regiments gave way, Captain John Lilburne, with William Prynne the Royalists' most prominent authorial adversary, was also taken prisoner.

Hampden's foot regiment, hastily sent for and newly arrived to reinforce the defence, covered the retreat of some Parliamentarian infantry. Many, less fortunate, were recorded in Whitelocke's account as 'divers driven into the river and drowned'. A Royalist officer, Matthew Smallwood, said these 'poor men', numbering about two hundred, had chosen their own miserable fate: 'What was most pitiful was to see how many . . . lost their lives striving to save them, for they ran into the Thames.'

The Royalists captured fifteen guns, eleven colours, and 500 prisoners including Lilburne, who alone was worth perhaps another 500 in propaganda value. The captured Parliamentarians were stuffed for the time being in the town's cattle pound. The victorious Royalist troops proceeded at Prince Rupert's direct order thoroughly to sack the town. Civilian casualties were few, yet England had not tasted such pillage in living memory, and it was easy for word to spread confirming the malpractices of the foreign robber prince. Whitelocke as so often provides a barometer of well-informed opinion. By evening, after the news had suffused the capital, he was appointed to a deputation urging the Lord Mayor to mobilize the Trained Bands, in reality London's scarcely trained reservists, in the city's urgent defence. In Parliament, Rupert's coup was spoken of as a 'bloody and treacherous design'. The prince's achievement at Brentford had been to carry off in miniature what he had hoped to inflict upon London itself after Edgehill. There could in fact have been no more perfect nor conspicuous method of uniting and galvanizing the capital against the King.

## 'Battalia' – The City, Chelsea Field, Turnham Green, Acton, Oxford, 12–13 November 1642

Bulstrode Whitelocke's *Memorials* describe the city on the night of 12 November as altered out of its familiar shape, cast by the confusion into 'much trouble and different appearance'. The atmosphere was, however, steadied by the 'resolution' of the determined and

## Friends in Youth

godly Lord Mayor, Isaac Penington, who had replaced the Royalist Sir Richard Gurney in August. Penington had sat in the Short Parliament and been elected to the Long Parliament, in both cases for the City of London; he held a colonelcy in the Trained Bands now being so urgently marshalled in response to the pleas of the Commons. Like Governor Venn at Windsor Castle, Penington was one of the select few excluded by the King from pardon in the event of peace. If his militarism was partly self-interested, it was nonetheless sincere.

Under Penington's influence the capital gave its consent to the calling out of the Trained Bands under officers nominated by Parliament. The chief command was allotted to the professional soldier and amateur devotional writer Sir Philip Skippon, in his early forties but with an older, more fatherly air, courageous, cheerful, knowledgeably attuned to soldierly psychology, with all the unflappability of eighteen years' doubtfully successful, unwaveringly dutiful service to the Protestant continental cause. His was an indispensable ballast to Parliament's aristocratic commanders, the morose, stolid Earl of Essex and his cousin, the charming popinjay Lord Holland. In a strategic landscape populated by excitable amateurs and cautious mercenaries, answering to ambitious, careful politicians of the great nobility, Skippon was the nearest thing to a man who both knew what he was doing and did it with enthusiasm.

Skippon's fighting spirit swept up even the hitherto torn and prudent Whitelocke. On the morning of 13 November, as Captain-General of the Trained Bands, Skippon drew up six regiments on the lush meadows of Chelsea, in rendezvous with Essex's weathered ranks, the warriors, if not quite victors, of Edgehill. The new combined army of Parliament presented a series of dichotomies, the hardened and the fresh, the trained and the raw, seasoned but battered fighters beside well-equipped notional soldiers who had never fought in anger. Numerical strength they unquestionably had, to about 24,000 men, almost twice the royal army's size (though none yet knew this). The Trained Bands had served only in ceremonies since the advent of the Stuart dynasty. They were youthful, brightly and variously attired in new regimental uniforms, with a merrily demotic tradition of marching songs, the old reputed royal wooing ballad 'Greensleeves' among them.

Among the most prominent of the latest, least soldierly-looking recruits was Bulstrode Whitelocke. Although a deputy lieutenant in two counties and a captain by a vote of the Commons, he had not served in the Edgehill campaign. Whitelocke's decision to join the muster in Chelsea as a recruit, rather than – as an inconveniently large number of Londoners were thronging to do – as a spectator, was upon a momentous, spontaneous, unanswerable impulse. He deliberately omitted to consult his wife Frances, who was, he states elsewhere, in every other context his entire and equal confidante, including in business and politics.

Whitelocke had been invited by his fellow Commons man Sir Philip Stapleton to join his mounted Life Guards. Like the King's equivalent Guards, with whom Lord Spencer served, though notionally responsible for the protection of Lord General Essex, Stapleton's Life Guards in fact insisted on serving in the van as regular cavalry. But various motives led Whitelocke instead 'to trail a pike' in the foot regiment of the great orator with whom he claimed kinship, John Hampden. These motives included Whitelocke's respect and liking for Hampden, an unstated but possible nervousness about fighting on horseback after the lasting injury caused by his Oxford hunting accident, and a romantically antiquarian feeling that it was more properly English to defend one's country on foot.

Whitelocke was now confident, optimistic, and defiant, most likely impelled by his fury at the deeds of Prince Rupert, at Brentford and, supremely, Fawley Court. He noticed Parliament's advantage and care in disposing of its artillery, 'great guns' stationed 'beyond Hammersmith', 'about a mile' from the looting Royalist victors of Brentford. Describing the muster at Chelsea, in his *Memorials* Whitelocke details the army's strengths but none of its limitations: 'above 24000 . . . stout, gallant, proper men . . . as well habited and well armed as were ever seen in any army . . . seemed to be in . . . good courage to fight the enemy'.

Whitelocke was impressed by the highest ranks of the army's command and trusted the competence of their arrangements. He believed that the parliamentary forces' 'order and marshalling' was conducted 'chiefly by the earl of Holland', who 'took great pains' and 'shewed good skill in martial affairs'. Although Holland's record was tainted in the eyes of any true soldier by his abysmal timidity in the Bishops' Wars against the Scots, the earl had long and successfully cultivated, as he had been cultivated by, Whitelocke (and indeed Lord Holland had maintained cordial relations with Hyde until early that year). An excellent rider with a fine stable and a superb wardrobe, his birth, carriage, amiability, wealth, and eloquence combined to ensure that Holland looked the part in Whitelocke's terms. Lord Holland was merely the best turned out of a representation upon Chelsea Field that to Whitelocke was encouragingly broad, consisting of peers, including the ever-powerful Northumberland, and 'divers' MPs, all in arms. Northumberland's presence was critical proof that the recent leader of the peace negotiations was now actively committed to resisting the King and protecting the capital.

Less elegant than Holland, but more heartily received by the troops, were Captain-General Skippon and the Lord General Essex. Whitelocke, a smooth if seldom a passionate public speaker, and a perceptive judge of rhetoric, noted how well Skippon the long-time soldier knew his audience in addressing the army before battle. Parliament's men seemed 'more taken' with his 'short and encouraging speeches' 'than with a set, formal oration'. Although Essex by contrast was stiff, solemn, melancholy, and taciturn, he was acknowledged and respected as the supreme commander. To Whitelocke, Essex seemed as diligent as Holland, as well liked by the men as Skippon. Parliamentary soldiers cheered and expressed their affection for their veteran general Essex (if not with the sort of awe of which Prince Rupert was in increasing receipt from both his troops and his enemies), crying: 'Hey for old Robin!' Robert Devereux, Earl of Essex, was just over fifty, about a decade older than the vigorous Skippon and perhaps showing it.

## Vulgar Intelligence, Vigorous Defence

Thus led, the defenders of London marched westwards and encountered the King's army coming from Brentford at the quietly fateful open ground of Turnham Green. Whitelocke the would-be cavalry officer in French service described Essex's armament 'drawn up in battalia'. Here thronged not only regiments of soldiers, experienced, trained, or otherwise, but an even more conspicuous array of civilian bystanders, already greatly in evidence at Chelsea and ever increasing since, many mounted or in carriages, the better to disseminate news of triumph or disaster.

Both Whitelocke, himself present, and Hyde, left in Oxford but kept informed by Falkland, who was attending the King in the midst of the royal army before Turnham Green, emphasize the presence of the non-combatant multitude behind Parliament's army, but invest it with quite different significance. To Whitelocke these war tourists were a nigh-on disastrous hindrance. At every blast of the King's comparatively scarce guns, Whitelocke records crowds of watching Londoners taking to saddle and stagecoach, each time bearing away with them dribs and drabs of true, if irresolute, soldiers, just as deserters had taken the chance to creep away from Essex's colours after Edgehill, to the inevitable 'discouragement of the parliament's army'. But for Hyde or his informants, as he later recalled in his *Life*, these watchful citizens provided all too obvious proof of the city's sympathies and the enemy's unstaunchable supply of 'all things proportionable . . . that could be of use to so numerous an army'. Worse still, both the people of London and the soldiers of Parliament now had an unrivalled, panoramic view 'of the whole miserable forces which had given them that alarum . . . and so recovered easily their own courage'.

It was *Twelfth Night*'s farcical duo of Cesario/Viola versus Sir Andrew Aguecheek writ large – both sides startled at the sight of one another and disinclined to try a reckless gamble. As it happened, the Royalist caution so volubly represented by Hyde, to the intense frustration of Prince Rupert, prevailed before the countervailing jitters of Parliament's troops or taxpayers intensified to any crisis of importance. The King was advised and agreed to withdraw,

## Friends in Youth

ending what might have been the largest, most decisive confrontation of a much shorter civil war, before it had truly begun.

When Whitelocke was acting as a peace negotiator in Royalist Oxford early in the succeeding year, with Hyde temporarily as in old times among his constant intimates and foremost sources, the Parliamentarian envoy recalled that 'some of the King's party did afterwards confess to me and others, that ... they had not bullet enough to have maintained fight for a quarter of an hour', if they had indeed fully engaged. Hyde, along with other civilian advisors committed to a conciliatory strategy, doubtless believed this, and may well have been right. Ammunition aside, the Royalists remained massively outnumbered; their victory, however still narrowly possible, would have been in any case politically far more potentially devastating to their cause than even Brentford had been, polluting the capital they hoped to gain with the blood of its reservist soldiers and quite probably a large number of civilian witnesses.

This is one of the instances where these two reluctantly opposed friends' shared political perspective shapes their mutually corroborative histories. From Whitelocke's actual experience of the almost-battle, as he witnessed it without the benefit of Hyde's later inside information, it seems clear that there was indeed a moment of doubt where Parliament's army was credibly felt to waver: even if this was a doubt his Royalist friend later hurried to assuage. For Hyde surely hoped Whitelocke would carry back to Parliament's peacemakers the soothing insistence that a reasonably disposed King Charles neither in fact could have, nor would ever have, wanted to turn his soldiers loose on London proper.

On the field itself as he watched the Royalist retreat, Whitelocke's sanguine character reasserted itself. He quickly involved himself in, and may even have suggested, an aggressive expedient of John Hampden's to take the fight to the retiring enemy. Like the Royalist advance itself, this was a serious but calculated military risk that had a chance of greatly curtailing the war. Hampden, loudly supported by Whitelocke, as well as unspecified 'lords' and 'others with Essex', urged the Lord General to send two regiments of horse and four of foot, including Hampden's in which Whitelocke had volunteered, to 'march about from the green by Acton', moving through wooded terrain to attack the King's flank. Whitelocke also seems to have been among those who proposed another suggestion of moving 3,000 foot and horse from their garrison at Kingston to attack the King from the south at Hounslow Heath.

In general, there was a large and revealing body of political opinion in favour of pursuit of some kind:

> It was then consulted whether the parliament's army should advance, and fall upon the king's forces . . . [this was the] opinion of most of the parliamentary men and gentlemen.

Whitelocke, by temperament pacific and unaligned, had now in the remarkable hurly-burly of civil war become part of a tactical tendency that was the equal balance to Prince Rupert, despoiler of Fawley Court, in urging an immediate, high-stakes assault. He portrays this group as socially as well as morally superior, composed of courageous political idealists and patriotic, well-born amateurs, opposed by the hesitant Lord General and his uncommitted mercenary advisors, 'the old soldiers of fortune, upon whose judgment the general most relied . . . their reasons were, that it was too hazardous to follow the enemy . . . [that it was] honour and safety enough to the parliament . . . [that the] king was retreated'.

Like Charles, the Earl of Essex at first inclined to the suggestions of the fire-eaters. The proposed detachment of horse and foot, Hampden, with Whitelocke, in its van, was sent as far as the woods of Acton before one of the 'soldiers of fortune', Sir John Meyrick, galloped up to the putative flankers and countermanded their orders. Whitelocke, though on fair enough terms with Meyrick, casts doubt on Sir John's loyalty in his *Memorials*, and continued at the time to be so fluently insubordinate that Hampden rather grimly joked that he had better accept the situation or else be shot for mutiny. Meanwhile, the Kingston men, by the advice again of Meyrick and of the unideological foreign mercenary Dalbier, rejoined the main force by a longer route, arriving too late for any action. The King's army escaped unscathed 'while we were consulting'.

Whitelocke's eager military instincts, as in the question of a parliamentary garrison at Oxford, had been overridden, though on this occasion he, Hampden, and the rest may indeed have been more impetuous than realistic. Whatever frustration Whitelocke felt, the mood among the colleagues of Hyde was lower yet. In the opinion of the most peaceable Royalist counsellors, complete disaster had, with the 'battle' of Turnham Green's rapid cessation and the ultimate return of the King to Oxford, been just barely averted, at great and needless cost. Starting from a promontory of strength and a rising reputation after Edgehill, the King and his nephew had succeeded in alienating many natural Royalists in Parliament and London, and exposing the continuing numerical feebleness of their principal army. As a result, 'his majesty returned to Oxford, unsatisfied with the progress he had made, which had likewise raised much faction and discontent amongst the officers, every man imputing oversights which had been committed to the rashness and presumption of others'.*

As the unfortunate Falkland busied himself with a half-hearted, propagandistic justification for the King's decisions at Brentford, one of Charles's formal declarations that Hyde would always be proud to disavow, there was, for Hyde, one consolation, and for Whitelocke, one burdensome yet evident expedient. It was mid-November, the campaigning season had long outlasted its proper span, and the moment had returned for the well-placed on both sides, all too well-known to one another, to resume the thankless work of reconciliation.

---

* In particular Clarendon, writing here in the *Life*, alludes to the over-boiling rivalry and tension between the similarly hot-tempered, hard-living cavalry generals Prince Rupert and Henry Wilmot.

## II.

# The Percy's Peace and the Poet's Plot

*Such a complement* Hanniball *in* Livy *bestowes upon* Scipio:
My comfort is, that by thee I am inforced to sue for a peace.

George Sandys, 'Upon the Ninth Book',
*Ovids Metamorphosis Englished*

## 'Great plenty and choice fowl' – Royalist Oxford, the Postmasters' Hall, the New Inn Hall, Merton and All Souls Colleges, the Court at Christ Church, December–January 1642–3, February–March 1643

A couple of months after the stand-off at Turnham Green, the defiant, claustrophobic grandeur of Oxford's improvised royal court concealed shady patches of day-to-day grief. One such spilled out on 19 January at a little house of recent construction, placed at the bottom of the garden belonging to the large, comfortable, handsome Postmasters', or Portionists', Hall. The Hall itself was an 'ancient stone-house' opposite Merton, one of the oldest colleges of the university. Named after the Mertonian term for senior undergraduates, the Postmasters' Hall had been occupied, since the arrival of the court late in the previous October, by Sir John Colepeper, Privy Counsellor, Chancellor of the Exchequer, third man, with Falkland and Hyde, in the moderate Royalist triumvirate. This important lodger had pushed the Hall's usual tenants, the Wood family, into the garden outhouse erected by their lately prosperous patriarch, the Oxonian lawyer and landlord Thomas Wood. Mr Wood's 'fat and corpulent' corpse now ripened in his new-built

*Friends in Youth*

lesser property, a natural death, but one plausibly hastened by unwonted wartime perturbances. One of the deceased's several sons feelingly recorded the predicament in which the family found itself: 'no body left (because of the raging of civil war) to take care of them, only a [serving] woman . . . the elder brother Thomas . . . a rude and boisterous soldier . . . 2nd brother Edward . . . a young scholar at Trinity . . . did in this or next year bear arms for his majesty . . . so far from being a governor to others, that he could scarcely govern himself'.

Anthony Wood, younger brother of these belligerent recent Royalist volunteers, later to become a famously acerbic antiquarian, uneasy collaborator of the more amiable John Aubrey, was at the time of his father's death an observant schoolboy of eleven. He would begin writing the autobiography and diaries that recall Royalist Oxford in the 1650s, though (like Clarendon's works) they were not published until the eighteenth century.

Young Wood's perspective on the King's wartime capital is poignantly domestic. His father had flourished sufficiently by the 1630s to be fined in lieu of accepting the honour and obligations of knighthood, one of Charles I's antiquarian expedients for raising extra-parliamentary revenue. Thomas Wood was a provincial miniature of Sir James Whitelocke in London and Berkshire, converting legal industry into landed substance. He acquired the lease of an inn among other sound urban property investments; the Flower de Luce stood opposite St Alban's Hall on Merton Street, once a medieval hall of the university, by the seventeenth century a satrapy of Merton. Before the war Thomas Wood thus stood high in Merton Street, a respectable landowner after the college itself, and, like the college, not instinctively disposed to love the King. By January 1643, Merton, all but empty of its Parliamentarian dons, was given over to the royal court. The Postmasters' Hall was Colepeper's berth, those Wood boys of age were Royalist soldiers, and the one-time landlord of the Flower de Luce was rotting in his garden house.

Anthony Wood naturally felt more dislocation than enthusiasm at the presence of the court. At New College's boys' school he endured lessons in a 'choristers' chamber . . . a dark nasty room and very unfit for such a purpose', while the stately college cloister and tower of which the pupils had once had the use now housed His Majesty's none too formidable powder magazine. Wood particularly resented the supererogatory insult that the 'plate which had been given . . . at his christening by his Godfathers & Godmother, which was considerable, was (with all other plate in Oxon) carried by his majesty's command to the mint at New Inn'.

Sir John Colepeper, the Woods' powerful lodger, oversaw as Chancellor of the Exchequer the initial levy of the city's plate. The improvised Royal Mint that transformed it into a much-admired coinage, well struck by established medallists, of unimpeachable fiscal quality, was under the direction of Sir Thomas Aylesbury, Master of Requests and of the Mint, and Ned Hyde's father-in-law. A court intrigue and scurry for office was about to propel Hyde himself more tightly into these ad hoc provisions, supplying an armed faction in a civil war with a makeshift system for raising taxes from civilians.

By December, Hyde was known to be the preeminent author of the King's declarations. He was also quietly composing a necessarily unquantifiable but certainly vast body of unsigned or falsely attributed Royalist propaganda and disinformation. He was among the royal advisors most reviled by Parliament, specifically exempted from any potential pardon that might result from a peace, at the furious behest of many of his most powerful former allies. Yet Hyde still lacked any formal post under the King, or a seat on the Privy Council.

This anomaly had not escaped the conscientious attention of his sovereign. King Charles's true attitude to his officially unaccredited advisor was revealed when one of the King's letters to his consort Queen Henrietta Maria, still abroad raising funds, arms, and sympathy in the Netherlands, was intercepted and published. 'I must make Ned Hyde secretary of state,' Charles confided, boldly given what he must have known to be his wife's contrary view of the matter, 'for the truth is I can trust nobody else.' But the King's existing Secretaries of State were Hyde's inseparable friend Falkland and

## Friends in Youth

Sir Edward Nicholas, an ageing family acquaintance of limited competence but absolute loyalty, whom Hyde felt himself bound in honour not to displace. So Hyde once more ducked the honour of office, just as he had previously declined to supplant Oliver St John as Solicitor-General.*

The situation resolved itself in a manner whose tremors intrigued and affected the whole Royalist university-court, and especially the limb of it lodged at the Postmasters' Hall. The answer had begun, unnoticed, to emerge, while the royal army marched to Reading on 2 November, with the death from smallpox of a little girl in Hertfordshire. In December her eldest brother and her father, Sir Charles Caesar, also died. Caesar had since 1639 been Master of the Rolls, second judge in the land after the Lord Chief Justice.

Sir Charles Caesar was the grandson of Cesare Adelmare, Trevisan doctor of the Tudor Queens Mary and Elizabeth. This Italian physician's Tottenham-born heir rose to become Sir Julius Caesar, Master of the Rolls. His son Sir Charles purchased the same office after Archbishop Laud meaningfully advised that it was 'not like to go without more money than he thought any wise man would give for it'. Declaring his indifference to such wisdom, as Laud had doubtless intended, Caesar offered the King £17,000 (about £2 million in contemporary purchasing power), much needed in 1639 to fund the Bishops' Wars. Hyde, revolted by this too naked act of state larceny and corruption, despite his friendship for Laud blamed him severely for brokering the sale.

Now, with Sir Charles Caesar dead, the King moved swiftly to confer his office upon Colepeper, who had long sought it. Colepeper, at first delighted, was then made to understand that his existing office, the Chancellorship of the Exchequer, technically less prestigious but potentially far more influential, was to be granted to Hyde. The current Chancellor's protests were unavailing against

---

* On that earlier occasion he had acted not from personal affection, but political considerations, including his desire to avoid incurring any political debt to the Queen.

the voices of Falkland and Digby, and the unusually determined desire of the King himself. Over the course of February and March, Ned Hyde was by degrees elevated into Sir Edward, Privy Counsellor, and Chancellor of the Exchequer, at last on equal terms with the King's official advisors.

This well-deserved promotion marked the high point of an unexpectedly pleasant interlude for Hyde. Now surpassing Colepeper in office, he had long since enjoyed superior lodgings. Although the Postmasters' Hall was spacious, comfortable, and dignified enough – and much missed by its peacetime Wood tenants – Hyde had, with his wife Frances, taken up permanent residence in what had previously been his occasional perch, All Souls College. There Gilbert Sheldon, the most iron-spirited disputant at Great Tew, who was to Chillingworth what Hyde was to Falkland, had for six years held sway as Warden.

The mischievous, always entertaining Lord Digby, still Hyde's unfailing if at times incongruous supporter and friend, also made the college his base of operations, exercising loose control over his latest wheeze, the new Royalist newspaper *Mercurius Aulicus*, from January 1643. Digby was a hands-off 'proprietor'; the All Souls don and Laudian protégé John Birkenhead was Digby's relaxed 'editor' and an 'exceedingly bold, confident and witty' star writer, prone, according to John Aubrey, still an undergraduate resident at Trinity, to 'lie damnably'; the tireless, obsessive propagandist Peter Heylyn their invariable dogsbody and delegatee.

Although in private Hyde grumbled about the ludicrous prices of this squashed, improvised court town, he soon had a particular, political motive to celebrate the quality of life in Oxford at the turn of 1642–3. Clarendon's *Life* attests to:

> . . . the great plenty in the markets, not only of the usual common fare, but of those choice fowl, of pheasants, partridge, cocks, snipes, in that abundance, as they were not so furnished in London; besides the best fish and wild fowl, which was brought in every day, from the western part, in such plenty, that it can hardly be imagined.

This bountiful description is not itself implausible. Oxford was only briefly to be subjected to anything resembling a true military blockade (at the end of the first English Civil War in 1646). In early 1643 the Royalists were relatively bullish, had they but known it, at more of a precarious height than a promising start. The university city was surrounded by well-forested and bountifully stocked Oxfordshire estates, many modest individually, but collectively extensive; their landowners were either, like Falkland, with the King in person, or in sympathy with him, or else, like Speaker Lenthall, owner of Burford, or Lord Saye, of Broughton, presently powerless to resist the local dominance of Royalist forces.

The royal army controlled the country south-east of Oxford, towards London, as far as Reading, and maintained safe communications with most of the West Country, and Wales. The coins minted and medals struck at Oxford's New Inn Hall were Cornish-mined. The colleges of the university, with their persistently pre-Reformation habits of mind and customs of body, had long made Oxford an inland city whose high tables boasted superb piscine banquets; the presence of a court, a war, and an emergency made such deliveries of marine and riverine luxury a still higher priority.

By the time Hyde, as Clarendon, came to write about the game and fish of Royalist Oxford, after his second exile in 1667, he had experienced much leaner times. By comparison the unbeaten, courtly, still vestigially academic Oxford of 1642–3 retained in his fond memories a splendidly royal flavour. But Hyde, though a good trencherman, remembered his Oxford diet for a cogent rhetorical, rather than merely descriptive, purpose. His gastronomic recollections made a light and correspondingly effective political point, as he called to mind the visit of the parliamentary Peace Commissioners, his old friend Whitelocke among them, to the Oxford court.

The delegation from both Houses of Parliament had arrived at Oxford late in January, furnished, to a degree that Hyde in the *History* claimed 'occasioned some mirth' among Royalists, with 'a great quantity of provisions':

## The Percy's Peace and the Poet's Plot

> The common people of London were persuaded that there was so great scarcity of victual and provisions at Oxford, and in all the King's quarters, that they were not without danger of starving, and that, if all other ways failed, that alone would in a short time bring the King to them. To make good this report, provisions of all kinds, even to bread, were sent in waggons and on horses from London to Oxford for the supply of this committee, when, without doubt, they found as great plenty of all things when they came as they had left behind them.

Hyde implies that this mistaken impression in Parliamentarian London was caused equally by Pymite propaganda and by the unimpressive effect of viewing the King's army at Turnham Green, after the advance Hyde himself had so urgently opposed. Elsewhere he emphasizes the continuing porousness of communication, correspondence, rumour, and conversation across the kingdom's still half-notional political declivity; a scarcely covert channel of uncontrollable gossip, conveying more human sympathy than military accuracy.

Like the parliamentary deputation that had negotiated with King Charles between Edgehill and Turnham Green, the two Houses' latest peace mission was led by Algernon Percy, 10th Earl of Northumberland, who took up grand lodgings opposite Colepeper at the mostly vacated Merton College. Hyde did not count Northumberland among his several personal friends or even casual acquaintances from the highest nobility. He observed and assessed the earl's character and motives with all his perceptive faculties, inborn and hard learnt. Whitelocke, on the other hand, paid more attention, and respect, to the great Percy's pocket. While he generally corroborates his Royalist friend's ironies on the well-stocked Parliamentarian provender, Whitelocke arrives at a separate, equally persuasive conclusion:

> The Earl of Northumberland carried with him his own plate, linen, provisions and wine, & [the parliamentary Commissioners] lived in

Oxford in as much state, and nobleness, as ... Northumberland useth to do, & that is hardly to be exceeded by any subject ... General [Patrick] Ruthven [to Royalists now Earl of Forth] & divers of [the King's] Lords & officers frequently came to their Table, & they had friendly discourses & treatments together, though enemies, & the King received Wine & provisions from the Earl when he had anything extraordinary brought from London.

With his decorous, enduring respect for the King's person and character as well as office, Whitelocke suggests, rather than asserts, that Northumberland lived in higher style, upon more abundant and stable means, than Charles himself could maintain. The royal residences in London, Westminster, and Windsor were all now under Parliament's control; the Navy was also loyal to Parliament. The King had access to whatever college cellars had not been sold off to fund his war, but both his own best vintages and the fruits of his kingdoms' commerce were denied him.

Crucially, though Northumberland had been removed as Lord High Admiral in June 1642 by Charles's command, Parliament had not reappointed him, instead replacing him with his cousin, the more radical Earl of Warwick. Here, in the form of the wine transported by the implacable Warwick's navy, delivered by the ambiguous, conservative, basically pacific Northumberland's generosity, was a potential gesture towards very particular political common ground.

That Charles graciously accepted wine offered by Northumberland in chivalrous spirit is hardly surprising, yet perhaps revealing of a circumstantial lack of luxury that overrode strict considerations of rank. That the bibulous Lord Forth, alias 'Father Red Wine', and other Royalist courtiers and soldiers, 'though enemies', accepted frequent, comfortable invitations to Northumberland's table at Merton is even more characteristic. It is overwhelmingly likely that the companionable Hyde attended such 'friendly discourses & treatments', even if he himself preferred later to recall enjoying less politically pungent Oxfordshire game and West Country fish.

## 'A Stout and Sober Carriage' – Parliament's First Peace Commissioners in Royalist Oxford; An Ominous Road, a Plague-Ridden Inn, and the Gardens of Christ Church, Late January 1643

After Whitelocke's safe return from Turnham Green to his worried but remarkably good-tempered wife Frances, who had remained in ignorance of his movements throughout the day of the contention, he had settled into a comfortable, if busy, winter in London. Obedient to the advice his father had given him in 1626, he maintained a range of politically various patrons, kept his private views discreet, and avoided entire commitment to any party, following 'the dictates of my own reason and conscience', 'which made him the more courted by all'. Already accepted as a kinsman by Hampden, Whitelocke was now also jocularly claimed as a distant relation by the friendly Yorkshire general Ferdinando, Lord Fairfax.* Whitelocke was, he reports in his diary, 'intimately' friendly with the bellicose but gracious Stapleton, the pacific if dour Holles, and even the old professional soldier Meyrick, with whom Whitelocke had quarrelled at Turnham Green. Above all Whitelocke was liked, respected, and trusted by the Lord General, Essex himself. 'Taking', as he did, 'all occasions to advise for peace', it was natural that Whitelocke be included among the all-important party with the delicate and difficult task of coming to terms with the King, or at least being seen to have tried so to do.

The parliamentary Peace Commissioners who conveyed preliminary propositions late in January were made up of four great nobles and eight Members of the Commons. Of the four peers, all three of Northumberland, Pembroke, and Holland were well known to Whitelocke. Hyde, who had entered politics as Pembroke's client

---

* In his *Memorials*, Whitelocke records Lord Fairfax's etymologically broadminded conviction that 'his name and mine [i.e. 'Fairfax' and 'Whitelocke'] were all one; his was French and mine was Saxon.'

and was still in friendly communication with him, knew, and thoroughly distrusted, Holland, and kept a distant, vigilant eye on Northumberland. Neither of the friends had any great estimate of the fourth peer, Salisbury, important only for his fortune's solidity and his name's lustre, a pedestrian, cautious, indifferent heir to his famous father, old King James's chief minister.

The seven Commons men who accompanied Whitelocke among the initial delegation were more akin to Hyde and Whitelocke by background, profession, and pattern of life than were the great peers, and in several cases connected to one or both of the two friends in personal as well as political life. Thomas, Viscount Wenman in the Irish peerage, was a cousin of the amiable Sir Francis Wenman, Falkland's neighbour, friend, and fellow scholar-amateur, who had died in 1640. Like Whitelocke, Lord Wenman was to be characterized by his political enemies as a moderate Royalist posing as a moderate Parliamentarian. During a later ill-starred peace treaty, Wenman's viscountess was lodged by Warden Pincke of New College. Pincke had himself, while acting as Vice-Chancellor of the University and trying to treat with Parliament, been imprisoned on its orders and did not forget this. He extended hospitality to no other parliamentary wives, suggesting that, after the war had blazed on for two more years, the Warden shared the prevalent view of the Wenmans as crypto-Royalists.

Richard Boyle, Viscount Dungarvan, was heir to the Earl of Cork, the Canterburian climber of genius who had made his family the richest and most powerful in Ireland. Dungarvan's younger sister Katherine had been a playmate and potential bride for the young Lucius Cary, and, as Lady Ranelagh, remained a trusted friend to both Falkland and Hyde within parliamentary London. Lord Cork had been one of Strafford's bitterest enemies; his eldest son notionally sat in the Long Parliament in the interest of Pym's reformers. But the parallel, ongoing, overshadowed, much more bitter conflict in Ireland had left Dungarvan little time in London. In September 1642 he and his younger two brothers had fought against the Catholic rebels at the rare Dublin government victory of

18. This portrait of a youthful King Charles also implies the dandiacally pensive intimacy that seems to have characterised the monarch's first private meeting with Hyde, at Whitehall in 1641.

19. The 3rd Earl of Essex, son of the Elizabethan hero and rebel, was an experienced soldier and genuinely popular national figure who had met with repeated humiliations at court. As Parliament's Lord General he was respected, if hardly inspiring.

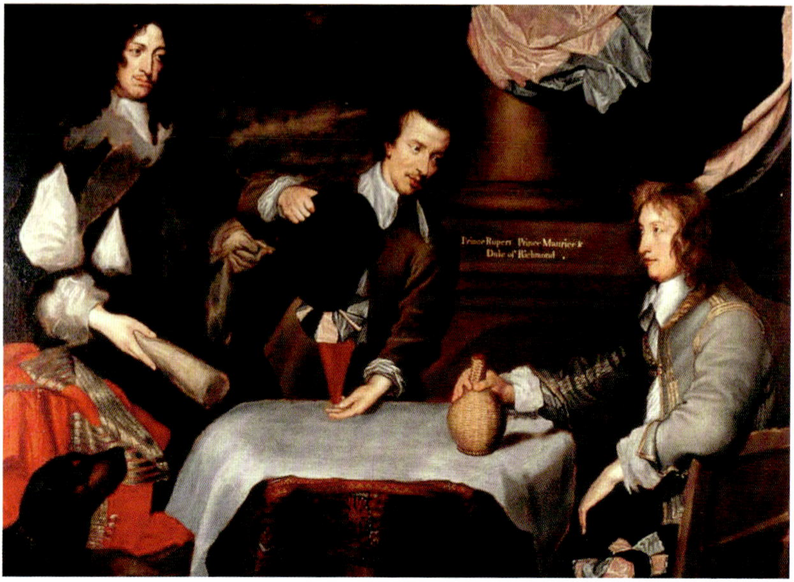

20. Prince Rupert of the Rhine (*left*), King Charles's nephew, alias 'Prince Robber'; Rupert's tactlessness, aggression and pitiless raids (one on Whitelocke's country seat), attracted the censure of both camps' moderates.

21. Sir John Byron, Royalist cavalry commander at the First Battle of Newbury in 1643, concisely and erroneously reported the death there of Lord Falkland to be the consequence of bungled enthusiasm.

22. Sir Edmund Verney, the King's knight-marshal and doomed standard bearer at Edgehill, before the battle confided to Hyde his profound personal misgivings about the Royalist cause.

23. This portrait of the Prince of Wales was commissioned by the King as a gift to Dr. William Harvey, who, along with Hyde, precariously ensured the Stuart princes' safety at Edgehill.

24. Hyde, by now a knight, Privy Counsellor and Chancellor of the Exchequer, seems here more sybarite than warrior; the Oxford courtiers, despite the war, lived well, if 'chargeably'.

25. Whitelocke, plainly but richly dressed in the Puritan fashion and looking well preserved in his middle years, as a grandee of the Commonwealth governing class.

26. One of the most powerful of the great 'popular peers' who formed the Parliamentarian 'Junto', the 10th Earl of Northumberland would prove profoundly equivocal in his attitude to the civil war.

27. Lady Dorothy Sidney, wooed under the name of 'Sacharissa' by the poet Edmund Waller, instead married Henry, Lord Spencer. Both of her suitors were associates of Great Tew.

28. Lucy, Countess of Carlisle, Northumberland's notoriously intriguante sister, was reputed to have been the lover in succession of Buckingham, Strafford and Pym during their respective ascendancies.

29. After a varied and chequered career, Sir Henry Vane the Younger emerged as the leading man in the Commons after Pym's death. Lady Ranelagh commented that his tyranny was palpably worse than the King's.

30. Unlike the seventeenth-century manor of Great Tew, the nearby church still stands. Falkland was buried in its cemetery in an unmarked grave, presumably owing to the suspicion of suicide.

Liscarrol; the middle Boyle brother was killed. Dungarvan had an especially urgent reason to wish for peace in England as a precondition for the restoration of order in Ireland (like Sir Faithful Fortescue, defector to the Royalists at Edgehill, another bereaved, Protestant Anglo-Irish soldier and landowner). Dungarvan soon returned to Ireland, but would later show his true colours, bringing over his troops to the King's side in England.

Like all his family, Dungarvan had been a friend of Falkland since the latter's Irish youth, and with his wife he had frequented Great Tew. Elizabeth, Lady Dungarvan, sole heiress to the Earl of Cumberland, was a witty and lettered woman of strong character. Parliamentarian broadsheets would stretch these facts to suggest an adulterous relationship between Lady Dungarvan and Falkland; almost certainly falsely, though as will be seen in a more notable case, the suggestion that Falkland in Oxford chafed at the bonds of his romantic marriage to the saintly Lettice is not wholly unsupported.

Sir John Holland was friendly to Whitelocke in politics and person, an innate moderate whose ecumenical politics were, like Falkland's, partly formed by a family of mixed confessional allegiance. His wife was a Catholic, whose right to private practice of her religion he openly defended at some personal risk, while he unsuccessfully strove against her proselytization to their children. Sir William Lytton, a nostalgic, Elizabethan veteran MP, like Falkland had resisted the payment of Ship Money by legal means in the 1630s. William Pierrepont would work closely alongside Whitelocke and is particularly noted by Hyde as an active and able Peace Commissioner willing to negotiate with him in earnest, if also deep secrecy. His hugely rich father, the Earl of Kingston, was a very reluctant Royalist, his elder brother somewhat more committed to the King but still clearly, and in the circumstances naturally, predisposed to an early peace. Richard Winwood, Whitelocke's fellow Deputy Lieutenant, was a good enough friend first to share his coach and horse (replacing the carriage and horses plundered by Prince Rupert's men), and later to rent a new town house alongside him (after circumstances had rendered Whitelocke's unambiguously Royalist fellow tenants the Hales and Palmers imprudent living companions even for the most open-minded Parliamentarian).

Edmund Waller, last of the delegation according to precedence, had long been friendly and politically sympathetic to Whitelocke, but had connections of the longest standing and closest sort to Hyde and Falkland, as well as, it was soon to become mysteriously apparent, more exalted secret channels. An attested companion of Great Tew, Waller was the greatest poet to be counted of the circle (unless the elderly Ben Jonson, who probably died before ever visiting Great Tew, is to be included). In the Short and Long Parliaments, Waller had been among Falkland and Hyde's most consistent and eloquent supporters.

During the Personal Rule, Waller had wooed 'Sacharissa', Lady Dorothy Sidney. In 1635 he had lost her to Lord Spencer, another occasional visitor at Great Tew, entirely in sympathy with the group's prevalent politics. A picturesque story circulated with suspicious speed that Sacharissa's rejection had driven Waller mad. This was in fact so far from being the case that the poet almost immediately began to shift his overtures, with characteristic doublesidedness, to 'Amoret':

*All that of my self is mine,*
*Lovely* Amoret, *is thine;*
Sacharissa*'s Captive fain*
*Would untie his Iron chain . . .*

It was to this lady that Waller in 1640 addressed what turned out to be an equally disingenuous sonnet, permanently renouncing poetry in favour of politics.

Amoret, according to the earliest and most interesting identification, was Lady Sophia Murray, daughter of the Earl and Countess of Annandale; both themselves, rather than great nobles, judiciously poetic courtiers who had risen under the word-addicted

King James.* She was at the Oxford court with her mother in 1643, where she caught the attention of Hyde, who would write in the highest terms of praise of her learning and moral character, and Falkland, who became at the very least her fellow philosophical disputant and intimate friend. All too quickly, with tragic consequence, she would be enmeshed in intrigue – possibly amatory, certainly political.

As for Waller, during his sojourn in Oxford with his fellow Parliamentarian Commissioners, he speedily located a third muse. Lady Isabella Thynne, by birth Rich, was the daughter of one of the poet's lordly senior colleagues on the peace commission, the Earl of Holland. Unhappily married to the Royalist MP Sir James Thynne, Lady Isabella had chosen Balliol College, ancient, poor, popish by repute, for her independent lodging. Her main reason for residing there was the presence next door, at the grander but equally crypto-Catholic Trinity College, of her friend Dorothea Fanshawe. John Aubrey remembered the havoc caused by these two beautiful and sportive young court ladies in college gardens and chapels alike. They affronted Ralph Kettell, the venerable President of Trinity who had saved its paintings from Lord Saye, by their carefully negligent attire, 'half dressed, like Angels', as Aubrey put it, using with false tact a habitual euphemism for courtesans. Kettell was especially blunt to Mrs Fanshawe: 'I know you for a gentlewoman, I will not say you are a Whore; but get you gone for a very woman.'

In Waller, Lady Isabella had a far more urbane and appreciative votary, as his verse declares:

---

* Lady Sophia Murray had been betrothed, as a small, well-dowered child, to Robert, Lord Maxwell, heir of the Catholic Earl of Nithsdale (later a fierce Royalist). Lord Maxwell shared some of his intended bride's interests – as the 2nd Earl of Nithsdale he would be known as 'the Philosopher' as well as 'the Astrologer' – but the engagement seems to have been broken off by the mid-1630s, whether over the couple's differing religious allegiance, or, more likely, Lady Sophia's delicate health.

> *Such moving sounds, from such a careless touch*
> *So unconcern'd her self, and we so much!*
> *What Art is this, that with so little Pains*
> *Transports us thus, and o'er our Spirits reigns!*
> *. . . So Nero once, with Harp in hand, survey'd*
> *His Flaming Rome, and as it Burnt he Play'd.*

Behind these lines' immaculate verbal polish – as surely Waller's signature as musical beguilement in fashionably disarrayed costume was Lady Isabella's – can easily be discerned assessments not so far removed from the ever-mischievous Aubrey and his cantankerous President Kettell. Waller's emphasis on Isabella's assumed artlessness is part of the Horatian tradition of lyrical admiration, whose light irony conveys its exact opposite, that the poet is perfectly aware of, and amusedly taking pleasure in, his subject's flirtation for devastating effect. At the same time Waller's invocation of Nero, in the midst of what was still, for all its setting's collegiate and horticultural elegance, a temporary court in a makeshift capital within an escalating civil war, is hardly auspicious. But Waller's great and lifelong skill renders hardly possible the extraction of any unambiguous political point from his image. Nero might as easily be either Charles I himself, or the parliamentary grandees among whom Isabella's father Holland still meandered in his own stylish, slippery way, or both.

Before Whitelocke, Waller, and the rest of Parliament's Commissioners could disport themselves within these woods of academical Arcady, they had to contend with certain embarrassments on the road from London to Oxford. The Parliamentarian soldiers guarding the Peace Commissioners' passage stopped a coach containing a senior official of the Exchequer, Sir Edward Wardour, Clerk of the Pells, and five city clergymen. In vain did Sir Edward produce a quite genuine pass from the House of Lords, authorizing him to present a petition to the King from the parishes of Westminster, in the hope of furthering an accommodation. The troops searched his party anyway, and discovered, as well as 'two scandalous books arraigning the proceedings of the House', ciphered letters to Lords Falkland and Spencer. It was a timely reminder to the peace negotiators that however much Falkland and Spencer might be private friends to several of them, with all but identical political interests and desires, they were still enemies at war.

Wardour and his clerical friends were released after a couple of months' imprisonment. One of them, the silver-tongued preacher Thomas Fuller, minister of the Savoy Chapel, was said to command 'two audiences, one without the pale, the other within; the windows of that little church, and the sextonry so crowded, as if bees had swarmed to his mellifluous discourse'. Fuller had predictably but evocatively chosen 'Blessed are the peacemakers' as his text on Holy Innocents' Day, 28 December 1642. After his release, by which time the peace negotiations had commenced a more advanced stage, Fuller was still less oblique, preaching from Samuel: 'Yea, let him take all, so my Lord the King return in peace.'

Meanwhile Whitelocke travelled, according to precedence, in the coach of the delegation's junior earl, Holland; arguably the best connected of the Commissioner Lords, and certainly the most charming personality among them. This urbane carriageful was completed by Edmund Waller. But on their arrival in Oxford, the Commissioners' perceived safety in company was rapidly diluted. Although Northumberland was immediately offered the ancient tranquillity of Merton College, Whitelocke by contrast was directed, alone, to a lowly inn, 'where they confessed that some in his chamber, not many days before had died of the plague, yet God preserved him, and,' he adds, not entirely convincingly, 'kept him from fear'. Whitelocke seems to have had Colonel Lewis Kirke, acting Governor of Oxford, to thank for this bad turn. Kirke, in a varied and adventurous career, had taken part in a brief seizure of Quebec from France, been convicted, possibly unjustly, of murdering a brother officer, and verified the apparition of Sir Edmund Verney's ghost on the field of Edgehill.

As the Commissioners prepared to be presented to the King at Christ Church, they were confronted by a large, disorderly group,

*Friends in Youth*

which Whitelocke drily described in his *Memorials* as 'some of the soldiers and of the rascality of the town, and others of better rank though of like quality'. These miscellaneous hecklers 'reviled them with the names of Rogues, Traitors, & Rebels', 'but we took no notice of them, only we acquainted some of the King's officers therewith, who seemed to be very angry at it'. With prices high and the army and court the most obvious commercial markets available, it is hardly surprising that a noisy and conspicuous part of the populace sought to cling to prosperity by vocal support for the King, despite the town's previous Parliamentarian sympathy. Indeed the irony of economics had rendered the court's presence as profitable to the recently Parliamentarian-inclined town as disastrous to the devotedly Royalist University. Whitelocke's low estimate of the Royalist troopers is that of a pacific, cultivated civilian landowner, only two months after the ransacking of Fawley Court; an event that still inconvenienced as much as angered him, of which he was shortly to be reminded in an even more obnoxious fashion.

The Commissioners were led into the Cathedral Garden at Christ Church, and the presence of Charles I. The King was attended at this first Oxford meeting by 'many Lords & others'; most prominently and ominously, he entered 'walking with the Prince'. Whitelocke saw no need to further identify which prince, but clearly referred not to Charles, Prince of Wales, a personally amiable teenager, but to the tactless, overbearing, foreign-born destroyer of Bulstrode's own patrimony, Prince Rupert. As for the 'Lords & others', Whitelocke indicates that they included the Earl of Southampton, the Lord Keeper Littleton, the Lord Chief Justice, Sir John Bankes, and other unspecified Privy Councillors, mostly peers. Falkland was possibly but not certainly present, Hyde, not yet elevated to the Exchequer or formally of the Privy Council, almost certainly absent. Of the senior counsellors mentioned by Whitelocke, Littleton and Southampton were very much in sympathy with Falkland and Hyde, Bankes distinctly less so.

Whoever exactly the witnesses were to this first pivotal meeting in those apparently promising precincts of Christ Church's gardens, regal, ecclesiastical, ordered, and peaceful, Whitelocke records its disruption by a few alarming glimpses of Stuart personality. The first occurred just after he had kissed the hand of the King, his first formal presentation to Charles I since that following *The Triumph of Peace* in 1634. Charles and his French Queen had both remained aware of the accomplished, courtly, rising lawyer since then, and kept a good opinion of him even (indeed especially) during his prosecution of Lord Strafford.

It may have been Charles's assumption, perhaps even encouraged by a friendly briefing from Ned Hyde, that Whitelocke was basically well disposed towards him, that led the King to whisper to Whitelocke's last colleague, Edmund Waller, while Whitelocke (alone of the other Commissioners) was still close enough to pick up his words: 'Though you are the last, yet you are not the worst, nor the least in my favour.' What, if anything, the King did or did not whisper to Whitelocke himself, the diarist does not impart. Whitelocke states that he reported this royal drop of syrup, 'the King's courtship to Waller', to 'some of his fellows, & they wondered at those words'. That 'some' forms a lawyerly provision against the remote possibility that one of his few colleagues to survive into the 1660s might contradict his testimony. Whitelocke's implication is that the King was either (rashly) referring to an existing complicity with Waller, or attempting his recruitment. Crucially, and carefully, if not necessarily truthfully, Whitelocke disassociates himself from this thread of understanding between Waller and the King.

Whether or not Whitelocke as well as Waller was covertly subjected to King Charles's charm, he unambiguously recalls treatment of the opposite kind from the King's nephew. After all the Commissioners had kissed Charles's hand, Prince Rupert extended his own. Whitelocke represents himself with coolly implausible politeness as passively 'cast back from the Crowd', but notes that Rupert did not accept this evasion from the grieving squire of Fawley Court. 'The Prince came to him and gave him his hand to kiss likewise,' leaving Bulstrode with no choice but bitter compliance.

Whitelocke's account of the meeting concludes with an admiring description of his superior Northumberland's haughty unflappability: 'Northumberland read the propositions to the King with a stout and sober Carriage, and being interrupted by the King ... said smartly, your Majesty will give me leave to proceed, the King said, Aye aye, & the Earl read them through.' Hyde interpreted Northumberland's sang froid very differently. Whitelocke implicitly conveys a touch of agreement with Northumberland's evident feeling that as private persons, the principal Stuart and the head of the Percys, he and the King are more equal than not. The Earl's axiomatically English 'stoutness' and 'sobriety' are implicitly and favourably compared with Charles's impulsive interruption and persistently Scots intonation. Hyde, on the other hand, when contemplating and characterizing Northumberland, meditated on a dynastic history that his friend Whitelocke preferred to efface – the 'frequent blemishes' of the Percy family 'of want of fidelity to the Crown'. Small wonder that Whitelocke was apt to ignore such blemishes; his own uncle and godfather, Captain Edmund Whitelocke, to whom Bulstrode owed his conspicuous first name, had shared a protracted stay in the Tower with Northumberland's father, after dining with the so-called 'Wizard Earl' and his cousin Thomas Percy, a Gunpowder Plot conspirator.

Hyde was inclined to discern faults in Northumberland behind what Whitelocke admired as the earl's virtues. He pointed out in the *History* that Northumberland at the inception of Charles I's reign had benefited from 'such a quick succession of bounties . . . as had rarely befallen any man who had not been attended with the envy of a favourite'. No less pointed was his judgement that Northumberland was '*in all his deportment*, a very great man'. Hyde bestowed the accolade of greatness with care, notably and controversially insisting on the murdered Buckingham's right to it. For him, Northumberland possessed only a highly convincing, ultimately hollow simulacrum of that quality. Hyde saw Northumberland's painstaking dignity, in the end, as a cynical political technique: 'His notions [were] not large or deep, yet his temper . . . reservedness in discourse ... [and] unrashness in speaking, got him the reputation of an able and wise man.'

For Hyde, Northumberland was not, as for Whitelocke, a representative of English nobility at its best, rather an example of what had corrupted it: 'If he had thought the King as much above himself as he thought himself above other considerable men, he would have been a good subject.' For all this, Hyde soon came to believe, and argue, that the interests of the Earl, the King, and the kingdom overlapped so profoundly that they presented an all-important way forward to peace.

The proposals that provoked the King into interrupting Northumberland were more or less identical with the Nineteen Propositions that Whitelocke had warily helped to draft the previous year, including the total abolition of episcopacy, the complete transfer of power over the militia to Parliament, the appointment of every government office by Parliament, and the condemnation of a wide array of 'evil counsellors' ranging from Digby to Hyde. Whitelocke does not comment on the strictness of the parliamentary terms, merely offering the optimistic assertion that 'way was made for a treaty'. But if Hyde is to be believed his old friend Whitelocke, along with some of his colleagues, was less inhibited away from the formal and public negotiations:

> They who brought this petition and propositions spake to their friends at Oxford with all freedom of the persons from whom they came [i.e. Pym, Hampden in the Commons, war party politicians such as Warwick and Brooke in the Lords]; inveighed against their tyranny and unreasonableness, and especially against the propositions they themselves had brought; but positively declared that if the King would vouchsafe so gracious an answer (which they confessed they had no reason to expect) as might engage the two Houses in a treaty, it would not be then in the power of the violent party to deny whatsoever his majesty could reasonably desire. However ... the King expected little from those private undertakings, well knowing that they who wished best were of least power, and that the

greatest among them as soon as they were but suspected to incline to peace immediately lost their reputation . . .

Neither Northumberland nor Whitelocke remotely desired the destruction of the bishops. Northumberland, that disappointed but not yet despairing courtier, even maintained keen interest in one great office in particular, the Admiralty, being awarded at the King's pleasure, so long as it was in his own favour. Whitelocke had advocated a subtly intermediate position on the militia question in the Commons, and had no wish to sentence his close and long-standing personal friend and political ally, Hyde, to death or exile. Hyde's description of the Commissioners' private positions, and predicament, while couched in exaggeratedly courtly terms, makes sense in the topsy-turvy circumstances of early 1643. As for the measured expectations he sincerely ascribes to the King, they are indistinguishable from his own.

## *'Plain contempt and stratagem' – The Treaty of Oxford: Christ Church, Westminster, Merton, Streets of Oxford, Oxford Castle, February–15 April 1643*

Between the parliamentary Commissioners' first, January visit to Oxford, and the beginning of formal talks after the return there of a changed, smaller delegation two months later, the war's course did not alter decisively. Minor battles, sieges, and dispositions favoured the Royalists, but so narrowly that the peace party in Parliament could still not attain any secure upper hand. Falkland and Hyde were settled in the King's political trust and personal friendship, but their influence was threatened by the return of the Queen from the Netherlands in February, an event that the King had awaited with anxious excitement and that in large part explained his slowness to begin negotiating the proposed treaty. Although Henrietta Maria did not arrive at court in Oxford until the summer, she landed in Yorkshire well supplied with funds, arms, and fighting spirit, better placed to frustrate the hopes of aspiring peacemakers on both sides than was, so far, the faltering Parliamentarian campaign.

Further wrangling about the make-up of Parliament's new, smaller group of Commissioners, and disagreement regarding the desirability and practicability of a cessation in fighting before and during the talks (required by Parliament, but resisted by the increasingly confident King), further delayed the latest parliamentary negotiators' arrival in Oxford and the earnest beginning of their deliberations until 23 March.

The Earl of Northumberland, William Pierrepont, Sir John Holland, and Whitelocke had returned to Oxford; Lord Saye, voted by Parliament to the new deputation, had been, as on former occasions, vetoed by the King as a declared traitor. One new Commissioner, the MP and baronet Sir William Armine, had joined them; like his predecessor Sir William Lytton he was a respectable child of the old Queen's reign, past middle age, with a mild, politic record of seemly resistance to Buckingham and the Stuart Crown. Armine was especially concerned in diplomacy with the Scots, Sir John Holland a diligent, intelligent, and circumspect follower, Northumberland, Pierrepont, and Whitelocke the men of initiative and statecraft left to speak for Parliament. Of the three earls left behind this time, Salisbury was a nonentity, Holland suspect, and Pembroke now too openly desperate for peace. Among the MPs, Lytton and Richard Winwood carried small weight, Dungarvan was back in Ireland and more or less obviously Royalist, while Wenman and Waller were also suspected of Royalism (whether or not Whitelocke really reported the King's 'courtship' of Waller to any of his colleagues).

Whitelocke, on the other hand, though quite as openly in favour of peace as Pembroke, had achieved the considerable feat of making himself indispensable to the delegation by his intellectual capacity, while also trusted by his Parliamentarian masters for unspotted integrity. Pierrepont's useful Royalist connections, efficiency, and trustworthiness put him in the same position. As for Northumberland, however ambiguous his political interests might be, without his immense status and innate credibility the Treaty of Oxford, both sides knew, counted for nothing.

When the confirmed Commissioners reached Oxford they found northern counterparts, acting for the Scots Covenanters, preparing to depart, with no decision for or against the King definitively taken (Falkland had prevented a crisis in this respect, narrowly dissuading King Charles from lecturing the Scots on theology in the manner of his late father). The Parliamentarian Commissioners initially sought permission to invite the Scots to London as mediators, which the King, with Hyde's approval, firmly declined.

The Peace Commissioners' approach to the Scots is at first surprising given the views of their Five Members, most of them firmly against any Scots meddling in Church or State, none more so than Whitelocke himself. But the proposed invitation to the Scots demonstrates how closely the Peace Commissioners' public actions, whatever their private, personal political positions, were monitored and controlled by Pym and the war party, who had already co-operated with the Covenanters in 1640, and were more than ready to do so again.

Whitelocke's summary of his mission captures both his total commitment to the negotiations and his frustration with his limited remit:

> [His] labour in this Treaty was very great, according to his affections to the business . . . his fellow Commissioners finding his pen useful in the service, put him upon the drawing of most of their papers to the King . . . The Commissioners' Instructions were very strict, & tied them up to treat with none but the King himself . . .

For Hyde – who, as a full Privy Councillor and Chancellor of the Exchequer, was now included in official as well as private discussions – the parliamentary Commissioners were so hampered by their leadership as to make of their whole enterprise, at least in its public and formal shape, no more than a sham, lacking:

... power to recede, or consent to any alteration [in the impracticably strict January propositions], but only to publish it if the King consented ... and then, and not till then, to proceed to treat ... a plain contempt, and stratagem to make the people believe by their sending their committee that they did desire a treaty and a cessation, yet ... to frustrate both, and to cast the envy of it upon the King.

There remained for both Whitelocke and Hyde the subtler, *sub rosa* instrument of private friendship and understanding. The intransigence shown both by Parliament's leadership, and (when, as was usually and essentially the case, he was under the influence of his consort) by the King, put Hyde and Whitelocke's particular, long personal history at the centre of their joint hopes for the war's speedy conclusion. Hyde also had hopes of Pierrepont, whom he complimented as 'of best parts' and noted was 'most intimate' with Northumberland. However little Hyde liked or esteemed the overweening Northumberland, he accepted the earl's central importance if any progress was to be made.

As if compensating for his humiliatingly restrictive instructions, Whitelocke emphasizes his Commission's exalted status, and the King's willingness to hear it out upon its own terms: 'they often attended [the King] at Christ Church, and had access to him whensoever they desired it, & a free debate allowed with him'. The paradoxical consequence of this, presumably unintended by Whitelocke and not altogether justified by the evidence (in particular, not by Hyde's), is to make the King seem to be negotiating in better faith than the leaders of Parliament. At times in his journal Whitelocke indulges in the moderate Parliamentarian fantasy that he and his colleagues were, in fact, the King's natural, favourite, most influential counsellors. The actual Privy Councillors are contrastingly presented as subordinate near-mutes, who 'never debated any matter with the Commissioners, but gave their opinions to the King, when he asked them, & sometimes put him in mind of some things, otherwise they did not speak at all'.

## Friends in Youth

While Whitelocke admits the evident hierarchy within his own Commission (and he was now technically its junior member), he also portrays its workings as fundamentally democratic: 'Northumberland spake most of the Parliament's Commissioners & every one of them spake as they saw occasion.' In this connection, he preserves a vignette of an ambiguous Charles, half peremptory, nervous autocrat, half gracious, reasonable sovereign:

> ... the King mistaking the Course of the River Thames, Whitelocke told him that [it] was such a way, and not as his Majesty took it. The King replied, it is as I say, & to convince you, I will show you the map, which he presently fetched, & bid Whitelocke to look out the place, which he did, & showed his Majesty that it was as he had informed him, at which the King, with great ingenuity & meekness, said Indeed I was mistaken, you were in the right Mr Whitelocke, I see you know your own Country very well, which is commendable and fit for a gentleman to do.

The story displays in miniature how Whitelocke saw the reign, the war, and the King's and his own part in them to date. Charles I had gone accidentally astray through pardonable ignorance (of English rivers, or laws), been courteously corrected, had resisted with a small, forgivable display of imperious petulance, and could be guided back into customary rectitude by firm, polite guidance: guidance the King tended, Whitelocke believed, to accept easily and well because of underlying sympathy with 'gentlemen' who 'knew their own Country', whereas Charles had temporarily failed to know his own kingdom.

This vision of the King as a potentially benevolent super-squire, rightly advised by Parliament, that emblematic body of country gentlemen and city lawyers, had almost everything in common with Hyde's theoretical ideals. But Hyde, for his part, had through 1641 learnt harder truths about the extremist, 'violent' leaders of Parliament, and was also shortly to be disillusioned as to the squirearchical reasonableness of his royal master.

## The Percy's Peace and the Poet's Plot

The Peace Commission's smaller size, more urgent and continuous duties, and longer stay in Oxford, meant that all five remaining Commissioners – Northumberland, Pierrepont, Holland, Armine, and Whitelocke – now shared in the grandeur of their senior colleague's Merton lodgings. Here the King's best available hospitality was married to Northumberland's extensive means and ostentatious tastes. Yet, having endured in January the plague-haunted inn, at Merton Whitelocke now 'fell extreme sick of a violent fever'. Among the Commissioners, Sir John Holland assumed principal responsibility for ensuring the proper care and recovery of their nominally junior, in fact irreplaceable, colleague.

Whether on his own initiative or at the patient's request, Sir John summoned Whitelocke's former tutor, Dr Philip Parsons of St John's College, a physician and occasional playwright. Parsons brought along a second doctor, who dosed the patient with medicine of his own devising. As the attempted cure proceeded without obvious progress, the gregarious Parsons roosting in Whitelocke's now impressive Merton accommodation happened to admit 'accidentally' to his lodging yet a third practioner, one of the many retained by the King himself, and an old acquaintance of the patient: Dr Samuel Turner.

Turner, a 'very able man in his profession', was also a displaced MP who had sat in both the Parliaments of 1640, a successful Royalist captain and, most tellingly, an intimate friend of John Selden and the Countess of Kent.* He had often met Whitelocke at Lady Kent's London residence and 'had affection for [him]'. Turner's political record, as befitted a friend of Selden's, was complex.† He had earned

---

* Turner may have been victorious in a skirmish with men answering to Whitelocke as Deputy Lieutenant, on the latter's own home ground of Henley, late in 1643.

† Another of Turner's friends and correspondents was the rich and scholarly lawyer John Fountaine, a youthful associate of Whitelocke. Whitelocke considered Fountaine, with rare asperity, to be a cynic and hypocrite, whether despite or because of their not dissimilar trajectories.

the special wrath of the King by calling Buckingham (appositely) 'the cause of all [MPs'] grievances' at the very beginning of the reign, but had also, unlike Hyde, been one of the few bravely outspoken 'Straffordians' in 1641. His character was more archetypally 'Cavalier' than his career. Anthony Wood would call Turner 'a man of very loose principles', probably on account of his siring an illegitimate son; Whitelocke described him as 'much addicted to drollery . . . raillery & plain speaking'.

After questioning the invalid 'above an hour together over several pipes of tobacco' (probably shared with the patient Whitelocke was a lifelong enthusiast for the healthful effects of smoking, *pace* old King James), Turner brusquely contradicted Parsons and his assistant:

> . . . he told Whitelocke that he was very ill indeed, & in much danger, that the other Doctors gave him improper Physic, and would kill him . . . that although [Whitelocke] was a Traitor and a Rebel against his King, yet as to his own person he knew him to be an honest man, & would prescribe him that which would recover him.

Turner's distinction between Whitelocke's public identity as a 'Traitor and a Rebel' and his private person as an 'honest man' was a witty inversion of the Parliamentarian party line, that their forces fought for the King's rightful public office and against his aberrant private actions. Whitelocke's response to Turner's unremittingly caustic bedside manner was modulated, but he obeyed this volubly Royalist doctor's advice:

> . . . though contrary to the opinions of some of his friends [presumably Dr Parsons, Parsons's assistant and Sir John Holland], for Whitelocke knew the Doctor to be honest and one that loved him . . . within a few days after [he] was abroad [i.e. on his feet] again, so great mercy did God show him, though by the means of such a man as Dr Turner.

The parting note here sounds sententious, but makes a profound point: like Christ's Samaritan, Whitelocke implies, the Royalist doctor has a discouraging reputation and demeanour but an excellent character. Whitelocke's gratitude and friendship for Turner was lasting. While the Commissioners stayed at Merton, Turner often visited his former patient, complimenting Northumberland's 'furniture and massy plate' and dubbing the Parliamentarians 'the gallantest Rebels that ever were in the world'. Whitelocke mentions Northumberland, Pierrepont, and Armine as showing him 'much respect' after his recovery, and again distinguishes Sir John Holland as being 'extreme kind and careful of him'.

Hyde now mentions Whitelocke but little; he may once again be censoring their old association, or Whitelocke's indisposition may have kept him out of much business, whereas Hyde had quickly noted Pierrepont's useful closeness to Northumberland. Hyde had already all but abandoned hope in the Treaty's public, formal efficacy. He was frustrated by the King and court's complete 'aversion' to agree to the cessation of fighting requested by Parliament, being certain that an obliging answer would more than make up in political and moral terms what it might temporarily yield in military advantage. Hyde rightly considered the twenty days allotted for the Treaty to be ludicrously inadequate. He saw the King's main hope, though one intrinsically difficult to put into action, in the Peace Commissioners' own covert, but obvious, distaste for the terms they carried. Clarendon summarized this conflict of interest in the *Life*:

> The commissioners, who had all good fortunes and estates, had . . . a great desire of peace, but knew well there must be a receding mutually on both sides from what they demanded . . . if the parliament insisted on [the January terms], all of the power of the crown . . . would be thrown off the hinges . . . [the Commissioners] saw well enough . . . that themselves should be as much involved in the confusion as those they called their enemies.

## Friends in Youth

This is more hindsight than prophecy; no one in 1643, save, possibly, the self-confessed republican Harry Marten, desired or envisaged the overthrow of the monarchy, let alone the diminishment of the aristocracy. But it still makes sense of the parliamentary Commissioners' private actions: seeing Hyde and Falkland as their most amenable counterparts, and making them unofficial suggestions.

According to the *Life*, those among the Commissioners 'known to wish well to the King' (arguably, all of them), secretly urged Hyde and Falkland to persuade the King to accept the January terms 'in some degree', then let the triumphant Parliamentarian peace party implement a reasonable compromise. They did not consider it necessary or even desirable that the King give ground on questions of Church government (which, Clarendon maintains, in truth scarcely interested the parliamentary war party), concentrating instead on that old sticking point, the militia question. When agreement here, too, proved elusive (Hyde was tempted to consider a middle way, Colepeper particularly set against one), Pierrepont discreetly put to Hyde his senior colleague Northumberland's most modest, realistic, personally specific request:

> [Pierrepont] rather desired than proposed, that the king would offer to grant his commission to the earl of Northumberland, to be lord high admiral of England . . . restored to his office, which he had lost for [the parliamentary leaders'] sakes . . . without any signal prejudice to the king; since he should hold it only by his majesty's commission, and not by any ordinance of Parliament . . .
>
> . . . [Pierrepont] said, if the king would be induced to gratify [him and Northumberland] in this particular, he could not be confident that they should be able to prevail with both houses to be satisfied therewith, so that a peace might suddenly be concluded; but, as he did not despair even of that, he did believe, that so many would be satisfied with it, that they would from thence take the occasion to separate themselves from [the parliamentary leadership], as men who would rather destroy their country than restore it to peace.

## The Percy's Peace and the Poet's Plot

The proffered deal Clarendon describes is extraordinary, and yet, given the subsequent behaviour both of King Charles and of Northumberland, very likely genuine. What Northumberland, via Pierrepont, was requesting was unquestionably treasonous towards the parliamentary leaders who had dispatched him to Oxford. By Pierrepont's admission, it was a favour that would cost the King nothing – the bestowal of *de jure*, purely titular authority over a navy that in practice had gone over to Parliament. But this cheap price would be enough to persuade the greatly influential Northumberland to support a peace agreement. Even should such an agreement then fail to pass through Parliament, the certain political upheaval that would ensue would help the King either to win the war, or at least end it on far better terms than those of January.

Northumberland confirmed that the suggestion was made at his behest and with his authority in conversation with Sir Edward Nicholas, Falkland's colleague as Secretary of State, 'with whom,' Clarendon adds, 'he had as much freedom as his reserved nature was capable of'. The next question must be whether the Admiralty proposal was known to the other Commissioners, Sir John Holland, Armine, and Whitelocke. The voluminous diaries of Holland and Whitelocke give nothing away.

Whichever Commissioners were party to it, the idea was dashed upon the rock of Charles I himself. Nicholas, putting it to the King, met with his instant, unexplained refusal 'to hear more of it'. Falkland and Nicholas then designated Hyde as the most persistent, propitious messenger. Hyde seized the best possible opportunity, the King in buoyant mood, strolling the gardens of Christ Church this time alone, 'most willing to be entertained'.

Hyde 'related ... the whole discourse' 'ingenuously', like an extended joke, bringing in Pierrepont, Northumberland, Nicholas, Falkland, himself, and an open recital of their manifold discussions. Shrewdly, he made clear his own personal disapproval of Northumberland, speaking of 'the earl's demerit towards his majesty with severity enough, and what reason he had not to be willing to restore a man to favour, who had forfeited it so unworthily'.

The groundwork now laid, Hyde arrived at his true argument:

> Yet he desired [the King] to consider his own ill condition . . . how unlike it was to be improved by the continuance of the war . . . whether he could ever imagine a possibility of getting out of it upon more easy conditions . . . the offer of which . . . could not but bring him very notable advantages; for if the peace did not ensue upon it, such a rupture infallibly would, as might in a little time facilitate the other.

His principal point made, Hyde continued to demonstrate such relative good qualities, and a few pertinent bad ones, that would make of Northumberland, once bought, a reliable ally.

The King heard him out 'very quietly, without the least interruption', generally, with him, an encouraging sign. But, when Hyde's loquacity at last ran out, Charles's more considered answer was no more favourable than the blunt negative by which he had silenced Nicholas. Nor were the King's given reasons, at first, without substance. He doubted, with some justice, Northumberland's ability to get a peace agreement through the Houses whose only tangible benefit was to the earl himself. Charles's guess that even if Parliament decided on peace it would be blocked by its own army was eerily far-sighted (as well as betraying the King's preference, very unlike that of his counsellor Hyde, for dealing with soldiers rather than civilian politicians). Suddenly the King descended into a personal fury, 'pathetical style', and specious considerations, standing upon his honour, unfavourably and irrelevantly comparing Northumberland with his foppish cousin Lord Holland, protesting that he had 'courted Northumberland as his mistress' in the past already, and would not do so again (his recent 'courtship' of Waller being apparently quite a different matter).

Hyde did not even now despair. Whether because of the

## The Percy's Peace and the Poet's Plot

question's importance or his confidence in the King's trust, he dared to raise the subject 'more than once' during the coming days. At last, he managed to extract permission to imply to Northumberland that the earl might expect to become Lord High Admiral *after* any peace, or in the (now almost certain) event of the Treaty's total failure, if Northumberland 'performed . . . any eminent service', that is, changed sides. The King also expressed his desire, one ardently shared by Hyde (and Whitelocke), that the period allowed for the Treaty be extended by another ten days.

But at some point, when or how he does not quite detail, either in the *History* or the *Life*, Hyde came to understand with crushing disappointment the true reason for the King's blend of stonewalling and temporizing. Charles considered himself bound by a promise to his Queen, not to restore any 'person into any favour or trust, who had disserved him, without her privity and consent'. As a result, the King was, at best, stalling until Henrietta Maria's arrival at Oxford, and, at worst, unlikely to give way in any case.

Whitelocke had in the meantime undergone another picaresque Oxford adventure. Walking without a manservant, close to the security of Merton Street, he ran into 'some gentlemen, who had left the Parliament whereof they were members, & some Officers of the King's Army, whom he knew'. Whitelocke innocently greeted these old acquaintances.* In return they 'saluted him with scorn and anger in their countenance', anger less confected than the comical jibes of Dr Turner. Enquiring how Whitelocke dared to walk alone in Oxford 'without expecting to be cut in pieces', the Royalists 'laid their hands upon their swords'. Whitelocke was preserved by 'providence', this time not in the form of Dr Turner but of the Royalist cavalry colonel Sir Humphrey Bennet, brother of the unfortunate first Mrs Whitelocke, Rebecca. Luckily this

---

* Unfortunately Whitelocke does not name these Royalist MPs, though they would certainly not have included Hyde, whose presence, even if passive, would have been bitterly remembered by Whitelocke.

brother-in-law, unlike his avaricious mother, was still on excellent terms with Whitelocke, and saw off his aggressive comrades 'with a fierce countenance'. In a later 'passage . . . of Merriment', Whitelocke and Sir John Holland were spotted visiting Parliamentarian captives in Oxford Castle, whereupon rumour swept the town that the King had locked up Parliament's Peace Commissioners.

Given that there is no way they can have seen each other's writings, Hyde and Whitelocke are astonishingly united in their estimation of the King's character. 'The King', in Whitelocke's opinion:

> . . . in this Treaty showed great abilities . . . apprehension, reason, & judgement, but his unhappiness was to trust others' judgement much more than his own, to his prejudice.

This is all but identical to Clarendon's considered verdict on King Charles:

> He had an excellent understanding, but was not confident enough of it; which made him often-times change his own opinion for a worse and follow the advice of a man that did not judge so well as himself.

Both friends, susceptible to the King's charm, were willing to deceive themselves about his capabilities.

The story that illustrates Whitelocke's final character sketch of the King, however, does implicitly suggest Charles's underhand malleability:

> . . . [the King] having agreed with the Commissioners upon a point of the Treaty, they prayed his answer accordingly, but the King told them it was then too late to write it, being midnight, but bid them come back the next morning . . . they attended him the next morning & then he gave them his answer in writing, quite contrary to what he had agreed the night before, the Commissioners humbly expostulated with his Majesty upon his royal word to them . . . &

## The Percy's Peace and the Poet's Plot

> prayed that his answer might be as was ... agreed, which would tend very much to a happy issue of the Treaty, whereas this answer would much endanger the breach of it.
>
> The King told them that his mind was altered since the last night, & that he would give no other answer than this ... Some of the King's friends, of whom the Commissioners enquired ... informed them that after the Council were gone from the King, some of his bedchamber, & some higher than they, doubting [i.e. fearing] that the answer which he had promised to us might bring the Treaty to a good effect ... prevailed with him to give that answer which was delivered to the Commissioners ...

What point this was under question, very nearly conceded by the King if Whitelocke is to be believed, is unknowable but can be somewhat narrowed down. Parliament's proposed cessation in fighting during the Treaty had been rejected already. The Church issues, not seriously pursued by the Commissioners, would never at this point have been yielded by Charles. The other serious matters under discussion at the Treaty of Oxford were the militia question, and the Admiralty proposal. There were, of course, innumerable less serious questions, such as whether the rigid Royalist Bankes ought to be replaced as Lord Chief Justice by the more constitutionally minded Bramston, father of another Middle Temple friend of Hyde. The 'King's friends' whose advice the Commissioners sought are very tempting to identify as Falkland and Hyde, ever fearful of the peace's sabotage by their own notional side, and always suspicious of 'bedchamber, & some higher' courtly influence, emanating ultimately from the French, Catholic Queen, even when she was as far off as York.

Both Hyde and Whitelocke put the principal blame on each other's camps, but secondarily on their hard-line war parties, for the failure to extend the Treaty, which thus expired, with nothing agreed, on 15 April. For the two friends this was an outcome as regrettable as it had been avoidable.

## 'Non in faece Romuli' – Oxford, London, Highgate, and Petworth, Spring and Summer 1643

In his *History*, Ned Hyde's portrait of Falkland in 1643, as a wartime Secretary of State, is as memorable as it is improbable, and indeed, read literally, it amounts to an allegation of political incompetence and irresponsibility. According to Hyde, Falkland behaved 'as if he had lived *in republica Platonis, non in faece Romuli*' (in Plato's Republic, not the Midden of Romulus – a tag plundered from Cicero). Hyde claims that Falkland neither employed intelligence agents – as opposed to military scouts – nor consented to read opened enemy correspondence himself, though he allowed subordinates to do so. His depiction of Falkland's motives in the practice of politics is delicately quixotic; his friend sounds alarmingly responsive in all his actions to public shame – shame of being thought servile, fearful, dishonourable, or inconsistent.

For literary, moral, and personal reasons, Hyde prefers to commemorate, indeed to canonize, Falkland the contemplative, the philosopher, the pacifist, adrift in cruel waters. The result is to emphasize by contrast Hyde the practical politician, a peacemaker rather than pacifist, alert to the possibilities of prosecuting war for the eventual advantage of achieving peace. Yet plentiful evidence makes it plain that this beguiling dichotomy, which exudes a miasma of ineffectual sanctity from which Falkland's conduct has never escaped, is a serious, and deliberate, misrepresentation on Hyde's part.\*

---

\* It is worth noting here Clarendon's complete censorship of his sister Susan's later activities as a Royalist intelligence agent in 1653–6, despite, or because of, the fact she lost her life in this endeavour. Whatever the *History* and *Life*'s psychological depth and candour, and their author's willingness to unveil high political intrigue, when it comes to writing about (as opposed to practising) espionage, Clarendon shows the very distaste that he attributes to Falkland. Similarly, in his discussion of the illness and death of the unnamed lady almost certainly meant to be Falkland's close friend Lady Sophia Murray, Clarendon omits both the fact

## The Percy's Peace and the Poet's Plot

There are those ciphered letters from London Royalists to Falkland and, more surprisingly yet, to that painstakingly honourable private subject and volunteer lifeguard Lord Spencer, intercepted by the Peace Commissioners' guards in January 1643; there is Falkland's identification, with Hyde, as the best private channel of communication for those Peace Commissioners who sought to conduct less official negotiations; but most important is Falkland's overarching involvement, far surpassing that of Hyde (as was natural to Falkland's post of Secretary, compared to Hyde's as Chancellor) in the puzzling scheme of late spring 1643 that confusedly entered history under the name of Waller's Plot. With whatever personal reluctance, Falkland was very far from being a Platonist, as opposed to Romulan, Secretary of State and spymaster.

It is clear that Pym and his closest associates had agreed to employ as Peace Commissioners those Parliamentarians most notorious for favouring peace (even if some were then removed from the Treaty of March to April). Allowing the peace party to own any peace, or lack of one, was a calculated risk. On the one hand, as Pym had no real intention of allowing the King to come to terms, to dispatch the leaders of the peace party to Oxford was an immediately effective way to increase the war party's power, both during the Commissioners' absence, and after their almost certainly unsuccessful return, as a now discredited force. But on the other hand, Pym was entrusting the enactment of his unpalatably strict instructions to precisely those moderates most susceptible to a conflict of loyalties. From this sophisticated gamble was to be born the enigmatic plot of that sophisticate *par excellence*, Edmund Waller.

For reasons of his own, Whitelocke implies that he had suspected Waller of already being in collusion with the King during the Peace Commission's visit to Oxford in January. This accusation is so obvious as to be hardly credible. Waller emerges from D'Ewes's parliamentary diary as a constant partisan of the moderate

---

and the circumstances of her imprisonment in London (accused of corresponding with Falkland in cipher).

## Friends in Youth

reformist faction to which Hyde, Falkland, Colepeper, Whitelocke, Geoffrey Palmer, and others belonged between the Irish Rebellion and the Grand Remonstrance. Hyde's *History* describes Waller's conduct in the Commons during the still more divisive year of 1642 with plausible, personally informed detail, and profound underlying cynicism:

> [Waller] had from the beginning of the Parliament been looked upon by all men as a person of very entire affections to the King's service, and to the established government of Church and State, and by having no manner of relation to the Court had the more credit . . . to promote the rights of it.
>
> When the ruptures grew so great between the King and the two Houses that very many members [of Parliament] withdrew . . . he . . . with equal dislike, absented himself; but . . . having intimacy and friendship with some persons now . . . about the King [Falkland and Hyde], with the King's approbation he returned again to London, where he spake upon all occasions with great sharpness and freedom; which (now there were so few there that used it, and . . . no danger of being outvoted) was not restrained, and . . . used as an argument against those who were gone upon pretence that they were not suffered to declare their opinions freely . . . which could not be believed when all men knew what liberty Mr. Waller took, and spake every day with impunity against the sense and proceedings of the House.
>
> This won him a great reputation . . . as the boldest champion the Crown had in both Houses . . .

By Hyde's astute reading, Waller remained in London as the King's 'approbated' spokesman, and Pym's licensed, toothless Leader of the Opposition, a bargain from which Hyde had, by the time of the *History*'s writing after 1646, come to think Pym derived more political capital. Waller's inclusion as a Peace Commissioner would seem to support his view. But as himself one of Waller's 'intimate friends' 'about the King' in 1642, by implication Hyde must have agreed at that time with Waller's lingering presence in the Commons as a royal advocate.

Waller was one of a group of prominent formerly close friends whom Hyde never forgave. Others included the quietly Royalist, personally obnoxious lawyer John Vaughan; the silver-tongued, to Hyde supremely deceptive, Parliamentarian leader John Hampden; the absolutist theorist, later to turn Cromwellian stooge, Thomas Hobbes; the learned, drunken intellectual who sold his pen to Parliament, Tom May; and the Great Tew theologian converted to Rome, Hugh Cressy. There is a personal, specific character to the sense of betrayal that Hyde feels in these cases; he never consigned his old friend Whitelocke, his political patron Pembroke, or his and Whitelocke's mentor Selden (whose quiet support for Parliament he considered blameless), into this category of infamy.

Clarendon's character sketches of such 'false friends' reveal his disapproval and disgust back over the whole course of these relationships under question. This can make it difficult to pinpoint exact moments of disenchantment. To this general tendency Waller presents a revealing exception, because his perfidy manifested itself so spectacularly. In the first half of 1643, Hyde and Falkland still, and rightly, thought of Waller as a true and useful friend. Lack not of zeal, but judgement, would eventually undo Waller's good intentions on behalf of the King and of peace.

As Hyde and Whitelocke both reported, the greatest, most influential concentration of Royalist sentiment in England was still to be found, however counter-intuitively, in London itself. While Lord Mayor Penington and his Aldermen were fiercely Parliamentarian, an equally Royalist city corporation had been elected only in 1641. Although many Royalist peers, MPs, and substantial citizens had fled to the King, at least as many had kept their mouths shut and their London property undisturbed, while hoping for a rapid peace to the King's advantage. In Ivy Lane, with Whitelocke still at Oxford, his wife Frances and their two eldest daughters still lived with the Royalist Hales and Palmers, all tenants of the Royalist Sir Thomas

Fanshawe. The witty milieus of the Inns of Court, where Whitelocke and Hyde among so many others had come of age, nurtured sharp, irreverent young men of means and talent, who by 1643 were as inclined to scoff in private at the overreaching dominion of the Long Parliament as Hyde and Whitelocke had once been to mock the oppressions of the Star Chamber. Royalist MPs at the time of the Grand Remonstrance had been, on average, a decade younger than Pym's seasoned Elizabethan nostalgists, the men who had come to maturity protesting against Buckingham.

This youthful, literary, satirical, educated London Royalist world was one that Waller exemplified, and, as Hyde noted, it chose Waller as its safest, most admired, and convenient confidant:

> ... such Lords and Commons who really desired to prevent the ruin of the kingdom willingly complied in a great familiarity with [Waller], as a man resolute in their ends, and best able to promote them ... it may be they believed his reputation at Court so good, that he would be no ill evidence there for other men's zeal and affection; and so all men spake their minds freely to him, both of the general distemper, and of the passions and ambition of particular persons: all men knowing him to be of too good a fortune, and too wary a nature, to engage himself in designs of danger or hazard ...

The problem, as Hyde cannot quite bring himself to admit through his fog of retrospective contempt, was that Waller turned out to be less wary or circumspect than his witty, worldly friends expected him to be.

Waller was careful enough to carry on a correspondence with Falkland, his old friend and Great Tew host, exclusively through an intermediary: his brother-in-law, Nathaniel Tomkins. Tomkins was not an ideal choice, himself tainted by the hottest strain of Royalism; a former MP, he had long ago been George Digby's tutor, and as a clerk even now handled some of the Queen's business affairs. Hyde, though keen to distance Falkland from the whole affair, concedes his friend's letters to and from Tomkins, behind him, by implication, being Waller:

> [Tomkins] sometimes writ ... and by messengers signified to [Falkland], that the number of those who desired peace, and abhorred the proceedings of the Houses, was very considerable, and that they resolved, by refusing to contribute to the war and to submit to their ordinances, to declare and manifest themselves in that manner that the violent party in the city should not have credit enough to hinder an accommodation. And the lord Falkland always returned answer that they should expedite those expedients as soon as may be, for that delays made the war more difficult to be restrained.

Thus even Hyde admits that by the spring of 1643, if not earlier, Falkland, as Secretary of State, had sanctioned and urged on, if not actually planned, a non-violent scheme for impeding the revenue that Parliament needed for its war, and strengthening the hand of the peace party in the two Houses: to be carried out by Waller, Tomkins, and a potentially large, highly placed body of sympathizers.

To encourage or to originate this imaginative and bloodless plan seems wholly in character, if not for the martyr-saint of Great Tew, then for Falkland as the scraps of direct evidence beyond Hyde himself show him – impulsive, intelligent, ecumenical, industrious, a dedicated opponent of armed conflict and civil strife, partly because he had himself suffered from the confessional divisions in his family and the violence dormant in his own nature.

Waller, Tomkins, a third confederate, the linen draper Richard Chaloner, and other more exalted if less definite plotters now began to conduct a sort of census of inner and outer London.* From their by necessity fragmentary enquiries, they estimated that Parliament had a narrow advantage within the City walls, but the King an

---

* Chaloner was not related to Hyde and Whitelocke's youthful companion, the future regicide Thomas Chaloner.

## Friends in Youth

overwhelming majority of enthusiastic, if currently cowed, supporters directly outside them. Hyde argues that the purpose of this exercise was consistent with the project Waller, via Tomkins, had mooted to Falkland:

> . . . to beget such a combination amongst the party well affected [i.e. the City Royalists], that they would refuse to conform to those ordinances of the twentieth part, and other taxes, for the support of the war; and thereby . . . to prevail with the Parliament to incline to a determination of the war.

Perhaps it began in this way. But Hyde also associates this improvised and anecdotal headcount with the direct involvement in the plot of one Irish peer, Viscount Conway, and the plotters' rumoured communication with two magnates of far greater importance: the Earl of Portland, the Royalist, possibly Catholic peer who had recently fomented public, undignified dissension between the pacific Pembroke and the leading war-party peer Lord Brooke; and Northumberland himself.

Conway was the cultivated, epicurean commander, inevitably another friend of Selden, who had been bested by the Scots at Newburn in 1640. Hyde allows that 'being more of a soldier', Conway 'administered questions and considerations necessary to be understood by men that either meant to use force or to resist it'. Nor would men with so much to lose as Portland and Northumberland be prevailed upon to listen to a plan that did not account for uglier contingencies than adverse votes in Parliament. It is possible to envisage how a peaceable, political plan, in part initiated by Falkland, developed momentum, through the pressure of its most powerful, but least committed, possible backers, into becoming an attempted coup in the capital.

Waller's plot was discovered, or at least dramatically revealed, by Pym during a perfectly timed parliamentary fast-day at the end of May. Pym's informant was named as a servant of Tomkins, who had apparently eavesdropped on his master's plan while concealed behind a wall-hanging. Waller, Tomkins, Chaloner, two innocent Royalist messengers, one of them a young cousin and namesake of Hampden, and even Conway and Portland, were all arrested, then interrogated by a parliamentary committee. Northumberland avoided any such indignities, even though Waller did his panicked, imprudent best to insist on the earl's entanglement. Portland was soon released on bail, Conway imprisoned for a short period, but Tomkins and Chaloner hanged outside their own thresholds.

Waller named many names to his examiners, indeed according to the well-informed and impartial Venetian ambassador, whom Hyde echoes, 'whatever he had said heard, thought or seen, and all that he knew . . . or suspected of others'. By blaming Northumberland, as well as Lord Holland, Waller perhaps hoped to deflect attention from his own culpability through the drama and magnitude of his disclosures. To the whole Commons he now delivered an excellent speech on the perils of letting any MP be sentenced to death at the say-so of soldiers. He consented to pay a fine to the parliamentary government of £10,000, about £1.25 million pounds in today's purchasing power, and reportedly dispensed untold further quantities in bribes throughout the Commons. Waller was released in 1644 and allowed to depart with his 'dear-bought life', and a newly married wife, into mildly inglorious, fairly comfortable French, Swiss, and Italian exile. In 1652 he would be permitted to return to Commonwealth England by the purged, regicidal Parliament. Hyde's parting comment on Waller in the *History* is almost admiring in its elegant disgust:

> . . . there cannot be a greater evidence of the inestimable value of his parts, than that he lived after [the Plot] in the good affection and esteem of many, the pity of most, and the reproach and scorn of none.

Indeed, Waller survived – to be renowned both for his conciliatory wisdom as an MP and his mellifluous flattery as a poet – into the reign of James II. At his death in 1687 his estate was worth £40,000, almost £5 million in today's money.

Northumberland's association with the conspirators was deeply inconvenient for Parliament to acknowledge. The earl had returned from Oxford diminished, but formidable, as Hyde's former neighbour in legal chambers, and once amiable acquaintance, the iconoclastic republican Harry Marten, one of the fieriest of the war party opposed to Northumberland, had discovered. Marten, a notorious womanizer, presumed to open a letter between Northumberland and his young wife, suspecting its contents to be politically subversive. Northumberland chose to regard this intrusion as an insult to his Olympian conception of his personal honour. He took Marten aside in Westminster's Painted Chamber during a meeting of committees from the Lords and Commons, and to the astonishment and consternation of many powerful witnesses 'cudgelled' him with his cane. Had the mercurial Pembroke rather than the saturnine Northumberland so departed from his aristocratic composure, no one would have been in the least surprised, but from a great peer of such renowned pride and self-control this action was truly remarkable. Northumberland had deigned to show the political world that even a 'peace lord' had his limits.

The awkward truth remained that Northumberland had been the principal parliamentary representative in the recent Treaty. A cloud upon his name put the loyalty and actions of his whole delegation, with their crucial, delicate responsibilities and unrivalled opportunities for confidential contact with the enemy, in doubt. It is partly for this reason that Whitelocke is so shrilly insistent on his own distance from Waller, and on the earliest signs in January of Waller's guilt. But in the immediate aftermath of the scandal, three suspects were, for whatever reason, of peculiar interest to the parliamentary interrogators – Whitelocke himself, his colleague Pierrepont, and that epitome of political experience and even-handedness, John Selden.*

Whitelocke, on the defensive, takes up the tale in his diary:

---

* Thomas, Viscount Wenman, one of Waller and Whitelocke's January colleagues, was also fleetingly mentioned in connection with the plot, probably

## The Percy's Peace and the Poet's Plot

> Mr Waller ... being examined about the Plot ... was particularly asked whether Selden, Pierrepont, Whitelocke & others [most likely Wenman, perhaps Dungarvan, Sir John Holland, Lytton and Armine, possibly even Lords Holland, Pembroke and Salisbury, perhaps Northumberland's sister the Countess of Carlisle] ... were not acquainted with it.
>
> He answered that he came one evening to Selden & found with him in his study, Pierrepont & Whitelocke & then intended to advise with them about the Plot, & began to mention such things in general, but they all inveighed so much against anything of that nature as baseness & treachery, that he said nothing to them of any of the particulars, & had such respect for them, that he was almost persuaded himself to give it over.

This fascinating scene is consistently presented, with all its author's juridical care, as Waller's testimony, at one remove, Whitelocke keeping silence on his own behalf as to whatever conversation may have occurred. Some of the sparse details Whitelocke gives have the ring of reality. Selden was generally his circle's city host (with Lady Kent its country hostess), his study a constant, open harbour for his friends and pupils. That Waller should turn up on a whim and find Whitelocke and Pierrepont there by chance sounds likely enough. That so important a topic should have been raised and quickly set down in such company, is less believable. Least tenable of all is the idea that Waller protected, rather than denounced, Selden, Whitelocke, and Pierrepont. He showed himself willing to pay out irretrievably vast sums of money and redirect blame onto anyone else whatsoever – especially Northumberland, the uncle of Waller's lost muse 'Sacharissa' (Lady Dorothy Sidney), who had arguably been his chief political and poetic patron.

A couple of details in Whitelocke's later *Memorials* suggest further clues. According to these Waller visited Selden, knowing

---

because he was Waller's marital kinsman as much as because of his rumoured Royalist leanings.

Whitelocke and Pierrepont to be there, 'on purpose to impart' the plot. The objection of his friends did not just concern 'baseness & treachery', but the likelihood that any such attempt on the city would be bound to become 'the occasion of shedding much blood'. Finally Selden is singled out as the main object of Waller's veneration – 'he durst not, for the awe and respect which he had for Selden, communicate' the whole design.

Sewing these snatches together, a narrative can be faintly made out. Waller's first intention, probably under Falkland's guidance, was to organize resistance by the large, rich, well-connected, discreet body of opinion in London that ranged from covert Royalism to simple pacifism. He planned a civilian and political protest against paying the taxes that financed Parliament's war, thus hoping to attain a resolution for peace in the two Houses. Waller reached out across his dazzling social acquaintance, including two groups, both partly involved with the approaching, or recently failed, Treaty of Oxford – the scholarly MPs, Whitelocke, Pierrepont, and Selden, and the soldier-peers, Conway, Portland, Holland, and Northumberland. The intellectuals approved of the plan as long as it remained exclusively political; the peers, Northumberland still smarting from the King's refusal to meet his secret offer and return to him the office of Lord Admiral, insisted on a practical scheme for taking London by force; whereupon the intellectuals, led by Selden, abhorring the prospect of violence in the city, withdrew their support. Waller, when examined, implicated everybody involved and many besides, but the embarrassed parliamentary leaders covered up the active consent of any recent Peace Commissioners apart from the transparent guilt of Waller himself, carefully exonerating Whitelocke, Pierrepont, and Northumberland.

From Hyde and Falkland's point of view, the abortive Plot was another promising but bungled chance for peace. They did not blame the pacific moderates, Whitelocke, Pierrepont, and Selden, for preventing what would almost certainly have been a futile episode of street-fighting, further alienating the capital from the King. Instead their disenchantment and anger fell on Waller, who had proved weak and unprincipled, all too willing to let a good prospect for peace become a farcical footnote of war.

The King had meanwhile granted a Commission of Array to be issued in London, by the Royalist merchant of Hammersmith, and West African slave-trader, Sir Nicholas Crispe: a hare-brained attempt to raise troops in, and release them upon, the city. Clarendon is at pains to disassociate this manoeuvre from Falkland and Waller's stratagem entirely, but his presentation of the matter does not convince. For one thing the luckless Tomkins was also used as an agent in the dissemination of the Commission of Array. For another, Waller, upon his arrest, had also implicated two ladies of the court well known to and admired by both Hyde and Falkland, both in connection with the Commission of Array once again.

The first, Lady D'Aubigny, née Lady Katherine Howard, was the widow of the King's cousin, Lord George Stuart, Seigneur d'Aubigny, who had been killed fighting in the King's Life Guards at Edgehill the previous year. Hyde esteemed her as 'a woman of very great wit'. She was permitted into London to settle her late husband's affairs, a request that Parliament could not turn down, owing to the dead nobleman's family and property, without offending France. She was reputed to have hidden the Commission's actual document in her abundantly curling dark hair. Most pertinently, Clarendon would call Lady D'Aubigny 'trusted and conversant in those intrigues which at that time could be best managed and carried on by ladies'. In this special role of secret courier, she was one of several Royalist heroines, but on this occasion she was to be associated with one in particular. Lady Sophia Murray, Falkland's particular friend, and probably, as 'Amoret', Waller's sometime muse, was now simultaneously arrested and interrogated by Parliament, along with Lady D'Aubigny, at least partly on Waller's ungallant evidence. The poet accused Lady Sophia of receiving a ciphered letter from Falkland that provided evidence of Northumberland's role in the conspiracy.

Astonishingly, Waller had previously managed to involve his original muse, Lady Dorothy Sidney ('Sacharissa'), by 1643 Lady

## Friends in Youth

Spencer, in his schemes, as early as that February, when he was still acting as a Parliamentarian Peace Commissioner. Lady Spencer was apprehended by Parliamentarian soldiers on her way from London to Oxford with a list of likely London Royalists among her possessions. Her excuse that it had been placed there without her knowledge was accepted: probably because two of her brothers were Parliamentarian officers, her father the Earl of Leicester was the most lukewarm of Royalists, her aunt was the always powerful Countess of Carlisle, her uncle Northumberland was then at the height of his credibility as leader of Parliament's Peace Commission, while even her actively Royalist husband, widely respected throughout Parliament, was known to favour peace.

Treated less courteously than her forerunner in Waller's verses, Lady Sophia altogether refused to condescend to answer her Parliamentarian accusers on the Committee of Safety as to the contents or even existence of her correspondence with Falkland, declaring that 'I do not mean to give an account to such fellows as you are'. Lest she be criticized for hauteur rather than praised for courage, it should be emphasized that the Committee included the Earls of Essex, Northumberland (despite his own compromised position), Holland, and Pembroke, as well as Lord Saye. In any case, the impression of two wholly unconnected schemes emphatically described by Clarendon is hardly believable.

It was thus probably with some justice, as well as the greatest of ease, that Pym depicted the Royalist plans involving London as a single diabolical, sanguinary Plot: precisely the emergency that the struggling war party in Parliament required. In early June, members of the Commons and then the Lords were heavily pressured to take the 'Vow and Covenant', a significant, candid development from the theoretical Parliamentarian position up to this time, that Parliament fought for the King's true, traditional interest. The 'Vow and Covenant' committed those who took it to 'Defence of the true Protestant Religion, and Liberties of the Subject', by uttermost resistance to the 'Popish Army', crucially and frankly described as 'raised by the King'.

Whitelocke was 'one of the last in the House that took the Covenant', among those 'looked upon as ill affected [to Parliament] who were backward to take it'. But like other moderate Parliamentarians, he had little choice since the disaster of Waller's Plot, considering how closely it had come to tarnishing him. To distance himself personally and geographically from his quasi-Royalist reputation, Whitelocke had already moved his family's city residence from Ivy Lane, with the Hales and the Palmers, to reside in Highgate, north London, with the Winwoods, despite the 'troublesome' greater distance from Westminster and the City. (Yet a hedging consideration subtly persisted: the Whitelockes' and Winwoods' landlord, Sir Robert Payne, was still a Royalist, and Highgate boasted many others of note.)

Two acts of kindness subtly served to illustrate the quality of the change that had now calcified upon the war, the city, and the kingdom. Whitelocke had been obliged to share his colleague and fellow lodger Winwood's coach since the loss of his own at Fawley Court, all the more often since removing to Highgate. Now his 'friend and client', the rich, bibliomane peace-party MP Sir William Drake, who had also long admired the capacities of Ned Hyde, 'bestowed upon him a Coach and a pair of good horses'; in return, Whitelocke was to handle Drake's business affairs while he stayed on the continent for an indefinite period, the latest peace-loving Englishman to despair of his country. About the same time the Speaker of the House of Commons, William Lenthall, gave Whitelocke a blank pass to take parliamentary leave out of London, however and wherever he wished, not so dissimilar to the medical pass Hyde had been granted in May 1642. Of this privilege Whitelocke optimistically states, 'such confidence [Lenthall] had in Whitelocke's friendship and faithfulness', probably to head off the more obvious conclusion that the Speaker, a humane man to his friends, was hinting to Whitelocke that the city might be too hot for him.

Falkland had warned Tomkins and Waller to 'expedite those expedients as soon as may be, for that delays made the war more difficult to be restrained.' This had in a way been percipient, but

Waller's miscarried 'expedients' had proved instead the very agency to extinguish the city's underlying yearning towards conciliation.

Northumberland, further insulted by the Lord Mayor Penington's rash attempt to have him arrested, sounded out none other than the Lord General Essex, his cousin, about both of them going over to the King. Meeting with no success there, he sulkily retired to his favourite seat of Petworth in Sussex in August. Three other 'peace lords' – the Earl of Bedford whose father had attempted to save Strafford and achieve compromise; the Earl of Clare, Strafford's brother-in-law, brother of the peace-party leader Denzil Holles; and that glistening weathervane the Earl of Holland – proceeded to Oxford at the same time. There Hyde and Falkland, but not the King, welcomed them. Their conspicuous, temporary defections were to bring peace no nearer.

## 12.

# Our Utmost Endeavours

> *... Till thou the bound*
> *Of pale* Avernus *passe, if back thou cast*
> *Thy carefull eyes, thou losest what thou hast.*
>
> George Sandys, Book X,
> *Ovids Metamorphosis Englished*

## 'An end to the carnage' – Uxbridge, January 1645; Westminster, Oxfordshire, Oxford, November–December 1644

Little of national or historical note, whether remote or recent, had ever transpired in Uxbridge, the Middlesex township west of London. In the mid-sixteenth century the antiquary John Leland had described it as 'but one street, but that, for timber, well builded'. 'The hamlet of Hillingdon' was a modest, quietly prosperous place, feeding upon the capital, boasting both church and market, neighbours of impeccable thirteenth-century lineage. Its small, kempt inns made of Uxbridge a sort of Brentford in miniature, but its civil-war experience, two and a half years into the English conflict, had been happier. The Royalist advance to Turnham Green had passed harmlessly by to its south. The town remained under Parliament's undisputed control, neither important nor imperilled enough to be encumbered with a governor and garrison.

Then, in January 1645, Uxbridge's every spare house and room suddenly teemed with royal counsellors, parliamentary grandees, subtle divines, charismatic preachers, interested and well-connected observers, Scottish dignitaries, industrious secretaries, assiduous retainers, and severally opinionated journalists; an official influx of 216 individuals, with an unknowable multitude besides. In sentiment as in geography, Uxbridge was well suited to a fresh treaty between Oxford and London. To Hyde it seemed that the mood of the town was all but Royalist:

> ... it was observed by the town and the people that flocked thither that the King's commissioners looked as if they were at home and governed the town, and the other [i.e. Parliament's Commissioners, and the representatives of their fractious Scottish allies] as if they were not in their own quarters: and the truth is, they had not that alacrity and serenity of mind as men use to have who do not believe themselves to be at fault.

But for Whitelocke this was a matter of simple decorum rather than underlying sympathy; the King's envoys were 'more civilly treated than the Parliament's Commissioners [had been] at Oxford', a comparison upon which, as a Peace Commissioner past and present, he had ample reason to meditate.

The year since Parliament's Vow and Covenant, in the summer of 1643, had not, on balance, tended to the King's advantage. Although Parliament lost its two most prominent leaders in 1643, Hampden mortally wounded in June, Pym succumbing to cancer in December, Pym had bequeathed an all-important legacy: a militarily committed, if inherently unstable, alliance with the Scots Covenanters. This chimerical compact produced bloody results in July 1644, at Marston Moor in Yorkshire. There the Scots shared, not without acrimony, the glory of defeating Prince Rupert and the Marquess of Newcastle with the Parliamentarian generals Sir Thomas Fairfax and Oliver Cromwell, so ending the long Royalist dominance of northern England.

But in September 1644 King Charles fought back, personally defeating the Earl of Essex at Lostwithiel in Cornwall. Encouraging news then reached him of the repeated success in Scotland of his most startling, virtuosic champion, the Marquess of Montrose, a disillusioned Covenanter. Meanwhile, the Royalist 'Parliament' summoned by the King, at Hyde's pressing suggestion, to convene at Christ Church and the Bodleian Library in Oxford, was continually urging Charles to consider a new treaty. The King was more irritated by the presumption of his Oxford MPs in matters of policy than Hyde would have liked, dismissing the Oxford assembly to his Queen, herself safe in France since July, as a 'mongrel Parliament'. Charles thus showed his Oxford Lords and Commons even less respect than Whitelocke and his Westminster colleagues, who termed them 'the Anti Parliament'.

Such a label, carrying with it Scriptural and antiquarian echoes of Revelation and of imperial and papal struggle, at least paid the Oxford Parliament the considerable compliment of hostile fear. By contrast Charles seems to have felt for his loyally schismatic Oxonian Parliamentarians an all too characteristic underlying contempt. But the King still realized the value of Hyde's constitutionalist device, both as political cover and as an instrument for bolstering his increasingly scarce revenue. Both these assets were naturally emphasized by Hyde, not just a constant and sincere upholder of English parliamentary precedent, but also as the long-suffering civil-war Chancellor of the Exchequer. So when Oxford spoke for peace, Charles felt obliged to adopt at least the appearance of listening.

Despite the frustrations Whitelocke had endured as a Peace Commissioner in 1643, he responded avidly to the fresh Royalist approach the next year: 'Upon a new Overture for . . . peace, Whitelocke spake passionately to further it'. Pleading for 'an end to the carnage', he showed his usual frank even-handedness, always so rhetorically (if not invariably politically) effective:

> God hath given you [i.e. the Parliamentarians] great successes . . . sometimes pleased to give our enemies successes . . . whether of one or the other party, the poor English are still sufferers . . .
>
> Whose goods, I pray . . . are plundered? Whose houses burnt? . . . Whose blood stains the walls of our towns and defiles our land?

## *Friends in Youth*

Is it not all English? And is it not then time for us, who are all Englishmen, to be weary of these discords, and to use our utmost endeavours to put an end to them?

... it was an unhappy mistake of those who told us in the beginning of our warfare, that it would be only to show ourselves in the field with a few forces, and then all would be presently ended.

... although we have Irish, French, Dutch, and Walloons, as well as other papists, engaged for the settlement of the protestant religion and laws of England, yet I am persuaded, that his majesty and you mutually endeavouring, (as it is both your interests,) none can hinder it.

... Let us consent to anything that is just, reasonable, and honourable, rather than in the least neglect *to seek peace* ...

It is one of Whitelocke's plainest speeches, unusually light on learned allusion, whether Biblical, classical, historical, or legal. The patriotic strain to which Whitelocke always had ready resort here approaches (understandable) xenophobia, in the speaker's distaste for foreign mercenary soldiery, from Princes Rupert and Maurice down, profiting while the natives of England continue to suffer. Whitelocke boldly questions the Providential confidence of the war party, acknowledging royal victories and implying that there is little to choose between the two sides in moral terms. He openly points out the error of the most militant Parliamentarian leaders in predicting a swift, almost bloodless war: that expedient complacency from which Whitelocke had correctly dissented at the outset. His ironical comment upon 'Irish, French, Dutch, and Walloons, as well as other papists, engaged for the settlement of the protestant religion and laws of England' applies to professional soldiers on both sides and makes dry mockery of both the Royalist and Parliamentarian party lines, yet bites hardest against Whitelocke's own theoretical colleagues, who by 1644 were all too open to the accurate allegation that they were altering, rather than defending, the long-established constitution. Whitelocke's own proposed course, vague but expansive, certainly makes potential concessions towards the King, in requesting the acceptance of 'anything . . . just, reasonable and honourable'.

In these sentiments Whitelocke represented, at least, a considerable and articulate body of Parliament's peace party. The war party, from whose ranks Marston Moor's English victor, Cromwell, was emerging as a leader, considered the peace-party moderates tamed since Waller's Plot. They opted to repeat the tactic of 1643, sending good-faith Peace Commissioners whose influence would be detached from Parliament for a time, and who would probably take the political discredit for a treaty's failure. Accordingly, in November 1644, Whitelocke got his dutiful if wearisome wish, a return to Royalist Oxford.

His companions on this latest mission included Wenman and Pierrepont: two seasoned and disillusioned peacemakers like himself; like Whitelocke, they were implicated, according to plausible rumour emanating from the war party, in Waller's Plot. There were also three Parliamentarians who had not gone to Oxford in 1643 – the Earl of Denbigh, Denzil Holles, and the young Baron Maynard. No relation to Whitelocke and Hyde's Middle Temple crony, Maynard had inherited significant property in Essex and Cambridgeshire. His later marriage to Margaret Murray, youngest daughter of the inveterate courtly intriguer, William Murray, Earl of Dysart, suggests Royalist inclinations. Holles, an always contradictory, stubbornly major figure – a long-time schemer with the Covenanters, yet a staunch defender of his deceased brother-in-law Strafford, one of the Five Members yet also tarnished by Waller's conspiracy, an incompetent soldier who dared to accuse Cromwell of personal cowardice – was the nearest thing the peace party had to a consistent leader. Denbigh, half Villiers through his mother, ambassador to Venice in the 1630s and attracted to the city-state's amalgam of oligarchy and strictly limited monarchy, had been a passionate friend of Hyde's before the war. At Edgehill he had led Parliament's cavalry, without great success, against his own father, who died of lingering wounds incurred that day. By 1644, Denbigh entertained clear doubts about the cause for which he had fought.

Parliament's envoys were now accompanied by a trio representing their Scots Covenanter allies: a minister, Robert Barclay, a laird, Sir Charles Erskine of Alva, and John, Lord Maitland, a fleshy, jumpy, pedantic young man of twenty-eight, prodigiously educated and politically duplicitous (traits of his able and avaricious family since the career of William Maitland of Lethington, Mary Queen of Scots's slippery Secretary of State).

Destined, as Duke of Lauderdale, to become Charles II's venally indispensable Scottish viceroy, Maitland was an experienced traveller (having studied at Geneva), a prolix speaker, and a proven schemer and negotiator. He had first acted as a Scots Commissioner sent to Charles I in 1640, at the age of twenty-four. Through 1643-4, Maitland had taken Whitelocke's measure as a fellow lay member of the Westminster Assembly of Divines, the body for deciding upon the structure of a new national Church, wherein Whitelocke, Selden, and John Glyn, another of Bulstrode and Ned's youthful companions, had eventually outmanoeuvred the Scots. To Maitland's credit, he seems to have felt more respect for, even deference to, Whitelocke, than enmity towards a triumphant adversary. This realistic ability to appraise an opponent and cooperate with him untribally as an efficient colleague was typical of Maitland: no fanatical Covenanter, but a flexible coming man of power.

The parliamentary and Scots Commissioners found the King unpromisingly difficult to run to ground, having been misinformed that he was at Marlborough in Wiltshire. Chasing Charles towards Wallingford on the latest information, 'very late & in bad ways & weather', they stopped for the night at the incommodiously named village of Nettlebed, not far from Whitelocke's own ravaged estate at Henley. Although in this 'small Country Village, they had very bad quarter, for so many great persons, Whitelocke shifted the better for being known in the place . . . they contented themselves & were cheerful'. Maitland, especially, noted his English colleague's resource.

At Wallingford the Royalist governor, Colonel Thomas Blagge, received them late and with ill grace, or, as Whitelocke delicately expressed it, 'not rudely, but with height enough'.* He offered Whitelocke and Maitland wine before informing them that their rural excursion had been unnecessary: 'he believed the King was returned to Oxford . . . it was more probable they might find him there, than in any other place'. Blagge then regaled Denbigh, the most military of the Commissioners, with a menacing, even insulting series of battle reminiscences, to which Denbigh replied in kind: 'some relations of passages of War, wherein both of them were actors, & neither of them could bear any diminution of themselves or their parties'. Unaligned in his journal as in the Commons, Whitelocke shows equal exasperation towards both braggart soldiers. But this edged exchange of war stories proved too much for Maitland, who turned for aid to the man he had identified as the coolest-headed and most effectual of the English Commissioners: '. . . both [Denbigh and Blagge] grew so high that the Lord Maitland looked very pale, & he & others feared their throats would be cut by the Garrison . . . they earnestly desired Whitelocke to be a means to bring them off from that place & peril'.

Whitelocke was perhaps still regarded among the Commissioners as having the smoothest relations with the Royalists. He failed, however, to smooth matters out between Denbigh and 'the haughty Governor', instead shepherding the delegation to the relative comfort of Bensington, an improvement on Nettlebed and boasting 'plenty of excellent fowl . . . good quarter, & entertainment which the Scots highly commended'. Over the next few months Whitelocke was to become well acquainted with Scots appetites.

The Commissioners re-entered Oxford after a pointedly uncomfortable and discourteous wait at the pleasure of another vindictive Royalist military governor, Sir Jacob Astley, 'about four hours . . . in the cold and open air'. Shadowed by menacing Royalist

---

* As the King's Groom of the Chamber, it is possible that Colonel Blagge played a role in hindering the Oxford negotiations of 1643, which Whitelocke noted were impeded both by bedchamber influence '& some higher than they'.

horse, the two English peers, four MPs, and three Scots, and their large combined retinue were all marched to the same billet, a step down even from Nettlebed, the Katherine Wheel, 'a poor Inn', 'little above the degree of an alehouse', with which it is however possible Whitelocke had picaresque prior acquaintance, nestled as it was in the majestic shadow of his, and Archbishop Laud's, Oxford college, St John's. The place was associated with Catholicism (it adjoined Balliol, another persistent haunt of Popery), having even played host to the Gunpowder Plotters. As lodging for Parliamentarian and Covenanter envoys professing patriotism, loyalty, and Protestantism, it invited scornful rebukes. Familiar catcalls drove the Peace Commissioners inside, as 'the people for whose sakes they did undergo all these hazards, called them Rogues, Traitors, & Rebels'.

The cavalry officer to whom Astley had entrusted his scarcely honoured guests 'slightly excused' the Katherine Wheel's lowliness, 'because the Town was so full of the King's forces'. Northumberland and Pembroke would never have been offered such 'mean quarter', and Denbigh, smarting from his quarrel with Blagge, felt his own shortage of prestige keenly (Maitland was, if less physically courageous, tougher-minded). In any case, the Commissioners' cramped and inauspicious new residence did not stop them from soon receiving visits of importance:

> Divers great Lords & others of the King's party came to visit them, & discoursed of the propositions, Sir Edward Hyde came to Whitelocke and they had much conference together.

Whitelocke's consistent acknowledgement of Hyde's Royalist knighthood is characteristically good-tempered but also significant. He even seems a little proud of his old friend's elevation, punctiliously calling him 'Mr Edward Hyde now knighted' at the first opportunity, however opposed their causes had become. Whitelocke first records Hyde's knighthood in almost the same quill-stroke as he commends his nephew, Roger Mostyn, for his exemplary gallantry as the *Royalist* governor of Flint Castle. That Whitelocke specifically mentions Hyde's 1644 approach is interesting; by contrast neither man referred to the other by name in their separate, detailed accounts of the 1643 Oxford Treaty. Whitelocke states that during this conversation Hyde 'professed his earnest desire and endeavour that [the peace proposals] might take effect'.

This 'conference' was not, however, one that Hyde, for his part, chose to recall. According to Whitelocke, both Hyde and Geoffrey Palmer had broken off private correspondence with him around the turn of 1643–4, amid the war's increasing polarizing influence after Waller's Plot and the Vow and Covenant. In that political context they might even have done so to protect Whitelocke's position as a possible peacemaker, as much as their own loyal credentials at Oxford. But Hyde's reticence may have been heightened by certain doubtful sequels to his visit to the Katherine Wheel.

Scarcely had Holles and Whitelocke – here associated together with particular closeness for the first, but not last, time – 'together waited on Sir Edward Hyde to the Inn door', when, 'returning back', they were alarmed by a considerable commotion in the inn's none too spacious main hall: 'a great noise . . . many in a great tumult . . . with swords drawn'. The increasing ill-discipline of the King's officers was telling once more. Obliged by the overcrowded conditions of the garrison-court-university-city, or by the Governor or the King's inhospitable orders, to share rooms with the Commissioners of the enemy, these ill-paid, doubtfully fortunate soldiers turned their anger on the Commissioners' servants. Holles, whose outstanding political bravery Hyde recognized, now showed personal calibre too, grabbing one officer, 'a tall, big, black fellow, & taking him by the Collar shook him, & told him, it was basely & unworthily done . . . to abuse the Commissioners' servants in their own quarters . . . contrary to the King's safe Conduct, & presently took the officer's sword from him'.

Whitelocke, despite his old leg injury and generally composed temperament seldom backward in pugilistic emergencies, and now bolstered by the doughty Holles, followed suit, '& did the same to another great mastiff fellow'. Both Commissioners, 'fearing some design upon them', sent an express message of complaint to Astley and had the inn's door secured. Before long their disarmed captives had been marched off to temporary imprisonment. The Commissioners were awarded a regular guard, having won their enemies' respect – 'this action of Holles & Whitelocke was commended by those of the King's party'. In 1643, similarly accosted, Whitelocke had been rescued by his Cavalier brother-in-law Sir Humphrey Bennet. This time he and Holles had fended for themselves, not without considering possible foul play. Whatever common ground Hyde and Whitelocke had agreed upon immediately beforehand, this was a discouraging aftermath.

The following day, Holles and Whitelocke, again inseparable, responded to the courteous invitation of a kinsman to both Holles himself and Frances Whitelocke: the Earl of Lindsey who had lost his father at Edgehill. After informing their colleagues, Holles and Whitelocke visited Lindsey at Christ Church, where Lindsey was himself bed-bound by a wound. Suddenly 'the King & divers Lords . . . came into the Room'; Hyde is not mentioned as being among them. Holles and Whitelocke were now in an awkward position. They had not cleared a private royal audience with the other Commissioners, and King Charles only increased their discomfiture, pressing them to tell him what terms they would advise him to accept, 'as from his private subjects & friends . . . in freedom of discourse'. Like so much personal Stuart diplomacy, the King's gambit possessed flair and imagination but no reliable, ballasting guarantee of good faith. Holles and Whitelocke extricated themselves with great difficulty and legalistic skill, leaving behind an unsigned statement written 'in an unusual hand', and letting slip only the apparently uncontentious verbal advice that the King should end the war by attending his Westminster Parliament in person.

The rest of the 1644 Oxford mission was passed in a week of quibbling bad temper, demonstrated particularly by Denbigh, Princes Rupert and Maurice, and the King himself. At the end of the month the Commissioners were obliged either 'themselves to break off the Treaty' without the 'judgement of their Masters', that is, both

Houses of Parliament, or to carry a message that the King had only reluctantly agreed to let them see, yet only deigned to address to them rather than to the Parliament they represented. At the 'earnest intreaty' of some Royalist 'lords', with whom Hyde would certainly have concurred, Whitelocke and his colleagues reluctantly agreed. They returned to London by way of Henley, Bulstrode's devastated patrimony, marred now by contending forts; Whitelocke's own Phyllis Court, the Royalists' Greenland, and Fawley Court in between, 'miserably torn & plundered by each of them'. Whitelocke complained that paradoxically 'they at [Parliamentarian] Phyllis Court did him much spoil & mischief, though he was a Parliament man, but brutish soldiers make no distinctions'. When told that the local woods belonged to his English colleague, Maitland, casting heavy-lidded eyes over the melancholy scene, declared with candid dismay in his scholarly East Lothian speech, 'In good faith man, these be nay woods, but broom closes', broom being a plant known to proliferate on uncultivated land.

The royal message grudgingly carried by Whitelocke and his fellows expressed Charles's 'earnest desire of peace', requesting a safe conduct for two emissaries of the highest rank, the King's cousin Richmond and the Earl of Southampton, both as genuinely devoted to the achievement of peace as Whitelocke himself. A protracted debate over whether the safe conduct should be conceded pitted the Scots and the English peace party against the war party, by now associated with 'Independent', varied, non-conformist religious toleration, as opposed to reformed national Church government on Presbyterian, quasi-Scottish lines. The most prominent Independent leaders were Sir Harry Vane the younger, Sir Arthur Haselrig, the ever-shifty Oliver St John, and, now coming to the fore, Oliver Cromwell. After the safe conduct was narrowly granted, the Earl of Essex, still Parliament's Lord General but now firmly with the peace party, colluded with Holles and the Scots in trying to employ Whitelocke, along with his and Hyde's old associate John Maynard, to have Cromwell prosecuted as an 'incendiary', kindling contention between Scotland and England. Whitelocke and Maynard adeptly avoided this dangerous brief; this demonstration of tactful neutrality would eventually commend their services to the grateful Cromwell.

To Hyde, his own, Richmond, and Southampton's view of the projected negotiations was clearly and substantially identical to that of the Parliamentarian peace party, so well represented by Whitelocke, his still not entirely former friend:

> [Richmond and Southampton] discovered that they who did heartily wish the peace did intend to promote a treaty between persons named by the King and . . . by Parliament, to meet at some third place, and not . . . to Oxford to treat with the King himself; which they had already found to be ineffectual . . .
>
> The method was not ingrateful to [Richmond and Southampton], who had the same conceptions, that, if sober men were named for commissioners, somewhat would result from the freedom of their communication.

In this way was hum-drum, hitherto passed-by Uxbridge discovered as the ideal 'third place', where Whitelocke and Hyde were both nominated among the 'sober men'. But before the negotiations proper could commence, the war party had an eloquently spiteful further point to make.

## 'Two hundred couple of black rabbits' – The Trial, Attainder, Pardon, and Execution of Archbishop Laud – Westminster 1643–5, Oxford 1644–5

During the autumn of 1643, one disheartening to both sides, Whitelocke had, with great difficulty and at some political risk, avoided a duty too opprobrious for his sometimes pragmatic and accommodating conscience.

Whitelocke had first come to national attention in 1641 by his crucial, prominent, ultimately unsuccessful role in preparing a capital charge of high treason against the Earl of Strafford. Although that legal case had collapsed, Parliament had voted through its desired, predetermined capital verdict anyway. Despite the fact that the impact of Strafford's trial on Whitelocke's political career was in the main positive, as a formative experience upon his personal character it was traumatic. Unlike Falkland and Hyde, he had no particular personal or political quarrel with Strafford; he recalls being treated well by him as a youthful MP, and though the date Whitelocke gives, 1626, cannot be correct, the encounter is likely enough to be transposed from some other time. Strafford's dignified bearing and powerful defence evidently affected Whitelocke, who was all too aware of the flaws in the case assembled, and at times articulated, by his committee colleagues.

As a private man called to condemn a largely admirable statesman and fellow human being upon patently unjust grounds, Whitelocke found the whole affair distasteful and guilt-inducing. Although he voted with the overwhelming majority for the attainder (unlike his mentor Selden, but like Hyde and Falkland), he cannot have done so happily. Whitelocke habitually felt empathy for great men brought low, great at any rate by office, whatever their actual qualities. Before Strafford's attainder, Whitelocke had, with Hyde and Falkland, pursued the impeachment of the corrupt, petty, and dictatorial Lord Keeper Finch, one of the 'grandees', with Selden and Noy, in the arrangement of the lawyers' masque. All three friends and allies were thanked by Parliament for this service, but while Hyde and Falkland had carried it out without compunction, Whitelocke experienced some sense of pathos at Finch's fall from worldly greatness, however much he deserved it. Finch, that bird of lesser stature, escaped into ignominious Dutch exile; Members of Parliament, including the nuanced and cautious Earl of Essex, were satisfied with nothing less than Strafford's blood. Although Whitelocke gave the attainder his prudent vote, he determined not to be forced to condemn a man against his conscience again. Indeed he avoided further capital charges of any kind, until the particular and obnoxious demands of October 1643.

Archbishop Laud, arrested alongside Strafford in 1641, bugbear of the Covenanter Scots and Parliamentarian English opposition to Charles I, had, in consideration of his age and office, been left to lie uncomfortably in the Tower, deprived of pen, paper, and books, but unharmed. Some lacklustre charges had been prepared against him during Strafford's trial, principally by Holles, who by showing zeal against Laud perhaps hoped to arrange a modicum of mercy for his brother-in-law. The prosecution had then lapsed for more than two years. But in late September 1643, Pym's long-sought alliance with the Scots came into being. It was felt needful to cover the awkwardness with which most Parliamentarians at Westminster swallowed the theocratic pledges of the Scots Solemn League and Covenant with some conspicuous sacrifice at the Presbyterian shrine. Thus, in October, was Whitelocke named to the committee ordered to draw up a substantive case for high treason against the archbishop of Canterbury.

Whitelocke's personal relations with Laud had been of much longer standing than Hyde's, but also of more variable warmth. His father the judge had been Laud's close, yet always qualified undergraduate friend at Oxford, prophetically considering him 'too full of fire, though a just and good man'. During Bulstrode's own career at St John's College, Laud was his benevolent president, a generous, interested, involved patron to his friend's son. At the death of Judge Whitelocke in 1632, Laud had summoned Bulstrode for a conversation during which he imparted quasi-paternal advice that was possibly also a veiled political threat. Late in 1634 Whitelocke had been reprimanded as Recorder of Abingdon for not enforcing Laud's regulations on religious ceremony, although he may also have been conducting intelligence work for the Privy Council at Laud's behest in the same period. After Whitelocke's runaway second marriage, the archbishop had ranted at him 'in his usual passion' for marrying above his rank. Peace had been effected through the good offices of Dr Richard Baylie, Laud's successor as President of St John's, but the relationship remained complex, however the highly coloured, emotional archbishop might insist what he felt for the younger Whitelocke was still at heart 'love'.

Neither Hyde nor Whitelocke had registered the slightest note of dissension at the archbishop's original arrest alongside Strafford, during the inception of the second Parliament of 1640. To them both it was an inevitable, at bottom necessary, political downfall (Falkland, for his part, was a constant and passionate critic of Laud's political influence and interference). But, considering both his attitude to the trial and attainder of Strafford and his personal history with Laud, Whitelocke was understandably horrified to be chosen to prosecute the archbishop in 1643. He could see that the case was as weak yet as politically preordained as had been Strafford's. Worse still, he knew that to try, convict, attaint, and execute Laud would be to inflict a cruel and needless wound upon the fragile prospect of peace. To cap it all, Whitelocke was being required to re-enact one of his most conspicuous and regretted briefs, and against someone whom, unlike Strafford, he had known intimately all his life.

At every exquisitely painful dilemma posed thus far by the civil war, Whitelocke had, often reluctantly and barely, come to identify the Parliamentarian position more closely with his duty (as it was very clearly with his material and professional interests) than the Royalist view. Now, for the first time, his duty and his interests were inextricably in conflict. He chose to take a moderate stand, befitting his general disposition:

> ... pressed by Mr [Miles] Corbet, the Chairman, to attend [the committee for Laud's prosecution] ... he declined, & gave his reasons to Mr Corbet for it. Nevertheless [Corbet] unkindly, complained to the house of Whitelocke's neglect in this business & moved that the house would order him to attend it. Whereupon Whitelocke acquainted the house, that when he was in Oxford the Archbishop Laud took care of his Education, & was very kind to him as his father's friend, & now for him personally to prosecute that man for his life, to whom he had been beholden for his education, he appealed to the house whether it were fit for him to do so, & prayed

their excuse in this, & his diligence should make it up for some other affairs in their service. The house unanimously excused him and Corbet was ashamed of his rugged accusation.

This made little or no difference to the archbishop's plight. Nonetheless Whitelocke's defence of Laud was brave in its way, intelligent in its form, and powerful in its symbolism, especially considering when it was delivered.

In late 1643 Whitelocke was a marked man to Westminster's war party, burdened by the failed Treaty of Oxford, sullied by the luxurious scent of Waller's Plot, separated by politics and religion from Parliament's new Scots allies. Yet he chose on this occasion to embrace his reputation as a moderate, near-neutral peacemaker. His offer to substitute for work arraigning the archbishop 'diligence . . . for some other affairs in their service', was transparently an offer to act in another treaty as soon as possible. By resisting the offensive duty of acting against Laud, he bested the war party, in the unlovely person of 'rugged' Miles Corbet (a future regicide and Cromwellian henchman in Ireland), to the gain, not directly of Laud himself, but, at least for the moment, of the entire peace party.

The trial of Laud proceeded during 1644, but for most of that year without urgency or immediate menace. Whitelocke recorded the most outlandish charges, wholly fictional intrigues between the archbishop and the Pope, in his much later *Memorials*, without any comment. Perhaps he was shocked by them; more likely he regarded them as so wild as to provide implicit evidence for the defence. He had old friends among both the prosecuting and defending counsel, John Maynard with the prosecutors, Matthew Hale and Chaloner Chute for the defence (all of these three, especially Chute, were friends of Hyde as well). Two regular enemies of Whitelocke's also prosecuted Laud: Samuel Browne, a relentless shadow of the war party's most exalted lawyer Oliver St John, and the pamphleteer William Prynne, masqued against a long decade ago, by now released, revered, and, as ever, voluminously productive.

At Oxford the latest charge against Laud was hardly noticed, considered, like its 1641 predecessor, to be an empty dead letter, until the new treaty to take place at Uxbridge was agreed upon in principle at the end of 1644, and Richmond and Southampton had been dispatched to London. In the late section of the *History*, Clarendon notes that:

> ... as soon as [the Parliamentarian leaders] received the King's message [requesting his lords' safe conduct], they proceeded upon their trial of the archbishop of Canterbury ... upon an impeachment of high treason, resolving likewise to give that evidence to the people of what resolution they had to make a peace.

He follows this bleak sarcasm with a revealing error, stating that '[Laud] had lain prisoner in the Tower from the beginning of the Parliament, full four years, without any prosecution'. But though Laud had in fact been prosecuted, strictly speaking, twice, once abortively, the second time ongoing since the preceding year, it was only now, with some reason, that the court was shocked into acknowledging Parliament's earnest, deadly intentions.

Whitelocke's references to the trial are impersonal in style and, but for the slenderest of implicit suggestions, impartial in content. Clarendon's version, after the reality of Laud's danger was accepted among the Royalists, is hot with outraged advocacy. He scoffs at the charges as 'several articles of high treason, which, if all that was alleged ... had been true, could not have made him guilty of treason'. This is a, perhaps half-conscious, inversion of the rhetorically effective, logically bankrupt doctrine of 'cumulative treason', which Falkland had invented to cover Strafford: 'How many hair's breadths makes a tall man?' In other words, even if no charges singly or collectively amounted to a technical definition of treason, the general impression of treason was conclusive enough. Laud's wittiest defence counsel, John Herne, put forward a similar argument to Clarendon's, again inverting Falkland's, with his own jocular-seeming question, whether 'two hundred couple of black rabbits' made a black horse.

Clarendon alludes to 'such . . . particulars as the consciences of his greatest enemies absolved him from'. Hyde was incandescently aware that such men as Oliver St John and Harry Marten, his own former friends and parliamentary and legal colleagues, did not believe Laud to be a crypto-Catholic, traitor, or anything but an ambitious, politically minded, meddling Protestant archbishop, indelibly hostile to their own political interests. Hyde knew all too well that Laud had fallen victim to a very particular political class, his own:

> [Laud was] prosecuted by lawyers . . . who, from their own antipathy to the Church and bishops, or from some disobligations received from him, were sure to bring passion, animosity and malice of their own, what evidence soever they had from others . . . they did treat him with all the rudeness, reproach and barbarity imaginable; with which his judges were not displeased.

Perfectly capable himself elsewhere both of understanding and acidly articulating anticlerical annoyance, Hyde perceived, analysed, reacted to, and returned the 'passion, animosity and malice' of the lawyers who brought down Laud, because he knew only very slight hazards of coincidence had separated him from their same opinion.

No one saw and described so lucidly as Hyde the human failings of Laud, his bad temper, his self-righteousness, tactlessness, touchiness, and ludicrous sense of his own and his office's importance. Few commentators lingered so emphatically as Hyde on the understandable irritation of the common lawyers, their professional interests increasingly impeded by the pretensions of Laud's emboldened ecclesiastical courts. Hyde, like Falkland, disapproved of Laud's wide-ranging excursions into the government of the state, and he put his criticisms to his archiepiscopal patron, if more politely, no less directly. He knew well that only chance had made him not, like so many of his colleagues, the recipient of Laud's 'disobligations' (like, for example, Hyde and Whitelocke's roistering

Inns of Court companion Tom Chaloner, who appeared as a witness against Laud to avenge his own persecution by the archbishop), but rather his ally, confidant, client, and friend. Among the prosecutors whom Hyde accuses of 'rudeness, reproach, and barbarity' was his old companion John Maynard, in the *Life* classed with Whitelocke as a man against whom Clarendon cannot muster any real blame or fury:

> ... though [Whitelocke and Maynard] did afterwards bow their knees to Baal, and so swerved from their allegiance, it was with less rancour and malice than other men: they never led, but followed; ... were rather carried away with the torrent, than swam with the stream ... failed through those infirmities, which less than a general defection and a prosperous rebellion could never have discovered.

Indeed Maynard, having played his political cards during the interregnum more carefully even than Whitelocke, would be promoted during the Restoration under Clarendon's Lord Chancellorship. Nonetheless, in the matter of Laud, Whitelocke stalwartly resisted any temptation to avenge the archbishop's real 'disobligations', whereas Maynard repaid them without compunction.

Clarendon forgivingly summed up Laud the man thus: 'his learning and piety and virtue have been attained by few, and the greatest of his infirmities are common to all'. His description of Laud's conduct at his trial is simply affectionate; the old man's faults forgotten in his desperate and almost heroic last situation (if all the more so by its inescapable association with the royal martyrdom that followed it five years later): '[Laud] defended himself with great and undaunted courage, and less passion than was expected from his constitution ... clearness and irresistible reason ... convinced all men of his integrity.' Laud's last stand, like his royal master's to come, is portrayed as his finest hour, purged of his temperamental flaws of character.

Clarendon goes on to attack the validity of the quorum of Parliamentarian peers that judged Laud, dismissing their number as 'not above twelve'. This is fairly accurate by the standards of Clarendon's usual patchily and partially remembered enumeration. There were indeed usually only about a dozen peers in attendance during the trial, although the Lords' Journal records twenty-one rounded up for the vote on the attainder. By contrast the 'Anti Parliament' in the Bodleian boasted forty-three continually active peers, eighty-two attending at its fullest.

It was immediately obvious to Hyde, as to Whitelocke, that once Parliament, buckling under the pressure of that ill-assorted alliance, the Scots and the Independent war party, had determined against the archbishop, Laud was doomed to suffer the fate of Strafford, his unlikely, dissimilar friend. Not all Maynard's ingenuity in what that wily barrister himself christened the *ars bablativa* would make the evidence against Laud sufficient. Yet the reality of Westminster in 1644 made certain the passing of a fatal attainder upon him. Nothing Hyde, even King Charles, could do at this stage would alter this. But, suitably instigated by Hyde, the King could still, like Whitelocke, make an effective political statement about this latest 'letter of blood':

> When the first mention was made of . . . bringing the archbishop to a trial for his life, the Chancellor of the Exchequer, who had always a great reverence and affection for him, had spoken to the King . . . and proposed to him, that, in all events, there might be a pardon prepared and sent to him under the Great Seal of England, to the end . . . he might plead the King's pardon, which must be allowed by all who pretended to be governed by the law; . . . if they proceeded in a martial, or any other extraordinary way, his majesty should declare his justice . . . to an old faithful servant . . . in having done all towards his preservation that was in his power.

Charles seized upon this plan with a relieved zeal whose inner motive soon and unattractively revealed itself. The King considered that by ineffectually trying to save Laud, he would be absolved of his earlier crime in sacrificing Strafford, his blood guilt transferred to his enemies. Laud himself, when the royal pardon reached him, showed, according to Clarendon, both gratitude and wisdom: '[Laud] received [the royal pardon] with great joy, as it was a testimony of the King's gracious affection to him ... without any opinion that they who endeavoured to take away the King's life would preserve his by his majesty's authority'.

The reference to 'take away the King's life' is again coloured by 1649 rather than representing 1644-5, but Laud's plausible reaction, if it is accurate, was astute. The archbishop knew the King and Ned Hyde, the counsellor he had once picked out as a talented young man, were powerless to save him, but he understood the impact of their gesture.

Clarendon concludes his account of the trial, attainder, and execution, which took place on 10 January 1645, with heavy, bitter sarcasm, auguring intentionally poorly for the negotiations at Uxbridge in which he was about to participate:

> When they had despatched this important work, and thereby received a new instance of the good affection and courage of their friends ... too many concurred in it without considering the heinousness of it, and only to keep their credits clear and entire, whereby they might with the more authority advance the peace ... they now enter upon the debate what answer they should send the King concerning a treaty ...

But at least Hyde could not, with justice, have included his old friend Whitelocke in the number of those who had proved party to the judicial murder of an aged archbishop in order to attempt a peace.*

---

* Whitelocke's behaviour during the trial of Archbishop Laud also prefigured his later refusal to become enmeshed in the trial and execution of the King, although he was not to display the same political and moral courage on that occasion. But then, unlike Hyde, he was not personally acquainted with and emotionally attached to King Charles to the same extent as Laud.

## The Treaty of Uxbridge – The Place House, St Margaret's Church, the Market Square, the Beerhouse, The George, The Crown, Uxbridge, January–February 1645

From the 1590s to the 1620s, Sir John Bennet, the lawyer, official, MP, scholarly patron, diplomat, would-be-statesman and large-scale speculator, had thrived but eventually fallen; an operator with a sprawling network within London, including Westminster and Whitehall, Oxford, York, and Uxbridge. By 1645, Sir John's late sixteenth-century town house, the 'Place House', was still Uxbridge's most obviously impressive, capacious residence.

Sir John's grandson, Henry Bennet, poet, linguist, and rising courtier at Oxford, had served his time in George, Lord Digby's stable of promising, amoral, witty, and useful young men. Digby was the one Royalist minister so obnoxious to Parliament that they made the proposed Treaty conditional on his not being named as a royal Commissioner, but that would have posed no obstacle to his protégé suggesting his family's large house as the ideal site for negotiations. Hyde, who would, two decades after the Restoration, find Henry Bennet, as the Earl of Arlington, a dangerous opponent, for the moment noted him for intelligence and industry.

Hyde also rated the bravery and military skill of Bennet's cousin, Sir Humphrey, who had done his brother-in-law Bulstrode Whitelocke a valiant good turn in Oxford. The Bennets of Uxbridge were thus, as the Middlesex geography of their holdings suggests, far more part of Whitelocke's world than Hyde's, kin to the deceased Rebecca Whitelocke, of the Mortlake and City Bennets. Judge Whitelocke had shared Sir John Bennet's profession, eminence, and social circle, though Sir James Whitelocke's popular party probity generally contrasted with Sir John's courtly venality. Their mutual friend Sir Ralph Winwood, another undergraduate companion of Laud, father of Bulstrode's fellow deputy lieutenant and 1643 Peace Commissioner Richard Winwood, had been among half-amused, half-embarrassed witnesses to Sir John's miserly table, and his thraldom to his corpulent Dutch third wife, Leonora Lady Bennet (whose fine monument still adorns St Margaret's Church, Uxbridge).

The southern half of Uxbridge was reserved for the Royalist Commissioners and their train to the total number of 108, with the two exceptions: the Place House itself, neutral ground where the Treaty itself was to be publicly negotiated, and additionally the characteristically comfortable residence of the Earl of Northumberland; and the nearby, also large Beerhouse, reserved by the more convivial, equally soft-living Earl of Pembroke. Both these grandees, seasoned and ambiguous politicians, perhaps appreciated both the company and the convenience provided by proximity to old friends and clients among the Royalist Commissioners. The separate headquarters of the Parliamentarian (and Scots) Commissioners was a handsome inn, the George, just to the north of the town's centre, whereas the Royalist equivalent, the Crown, stood opposite to the south. Hyde, the Royalist delegation's chief in industry and importance though not status, resided at the Crown.

Whitelocke, a valuable rather than dominant figure among the Parliamentarians, had been left to more circumscribed arrangements in the north of the town, sharing a chamber with his old associate in pacific sentiment, Lord Wenman, once again acting as a privately near-Royalist, yet conscientiously Parliamentarian, Commissioner. The lack of space, combined with Whitelocke's inferior social rank, obliged Bulstrode to sleep, on those short occasions during this unforgiving Treaty when any rest was possible, on a 'field-bed' lent to him by Sir John Meyrick. Whitelocke and Meyrick's tactical disagreement at Turnham Green had long since been forgotten in common loyalty to the cautious and conservative leadership of the Earl of Essex, as opposed to Cromwell, Parliament's belligerently scorching rising sun.

As the meeting point for the assembled Commissioners, the Place House had been chosen for subtler reasons than mere size and grandeur. Whatever young Henry Bennet's role, Clarendon and Whitelocke are agreed that the house itself and the dispositions of both sides' lodgings were chosen by Parliament, on whose territory the Treaty took place. In the late section of the *History*, Clarendon allows that Parliament was 'very civil in the distribution', offering 'accommodation . . . as good as the town would yield, and as good as the [Parliamentarians & Scots] had'. The same work describes the Place House's advantages of both display and discretion in considerable detail:

> . . . a fair house at the end of the town . . . was provided for the treaty, where was a fair room in the middle . . . handsomely dressed up . . . a large square table being placed in the middle . . . many other rooms on either side of this great room, for the commissioners . . . to retire to, when they thought fit to consult together . . . there being good stairs at either end of the house, they never went through each other's quarters, nor met but in the great room.

If Clarendon captures the Place House's practical assets, it is Whitelocke in his *Memorials* who is more alive to the occasion's deliberate symbolism. He significantly recalls the 'fair great chamber' with its 'large table . . . like that heretofore in the starchamber'. For the Parliamentarians and even for Hyde, who had played a substantial role in the Star Chamber's abolition, that court and its kindred prerogative institutions had been over-exploited instruments of arrant, and arid, tyranny, infamous as much for comically pedantic legal hair-splitting as for corruption and injustice. Yet here Whitelocke somehow, and surprisingly, writes in another strain, one of nostalgia, seeing legitimacy in a place and device that, however inimical its practices had become, possessed undeniable, lofty, ancient authority. In the troubled world of 1645, there was something reassuring about a makeshift Star Chamber, bringing back memories of a youthful, safer age. There is a quasi-Arthurian democracy about how Whitelocke goes on to describe the Treaty's table, 'almost square, without any upper or lower end'. With all too many prickly, egotistical characters among the Commissioners, this geometry was about to prove invaluable.

The Parliamentarian newsletters called the central treaty chamber 'well hanged' (i.e. with tapestries) and 'very spacious'. The upstairs wood-panelled rooms surviving in the former Place House, now the Crown & Treaty pub, would be distinctly crowded for twelve Parliamentarian Commissioners, ten Scots, and sixteen Royalists, plus secretaries, ecclesiastics, and various observers. Almost half the house has not survived the three and a half centuries since the Treaty, and it seems likely that the great chamber alluded to by the two Commissioner-historians was in this vanished portion.

The convergence of the Commissioners began with a public parade of commensal harmony, alongside a great number of more discreet and particular individual meetings, their exchanges more meaningful, but their guardedness a more accurate reflection of the true relations between the participants. The Royalist Commissioners' main advantage was their relative unity. Their shades of differing religious opinion concerned pragmatic political gain rather than deep feeling. Almost all of their Commissioners, with the possible exception of King Charles's meddling favourite Jack Ashburnham, an old sparring partner of Hyde, genuinely desired peace. What is more, a letter written at this time from the King to his more implacable consort suggests that their royal master had at last been persuaded, if with still dubious sincerity, to welcome a positive, pacific outcome:

> All, even my party . . . strangely impatient for peace, which obliged me all the more, at all occasions, to show my real intentions to peace . . . I am put in a very good hope (some hold it a certainty) that if I could come to a fair treaty, the ring-leading rebels would not hinder me . . . their own party almost weary of the war . . . great distractions . . . among themselves . . . in religion . . . and in point of command.

The King was correctly informed (especially by Hyde) about his enemies' division, contrasting with his own servants' uncharacteristic concord. The Royalists' counterparts included Parliamentarians and Scots, a majority of peace-party spokesmen overseen by a minority of war-party 'watch dogs', and a furious range of religious disputants – Scots Presbyterians, seeking nothing less than the imposition upon England of their Covenant and of a Church organized all but identically to theirs; English 'Presbyterians', a very different, amorphous group, just about still including Whitelocke at this time, some of whom, especially Bulstrode, hoped only for mild religious reform and 'Erastian' state control of the Church; and English 'Independents', all fierce war-party partisans, who preferred total religious toleration and little national Church structure of any kind. Finally, the Parliamentarians and the Scots were all in the midst of the torrid arguments that were to be the birth agonies of the New Model Army (a project to which Whitelocke was prominent and conservative in his opposition).

Whether Clarendon was in his retrospective account correct to infer Royalist sentiment in Uxbridge, it is demonstrable that peace itself was longed for: in Uxbridge and, still, for all the rising Independent and war-party position in Parliament, in the capital itself. But such peace was also hardly expected – as a London barrister John Greene wrote, 'wonderful improbable' and 'scarce to be hoped for'.

To the rapid consternation of the Royalist Commissioners, a young Presbyterian preacher, Christopher Love, chose 31 January, the day of the Royalists' arrival in the town, to draw upon and inflame this nagging pessimism. As Clarendon relates, the preacher:

> ... told his auditory, which consisted of all the people of the town ... who came to the market ... that they were not to expect any good from that treaty ... men of blood ... employed in it from Oxford ... intended only to amuse the people with the expectation of peace ... [Love] inveighed so seditiously against all cavaliers, that is ... all who followed the King, and ... the persons of the commissioners, that he could be understood to intend nothing else but to stir up the people ... to do some act of violence upon the commissioners ...

In Oxford, Whitelocke and his colleagues had faced popular abuse as well as actual violence, but Hyde, whose own considerable person had not been in any physical danger since Edgehill, can be forgiven for responding with some alarm to Love's fire-eating denunciation. What stung further for the Royalists was that they were debarred from worship in St Margaret's Church, as Parliament forbade the use of the Book of Common Prayer in a house of religion within its territory. Christopher Love had chosen the market square over the church for a different and, to the Royalists, galling reason – his 'auditory' being too large for the building's confines. Here, perhaps, is one implied refutation of Clarendon's portrait of a latently Royalist Uxbridge. Upon the Royalists' complaint, Love was instructed to return at speed to and remain at London, but the Parliamentarian Commissioners claimed to be unable to reprimand him further. In a strange twist of fate, grimly appreciated by Clarendon the historian, Love was to be executed six years later for plotting against Cromwell in favour of the exiled Charles II.

The Commissioners were theoretically led by their highest-ranking members, Richmond for the Royalists, Northumberland for the Parliamentarians, and the Earl of Loudoun, Chancellor of Scotland, for the Covenanters. Of these only Loudoun was in practice in charge of his delegation's policy, and indeed it was the Scots Chancellor who possessed the most coherent, if not realistic, aim for the Treaty. After an unedifying quarrel between Loudoun and Northumberland concerning differing English and Scots conventions of precedence, where Northumberland as usual prevailed, Loudoun, accurately identifying Hyde as the actual driving force behind the Royalist Commissioners, approached him through Richmond. Perhaps well briefed on Hyde's religious and temperamental aversion to the Scots, Loudoun attempted simultaneously to soften and intimidate him, emphasizing how hated Hyde was by his former parliamentary colleagues, and how it was only at the Scots' insistence that Parliament had acknowledged his safe conduct under his Royalist knighthood. Loudoun then attempted a high-flown sort of blackmail, informing Hyde 'that he had now a good opportunity to wipe off all those jealousies by being a good instrument in making this peace, and by persuading his majesty to comply with the desires and supplications of the Parliament'.

Hyde, by his own later testimony, rejected every item of this with courteous coldness, replying that though the King himself needed no convincing to further peace (on Hyde's own copious evidence, quite untrue, but politically an invaluable position to defend), no counsellor, himself included, would induce King Charles to accept any peace 'inconsistent with his honour or his conscience'. For his own part, 'without reflecting on the good or ill opinion Parliament might have of him', he would always counsel against any such dishonourable peace.

Hyde's reference to the King's 'honour or his conscience' showed that he was fully aware of what was afoot. Loudoun, in cooperation with Holles, the most senior and forceful of the English peace party, and with the passionately *intriguante* Countess of Carlisle, Northumberland's sister and once the Queen's closest friend, hoped to put to Charles a resolution at the expense of the Church of England as by law established: a 'Scottish peace', settling some form of Presbyterianism in England. Hyde considered the attitude of Holles, whom he personally respected, to this unholy alliance to be completely transactional, and correctly assumed the position and aspirations of Whitelocke, the other peace-party moderates like Wenman, and the still powerful, innately conservative, jealously self-interested Parliamentary peers – Northumberland, Pembroke, and the rest – to be in the same broad category. Clarendon would write that Holles, 'frankest amongst them in owning his animosity and indignation against all the Independent party . . . was no otherwise affected to the Presbyterians than as they constituted a party upon which he depended to oppose the other'.

Whitelocke, though less 'frank' and more diplomatic than Holles, was a political 'Presbyterian' at Uxbridge in this same, limited sense; opposed to the religious Independents insofar as they were the party of the war's continuance and the army's power, even if their religious ideals were closer to his (as they were, for example, to those of the similarly intellectually liberal Falkland). For this reason Whitelocke, like Holles, was prepared to work with the Scots on a more or less temporary basis, for want of a better, stronger, or more sympathetic ally, though his journal, later *Memorials*, and events to come all reveal how scant was his respect or affection for the Covenanters' nation, cause, and representatives.

The Holles-led scheme was to cede the Scots what they wanted on religion for the moment, and snatch back the advantage when working out the details later. But this was not a course Hyde was ever convinced could work. Although later both the first and second King Charles would in turn attempt in their desperation this same disingenuous policy and awkward alliance, for the present Charles I – despite the advocacy of his Queen, and of Hyde's colleague Colepeper – was unwilling to sacrifice his ecclesiastical principles for an uneasy alliance with the first of his peoples to rebel against him, a people, moreover, over whom his freshest partisan, the Scots Royalist general Montrose, was still achieving victories. Hyde was willing to concede a certain amount of ground on ecclesiastical matters, but not to surrender the Church of England altogether. Besides, he was already contemplating a different compromise, and noted with interest that Loudoun 'did as good as conclude that if the King would satisfy them in the business of the Church, [the Scots] would not concern themselves in any of the other demands'.

By Clarendon's account, however, Hyde and Loudoun ended their private 'conference' on bitter terms. From other, similar private exchanges, surely including some with Whitelocke, Hyde concluded that 'the Parliament took none of the points in controversy less to heart, or were less united in, than in what concerned the Church'. This being so, Hyde reasoned that even if, against his political judgement and moral principles, he was to accept Loudoun's proposal, he might gain little from it that would further peace – the good opinion of the Scots being only counterbalanced by the aggravation of the Independents, even perhaps of some English 'Presbyterians' in the longer run.

Whitelocke recalls that the first individual call Hyde paid at

*Friends in Youth*

Uxbridge was to him and Holles, revealingly jointly, probably at the relative privacy and comfort of the George Inn, where Holles was lodged. For his part, he visited, as far as he reveals alone, Hyde, Geoffrey Palmer, and Richard Lane, all old friends – or former friends – and all lawyers of the Middle Temple, Lane being a generation older than Whitelocke and the others.* It seems that Hyde was operating purely politically, wooing, in Whitelocke and Holles, the English 'Presbyterians', regardless of the fact that one was, in their history if not their present allegiances, perhaps his oldest remaining friend, while the other was a respected, cordial opponent.† By contrast Whitelocke sought to resume ties of fond personal association among the Royalists. But he also had good reason to sound out, in particular, the King's best lawyers.

Clarendon's version in some ways distinguishes Whitelocke in private from his Parliamentarian colleagues, and in other ways treats him as a characteristic example of their conflicted and cautious behaviour. Clarendon states that in general the Parliamentarian Commissioners treated, indeed were obliged to treat, their Royalist counterparts, including friends of old, with less candour and openness than they received from them in turn:

---

* For some time Whitelocke's London foothold had been Lane's own Middle Temple chambers, voted to him by Parliament. As an old friend of Lane before the civil war, Whitelocke claimed to be acting as a responsible steward of Lane's possessions. Lane died a penniless exile in 1650. After the Restoration, Lane's son accused Whitelocke of pilfering his father's valuable library, a charge that was substantially arguable and certainly politically motivated, but by some definitions very likely justified.

† Hyde had caused some annoyance for Holles in 1638, representing the other lawyer's mother-in-law in a private chancery case. Hyde admired Holles's oratory and prose, and could imitate him on paper with his usual facility, later writing at least one document from exile implied to be Holles's to spread misinformation among the Parliamentarians. As with his similar ventriloquization of the Earl of Pembroke, Hyde could divide and disorient his enemies by emphasizing controversial opinions that they genuinely held.

> Nor was there any restraint from giving and receiving visits apart, as their acquaintance and inclinations disposed them; in which those of the King's party used their accustomed freedom as heretofore; but on the other side there was great wariness and reservation, and so great a jealousy of each other that they had no mind to give or receive visits from their old friends whom they loved better than their new, nor would any of them be seen alone with any of the King's commissioners, but had always one of their companions with them, and sometimes one whom they least trusted.

By those 'least trusted', Hyde indicates the disproportionately powerful trio of Parliamentarian Commissioners of the Independent and war party, Oliver St John, Sir Harry Vane the younger, and Edmund Prideaux. These he interpreted as little-loved leaders and spies upon their notional colleagues, invigilating the peace party's doubtful loyalties. St John and the younger Vane were, before their eclipse by Cromwell, the nearest Pym and Hampden had to successors in orchestrating the whole Parliamentarian cause; Prideaux, if of lesser importance, was equally zealous and had crucial responsibility for Parliament's postal service.

It seems, however, that Clarendon exaggerates, as he also recalls many instances of Parliamentarian Commissioners, Whitelocke among them, arranging to meet Royalists without such supervision (thus backing up Whitelocke's *Diary* and *Memorials*). Considering Whitelocke's private words to him at Uxbridge, Clarendon would sum up his old, or former, friend's feelings, while conveying his own lasting judgement:

> from the beginning [Whitelocke] had concurred with [the Parliamentarian leaders] without any inclination to their persons or principles . . . all his estate was in their quarters, and he had a nature that could not bear or submit to be undone . . . yet to his friends who were commissioners for the King he used his old openness and professed his detestation of all their proceedings, yet could not leave them.

Whitelocke's lifelong political ambiguity is here simplified to mere self-interest, and a new criticism of his personality, or 'nature', is brought to light, one more understandable than accurate. It is a passage that feels hardened by the economic discomfort, heavy responsibility, and moral compromise Hyde was forced to endure in his first exile, beside which his old companion's life had come to feel soft, gutless, professionally ambitious, and self-protective at the cost of duty and conscience.

The proceedings at Uxbridge were divided into four days for each of the three most pressing matters: the Church, the militia, and the rebellion in Ireland. During the first of these sessions, Whitelocke and Hyde possessed similar religious opinions, but drew different political conclusions from them. It was a Royalist Commissioner, the Marquess of Hertford, Essex's brother-in-law and formerly himself among the reforming Junto of great noblemen, who most powerfully expressed Whitelocke's own view of the question:

> Hertford said, that he held neither [episcopacy] one nor the other [i.e. Presbyterianism] to be *jure divino* . . . nor any [Church] government whatsoever is *jure divino*; and I desire that we may leave this argument . . . proceed to debate upon the particular proposals . . . Pembroke . . . of the same judgment . . . many of the commissioners besides . . . willing to pass over this point.

This was the position of Great Tew, of Chillingworth, Falkland, and Hales; that questions of church government, whether by bishops, presbyters, elders, assemblies, all counted as 'inessentials' of Christian doctrine, which should be permitted to be arranged however a people desired them, but about which no theological dispute or schism was worthwhile.

Hyde still sympathized with this position to an extent he was to obscure in more partisan later writings. Yet his conduct at Uxbridge might suggest otherwise. Instead of facilitating agreement, he created objections with relish, criticizing Parliament's proposed Presbyterian solutions, with justice, as vague, obscure, and commanding no broad allegiance even within their own supposed side. As the Royalist Commissioners' most influential creator of policy and most articulate mouthpiece, as well as the Commissioner in most ways closest to his monarch's preferences on the Church, Hyde was not altogether unconstructive. But, as Loudoun had discovered, Hyde was not willing to entertain the Scots-English Presbyterian, Loudoun-Holles-Carlisle misalliance of convenience, even as a temporary measure for the most utilitarian, pacific motives.

Instead, Hyde eventually offered firmer rules against episcopal pluralism, obligations for bishops to preach and to be involved in the active administration of their sees, and, as Chancellor of the Exchequer, £100,000 to the coffers of the state to be paid out of the lands of the Church. As he well knew, these lands, episcopal residences, and estates, already threadbare, only partially fattened up by acquisitions under Laud, had already been thoroughly plundered and physically vandalized in many cases by Parliament and its army.

Whitelocke noted that moderate, aristocratic religious conservatism cut across the conflict's supposed party lines, embracing both Hertford and Pembroke. Hyde, Pembroke's long-time political client before the civil war, agreed. But he believed it was more practical to capture this interest, not by agreeing to some opaque and divisive new permutation of Anglo-Presbyterianism, but by proposing the mildly reformed variant on the status quo he saw the moderates supported with both head and heart, were they at liberty to say so. An anecdote Clarendon tells with much amusement about the bluff, unbookish Pembroke reveals Hyde's perspective upon that nobleman's true allegiance:

> ... a pleasant accident [occurred] on one of those days ... assigned for the matter of religion. The commissioners of both sides, either before their sitting or after their rising, entertaining themselves together by the fire-side, as they sometimes did, it being extremely cold, in general and casual discourses, one of the King's commissioners asking one of the other [i.e. a Parliamentarian], with whom he had familiarity, in a low voice, why there was not in their whole Directory

## Friends in Youth

[of Worship, Parliament's substitute for the Book of Common Prayer] any mention of the Lord's Prayer, the Creed, or the Ten Commandments ... Pembroke, overhearing ... answered aloud, and with his usual passion, that he and many others were very sorry that they had been left out; that the putting them in had taken up many hours' debate in the ... Commons, and that at last the leaving them out had been carried by eight or nine voices, and so they did not think fit to insist ... in the House of Peers ... he verily believed, if it were to do again, they should carry it for the inserting all three ...

Pembroke seemed wholly unflustered by the prospect of aggrieving two of his colleagues, the London minister Stephen Marshall and the Scot Alexander Henderson, who had been instrumental in the compilation of the plain, pared-back Directory he readily derided.* In matters of state, as opposed to religion, Clarendon portrays Pembroke as franker still in his private speech to his former Commons placeman:

One night, late ... Pembroke came to the Chancellor of the Exchequer's lodging to return him a visit, and sat with him some hours; all his discourse being to persuade him to think it reasonable to consent to all that the Parliament had demanded. He told him there was never such a pack of knaves and villains as they who now governed in the Parliament, who would so far prevail if this treaty were broke as to remove ... Essex, and then they would constitute such an army as should force the Parliament, as well as the King, to consent to whatsoever they demanded; which would end up in the change of the government into that of a commonwealth.

---

* The Prayer Book, as Hyde well knew, was one of the Royalists' most popular causes. Henry Hammond, Great Tew's foremost Biblical scholar, was among the divines attached to the Royalist Commissioners and actually changed the allegiance of the Parliamentarian minister Nathaniel Hardy in the midst of their discourse.

The Chancellor told him, if he believed this, it was high time for the Lords to look about them, who would then be no less concerned than the King. He confessed it, and that they were now sensible that they had brought this mischieve upon themselves, and did heartily repent it, though too late . . . in no degree able to prevent the general destruction which they foresaw: but if the King would be so gracious . . . as to preserve them by consenting to those unreasonable propositions . . . the other wicked persons would be disappointed by such his concessions; . . . Essex would still keep his power; and they should be able, in a short time after the peace concluded . . . to recover all for [Charles I] that he now parted with, and to drive those wicked men who would destroy monarchy out of the kingdom, and then his majesty would be greater than ever.

How extravagant soever this discourse seems to be, the matter of it was the same which the wisest of the rest (and there were men of very good parts amongst them) did seriously urge to other of the King's commissioners, with whom they had the same confidence: so broken were they in their spirits . . . so corrupted in their understanding, even when they had their own ruin in their view.

Clarendon implies that the opportunistic triumvirate of Northumberland, Holles, and Loudoun had selected particular Commissioners to win over individual Royalists, Pembroke being the one to sway Hyde himself.

The great Parliamentarian peers, about to be locked out of army commands by Cromwell's Self-Denying Ordinance, were desperate to come to an agreement with the Royalists, their more sympathetic foes. Hyde, sensing that desperation, was not prepared to reward it with the virtual capitulation required of him. Loudoun had tried to charm and threaten him, Pembroke to reason him into not just friendship but faith, and Hyde did not trust the capacity of either spokesman to deliver on their intentions or promises. In private writings he meditated that 'without faithful counsel tribute of friendship can never be given'. This precluded new 'friendship' with the Scots, and its logic demanded the withdrawal, with whatever regret, from true friendship with Pembroke, even, at last, with Bulstrode Whitelocke.

The subject of the second session at Uxbridge, the militia, was one to which Hyde brought a more genuine willingness to accommodate Parliament. While his and Falkland's third man, Colepeper, had always advocated giving ground on religion but standing firm on royal control of the militia at all costs, Hyde's instincts were exactly the opposite. Whereas for Colepeper, he who held the sword could dictate religious affairs to his own liking in due time, to Hyde, a complete betrayal of the monarchy's natural supporters in the Church undermined the Crown's good faith and so put the King's subsequent ability to wield the sword into question. Before war broke out he had privately, afterwards openly, sought some route to agreement on the militia. Whitelocke, for his part, had consistently advocated both the legality and the desirability of such a compromise since the outbreak of the Irish rebellion in 1641. Yet the two Commissioners in February 1645 who would most conspicuously clash over the militia question were to be none other than the fellow lawyers and divided friends, Whitelocke and Hyde.

Clarendon only elliptically alludes to his old friend's involvement in this part of the Treaty, and elides and obfuscates his own. It seems probable that the process and outcome of this argument caused Hyde regret, even shame. But his narrative in the *History* suggests, first, that the Parliamentarian peace party – the English 'Presbyterians', led by Holles and including Whitelocke – were unexpectedly more unreasonable even than the Independent war party (while the Scots were indifferent to the subject); second, that he himself changed his mind about the advisability of a deal on the militia at the critical moment.

Without mentioning any particular names, Clarendon concentrates on the counter-intuitive mentality of the peace party:

> . . . they of that [Parliamentarian] side (even they who most desired the peace) both publicly and privately insisting upon having the whole command of the militia by sea and land, and all the forts and

ships of the kingdom at their disposal; without which they looked upon themselves as lost and at the King's mercy, without considering that he must be at theirs if such a jurisdiction was committed to them ... in this particular, he who was most reasonable amongst them thought it very unreasonable to deny them that necessary security; and believed it could proceed from nothing else but a resolution to take the highest vengeance upon their rebellion.

Unquestionably Whitelocke was among 'they who most desired the peace', and it is possible that Clarendon refers to him as 'he who was most reasonable amongst them'. When describing the Royalist view of the King's ancient, incontestable, defining right over the militia, Clarendon effaces himself from the picture, exploiting the useful truth that there were many lawyers more learned than him among the Royal Commissioners: 'the commissioners of the King, whereof there were four very eminent in the knowledge of the law, Lane, Gardiner, [Orlando] Bridgeman and Palmer, made the demand appear to be without any pretence of law or justice'. But, if Palmer was Hyde's superior in depth of legal understanding, their friend Whitelocke was incontestably so. Perhaps this also explains Clarendon's unwillingness to recall the details of this confrontation; the skill in debate of his one-time boon companion may have left him smarting.

Whitelocke's rather different version puts them both to the fore, while bearing an interesting resemblance to the less contested shape of the previous argument, over religion:

> A debate passed ... betwixt Sir Edward Hyde [the Royalist knighthood here, as ever, acknowledged] & Whitelocke concerning the Militia, Sir Edward Hyde affirmed the power of the Militia to be by Law unquestionably in the King only, Whitelocke denied this, as reflecting upon the Parliament's propositions, & not clear by law where that power was; Hyde challenged the debate of this point with Whitelocke the next day, & he did not decline it, but the Earl of Southampton moved, that they might first see how near they could

*Friends in Youth*

come to a composure upon the business of the Militia. Hollis and others seconded the Earl & so the debate went off, & the Committees of both Kingdoms gave Whitelocke thanks for his encountering of Sir Edward Hyde & vindicating the honour & right of the Parliament.

As in the religious negotiations, representatives of the two sides had clashed over theory – the legal possession of the militia, like the divine legitimacy of bishops or presbyters – then been called off by senior moderates from both sides (Southampton and Holles, like Hertford and Pembroke). What is odd is that Whitelocke and Hyde should, in this instance, have acted in the roles, previously most unlike them both, of theoretical ideologues. Taken together, both these debates, enacted so publicly, formally, and grandly, have a performative, covertly consensual, all but prearranged structure (bringing to mind the stagey way in which Satan gains the unanimous consent of his devils for his mission early in *Paradise Lost*).

Whitelocke and Hyde were perhaps selected as their respective sides' principal spokesmen on the militia not because they were political extremists, but because, like the divines speaking on the previous days, they were the preeminent experts in this field. For, if Hyde was a less profound lawyer than Palmer, Lane, Gardiner, Bridgeman, or indeed Whitelocke, he was, by general consent, a clearer and better speechwriter and orator than any of them. On Parliament's side, Whitelocke's reputation as a clear and persuasive speaker approached Hyde's most nearly. It seems that, on this occasion, in his own opinion, that of his colleagues, and of their employers on the Committee of Both Kingdoms in the Lords and Commons – as well as, judging by Clarendon's touchy silence, possibly by the estimate of his old friend and opponent – Whitelocke did get the better of Hyde. In the following stage of the negotiations, the Royalists proved ready to offer an intermediate solution on the militia, such as Whitelocke had always supported, and Hyde long privately considered.

While, as far as Clarendon was concerned, Loudoun and the

Scots were entirely detached from the militia question except insofar as they could leverage compliance with the Royalist position to make gains on religion, Whitelocke notes that 'The Scots Commissioners took it as a neglect of their kingdom, that no answer was given . . . touching the Militia of Scotland.' Like the rest of Whitelocke's account, this rings truer than Clarendon's *History*. Whitelocke was living in fairly frequent, indeed irritatingly close company with the Scots; Hyde's distaste for the Scottish nation, even more pronounced than Whitelocke's, led him consistently to underrate or ignore Scots desires and concerns. The Scots, whose home army was being trounced by resurgent Scots-Irish, Catholic, and Episcopalian Royalists at this time, had pressing reasons to demand their right to their own defence (one that they were in any case exercising) as soon and as fully as possible. And they were always alert, as in the matter of Anglo-Scots precedence, to any sense that the English were treating England's affairs as of superior importance.

The third major topic before the Commissioners reversed the politics of the Treaty so far. On Ireland, the Parliamentarian war and peace parties, Independents, and Scots and English Presbyterians were all at one; the Royalists, on the other hand, were divided, unhappy, uncertain, distrusted, unpopular, and all too aware of so being. The King's Irish policy or 'cessation', a negotiated ceasefire with the Catholic rebels in order to bring more troops back to England to fight Parliament, was one to which Hyde had never been party. Its chief supporters, Lord Digby and the Queen, were two of the hate-figures whose ill repute Parliament had so skilfully exploited.

Most of the Royalist Commissioners present were in truth appalled by the Irish cessation, and none more so than Hyde himself. He was now obliged to prepare both his own and the Duke of Richmond's case and papers, for a brief he called in confidence 'inexcusable to justice, piety, and prudence'. In the *History*, Clarendon admits that when it came to Ireland 'the people generally concurred with [Parliament]'. His mission in communicating, defending, and executing the King's will in this arena was innately, almost comically impossible. Perhaps the very direness of the

## Friends in Youth

situation lent Hyde strength. With political victory out of reach, he settled upon an argument of ruthless logic, rhetorical flair, and transcendent, tactless accuracy, which confuted and outraged his adversaries far more emphatically than Whitelocke could have wrong-footed him on the militia:

> . . . he put them in mind of their bringing those very troops which were levied by the King's authority for the suppression of the rebellion in Ireland, to fight against the King at Edgehill: of their having given over the prosecution of that war, or sending any supply . . . thither, having employed those magazines which were provided for that service against his majesty . . . £100,000 brought in by the adventurers for Ireland had been sent into Scotland, to prepare and dispose that kingdom to invade this . . . and till then his majesty had not in the least degree swerved from the observation of that Act of Parliament [for suppressing the Catholic rebels]: but when he saw that the Parliament, instead of prosecuting . . . the intention of that statute, apply it wholly to the carrying on the war against him, he thought himself absolved . . . supplies his majesty could not, and the Parliament would not, send . . . all the mischieves and misery that must attend [the Protestants] would, before God and man, be put to the account of the Parliament, which had defrauded them . . .
>
> . . . if the Parliament would yet give his majesty sufficient caution that the war shall be vigorously prosecuted there against the Irish, by sending over strong supplies of men and money, he would put an end to that cessation . . .

On this remarkable defence of the Irish cessation Whitelocke is as tellingly silent as Clarendon is about Whitelocke's successful assertion of the militia's ambiguous status. Whitelocke merely blusters out the stale canards by which Parliament had for years increasingly and exponentially exaggerated the atrocities committed by Catholics. He was, after all, himself one of the most substantial investors in the Irish Adventure, well aware of the use to which its funds had been put in England. Hyde's insultingly clever counter-proposal, that the King would start taking Ireland seriously when Parliament did, was too inconvenient and palpable a charge of hypocrisy to recognize, and the Parliamentarians and Scots behaved as if it had not been spoken. After hearing enough of the plaintive Parliamentarian horror stories about Irish rebels, Hyde pointedly, unanswerably remarked that he 'wished it were in the King's power to punish all rebellion with that severity which was due to it; but since it was not so, he must condescend to treaties.'

Hyde's merciless handling of his opposition was positively destructive to the Treaty's prospects. Its truthfulness did not stop the inefficacy of the King's cessation; the troops the Royalists gained proved of doubtful use, the political damage to the King's cause lasting and catastrophic. But, though Hyde's bravura performance on Ireland may not even have convinced its own speaker, its candour is refreshing to the ears of posterity.

During the Treaty's first fortnight, news of the continuing war throughout the three kingdoms percolated into Uxbridge, affecting the morale of the Commissioners first one way, then another. First the King was on the point of taking Weymouth, and his forces gained a windfall of Spanish bullion; then Parliament had seized Shrewsbury, once a small but gallant and hopeful capital to the embryonic Royalist army. From Scotland the still-victorious Montrose, whose nemesis, the Marquess of Argyll, had briefly been a Commissioner at Uxbridge before returning north to face defeat at his old enemy's hand, wrote to stiffen King Charles against any concessions whatsoever:

> The more your Majesty grants, the more will be asked; . . . in my poor opinion, it is unworthy of a King to treat with rebel subjects, while they have the sword in their hands. And though God forbid I should stint your Majesty's mercy, yet I must declare the horror I am in when I think of a treaty . . . unless they disband, and submit themselves entirely to your Majesty's goodness and pardon . . .

Well might Montrose plead in this vein, for the Scots Covenanters at Uxbridge were his former allies and mortal enemies. The relationship was similar to the irretrievable venom between Hyde and the likes of Oliver St John and Harry Marten, Hyde's one-time fellow reformers in the Commons.

One letter captured by the Royalists embarrassed Parliament, laying bare the worsening dissensions between the peace party and the Scots on the one hand, the rising Independent, army, war party on the other. Written by the war-party MP John Pyne to the Independent naval officer Colonel Popham, it contained a 'bitter invective against . . . Essex and all those who advanced the treaty of peace . . . very indecent expressions against the King himself and all who adhered to him . . . the Scots . . . likewise inveighed against'. In Hyde's view, the 'great discovery of the faction' made by this letter revealed 'many', even a possible majority, in Parliament 'who desired to have peace, without any alteration of government, [as long as] they might be sure of indemnity and security for what was past'. Pyne's letter added to the evidence that the Scots would make no concession on the Church, but no demands outside it; it further showed that the Independent minority 'would have no peace upon what conditions soever' and 'did resolve to change the whole frame of the government in State as well as Church'.

Pyne, in happier days Whitelocke's close friend, whose elopement he had actively assisted (just as Ned Hyde had been party to his own), had become 'Whitelocke's enemy in Parliament . . . of the more rigid [that is, the Independent and war] party'. If the Pyne incident revealed bitter insubordination among Independent MPs and military officers serving Parliament, Whitelocke also noted troubling unruliness and antagonism towards MPs from Parliament's common troops at this time. These had committed 'several murders, rapes and other cruelties . . . some servants slain . . . of Mr Hoby's, a member of the house [in fact Whitelocke's fellow MP for the borough of Great Marlow, elected alongside him in the disputed elections of 1640–41], and [Hoby] called [by the troops] . . . *a parliament dog*'.

With the first twelve days passed, the three great controversies undertaken, it had become clear that on the first, religion, there was an impasse. The Scots and some of the English peace party (Holles, but not Whitelocke or Pembroke) demanded full Presbyterian reform; the Royalists, led by Hyde, countered with only modified episcopacy. On the third subject, Ireland, antagonism was total. That left grounds for true compromise only on the question of the militia, that nagging, obscure, existential problem, the *arcanum imperii* in whose shadow Whitelocke had first parted company from Hyde and Geoffrey Palmer in 1642, whether the armed forces of the realm ultimately answered to King or Parliament.

Clarendon acidly observed of the peace party, including Whitelocke, that 'In the militia they who most desired peace would adhere to that which most concerned their own security.' According to the *History*, Hyde himself had already despaired of a positive result to the Treaty, and agreed to offer terms to Parliament on the militia in a spirit of dubious faith and thorough realpolitik:

> Some of them [i.e. the Parliamentarian Commissioners of the peace party, including Whitelocke], who knew how impossible it was to prevail [in achieving a breakthrough in the Treaty] . . . did wish that in order to get the time of the treaty prolonged some concessions might be made in the point of the militia, in order to [i.e. to guarantee] their security . . . this seemed such an expedient to those to whom they proposed it, that they thought fit to make a debate amongst all the commissioners . . . if it did produce no other effect than . . . getting more days to the treaty, and more divisions in the Parliament . . . the benefit was not small that would attend it; for as long as the treaty lasted there could be no advance made towards new modelling the army . . .

But this descent into pure, utilitarian cynicism sits peculiarly with Clarendon's description in the *History*'s manuscript of the passionate industry he continued to commit to the Treaty: '[Hyde was] wont to say that in his life he never underwent so great fatigue for twenty days together.'

With whatever sincerity, the Royalist Commissioners initially agreed on an offer to Parliament for the militia to be devolved to the control of a mixed body for some years, ten of the proposed committee to be nominated by Parliament, ten by the King.* Any controllers who outstayed their terms were to be charged with high treason. Among the Parliamentarian controllers of the militia the Royalist side signalled willingness to accept Essex, Northumberland, Warwick, Manchester, Fairfax, and Cromwell. This was an apparently generous selection, including the leading Independent peer, Warwick, and MP, Cromwell, as well as Fairfax, who though he would emerge as more pacific, moderate, and 'Presbyterian', was at this point wholly identified with the war party and the new modelling of the army. Whitelocke, always on good terms with the Fairfax family, would have been in a position to reassure Hyde, had his old friend cared quietly to consult him, that these were men who could be expected to hear reason. But the strong Royalist hint that any proposed agreement would involve the continuance of Essex and the other traditionalist Parliamentarian peers' primacy rendered irrelevant their acceptance of some Independents, as the war party immediately perceived.

As for the Royalist nominees, the King himself, Clarendon says, pressed for the inclusion of his Chancellor of the Exchequer. But the decidedly unmilitary Hyde 'was troubled at the honour, and writ very earnestly to the King to exempt him from the envy of such a trust'. In the end the Royalist Commissioners, reserving the King's right to name ten voices over the militia, deliberately specified none, so that Parliament 'might see a greater condescension from the King . . . than he had ever yet been induced to'. By implication it might be guessed that the Royalist ten were to include Arthur, Lord Capel, a Royalist soldier who shared Hyde's political background, as a reformist MP turned conciliator yearning for peace, and Jack Ashburnham, an acquisitive and interfering courtier of countervailingly bellicose politics. These two, perhaps to balance

---

* The time period offered by the Royalists was indistinct; seven or eight years were at first spoken of, but only three guaranteed in the proposals extended to Parliament.

each other, were the Commissioners chosen, Hyde having declined, to carry messages on the militia to and from the King at Oxford. Yet at some point while all these minutiae were decided upon, Hyde, according to the *History*, crucially but mysteriously lost faith in even this limited offer, 'having in the debate changed his mind, and, upon somewhat that was foreseen to fall out, was against the making any proposition at all'.

Like Clarendon's assertion that he was by this point no longer treating in earnest, but only to gain time, this later, pessimistic application of hindsight should be regarded with extreme care. To abandon even an attempted agreement at this point on the militia, the only subject on which Hyde had always contemplated real concessions, would certainly have been to abandon the treaty itself, which Hyde's previous history, his extreme commitment of time and work, even his Machiavellian stated intentions to delay the legislation regarding the New Model Army, all suggest he was not yet ready to do.

From the parliamentary side, Whitelocke noted the Royalist performance of spiritual sincerity – 'in all [the Royalist] quarters a solemn fast was kept for the good success of the Treaty'. However, his colleagues were predictably dissatisfied by the substance of their opposites' proposals, finding:

> ... nothing satisfactory [in the Royalist militia offer] ... Northumberland, Holles, Pierrepont, Whitelocke and others advised together about it, & endeavoured by private applications to their friends of the King's Commissioners to get a better answer to that point, but could not obtain it, [the Royalist Commissioners] hinting themselves to be bound by their Instructions that they could go no further, but they promised to send to the King for further power but nothing came of it, All the papers were sent to the Parliament and they were much troubled at this answer ...

It seems that Whitelocke counted himself as included in the inmost councils of the Parliamentarian peace party. He had established himself as his delegation's expert on the militia. If Northumberland was the group's dignified figurehead and Holles their most forceful politician, Whitelocke was at least the equal of the ever subtle and influential Pierrepont. Pierrepont was, however, now despaired of by Hyde as a friendly means of communication among the enemy. Clarendon was to note that Pierrepont, though he 'had always been of the greatest moderation in their counsels . . . appeared now to have contracted more bitterness and sourness . . . more reserved towards the King's commissioners'. Holles, meanwhile, was fully invested in the Scots religious offer to which Hyde and his King had given a granitic response. The Royalists had mustered only a lukewarm suggestion, which mostly fell on deaf ears.

As Capel and Ashburnham had been picked to go to the King, so Whitelocke was now chosen to go to the Parliamentarian Commissioners' many masters at Westminster. Unlike his Royalist friend Hyde, Whitelocke neither then nor later cast doubt upon his own honestly pacific intentions and persistent optimism. At Parliament he secured three more days for the Treaty, and brought back adjusted proposals from Westminster and the Committee of Both Kingdoms, 'not doubting but that it would have been agreed unto'. Parliament had agreed to deliberate upon:

. . . passing a bill for settling the militia in the power of parliament until such time as the 3 kingdoms shall be reduced to peace, and so declared by parliament, and 3 years after; or else for 7 years . . . after that his majesty to take advice of both houses for the settling thereof.

It is hard to see Whitelocke's good spirits about this counterproposal as justified, as, though courteously couched, it indefinitely denied the King full control over the militia. It was Pembroke's advice to Hyde in a legislative form; that if Charles would only give the Parliamentarian peace party all it asked for, it would do the King right in its gratitude. Yet Whitelocke still maintains he and his colleagues were 'full of hopes that [the Royalist Commissioners] would have consented to it'.

When Whitelocke and the rest received an answer, it was one that they had not expected but to which they could hardly object. The King offered no definite response to the terms at all. The Royalist Commissioners only asked for more time to consider the issue. But the King requested a safe conduct to come himself to Westminster and discuss matters further there: the very advice Whitelocke and Holles had, at his private but urgent request, given him at Oxford in verbal and perhaps written, if unsigned, statements. It was for Parliament to consent to or deny this flourish of royal bravura, in a long, narrow, inconclusive debate from which Whitelocke, returned to Uxbridge, was absent. His contribution was limited to a signature on the melancholy communication by which the Parliamentarian and Scots Commissioners admitted to Parliament that there was no sign of any concession whatsoever close at hand. The failure of the Lords and Commons to extend the Treaty greatly dashed Whitelocke's spirits and those of others like him:

> Upon this the house of commons did rise, without doing anything in the business; . . . this night till 12 o' clock the commissioners may treat, and no longer . . .
>
> This caused much trouble in the minds of many honest men, lovers of their country's peace; and divers of the King's commissioners, as well as the other, seemed sorry that all their endeavours to so good an end should prove so fruitless . . .
>
> Various judgments were passed by all persons, according to their own fancies and interests, most sober men lamented the sudden breach of the treaty.

Even to the end of the first English Civil War's last, strained after, stillborn treaty, Whitelocke continued to see the wholehearted members of his own political persuasion, the 'sober men', as persisting in both camps. It is almost certain, despite the later, more cynical reflections of Clarendon, that Whitelocke persistently and rightly included Hyde in this category.

13.

# England Commits

*BENVOLIO*

*O Romeo, Romeo, brave Mercutio's dead!*
*That gallant spirit hath aspired the clouds,*
*Which too untimely here did scorn the earth.*

*ROMEO*

*This day's black fate on more days doth depend;*
*This but begins the woe, others must end.*

William Shakespeare,
*Romeo and Juliet*, Act 3, Scene 1

## 'His Nimble Pegasus' – Falkland in 1643, 'Sortes Virgilianae', Abraham Cowley, and 'Mrs Moray'

Hyde's labours at Uxbridge, whether Machiavellian, sincere, or some combination of the two, ultimately perhaps unknowable even to himself, were not just all-important and unstinting, but for him innately melancholy and lonely. By the time of the Treaty early in 1645, Hyde had already long been deprived of the help and company of the partner of his hopes within the Royalist camp: Sir Lucius Cary, 2nd Viscount Falkland, since at least the downfall of Strafford his closest personal as well as political friend, if also an occasional foil. Falkland's death, at the first Battle of Newbury on 20 September 1643, was always subsequently stated by Hyde to have been the greatest tragedy of his own life.

Hyde portrays his bosom friend's darkening psychological

condition from the outset of the civil conflict with haunting plausibility. 'From the entrance into this unnatural war, [Falkland's] natural cheerfulness and vivacity grew clouded, and a kind of sadness and dejection of spirit stole upon him.' This sense of an 'unnatural' civil war, which Hyde so sharply contrasts to his friend's lost 'natural cheerfulness', was felt with equal intensity on the Parliamentarian side. Whitelocke's frequent, regular, unflagging speeches advocating peace negotiations at the increasing cost to his own political influence, or the celebrated remark of the parliamentary commander Sir William Waller, written in July 1643 to his old friend turned Royalist opponent Sir Ralph Hopton, 'with what a perfect hatred I detest this war without an enemy', bear witness to the sentiments of Hyde's most sympathetic adversaries.

The theatrical profundity of Falkland's grief as described by Hyde brings to mind such a figure as Shakespeare's King Henry VI, sitting beneath a tree to mourn his people's fathers and sons, slain by one another's hands. As Hyde said of his friend, 'Sitting among his friends, often, after a deep silence and frequent sighs, [Falkland] would, with a shrill and sad accent, ingeminate the word *Peace, Peace* . . .' Yet this emphatically sombre mood effaces some of what seems to have been the reality of a lighter, more hopeful and sprightly mood during Falkland's wartime Secretaryship, and the last year of his life. Just as Falkland was not the honour-shackled naif described by Hyde, over-scrupulously recusing himself from his crucial duty to oversee Royalist intelligence, so his life at the Oxonian court seems to have been more fulfilled, variable, and highly coloured than Hyde's funereal summary.

Even the wartime Falkland of Hyde's *History* and Clarendon's *Life* is sporadically but persistently visible in a lighter temper. It seems from Hyde's testimony that the affection and good spirits of the King at Royalist Oxford, jocular in adversity, familiar with men he had identified as kindred souls regardless of rank, had an infectious, optimistic impact on both friends. Elsewhere notorious for his shyness, pomposity, insecurity, and touchiness, in Hyde's writings Charles I appears willing to engage in (and pay for) wagers with his counsellors and friends, take sophisticated jokes against himself in good part, and accept advice running counter to his passionate instincts. It is an attractive picture, and one that Whitelocke, in part, corroborates.

Hyde's account of King Charles is especially persuasive because he is also open about the all-important flaw in the King's mostly genuine friendship – that it never extended to complete honesty, an omission with ever more serious consequences. Here, and with strikingly similar observations and phraseology, Hyde's friend Whitelocke is at one with him in his assessment both of the King's theoretical, potential, at times even actual virtues, and of Charles's besetting, tragic weakness.

Before his advancement to the Exchequer in March 1643, Hyde was still employed by the King – as was Whitelocke for Parliament – partly due to his unflagging efforts in drafting declarations addressed to the adverse side, in truth for the benefit of the still unpersuaded, uncommitted majority. Such duties gave rise to Hyde's most substantial and vivid passage concerning his and Falkland's personal relationship with the King. He remembers King Charles conversing with Falkland about Hyde's 'peculiar style' of prose, declaring that '[Charles] could know any thing written by [Hyde], if it were brought to him by a stranger, amongst a multitude of writings by other men'. Falkland, himself the King's supplementary speechwriter and propagandist when Hyde was unable or unwilling to serve, politely demurred, pointing out Hyde's flair for dissimulation: '[Falkland] doubted [i.e. feared] his majesty could hardly do that . . . [as Falkland] himself, who had so long conversation and friendship with [Hyde], was often deceived'.

So the King and his Secretary of State entered into a private bet as to whether Charles would indeed recognize Hyde's prose unsigned. The stake was to be a single golden angel, the highest-value coin minted in England before the Restoration striking of the guinea, worth 10 shillings since King James's day. Those minted by Charles I before the civil war bore the legend *Amor populi praesidium regis*, 'The people's love is the king's protection'. However much bitter, bellicose Royalists of the Queen's party might dismiss it as cant, this doctrine sincerely united Hyde, Falkland, Whitelocke and, erratically but persistently to his tragic, eloquent end, Charles himself.

Falkland then displayed his underrated capacity for subterfuge. He waited several days before handing the King 'several packets... from London':

> ... prints of diurnals [daily newsletters] ... speeches, and the like ... every day printed at London, and as constantly sent to Oxford ... amongst the rest ... two speeches ... one made by the lord Pembroke for an accommodation ... the other by the lord Brooke against it ...

The King was delighted by Pembroke's fluency in attempting a peaceful 'accommodation', though a little puzzled, as that wavering earl was considered no great orator. 'He did not think that Pembroke could speak so long together; though every word he said was so much his own, that nobody else could make it.' Thus did Falkland cheerfully claim his angel, having in fact shown to his monarch two outstanding specimens of Hyde's misleadingly convincing ventriloquism. The King 'willingly' accepted his defeat in a 'very merry' fashion.

According to a second story, less well attested but in currency from at least the late 1670s, Falkland, both as Secretary of State and as a scholarly personal friend, accompanied King Charles to the Bodleian Library, not as yet in use as the Oxford Parliament. As Charles was this time feeling altogether less merry, Falkland attempted to cheer him up, light-heartedly experimenting with the ancient custom of the *Sortes Virgilianae*. Virgil, Augustan Rome's greatest epic poet, had become regarded by medieval schoolmen as a prophetic magus, who had anticipated the coming of Christ, and whose *Aeneid* held infallible keys to the secrets of the future. Twice Falkland dipped into the heroic epic; twice he found extracts of dire significance – Dido's curse upon Aeneas, and King Evander's lament for his slain son Pallas.

This tale seems on the whole more probably transposed from

a later learned display to Charles II, by the poet Abraham Cowley, a known devotee of the *Sortes*. Cowley was, however, a constant admirer of Falkland, much in his and the King's company at Oxford in 1643. In 1639, aged scarcely twenty, Cowley, then a Cambridge undergraduate, had composed an epistle in Falkland's honour when Falkland, then a more celebrated poet as well as patron, had departed for Scotland as a volunteer soldier in the First Bishops' War:

> *Great is thy charge, O North; be wise and just;*
> *England commits her Falkland to thy trust.*
> *Return him safe: learning would rather choose*
> *Her Bodley or her Vatican to lose.*
> *All things that are but writ or printed there*
> *In his unbounded breast engraven are.*
> *There all the sciences together meet,*
> *And every art does all his kindred greet,*
> *Yet justle not, nor quarrel; but as well*
> *Agree as in some common principle.*
>
> *. . . And this great prince of knowledge is by Fate*
> *Thrust into th'noise and business of the State . . .*
>
> *While we, who can no action undertake,*
> *Whom Idleness itself might learned make, –*
> *Who hear of nothing, and as yet scarce know*
> *Whether the Scots in England be or no, –*
> *Pace dully on, oft tire, and often stay,*
> *Yet see his nimble Pegasus fly away . . .*
>
> *He is too good for war, and ought to be*
> *As far from danger as from fear he's free . . .*

Cowley's youthful, joyous flattery was ultimately to become (whether or not by Virgil's assistance) all too prophetic. It also hints at an early personal knowledge of Falkland, or his reputation; for example, of his habit at Great Tew of quoting authorities to friends from memory rather than, in their company, ever consulting his famously extensive library. Whether or not Cowley and Falkland were already acquainted in 1639 – it would have been an exceptional stroke of talent-spotting by Falkland if they had been, if not one beyond Great Tew's nurturing capacities – by 1643 they were frequently together, with Hyde, at Oxford, all as intimates of the King. The *Sortes Virgilianae* anecdote has significance less as proleptic irony than as evidence towards a certain atmosphere: bookish, civilized, at times surprisingly carefree, at others shaded by intimations of more or less probable disaster.

To this time and setting also belongs a controversial, tenacious rumour about Falkland's private life, to the effect that amid the febrile glories of the Oxford court, the proverbially honourable Falkland was nonetheless straining his marriage vows to Lettice, Lady Falkland, left at home in Great Tew. Lady Falkland was pious, charitable, emotional, personally persuasive, and at least according to Clarendon, beautiful. The sister of Sir Harry Morison, Falkland's deceased friend and Ben Jonson's fellow patron, she was the penniless bride for whose sake Falkland had finally fallen out with his spendthrift, irascible father. John Aubrey, elsewhere muddled enough about different generations of Carys and Falklands, gleefully states that a certain 'Mrs Moray', 'a handsome Lady at court', became Falkland's 'mistress . . . whom he loved above all creatures'. This story was evidently at large after the Restoration, for Clarendon regretfully confronts it in the *Life*:

> . . . they who knew either the lord or the lady [i.e. 'Mrs Moray', rather than Lady Falkland], knew well that neither of them was capable of an ill imagination. She was of the most unspotted; unblemished virtue; never married; of an extraordinary talent of mind, but of no alluring beauty; nor of a constitution of tolerable health, being in a deep consumption, and not like to have lived so long by many months. It is very true, the lord Falkland had an extraordinary esteem of her, and

exceedingly loved her conversation, as most of the persons of eminent parts of that time did; for she was in her understanding, and discretion, and wit, and modesty, above most women; the best of which had always a friendship with her. But [Falkland] was withal so kind to his wife, whom he knew to be an excellent person, that, though he loved his children with more affection and fondness than most fathers used to do, he left by his will all he had to his wife . . .

Clarendon's loyal protestations were, to posterity, entirely counter-productive, supplying Aubrey's gossip with material otherwise lacking in authority and substance. A recitation of Falkland's sensible arrangements for the custody of his underage sons' estate hardly refutes the sense that, at least, a complicated romantic friendship is under discussion (a similar connection is tangible in Hyde's correspondence with his Villiers marital relation, Anne, Lady Dalkeith). But almost every single detail asserted by Aubrey is contradicted by those let slip by Clarendon.

For Aubrey, Mrs Moray was 'handsome', for Clarendon 'of no alluring beauty'. And for Clarendon, indeed, the unnamed lady sounds much more than a mere beauty about court, high ranking, but also highly conspicuous for wit and learning, enough so, as in the case of Lady Ranelagh, Lady Dalkeith, and Lady Falkland herself, to pierce his frequently all-encompassing suspicion of womankind. In sum, Clarendon all but reveals to well-informed eyes – and there must have been many more of them when his *Life* was written, even when it was published in the early eighteenth century – that the handsome Mrs Moray of Aubrey's scurrilous anecdote is none other than the high-minded, great-spirited, yet sadly frail Lady Sophia Murray. Lady Sophia, Edmund Waller's kind-hearted 'Amoret', was soon to be imprisoned in London during her last three months of declining health. This was as a consequence of the foiled London Royalist plots in which both her poetical suitor, Edmund Waller, and her rumoured lover, Falkland, had played incompetently clandestine parts, and on the actual evidence of the supremely perfidious Waller.

It is unlikely to be ascertained whether, or in what sense, Lady Sophia Murray and Falkland were ever lovers (Aubrey's story is, incidentally, quietly believed in the present Cary family). Like Lady Dungarvan, Lady Sophia is called Falkland's mistress in Parliamentarian pamphlets that tend to make the tale less rather than more persuasive; yet the effort and detail with which Clarendon tries to arrest the gossip is still more telling. Either way, it still seems that, as Secretary of State in the first half of 1643, Falkland, far from being sunk in torpid apathy, was stimulated not just by Hyde's constant intellectual ballast, and by the wit of lively, curious, artistic companions such as Cowley, but by an intense, possibly illicit, in every sense delicate friendship with a woman who appears to have been his intellectual and moral, as well as social, equal.

## 'View of a kingdom in war' – Bristol, Gloucester, the Gloucester Campaign, Summer to Autumn 1643

As Secretary of State, Falkland – unlike Hyde – sat on the inner committee of the Privy Council that concerned itself with the King's foreign policy and military dispositions. Like his friend Hyde, Falkland was truly depressed by many of the decisions the King made, in this inner council as in Charles's still more private correspondence. In three kingdoms, Charles was carrying on a more belligerent strategy than Falkland favoured. In one crucial case, Falkland's attempt to moderate the King's instincts (or the Queen's, after her return to Oxford that summer) may have disastrously miscarried. Aubrey, as always tending to complicate Falkland's lofty reputation with a mixture of humanistic admiration and mischievously iconoclastic scepticism, lodges the crucial accusation:

> ... Charles I ... made [Falkland] Principal Secretary of Estate ... which he discharged with a great deal of Wit and Prudence, only his advice was very unlucky to his Majesty, in persuading him (after the victory of Roundway-down, and the taking of Bristol) to sit down

before Gloucester, which was so bravely defended [ . . . the siege] so broke and weakened the King's Army, that 'twas the procatractic [i.e. original] cause of his ruin.

The council of war where this pivotal decision was made took place at Prince Rupert's new and costly acquisition, Bristol, the second port of England. Here Falkland certainly spoke boldly to the King on Hyde's behalf, facing down the third of their strained triumvirate, Colepeper, and the King's Bedchamber favourite Jack Ashburnham, by channelling Bristol's revenues into Hyde's purview as Chancellor of the Exchequer, where they properly belonged. Falkland certainly supported, and perhaps originated, the intermediate military policy that emerged at the Bristol council, hesitantly chosen by King Charles over two more definitive, bloodier expedients.

Prince Rupert, fresh from bloody victory at Bristol, wished to storm the less heavily defended Gloucester in turn, and at once. The Queen and her by now numerous, if themselves endemically squabbling, supporters – including Ashburnham, Colepeper, Digby, Harry Jermyn, George Goring, and Henry Wilmot – saw little point in this Midlands foray, pushing instead for another advance on London. Both of these courses involved bloodshed and political aggression from which the King, seconded by Falkland, shrank. When the governor of Gloucester, Colonel Edward Massey, secretly intimated that he would surrender to the King if Charles led his army against him in person, Falkland was among the voices – perhaps the decisive one – in favour of this apparently bloodless opportunity.

If so, Falkland was all too soon proven wrong: Massey held out and received no more negotiations. Falkland determined, against all Hyde's solicitous urgings, to take a conspicuous part in the siege of Gloucester himself:

> . . . when his friends passionately reprehended him for exposing his person unnecessarily to danger (as he delighted to visit the trenches

and nearest approaches, and to discover what the enemy did), as being so much beside the duty of his place [as Secretary] that it might be understood against it, he would say merrily, that his office could not take away the privileges of his age, and that a Secretary in war might be present at the greatest secret of danger; but withal alleged seriously that it concerned him to be more active in enterprises of hazard than other men, that all might see that his impatiency for peace proceeded not from pusillanimity or fear to adventure his own person . . .

Falkland was already displaying ostentatious physical courage at Gloucester with mixed motives. He had always been prone to precipitate, combative action in a crisis – his rash challenge in his youth to the officer who relieved him of his troop of Irish horse, his ineffectual period of volunteer service in the Netherlands, and his more active part in the First Bishops' War all come to mind. He felt, as Hyde evidently did not, that his preference for peace made it doubly necessary to prove himself in war. He probably blamed himself for the unfortunate consequences already resulting from the protracted siege of Gloucester. And his distaste for the war and the times was, perhaps, beginning to make itself felt in an increasingly general disregard for his own safety.

As a volunteer soldier in a cause he half-doubted, Falkland shared common ground with his friend Lord Spencer, lately risen to Earl of Sunderland, who envisaged going into exile should the cause for which he fought actually come to prevail. Falkland, like Whitelocke, also had a generally more ardent response to the military bugle than did Hyde. For Hyde, the most 'lively representation & emblem' of hell was a 'view of a kingdom in war'. But Falkland and Whitelocke, while fully sharing this belief in war's unnecessary barbarity, were also drawn to the public distinction, the time-hallowed, defining sense of honour, the sheer glamour of martial service.

At Gloucester, Falkland's keenness to act could not ameliorate the misstep for which he may have been responsible. The Earl of Essex, unexpectedly well resupplied, performing at his rare best, outmanoeuvred the King to relieve the city. He then took upon himself, and what was then Parliament's only remaining full army, the risk of what seemed sure, one way or the other, to be a decisive encounter. It was to take place before the Berkshire town of Newbury.

## *The First Battle of Newbury and Its Issue,*
## *19 September 1643–March 1644*

The night before the first Battle of Newbury, Falkland took communion – as he may or may not have predicted, his last – from the town's Rector, Dr William Twisse. Those, like Aubrey, who assumed Falkland to be of 'the Polish' or 'Socinian' theological persuasion (that is, a denier of the Trinity), might have been surprised enough at this decision, but its real peculiarity was less theological than political. Dr Twisse, a Newbury man of German descent, was a clergyman so committedly Parliamentarian that the two Houses had named him prolocutor, or chairman, of the Westminster Assembly. There the extremity of his Calvinism was remarked upon; he frequently expressed his aversion to Archbishop Laud (one, indeed, consistently shared by his unlikely Royalist communicant). It is understandable that the pious, ecumenical Falkland should have accepted the service of any divine to hand, but that Twisse was content to officiate for the absolution of the King's Secretary of State, riding in the army lately pronounced 'popish' by Parliament's Vow and Covenant, is testament both to the individual respect that Falkland commanded and to the sense of indecision still at large in the country.

What sins or memories weighed on Falkland's conscience may depend again in part on Aubrey's 'Mrs Moray', Clarendon's unnamed but fairly clearly identified Lady Sophia Murray. Aubrey considered 'Mrs Moray' to have died a short while before Falkland, to her lover's certain, grief-stricken knowledge. But Clarendon's *Life* is still more dramatic: 'she died the same day, and as some computed it, the same hour' as did Falkland. The first Battle of Newbury was fought on 20 September 1643. On that same day, Parliament issued orders for a certain Robert Kincade to 'pass to Oxford, to obtain a pass for the Lady Annandale, to pass with the Corpse of her Daughter into Scotland'.

Clarendon's account is thus in this instance mostly upheld: Falkland can scarcely have heard of his friend, or lover's, death. In the same passage, Clarendon emphasizes the fateful fitfulness of wartime communications, pointing out that Falkland's reply to his concerned letter written to Gloucester only reached Oxford at the same time as news of his friend's death at Newbury, the day after that battle. In Clarendon's unintentionally revealing account it was not the death of Falkland's mistress, but the relationship itself that was thought (wrongly, he protests) to have played a part in his friend's depressed state of mind:

> He died as much of the time as of the bullet: for, from the beginning of the war, he contracted so deep a sense of sadness and melancholy, that his life was not pleasant to him; and sure he was too weary of it. Those who did not know him well imputed, very unjustly, much of it to a violent passion he had for a noble lady . . .

The 'deep consumption' (another point strongly suggesting Lady Sophia Murray) of this 'noble lady', an illness mentioned by Clarendon as a fact making her an unlikely object of romance, lacking 'tolerable health', does after all explain why, even without any sure news of his lover's actual death, Falkland's melancholy might have been deepened by the connection.

Clarendon, as ever both protecting what he imagines to be the best interests of his dead friend's reputation and averting his gaze from espionage in general for reasons both of state and distaste, does not mention the sorrow Falkland must have additionally felt at Lady Sophia's imprisonment in London, whether or not he was her lover, given their evidently intimate friendship and the measure of responsibility he himself bore for her plight. She had been exposed to danger in London, probably engaged in the ciphered correspondence that condemned her, and been betrayed by Waller, the self-serving poet who had once, if equivocally, hymned her, all because of decisions that Falkland had, if not initiated, then sanctioned as Secretary of State.

Writing before Aubrey's version was published, yet already fighting against the tide to quell existing tittle-tattle, in the *History* Clarendon pronounced his friend 'in the morning before battle, as always upon action . . . very cheerful'. This sanguine verdict was, however, contradicted by its author's other great friend, Whitelocke, in the *Memorials*:

> The lord Falkland, secretary of state, in the morning of the fight called for a clean shirt, and being asked the reason of it, answered, that if he were slain in the battle they should not find his body in foul linen.
>
> Being dissuaded by his friends to go into the fight, as having no call to it, and being no military officer, he said he was weary of the times, and foresaw much misery to his own country, and did believe he should be out of it ere night, and could not be persuaded to the contrary . . .

The archetypally 'Cavalier' bravado of Falkland's calling for 'a clean shirt' brings to mind the second shirt worn by his King at his execution six years later, so that the crowds would not see him shiver and think him afraid. The stories resonated, got about, and persisted perhaps for similar reasons, whatever their veracity (and the King's shirt is well attested); they were playing a part in early martyrologies, King Charles's of Anglican religion and sacramental monarchy, Falkland's of theological and political liberalism, evoked by the two syllables of Great Tew. But the second half of Whitelocke's version reads like a response to whatever his old friend Hyde had told him in person. Whitelocke reinterprets Hyde's account of Falkland driven to fight by political duty, transforming, perhaps distorting it into courageous, Stoical, terminal despondency.

## England Commits

In the *Life*, Clarendon does not dispute Falkland's deliberate impetuosity at Gloucester, or his general weariness of the war, the era, and his part in it. He notes also Falkland's particularly hotheaded choice of regiment, commander, and position at Newbury, but as part of a general attitude, rather than a single act of premeditated self-destruction:

> ... the lord Falkland, hurried by his fate, as he was naturally inquisitive after danger, put himself into the head of Sir John Byron's regiment, which he believed was like to be in the hottest service ...

Compared to Whitelocke this is a providentialist reading, more elevated and heroic; not an act of individual surrender to unhappiness, but the workings of a tragic larger destiny: 'as much of the time as of the bullet' in a larger, more deterministic sense.

Falkland was riding against an enemy commander, the Earl of Essex, whom he, Hyde, and, from within the same camp, Whitelocke all essentially admired as a decent man. In the Scots war of 1639, Falkland had proudly served under Essex. Falkland's gentle sense of irony might have responded to his chief opponent's identity, as to the convictions of the previous night's clergyman, Dr Twisse. Certainly Falkland had higher regard for the Parliamentarian Lord General than for Prince Rupert, his own chief commander as general of the King's horse. Falkland's more immediate superior was the inevitable Sir John Byron, the opportunistic raider of Oxford and the ineffectual disciplinarian at Fawley Court.

Byron's own account of Falkland's death deserves the respect due to immediacy and proximity of experience, if not formal elegance:

> The service grew so hot, that in a very short time, of twelve ensigns that marched up ... eleven were brought off the field ... Upon this a confusion was heard among the foot, calling, horse! horse! whereupon I advanced with those two regiments I had ... went to view

> the ground . . . which I found to be enclosed with a high quick hedge and no passage into it, but by a narrow gap through which but one horse at a time could go and that not without difficulty. My Lord of Falkland did me the honour to ride in my troop this day, and I would needs go along with him, the enemy had beat our foot out of the close, and was drawn up near the hedge; . . . as I was giving orders for making the gap wide enough, my horse was shot in the throat . . . in the meanwhile my Lord Falkland (more gallantly than advisedly) spurred his horse through the gap, where both . . . were immediately killed.

Byron's narration of the battle, undertaken for Hyde's benefit but of which the historian-counsellor made tersely selective use, illustrates more clearly than Whitelocke's evocative, but rhetorical, partial, and rumour-spun parable, that Falkland's end was, according to the man who was in the best position to know, his own doing. Sir John's note of frustration is definite and comprehensible. In the grand scheme of the battle, his horse's advance through high hedges against Parliamentarian foot had been a rare Royalist success, yet he now knew it would be remembered mainly for the death of the King's advisor and the Chancellor of the Exchequer's dearest friend.* Next to overruling military plans, the most maddening habit of powerful civilians was to volunteer and get themselves killed.

Byron judges Falkland in four efficient words, 'more gallantly than advisedly'. Falkland had achieved his wish – gaining notice for an indisputably, insanely brave death – but the more hardened soldier thought his volunteer more of an incompetent than a hero. In this, however, Byron was mistaken. Falkland had showed both ability and prudence sorely lacking among Royalist commanders at Edgehill, urging Wilmot to keep the cavalry in good order, only to

---

* The battle itself was tactically undecided, but strategically, along with the persistence of Massey at Gloucester, it arguably constituted a turning point against the King.

## England Commits

be dismissed with that dissolute officer's characteristic, languid complacency. At Newbury, too, he knew what he was doing, and so Whitelocke's analysis, for all its folkloric character, is in the end to be preferred to Hyde's as faithful to Falkland's final intentions.

Where Whitelocke cannot approach Hyde is in his strength of feeling as an elegist. Whitelocke knew and greatly revered 'that ingenious Lord Falkland, [my] great friend', and was proud of their relatively slight, mainly professional connection. Later in his life Whitelocke supported Falkland's clerical protégés, attempted (unsuccessfully) to act as a generous patron to Falkland's son, and collected what Falkland himself would have hoped was his most durable legacy, his theological writings. His compact obituary of Falkland in the *Memorials* is precise, proportionate, fair but bloodless, its regret cool-headedly political:

> His death was much lamented by all that knew him, or heard of him; being a gentleman of great parts, ingenuity and honour, courteous and just to all, and a passionate promoter of all endeavours of peace betwixt the king & parliament.

He makes Falkland sound like a less fortunate version of himself. Hyde, on the other hand, can hardly make his lost friend out through successive waves of emotion that overwhelm him by turns. First of all comes deluded hope:

> . . . in the instant falling from his horse, his body was not found till the next morning, till when there was some hope he might have been a prisoner; though his nearest friends, who knew his temper, received small comfort from that imagination.

Hyde's reader is carried far from the field of Newbury witnessed by Byron, back to the civilian royal counsellors at Oxford, anxiously waiting for news. Where Falkland is concerned, the ambiguity that accompanies, threads through, and in places undermines Hyde's *History* and Clarendon's *Life* suggests that 'his temper' can refer either to Falkland's mettlesome courage, or his bleak final mood, with a growing prejudice towards the second. Overstretched hope gives way to underlying, all too cognizant grief, the heart-breaking, if still unacknowledged realization of Falkland's chosen destiny.

Falkland had one way to reply to his encomiasts – his will. In it, as Clarendon emphasized, he left his estate to his famously saintly wife, as guardian of their children with full responsibility, but to be guided and advised by the most prominent, loyal survivors of Great Tew – Hyde himself, Gilbert Sheldon, George Morley, and John Earle. Much more unexpectedly, Falkland left a small physical bequest, a ring, to Bulstrode Whitelocke, engaged with the cause against which he had just died fighting. Given the always formal, political, rather than fully personal nature of their association, this was a powerful parting vote in favour of national reconciliation, lying however far ahead.

Almost half a year later, in March 1644, Hyde received what he considered 'a very sensible letter' on the subject of Falkland's death, embodying the same peace-making desire and duty, and written from the parliamentary London of Whitelocke and his colleagues. It was from Katherine Jones, Viscountess Ranelagh, *née* Boyle, Falkland's friend since their Irish youth, possibly even at one point a candidate for his hand. She was both his and Hyde's constant correspondent, in defiance of civil war, in their maturity. To Hyde, Lady Ranelagh wrote with sincerity, courtesy, sympathy, respect, and a solemn charge that she urged him, in their friend's name and cause, to undertake:

> When I consider that gallant man, to whom you were a friend, and remember how passionate he was for the peace of this kingdom, and think how impossible it is that there should be a friendship where there is not some agreement in humour and opinions; I cannot but hope you had an agreement with him in those inclinations that carried him on so strongly to endeavour the peace and preservation of his country . . .

## England Commits

My hope assures me you may now have peace at an easier rate than ever you yourselves offered for it, whilst we still had the blessing of his life . . .

For we have learnt at last that it is an easier thing to be weary of the government we have, than to mend ourselves by a change, and that our own disorders have brought us into this middle, that we must either submit to one or be tyrannized over by hundreds . . . Those that did with the greatest violence pull themselves from under the king's government, when they looked upon it in comparison with Queen Elizabeth's, would with as much greediness crouch to it, now they are able to compare it experimentally with Sir Henry Vane's . . .*

. . . all this is spoken to my Lord Falkland's friend, from one that was to him, and is to you upon his score, a very faithful humble servant.

Lady Ranelagh's proposed course of action, that if the King were simply to acknowledge the Long Parliament as incontestably legitimate, that would in itself be sufficient to set a lasting peace in motion, reflected opinion in the capital, the City, amid the gentry, the nobility, and in Parliament, but did not reckon sufficiently with the political strength of Vane and the Independents. Yet her letter shows that while King Charles was hardly loved, his pacific Secretary of State was still cherished in memory by the peace-party Parliamentarians, and Hyde, though officially a warmongering *persona non grata* exempted by Parliament from any hope of a pardon, could for all that be looked to as Lord Falkland's heir.

'If the celebrating the memory of eminent and extraordinary persons,' Hyde begins his threnody as he turns aside in his *History*:

---

* Lady Ranelagh probably meant the younger Henry Vane, in March 1644 emerging as a powerful Independent leader in Parliament after the deaths of Pym and Hampden.

> ... and transmitting their great virtues for the imitation of posterity, be one of the principal ends and duties of history, it will not be thought impertinent in this place to remember a loss which no time will suffer to be forgotten, and no success or good fortune will repair ... if there were no other brand upon this odious and accursed civil war than that single loss, it must be most infamous and execrable to posterity.

Time has, on the whole, suffered Lucius Cary, Lord Falkland, that 'person of such prodigious parts of learning and knowledge, of that inimitable sweetness and delight in conversation, of so flowing and obliging a humanity and goodness', to be forgotten indeed. Sir Edward Hyde is scarcely now more remembered, and still more rarely for his lean years of labour against impossible odds for peace and moderation. As for Bulstrode Whitelocke, he is left – as he probably expected, and as might have pleased the less vainglorious part of his prudent, precise nature – to scholars, diplomats, and lawyers.

These men are doubly lost: in the gigantic shadow of Cromwell, soon to overtake them, their native monarch, and all their compatriots; and in the drum-and-trumpeted national saga that came to terms with the trauma of the civil wars, by identifying in them, however unpleasant they were to undergo, the necessary, ultimately 'progressive' adolescence of a sophisticated, democratic modern British polity. For Hyde, for Whitelocke, for Falkland, for the wearily wise, unanswerably authoritative voice of John Selden and of civilization behind all three, the civil wars were an excrescence, not an education. As these men strove, and for all their conscientious and abundant skill failed, in statecraft, they succeeded, at least, in incarnating for as long as they could, and by preserving for whoever is inclined to identify it, an attractive common world: an alternative to the ravages of party enmity and sealed-off thought. For Falkland a pale afterlife as a 'Martyr of Peace' awaited; Hyde and Whitelocke had long, busy, still strangely, paradoxically entwined careers yet to run. But the hope with which both men had entered public life in 1640, burning with earnest, honourable ambition, was in truth quenched long before the onerous futility of the Treaty of Uxbridge in early 1645. The standard of hope fell, with their friend and by his preference, at the first Battle of Newbury on 20 September 1643.

# List of Notable Characters

### The Scene

England, briefly France.

### The Time

Loosely 1628 to specifically 1645.

### The Protagonists

Edward, otherwise Ned, Hyde, of Dinton and Purton in Wiltshire. Born at Dinton in 1609. Educated at Magdalen Hall, Oxford, and the Middle Temple. Literary hanger-on, failed poet, amateur historical essayist. Called to the bar 1633. MP for Wootton Bassett in the Short Parliament and Saltash in the Long. Knighted, made Privy Councillor and appointed Chancellor of the Exchequer in 1643. Royalist Peace Commissioner at Uxbridge, 1645.

Later historian and statesman, Lord Chancellor under Charles II and first Earl of Clarendon. Author of *The History of the Rebellion*, generally referred to in this book as the *History*, as Sir Edward Hyde, 1646–8; author of his *Life* and a continuation of the *History* as Earl of Clarendon, after his political downfall and exile in 1667. His title is thus employed here mostly when drawing upon, and emphasizing, later writings and perspectives.

Bulstrode Whitelocke, of Fawley and Phyllis Courts in Buckinghamshire and Oxfordshire. Born 1605, Fleet Street. Educated at Eton, the Merchant Taylors', St John's College, Oxford, and the Middle Temple, at which last elected Master of Revels and Treasurer. Called to the

*List of Notable Characters*

bar 1626. Successful amateur composer. Historical and antiquarian dabbler. Briefly MP in 1626, recorder of Abingdon from 1632, MP for Great Marlow in Long Parliament, prosecutor of Earl of Strafford 1640–41, drafted 'Perpetual Parliament' Act, Deputy Lieutenant for Buckinghamshire and Oxfordshire, would-be Governor of Oxford, captain, would-be colonel, Peace Commissioner in 1643 and 1645, lay member of the Westminster Assembly of Divines from 1643.

Later Lord Keeper of the Great Seal and Ambassador to Sweden for the Commonwealth, knighted during the Protectorate, historian, memoirist, and diarist. Almost all of his surviving writings were composed in his enforced retirement after the Restoration.

## Other Members of the House of Commons

Sir William Armine, Parliamentarian Peace Commissioner in 1643.

John, otherwise Jack, Ashburnham. Courtier, Royalist MP and army plotter, defended by Hyde in 1641. Afterwards Hyde's political opponent and a supporter of the Queen. Royalist Commissioner at Treaty of Uxbridge.

Sir Lucius Cary, 2nd Viscount Falkland. Born c. 1610 at Burford. Entered briefly at Cambridge, largely educated at Trinity College, Dublin. Patron of letters, minor poet, thwarted duellist, volunteer soldier, amateur theologian. Lord of the manor of Great Tew, and host there of charmed circle of scholarly, literary, and clerical friends, notable for culturally refined, politically heterogeneous religious ecumenism. MP for Newport on the Isle of Wight from 1640, Secretary of State to King Charles from January 1642. Killed at first Battle of Newbury, 1643.

Sir John Colepeper, later 1st Baron Colepeper. Colleague, though not personal friend, of Falkland and Hyde, with them leader of moderate Royalists. Less concerned about Church than Hyde, firmer on militia. Chancellor of the Exchequer for a year, then

## List of Notable Characters

grudgingly made way for Hyde. Increasingly a partisan of the Queen. Attended Treaty of Uxbridge.

Oliver Cromwell, rustically attired, particularly uncompromising follower of Pym. On civil terms with Falkland, but not Hyde. Most admired English victor of Marston Moor in 1644; thereafter ascendant leader of Independent religious faction, and war party in Parliament.

Sir Simonds D'Ewes, moderate supporter of Pym, antiquary and diarist. Probably envious, certainly shockable, critic of Selden. Fairly respectful towards Hyde, Falkland and Whitelocke. One of the first observers to identify an 'episcopal party' led by Hyde. Prone to prudent departure before heated divisions of the House.

Sir John Eliot, foremost opposition leader in the Commons up to 1629, died in 1632, in royal captivity.

Sir Walter Erle, veteran of a brief Low Countries campaign, amateur military enthusiast. Commons client of Lord Saye. Inept prosecutor of Strafford.

Nathaniel Fiennes, second son of Lord Saye. The bitterest enemy of the bishops in the 1640 Parliaments. Associate turned enemy of Hyde. Unsuccessful Parliamentarian soldier.

John Glynne, Welsh lawyer. Prosecutor of Strafford. Like Hyde, Commons client of the Earl of Pembroke. Supporter of Parliament over the Militia. Moderate, peace party Parliamentarian.

John Hampden, hugely rich Ship Money rebel, Pym's most persuasive lieutenant, related distantly to Bulstrode Whitelocke, more closely to Edmund Waller and Oliver Cromwell. Died from wounds incurred at Chalgrove Field, June 1643. One of the 'Five Members' whom King Charles I, in January 1645, unsuccessfully attempted to seize, in breach of Parliament's privilege.

## List of Notable Characters

Sir Arthur Haselrig, belligerent opposition leader, later Parliamentarian cavalry commander. One of the Five Members.

Sir John Holland, diarist, similar to Whitelocke in moderate support for Parliament and primary desire for peace. Married to a Catholic. Parliamentarian Peace Commissioner sent to Oxford in 1643, cared for Whitelocke during an illness there.

Denzil Holles, Commons opposition leader. Brother-in-law of royal government strongman Thomas Wentworth, Earl of Strafford. Peace party leader, Peace Commissioner in 1644–5. Admired but disliked by Hyde, perhaps owing to legal differences in their profession. One of the Five Members.

William Lenthall, squire of Burford, Oxfordshire, Speaker of the House of Commons from 1640.

Sir William Lytton, Parliamentarian Peace Commissioner in 1643.

Henry, or Harry, Marten, lawyer, neighbour, and friendly acquaintance of Hyde. Increasingly open republican, loose-living character, war party firebrand, unsuccessful soldier, incautious politician.

John Maynard, Middle Temple companion of Whitelocke and Hyde, lawyer, MP, with Whitelocke prosecuted the Earl of Strafford, later prosecuted Archbishop Laud.

Geoffrey Palmer, early and close Middle Temple friend of Bulstrode Whitelocke (his distant relation) and of Ned Hyde. Barrister, with Whitelocke one of the prosecutors of Strafford. Subsequently unswerving, vocal Royalist MP. Fellow tenant with Whitelocke in Ivy Lane 1642–3. Royalist Peace Commissioner at Uxbridge in 1645.

Isaac Penington, clothier, wine merchant, and brewer. MP for the City of London. Hard-line Pymite in politics, hot Protestant in religion. Lord Mayor of London from 1642. Ensured Parliamentarian control of the city's militia and armaments. Attempted to arrest the Earl of Northumberland for treason in 1643.

Henry Percy, younger brother of 10th Earl of Northumberland. Courtly rival of Cary family over military preferment in Ireland. Favourite of the Queen. One of the contrivers of the ultra-Royalist 'First Army Plot', but betrayed it to his brother. Unexpected first intermediary between Hyde and the King.

William Pierrepont, moderate Parliamentarian, close ally of Whitelocke. Son and brother of moderate Royalists. Peace Commissioner in 1643 and 1645. At first respected, then condemned by Hyde.

John Pym, procedural parliamentary mastermind, inexhaustible speaker, would-be Chancellor of the Exchequer, effective leader of the House of Commons in opposition to the court from 1640 to his death from natural causes in December 1643. Most prominent of the Five Members.

John Selden, greatest authority of his age on constitutional and legal history, foremost English scholar of Hebrew, lawyer, MP for Oxford University, antiquarian, author, collector, host, wit. Sometime political prisoner at Charles I's pleasure. Exceptionally various political record and assortment of friends. According to rumour, first lover, then common-law husband of the Countess of Kent. Mentor and exemplar to Whitelocke and Hyde. Lay member of Westminster Assembly from 1643.

Oliver St John, close ally of Pym, client of the Earl of Bedford, legal counsel of Hampden, marital relation of Cromwell. Instrumental in the downfall of the Earl of Strafford. In 1641 named Solicitor-General to the King to appease the opposition. Parliamentarian Peace Commissioner at Uxbridge, 1645. Continued to be powerful leader of Parliament's war party, though never a republican.

## List of Notable Characters

Sir Philip Stapleton, Yorkshire MP, firm, courteous Pym supporter while also one of Hyde's 'Northern friends'. After the outbreak of the English Civil War, Commander of Essex's Life Guards. Ally of Essex, friend of Whitelocke, ultimately inclined towards Parliamentarian peace party.

William Strode, extreme, inarticulate, long-time opposition leader. Not to be confused with his kinsman, the Laudian religious poet and academic of the same name. One of the Five Members.

Nathaniel Tomkins, brother-in-law of Edmund Waller. Implicated in Waller's Plot and hanged for treason by order of Parliament in 1643.

Sir Henry, or Harry, Vane the younger, son of the sometime courtier of the same name. Played crucial part, with his father, in downfall of Strafford. Hard-line opponent of bishops. With Pym, architect of the Parliamentarian-Covenanter alliance. Lay member of the Westminster Assembly. After the deaths of Hampden and Pym in 1643, arguably the most powerful single man in the Commons at Westminster. Attended, and helped to scupper, the Treaty of Uxbridge.

Edmund Waller, like Bulstrode Whitelocke youthful MP in the 1620s. Of exceptionally large property and income. Poet. Pupil and creditor of Dr George Morley; consequently companion at Great Tew. Unsuccessful suitor of Lady Dorothy Sidney. MP in 1640, apparently open Royalist but remained in London. Peace Commissioner in 1643. Prime mover of 'Waller's Plot' against Parliament later that year. Imprisoned and subsequently exiled.

Sir William Waller, veteran soldier and MP. Parliamentarian general, frequent opponent of his old friend Sir Ralph Hopton.

Philip Warwick, bold and rare Commons supporter of the Earl of Strafford in 1640–41. Delicate taste in dress. Royalist, memoirist.

## List of Notable Characters

Richard Winwood of Ditton Park, family friend and moderate Parliamentarian ally of Whitelocke. As fellow Deputy Lieutenant for Buckinghamshire, received with Whitelocke news of Edgehill. Shared his coach and horses with Whitelocke. Parliamentarian Peace Commissioner in 1643. Co-tenant with Whitelocke in Highgate later that year.

### Other Lawyers

Tom Chaloner, riotous youthful companion of Whitelocke and Hyde. Fell foul of Archbishop Laud and fled abroad, most likely to Turkey. Testified against Laud at his trial in 1644, thereafter Independent MP.

Robert Cole of the Middle Temple, Whitelocke's travelling companion in France in 1634.

Matthew Hale, companion of young Whitelocke, friend of John Selden, renowned jurist, moderate Royalist, fellow tenant with the Whitelockes in Ivy Lane 1642–3, defence counsel for both the Earl of Strafford and Archbishop Laud.

Sir Richard Lane, old Middle Temple associate of Whitelocke and Hyde. Moderate Royalist. Commissioner at Treaty of Uxbridge. Stated by Hyde to be especially learned in the law (more so than Hyde himself).

William Noy, King's Attorney-General from 1631, a legal patron of Whitelocke who predicted great things for his future. Primary organizer of the lawyers' masque for the King and the Queen, *The Triumph of Peace*, performed in 1634.

William Prynne, unsuccessful barrister, prolific, prolix, and popular pamphleteer. Prosecuted in the Star Chamber, mutilated and imprisoned for insulting the Queen among other charges, partly at the urging of Archbishop Laud. Released by parliamentary order in 1640 and regarded as popular hero. Later solicitor for Laud's prosecution.

## *The Court*

Anna, Countess of Caernarvon, daughter of Philip Herbert, 4th Earl of Pembroke and 1st of Montgomery.

Tom Carew, Gentleman of the Bedchamber. Celebrated erotic poet and 'son of Donne', writer of court masques. Friend of Hyde, Selden, and John Hales, claimed as cousin in jest by Falkland. Courtly rake, reluctant soldier in late 1630s Scottish wars, possibly reformed character late in life, died obscurely, probably shortly before the first English Civil War.

Francis, Baron Cottington. Chancellor of the Exchequer, Privy Counsellor. Old adversary of Laud and Strafford but defended Strafford at his trial from Sir Harry Vane's insinuations. Later willing to step aside to allow Pym to accept office as Chancellor.

Sir Nicholas Crispe, trader in West African slaves, tax farmer. Irish 'Adventurer', investing in future conquest of Catholic rebel lands. Royalist plotter in 1643 aiming to return London to King's allegiance, a scheme unconvincingly characterized by Hyde as separate from Waller's Plot.

Robert Dormer, Earl of Carnarvon, Catholic addict of the chase and the card tables, killed at first Battle of Newbury, September 1643.

Sir John Finch, Speaker of the House of Commons 1628–9, restrained in his chair by opposition MPs, including John Selden, at the dissolution of Parliament. Chief Justice of the Court of Common Pleas 1634, and as such persecutor of William Prynne; involved in the planning of *The Triumph of Peace* lawyers' masque.

## List of Notable Characters

Baron Finch and Lord Keeper of the Great Seal 1640–41. Forced abroad by parliamentary committee including Hyde, Falkland, and Whitelocke.

James Hamilton, 1st Marquess of Hamilton and 1st Earl of Cambridge. The King's cousin and at times a favourite. Premier Scots peer. Unreliable intermediary between King and Covenanters. Possible target of royally sponsored kidnap or assassination plot known as 'the Incident'. Consistently distrusted by Hyde.

Lucy Hay, née Percy, Countess of Carlisle. Related to most of the leading opposition 'popular peers'. Favourite of the Queen. Rumoured to be the lover first of Strafford, then of Pym, in their respective days of power. Later favoured the peace party and intrigued with the Scots and English Presbyterian factions.

Henrietta Maria, Princess of France, Queen of England, Scotland, and Ireland, admirer of Whitelocke as composer, dancer, and advocate. Always suspicious of Hyde's influence, heartily disliked by him in return.

Philip Herbert, 4th Earl of Pembroke and 1st of Montgomery, once a favourite of old King James, Lord Chamberlain 1625–41, amiable to Whitelocke, long-standing patron of Hyde, Peace Commissioner in 1643 and 1645.

Simon Ives, composer and musician to the Queen.

Henry (Harry) Jermyn, courtier, seducer, duellist, favourite of the Queen. Hated by Hyde with personal intensity.

Henry and Will Lawes, Wiltshire and Dinton countrymen of Ned Hyde, tenants of his father Henry Hyde the elder. Composers and musicians to the King and Queen.

## List of Notable Characters

Sir Humphrey May, Chancellor of the Duchy of Lancaster, close university friend of William Laud, later Archbishop of Canterbury, and of Sir James Whitelocke, father of Bulstrode. The younger Whitelocke's first political patron and arranger of his first marriage, to May's niece.

Walter, or Wat, Montagu, courtier, brother of Parliamentarian Earl of Manchester. Favourite of the Queen, spy, elaborately inept poet of pastoral masque, Catholic convert, monk, and priest.

William (Will) Murray, later 1st Earl of Dysart. King Charles's constant companion since childhood and one of his least reliable confidants – reportedly secretive when (often) drunk, but indiscreet once sober.

Sir Edward Nicholas, a devoted royal counsellor. Secretary of State from 1641. Old family friend of the Hydes.

James Stewart, Duke of Richmond, the King's cousin and close, loyal companion. Courteously refused to leave the King's side at Edgehill. Inclined towards moderation and peace, became an ally and friend of Hyde. As a royal envoy to Parliament in 1644, demonstrated substantial common ground with Parliamentarian peace party. Highest-ranking Royalist representative at Uxbridge in 1645, and the delegation's figurehead, with Hyde as its executive leader.

Charles Stuart, King of England, Scotland, and Ireland, ascended the throne in 1625. Received Whitelocke and Hyde with cordiality in 1634. Increasingly intimate with Hyde from 1641 onwards. Treated Whitelocke with signal courtesy at Oxford in 1643 and 1644.

Charles Stuart, Prince of Wales, the King's eldest son and heir. Witnessed Edgehill.

James Stuart, Duke of York, the King's second son. Witnessed (and later described) Edgehill.

## List of Notable Characters

Sir Henry, or Harry, Vane the elder, an ambitious, proud and faithless royal counsellor. Comptroller of the Household 1629–39, Secretary of State 1640–41.

George Villiers, 1st Duke of Buckingham, ubiquitous, omnipotent, ill-fated favourite of James I and Charles I, assassinated 1628. Both Whitelocke and Hyde would proudly claim marital connection to his family. His reputation defended by Hyde.

Sir Thomas Wentworth, MP, later Baron Wentworth, later 1st Earl of Strafford. Lord President of the Council of the North, Lord Deputy and then Lieutenant of Ireland. Former enemy of Buckingham and parliamentary reformer turned royal strongman. Greatly feared by the reforming MPs of 1640. Attacked by broad coalition with links to Buckingham's circle, parliamentary opposition, and personal enemies in Ireland. Tried unsuccessfully by a prosecution team including Whitelocke in 1640–41. Convicted by parliamentary Act of Attainder and executed May 1641.

Sir John Wolstenholme the younger, of Nostell Park. Royal financier, customs farmer, MP in Short Parliament. Aided Hyde's journey to the King's court at York. Retained Whitelocke on private business.

### Fathers

Sir Henry Cary, 1st Viscount Falkland, father of Sir Lucius Cary, 2nd Viscount Falkland. An unlucky soldier, improvident spender, and ineffectual Lord Deputy of Ireland. Patron of Ben Jonson. Client of George Villiers, 1st Duke of Buckingham.

Henry Hyde the elder, Ned Hyde's father. Younger son of a notable legal dynasty, unenthusiastic student of law, traveller, briefly MP, amateur scholar, charitable and conscientious Wiltshire squire.

## List of Notable Characters

James VI of Scotland and I of England, King Charles's father. Pedantic but pragmatic ruler in Church and State, regarded with nostalgic fondness by Hyde.

Sir James Whitelocke, Bulstrode Whitelocke's father. Younger son of purportedly old but impoverished family. Lawyer, MP, Judge of the King's Bench. Keen musician, Puritanical inclinations in religion, squire of Fawley and Phyllis Courts by Henley.

### Mothers

Dorothy Bennet, widow of Alderman Thomas Bennet, of Mortlake. Bulstrode Whitelocke's first mother-in-law, a woman of strong, enterprising, unscrupulous character.

Elizabeth Cary, Viscountess Falkland, née Tanfield, heiress of notoriously grasping Oxfordshire parents, child prodigy, playwright, proselytizing Catholic convert.

Mary Hyde, née Langford, Ned Hyde's mother. Daughter and heiress to a rich clothier, heartily disliked London.

Elizabeth Whitelocke, née Bulstrode, Bulstrode Whitelocke's mother. Born into two ancient families of legal gentry, the Bulstrodes and Crokes. Musical, Puritanical, French speaking, devoted to the nursing, health, and care of her son.

Frances Willoughby, Lady Willoughby of Parham, née Manners. Whitelocke's second mother-in-law, confidante of Bishop Williams.

### Wives

Anne Ayliffe, Ned Hyde's soon lost, lamented first wife, a relative of the Villiers family. Married in 1629, died of smallpox while pregnant the next year.

*List of Notable Characters*

Frances Hyde, daughter of Sir Thomas Aylesbury, became Hyde's second wife in 1634, mother of his many children. In 1642 joined her husband at Nostell in Yorkshire on his way to the King's northern court. Lived with him in Oxford during the first English Civil War.

Lettice, Lady Falkland, née Morison, sister of Falkland's youthful best friend Sir Harry Morison. Impulsively wedded by Falkland against the will of his father. As mistress of Great Tew, especially remembered for piety and good works. Her character and beauty praised by Hyde. Entrusted with the care of Falkland's estate in his will, with Hyde and other survivors of Great Tew appointed to advise her.

Frances Whitelocke, née Willoughby, niece of the Catholic Countess of Sunderland and the Puritan Earl of Rutland. Wooed and won, against her uncle's preference, as Whitelocke's second wife in 1635. Mother of many of Whitelocke's children, close confidante of his private and public thoughts.

Rebecca Whitelocke, née Bennet, niece of Sir Humphrey May, married Bulstrode Whitelocke in 1630, mother of his eldest son and heir, James Whitelocke the younger. Subject to increasingly severe fits of insanity, confined and died in 1634.

## Other Relations

Sir Thomas Aylesbury, Ned Hyde's second father-in-law, Master of Requests, Surveyor of the Navy, Master of the Mint, Keeper of Cranbourne Chase, bibliophile, and patron of mathematicians, numismatists, astronomers, and astrologers.

Sir Humphrey Bennet, Whitelocke's brother-in-law by his first marriage. Royalist officer, but true friend in need to his Parliamentarian marital kinsman.

## List of Notable Characters

Edward Bulstrode, Bulstrode Whitelocke's maternal uncle, bencher and reader at the Inner Temple. An inconspicuous, hard-working, circumspect man. Father of Captain Richard Bulstrode, a Royalist officer.

Sir George Croke, eminent judge, kindly maternal great-uncle to Bulstrode.

Anne Hyde, Ned Hyde's first-born child with his second wife, named for his first wife.

Henry Hyde the younger, loose-living, prematurely deceased elder brother of Ned.

Sir Nicholas Hyde, Lord Chief Justice, one of Ned's formidable legal paternal uncles, kept his nephew studying hard by night as a young student of law.

Elizabeth Mostyn, Bulstrode Whitelocke's sister, married into a family of Welsh Royalists.

Elizabeth Scrope, Countess of Sunderland, née Manners, Whitelocke's friendly neighbour and after 1635 equally friendly aunt by marriage, crypto-Catholic in religion.

Captain Edmund Whitelocke, uncle and godfather of Bulstrode, soldier, parasite, and fellow prisoner of various rebellious noblemen.

James Whitelocke the younger, Bulstrode Whitelocke's first-born child and heir, by his first wife.

## Other Peers

Montagu Bertie, Lord Willoughby of Eresby, later 2nd Earl of Lindsey. Surrendered at Edgehill to superintend his wounded father's

## List of Notable Characters

care, later released. Marital kinsman of Whitelocke, and his courteous host, while himself recovering from a wound, at Oxford. May have been used by the King to facilitate unofficial contact with Whitelocke.

Robert Bertie, 1st Earl of Lindsey. Veteran soldier, the King's first choice as general-in-chief at Edgehill. Old friend of the Earl of Essex. Following a quarrel with Prince Rupert and Patrick, Lord Ruthven, who both favoured more modern Swedish over traditional Dutch tactics, resigned to serve as colonel of his regiment. Wounded at Edgehill, captured, died of his wounds.

Richard Boyle, 1st Earl of Cork. Canterburian self-made Anglo-Irish plutocrat, made and broke successive Lords Deputy of Ireland, mortal enemy of Strafford.

Edward Conway, 2nd Viscount Conway, soldier, civilized voluptuary. Friend of Selden. Defeated by Covenanters in 1640. Compromised by Waller's Plot in 1643. Lay member of Westminster Assembly of Divines.

Robert Devereux, 3rd Earl of Essex. Son of the famous rebel Earl in Elizabeth's reign. Humiliated in two marriages. Experienced if not brilliant professional soldier. International Protestant hero. Awkward, thwarted courtier, but genuinely popular peer. Served against Scots in 1639, but denied overall command in favour of his cousin Holland. Determined upon death of Strafford in 1641. Cordial to Hyde, friendly to Whitelocke. Parliamentary Lord General from 1642, focus of hope for both Parliamentarian peace party and moderate Royalists.

George (Lord) Digby. Lord Bristol's heir. Brought up in Spain, Spanish speaking. Initially reform-minded MP in 1640 and originator of the 'Grand Remonstrance'. With Whitelocke on committee for Strafford's prosecution but spectacularly changed sides, also betraying its

## List of Notable Characters

minutes. Encouraged Hyde's decisive, if secret, entry into Charles's service after the passage of the Grand Remonstrance. Tarnished by ambivalent involvement in attempted arrest of the Five Members. Debarred from attending Treaty of Uxbridge because of the Commons' fear and distrust of him.

John Digby, 1st Earl of Bristol. Once a favourite of King James, former ambassador to Spain. Enemy of Buckingham and of Strafford, who mocked him as 'the Scots' Mercury' for his desire to negotiate with the Covenanters. Moderate reforming peer. With the Earl of Bedford, tried in vain to save Strafford in 1641. Moderate Royalist in the civil war.

William Fiennes, 1st Viscount Saye and Sele. Thwarted courtier, colonial investor in the Caribbean, anti-episcopal hot Protestant. Parliamentarian Lord Lieutenant of Oxfordshire, Gloucestershire, and Cheshire. Luckless chatelain of Broughton. Intense pride of blood; as descendant of William of Wykeham, Bishop of Winchester 1367–1404, proudly claimed rights as founder's kin of New College, Oxford. High Steward of that university. Personal enemy of Whitelocke from 1640.

Robert Greville, 2nd Baron Brooke. Kinsman, heir and adopted son of Elizabethan poet, soldier, and intellectual, Fulke Greville. The fiercest enemy of the bishops in the Lords. Chatelain of Warwick Castle. Popular rival of Essex for overall Parliamentarian command. Colonel of one of the foot regiments routed at Brentford. Fierce war-party advocate and political enemy of Pembroke. His belligerent speaking style successfully caught in 'unchristian' version of his oratory circulated as disinformation by Hyde. Shot dead by a Royalist sniper at Lichfield shortly before beginning of 1643 Treaty of Oxford, amid great rejoicing in the King's party.

Henry Grey, 8th Earl of Kent. Scholarly, genial host in indifferent health. Employer and friend of John Selden, probably his wife's lover. Died in 1639.

## List of Notable Characters

Thomas Howard, 1st Earl of Berkshire. Royalist Commissioner of Array, arrested by Whitelocke in 1642 and always despised by Hyde.

Thomas Howard, 14th Earl of Arundel. England's foremost collector of antiquities. Earl Marshal, and as such head of a prerogative court concerning heraldry. Personal enemy and political target of Hyde.

Edward Littleton, 1st Baron Littleton, Lord Keeper of the Great Seal from 1641. Highly distinguished, politically ambivalent lawyer, friend of Whitelocke and Hyde through John Selden.

George Manners, 7th Earl of Rutland. Jovial but choleric, Puritan in religion, became Bulstrode Whitelocke's reluctant uncle by marriage in 1635.

Edward Montagu, Lord Mandeville, later 2nd Earl of Manchester. Along with the Five Members, attempted target of Charles I's mishandled arrest. Liked and respected by Hyde. Considered as one of the committee to take charge of the militia for a fixed time in the event of a peace settlement.

Henry Pierrepont, Viscount Newark, later 2nd Earl of Kingston. Moderate Royalist, cholerically tempered heir of an enormously rich and famously lukewarm Royalist. Elder brother of William Pierrepont, parliamentary Peace Commissioner. Himself Royalist Commissioner at Treaty of Uxbridge.

Henry Rich, 1st Earl of Holland. Cool acquaintance of Hyde, friend of Whitelocke. Former favourite of Queen Henrietta Maria. Matchless wardrobe and stable. Military peacock, political weathercock.

Robert Rich, 2nd Earl of Warwick. Most powerful and radical of the Parliamentarian peers. Elder brother of the more ambivalent Earl of Holland. Consistent leader of Parliament's war party. Replaced his cousin the Earl of Northumberland as Lord

Admiral by parliamentary nomination, to Northumberland's lasting resentment.

Francis Russell, 4th Earl of Bedford. Patron of Pym, initially secret ally of Covenanters. On good terms with Hyde. Father-in-law of Lord Digby. Architect of plan to bring Pym and his allies into government. Attempted broker of a compromise to save Strafford's life. Died of smallpox in May 1641, three days before Strafford's execution.

Edward Sackville, 4th Earl of Dorset. Duellist and rake in his youth. Soldier, adventurer, colonialist, diplomat, dabbler in political opposition and ecumenical theology. Moved into Royalist camp around same time as Hyde in 1641. Joined the King at York in 1642. Angrily refused to court the charge of cowardice by obeying the King's request to leave his side and escort the princes from the field of Edgehill. Consistently advocated peace. Suggested by the King as a commissioner of the militia for a fixed time, in the event of a settlement at Uxbridge. Greatly admired by Hyde.

William Seymour, 2nd Earl, later 1st Marquess of Hertford. Part of the reforming noble group of marital and blood relations including Warwick, Holland, Northumberland, and Essex (his brother-in-law). Assisted Bedford's attempt to save Strafford. Afterwards broke definitively from the rest of the 'Junto', and remained a moderate Royalist throughout the civil wars. Powerful advocate for compromise, especially in church government, at the Treaty of Uxbridge. Admired by Hyde.

Robert Sidney, 2nd Earl of Leicester. Enjoyed company of Edmund Waller, but preferred Lord Spencer as a son-in-law. Compromise candidate agreed by King and Parliament to succeed Strafford as Lord Lieutenant of Ireland. Deeply reluctant to take up his post there; resigned without having left England in 1643. Father of two Parliamentarian sons, himself as non-aligned as possible.

## List of Notable Characters

Henry Somerset, 5th Earl, later 1st Marquess, of Worcester. Very rich Catholic convert, munificent and influential Royalist. Rumoured in hot Protestant circles, probably falsely and for Pym inconveniently, to be intriguing with the French (who were actually closer to Pym). Good opinion of Hyde despite their religious differences.

Henry Spencer, 3rd Baron Spencer, later 1st Earl of Sunderland. Great Tew associate, successful rival of Edmund Waller for the hand of Lady Dorothy Sidney. Initially favoured Parliament, for which he raised troops, then chose to serve as volunteer in King's lifeguard to satisfy personal honour. Companion of Falkland both in diplomacy and subterfuge. Loathed the war and contemplated self-imposed exile in the event of Royalist victory. Killed, like Falkland, at the first Battle of Newbury.

William Villiers, 2nd Viscount Grandison. Relative of Hyde's first wife, Hyde's friend and ally, brave and competent Royalist soldier.

Thomas Wenman, 2nd Viscount Wenman, cousin of the Great Tew companion Sir Francis Wenman. Peace Commissioner for Parliament in 1643 and 1645.

Jerome Weston, 2nd Earl of Portland, rich, Royalist, crypto-Catholic, cautious in politics, childhood friend and later patron of Falkland.

Richard Weston, 1st Earl of Portland, a hated Lord Treasurer, father of Jerome Weston, died a Catholic.

Francis Willoughby, 5th Baron Willoughby of Parham. Whitelocke's friendly, hot-headed brother-in-law, Parliamentarian soldier of some ability, political moderate.

Thomas Wriothesley, 4th Earl of Southampton. Loyal Royalist political moderate, trusted and admired by Hyde. Envoy to Parliament in 1644, Royalist Commissioner at Treaty of Uxbridge.

## List of Notable Characters

### The Scots

John Campbell, 1st Earl of Loudoun, Lord Chancellor of Scotland. Leader of the Scots Commissioners at Uxbridge. Prickly about his rank. A wily diplomat, ready to reach out to English Presbyterians and moderate Royalists to thwart the Independent Parliamentarian war party.

James Graham, 1st Marquess of Montrose. Covenanter turned Royalist, won astonishing string of victories for the King in Scotland over 1644–5. Urged King Charles against any concessions at Uxbridge.

Alexander Leslie, mercenary general experienced in Swedish service, military commander of the Covenanters during the Bishops' Wars. Later Earl of Leven. One of the victors of Marston Moor in 1644.

John, Lord Maitland, heir of the Earl of Lauderdale, President of the Scots Parliament. Well educated in Latin, Greek, and Hebrew. Experienced theological negotiator, politician, and diplomat. Outwitted, or at least outlasted, by Bulstrode Whitelocke, Selden, and Glynne, and the English Erastians while attending the Westminster Assembly of Divines as Scots representative, but appeared to hold no grudge. Peace envoy with Whitelocke to Oxford in 1644.

### The Church

Dr William Chillingworth, godson of Dr William Laud, undergraduate star of Trinity College, Oxford, renegade successively from Churches of England and Rome. Fleeting seminarian, distracted tutor, rumoured informer and heretic, leading philosopher and theologian of Great Tew Circle, author of *Religion of Protestants*. Political meddler of strong Royalist convictions if slippery stated principles. Detained by Parliament for loose language in 1642. Aided Hyde in his journey to the King at York. Died in parliamentary captivity, harangued in his decline by a theological opponent, in 1644.

## List of Notable Characters

Hugh Cressy, companion of Great Tew, friend of Hobbes, Laudian, later Catholic convert.

John Hales, Fellow of Eton. Unofficial attendant at Synod of Dort in 1618–19. Ecumenical theologian. Youthful friend of William Laud. Companion of Great Tew, particular admirer of William Shakespeare.

Dr William Juxon, Fellow and from 1621 President of St John's College, Oxford, Bishop of London from 1633, Lord Treasurer from 1636.

Dr Ralph Kettell, President of Trinity College, Oxford. Protected his college chapel from Lord Saye with great coolness. Unhappy with the gallant, courtly goings-on at Royalist Oxford.

Dr William Laud, undergraduate friend of Bulstrode Whitelocke's father, President of St John's College, Oxford 1611–21, Bishop of London from 1628, Archbishop of Canterbury from 1633, Lord Treasurer 1635–6. Patron of Ned Hyde, friend of John Selden, fond of Cypriot tabby cats and of the Duke of Buckingham. Fell from power and imprisoned by parliamentary order in 1640. In 1644 unsuccessfully tried, then attainted, by Parliament for treason, and in January 1645 executed.

Dr George Morley, traditional Calvinist theologian, wit, noted for high living, in debt to his pupil Edmund Waller, well-informed in politics, companion of Great Tew. Helped Hyde escape parliamentary arrest in 1642.

Gilbert Sheldon, inseparable university friend of Chillingworth, companion of Great Tew. Not a Laudian but also denied Calvinist identification of the Papacy with Antichrist. Warden of All Souls from 1636, Hyde's frequent host thereafter.

John Williams, Bishop of Lincoln, later Archbishop of York. Aristocratic Welshman, bibliophile, conservative Calvinist. Favoured by

## List of Notable Characters

King James despite slowness to adapt to rise of Buckingham. Enemy of Laud and Strafford. Friend of the Whitelockes. Unlike Laud, eloquently and usefully supported Bulstrode's second marriage.

### Physicians

Dr Bartlett of Bow, expensive physician specializing in the care of mentally disturbed women.

Dr William Harvey, younger brother of an important private client of Hyde. Friend of Selden and Hobbes. Royal doctor, guardian of the princes at Edgehill. Sceptical about witchcraft. Pioneering theorist regarding the circulation of the blood, made observations based on the battlefield. Lost an entomological treatise as a result of the war's opening upheavals. Early English consumer of coffee.

Dr John Hinton, young physician to the Queen, but favoured political compromise. By his own, somewhat self-glorifying account, helped protect the young princes at Edgehill.

Dr Philip Parsons of St John's College, Oxford. Formerly Bulstrode Whitelocke's tutor. Conservative physician, occasional playwright.

Dr Samuel Turner, anti-Buckingham and Straffordian MP. Royalist soldier, advanced physician. Friend of Selden. Said by Wood to be of 'loose principles'; certainly fond of good living, wine, and tobacco. Brusque wit, loyal friend across party lines.

Dr Thomas Winston, of ambivalent politics, colluded with Ned Hyde to obtain latter's leave from Commons.

### The Ever-Extending Connections of the Villiers Family

Anne Douglas, Lady Dalkeith, Anne Ayliffe's cousin, Ned Hyde's friend and confidante, object of his courtly devotion.

*List of Notable Characters*

Anne, widowed Lady Lee, née St John, cousin of Hyde's first wife Anne Ayliffe, Puritan in religion, chatelaine of Ditchley in Oxfordshire.

Basil, Lord Feilding, later 2nd Earl of Denbigh. Nephew of Buckingham. Close friend of Hyde before the civil war. Ambassador to Venice in 1630s. Parliamentarian cavalry commander, fought against his father at Edgehill. Parliamentarian Peace Commissioner at Uxbridge, expressed gloomy opinions of his own side to Hyde.

Barbara Villiers, aunt of Anne Ayliffe. Well disposed to Hyde, whom she continued to treat as a nephew after her niece's untimely death.

Eleanor Villiers, Barbara's daughter, lady-in-waiting to the Queen, at centre of a court scandal.

## Writers

John Aubrey, a well-connected, bookish gossip, at Trinity College, Oxford, on and off during the first English Civil War.

Abraham Cowley, prodigious young Royalist poet. Admirer of Falkland. Practitioner of the *Sortes Virgilianae*.

Will Davenant, poet, godson, and self-hinted bastard of Shakespeare, lodger and sometime hanger-on of Hyde, also friend of Whitelocke.

Sir Kenelm Digby, privateer, natural philosopher, romancer, Catholic, courtier, diplomat, lover. Kinsman of Earls of Bristol. Friend of young Ned Hyde through Ben Jonson.

Sir Richard Fanshawe, diplomat, linguist, translator, and poet. Close friend of Tom May. Brother of the King's Remembrancer, but chose the King's side sceptically and with difficulty. Close friend of Hyde.

## List of Notable Characters

Thomas Hobbes, Wiltshire fellow countryman of Hyde, sometime companion of Great Tew, political philosopher. Initially Royalist authoritarian in politics, fled to France in anticipation of Parliament's wrath after November 1640.

Lucy Hutchinson. Connection by marriage of Hyde. Wife of Parliamentarian Colonel John Hutchinson. Comprehensive and fairly reliable historian.

Ben Jonson, survivor of Elizabethan and Jacobean age, poetic father of the Tribe of Ben, playwright, poet of lyrics and masques, unofficial and ageing laureate, Hyde's friend and mentor for a time, recipient of charity from 1st Viscount Falkland and his heir Sir Lucius Cary.

Tom May, poet, translator, and historian, friend of Selden and Hyde.

John Milton, self-conscious prodigy as poet, mutable as a young man in religion and politics.

George Sandys, poet, travel writer, translator, and theologian. Arminian religious views. Like many of his family, associated with the Great Tew circle.

James Shirley, professional poet, the King's favourite playwright, friend to lawyers, Catholic inclinations.

Aurelian Townshend, poet of masque and lyric.

Izaak Walton, companion of Great Tew, writings admired by Bulstrode Whitelocke.

Anthony Wood, Oxford antiquary, traumatized child witness of the wartime Royalist capital.

## List of Notable Characters

### Soldiers

Sir Jacob Astley, Royalist infantry general, former tutor of Prince Rupert in the art of war. As governor of Oxford, treated Whitelocke and other Parliamentarian and Scots envoys brusquely in 1644.

Sir William Balfour, Scots professional commanding reserve cavalry in parliamentary service at Edgehill. All but retrieved a parliamentary victory single-handed.

Colonel Thomas Blagge, Groom of the Bedchamber, then governor of Wallingford. Hot-tempered Royalist. May have covertly hampered peace talks in 1643. Menaced Whitelocke and his fellow Parliamentarian and Scots envoys in 1644.

Richard Boyle, Viscount Dungarvan, the Earl of Cork's heir. Anglo-Irish soldier, Parliamentarian Peace Commissioner in 1643 but later in arms for the King.

Sir John Byron of Newstead Abbey, later 1st Baron Byron. Eldest of seven redoubtable brothers, all Royalist soldiers. Raided Oxford, pursuit by Parliamentarians resulted in Royalist victory at Powicke Bridge. Impetuous at Edgehill. Failed to restrain his troops' appetite for plunder at Fawley Court. Accepted Falkland as a volunteer in his regiment at the first Battle of Newbury, regarded his death as caused by amateurish incompetence.

Sir Thomas Byron, one of Sir John's many soldier younger brothers. Saved the life of Bulstrode Whitelocke's Royalist cousin, Captain Richard Bulstrode, at Edgehill. Praised by Whitelocke for humane treatment of the younger Whitelocke children while occupying Fawley Court. Possibly inspired the celebrated nineteenth-century W.F. Yeames historical painting, *And When Did You Last See Your Father?*

## List of Notable Characters

Colonel Jan Dalbier, continental mercenary paymaster. Released from debtors' prison to serve Parliament. One of Essex's cautious professional military advisors, resented as such by more impetuous Parliamentarian MPs and gentlemen amateurs such as Whitelocke.

Ferdinando Fairfax, 2nd Lord Fairfax of Cameron. Yorkshire magnate, moderate Parliamentarian. Attempted to arrange treaty of neutrality in north with Royalist Belasyse family. Soldier of mixed success. Friendly to Whitelocke, whom he claimed as a cousin, probably a genial pun on their surnames. Father of the more famous Sir Thomas Fairfax.

Sir Thomas Fairfax, Parliamentarian general. Victor of Marston Moor in 1644. At Uxbridge proposed as a commissioner controlling the militia in the event of a peace settlement.

John Felton, ensign. Melancholy, radical, embittered assassin of Buckingham. Hanged in chains in 1628.

Sir Faithfull Fortescue, Anglo-Irish soldier. Disillusioned by Parliament's redirection of Irish Adventurers' forces against the King. Defected to Royalists on the field of Edgehill after secret approach from Prince Rupert.

George, Lord Goring, able soldier, fickle schemer. Hated by Hyde and Falkland. Favourite of the Queen.

Sir William Howard, elderly commander of the Gentlemen Pensioners, an honourable but small and un-combatworthy bodyguard to the young Stuart princes at Edgehill.

'Freeborn' John Lilburne, prolific radical pamphleteer, with Prynne Parliament's most prominent propagandist author. Captain in Lord Brooke's foot division, captured by Prince Rupert's forces at sack of Brentford.

*List of Notable Characters*

Sir John Meyrick. One of the professional soldiers whose advice Essex favoured over hotter heads. Quarrelled with Whitelocke in the woods of Acton after the stand at Turnham Green, but afterwards on good terms with him.

Sir Henry, or Harry, Morison, educated and knighted at Dublin. Falkland's dearest friend in youth and brother of his later wife, Lettice. Admired in verse by Jonson, died c. 1630.

Sir James Ramsay, Scottish professional in Parliamentarian employ. Cavalry commander at Edgehill, routed and brought premature news of defeat to London.

Patrick, Lord Ruthven of Ettrick, later 1st Earl of Forth (and Brentford, later still). Talented Scots veteran of Swedish service. Replaced Lindsey as Royalist general at Edgehill after backing Prince Rupert in a quarrel over tactics. Charismatic if drink-sodden commander known as 'Pater Rothwein' (Father Red Wine).

Edwin Sandys the younger. His father the MP and uncle the poet both admired by Hyde. Parliamentarian colonel. Accused of numerous grave misdeeds. Badly wounded at the Battle of Powicke Bridge, possibly by opposing commander Henry Wilmot in person. Briefly captured, said by Royalists to have recanted his support for Parliament, released, said by Parliamentarians to have confirmed his constant support for Parliament on his deathbed soon after.

Sir Philip Skippon, veteran Captain-General of the London Trained Bands, loved by his men. Crucial to the firm stand of the Parliamentarian 'battalia' at Turnham Green.

Captain John Smith, English Catholic. Royalist officer under Lord Grandison, one of the heroes of Edgehill, more frequently credited with the recapture of the Royal Banner by gallant action. The moderate Royalist peace party's favourite candidate for this feat.

Sir Edmund Verney, the King's Knight-Marshal and bearer of the Banner Royal. Privately detested civil war, serving the King solely out of personal loyalty. Head of a sadly divided family. Killed at Edgehill, said to have haunted its field.

Sir Robert Welch, Irish Catholic. Royalist officer, fierce adherent of Prince Rupert. Likely in fact to have recaptured the Royal Banner by trickery. The politically inconvenient hero of the belligerent Royalist 'Swordsmen'.

Colonel Henry Wilmot, later Royalist Commissary-General, Baron and Viscount Wilmot. Capable but impetuous commander, drunken braggart.

## The Painter

Sir Anthony van Dyck, pictorial master of the age so universal as to cause coinage of the verb 'to vandike', or doodle. So much in demand that, despite a factory of assistants, in 1641 he died of a serious illness brought on by overwork, aged just 42.

## Patronesses

Elizabeth Grey, Countess of Kent, née Talbot. Very rich and cultivated noblewoman. Possibly married John Selden in her widowhood, probably his lover during her husband's life. Hostess of Selden, Tom Carew, Whitelocke and Dr Samuel Turner among many others.

Katherine Jones, Viscountess Ranelagh, née Boyle, friend of Falkland since childhood, friend in maturity of Falkland and Hyde.

*List of Notable Characters*

## *Muses*

Elizabeth, Lady Dungarvan, née Clifford. Associate of Great Tew with her husband; called Falkland's mistress by the Parliamentarian press, almost certainly without substance.

Lady Sophia Murray, daughter of the Scottish courtiers John Murray, created Earl of Annandale by James VI and I, and Elizabeth, née Schaw, lady-in-waiting to King James's consort Anna of Denmark. Wooed by Waller, after his rejection by 'Sacharissa', as 'Amoret'. Her learning, more than her beauty, admired by Hyde. Imprisoned as a result of her former suitor Waller's plot to arrange a Royalist uprising in London; boldly refused to cooperate with the Parliamentarian Committee of Safety. Rumoured, with somewhat more plausibility than Lady Dungarvan, to have engaged in a secret love affair with Falkland. Died of consumption in Parliamentarian captivity at London.

Lady Dorothy Sidney, daughter of the Earl of Leicester. Beloved of Edmund Waller, who dubbed her 'Sacharissa'. Married Henry, Lord Spencer.

Lady Isabella Thynne, née Rich. Beautiful, unhappily married daughter of the Earl of Holland. Lodged at Balliol College in Royalist Oxford, next to her friend Dorothea Fanshawe at Trinity College. Annoyed Dr Kettell of Trinity by flirtatious conduct. Like 'Sacharissa' before her, inspired Waller. Alluringly skilful musician.

## *Great Foreign Personages*

Charles Louis, Elector Palatine, known in England as 'the Palgrave', eldest son and heir of Frederick V and Elizabeth of Bohemia. Gloomily accompanied his uncle, King Charles, to the attempted arrest of the Five Members. Subsequently openly favoured Parliament, which paid him a pension.

## List of Notable Characters

Elizabeth of Bohemia, the 'Winter Queen', wife of Frederick V, by birth a Stuart, King Charles's sister.

Frederick V, Elector Palatine, exiled 'Winter King' of Bohemia.

Gustavus Adolphus, King of Sweden. Protestant hero killed and widely mourned in 1632.

Henri, duc de Rohan, King Charles's godfather. Celebrated French Protestant soldier and much admired author. Died of battlefield wounds in 1638.

Louis XIII, King of France, Queen Henrietta Maria's brother.

Prince Maurice, another younger son of the Winter Queen, lieutenant and companion to his brother Prince Rupert. Fought at Powicke Bridge without armour. Like Rupert, abrasively inimical to Hyde, and curt with Whitelocke and his colleagues during the Parliamentarian peace initiatives of 1643 and 1644.

Cardinal Richelieu, Louis XIII's chief minister. Expressed interest in employing Whitelocke.

Prince Rupert of the Rhine, the Palgrave's younger brother. Already a veteran of glorious defeat on the continent. Like his parents, firm Calvinist in religion. Gifted, aggressive cavalry commander, but too young, inexperienced, and foreign to act with tact on the English political, or military, scene. His careless, lucky, and ferocious victory at Powicke Bridge brought into being a formidable reputation. Quarrelled with his uncle's first choice as general, the Earl of Lindsey. All but won, then threw away, victory at Edgehill. In command of cavalry who cruelly sacked Whitelocke's seat, Fawley Court. Sacked Brentford and alienated London. Insulting and intimidating to Whitelocke at Oxford in 1643. Took Bristol that summer. Overruled, possibly by Falkland's advice, over siege of Gloucester,

*List of Notable Characters*

with unfortunate results. Lost Marston Moor the next year. Once again discourteous to Whitelocke and other Parliamentarian peace envoys in 1644. Disliked and often opposed by Falkland and Hyde.

## *Diplomats*

René Augier, Dauphinois Huguenot, lutenist, Franco-English diplomat posted to Paris until 1640, and again after 1644.

Jacques d'Éstampes, Marquis de la Ferté-Imbault, mostly known simply as La Ferté in England. Ambassador from France to England, 1641–3. Schemed with the Scots and with Pym, despite provocation by some of the latter's less statesmanlike anti-Catholic adherents.

## *Country Folk and Domestics*

John Cely, Whitelocke servant in town.

William Cooke, tenant-farmer at Whitelocke's estate of Fawley Court.

Piccart, usefully monoglot French page boy, skilful lutenist.

Theodosia Thynne, twice widowed, gentlewoman companion of the Countess of Sunderland.

# Further Reading

This book draws principally on the following works either by its protagonists, or written to or about them contemporaneously:

Edward Hyde, Earl of Clarendon, *History of the Rebellion* (Oxford University Press 1969), vols 1, 2, 3, 6
*Life of Edward Earl of Clarendon* (Oxford University Press 1827), vol. 1

Clarendon Papers, Bodleian Library, Oxford

Sir Bulstrode Whitelocke
*Memorials of the English Affairs* (Oxford University Press 1853)
*Diary of Bulstrode Whitelocke* (ed. Ruth Spalding) (Oxford University Press 1990)

Whitelocke Papers, Longleat House (microform edition)

Sir Bulstrode Whitelocke, *Annals*, British Library

Sir James Whitelocke, *Liber Famelicus* (Camden Society 1857)

I have made liberal use throughout of the invaluable *Oxford Dictionary of National Biography* online.

There follows a select (not, I hope, too select) bibliography of sources, primary, secondary or, quite often, something of both, which were of particular assistance in the writing of individual chapters.

## Prelude: The Pit's Brink

John Aubrey, *Aubrey's Brief Lives*, ed. Oliver Lawson Dick (Penguin Classics 1987)

George Peele lyric, 'His golden locks', quoted from Sir Arthur Quiller-Couch, *The Golden Pomp: A Procession of English Lyrics from Surrey to Shirley* (Methuen 1895)

Samuel Pepys's *Diary* is my most specific authority for Clarendon's melodious yet authoritative speaking voice. Ned Hyde's ease, eloquence, fluency, and confidence as a younger man, both in private conversation and public oratory, were noticed by figures including the merchant Daniel Harvey, the MP-antiquary Sir William Drake, and his family friend the courtier Sir Edward Nicholas. It does not seem to me an outrageous stretch to consider this euphony an attribute he acquired (unlike, he says, his friend Sir Lucius Cary) very early on.

## 1. *The Making of the Moderates*

John Aubrey, *Aubrey's Brief Lives*, ed. Oliver Lawson Dick (Penguin Classics 1987)

Charles Carlton, *Charles I: The Personal Monarch* (Routledge 1983)

Lady Georgiana Fullerton, *The Life of Elisabeth Lady Falkland, 1585–1639* (Burns & Oates 1883)

Alfred Harbage, *Sir William Davenant: Poet, Venturer, 1606–1668* (Octagon Books 1935)

George Herbert, *Herbert's Poetical Works*, ed. Rev. A.B. Grosart (George Bell & Sons 1891)

James Howell, *The Familiar Letters of James Howell*, ed. Joseph Jacobs, vol. 1 (David Nutt 1892)

Ben Jonson, *The Poems of Ben Jonson*, ed. Tom Cain and Ruth Connolly (Routledge 2021)

T. H. Lister, *The Life and Administration of Edward, Earl of Clarendon*, vol. 1 (Longman 1838)

David Lloyd, *The Statesmen and Favourites of England since the Reformation* (Peter Parker 1679)

Roger Lockyer, *Buckingham* (Longman 1981)

Royce MacGillivray, *Restoration Historians and the English Civil War* (Springer Netherlands 1974)

## Further Reading

Noel Malcolm, *The Origins of English Nonsense* (HarperCollins 1997)

Joe Moshenka, *A Stain in the Blood: The Remarkable Voyage of Sir Kenelm Digby* (Windmill Books 2017)

Arthur H. Nethercot, *Sir William D'Avenant: Poet Laureate and Playwright Manager* (University of Chicago Press 1938)

Richard Ollard, *Clarendon and His Friends* (Oxford University Press 1988)

John Selden, *The Table-Talk of John Selden* (C. Whittingham 1818)

Hugh Trevor-Roper, 'A lecture delivered before the University of Oxford on 2nd December, 1974 to mark the tercentenary of Clarendon's death' (Oxford University Press 1975)

Kurt Weber, *Lucius Cary, Second Viscount Falkland* (Columbia University Press 1940)

## 2. The Lawyers' Interlude

John Adamson, *Noble Revolt: The Overthrow of Charles I* (Weidenfeld & Nicolson 2009)

John Aubrey, *Aubrey's Brief Lives*, ed. Oliver Lawson Dick (Penguin Classics 1987)

Thomas Carew, *Poems of Thomas Carew*, ed. Rhodes Dunlap (Oxford University Press 1949)

Charles Carlton, *Charles I: The Personal Monarch* (Routledge 1983)

Sir Edward Coke, *Institutes of the Laws of England*, vol. 4, accessed via Wythe's Library Online 2023

William Lamont, *Puritanism and Historical Controversy* (Routledge 1996)

Leanda de Lisle, *Henrietta Maria: Conspirator, Warrior, Phoenix Queen* (Chatto & Windus 2022)

Ben Jonson, *The Poems of Ben Jonson*, ed. Tom Cain and Ruth Connolly (Routledge 2021)

Walter Montagu, *The Shepherd's Paradise*, c. 1632, MS, British Library

Alison Plowden, *Henrietta Maria: Charles I's Indomitable Queen* (Sutton Publishing 2001)

William Prynne, *Histrio-mastix: the players scourge, or actors tragedie* (Michael Sparke 1632), Bodleian Library, Oxford

*Further Reading*

—*The Unloveliness of Lovelocks* (1628), Bodleian Library, Oxford
Kevin Sharpe, *Criticism and Compliment: The Politics of Literature in the England of Charles I* (Cambridge University Press 1987)
James Shirley, *The Triumph of Peace* (William Cooke 1634), accessed via Early English Books Online 2023
Ruth Spalding, *Improbable Puritan: Life of Bulstrode Whitelocke, 1605–1675* (Faber & Faber 1975)
Aurelian Townshend, *Aurelian Townshend's Poems and Masks*, ed. E. K. Chambers (Clarendon Press, 1912)
Hugh Trevor-Roper, *Princes & Artists: Patronage and Ideology at Four Habsburg Courts 1517–1633* (Thames & Hudson 1991)
Kurt Weber, *Lucius Cary, Second Viscount Falkland* (Columbia University Press 1940)

## 3. Tragedy, Adventure, and Romance

John Aubrey, *Aubrey's Brief Lives*, ed. Oliver Lawson Dick (Penguin Classics 1987)
M. W. Brownley, 'The Women in Clarendon's Life and Works', *The Eighteenth Century*, vol. 22, no. 2, 1981
Gilbert Burnet, *Bishop Burnet's History of His Own Time* (T. Ward 1724)
Peter Levi, *Eden Renewed: The Public and Private Life of John Milton* (Macmillan 1996)
T. H. Lister, *The Life and Administration of Edward, Earl of Clarendon*, vol. 1 (Longman 1838)
Ruth Spalding, *Improbable Puritan: Life of Bulstrode Whitelocke, 1605–1675* (Faber & Faber 1975)
Sir John Suckling, *The Poems, Plays and Other Remains of Sir John Suckling*, ed. William Carew Hazlitt (F. & W. Kerslake 1874)
Hugh Trevor-Roper, *Catholics, Anglicans and Puritans: Seventeenth-Century Essays* (Secker & Warburg 1987)
—*Europe's Physician: The Various Life of Sir Theodore de Mayerne* (Yale University Press, 2006)

Kurt Weber, *Lucius Cary, Second Viscount Falkland* (Columbia University Press 1940)

## 4. Prelates, Predestination, and Parliament

John Aubrey, *Aubrey's Brief Lives*, ed. Oliver Lawson Dick (Penguin Classics 1987)
Thomas Carew, *Poems of Thomas Carew*, ed. Rhodes Dunlap (Oxford University Press 1949)
Justin Champion, John Coffey, Tim Harris, and John Marshall, *Politics, Religion & Ideas in Seventeenth- and Eighteenth-Century Britain* (Boydell Press 2019)
William Chillingworth, *The Religion of Protestants* (John Clarke 1638)
Edward Fairfax, *Tasso's Jerusalem Delivered*, ed. Henry Morley (Routledge 1890)
John Hacket, *Bishop Hacket's Memoirs of the Life of Archbishop Williams* (Sam Briscoe 1715)
John Hales, *The Way towards the Finding of a Decision of the Chief Controversie now debated concerning Church Government* (1641), Eton College Library
—*A Tract concerning Schisme and Schismatiques* (1642), Eton College Library
—*Golden Remains of the Ever Memorable Mr. John Hales* (1659), Eton College Library
—*Sermons Preached at Eton* (Richard Marriot, 1660), Eton College Library
R. W. Harris, *Clarendon and the English Revolution* (Chatto & Windus 1983)
T. H. Lister, *The Life and Administration of Edward, Earl of Clarendon*, vol. 1 (Longman 1838)
Richard Ollard, *Clarendon and His Friends* (Oxford University Press 1988)
William Prynne, *Breviate of the Life of William Laud* (Michael Sparke 1644), accessed via EEBO 2023
John Selden, *Titles of Honour* (John Helme 1614), accessed via EEBO 2023
Ruth Spalding, *Improbable Puritan: Life of Bulstrode Whitelocke, 1605–1675* (Faber & Faber 1975)
John Stubbs, *Reprobates: The Cavaliers of the English Civil War* (Viking 2011)

*Further Reading*

Sir John Suckling, *The Poems, Plays and Other Remains of Sir John Suckling*, ed. William Carew Hazlitt (F. & W. Kerslake 1874)

Victor D. Sutch, *Gilbert Sheldon: Architect of Anglican Survival in England 1640–1675* (Springer 1973)

Hugh Trevor-Roper, *Archbishop Laud, 1573–1645* (Macmillan 1940)

—*Catholics, Anglicans and Puritans: Seventeenth-Century Essays* (Secker & Warburg 1987)

—'A lecture delivered before the University of Oxford on 2nd December, 1974 to mark the tercentenary of Clarendon's death' (Oxford University Press 1975)

John Tulloch, *Rational Theology and Christian Philosophy in England in the Seventeenth Century*, vol. 1 (W. Blackwood 1872)

Stefania Tutino, *Thomas White & the Blackloists: Between Politics and Theology during the English Civil War* (Routledge 2008)

C. V. Wedgwood, *The King's Peace* (Collins Fontana 1970)

B. H. G. Wormald, *Clarendon: Politics, History & Religion 1640–1660* (Cambridge University Press 1964)

Kurt Weber, *Lucius Cary, Second Viscount Falkland* (Columbia University Press 1940)

## *5. Pulling Down Cobwebs*

Earl of Birkenhead, *Strafford* (Hutchinson 1938)

Justin Champion, John Coffey, Tim Harris, and John Marshall, *Politics, Religion & Ideas in Seventeenth- and Eighteenth-Century Britain* (Boydell Press 2019)

John Heneage Jesse, *Memoirs of the Court of England* (R. Bentley 1846)

J. P. Kenyon, *The Stuarts* (Fontana 1976)

Lady Theresa Lewis, *Lives of the Friends and Contemporaries of Lord Chancellor Clarendon* (John Murray)

T. H. Lister, *The Life and Administration of Edward, Earl of Clarendon*, vol. 1 (Longman 1838)

Richard Ollard, *Clarendon and His Friends* (Oxford University Press 1988)

Sir Thomas Roe, letter to the Queen of Bohemia, 1634, *Calendar of State Papers, Ireland* (1600–1659)

Ruth Spalding, *Improbable Puritan: Life of Bulstrode Whitelocke, 1605–1675* (Faber & Faber 1975)

William Charles Townsend, *Memoirs of the House of Commons*, vol. 2 (Henry Colburn 1844)

Hugh Trevor-Roper, *Archbishop Laud, 1573–1645* (Macmillan 1940)

Sir Philip Warwick, *Memoires of the Reign of King Charles I* (Ri. Chiswell 1703)

Kurt Weber, *Lucius Cary, Second Viscount Falkland* (Columbia University Press 1940)

C. V. Wedgwood, *Thomas Wentworth, First Earl of Strafford: A Reevaluation* (Jonathan Cape 1964)

—*The King's Peace* (Collins Fontana 1970)

B. H. G. Wormald, *Clarendon: Politics, History & Religion 1640–1660* (Cambridge University Press 1964)

## 6. Differences in Opinion

John Adamson, *Noble Revolt: The Overthrow of Charles I* (Weidenfeld & Nicolson 2009)

M. W. Brownley, 'Why Clarendon Served the Stuarts', *Biography*, vol. 4, no. 2, Spring 1981

John Campbell, 1st Baron Campbell, *Lives of the Chancellors and Lord Keepers*, vol. 3 (Cornell University Library, 2009)

Justin Champion, John Coffey, Tim Harris, and John Marshall, *Politics, Religion & Ideas in Seventeenth- and Eighteenth-Century Britain* (Boydell Press 2019)

Sir Simonds D'Ewes, *The Journal of Sir Simonds D'Ewes*, ed. Willson Havelock Coates (Yale University Press 1942)

T. H. Lister, *The Life and Administration of Edward, Earl of Clarendon*, vol. 1 (Longman 1838)

Richard Ollard, *Clarendon and His Friends* (Oxford University Press 1988)

Dorothy Osborne, *Letters to Sir William Temple, 1652–54*, ed. Kenneth Parker (Ashgate 2002)

*Further Reading*

Paul Seaward, 'Clarendon, Tacitism and the Civil Wars of Europe', *Huntington Literary Quarterly*, vol. 68, nos 1–2, March 2005

Ruth Spalding, *Improbable Puritan: Life of Bulstrode Whitelocke, 1605–1675* (Faber & Faber 1975)

Kurt Weber, *Lucius Cary, Second Viscount Falkland* (Columbia University Press 1940)

C. V. Wedgwood, *The King's Peace* (Collins Fontana 1970)

B. H. G. Wormald, *Clarendon: Politics, History & Religion 1640–1660* (Cambridge University Press 1964)


## 7. A Tedious Debate

John Adamson, *Noble Revolt: The Overthrow of Charles I* (Weidenfeld & Nicolson 2009)

Sir Simonds D'Ewes, *The Journal of Sir Simonds D'Ewes*, ed. Willson Havelock Coates (Yale University Press 1942)

T. H. Lister, *The Life and Administration of Edward, Earl of Clarendon*, vol. 1 (Longman 1838)

Donald Nicholas, *Mr Secretary Nicholas: His Life and Letters* (Bodley Head 1955)

Richard Ollard, *Clarendon and His Friends* (Oxford University Press 1988)

Ruth Spalding, *Improbable Puritan: Life of Bulstrode Whitelocke, 1605–1675* (Faber & Faber 1975)

Adrian Tinniswood, *The Verneys: A True Story of Love, War and Madness in Seventeenth-Century England* (Jonathan Cape 2007)

Kurt Weber, *Lucius Cary, Second Viscount Falkland* (Columbia University Press 1940)

C. V. Wedgwood, *The King's Peace* (Collins Fontana 1970)

Blair Worden, *God's Instruments: Political Conduct in the England of Oliver Cromwell* (Oxford University Press 2012)

B. H. G. Wormald, *Clarendon: Politics, History & Religion 1640–1660* (Cambridge University Press 1964)

*Further Reading*

## 8. Sober Men, Authors of Counsels

Robert Martin Adams, *Liberal Anglicanism: 1636–1647* (Acorn Press 1944)

John Adamson, *Noble Revolt: The Overthrow of Charles I* (Weidenfeld & Nicolson 2009)

John Aubrey, *Aubrey's Brief Lives*, ed. Oliver Lawson Dick (Penguin Classics 1987)

Gilbert Burnet, *Bishop Burnet's History of His Own Time* (T. Ward 1724)

John Campbell, 1st Baron Campbell, *Lives of the Chancellors and Lord Keepers*, vol. 3 (Cornell University Library, 2009)

Justin Champion, John Coffey, Tim Harris, and John Marshall, *Politics, Religion & Ideas in Seventeenth- and Eighteenth-Century Britain* (Boydell Press 2019)

Sir Simonds D'Ewes, *The Journal of Sir Simonds D'Ewes*, ed. Willson Havelock Coates (Yale University Press 1942)

Clare Jackson, *Devil-Land: England under Siege 1588–1688* (Allen Lane 2021)

*Journals of the House of Commons*, vol. 2, accessed via British History Online 2023

T. H. Lister, *The Life and Administration of Edward, Earl of Clarendon*, vol. 1 (Longman 1838)

Donald Nicholas, *Mr Secretary Nicholas: His Life and Letters* (Bodley Head 1955)

Richard Ollard, *Clarendon and His Friends* (Oxford University Press 1988)

J. P. Prendergast, *The Cromwellian Settlement of Ireland* (Longmans 1870)

Conrad Russell, *The Origins of the English Civil War* (Macmillan 1973)

—*The Fall of the British Monarchies, 1637–1642* (Clarendon Press 1991)

Ruth Spalding, *Improbable Puritan: Life of Bulstrode Whitelocke, 1605–1675* (Faber & Faber 1975)

B. H. G. Wormald, *Clarendon: Politics, History & Religion 1640–1660* (Cambridge University Press 1964)

## 9. Hurry and Smoke

John Aubrey, *Aubrey's Brief Lives*, ed. Oliver Lawson Dick (Penguin Classics 1987)

## Further Reading

John Campbell, 1st Baron Campbell, *Lives of the Chancellors and Lord Keepers*, vol. 3 (Cornell University Library, 2009)

Henry Craik, *English Prose Selections: Volume Two, Sixteenth Century to the Restoration* (Macmillan 1894)

—*Life of Edward, Earl of Clarendon*, vol. 1 (Macmillan 1911)

Anne, Lady Fanshawe, *Memoirs of Lady Fanshawe*, accessed via Project Gutenberg 2023

C. H. Firth, *Oliver Cromwell and the Rule of the Puritans in England* (G. P. Putnam's Sons 1908)

Elizabeth Lane Furdell, *The Royal Doctors, 1485–1714: Medical Personnel at the Tudor and Stuart Courts* (University of Rochester Press, 2001)

Tristram Hunt, *The English Civil War at First Hand* (Weidenfeld & Nicolson 2002)

Lucy Hutchinson, *Memoirs of the Life of Colonel Hutchinson* (Longman 1806)

Ronald Hutton, *The Royalist War Effort 1642–1646* (Routledge 1982)

Geoffrey Keynes, *The Life of William Harvey* (Oxford University Press 1966)

Peter Levi, *Eden Renewed: The Public and Private Life of John Milton* (Macmillan 1996)

T. H. Lister, *The Life and Administration of Edward, Earl of Clarendon*, vol. 1 (Longman 1838)

John Milton, *The Major Works*, ed. Stephen Orgel and Jonathan Goldberg (Oxford University Press 2008)

Lucy Moore, *Lady Fanshawe's Receipt Book* (Atlantic Books 2017)

Richard Ollard, *Clarendon and His Friends* (Oxford University Press 1988)

George Sandys, *Ovid's Metamorphosis* (London 1640)

John Selden, *The Table-Talk of John Selden* (C. Whittingham 1818)

*Sidney Papers*, vol. 2 (John Murray 1825)

Ruth Spalding, *Improbable Puritan: Life of Bulstrode Whitelocke, 1605–1675* (Faber & Faber 1975)

Charles Spencer, *Prince Rupert: The Last Cavalier* (Phoenix 2008)

Adrian Tinniswood, *The Verneys: A True Story of Love, War and Madness in Seventeenth-Century England* (Jonathan Cape 2007)

John Webb, *Memorials of the Civil War between King Charles I and the Parliament of England as It Affected Herefordshire and Adjacent Counties* (Longmans 1879)

*Further Reading*

C. V. Wedgwood, *The King's War* (Collins Fontana 1970)

B. H. G. Wormald, *Clarendon: Politics, History & Religion 1640–1660* (Cambridge University Press 1964)

## 10. Vulgar Intelligence, Vigorous Defence

John Eric Adair, *By the Sword Divided: Eyewitnesses of the English Civil War* (Century 1983)

Sir Richard Bulstrode, *Memoirs and Reflections upon the Reign and Government of Charles I*, accessed via Eighteenth Century Collections Online 2023

Charles Carlton, *Going to the Wars: The Experience of the British Civil Wars 1638–1651* (Routledge 1994)

Neil Chippendale, *The Battle of Brentford* (Partisan Press 1991)

Geoffrey Keynes, *The Life of William Harvey* (Oxford University Press 1966)

Chris Laoutaris, *Shakespeare's Book* (William Collins, 2023)

T. H. Lister, *The Life and Administration of Edward, Earl of Clarendon*, vol. 1 (Longman 1838)

Richard Ollard, *Clarendon and His Friends* (Oxford University Press 1988)

William Shakespeare, *Complete Works* (HarperCollins 1994)

Raymond South, *Royal Castle, Rebel Town: Puritan Windsor in Civil War & Commonwealth* (Barracuda Books 1981)

Ruth Spalding, *Improbable Puritan: Life of Bulstrode Whitelocke, 1605–1675* (Faber & Faber 1975)

Charles Spencer, *Prince Rupert: The Last Cavalier* (Phoenix 2008)

Adrian Tinniswood, *The Verneys: A True Story of Love, War and Madness in Seventeenth-Century England* (Jonathan Cape 2007)

C. V. Wedgwood, *The King's War* (Collins Fontana 1970)

## 11. The Percy's Peace and the Poet's Plot

Nadine Akkerman, *Invisible Agents* (Oxford University Press 2018)

John Aubrey, *Aubrey's Brief Lives*, ed. Oliver Lawson Dick (Penguin Classics 1987)

## Further Reading

Mark Bence-Jones, *The Cavaliers* (Constable 1976)

Sir John Bramston, *The Autobiography of Sir John Bramston*, ed. Richard Griffin, Baron Braybrooke (Camden Society 1845)

Sir Simonds D'Ewes, *The Journal of Sir Simonds D'Ewes*, ed. Willson Havelock Coates (Yale University Press 1942)

Letter from John Fountaine to Dr Samuel Turner, British Library

Thomas Fuller, *Collected Sermons 1631–1659*, ed. John Eglington Bailey and William Edward Armytage Axon, vol. 1 (Gresham Press 1891)

S. R. Gardiner, *History of the Great Civil War, 1642–1649*, vol. 1 (Longmans 1893)

Clare Jackson, *Devil-Land: England under Siege 1588–1688* (Allen Lane 2021)

Anna Keay, *The Restless Republic: Britain without a Crown* (HarperCollins 2022)

Raymond Lamont-Brown, *Phantom Soldiers* (Drake Publishers 1975)

Sir Tresham Lever, *The Herberts of Wilton* (John Murray 1967)

T. H. Lister, *The Life and Administration of Edward, Earl of Clarendon*, vol. 1 (Longman 1838)

Royce MacGillivray, *Restoration Historians and the English Civil War* (Springer Netherlands 1974)

W. E. Mahaney and W. K. Sherwin, *Two University Latin Plays* (University of Salzburg 1973)

Richard Ollard, *Clarendon and His Friends* (Oxford University Press 1988)

*Papers of the Manchester Literary Club*, vol. 43 (H. Rawson & Co. 1917)

Ruth Scurr, *John Aubrey: My Own Life* (Chatto & Windus 2015)

Charles Kirkpatrick Sharpe, *Memorialls, Or, The Memorable Things that Fell Out Within this Island of Brittain from 1638 to 1644* (A. Constable 1818)

Kevin Sharpe, *Reading Revolutions: The Politics of Reading in Early Modern England* (Yale University Press 2000)

Ruth Spalding, *Improbable Puritan: Life of Bulstrode Whitelocke, 1605–1675* (Faber & Faber 1975)

*Survey of London*, vol. 17 (London County Council, 1936)

Hugh Trevor-Roper, 'A lecture delivered before the University of Oxford on 2nd December, 1974 to mark the tercentenary of Clarendon's death' (Oxford University Press 1975)

Edmund Waller, *Poems of Edmund Waller*, ed. George Thorn-Drury (Lawrence & Bullen 1893)

Kurt Weber, *Lucius Cary, Second Viscount Falkland* (Columbia University Press 1940)

C. V. Wedgwood, *The King's War* (Collins Fontana 1970)

Anthony Wood, *The Life of Antony Wood in His Own Words*, ed. Nicholas K. Kiessling (Bodleian Library 2009)

B. H. G. Wormald, *Clarendon: Politics, History & Religion 1640–1660* (Cambridge University Press 1964)

## 12. Our Utmost Endeavours

John Buchan, *The Marquis of Montrose* (T. Nelson 1928)

—*Oliver Cromwell* (Hodder & Stoughton 1934)

John Campbell, 1st Baron Campbell, *Lives of the Chancellors and Lord Keepers*, vol. 3 (Cornell University Library, 2009)

Justin Champion, John Coffey, Tim Harris, and John Marshall, *Politics, Religion & Ideas in Seventeenth- and Eighteenth-Century Britain* (Boydell Press 2019)

Doreen Cripps, *Elizabeth of the Sealed Knot: A Biography of Elizabeth Murray, Countess of Dysart* (Roundwood 1975)

John Leland, *Itinerary* (Printed at the Theater, London 1711)

Sir Tresham Lever, *The Herberts of Wilton* (John Murray 1967)

T. H. Lister, *The Life and Administration of Edward, Earl of Clarendon*, vol. 1 (Longman 1838)

John Milton, *The Major Works*, ed. Stephen Orgel and Jonathan Goldberg (Oxford University Press 2008)

Richard Ollard, *Clarendon and His Friends* (Oxford University Press 1988)

*Oxford Historical Society*, vol. 87 (1928)

Ruth Spalding, *Improbable Puritan: Life of Bulstrode Whitelocke, 1605–1675* (Faber & Faber 1975)

Charles Spencer, *Prince Rupert: The Last Cavalier* (Phoenix 2008)

Hugh Trevor-Roper, *Archbishop Laud, 1573–1645* (Macmillan 1940)

C. V. Wedgwood, *The King's War* (Collins Fontana 1970)

Blair Worden, *God's Instruments: Political Conduct in the England of Oliver Cromwell* (Oxford University Press 2012)

B. H. G. Wormald, *Clarendon: Politics, History & Religion 1640–1660* (Cambridge University Press 1964)

## 13. England Commits

John Aubrey, *Aubrey's Brief Lives*, ed. Oliver Lawson Dick (Penguin Classics 1987)

Ian F. W. Beckett, *Wanton Troopers: Buckinghamshire in the Civil Wars, 1640–1660* (Pen & Sword 2016)

A. H. Burne, *The Battlefields of England* (Pen & Sword 2005)

Abraham Cowley, *Complete Works in Prose and Verse of Abraham Cowley*, ed. Alexander Balloch Grosart (T. & A. Constable 1881)

David Cressy, *Charles I and the People of England* (Oxford University Press 2015)

Johanna Harris and Elizabeth Scott-Bauman, *The Intellectual Culture of Puritan Women* (Macmillan 2010)

*Journals of the House of Commons*, vol. 3 (House of Commons 1803)

Thomas Longueville, *Falklands* (Longmans 1897)

J.A. Marriott, *The Life and Times of Lucius Cary, Viscount Falkland* (G. P. Putnam's Sons 1907)

Richard Ollard, *Clarendon and His Friends* (Oxford University Press 1988)

—*This War Without an Enemy: A History of the English Civil Wars* (Hodder & Stoughton 1976)

Carol Pal, *Republic of Women: Rethinking the Republic of Letters in the Seventeenth Century* (Cambridge University Press 2012)

William Shakespeare, *Complete Works* (HarperCollins 1994)

Kevin Sharpe, *Reading Revolutions: The Politics of Reading in Early Modern England* (Yale University Press 2000)

Charles Spencer, *Prince Rupert: The Last Cavalier* (Phoenix 2008)

Hugh Trevor-Roper, *Catholics, Anglicans and Puritans: Seventeenth-Century Essays* (Secker & Warburg 1987)

## Further Reading

—'A lecture delivered before the University of Oxford on 2nd December, 1974 to mark the tercentenary of Clarendon's death' (Oxford University Press 1975)

Kurt Weber, *Lucius Cary, Second Viscount Falkland* (Columbia University Press 1940)

C. V. Wedgwood, *The King's War* (Collins Fontana 1970)

James Welwood, *Memoirs of the most Material Transactions in England for the last Hundred Years preceding the Revolution in 1688* (London 1700)

Blair Worden, *God's Instruments: Political Conduct in the England of Oliver Cromwell* (Oxford University Press 2012)

B. H. G. Wormald, *Clarendon: Politics, History & Religion 1640–1660* (Cambridge University Press 1964)

# *Acknowledgements*

This book ended up, in effect, with two endings – chronological, at the failure of the Treaty of Uxbridge, and emotional, in the death of Falkland – but it had many more beginnings.

A half-Scottish native of Oxford, the Royalist capital, I grew up a passionate partisan of the Stuart dynasty. In this I differed from my father, a faithful exegete of George Herbert's Jacobean Protestantism who, in his day job as a college bursar, saw his mission as essentially Parliamentarian, versus the overweening and often uncomprehending Crown of the University. It was, I think, because of rather than despite such differences that I first learned from him to love the wit, complexity and beauty of seventeenth-century England.

This book is dedicated to him, but also to my wife, Flora Scrymgeour. Her endeavours in portraiture have dovetailed mine in non-fiction, as we strive to perform the mysterious alchemy that unites artist and subject in a third presence. Every day she has heard out my overexcited ruminations, unravelled my besetting problems, and helped me to discern the often elusive path ahead.

Writing in the aftermath of Brexit, I thought constantly and unavoidably of my father and of my Scots Episcopalian Jacobite mother, but also of my Lexiteering, Grecian step-brother, Xavier Buxton, and of Sammy Jay, whose family allegiance to the Labour Party might be described as anything from Whig to Shintoist. Xavier and Sammy, both godfathers to my son, are friends with whom I have never genuinely or fundamentally disagreed about anything, yet I can all too easily imagine each of them as arbitrary, involuntary, entirely notional adversaries, in the sad tradition of Whitelocke and Hyde.

In retrospect, the first years of Brexit were, though at times fascinating, consistently deranging, but I do not regret for a moment identifying Rory Stewart as the most clarifying and historically

## Acknowledgements

conscientious presence in that whole *Kalevala* of a national conversation. The Covid pandemic, about which he was characteristically far-sighted, spoilt the efforts of a merry company of volunteers to win him, if not Britain, then London, but, during the lowering depths of lockdown, Rory's evident appreciation for Falkland and Clarendon provided a rare element of good cheer.

Simon Winder, editor *sans reproche* and also *sans peur*, has overseen this book from its insanity-inducing initial brief as a general overview of moderate politics in the seventeenth century, to its current comparatively focused shape as a study of a particular friendship against the background of an extremely peculiar time. He also rowed behind the title I had always wanted, for which I must thank Samuel Taylor Coleridge (whose own early admiration for Clarendon sadly curdled to disgust).

Like both my subjects, I am an amateur as a writer of history. I have benefited inexpressibly from the edification and entertainment provided by scholars resident in this world and the next – most transcendently Hugh Trevor-Roper, Brian Wormald, Ruth Spalding, Richard Ollard, Kevin Sharpe, John Adamson, Blair Worden and Anna Keay. I wish, however, to single out Blair Worden for his unique generosity as the editor, representative and medium of Lord Dacre of Glanton, and for his own penetrating writing on the Civil Wars, his fascinating company, and unwavering personal kindness.

In the late stages of this book's materialization, I owe thanks for the diligence and reassurance provided by Richards Duguid and Mason in perfecting the text, Olivia Kumar for her indispensable insights, and Marian Aird for work on the index. Without the gloriously hydra-headed team of agents who backed both this book and its predecessor, Caroline Dawnay, Sophie Scard and Kat Aitken, almost no element of my adult life is imaginable.

Rebecca Bullard first advised me to read Clarendon's *History of the Rebellion* about fifteen years ago, on the most honourable and accurate grounds that I would enjoy it.

My father-in-law Alexander Dundee, who lived with us during one of lockdown's most compensatory interludes, gave kind,

## Acknowledgements

serious and extended consideration to the nature of the ending, as well as introducing me to the present Viscount Falkland. Charlie Dudbridge at a very late stage helped me to decode the riddle of Aubrey's 'Mrs Moray'.

George Wyndham is both a friend and an employer of rare quality at Special Rider Books & Records, Shepherd's Bush Market. Matthew Walther, editor of *The Lamp*, has been my most ardent transatlantic champion. The secret disquisitions of the *Pussshkin* discussion group have, since 2020, served as whetstone and pick-me-up by turns.

The London Library and the Academy Club have been the twin pillars of my metropolitan existence for what is now very nearly half my life. The Great Tew-like household of James, Maggie, Flora and Izzy Fergusson has for the last seven years become a third such pillar. Flora Fraser, Artemis Cooper and Frances Wilson have been stimulating examples and steadfast friends. Dick Elcho guided me around the Elizabethan splendour and Second World War endurance of Middle Temple Hall.

My parents, Fram Dinshaw and Candia McWilliam, and my friends Ann Shukman, Oliver Rowse, Sammy Jay, Paul Dean, Charlotte Goldney and Anna Kullmann, all read parts or the whole of the book in the course of its writing, and offered their encouragement and assistance. My step-mother Claudia Fitzherbert, on the other hand, rallied me in hours of doubt and difficulty by her refusal to read any text until the manuscript was complete.

My son Orfeo, this time pipped by his mother and grandfather to a formal dedication, can rest content as an additional, all-important recipient. The past may be no handbook to the future, but it is my hope it may hang on as its friend, companion and consolation.

# Index

Abbot, George, Archbishop of Canterbury, 115, 115n
Abingdon, Oxfordshire, xxxi, 128, 133, 135, 285; Bulstrode Whitelocke as Recorder of, 104, 127, 133, 284, 370
Adventurers' Act (1640), 219–21
All Souls College, Oxford, 120, 281, 313; Gilbert Sheldon as Warden of, 13, 120, 239, 281, 313
Allen, William, 90n
Anglesey, Arthur Annesley, 1st Earl of, xxvii, 42
Antichrist, Papacy as, xv, 114, 120, 236, 245
Antrim, Randal MacDonnell, 2nd Earl (*later* 1st Marquess) of, 107n, 182
Apollo Chamber, Devil and St Dunstan Tavern, 48–51, 53, 76, 98, 129, 260
*arcanum imperii*, 4, 8, 192, 399
Argyll, Archibald Campbell, 1st Marquess of, 397
Armine, Sir William, Peace Commissioner, 329, 333, 335, 337, 351
Arminianism, xv, xviii–xix, 16, 114–18, 119–21, 130
Arminius, Jacobus, 114
Arundel, Thomas Howard, 14th Earl of, 130–1, 165
Ashburnham, John, otherwise Jack, 180, 381, 400, 402, 412
Astley, Sir Jacob, 264, 363–4, 366
Aston, Sir Arthur, 247
Attainder, Act of: as applied to the 1st Earl of Strafford, 154–9, 160–1, 163, 184, 187; as applied to Archbishop Laud, 368–9, 371, 376–7
Aubigny, Katherine, Lady d', 353
Aubigny, Lord George Stuart, Seigneur d', 353
Aubonne, Henry d', 91
Aubonne, Theodore Turquet de Mayerne, baron d', 91
Aubrey, John, 29n, 33, 34n, 46n, 50n, 71n; on Great Tew, 3, 83; on William Chillingworth, 16, 37, 116; on John Selden, 43n, 44, 83n; and Royalist Oxford, 237, 310, 313, 321–2; on William Harvey, 266, 268, 277; on 'Mrs Moray', 409–11, 414, 416; on Socinian and Pelagian heresies, 16, 414
Augier, Réné, 89, 89n
Austrey, Elizabeth, 220
Aylesbury, Buckinghamshire, xxxi, 284
Aylesbury, Sir Thomas, 1st Baronet, 97, 112, 147, 292, 311; his family clients of 1st Duke of Buckingham, 140
Aylesbury, Will, 97n
Ayliffe, John, 16, 17
Ayliffe, Sir George, 37
Aynho, Northamptonshire, 279

Balfour, Sir William, 269–70, 273
Balliol College, Oxford, 266, 321, 364
Bankes, Sir John, 324, 341
Banqueting House, Whitehall, 71, 73, 73n, 74

## Index

Barclay, Robert, 362
Bartlett, Dr, 88, 92–3
Bassano, Aemilia, 76n
Baylie, Richard, 111, 370
Bedford, Francis Russell, 4th Earl of, xx; conversation with Edward Hyde in Piccadilly, 156–9, 200; hopes for political compromise dashed by death of, 161, 165, 171, 174, 200, 210, 213, 226, 356; patron of John Pym, xx, 157–8, 165, 174
Bedford, John, 1st Duke of, Regent of France, 90
Bedford, William Russell, 1st Duke of (and 5th Earl), 210, 356
Bennet, Dorothy, 57, 79, 88, 92–6
Bennet, Henry (*later* 1st Earl of Arlington), 378
Bennet, Leonora, Lady, 379
Bennet, Sir Humphrey, 339–40, 366, 378
Bennet, Sir John, 378–9
Bennet, Thomas, 79
Berkeley, Sir John (*later* 1st Baron Berkeley), 180
Berkshire, Thomas Howard, 1st Earl of, 231–4
Birkenhead, John, 313
Bishops' Wars, xix, 123–6, 133–4, 211, 234, 304, 312, 408, 413; Lord Falkland's service as volunteer in, 125, 408, 413
Blagge, Colonel Thomas, 362–4
Bohemia, xvi, xxii, 22, 69, 137
Brackley, Northamptonshire, 234–5
Brentford, Middlesex, xxxi, 298–9, 305, 357; battle and sack of (1642), xxiii, 298–301, 303, 306, 308
Bridgeman, Sir Orlando, 1ater 1st Baronet, 393

Bridgewater, John Egerton, 1st Earl of, 142n
Bristol, xxxii, 256; Prince Rupert's capture of (1643), xxiii, 411–12
Bristol, John Digby, 1st Earl of, 147, 153, 155, 161, 211, 213, 279
Brooke, Fulke Greville, 1st Baron, 32, 33–4
Brooke, Robert Greville, 2nd Baron, 33, 166, 277, 298, 300, 327, 348, 407
Broughton Castle, 280, 314
Brown, Colonel John, 249
Browne, Samuel, 372
Buckingham, George Villiers, 1st Duke of, xiv, xvi–xvii, xix–xx, xxviii–xxix, 30–1; assassination of, 33–7, 38, 40, 41n, 47, 51, 60, 96–7; family of, 102–3, 108, 109, 116, 114n, 139–41, 143; political legacy, 149, 161, 211, 213n; Edward Hyde's essay on, 60, 169, 326; opposition to, 329, 334, 346
Buckingham, Katherine, Duchess of (*later* Countess, then Marchioness, of Antrim), 102, 106, 106n, 109
Bulstrode, Captain (*later* Sir) Richard, 290–1
Bulstrode, Colonel Henry, 284
Bulstrode, Edward, 81, 291
Burnet, Gilbert, Bishop of Salisbury, 98, 215
Butler, William, 31n
Byron, Sir John (*later* 1st Baron Byron): raid on Oxford (August 1642), 234–6, 239, 244; and Powick Bridge (September 1642), 249, 250–1, 273; raid on Fawley Court (November 1642), 286–7, 289; and Lord Falkland's death, 417–19
Byron, Sir Thomas, 290, 291n

478

# Index

Caernarvon, Anna Dormer, Countess of (*née* Herbert), 74

Caernarvon, Robert Dormer, 1st Earl of, 74, 242

Caesar, Sir Charles, 312

Caesar, Sir Julius, 312

Calvin, John: Frenchness of, 68; bade Good Night by John Hales, 121

Calvinism, xv, 16, 65, 68, 71, 82, 108, 110, 123, 137, 138, 244, 414; traditional English doctrine as 'high Calvinism', 14, 37, 115, 236; Double Predestination and identity of papacy with Antichrist as tenets of, 114; dissenters from, 52, 114, 121, 237; and Great Tew, 119–20

Cambrensis, Giraldus, 221

Cambridge University, 240, 249; Trinity College, 30

Camden, William, *Annals*, 34

Capel, Arthur, 1st Baron, 400–402

Carew, Thomas, 51, 66–7, 68, 70–1, 210; gossips about the Queen, 61; claimed in jest as cousin by Sir Lucius Cary, 67; exchanges epistles with Aurelian Townshend, 71; *Coelum Britannicum*, 76; disapproved of by Hyde, 85; and by Hales, 121; epistle to 'Ghibi' regarding Scottish wars written from Wrest Park, 123–4

Carlisle, Lucy Hay, Countess of, 215, 351, 354, 384, 389

Cary, Patrick, 116–17, 117n

Cely, John, 92

Chaloner, Dr Thomas, headmaster of Shrewsbury School, 244

Chaloner, Richard, Royalist conspirator, 347, 347n, 349

Chaloner, Thomas ('Tom'), 244; youthful companion of Whitelocke and Hyde, 46–47n, 244; witness against Archbishop Laud, 375; circle of freethinking friends, lack of Puritanical character summed up by Aubrey, 46n

Chancery, courts of, 130, 130n, 386n

Charles, Prince of Wales (*later* Charles II), xxix, 246, 265, 268–71, 324

Charles I, King of England, Scotland and Ireland: as King: xvi, xxviii–xxix, 2, 4, 36, 38, 75, 91, 109, 122, 142, 143, 173, 213, 228, 310, 322, 362, 370, 385, 391, 411, 414; as Prince of Wales, xv; accepts Petition of Right and dissolves 1629 Parliament, 47–8; policy of peace, 69–70; appoints Laud Archbishop of Canterbury, 115; and the Scottish wars, 125, 134; summons Parliament (1640), 126; dissolves Short Parliament, 132–3; and the Earl of Strafford, 137–8, 150, 159; consults Hyde on 'Root and Branch' bill, 168–71; attempt to arrest Five Members of Parliament, 214–15; leaves London for York, 216; raises standard at Nottingham, 217–18; consents to the Adventurers' Act (1640), 219; Commissions of Array, 224, 353; royal court at Shrewsbury, 243–4; at the Battle of Edgehill, 263–5, 269; royal court at Oxford, 280–3, 324–8, 331–2, 337–9, 359, 366; elevation of Edward Hyde, 311–13; character, 340–1, 405–7; grants royal pardon to Laud, 375–6; and the Treaty of Uxbridge, 381, 384–7, 389–93, 395–403; and Lord Falkland, 405–7, 409, 411–12, 416–19, 421

Charles Louis, Elector Palatine, 214

Chillingworth, Dr William, aids Hyde's flight to York, 15–18, 37; and Great Tew Circle, 84, 126, 211, 240, 388; religious beliefs, 115–19, 117n, 245, 251n; royalist loyalties, 120; arrested and held in the Tower, 207–9; *The Religion of Protestants*, 117, 207–8; friendship with Gilbert Sheldon, 211, 237, 240, 313; controversy-wracked deathbed of, 251n

Christ Church, Oxford, 283, 323–4, 331, 337, 359, 366

Chute, Chaloner, 372

Clare, John Holles, 2nd Earl of, 356

Clarendon, Edward, otherwise Ned, Hyde, (*later* 1st Earl of), xiii–xv, xvii–xxv, xxviii–xxx, 219–20, 225; contrasted with Bulstrode Whitelocke, 7, 80, 224, 292, 369; family and education, 28–9; foreign travel of father of, 89–90; friendship with Whitelocke, 4, 9, 23, 25–8, 45, 47, 52, 62–3, 87–8, 92–6, 99, 102–3, 105–7, 255, 259, 277, 280; entry to the Middle Temple, 30–2; Will Davenant lodger of, 32–3, 46; and assassination of Duke of Buckingham, 34–7; first marriage to Anne Ayliffe a love-match, 37, 59–60, 95; literary friendships amid 'Tribe of Ben', 21, 41–4, 48–51, 123–4, 126, 258, 260; and first acquaintance with Sir Lucius Cary, 52–6; first exposure to royal court, 60–1; organizes *The Triumph of Peace* (masque), 64–77; and Great Tew Circle, 83–6, 115–22, 126, 260–1; second marriage to Frances Aylesbury, 96–9; employment by and friendship with Archbishop Laud, 112–14, 138–9; birth of daughter Anne, 122; on the First Bishops' war, 125, 134; takes seat in Short Parliament (1640), 6, 127–33; member for Saltash in Long Parliament, 2, 136; detestation then abolition of extra-parliamentary courts, 137, 141, 145, 149, 165, 380; natal and marital kindred of, 140, 235n; and the militia debate, 10–12; relations with Pym and Hampden, 142–3, 164–5, 174–5; and Strafford's downfall, 141, 144–5, 148–9, 154–61, 334; family and domestic life, 146–7, 292, 293n; and bishops' voting rights, 166–8, 172, 177–8; private audience with the King (1641), 168–71; on the Irish Rebellion, 173, 180–3; nuanced impression of in D'Ewes's diary, 177–9; and the Grand Remonstrance, 184–207, 209; and George Lord Digby, 210–11; 'ghost writer' for the King, 212, 311; influence on the King, 213, 215–16, 221; horror at attempted arrest of Five Members, 214–15; leaves London to join the King, 1–4, 223; shelters at Ditchley, 13–17; shelters at Nostell Priory with family, 18; at the royal court in York, 19, 217, 222; death of son Edward, 218; arranges defection of Lord Keeper Littleton, 226–8; and Earl of Essex, 230; brief pre-war visit to Oxford, 240–1; outlawed by Parliament, 242; at Nottingham, 243; arranges friendly reception for the King at Shrewsbury, 243–4; and Lord Feilding, later 2nd Earl of Denbigh, 257, 361; religious inclination, 245–6;

*Index*

collects Catholic contributions for the Royalist cause, 246–8; on Powick Bridge, 249–52; lukewarm Royalism of several friends of, 261–4; in charge of Stuart princes at the Battle of Edgehill, 264–76; disapproves of Royalist advance on London, 285–6, 291, 293, 299–300; and Earl of Holland, 304, 317; Privy Counsellor and Chancellor of the Exchequer, 311–13; at the royal court in Oxford, 281, 305–6, 308–9, 313–16; 'false friends' of, 345; peace negotiations in Oxford, 318–21, 324–8, 330–2, 335–41, 356, 364–8; and misrepresentation of Royalist intelligence, 342; and Waller's Plot, 343–53; and Sir William Drake, 355; persuades the King to summon Royalist Parliament to Oxford, 359; on Laud's trial and execution, 370–7; and the Treaty of Uxbridge, 358, 378–9, 381, 383–404; on death of Falkland, 404–5, 416–22; his friendship with the King, 406–7; and intimacy of Oxford court, 409–11; and Lord Falkland between Bristol and Gloucester, 412–13; like Whitelocke, survives the civil wars but does not live to see their decisive political resolution, 22

*Writings:* essay on the Duke of Buckingham, 60; *History of the Rebellion*, xxviii–xxx, 20, 35–6, 53–4, 64, 123, 131, 133, 143–4, 150, 151n, 153, 156, 163, 165–6, 173, 175–6, 178, 179, 192–3, 200–5, 218, 233–4, 246–7, 272, 278–9, 280, 282–3, 294–7; *Life*, xxix–xxx, 25, 29, 34, 40, 41–2, 42–3, 49–50, 53–4, 61, 96, 143–4, 166, 185–6, 188–90, 193–4, 200–201, 211, 261, 271, 294, 305

Clarendon, Frances Hyde, Countess of (*née* Aylesbury), 18, 96–8, 122, 217, 267, 292, 313

Coke, Sir Edward, 40, 64

Cole, Robert, 88–91, 95

Colepeper, Sir John (*later* 1st Baron Colepeper), royalist supporter, 172, 176, 215, 216, 222–3; and the Grand Remonstrance, 190, 191–3, 197; 'Irish Adventurer', 219; and the Irish rebellion, 183; Chancellor of the Exchequer, 213; joins royal court in York, 217; with Falkland and Hyde, urges compromise over the militia, 221; at the Battle of Edgehill, 268–9, 272; in Royalist Oxford, 310–11, 315; Master of the Rolls, 312–13; hardens against a militia compromise, 336; as political moderate, 344; and the Treaty of Uxbridge, 385, 392; supports the Queen's party at the siege of Gloucester, 412

Colnbrook, Buckinghamshire, 293–4, 296–8

Commissions of Array, 19, 224, 229, 231–2, 234, 353

Commons, the, lower House of Parliament of England, xvii, xxi, xxii, 2, 4–5, 7–8, 10, 19, 21, 28, 34, 38–40, 50, 67, 73, 82, 128–9, 131–2, 134–5, 143, 145, 147, 151, 164–6, 168–9, 171, 173–4, 178, 201, 207–8, 211–14, 218, 220, 222, 224, 227, 230, 232, 249, 251, 254, 285, 302–3, 317–18, 327–8, 349–50, 354–5, 359, 363, 390, 394, 398, 403; and Bill of Attainder, 154–6; aftermath of Strafford's execution, 164–6; and Irish Rebellion, 180–2; and Grand

481

Commons – *cont'd*.
  Remonstrance, 184–9, 193, 196–9; George Lord Digby escapes from into Lords, 211–14; Edmund Waller's role in after outbreak of English civil war, 344–6
Conway, Edward, 2nd Viscount Conway, 134, 142, 348, 349, 352
Cooke, William, 99–100, 102, 104–5, 255, 290–1
Cooper, Sir Anthony Ashley, 220
Corbet, Miles, 371–2
Cottington, Francis, 1st Baron, 152–3
Council of the North, 47, 52, 101, 130, 137, 141, 144, 165–6, 217
Court of Honour *see* Earl Marshal's Court
Court of Requests, 97n, 130, 191
Covenanters, Scots, xix, xxiv, 134, 150, 189n, and the Bishops' Wars, 123–6; and English peers, xix; and the Irish rebellion, 180–1; Parliament seeks aid from, 294, 330; alliance with Parliament, 358, 362, 382; and allied victory over Prince Rupert at Marston Moor, 358; and the Treaty of Uxbridge, 361, 383, 395, 397–8
Coventry, Thomas, 1st Baron Coventry, 126, 220
Cowley, Abraham, 408–9, 411
Cranbourne Lodge, Windsor, 87, 217, 292–3
Crane, John, 31n
Cressy, Hugh, 85, 345
Crispe, Sir Nicholas, 220, 353
Critz, Emanuel de, 259
Croke, Judge George, 38, 48, 146, 164; family of, 27–8
Cromwell, Oliver (*later* Lord Protector of England, Scotland and Ireland), xxiv, xxviii, 87, 117n, 130n, 170, 220, 230, 230n, 258, 277; dispute with Hyde over tenants' rights, 144; and bishops' voting rights, 178; and the Militia Ordinance, 182; and the Grand Remonstrance, 189–90, 199–200; prevents Cambridge from offering financial support to the King, 240, 249; contempt for Parliamentary forces, 273; at the Battle of Marston Moor, 358; leader of Independent MPs, 361, 367–8, 379, 387, 400; Self-Denying Ordinance, 391; evicts Hyde's children from Cranbourne Lodge, 293n; plotted against as Protector, 383; overshadowing place in period's historical memory, 422
Cromwell, Thomas, 1st Earl of Essex, 3n, 214n
Cumberland, Henry Clifford, 5th Earl of, 242

Dalbier, Colonel Jan, 277, 307
Dalkeith, Anne Douglas, Lady, 61, 410
Davenant, Will, 32–3, 37, 46, 48–9, 53, 67, 98, 122–3, 211
Dawes, Sir Abraham, 112n
Denbigh, Basil Feilding, 2nd Earl of (*formerly* Viscount Feilding), 256–7, 267, 272–3, 361, 363, 364, 366
Denbigh, William Feilding, 1st Earl of, 272
Dering, Sir Edward, 176, 187, 190
Devil and St Dunstan Tavern, Fleet Street, 49, 52
D'Ewes, Sir Simonds, on Dr Chillingworth, 209; and the Irish Adventurers, 220; parliamentary diarist, 176–83, 185–7, 189, 190, 193, 194, 195, 197–9, 201, 209, 220, 224, 343

## Index

Dieppe, France, 89–90, 104
Digby, George, Lord (*later* 2nd Earl of Bristol), x, 147, 148, 152–3, 155–7, 156n, 160–1, 184, 209–15, 250, 267, 272–3, 279, 313, 327, 346, 378, 395, 412
Digby, Sir Kenelm, 34, 34n, 36, 51, 116n, 148, 210
Digges, Sir Dudley, 40
Ditchley, Oxfordshire, 13–17
Ditton Park, Berkshire, 253-6
Dordrecht (Dort), Synod of, xv, 121
Dormer, Sir Robert, 232
Dorset, Edward Sackville, 4th Earl of, 265, 267, 269–70, 279
Dowland, John, 13
Drake, Sir William, 355
Dryden, John, 121
Dublin, xxxii, 3, 51–2, 55–6, 126, 140–2, 173, 318; Trinity College, 52
Dumas, Alexandre, 36
Dungarvan, Elizabeth Boyle, Viscountess, 319, 411
Dungarvan, Richard Boyle, Viscount, 318–19, 329, 351
Dysart, William Murray, 1st Earl of, 215–16, 361

Earl Marshal's Court, 47, 130–1, 141, 165
Earle, John, 85, 420
Edgcote House, 276–7, 279
Edgehill, Battle of (1642), xxii, xxxii, 319, 361, 366, contemporary Parliamentarian responses to, 257–9, unfolding of, 263–75, aftermath of, 276–7, 280, 282–3, 290, 294, 300–303, 305, 308, 315, 353, Sir Edmund Verney's ghost confirmed as haunting field of, 323, Hyde's unique exposure at, 383, Parliament's legally dubious impressment of Irish Adventurer forces at recalled by Hyde, 396, Lord Falkland's initiative at, 418
Edinburgh, xxxii, 123, 172, 177, 184, 216
Edward I, King of England, 228
Edward III, King of England, 9
Edward IV, King of England, 293
Edward VI, King of England and Ireland, 5, 228, 244
England, Kingdom of, xiii, xviii–xix, xxv, xxxii, 4–5, 10–11, 14, 21–2, 31, 35, 37, 41, 43, 51, 53, 56, 60, 70, 75, 76n, 91–2, 94, 110, 122–3, 133, 138, 142, 150, 167, 173, 182, 193, 200, 206, 220–1, 244–5, 256, 278, 280–1, 287, 319, 345, 360, 408; queen consort of, 20, 188; Hyde Lord Chancellor of, 27; Church of, 95, 119, 170, 243, 245, 260, 266, 274, 360–1, 384–5; Thomas Wentworth imagined as king of, 139; laws of, 174–5, 289, 332, 359, 360; Parliament of, 180, 359; and Ireland, 174, 183, 396; 'mixed monarchy' of, 224–5; Elizabeth I as monarch of, 245; long peace and outbreak of civil war in, 248, 250–1, 258, 301; ideal subject of, 262; and soldier of, 264, 326; and nobleman of, 327; political norms of and military service, 267; civil war conducted in, 271n, 283–5, 314, 403; diplomacy of, 272; and Jan Dalbier, 277; admiralty of, 336; Commonwealth or Republic of, 260, 349; opinions regarding foreign soldiery in, 285, 287; and dogs, 288; and King Cassivellaunus, 298; tradition of infantry in, 303; rivers of, 332; despairing exile of patriotic natives of, 355; north of, 358; and Scotland, 362–4, 367, 370,

*Index*

England, Kingdom – *cont'd.*
382–3, 395, 398; 'Presbyterianism' in, 382, 386, 389, 392, 395; peace party in, 384, 398; Great Seal of, 376; coinage of, 406; Bristol second port of, 412

Eliot, Sir John, 39, 40, 47, 48, 126–7

Elizabeth I, Queen of England and Ireland, 14, 32, 35, 39, 60, 100, 139, 222, 236, 243, 245, 312; as 'Gloriana', the 'Faerie Queene', and the 'Virgin Queen', xiii; remembered favourably, according to Lady Ranelagh, by comparison to Charles I, 421; her era, 13, 33, 65, 119, 245, 263, 346; obstacles to continental travel during reign of, 89

Elizabeth, Queen of Bohemia ('Winter Queen'), xv–xvi, xxii, 69, 137–8

Erle, Sir Walter, 147, 150–4, 177, 207

Erskine of Alva, Sir Charles, 362

Essex, Robert Devereux, 2nd Earl of, xxviii, 60; rebellion of against Elizabeth I, 100, 243

Essex, Robert Devereux, 3rd Earl of, xix, xxiv, 182, 213, 277, 279, 294, 388; and the Earl of Strafford, 158–9, 160, 200, 369; Lord Chamberlain, 165; and Charles' attempt to arrest the Five Members, 215; enters royal presence despite oppositional politics, there encountering Hyde, 216–7; Lord General of the Parliamentary troops, 230, 239, 242, 248–9, 256, 259, 285, 293, 379; country house at Chartley, 243; blamed for defeat at Powick Bridge, 253; at the Battle of Edgehill, 257, 263, 265, 267–9, 273–4; conduct on retreat, 276, 276n; marches from Coventry to London, 295–7; bearing towards troops, 302; at Turnham Green, 303–7; and Bulstrode Whitelocke, 317; and Lady Sophia Murray, 354; and his cousin Northumberland, 356; defeat at Battle of Lostwithiel, 358; attempts to prosecute Cromwell, 367; invoked by *politiques* of peace party at Uxbridge, 390–1, 400; resented by war party, 398; at the siege of Gloucester, 413; at the Battle of Newbury, 417

Evelyn, Sir John, 294, 295, 296

Fairfax, Edward, 121

Fairfax, Ferdinando, 2nd Lord Fairfax of Cameron, truce in Yorkshire proposed by family of, 218; cordial relations and putative kinship with Whitelocke, 317, 400

Fairfax, Sir Thomas (*later* 3rd Lord Fairfax of Cameron), 358, 400; great-nephew of Waller's poetic master, 121

Falkland, Elizabeth Cary, Viscountess, 52, 76n, 84, 116–7

Falkland, Henry, 1st Viscount Falkland, 51–6, 82, 140, 299; family of, 86n, 97

Falkland, Lettice Cary, Viscountess, 54–6, 59, 319, 409–10

Falkland, Lucius Cary, 2nd Viscount, family of, xiv; Oxfordshire property of, 4, 13 127; background and marriage, 52–6; and Great Tew Circle, xv, xviii, 3, 82–6, 98, 118–24, 235n, 239, 249, 320, 388, 409; politics of, xix–xxiii, 10, 126, 132, 210–19, 221, 228, 245, 253, 260–1, 279, 371, 374, 385, 392; and developing closeness to

484

## Index

Hyde, 11, 59–60; friendships with poets, 66–7, 76, 123; abortive military service in Low Countries, 92; and William Chillingworth, 14–17, 115–16, 207, 209; Parliamentary seats of in 1640, 6n, 128–9; volunteer military service under Earl of Essex in Scotland during First Bishops' War, 125, 408; shrill speaking voice, 131; youthful conflict with Wentworth faction, 140, 169; and Strafford's downfall, 138–41, 144–5, 148–9, 155–6, 160–1, 369, 373; and bishops' voting rights, 167–8, 172, 176–8; and emerging Royalist party, 180–1, 183; and the Grand Remonstrance, 187, 189–90, 191, 199–200, 205–6; appointed King's Secretary of State, 213, 222; joins King at York, 18–19, 217; outlawed by Parliament, 242; and aftermath of Powick Bridge, 251; at the Battle of Edgehill, 267–9, 272, 275; at the royal court in Oxford, 281, 314, 318–19, 321, 324, 336, 341; clashes with Prince Rupert, 263–4, 285, 300; as Secretary of State, 3n, 223, 305, 308–9, 311, 313, 323, 330, 337, 342–8, 352–6, 411–13; portrayed by Clarendon, 404–7; relationship with Charles I, 328, 406–7; rumoured mistress, 409–11; in the siege of Gloucester, 412–14; death at Battle of Newbury (1643), xxiii, 404, 414–23

Fanshawe, Dorothea, 321
Fanshawe, Sir Richard, 259–61, 263, 345–6
Fanshawe, Sir Thomas, 255, 259
Fawley Court, Buckinghamshire (principal seat of Bulstrode Whitelocke), 81, 92, 95, 99–100, 104–5, 109–10, 133, 225, 231, 254–55, 303, 307, 324–5, 355, 417; sack of by Prince Rupert's horse, 285–92; and pillage by Parliamentarian soldiers also, 367
Feilding, Basil, Viscount *see* Denbigh, Basil Feilding, 2nd Earl of
Felton, John, xvii, 33–7, 47
Fiennes, Nathaniel, 166–7, 171–2, 249, 253, 298, 300
Finch, Sir John, 48, 67–8, 73, 76, 127, 178, 369
Five Members, Charles' attempt to arrest, 214–15, 229, 295; Holles as one of, 298, 361
Fleetwood, Charles, 273
Fortescue, Sir Faithfull, 256, 269, 319
Fountaine, John, 26, 333n
France, xvi–xvii, xxix, 22, 31, 33–4, 61n, 71, 75, 86, 88–92, 104, 115, 117, 140, 151, 189n, 208, 266, 323, 325, 341, 349, 353, 359; fashion and music of, Whitelocke's taste for, 7, 20, 69, 75, 91; language of, 68, 317n; Whitelocke's journey in, 88–96; cavalry of, 94–5, 230, 267, 305; mariners of, 96; young lutenist Piccart from, 101, 103; ambassador of, 188, 215; mercenaries from, 360
Frederick V, Elector Palatine and King of Bohemia ('Winter King'), xv–xvi, 22, 69
Fuller, Thomas, 323

Geddes, Jenny, 123
Germany, xv, 22, 45, 70, 89, 214, 250, 252, 254, 263–4, 284, 414
Gibbons, Sir Richard, 243, 244
Gill, Alexander, the Younger, 37, 116
Gloucester, siege of, 412–14

*Index*

Glynne, John, 148, 153, 228–9, 362
Goodwin, Colonel Arthur, 232, 233
Goring, George, 210, 412
Graham, Sir Richard, 271
Grand Remonstrance (1641), xxi, 184–205, 206, 212–13, 229, 344, 346
Grandison, William Villiers, 2nd Viscount, 61, 103–4, 106, 169, 267, 272–273
Great Marlow, 6, 6n, 135, 145, 229, 398
Great Seal, 26, 109, 376; Littleton sends to the King, 16–17, 19, 217, 223, 228
Great Tew, circle at, xv, xviii, xxiii, 3, 13, 16, 29n, 52–3, 56, 61, 82–7, 90, 93, 98, 116–22, 124, 126, 129, 138–9, 160, 181, 209–10, 220, 235n, 240, 245, 249, 269, 281, 313, 319–20, 345–7, 388, 390, 409, 416, 420
Greene, John, 382
'Greensleeves', song, 303
Greenwich, palace of, 61, 169, 216
Grimston, Harbottle, 26, 38, 45–7, 228–9
Gunpowder Plot (1605), xiii–xiv, 326, 364
Gurney, Sir Richard, 302
Gustavus Adolphus, King of Sweden, 70, 264

Hale, Matthew, 26, 156n, 255, 300, 372; personal character of, 255; family and living arrangements of, 255, 280, 282, 320, 345, 355
Hales, John, xv, 32, 49, 85, 121–2, 138, 388
Hall, Bartholomew, 26, 93
Hamilton, James Hamilton, Marquess of (*later* 1st Duke), 216–17
Hammond, Henry, 390n
Hampden, John: as one of the Five Members, 2; primacy in the 'anti-court' party, 6, 39, 40; opposes 'Ship Money' tax, 121; Whitelocke works for, 126; Hyde's friendship with, 132–3, 139, 143, 146; and Strafford's downfall, 147–8, 152–9; and bishops' voting rights, 166, 168, 172; and the Grand Remonstrance, 188, 196, 199; King's attempt to arrest, 214–15; leads infantry at skirmish at Watlington, 232–3; military role, 267–8; not present at Edgehill, 277; regiment at Brentford, 301; at Turnham Green, 303, 306–8; Whitelocke's friendship with and claim of kinship to, 317; secretly reins in peace party, 327; Clarendon's hostility to, 345; young cousin of arrested as Royalist courier, 349; death, 358; eminence among Parliamentarians, 387, 421n
Hampton Court, palace of, xxii, xxxii, 216
Hannay, James, 123
Hardy, Nathaniel, 390n
Harrington, John, 46n
Harvey, Daniel, 112, 266
Harvey, Dr William (royal physician), 266, 268–70, 277–9, 288
Haselrig, Sir Arthur, 2, 214, 367
Henderson, Alexander, 390
Henley, Oxfordshire, xxii, xxxi, 3, 12, 58, 87, 105, 219n, 233, 235, 254, 286, 333n, 362, 367
Henri IV, King of France and Navarre, 90
Henrietta Maria, princess of France, Queen of England, Scotland and Ireland, 90, 185, 188, 265, 346, 384; Charles' marriage to, xvi–vii;

## Index

attached by rumour to Irish rebellion, xxi, 175, 206, 221; and the Eleanor Villiers affair, 60–1; enjoyment of musical entertainment and dramatic art, xviii, 63–4, 66–9, 74–7, 89n, 91, 101; sponsor of aggressive foreign policy through poetry, 71; libelled by William Prynne, xviii, 63–5; and Henry Percy, 169, 170–1; influence on the King, xvii, 69, 132, 137, 192, 214–17, 228, 246, 328–9, 339, 341, 385, 411; interest in Bulstrode Whitelocke, 7, 20, 87, 106, 162; at Strafford's trial, 150, 152, 153, 325; and Harry Jermyn, 210; seeks financial support and arms in the Netherlands, 221–2, 311, 328–9; and supporters at Royalist court, 239, 242, 395, 407, 412; in France, 359

Henry VI, King of England and France, 228; as dramatized by William Shakespeare, 405

Henry VIII, King of England and Ireland, 3n, 18, 39, 76n, 214n, 293

Henry Stuart, Prince of Wales, elder brother of Charles I, xv–xvi

Herbert of Cherbury, Edward, 1st Baron, 89n

Herbert, George, 35n, 72, 89n

Herne, John, 373

Hertford, William Seymour, Marquess of, 158, 200, 207, 213, 388–9, 394

Heylyn, Peter, 313

Highgate, Middlesex, 355

Hinton, Dr John (royal physician), 265, 269–72

Hobbes, Thomas, 29n, 85, 128, 245, 266, 345

Holland, Henry Rich, 1st Earl of, 227, 349; in the Scots war, 125–6; Puritan grandee, 213, 216–17; as soldier, 267, 302, 304; Peace Commissioner, 317–18, 321–23; the King's disgust with, 338; and Waller's Plot, 349, 351–2, 354; defects to Oxford, finding cool reception there, 356

Holland, Sir John: parliamentary diarist, 176, 182, 186, 190–1, 193, 351; Peace Commissioner, 319, 329, 333–5, 337, 340

Holles, Denzil: claims compensation for imprisonment, 146; on Strafford impeachment committee, 147, 148, 150, 152; King's attempt to arrest, 2, 214; misses Edgehill, 277; troops of at Brentford garrison, 298, 300; in the 'peace party', 317, 356, 361, 365–6, 367, 389, 391–2, 394, 398, 401; and prosecution of Laud, 370; plots with the Scots, 384–6, 402; and Edward Hyde, 386n; and Whitelocke in connection with secret peace approach to the King, 403

Hopton, Sir Ralph, 405

Horton, Buckinghamshire, 81n

Horton, Colonel Thomas, 271

Hotham, Sir John, 202, 209

Howard, Sir William, 265, 270–1

Hutchinson, Lucy, 258

Hyde, Anne (daughter of Edward; *later* Duchess of York), 122, 217, 292–3

Hyde, Anne (first wife of Edward), 13, 37, 59–60, 95-7

Hyde, Edward *see* Clarendon, Edward Hyde, 1st Earl of

Hyde, Frances (second wife of Edward) *see* Clarendon, Frances Hyde, Countess of

Hyde, Henry, the Younger (elder brother of Edward), 28–9, 31

487

## Index

Hyde, Henry (eldest son of Edward; *later* 2nd Earl of Clarendon), 217, 292–3

Hyde, Henry the Elder (father of Edward), 28, 29–30, 34, 60, 69, 89, 90, 90n, 97, 98

Hyde, Lawrence, progenitor of the Hyde legal dynasty, 102

Hyde, Sir Lawrence (uncle of Edward), Queen's Attorney-General, 32

Hyde, Lawrence (younger son of Edward; *later* 1st Earl of Rochester), xxx, 217, 292–3

Hyde, Mary (mother of Edward), 97, 97n

Hyde, Sir Nicholas (uncle of Edward), 30, 41, 48, 59

Hyde, Robert (cousin of Edward), 26

Hyde, Susan (sister of Edward), 28, 28n, 342n

'Independents', 367, 376, 382, 384–5, 392, 395, 398, 400, 421

Ireton, Henry, 273

Ireland, Kingdom of, xx–xxi, xxiv, xxxii, 4, 21, 51, 53–4, 56, 126, 137–8, 140, 142, 150, 160, 206, 216, 218, 221, 225, 241, 256, 293, 318–19, 329, 372, 388; and rebellion in, 173–5, 181–3, 188–90; discussed at Uxbridge, 395–9

'Irish Adventurers', 219–21, 256; alluded to by Hyde, 396

Irish Rebellion (1641), xxi, xxiii, 4–5, 173–5, 180–3, 188–9, 206, 256, 344, 392, 397

Italy, 312; music of, 20; language of, 97

Ives, Simon, 69, 76, 101

Jackson, Gilbert, 108

James VI & I, King of England, Scotland and Ireland, xiii–xvi, 8, 43, 71, 100, 114n, 115n, 245, 318, 321, 334, 406; and Bishop Williams, 108–10

Jermyn, Harry (*later* 1st Earl of St Albans), 61, 210–11, 214, 217, 412

Johnson, Cornelius, 54

Jones, Inigo, 68, 73

Jonson, Ben, xxviii, 32, 48–50, 50n, 51–3, 55, 59, 70, 76, 98, 121–3, 160, 187, 210, 245, 320, 409; Pindaric Ode to Cary & Morison, 53; *Chloridia*, 70

Juxon, William, Bishop of London and Lord Treasurer, 7, 28, 78, 113, 158, 236

Kent, Elizabeth Grey, Countess of, 43, 43n, 123, 333, 351, 429

Kent, Henry Grey, 8th Earl of, 43, 123

Kettell, Ralph, 237, 321–2

Kincade, Robert, 415

Kineton, Warwickshire, 256–7, 265, 276

King's Men (theatre company), 298–9

Kirke, Colonel Lewis, 323

Kirton, Edward, 207

Knights of the Shire, 134, 134n, 183

Lambeth Palace, 111, 141

Lane, Sir Richard, 122n, 156n, 386, 386n, 393–4

Lanier, Nicholas, 76, 76n

Laud, William, Archbishop of Canterbury, and Arminianism, xv, 115; aesthetic common ground of with Charles I over ceremony and hierarchy, xvi; godfather of Chillingworth, 15, 84, 207; appointed Archbishop of Canterbury, 115; relations with Great Tew, 16, 119–20, 129, 414; and Oxford, 28, 37–8, 236–7, 240, 364; old friendship of with Sir James

488

Whitelocke, 48, 110, 139, 378; and with John Hales, 122; quasi-paternal interest in and occasionally fractious relationship with Bulstrode Whitelocke, xiv, xix, 27, 58–9, 65, 104, 111–12, 135, 139; employment of and friendship with Edward Hyde, xix, 112–14, 136, 138–9, 149, 172, 245, 266; and prosecution of Prynne, xviii, 63; perceived sympathy with and modulated actual attitude to Catholicism, 113–14; and Bishops' Wars with Scots, xix, 123; and the Short Parliament, 132; allied to, then brought down with, Strafford, xx, 152, 158, 186; committed to the Tower, 149, 160, 167; his Church criticized by his godson in abortive appeal to Pym, 207–8; persecutor of Tom Chaloner, 244; underexplored affinities of John Milton with, 254; implicit political corruption of, 312, 389; journalistic protégé of, 313; trial and execution, xxiv, 192, 255, 368–77

Lawes, Henry, 69

Lawes, Will, 69, 76

Le Neve, Sir William, 276

Lee, Lady Anne, 13–17

Lee, Sir Henry, Queen's Champion, 14

Lee, Sir Henry, the champion's cousin and heir, married to Anne, Lady Lee, 14

Leicester, Robert Sidney, 2nd Earl of, 173, 260, 354

Leland, John, 357

Lenthall, William, Speaker of the House of Commons, 2–3, 13, 82, 201, 215, 314, 355

Leslie, General Alexander (*later* 1st Earl of Leven), 126, 134

Levant Company, 34, 39, 127

Lilburne, Captain John, 298, 300, 301

Lilly, William (astrologer), 174

Lindsey, Robert Bertie, 1st Earl of, 263–4, 273, 274, 276, 278–9, 366

Lindsey, Montagu Bertie, 2nd Earl of (*formerly* 15th Baron Willoughby of Eresby), 273, 274, 278–9, 366

Lisle, Philip Sidney, Viscount, 260

Littleton, Edward, 1st Baron Littleton, 11, 16–17, 41, 43, 220, 223, 226, 228, 324

London, xxxi–xxxii, 1, 8, 10–13, 37–8, 40, 43, 52, 54, 56–7, 59, 63, 65, 73, 83, 89, 92, 97, 104, 106, 115, 131, 173–4, 188, 217–20, 223, 233–4, 238, 243, 248, 253, 268, 297, 310, 318, 322, 330, 333, 367, 373, 378, 382–4, 390, 407, 410, 412, 420; in 1620s, xvii, 31–4; Charles I's alienation of, xxii–xxiii; Royalists decamp from, 3–4, 18–19; and calling of Parliament in 1640, 126–8; return of the King from Scotland to, 184–5; popular unrest in, 206–8; trepidation on approach of Royalist army to, 255–7; Royalist communications with, 279–80; continued Royalist advance upon, 282–6, 291–5; Turnham Green campaign, 300–8; perception within of short provisions at Oxford, 313–17; and Waller's Plot, 342–7, 352–5; Uxbridge meeting point between Oxford and, 357–8; Lady Sophia Murray's captivity in, 415–6

Long, Sir Walter, 146

Long Parliament, xix, 139; assembled, 136; Bill of Attainder and execution of Strafford, 154–61, 262; exclusion of

*Index*

Long Parliament – *cont'd.*
  Court-aligned former MPs, 164;
  Whitelocke draws up act for
  'Perpetual Parliament', 163–4; and
  Bishops' voting rights, 166–8;
  documented by diarists, 175–6;
  initially embraced by Hyde, 178, 186;
  Grand Remonstrance (1641), 184–205;
  militia debate, 216, 221; Nineteen
  Propositions, 223; hardliners in, 302;
  waverers in, 318; sends Peace
  Commissioners to royalist Oxford,
  314–28; criticism of in London legal
  circles, 346; Vow and Covenant, 354–5,
  358; Lady Ranelagh's view of, 421
Lords, the, upper house of Parliament
  of England, xxi, 10, 33, 67, 120, 145,
  154, 156, 159, 177–8, 191–2, 197, 218,
  220, 224, 230, 322–3, 327, 346, 350, 354,
  391, 394, 403; and voting rights of
  bishops, 165–8; George Lord Digby
  accelerated to, 211–14; Royalist
  Lords at Oxford, 359
Lostwithiel, Battle of (1644), xxiv,
  xxxii, 358
Loudoun, John Campbell, 1st Earl of,
  383–5, 391, 394–5
Louis XIII, King of France and
  Navarre, 89
Love, Christopher, 382–3
Lowin, John, 298–9
Lucan, poet, 21, 51
Ludlow, Shropshire, 69, 141
Lytton, Sir William, Peace
  Commissioner, 319, 329, 351

Magdalen College, Oxford, 29
Magdalen Hall, Oxford, 29, 29n
Maitland, John, Lord (*later* 1st Duke of
  Lauderdale), 362–4

Maitland of Lethington, William, 362
Mandeville, Edward Montagu,
  Viscount *see* Manchester, Edward
  Montagu, 2nd Earl of
Mare, Pierre de la, 91
Marshall, Stephen, 390
Marston, John, 63
Marston Moor, Battle of (1644),
  xxiii–xxiv, xxxii, 358, 361
Marten, Henry, otherwise Harry, 46n,
  167, 171–2, 209, 245, 285, 336, 350, 374,
  398
Marvell, Andrew, 260
Mary I, Queen of England, 237n, 312
Mary I, Queen of Scots, 243, 362
Mary II, Queen of England, Scotland
  and Ireland, 22
Massey, Colonel Edward, 412, 418
Matthews, Miles, 271
Maurice, Prince Palatine of the Rhine,
  250, 360, 366
May, Sir Humphrey, xvii, 38, 39, 44, 48,
  57, 79, 140
May, Thomas, otherwise Tom, 21, 46n,
  51, 85, 123, 258, 259–60, 345
Maynard, William, 2nd Baron, 361
Maynard, John, 26, 136, 148, 152–3, 180,
  228–9, 361, 367, 372, 375–6
Merchant Taylors' school, 20, 28, 51, 76
Merton College, Oxford, 309–11, 315–16,
  323, 333, 335, 339
Meyrick, Sir John, 307, 317, 379
Middle Temple, Inn of Court, 2, 10, 19,
  25–8, 30, 32, 41, 44–5, 50, 62, 66, 85,
  88, 92, 99, 112, 125, 129, 136, 148, 180,
  198, 201, 341, 361, 386; colours of, 73
Militia Ordinance, 10–11, 17, 19, 182,
  224, 226–7, 229
Milton, John, 81, 117n, 142n, 253–4, 283;
  *Comus*, 69; 'Captain or Colonel or

## Index

Knight at Arms', 254; *Paradise Lost*, 394

Montagu, Walter, otherwise Wat (*later* abbé), 63, 67, 68; *The Shepherd's Paradise*, 63

Montgison, Balthasard de, 91

Montigny, Guillaume, Colonel de, 89–90, 104

Montrose, James Graham, 1st Marquess of, xxiv, 358–9, 385, 397

Morison, Sir Harry, 53–6, 59–60, 409

Morley, Dr George (*later* Bishop of Winchester), 16, 17, 85, 119–20, 120, 420

Mostyn, Roger, 364; family of, 78

Murray, Lady Sophia, 320–1, 321n, 342–3n, 353–4, 409–11, 414–16

Murray, Margaret, 361

Murray, William, otherwise Will *see* Dysart, William Murray, 1st Earl of

Mytens, Daniel, 170

Nettlebed, Oxfordshire, 362–4

Neville, Henry, 46n

New Model Army, 382, 399, 400–1

Newark, Henry Pierrepont (*later* 2nd Earl of Kingston-upon-Hull, 1st Marquess of Dorchester), Viscount, 242

Newburn, Battle of (1640), xxxii, 134

Newbury, First Battle of (1643), xxiii, xxxi–xxxii, 85, 404, 414–23

Newcastle-upon-Tyne, xix, xx, xxxii, 134

Newcastle, William Cavendish, 1st Earl, *later* 1st Duke of, 242, 358

Nicholas, Sir Edward, 3n, 172, 185, 196, 197, 207–8, 213n, 242, 251, 312, 337

Nineteen Propositions, xxii, 223, 327

Nithsdale, Robert, 2nd Earl of, 321n

North, Gilbert, 123

Northumberland, Algernon Percy, 10th Earl of, brother of Henry Percy, 169; at Turnham Green, 304; Peace Commissioner, 296, 298, 315–16, 317–18, 323, 326–8, 329, 331–9; and Waller's Plot, 348–56; and the Treaty of Uxbridge, 364, 379, 383, 391, 400, 402

Northumberland, Henry Percy, 9th Earl of ('Wizard Earl'), 100, 326

Nostell Priory, Yorkshire, 18, 217

Nottingham, xxxii; King's court at, 217–18, 241, 243–4, 261, 263

Noy, William, 41, 43, 62, 63, 66–7, 74

Osborne, Dorothy, Lady Temple, 176

Ottley, Sir Francis, 243

Oxford, xviii, xxxi, 32, 58, 81, 83, 266, 278–9, 284, 292, 294, 308, 322–3, 354, 358, 378, 407, 411, 415, 417; fleeting Parliamentarian occupation of, 235–49; royal court at, xxii, 233, 268, 280–6, 305–6, 309–16, 319, 321, 324, 327, 356, 359, 361, 363–6, 368, 378, 382–3, 401, 403, 405, 408–9, 419

Oxford, Treaty of, 328–41, 343, 345, 350, 352, 372

Oxford University, xiv, 13–15, 38, 58, 83, 370; college plate, 235, 239–40, 249, 311; monarchist and Catholic sympathies, 236–8; religious inclinations, 37, 119–20; Whitelocke and Hyde attend, 7, 26, 28–9, 45, 50, 58–9, 303, 371

Paget, William, 6th Baron Paget, 227, 256

Palmer, Geoffrey (*later* 1st Baronet), 19, 26, 45, 148, 153, 194, 198–203, 205–9,

## Index

Palmer, Geoffrey – *cont'd*.
216, 219, 222–3, 229, 255, 283, 344, 365, 386, 393–4, 399; with Hyde, regretfully parts ways from Whitelocke over militia question, 10–12; protestation of in House of Commons over Grand Remonstrance, 198–203, 205; detention at Tower, 206–9; family of, co-tenancy with Whitelocke and Hale families at Ivy Lane, 255, 280, 282, 320, 345–5

Parsons, Dr Philip, 333, 334

Payne, Sir Robert, 355

Peace Commissioners, 12, 315, 317–28, 344, 358–9, 378

Pembroke, Mary Herbert, Countess of, 72n

Pembroke, Philip Herbert, 4th Earl of, Hyde's political patron, 2–3, 73, 89, 128, 149, 157, 242, 292, 345; Lord Chamberlain, 71–2, 107; replaced as Lord Chamberlain, 165; and the Irish Adventurers, 220; Peace Commissioner, 296, 317, 329, 364, 379, 384, 388–90, 391–2, 394, , 399, 402; peace party leader, 348, 351, 354; temper, 350; Hyde's facility for imitation of, 386n, 407

Penington, Isaac, 301–2, 345, 356

Pennington, William, 174

Percy, Henry (*later* Baron Percy of Alnwick), 168–70

Percy, John (aka Fisher), 116n

Percy, Thomas, 326

Percy, Mrs, Fleet Street landlady, 45–7, 49, 51, 63

Personal Rule (of Charles I), xx, 8, 102, 129, 130, 246, 320

Petition of Right, 33, 47

Peyton, Sir Thomas, 176, 194, 199

Piccart (French lutenist), 101, 103, 106

Pierrepont, William, Peace Commissioner, 242, 319, 329, 331, 333, 335, 336–7, 350–2, 361, 401–2

Pincke, Dr Robert, Warden of New College, Oxford, 318

Pollard, Sir Hugh, 180

Popery, 185, 193, 237, 364, 372

Popham, Colonel, 398

Porter, Sir Endymion, 242

Portland, Richard Weston, 1st Earl of, 112–13, 193

Portland, Jerome Weston, 2nd Earl of, 3, 348–9, 352

Postmasters' Hall, Oxford, 309–10

Powick Bridge, Battle of (1642), xxxii, 248–53

Prayer Book, 185–6, 383, 390n; ill-fated Scottish version, xix, 123

Prideaux, Edmund, 387

Prynne, William, xviii, xx–xxii, 65n, 75, 111, 149, 298, 300, 372; *Histrio-mastix: the players scourge*, 62–6, 68

Pym, John, dominance in the Commons, 2, 5–6, 13, 16, 21, 175; and the Militia Ordinance, 9–11, 23; determination to prosecute Hyde, 17; anti-Catholic belligerence of, 20; emerging as parliamentary leader, 39, 40; in the Short Parliament, 126, 128–33; Hyde, Whitelocke and Falkland's initial compatibility with, 139–41, 172, 245; and Strafford's downfall, 141–5, 147–9, 153–8, 160; financial difficulties, 164–5; and bishops' voting rights, 166, 171; Harry Marten's support of cynical, 167; client of Earl of Bedford, 174; moderate supporters of, 176–7, 179, 242, 248, 252, 261, 318; and the Irish

492

## Index

rebellion, 181–3; and the Grand Remonstrance, 184–6, 188–97, 200–212; offered post as Chancellor of the Exchequer, 213; King's attempt to arrest for treason, 214–15; victory over militia assured, 216; and Irish Adventurers, 219; and Oliver St John, 226; and continuing scepticism among allies over militia, 228–9; increasingly narrow support of , 283, 346; radical 'war party' supporters of, 294, 327; propagandistic ability of, 315; and the Peace Commissioners, 330, 343; and Waller's Plot, 344, 348, 354; death, 358; legacy of Parliamentarian alliance with Scots, 370; successors of, 387, 421n

Pyne, John, 38, 398

Ramsay, Sir James, 256–7, 269
Ranelagh, Arthur Jones, 2nd Viscount, 55, 145, 160
Ranelagh, Katherine Jones, Viscountess, 55, 98, 145, 318, 410, 420–1
Richard II, King of England, 183
Richard III, King of England, 209
Richelieu, Cardinal, 89, 90, 91, 188
Richmond, James Stewart, 1st Duke of, 242, 265, 269–70, 367–8, 373, 383, 395
Ripon, Treaty of, 134
Rivers, John Savage, 2nd Earl, 242
Rochester, Henry Wilmot (*later* 1st Earl of), 14, 180, 250, 251, 268–9, 272–3, 308n, 412, 418
Rochester, John Wilmot, 2nd Earl of, 14
Rodes, Elizabeth, 148n
Roe, Sir Thomas, 137–8
Rohan, Henri, duc de, 22

Rome, 20, 35, 55, 90n, 114, 117n, 236, 245, 345; ancient, 8, 322, 407
'Root and Branch' bill, 166–72, 186–7
Rouen, Normandy, France, 90, 95
Rowse, A. L., 76n
Royal Library, 122n
Rudyerd, Sir Benjamin, 187, 190, 191, 194, 196
Rupert of the Rhine, Prince, xxii–xxiii; bellicose disposition of, 239; at the battle of Powick Bridge, 249, 250, 251, 252–3; associated with looting and violence, 272, 284–9; before and during the Battle of Edgehill, 256, 263–4, 269, 273–4, 276, 278; family cause of, 277; advocates attack on London, 279, 282–6, 297; his troopers ransack Fawley Court, 287–9, 303, 319; Yorkist ancestry of, 293; bombards Windsor, 295; as Governor of Windsor Castle, 289n; and the battle of Brentford, 298–301, 303; increasing legend of, 304; thwarted at Turnham Green by more cautious strategists, 305; Parliamentarian strategic counterparts of, 307; with Charles I in Oxford, 324, 325, 366; conflict with Henry Wilmot, 308n; defeated at Marston Moor, 358; Whitelocke's view of as foreign mercenary, 360; victory at Bristol, 412; Lord Falkland's greater regard for Parliamentarian Lord General Essex than, 417

Russell, Francis, 235
Ruthven, Patrick, 3rd Lord (*later* 1st Earl of Forth and of Brentford), 263–4, 269, 316
Rutland, Francis Manners, 6th Earl of, 100, 102, 109, 109n, 111

## Index

Rutland, George Manners, 7th Earl of, 100, 103–7, 111, 226
Rutland, Roger Manners, 5th Earl of, 100

St John of Bletso, Baron, 235
St John, Oliver, 6, 13, 133, 143, 148, 158, 177, 226, 228–9, 235, 312, 367, 372, 374, 387, 398
St Stephen's Chapel, Westminster, 5, 39, 177, 190, 196
Salisbury, Wiltshire, xxxii, 97
Salisbury Court, west of St Paul's Cathedral, London, 68, 87, 99
Salisbury, Sir Thomas, 300
Salisbury, Robert Cecil, 1st Earl of, 318
Salisbury, William Cecil, 2nd Earl of, 318, 329
Sandys, Colonel Edwin, 249–52
Sandys, Sir Edwin, 41n, 250
Sandys, George, 249, 252; *Ovids Metamorphosis Englished*, 1, 25, 62, 78, 108, 137, 163, 184, 206, 241, 276, 309, 357
Savile, Sir John, 41n
Saye and Sele, James Fiennes, 2nd Viscount, 134–5, 227
Saye and Sele, William Fiennes, 1st Viscount, 134–5, 146–7, 150–1, 166, 227, 229, 232, 235–40, 248–9, 253, 280, 282, 298, 314, 321, 329, 354
Scotland, Kingdom of, xiii, xix, xxxii, 4, 123–5, 138, 150, 160, 171, 175, 177, 180, 182, 186, 200, 294, 358, 367, 383, 395–7, 408, 415; *see also* Bishops' Wars; Covenanters, Scots
Scrope, Adrian, 278
Scrope, Sir Gervase, 277–8
Selden, John, mentor to Hyde and Whitelocke, xvii, xx, 11–12, 41–4, 49–50, 59, 98, 119, 300, 348, 422; various friends of, 21, 134, 210, 266, 333; arrested and imprisoned for resisting dissolution of Parliament (1629), 48, 57, 127, 178; and the *Triumph of Peace*, 67; library of, 83n, 122, 260; political opinions of, 118, 124, 126, 128, 172, 174, 209, 224; admiration and affection for Laud, 120, 138–9, 245; rumoured lover of Countess of Kent, 123; makes claim for compensation from Whitelocke, 145–7, 164; appointed to the Strafford committee, 148, 152; opposes Strafford's execution, 155–6, 160, 369; and bishops' voting rights, 167–8; D'Ewes suspicious of, 176; integrity of intact in Hyde's view, 180, 345; and the Grand Remonstrance, 187, 194; and the militia debate, 228–9; sedentary self-image, 267; and Waller's Plot, 350–2; and Westminster Assembly, 362; *Titles of Honour* (1614), 130–1; *Table Talk*, 42

Shakespeare, William, 32, 49, 67, 72, 76, 121, 170, 187, 298–9, 404, 405; *The Tempest*, 67–8; First Folio, 72, 187; sonnets, 72n; *The Merchant of Venice, A Midsummer Night's Dream, Twelfth Night*, 170; *The Merry Wives of Windsor*, 299; *Romeo & Juliet*, 299; *Henry VI* part 3, 405
Sheldon, Gilbert (*later* Archbishop of Canterbury), 13, 85, 116, 120, 126, 237, 239–40, 281, 313, 420
Ship Money (tax), xviii, xx, 121, 126–7, 135, 179, 184, 220–1, 228, 319
Shirley, James, 68, *The Triumph of Peace*, 69–71, 73, 75–6

# Index

Short Parliament (1640), xix, 128–34, 142, 150

Shrewsbury, Shropshire, xxxii, 249, 264; King's court at, 238, 242–4; falls to Parliament, 397

Shrewsbury School, 244

Sidney, Colonel Algernon, 260

Sidney, Lady Dorothy *see* Sunderland, Dorothy Spencer, Countess of

Sidney, Sir Philip, 32, 72n, 244

Skippon, Sir Philip, 302, 304

Smallwood, Matthew, 301

Smith, Captain John, 273–4

Socinians, 16, 117, 414

*Sortes Virgilianae*, 407–9

Southampton, Thomas Wriothesley, 4th Earl of, 324, 367–8, 373, 393–4

Spain, xvi, 31, 67, 140, 189, 210–11, 222, 397; armada of, 90n, 250; 1st Earl of Bristol's fondness for, 279

Spalding, Ruth, xxvii

Spencer, Henry, 3rd Baron Spencer *see* Sunderland, Henry Spencer, 1st Earl of

Spenser, Edmund, *The Faerie Queene*, xiii, 74

Stapleton, Sir Philip, 202, 303, 317

Star Chamber, court of, xviii, xx, 37, 46–7, 63–4, 122, 130, 141, 165, 178, 244, 346, 380

Stonehouse, Sir George, 127

Strafford, Thomas Wentworth, 1st Earl of, x, xix-xx, 318; opponent of Buckingham, 40; and the Petition of Right, 47–8; Lord Deputy of Ireland, 51–2, 137–8, 141–2; with Laud, minister responsible for 'Thorough' royal government, 59; unpopularity with Great Tew Circle, 138–41; urges King to summon parliament, 126; Pym's hatred of, 142–4; family of, 148, 148n, 298, 356, 361; trial and execution, 145–67, 184, 186–7, 192, 194, 200–201, 203–4, 207, 211–12, 228, 262, 325, 369–71, 373, 404; abortive plots for his rescue, 169, 214; failed compromise to save life of, 200, 213, 356; Irish Rebellion a consequence of downfall of, 173; and unrest at York also, 241–2; Pym all too aptly likened to by Waller, 182; and by Chillingworth, 209; rumoured affair with Lady Carlisle, 215; and Manor House at York, 217; Hale defence counsel of, 255; few defenders of, 334; similar fate of his friend Laud, 376

Strickland, Walter, 222

Strode, William, 2, 146, 147, 214

Suckling, Sir John, 211

Sunderland, Dorothy Spencer, Countess of (*formerly* Lady Dorothy Sidney), 260, 320, 351, 353–4

Sunderland, Elizabeth, Countess of, 101–2, 103, 105, 111, 224–5

Sunderland, Emanuel Scrope, 1st Earl of, 101–2

Sunderland, Henry Spencer, 1st Earl of, 260–2, 263, 265, 267, 269, 272, 303, 343, 413

Switzerland, xv, 349

Taylor, Joseph, 298–9

Thirty Years War, 69, 200

Thynne, Lady Isabella, 321–2

Thynne, Sir John, of Longleat, 102

Thynne, Theodosia, 102–3, 105–6

Tomkins, Nathaniel, 346–9, 353, 355

Townshend, Aurelian, 70–1

## Index

Trained Bands (London reservists), 182, 301, 302–3
Trinity College, Cambridge *see* Cambridge, University of
Trinity College, Dublin *see* Dublin
Trinity College, Oxford, 15, 37, 237, 237n, 240, 310, 313, 321
Triplett, Thomas, 85–6, 118
*Triumph of Peace, The* (masque), xviii, 64–77
Turner, Dr Samuel, 333–5, 333n
Turnham Green, 'battle' of, xxiii, 305–8, 315, 317, 357, 379
Twisse, Dr William, 414

United Provinces, 222, 369, 379; theology of, xv, 114; art of, 54; military of, 56, 92; English volunteers serving in, 151; old-fashioned infantry tactics of, 263–4; mercenaries from, 360
Ussher, James, Archbishop of Armagh, 52
Uxbridge, Middlesex, xxxi–xxxii, 256, 357–8, 368, 373, 377
Uxbridge, Treaty of (1645), xxiv, 378–403, 404, 423

Valentine, Benjamin, 146
Vane, Sir Harry the Elder, 3n, 71–2, 135, 150–3, 150n, 166, 213n
Vane, Sir Harry the Younger, 151, 151n, 155, 166, 220, 367, 387, 421, 421n
Vaughan, John, 345
Venice, xv, 272, 361; and Lanier family, 76n; ambassador of, 349
Venn, Colonel John, 294
Verney, Sir Edmund, 261–3, 272–4, 276, 278, 323
Verney, Sir Ralph, 261, 276

Villiers, Eleanor, 60–1
Villiers, Barbara, Lady, 60–1
Virgil, 278, 407–9, *Aeneid*, 407
Vivers, Captain Robert, 300

Wadland, Thomas, 207, 208
Wales, Principality of, xxxii, 47, 53, 69, 78, 108, 115, 130, 139, 142n, 148, 246, 271, 300, 314
Wall, Moses, 220
Waller, Edmund, xxiii; in the 1626 parliament, 40; in the Great Tew circle, 85, 120–1; in the Short Parliament, 126, 128, 129; in the Long Parliament, 172, 181–2, 209; D'Ewes' comment on, 179n; courtship of 'Sacharissa', 260; Peace Commissioner, 320–2, 323, 325, 329, 338; eponymous Plot, 343–56, 361, 365, 372; and Lady Sophia Murray, 410, 416
Waller, Sir William, 134, 405
Wallingford, Oxfordshire, xxxi, 362–3
Walton, Izaak, 93
Wandesford, Christopher, 138, 173
Wardour, Sir Edward, 322–3
Warwick, Sir Philip, 144, 155, 161
Warwick, Robert Rich, 2nd Earl of, 213, 316, 327, 400
Warwick Castle, 276
Watlington, Oxfordshire, xxxi, 231–4
Welch, Sir Robert, 274
Wenman, Sir Francis, 235n, 318
Wenman, Margaret, Viscountess, 318
Wenman, Thomas, 2nd Viscount, 235, 235n, 318, 329, 350n, 351, 361, 379, 384
Wentworth, Arabella, Lady, 148n
Wentworth, Sir Thomas *see* Strafford, Thomas Wentworth, 1st Earl of
Wharton, Philip, 4th Baron, 227n, 256

## Index

Whitelocke, Bulstrode, xiii–xiv, xvii–xx, xxii–xxv, xxvii–xxx, 120, 142n, 347n; family and education, 20, 27–8, 30–1; leg injury, 7, 78; friendship with Edward Hyde, 4, 19, 25–7, 47–9, 52–3, 61–2, 84, 86, 92–6, 98, 169, 172, 179–80, 209, 222–3, 275, 296, 345; musical taste and ability of, 13; political and religious tendencies of, 14, 382; Royalist clients of, 18, 164; sympathy for Buckingham's assassin, 35–7; in the 1626 Parliament, 37–44, 132; Master of Revels for the Middle Temple, 44–6, 50, 57; oratorical style of, 51; marriage to Rebecca Bennet, 57–8, 78–82, 86–8, 92–6; death of father of, 59; organises *The Triumph of Peace* (masque), 64–77, 131–2, 169; amateur composer, 69, 75–6, 81–2, 87; and Lord Falkland, 56, 85–6; journey to France (1634), 88–96; troubles with mother-in-law of, 97; second marriage to Frances Willoughby, 99–108, 110–11; and Bishop Williams, 108–10, 159; and Archbishop Laud, 59, 111–113, 138, 245, 373–6; Erastianism, 118; advises John Hampden regarding Ship Money, 121; children of, 122, 290–1, 291n; and John Selden, 123–4; on the Scots Covenanters, 125, 133; and 'Ship Money', 121, 126–7; fails to gain place in Short Parliament, 127–8, 133; and Star Chamber, 130, 346; gains seat in Long Parliament, 134–6; speeches in the militia debate, 6–12, 17, 19–23, 192, 216, 226; and the Earl of Strafford, 138–41, 147–56, 161–2, 203; defends claims of compensation against his father, 145–6; draws up Act for Long Parliament, 163–5; and John Pym, 166; and bishops, 167–8; and the Irish rebellion, 173–4, 182; consults astrologer to cure illness, 174; impression of in diary of D'Ewes, 176–7; and the Grand Remonstrance, 187, 194–5, 196, 198, 201, 203, 205; chosen to reassure the City regarding Irish loan, 189; and the 'Irish Adventurers', 218–21; assists in preparation of Nineteen Propositions, 223; teased by his wife's aunt, 224–5; Deputy Lieutenant for Berkshire and Oxfordshire, 227–30; in command of skirmish at Watlington, 231–4; recommends taking Oxford for Parliament, 235–40, 248, 282; notes outlawry of Hyde, 242; and Tom Chaloner, 244, 374–5; reacts to Powick Bridge, 249–53; and mood in London, 254; Catholic family and friends, 224–5, 247; at Ditton Park, 254–5; and Ivy Lane, 254–5, 280, 355; on the battle of Edgehill, 256–9; on battle in general, 271n; preference for achieving peace by aggressive strategy, 277, 297; end of surviving, though apparently not actual, correspondence with Hyde, 280; sensitivity to mood at Oxford, 281; and in London, 283; family of and Oxfordshire skirmishes, 284; looting of his home Fawley Court, 285–91; Governor of Windsor Castle, 289n; Hyde's view of conduct of, 292, 296, 375; eldest son of, 293n; and Denzil Holles, 298; friends among London Royalists, 300; on sacking of Brentford, 301; at standoff at

## Index

Whitelocke, Bulstrode – *cont'd.*
  Turnham Green, 302–8, 217; Peace Commissioner, 314–20, 322–35, 337, 339–41, 343, 358–67, 383; and Waller's Plot, 350–52, 355; and Laud's trial and execution, 368–73, 377n; and the Treaty of Uxbridge, 378–80, 384–9, 392–6, 398–403; expends waning influence advocating peace in Commons, 405; on Charles I, 406–7; personal martial impulse shared with Falkland but not Hyde, 413; on death of Lord Falkland, 416–419; Falkland's bequest to, 420; legacy of, 422; *Diary*, xxvii–xxviii; *Memorials of English Affairs*, xxvii–xxviii, xxx, 42, 65, 253, 294, 301, 303, 324, 351–2, 372

Whitelocke, Captain Edmund (uncle of Bulstrode), xiv, 28, 100, 109n, 326

Whitelocke, Elizabeth (mother of Bulstrode), 27, 68, 78, 86–7; family religious tendencies of, 65

Whitelocke, Elizabeth (sister of Bulstrode), 78, 93; her son a Royalist governor, 364

Whitelocke, Frances (second wife of Bulstrode), 99–107, 110, 122, 128, 224–225, 231, 254–5, 290, 303, 317, 345, 366

Whitelocke, James, the Younger (eldest son of Bulstrode), 58, 80, 87, 92–3, 95, 99, 103, 122, 255–6, 293n

Whitelocke, Sir James, the Elder (father of Bulstrode), xiv, xvii, xxvii, 27, 28, 34, 37–41, 48, 57–9, 63, 65, 78–9, 87, 99–100, 102, 106, 109–10, 121, 127, 135, 145–6, 138, 164, 310, 370, 378

Whitelocke, Rebecca (first wife of Bulstrode), 57–8, 68, 79–82, 86–8, 93–5, 99, 105, 339, 378

Widdrington, Thomas, 26, 189

William I, King of England, 174

William III and Mary II, joint monarchs of England, Scotland and Ireland, 22

Williams, John, Archbishop of York (*formerly* Bishop of Lincoln), 108–11, 113, 115, 122, 159

Willoughby, Frances, Lady, 100, 103, 110–11, 128

Willoughby, Francis, 5th Baron Willoughby of Parham, 103–4, 106, 226, 277

Willoughby, Montagu Bertie, 15th Baron Willoughby of Eresby *see* Lindsey, Montagu Bertie, 2nd Earl of

Willoughby, William, 3rd Baron Willoughby of Parham, 100–101

Wilmot, Henry, Viscount *see* Rochester, Henry Wilmot (*later* 1st Earl of)

Windebank, Sir Francis, 193, 260

Windsor, xxxi–xxxii, 216, 292–3, 295, 316; Forest and Great Park of, 87, 217, 292, 295

Windsor Castle, 289n, 294–6, 302

Winston, Dr Thomas, 2

Winwood, Richard, 254, 256–7, 319–20, 329, 355, 378; family of at Highgate, 355

Winwood, Sir Ralph, 378

Wolstenholme, Sir John, the Elder, 18

Wolstenholme, Sir John, the Younger, 18, 19, 164

Wood, Anthony, 83, 310–11, 334

Wood, Thomas, 309–10

Woodstock, royal manor of, Oxfordshire, 280

Worcester, Henry Somerset, 5th Earl of (*later* 1st Marquess), 188, 246

*Index*

Wright, Robert, Bishop of Bristol, 109
Wycliffe, John, 18

Yeames, William Frederick, *And When Did You Last See Your Father?*, 291n
York, xxii–xxiii, xxxii, 37, 141, 144, 149, 156, 159, 166, 202, 222–3, 228, 231, 239, 260; King's court at, 13, 17–18, 157, 216, 217, 229n, 241, 244, 341, 378; Archbishop of, 250
York, Anne, Duchess of *see* Hyde, Anne
York, Prince James, Duke of (*later* James II), xxix, 265, 268–71
Yorkshire, xxiii, 15, 18, 38, 40, 126, 137–8, 160, 218, 317, 328, 358

ALLEN LANE
*an imprint of*
PENGUIN BOOKS

# Also Published

Quinn Slobodian, *Hayek's Bastards*

Didier Eribon, *The Life, Old Age, and Death of a Working-Class Woman*

Richard Overy, *Rain of Ruin: Tokyo, Hiroshima and the Surrender of Japan*

Herman Pontzer, *Adaptable: The Surprising Science of Human Diversity*

Michael Lewis, *Who is Government?: The Untold Story of Public Service*

Fara Dabhoiwala, *What Is Free Speech?: The History of a Dangerous Idea*

Owen Hatherley, *The Alienation Effect: How Central European Émigrés Transformed the British Twentieth Century*

Shon Faye, *Love in Exile*

Bill Gates, *Source Code: My Beginnings*

Emily Callaci, *Wages for Housework: The Story of a Movement, an Idea, a Promise*

Kenneth Roth, *Righting Wrongs: Three Decades on the Front Lines Battling Abusive Governments*

Selena Wisnom, *The Library of Ancient Wisdom: Mesopotamia and the Making of History*

Agnes Callard, *Open Socrates: The Case for a Philosophical Life*

Manu S. Pillai, *Gods, Guns and Missionaries: The Making of the Modern Hindu Identity*

Minoo Dinshaw, *Friends in Youth: Choosing Sides in the English Civil War*

Marcus Bull, *The Great Siege of Malta*

Stephan Malinowski, *The Hohenzollerns and the Nazis: A History of Collaboration*

Ariel Zeleznikow-Johnston, *The Future Loves You: How and Why We Should Abolish Death*

Lee Seong-bok, *Indeterminate Inflorescence: Notes from a poetry class*

Robin Wall Kimmerer, *The Serviceberry: An Economy of Gifts and Abundance*

David Graeber, *The Ultimate Hidden Truth of the World*

Andrew Roberts, *Churchill: Walking with Destiny*

Jordan B. Peterson, *We Who Wrestle With God: Perceptions of the Divine*

Tim Blanning, *Augustus The Strong: A Study in Artistic Greatness and Political Fiasco*

Lionel Barber, *Gambling Man: The Wild Ride of Japan's Masayoshi Son*

Caleb Carr, *My Beloved Monster*

Helen Castor, *The Eagle and the Hart: The Tragedy of Richard II and Henry IV*

James Rebanks, *The Place of Tides*

Jean-Baptiste Fressoz, *More and More and More: An All-Consuming History of Energy*

N A M Rodger, *The Price of Victory: A Naval History of Britain: 1815 – 1945*

Lluís Quintana-Murci, *Human Peoples: On the Genetic Traces of Human Evolution, Migration and Adaptation*

Sunil Amrith, *The Burning Earth: An Environmental History of the Last 500 Years*

Diarmaid MacCulloch, *Lower than the Angels: A History of Sex and Christianity*

Claude Béata, *The Interpretation of Cats: And Their Owners*

Jerry Brotton, *Four Points of the Compass: The Unexpected History of Direction*

Serhii Plokhy, *Chernobyl Roulette: A War Story*

Richard J. Evans, *Hitler's People: The Faces of the Third Reich*

Alexis Pauline Gumbs, *Survival is a Promise: The Eternal Life of Audre Lorde*

Nate Silver, *On the Edge: The Art of Risking Everything*

Webb Keane, *Animals, Robots, Gods: Adventures in the Moral Imagination*

Helen Charman, *Mother State: A Political History of Motherhood*

Anne Applebaum, *Autocracy, Inc.: The Dictators Who Want to Run the World*

Anil Ananthaswamy, *Why Machines Learn: The Elegant Maths Behind Modern AI*

Stephen Alford, *All His Spies: The Secret World of Robert Cecil*

Rob Jackson, *Into the Clear Blue Sky: The Path to Restoring Our Atmosphere*

Clare Hammond, *On the Shadow Tracks: A Journey through Occupied Myanmar*

Elias Dakwar, *The Captive Imagination: Addiction, Reality and our Search for Meaning*

Matt Parker, *Love Triangle: The Life-changing Magic of Trigonometry*

Paul Collier, *Left Behind: A New Economics for Neglected Places*

Andrew Hindmoor, *Haywire: A Political History of Britain since 2000*

Neil D. Lawrence, *The Atomic Human: Understanding Ourselves in the Age of AI*

Ruchir Sharma, *What Went Wrong With Capitalism*

Mark Gilbert, *Italy Reborn: From Fascism to Democracy*

Oleksandr Mykhed, *The Language of War*

Kelly Clancy, *Playing with Reality: How Games Shape Our World*

Shami Chakrabarti, *Human Rights: The Case for the Defence*

George Monbiot and Peter Hutchison, *The Invisible Doctrine: The Secret History of Neoliberalism (& How It Came to Control Your Life)*

Corinne Fowler, *Our Island Stories: Country Walks through Colonial Britain*

Oswyn Murray, *The Muse of History: The Ancient Greeks from the Enlightenment to the Present*

Andy Beckett, *The Searchers: Five Rebels, Their Dream of a Different Britain, and Their Many Enemies*

Sulmaan Wasif Khan, *The Struggle for Taiwan: A History*

Salman Khan, *Brave New Words: How AI Will Revolutionize Education (and Why That's a Good Thing)*

Eugene Rogan, *The Damascus Events: The 1860 Massacre and the Destruction of the Old Ottoman World*

J. Doyne Farmer, *Making Sense of Chaos: A Better Economics for a Better World*

Joseph E. Stiglitz, *The Road to Freedom: Economics and the Good Society*

Lisa Kaltenegger, *Alien Earths: Planet Hunting in the Cosmos*

Harriet Baket, *Rural Hours: The Country Lives of Virginia Woolf, Sylvia Townsend Warner and Rosamond Lehmann*

Nasser Abu Srour, *The Tale of a Wall: Reflections on Hope and Freedom*

Clayton Aldern, *The Weight of Nature: How a Changing Climate Changes Our Minds, Brains and Bodies*

Fareed Zakaria, *Age of Revolutions: Progress and Backlash from 1600 to the Present*

Daniel Susskind, *Growth: A Reckoning*

Judith Butler, *Who's Afraid of Gender?*

Chris Thorogood, *Pathless Forest: The Quest to Save the World's Largest Flowers*

Jonathan Haidt, *The Anxious Generation: How the Great Rewiring of Childhood Is Causing an Epidemic of Mental Illness*

Gary Stevenson, *The Trading Game: A Confession*

Justine Firnhaber-Baker, *House of Lilies: The Dynasty that Made Medieval France*

Henry Louis Gates, Jr., *The Black Box: Writing the Race*

Hanif Abdurraqib, *There's Always This Year: On Basketball and Ascension*

Richard Sennett, *The Performer: Art, Life, Politics*

Steve Coll, *The Achilles Trap: Saddam Hussein, the United States and the Middle East, 1979-2003*

Ingrid Robeyns, *Limitarianism: The Case Against Extreme Wealth*

Erica Benner, *Adventures in Democracy: The Turbulent World of People Power*

Patrick Joyce: *Remembering Peasants: A Personal History of a Vanished World*

Vincent Dreary, *How We Break: Navigating the Wear and Tear of Living*

Christopher Harding: *The Light of Asia: A History of Western Fascination with the East*

Kate Manne, *Unshrinking: How to Fight Fatphobia*

Michèle Lamont, *Seeing Others: How to Redefine Worth in a Divided World*

Clair Wills, *Missing Persons, Or My Grandmother's Secrets*

Anthony Grafton, *Magus: The Art of Magic from Faustus to Agrippa*

Richard Whatmore, *The End of Enlightenment: Empire, Commerce, Crisis*

Slavoj Žižek, *Too Late to Awaken: What Lies Ahead When There is No Future?*

Robert Skidelsky, *The Machine Age: An Idea, a History, a Warning*

Peter Biskind, *Pandora's Box: The Greed, Lust, and Lies That Broke Television*

Robert Darnton, *The Revolutionary Temper: Paris, 1748–1789*

Frank Trentmann, *Out of the Darkness: The Germans, 1942-2022*

Joachim C. Häberlen, *Beauty is in the Street: Protest and Counterculture in Post-War Europe*

Nathan Thrall, *A Day in the Life of Abed Salama: A Palestine Story*

Benjamin Moser: *The Upside-Down World: Meetings with the Dutch Masters*

Y-Dang Troeung: *Landbridge: Life in Fragments*

David Brooks, *How to Know a Person: The Art of Seeing Others Deeply and Being Deeply Seen*

Alice Albinia, *The Britannias: An Island Quest*

Jackie Wullschläger, *Monet: The Restless Vision*

Michael Lewis, *Going Infinite: The Rise and Fall of a New Tycoon*

Carlo Rovelli, *White Holes*

Greg Lukianoff & Rikki Schlott, *The Canceling of the American Mind: How Cancel Culture Undermines Trust, Destroys Institutions, and Threatens Us All*

Daniel C. Dennett, *I've Been Thinking*

Naomi Klein, *Doppelganger: A Trip Into the Mirror World*

Ludovic Slimak, *The Naked Neanderthal*

Camilla Nord, *The Balanced Brain: The Science of Mental Health*

John Gray, *The New Leviathans: Thoughts After Liberalism*

Michèle Lamont, *Seeing Others: How to Redefine Worth in a Divided World*

Henry Farrell and Abraham Newman, *Underground Empire: How America Weaponized the World Economy*

Yascha Mounk, *The Identity Trap: A Story of Ideas and Power in Our Time*

Kehinde Andrews, *The Psychosis of Whiteness: Surviving the Insanity of a Racist World*

Ian Johnson, *Sparks: China's Underground Historians and Their Battle for the Future*

Diarmuid Hester, *Nothing Every Just Disappears: Seven Hidden Histories*

David Sumpter, *Four Ways of Thinking: Statistical, Interactive, Chaotic and Complex*

Philip Gold, *Breaking Through Depression: New Treatments and Discoveries for Healing*

Wolfram Eilenberger, *The Visionaries: Arendt, Beauvoir, Rand, Weil and the Salvation of Philosophy*

Giorgio Parisi, *In a Flight of Starlings: The Wonder of Complex Systems*

Klaus-Michael Bogdal, *Europe and the Roma: A History of Fascination and Fear*

Robin Lane Fox, *Homer and His Iliad*

Jessica Rawson, *Life and Afterlife in Ancient China*

Wesley Lowery, *American Whitelash: The Resurgence of Racial Violence in Our Time*

Lucy Jones, *Matrescence: On the Metamorphosis of Pregnancy, Childbirth and Motherhood*

Julian Jackson, *France on Trial: The Case of Marshal Pétain*

Rachel Chrastil, *Bismarck's War: The Franco-Prussian War and the Making of Modern Europe*

Peter Turchin, *End Times: Elites, Counter-Elites and the Path of Political Disintegration*

Paul McCartney, *1964: Eyes of the Storm*

Scott Shapiro, *Fancy Bear Goes Phishing: The Dark History of the Information Age, in Five Extraordinary Hacks*

John Romer, *A History of Ancient Egypt, Volume 3: From the Shepherd Kings to the End of the Theban Monarchy*

Michio Kaku, *Quantum Supremacy: How Quantum Computers will Unlock the Mysteries of Science – and Address Humanity's Biggest Challenges*

Elizabeth-Jane Burnett, *Twelve Words for Moss*

Martin Daunton, *The Economic Government of the World: 1933-2023*

Martyn Rady, *The Middle Kingdoms: A New History of Central Europe*

Andy Clark, *The Experience Machine: How Our Minds Predict and Shape Reality*

Serhii Plokhy, *The Russo-Ukrainian War*

John Rapley and Peter Heather, *Why Empires Fall: Rome, America and the Future of the West*

Theresa MacPhail, *Allergic: How Our Immune System Reacts to a Changing World*

Christopher Clark, *Revolutionary Spring: Fighting for a New World 1848-1849*

Daniel Chandler, *Free and Equal: What Would a Fair Society Look Like?*

Jonathan Rosen, *The Best Minds: A Story of Friendship, Madness, and the Tragedy of Good Intentions*

Nigel Townson, *The Penguin History of Modern Spain: 1898 to the Present*

Katja Hoyer, *Beyond the Wall: East Germany, 1949-1990*

Monica Potts, *The Forgotten Girls: A Memoir of Friendship and Lost Promise in Rural America*

Quinn Slobodian, *Crack-Up Capitalism: Market Radicals and the Dream of a World Without Democracy*

Clare Carlisle, *The Marriage Question: George Eliot's Double Life*

Sara Ahmed, *The Feminist Killjoy Handbook*

Matthew Desmond, *Poverty, by America*

Bernie Sanders, *It's OK To Be Angry About Capitalism*

Mariana Mazzucato and Rosie Collington, *The Big Con: How the Consulting Industry Weakens our Businesses, Infantilizes our Governments and Warps our Economies*

Martin Wolf, *The Crisis of Democratic Capitalism*

Bernard Wasserstein, *A Small Town in Ukraine: The place we came from, the place we went back to*

David Graeber, *Pirate Enlightenment, or the Real Libertalia*

Leonard Susskind and Andre Cabannes, *General Relativity: The Theoretical Minimum*